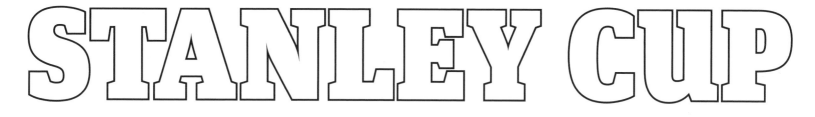

STANLEY CUP

120 YEARS OF HOCKEY SUPREMACY

STANLEY CUP

120 YEARS OF HOCKEY SUPREMACY

ERIC ZWEIG

FOREWORD BY PHIL PRITCHARD,
THE KEEPER OF THE CUP

 HOCKEY HALL *of* FAME

FIREFLY BOOKS

A FIREFLY BOOK

Published by Firefly Books Ltd. 2012

FIRST PRINTING

Publisher Cataloging-in-Publication Data (U.S.)
Zweig, Eric.
   Stanley Cup : 120 years of hockey supremacy / Eric Zweig.
[352] p. : col. ill. ; cm.
Includes index.
ISBN-13: 978-1-77085-104-7
1. Stanley Cup (Hockey)—History.   2. National Hockey League.   I. Title.
796.962/648 dc23   GV847.7.Z945 2012

Library and Archives Canada Cataloguing in Publication
Zweig, Eric, 1963–
      Stanley Cup: 120 years of hockey supremacy / Eric Zweig.
Includes index.
ISBN 978-1-77085-104-7
1. Stanley Cup (Hockey)—History. I. Title.
GV847.7.Z845 2012   796.962'648   C2012-902191-1

Published in the United States by
Firefly Books (U.S.) Inc.
P.O. Box 1338, Ellicott Station
Buffalo, New York 14205

Published in Canada by
Firefly Books Ltd.
66 Leek Crescent
Richmond Hill, Ontario L4B 1H1

Cover and interior design: Gareth Lind/LINDdesign
Creative Direction/Editor: Steve Cameron

Printed in China

*The publisher gratefully acknowledges the financial support for our publishing
program by the Government of Canada through the Canada Book Fund as
administered by the Department of Canadian Heritage.*

Previous page: The simple
cup that started it all. This
is Lord Stanley's original gift
to hockey, with the many
distinctive markings that it
gained in hockey's early years.

The modern day Stanley Cup
— the Presentation Stanley
Cup — is the cup that is
brought to center ice every
year to be presented to the
NHL's best.

Contents

Dustin Brown takes in the roar of the crowd as he hoists the Stanley Cup during the Los Angeles Kings' victory parade on June 14, 2012.

Foreword

If the Cup could share its story, it would be a best seller.

Many share that sentiment when talking about the history of the Stanley Cup, and the "Keepers of the Cup" feel the same way. Even we don't know the whole tale!

When Frederick Arthur Stanley (Lord Stanley of Preston) donated the Dominion Hockey Challenge Cup in 1892, he wanted the prize to be awarded to the best hockey team in the dominion of Canada. Since then, hockey's top prize has taken on a life of its own.

It has been kicked, lost, stolen (then recovered) and dented; it has been to cemeteries, sauna parties and parades; and, most famously, people have eaten and drunk all manner of things from it. But most of all, the Stanley Cup has been respected.

Each year, as Craig Campbell and I prepare to walk the Stanley Cup down the red carpet after the final game of the playoffs, we watch the disappointment on the faces of one team and the shear joy on the faces of the other. After those teams do

the traditional handshake, it is time for us to bring the Cup to center ice, and it seems like time stands still. Step by step we hear the roar of the crowd (regardless of whether the Cup is won at home or on the road; the fans see themselves as being, first and foremost, at a Stanley Cup presentation game), and after we set the Cup down and it is presented to the new champion, the chills and thrills go down my spine — and it never gets old. The honor of being a part of an amazing hockey moment is the highlight of my season, as I'm a hockey fan too. I enjoy every minute of the NHL season, from the first puck drop in October to the last second of the Stanley Cup final — and my small role in helping make the dreams of hockey's best come true.

The tradition and aura of Lord Stanley's Cup is unmatched in all of sport. While the game has changed from the one Lord Stanley first witnessed, one thing has remained a constant in its 120 years of glorious

history: the will and desire to win the Stanley Cup.

Hockey in 2012 is played in over 70 countries around the world, and everybody who has picked up a stick and put on skates surely dreams of one day playing in the greatest league in the world, the National Hockey League, and winning the Stanley Cup. As of my writing this, the Cup has visited 24 of those 70 countries. Players, each year, win the right to have their day with the Cup, and many bring it home to share with their families, loved ones and countrymen.

From sauna parties in Finland to knighting ceremonies in Slovakia to traditional celebrations in Russia, the Cup has seen it all. It has climbed the Rockies of Colorado, gone fishing in Wawa Lake in northern Ontario and even spent some solemn time at a grave sight for a close family member of a Cup winner.

As one of the Keepers of the Cup, I am fortunate to have been up close

with the Cup for nearly a quarter century. I have traveled far and wide with Stanley, always riding the Cup's coattails. It is the same for me as it is for the other keepers. Craig, Mike Bolt, Bill Wellman, Howie Borrow and Walter Neubrand understand it is an honor and a privilege to escort the Cup to its various obligations and duties around the world. To those who carried the Cup before us, we say thank you. For those who's future is to join the ranks of the Cup Keepers, immerse yourself in this book, because knowing the history and tradition of the Stanley Cup is an important part of the job.

Each year, a new story unfolds in the NHL and a new team is crowned as Stanley Cup champions, and so goes the tradition of the Stanley Cup. Within these pages are those 120 years of history. Enjoy it and, like you, I can't wait to see who will win Lord Stanley's legacy next!

Phil Pritchard
Vice President, Curator
and Keeper of the Cup
Hockey Hall of Fame

Introduction

Hockey historians love to debate the origins of the game. Did it begin on Long Pond near Dartmouth, Nova Scotia, around 1800? Or do hockey's roots begin with the stick-and-ball games depicted in paintings from Holland in the 1500s? Perhaps hockey began in ancient Greece several thousand years before?

One thing most historians do agree on is that hockey finally moved indoors, off of the frozen lakes and rivers where it had been cultivated, in the city of Montreal. The first formal exhibition of an indoor game of hockey took place at the Victoria Skating Rink in Montreal on March 3, 1875. Though this game would bear little resemblance to the one played in Los Angeles, California, on June 11, 2012, there are enough elements of similarity that few would doubt that today's hockey could trace its roots back to that Montreal game in 1875.

Hockey players in the 19th century wore almost no protective equipment — even though they were expected to play the entire length of the game, which was 60 minutes, same as today. Goalies were there to stop the puck, but they weren't allowed to drop to the ice to do so. There were no $100 million contracts either. Not even $100 contracts. In fact, nobody was paid at all. The game, in its infancy, was strictly amateur. And yet, the trophy the 19th-century top players of the game would soon be after is the same one chased by the top stars of the 21st century.

The modern sport of hockey was less than 20 years old when the trophy won by the Los Angeles Kings in 2012 was first presented in 1893. That trophy, of course, is the Stanley Cup. This book will tell the tale of the winners and losers, all the changes in the game, and all the oddball adventures that have been a part of the Stanley Cup story for 120 years.

Like the game itself, the Stanley Cup has undergone a lot of changes. At first, it was simply a squat, silver bowl placed atop a small ebony base. But that base was fitted with a silver band on which each winning team could make an engraving. As the years went by, more bands were added, and the Cup began to grow. The game grew too.

As the prestige of winning the Stanley Cup increased in the early 1900s, teams began paying for the best players they could find. By 1906, the game's top leagues were becoming professional, and so the top prize in the game became a professional trophy. By 1914, the pro game was represented by two major leagues, so the challenge system that had been used to determine Stanley Cup winners in the early days was abandoned in favor of an annual World Series-like competition between the two league champions. Lord Stanley had donated his trophy to honor the best team in Canada, but when these top pro leagues began adding American teams, the trustees who oversaw Stanley Cup competition declared that the trophy would be symbolic of the world's professional hockey championship. By the 1926–27 season, the National Hockey League had emerged as the game's only major professional circuit. Since then, competition for the Stanley Cup has been held exclusively among the teams of the NHL.

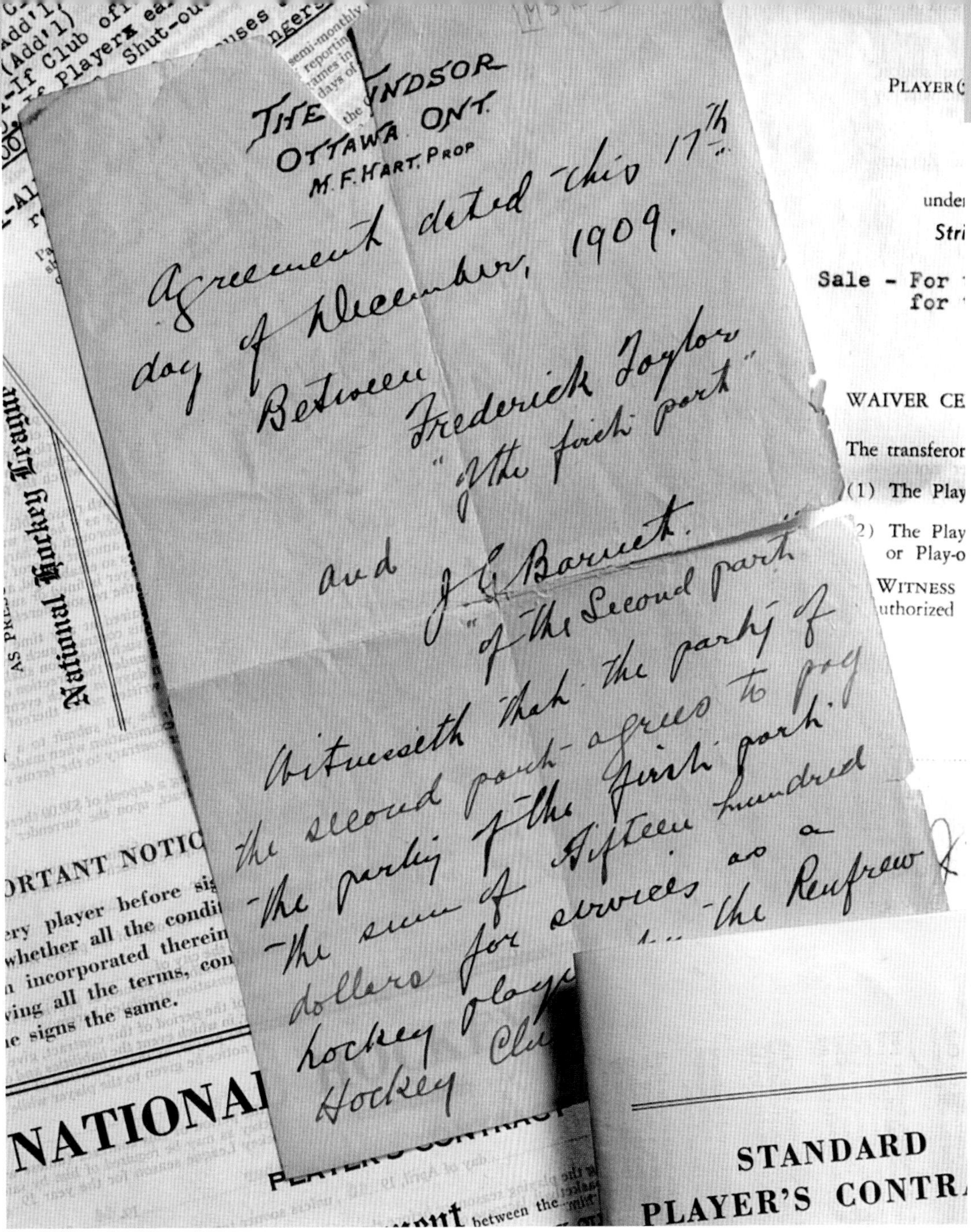

Today, the Stanley Cup is among the most famous and recognizable trophies in all of sports. His Lordship would likely be amazed at the attention given to the bowl purchased in England for the price of 10 guineas.

Even in 1893, guineas were more of a concept than a currency. Long since replaced by the British pound, the aristocracy still tended to quote prices in guineas for their more important purchases. Often, it is said that the price of the Stanley Cup was the equivalent of $48.67 in the colonies, but that price reflects the exchange rate for the pound. A guinea was worth 21 shillings to the pound's 20, and so a more accurate price would be $51.10. That may not sound like much, but the average working man in North America in 1893 would have counted himself lucky to take home a monthly salary of $50 or $60 so it was not an insignificant purchase.

It's said there are countless silver bowls in antique shops in England bearing a strong resemblance to the original Stanley Cup. They sell for between $2,000 and $3,000. The NHL has the trophy insured for $75,000 — but, in the words of the Mastercard commercial that made Cup keeper Phil Pritchard famous, the true value of winning it is "priceless."

Frederick "Cyclone" Taylor was one of hockey's early stars, and he was one of the first to make big money playing the professional game. The contract shown here guaranteed him $1,500 for suiting up for the Renfrew Hockey Club in 1909–10.

Steve Yzerman hoists the cup following Game 4 of the 1998 Stanley Cup final. The victory marked the second-consecutive Cup win for the Detroit Red Wings.

Expansion History since 1967

1967–68 Los Angeles Kings, Minnesota North Stars (Dallas Stars 1993–94 to present), Philadelphia Flyers, Pittsburgh Penguins, Oakland/California Seals (Cleveland Barons 1976–77 to 1977–78, merged with North Stars in 1978–79), St. Louis Blues

1970–71 Buffalo Sabres, Vancouver Canucks

1972–73 Atlanta Flames (Calgary Flames 1980–81 to present), New York Islanders

1974–75 Kansas City Scouts (Colorado Rockies 1976–77 to 1981–82, New Jersey Devils 1982–83 to present), Washington Capitals

1979–80 Edmonton Oilers, Hartford Whalers (Carolina Hurricanes 1997–98 to present), Quebec Nordiques (Colorado Avalanche 1995–96 to present), Winnipeg Jets (Phoenix Coyotes 1996–97 to present)

1991–92 San Jose Sharks

1992–93 Ottawa Senators, Tampa Bay Lightning

1993–94 Mighty Ducks of Anaheim (Anaheim Ducks 2006–07 to present)

1998–99 Nashville Predators

1999–2000 Atlanta Thrashers (Winnipeg Jets 2011–12 to present)

2000–01 Columbus Blue Jackets, Minnesota Wild

The Modern NHL: 1967–68 to Present

Today's 30-team NHL would shock the men who played hockey in its earliest days. The speed of the game would dazzle them. The big crowds and arenas would amaze them. The huge salaries would stun them.

Where once the game at the NHL level was populated nearly 100 percent by Canadian players, today there are enough different countries and languages represented in most dressing rooms to form a miniature United Nations.

Hockey's pioneers would surely be more comfortable with the NHL of 1967–68, the season the league doubled in size from six to 12 teams. While it had been decades since anyone played a full 60 minutes, as hockey's pioneers had, shifts in the 1960s and 1970s could still stretch more than two minutes. Helmets were rare, and other equipment offered only the simplest protection.

Other sports were quicker than the NHL to expand in the 1960s, and there was a fear that there were not enough talented players to grow beyond the league's six teams. It would take a few years before the new NHL teams were on par with the old ones, but it was quickly apparent that there was plenty of skill to go around. By the 1974–75 season, the NHL had tripled in size to 18 teams. (With the World Hockey Association, which started in 1972–73, reaching 14 teams that year, there were actually 32 pro hockey clubs that season.)

The game sped up, and scorers regularly topped 50 goals and 100 points, but the dynasty days of the six-team NHL continued. By the 1991–92 season, 25 years after expansion (and the same length of time the Original Six era had existed), only eight of the league's then 22 teams had won the Stanley Cup. Seven of those teams won it more than once, led by the Montreal Canadiens, who won nine postexpansion Cups in that 25-year span (their 10th would come in 1992–93). Since then, defense has come to dominate the NHL, and the economics of the game make it very difficult to keep a winning team together year after year. Twelve of the NHL's now 30 teams have won the Stanley Cup since the 1993–94 season, with Detroit (four times), New Jersey (three) and Colorado (two) the only teams to have won it more than once.

As the NHL has grown, the road to the Stanley Cup has gotten longer too. In the six-team era, a team required only two rounds of playoffs and eight victories over about four weeks to claim a championship. Today, the 16 wins needed in four rounds of intense action stretching over two full months makes the Stanley Cup the toughest test in all of sports.

Lord Stanley and the Cup

Frederick Arthur Stanley was born in London on January 15, 1841. He was the youngest of the six children (three of whom died at birth) of Edward George Geoffrey Smith-Stanley, the 14th Earl of Derby, and his wife, Emma. Lord Derby, as Edward Stanley was known, served as prime minister of England in 1852 and again in 1858–1859 and then from 1866 to 1868.

> **Like a great many British aristocrats of the day, Lord Stanley was an avid sportsman. His great-grandfather, the 12th Earl of Derby, had established the Epsom Derby (still one of the world's most famous horse races), and racing, shooting and cricket were all great passions of his.**

His son Frederick was educated at Eton and later at the Royal Military Academy Sandhurst. Frederick Stanley joined the Grenadier Guards after leaving Sandhurst in 1858. He served seven years in the military before resigning his commission on July 11, 1865, to follow his father and his older brother, Edward Henry Stanley, into politics.

Frederick Stanley remained a member of Parliament for nearly 20 years, holding such posts as financial secretary to the War Office and secretary to the treasury before succeeding his brother as secretary of state for the colonies for a brief time, from June 1885 to February 1886. Later in 1886, Frederick Stanley was offered a peerage, given the title Baron Stanley of Preston and entered the House of Lords. On February 1, 1888, Lord Salisbury, the British prime minister, acting on the advice of Queen Victoria, offered Lord Stanley the position of governor-general of Canada. He accepted on May 1st and sailed from Liverpool 30 days later with his wife, Lady Constance, and four of their eight children. (The Stanleys had seven sons and a daughter—all of whom would eventually join them in Canada—but they also lost a boy and a girl in infancy.) After arriving in Quebec City on June 9th, Stanley and his wife proceeded to Ottawa by special train, where he was officially sworn in as governor-general.

Described in the *Toronto World* newspaper of September 11, 1888, as being of medium height with a strong, well-built frame and graceful carriage, the blue-eyed Lord Stanley had thinning hair but a full beard streaked slightly with gray. He bore a slight resemblance to Queen Victoria's son the Prince of Wales (and future King Edward VII). Though somewhat shy, Stanley possessed expert diplomatic skills and was an important friend and ally to Canada's then prime minister, Sir John A. Macdonald. Lord Stanley was to serve as governor-general until September 1893, but after his brother's death in April of that year, he succeeded him as the 16th Earl of Derby and returned to England on July 15th. Stanley would serve as Lord Mayor of Liverpool in 1895 and of Preston in 1901. He then served as chancellor of the University of Liverpool from 1903 until his death at the age of 67 on June 14, 1908.

Like a great many British aristocrats of the day, Lord Stanley was an avid sportsman. His great-grandfather, the 12th Earl of Derby, had established the Epsom Derby (still one of the world's most famous horse races), and racing, shooting and cricket were all great passions of his. Lord Stanley and his family also enjoyed the many new sports they discovered during his posting to Ottawa. Snowshoeing and toboggan parties became a wintertime feature of life at Rideau Hall, the governor-general's official residence. On February 1, 1889, Lord Stanley presided over a costume carnival at the official opening of the Rideau Skating and Curling Club in Ottawa. He was not only the patron, but also an investor. Three nights later, Stanley and his family witnessed their first hockey game, at the Victoria Skating Rink in Montreal.

Hockey quickly became an obsession among the Stanley children, with daughter Isobel being among the first women to take up the game. Sons Edward, Arthur and Algernon became part of a team known as the Rideau Rebels, and their involvement helped to popularize the sport.

In November 1890, Arthur Stanley was one of 14 men who formed the Ontario Hockey Association—with his father again acting as the patron. Lord Stanley was also a patron of the Ottawa Amateur Athletic Association, and it was at a dinner that group held for the Ottawa Hockey Club on March 18, 1892, that the governor-general asked Lord Kilcoursie, one of his aides and a member of the Rebels hockey team, to read a letter on his behalf:

Gentlemen:

I have for some time been thinking that it would be a good thing if there were a challenge cup, which would be held from year to year by the leading hockey club in the Dominion [of Canada]. There does not appear to be any outward sign of the championship at present, and considering the general interest which hockey matches now elicit, and the importance of having the game played fairly and under rules generally recognized, I am willing to give a cup which shall be held from year to year by the winning club.

Captain Charles Colville, a former secretary to Lord Stanley in Ottawa who was now back in London, was asked to find a suitable trophy. He purchased a fine silver punch bowl crafted in Sheffield and sold by George Richmond Collis & Company, Regent Street, London. It was engraved with the name "Dominion Hockey Challenge Cup" on one side and the words "From Stanley of Preston" with the family coat of arms on the other. The cost was 10 guineas. And with that, the Stanley Cup was born.

CONFERENCE QUARTERFINAL
4 games to 1 over Vancouver

CONFERENCE SEMIFINAL
4 games to 0 over St. Louis

CONFERENCE FINAL
4 games to 1 over Phoenix

CONN SMYTHE TROPHY **JONATHAN QUICK** G – LOS ANGELES

FINAL   4 GAMES TO 2

MAY 30 ►	Los Angeles 2 at New Jersey 1 OT
JUNE 2 ►	Los Angeles 2 at New Jersey 1 OT
JUNE 4 ►	New Jersey 0 at Los Angeles 4
JUNE 6 ►	New Jersey 3 at Los Angeles 1
JUNE 9 ►	Los Angeles 1 at New Jersey 2
JUNE 11 ►	New Jersey 1 at Los Angeles 6

PLAYOFF SCORING LEADERS

Dustin Brown	GP	G	A	PTS
LOS ANGELES	20	8	12	20

Anze Kopitar	GP	G	A	PTS
LOS ANGELES	20	8	12	20

FINAL SERIES SCORING

LOS ANGELES	GP	G	A	PTS	PIM
Drew Doughty	6	2	4	6	2
Anze Kopitar	6	2	3	5	2
Jeff Carter	6	4	0	4	4
Justin Williams	6	2	2	4	0
Dustin Brown	6	1	3	4	10
Mike Richards	6	0	4	4	2
Trevor Lewis	6	2	1	3	0
Dwight King	6	0	3	3	2
Matt Greene	6	1	1	2	2
Alec Martinez	6	1	1	2	0
Colin Fraser	6	1	0	1	0
Willie Mitchell	6	0	1	1	6
Jordan Nolan	6	0	1	1	0
Dustin Penner	6	0	1	1	6
Jarret Stoll	6	0	1	1	4
Simon Gagné	4	0	0	0	2
Brad Richardson	2	0	0	0	0
Rob Scuderi	6	0	0	0	0
Slava Voynov	6	0	0	0	0

GOALTENDER	GP	W	L	MIN	GA	SO	AVG
Jonathan Quick	6	4	2	380	7	1	1.11

NEW JERSEY	GP	G	A	PTS	PIM
Bryce Salvador	6	1	2	3	10
Alexei Ponikarovsky	6	0	3	3	2
Adam Henrique	6	2	0	2	0
Patrik Elias	6	1	1	2	0
David Clarkson	6	0	2	2	12
Travis Zajac	6	0	2	2	0
Ryan Carter	6	1	0	1	12
Ilya Kovalchuk	6	1	0	1	0
Zach Parise	6	1	0	1	2
Anton Volchenkov	6	1	0	1	2
Steve Bernier	6	0	1	1	15
Petr Sykora	3	0	1	1	2
Marek Zidlicky	6	0	1	1	6
Dainius Zubrus	6	0	1	1	4
Mark Fayne	6	0	0	0	4
Stephen Gionta	6	0	0	0	0
Andy Greene	6	0	0	0	2
Peter Harrold	3	0	0	0	0
Jacob Josefson	3	0	0	0	0
Henrik Tallinder	3	0	0	0	0

GOALTENDER	GP	W	L	MIN	GA	SO	AVG
Martin Brodeur	6	2	4	380	15	0	2.37

ROSTER

Jonathan Bernier

Dustin Brown (captain)

Jeff Carter

Kyle Clifford

Drew Doughty

Colin Fraser

Simon Gagné

Matt Greene

Dwight King

Anze Kopitar

Trevor Lewis

Andrei Loktionov

Alec Martinez

Willie Mitchell

Jordan Nolan

Dustin Penner

Jonathan Quick

Mike Richards

Brad Richardson

Rob Scuderi

Jarret Stoll

Slava Voynov

Justin Williams

Dean Lombardi (general manager)

Darryl Sutter (head coach)

Turning on the Power

After going just 6-for-74 (8.1%) on the power play in the first three rounds of the playoffs, Los Angeles was 6-for-20 (30%) against New Jersey in the final. When Steve Bernier received a major penalty during the first period of Game 6, the Kings scored three power-play goals in a span of 3:48 to take command of the game and win the series. The fastest trio of power-play goals during the Stanley Cup final in NHL history was set by the Montreal Canadiens on April 6, 1954, when they scored three times in 56 seconds against the Detroit Red Wings.

Captain America

The meeting of Los Angeles and New Jersey marked the first time in Stanley Cup history that both teams in the final had American-born captains. The Kings' Dustin Brown is just the second American-born Stanley Cup–winning captain, after Derian Hatcher of the 1999 Dallas Stars.

Kings Coronation a Long Time Coming

The history of hockey in Los Angeles dates back a lot further than most people realize. The California Amateur Hockey Association was formed in 1925, and the California Professional Hockey League followed one year later. Though the pro league died during the Great Depression, teams from Los Angeles, Hollywood, San Diego, San Francisco and Oakland would all play in the Pacific Coast Hockey League and the Western Hockey League from the 1940s through the 1970s.

The man behind NHL hockey in Los Angeles is Jack Kent Cooke, a Canadian entrepreneur who moved to the United States in 1960. Cooke became a part owner of the Washington Redskins in 1961, bought the Los Angeles Lakers in 1965, paid $2 million for an NHL franchise to begin play when the league doubled from six to 12 teams for the 1967–68 season, and built the Los Angeles Forum. The Lakers would go on to great success, but the Los Angeles Kings would struggle to simply attract attention in a highly competitive sports market. Cooke eventually sold the Kings, the Lakers and the Forum to Dr. Jerry Bus in 1979. Bruce McNall became a partner in the Kings in 1986, and after buying out Bus in March 1988, McNall shocked the hockey world when he acquired Wayne Gretzky from Edmonton on August 9, 1988.

Gretzky brought Hollywood-style star power to Los Angeles hockey, and Kings tickets were suddenly hot. The team reached the Stanley Cup final in 1993, but the good times wouldn't last. New owners Philip Anschutz and Edward Roski Jr. would open the Staples Center in 1999, but the Kings missed the playoffs for six straight seasons between 2002 and 2008. Former Kings star turned general manager Dave Taylor drafted Dustin Brown in the first round in 2003 and Anze Kopitar in 2005 (along with Jonathan Quick in the third round), but he was replaced by Dean Lombardi in 2006. Lombardi selected Drew Doughty second overall in 2008. Before the 2011–12 season, Lombardi traded two top prospects for Philadelphia's Mike Richards and then acquired former Flyer Jeff Carter at the trade deadline. Darryl Sutter took over as head coach in December 2011, and the team played red-hot hockey down the stretch to finally nail down a playoff spot in the Western Conference.

After shocking the top-seeded Vancouver Canucks in the opening round, the Kings knocked off second-placed St. Louis and third-placed Phoenix before defeating the New Jersey Devils to become the first eighth-placed team to win the Stanley Cup.

To the Rescue

Darryl Sutter is just the fifth coach in NHL history to win the Stanley Cup after taking over a team midseason. The other four are:

1932 ► Dick Irvin (Toronto) replaced Art Duncan (defeated New York Rangers in final)

1971 ► Al MacNeil (Montreal) replaced Claude Ruel (defeated Chicago in final)

2000 ► Larry Robinson (New Jersey) replaced Robbie Ftorek (defeated Dallas in final)

2009 ► Dan Bylsma (Pittsburgh) replaced Michel Therrien (defeated Detroit in final)

Crazy Eights

Since the current playoff format was introduced in 1994, there have been 10 teams that were seeded eighth but knocked off the top seed in the opening round:

YEAR	TEAMS	SUBSEQUENT RESULTS
1994	San Jose over Detroit 4–3	lost conference semifinal
1995	New York Rangers over Quebec 4–2	lost conference semifinal
1998	Ottawa over New Jersey 4–3	lost conference semifinal
1999	Pittsburgh over New Jersey 4–3	lost conference semifinal
2000	San Jose over St. Louis 4–3	lost conference semifinal
2002	Montreal over Boston 4–2	lost conference semifinal
2006	Edmonton over Detroit 4–2	lost Stanley Cup final
2009	Anaheim over San Jose 4–2	lost conference semifinal
2010	Montreal over Washington 4–3	lost conference final
2012	Los Angeles over Vancouver 4–1	won Stanley Cup

Kings of the Road

The Kings went 10–1 on the road during the 2012 playoffs, winning an amazing 10 straight road games to set records for consecutive road wins in one playoff year and in multiple years with 12 straight dating back to 2011. The Kings' success on the road helped them become the first team in history to go up 3–0 in all four series in a single playoff year. The Kings were the fourth team in a row to win the Stanley Cup after opening the season on the road in Europe as part of the NHL's Premiere Series.

Working Overtime

The Kings were a perfect 4–0 in overtime during the 2012 playoffs. Jarret Stoll wrapped up the first-round series against Vancouver with the overtime winner in Game 5, while Dustin Penner clinched the Western Conference final with an OT goal against Phoenix. Anze Kopitar (Game 1) and Jeff Carter (Game 2) beat the Devils in overtime in the Stanley Cup final.

Quick Playoff Highlights
Jonathan Quick set NHL playoff records (minimum 15 games) with a 1.41 goals-against average and a .946 save percentage.

California Dreaming

Dustin Penner added his Stanley Cup win in Los Angeles to his 2007 Stanley Cup victory with the Anaheim Ducks.

CONFERENCE QUARTERFINAL	CONFERENCE SEMIFINAL	CONFERENCE FINAL
4 games to 3 over Montreal	**4 games to 0 over Philadelphia**	**4 games to 3 over Tampa Bay**

ROSTER

CONN SMYTHE TROPHY **Tim Thomas** G – BOSTON

Patrice Bergeron
Johnny Boychuk
Gregory Campbell
Zdeno Chara (captain)
Andrew Ference
Nathan Horton
Tomas Kaberle
Chris Kelly
David Krejci
Milan Lucic
Brad Marchand
Adam McQuaid
Daniel Paille
Rich Peverley
Tuukka Rask
Mark Recchi
Michael Ryder
Marc Savard
Tyler Seguin
Dennis Seidenberg
Tim Thomas
Shawn Thornton
Peter Chiarelli
(general manager)
Claude Julien
(head coach)

FINAL 4 GAMES TO 3

JUNE 1 ►	Boston 0 at Vancouver 1	
JUNE 4 ►	Boston 2 at Vancouver 3 OT	
JUNE 6 ►	Vancouver 1 at Boston 8	
JUNE 8 ►	Vancouver 0 at Boston 4	
JUNE 10 ►	Boston 0 at Vancouver 1	
JUNE 13 ►	Vancouver 2 at Boston 5	
JUNE 15 ►	Boston 4 at Vancouver 0	

PLAYOFF SCORING LEADER

David Krejci	GP	G	A	PTS
BOSTON	25	12	11	23

FINAL SERIES SCORING

BOSTON	GP	G	A	PTS	PIM
Brad Marchand	7	5	2	7	22
Mark Recchi	7	3	4	7	4
Michael Ryder	7	3	3	6	4
David Krejci	7	2	4	6	2
Patrice Bergeron	7	2	3	5	14
Rich Peverley	7	2	2	4	6
Zdeno Chara	7	0	4	4	20
Andrew Ference	7	2	1	3	22
Milan Lucic	7	2	1	3	20
Johnny Boychuk	7	0	3	3	6
Tomas Kaberle	7	0	3	3	0
Dennis Seidenberg	7	0	3	3	21
Chris Kelly	7	1	1	2	2
Daniel Paille	7	1	1	2	0
Gregory Campbell	7	0	1	1	0
Tyler Seguin	6	0	1	1	0
Nathan Horton	3	0	0	0	0
Adam McQuaid	7	0	0	0	14
Shawn Thornton	5	0	0	0	22
GOALTENDER	GP	W	L	MIN	GA	SO	AVG
Tim Thomas	7	4	3	417	8	2	1.15

VANCOUVER	GP	G	A	PTS	PIM
Daniel Sedin	7	1	3	4	24
Alexandre Burrows	7	2	1	3	28
Maxim Lapierre	7	2	1	3	12
Jannik Hansen	7	1	2	3	2
Raffi Torres	7	1	2	3	6
Alexander Edler	7	0	2	2	2
Henrik Sedin	7	1	0	1	6
Kevin Bieksa	7	0	1	1	14
Christian Ehrhoff	7	0	1	1	0
Christopher Higgins	7	0	1	1	0
Ryan Kesler	7	0	1	1	35
Sami Salo	7	0	1	1	0
Andrew Alberts	6	0	0	0	6
Keith Ballard	1	0	0	0	2
Alexandre Bolduc	1	0	0	0	0
Tanner Glass	4	0	0	0	0
Dan Hamhuis	1	0	0	0	0
Manny Malhotra	6	0	0	0	0
Victor Oreskovich	7	0	0	0	0
Mason Raymond	6	0	0	0	2
Aaron Rome	3	0	0	0	19
Jeff Tambellini	4	0	0	0	2
Christopher Tanev	3	0	0	0	0
GOALTENDERS	GP	W	L	MIN	GA	SO	AVG
Roberto Luongo	7	3	4	351	21	2	3.59
Cory Schneider	2	0	0	65	2	0	1.83

Rookie on a Roll

Brad Marchand's 11 goals during the 2011 playoffs were the most by a rookie since Jeremy Roenick scored 11 in 1990. Marchand was just three goals shy of the rookie record of 14, set by Dino Ciccarelli of the Minnesota North Stars in 1981.

German Imports

Boston's Dennis Seidenberg joined Uwe Krupp (Colorado, 1996) as the only German-born players to win the Stanley Cup.

Name Game

Though Marc Savard played only 25 games for the Bruins in 2010–11 and missed the entire playoffs due to injury, he still got his name engraved on the Stanley Cup. NHL guidelines state that a player must play at least 41 games in the regular season or one game in the final to have his name engraved on the trophy. However, since 1994 the league has allowed teams to petition Commissioner Gary Bettman to have other players listed in cases with extenuating circumstances.

Road to the Stanley Cup

Few people had the Boston Bruins listed as Stanley Cup favorites heading into the 2010–11 season. Two years earlier, in 2008–09, Boston had posted 53 wins and 116 points for the team's best season since their last Stanley Cup victory, in 1971–72. However, a second-round exit left many disappointed, and the Bruins struggled to make the playoffs the next season, in 2009–10. That postseason Boston became just the third team in NHL history to surrender a three-games-to-nothing series lead when Philadelphia eliminated them in the second round.

An off-season deal to acquire Nathan Horton and Gregory Campbell from Florida did little to boost enthusiasm heading into the 2010–11 campaign. Things began to look up, however, as Tim Thomas regained the form he had shown during his Vezina Trophy–winning season of 2008–09. Thomas posted a record of 35-11-9 in 57 games in 2010–11 and led the NHL with a goals-against average of 2.00. His save percentage of .938 was the best since the league had introduced the statistic back in 1976–77. In front of him, captain Zdeno Chara led the

NHL in plus-minus at plus-33 and was among the league's busiest blue-liners with an average of 25.26 minutes of ice time per game. Offensive talent Marc Savard missed most of the season, but Milan Lucic filled in admirably, leading the offense with a career-best 30 goals, while Patrice Bergeron ranked among the NHL's best faceoff men.

Boston finished the year first in the Northeast Division and third in the Eastern Conference with 103 points. In the playoffs, the Bruins eliminated Montreal on a Nathan Horton overtime goal in Game 7 and then avenged their 2010 loss to Philadelphia with a four-game sweep. In the Eastern Conference final, Horton scored the Game 7 winner again, this time late in the third period for a 1–0 victory over Tampa Bay. The Vancouver Canucks had been the best team in the NHL in 2010–11 and opened the Stanley Cup final with two home-ice victories over the Bruins. However, momentum switched dramatically early in Game 3, when Horton was knocked out of the series by a late hit. Boston rallied for an 8–1 victory and would go on to win a seven-game series that was both incredibly close and statistically one-sided.

Seventh Game Success

Boston became the first team in NHL history to win three seventh games en route to the Stanley Cup. The 1993 Toronto Maple Leafs and 2002 Colorado Avalanche are the only previous clubs to appear in three Games 7s, but both were eliminated in Game 7 of the conference final.

Over and Out At age 43, Boston's Mark Recchi became the oldest player to score a goal in the Stanley Cup final, which he did in Game 2 against Vancouver. The 22-year veteran finished the series with three goals and four assists and walked away on top when he announced his retirement moments after Game 7.

STANLEY CUP FINAL SERIES DECIDED IN GAME 7

YEAR	OUTCOME	KEY FACTS
1942	Detroit 1 at Toronto 3	Three goals in third period overcame 1–0 deficit
1945	Toronto 2 at Detroit 1	Babe Pratt's power-play goal in third period broke 1–1 tie
1950	New York Rangers 3 at Detroit 4 (2X OT)	First Game 7 in final decided in overtime
1954	Montreal 1 at Detroit 2 (OT)	Only other Game 7 in final decided in overtime
1955	Montreal 1 at Detroit 3	Alex Delvecchio scored two; Gordie Howe added the other
1964	Detroit 0 at Toronto 4	Leafs' third straight Cup win; Johnny Bower recorded shutout
1965	Chicago 0 at Montreal 4	All goals in first period; Gump Worsley recorded the shutout
1971	Montreal 3 at Chicago 2	Henri Richard scored game-winner in third period
1987	Philadelphia 1 at Edmonton 3	Oilers tallied one goal in each period to overcome early deficit
1994	Vancouver 2 at New York Rangers 3	Mark Messier scored game-winner in second period
2001	New Jersey 1 at Colorado 3	Alex Tanguay had three points; Ray Bourque gets first Cup
2003	Anaheim 0 at New Jersey 3	Home clubs won all games in final for the first time since 1965
2004	Calgary 1 at Tampa Bay 2	Ruslan Fedotenko scored both Tampa Bay goals
2006	Edmonton 1 at Carolina 3	Frantisek Kaberle scored the game-winner in second period
2009	Pittsburgh 2 at Detroit 1	Maxime Talbot scored both Pittsburgh goals
2011	Boston 4 at Vancouver 0	Tim Thomas the first to post a road shutout in Game 7 of final

Make Yourself at Home

After the first six games of the 2011 final were all won by the home team, Bruins assistant coach Geoff Ward asked members of the equipment staff to bottle up some shavings from center ice at the TD Garden to bring to Vancouver. Injured Bruins forward Nathan Horton poured the melted water onto the surface at the Rogers Arena two hours before the puck dropped for Game 7. "I was just trying to get some Garden ice here and make it our ice," Horton explained after CBC cameras caught him in the act.

Tom Terrific At the age of 37, Bruins goalie Tim Thomas became the oldest player to win the Conn Smythe Trophy. Thomas had 16 wins and nine losses in 25 games, and his 1.98 goals-against average and .940 save percentage led all playoff goaltenders. He set new playoff records for most shots faced in one playoff year (849) and most saves (798), and the 238 saves he made during the Stanley Cup final also set a new record. Thomas' 1.15 goals-against average in the final was the lowest mark in the modern era among goaltenders with at least five appearances until Johnathan Quick posted a 1.11 average in 2012.

Title Town The Bruins' Stanley Cup win in 2011 capped a decade of success that had seen the New England Patriots win the Super Bowl in 2002, 2003 and 2005, the Boston Red Sox win the World Series in 2004 and 2007, and the Boston Celtics win the NBA title in 2008.

Accidents and Incidents

As accidents go, it really wasn't all that bad. But this incident—unlike so many of the legendary misadventures of the Stanley Cup—was caught on camera and broadcast around the world. There was no place to hide.

With the Stanley Cup traveling as much as it does, there will always be the potential for accidents and unusual incidents. However, the true era of Stanley Cup mayhem likely came to an end in the summer of 1994 when members of the New York Rangers got up to all sorts of trouble.

On August 30, 2011, Michael Ryder, who had won the Stanley Cup with the Boston Bruins in 2011 and had already signed with the Dallas Stars over the offseason, brought the Stanley Cup to St. John's, Newfoundland, for his day with the Cup. During one of his early stops the Cup was placed on a small table, which promptly collapsed. The Mounties on hand did their best to bang things back into shape, but a large dent in the bowl was still noticeable two weeks later when the Stanley Cup visited the small town of Thornbury, Ontario, as part of the training camp for NHL referees and linesmen.

Since 1995, when the Hockey Hall of Fame began sending a "Keeper of the Cup" to safeguard the trophy during its summer vacation with members of the winning team, incidents involving the Stanley Cup have tended toward the cute and touching variety. For instance, many have eaten out of it: perogies for Marian Hossa of the Chicago Blackhawks in 2010; Frosted Flakes for Jordan Staal of the Pittsburgh Penguins in 2009; ice cream sundaes for Carolina Hurricanes player Doug Weight and his family in 2006; and dog food for the golden retriever of Anaheim Ducks player Jean-Sébastien Giguère in 2007. (Clark Gillies of the New York Islanders had let his German shepherd slurp champagne from the Cup back in 1980. When questioned about it, Gillies simply stated, "So what? He's a good dog.") Various babies have also been placed inside the Stanley Cup bowl over the years, and, on occasion, some have been known to do what babies do best.

Recent stories have also focused on the unusual places the Stanley Cup has visited, from an igloo at the Arctic Circle to a mountaintop in British Columbia and a beach in California. The Cup has also visited various historic sites, including the White House in the United States, Red Square in Moscow and the Eiffel Tower in Paris. And in both 2007 and 2008 the Cup and several NHL alumni traveled to army camps in Afghanistan to visit with troops from Canada, the United States and other North Atlantic Treaty Organization countries.

With the Stanley Cup traveling as much as it does, there will always be the potential for accidents and unusual incidents. However, the true era of Stanley Cup mayhem likely came to an end in the summer of 1994, when members of the New York Rangers got up to all sorts of trouble. It's never truly been clear whether Ed Olczyk really fed the Kentucky Derby–winning racehorse Go for Gin from the Stanley Cup at Belmont Park that summer. All Olczyk will admit is that he took the Cup to the track and posed for pictures with the champion horse.

In both 1991 and 1993, the Stanley Cup wound up in swimming pools of star players (Mario Lemieux of the Pittsburgh Penguins and Patrick Roy of the Montreal Canadiens, respectively) at team parties. While stories all say the Cup sank like a stone, it seemed to float when Lemieux held another team party for the Penguins in 2009.

It's pretty well known that the Edmonton Oilers celebrated in the 1980s by taking the Stanley Cup to "adult entertainment" establishments. The motives of the Canadiens' Guy Lafleur were much more innocent in 1978, when he

Dandurand's house for a party when they got a flat tire. When the players got out to make repairs, the Cup was placed on the curb by the side of the road. When they all finally got to Dandurand's home, the players realized they'd left the Cup behind! So they retraced their route through the streets of Montreal and found the Cup right where they'd left it.

Another famous story is of the Ottawa "Silver Seven" trying to kick the Cup across the Rideau Canal. The kicker may have been Harvey Pulford, and he might have done it after a Stanley Cup banquet following Ottawa's win over Dawson City in 1905. As the story goes, the Cup remained on the frozen canal overnight before someone from the team retrieved it the next day.

Are these stories true?

It's impossible to say.

If the Canadiens did leave the Cup by the road, it likely happened on April 1, 1924. That's the night the team was presented with the trophy at an official team banquet at the Windsor Hotel—an entire week after having won it. As for Ottawa, historian Paul Kitchen has searched the city's newspapers of the time for any reference to the canal incident. He's yet to find anything. However, the day after NHL president Frank Calder died in 1943, a Canadian Press report noted the legendary storyteller always maintained the Cup-kick was a fable.

Unlike with Michael Ryder, we'll never know for sure.

"stole" the Cup after a day of celebrations in Montreal. The trophy wound up on the lawn of Lafleur's home in Thurso, Quebec, while his excited father called family and friends to come over and see it.

During Lafleur's time —and dating all the way back to the 1930s—players didn't get to see much of the Stanley Cup after the on-ice presentation and maybe a team party or two. Perhaps that was the result of one of the most famous Stanley Cup incidents of them all, which occurred back in 1924.

According to legend, a carload of Montreal Canadiens players was taking the Stanley Cup to manager Léo

The Stanley Cup is guarded by Phil Pritchard and Craig Campbell prior to being presented to the Los Angeles Kings in 2012.

CONFERENCE QUARTERFINAL
4 games to 2 over Nashville

CONFERENCE SEMIFINAL
4 games to 2 over Vancouver

CONFERENCE FINAL
4 games to 0 over San Jose

ROSTER

CONN SMYTHE TROPHY **Jonathan Toews** C – CHICAGO

- Dave Bolland
- Nick Boynton
- Troy Brouwer
- Adam Burish
- Dustin Byfuglien
- Brian Campbell
- Ben Eager
- Colin Fraser
- Jordan Hendry
- Niklas Hjalmarsson
- Marian Hossa
- Cristobal Huet
- Patrick Kane
- Duncan Keith
- Tomas Kopecky
- Andrew Ladd
- John Madden
- Antti Niemi
- Brent Seabrook
- Patrick Sharp
- Brent Sopel
- Jonathan Toews (captain)
- Kris Versteeg
- Stan Bowman (general manager)
- Joel Quenneville (head coach)

FINAL 4 GAMES TO 2

MAY 29	► Philadelphia 5 at Chicago 6
MAY 31	► Philadelphia 1 at Chicago 2
JUNE 2	► Chicago 3 at Philadelphia 4 OT
JUNE 4	► Chicago 3 at Philadelphia 5
JUNE 6	► Philadelphia 4 at Chicago 7
JUNE 9	► Chicago 4 at Philadelphia 3 OT

PLAYOFF SCORING LEADER

	GP	G	A	PTS
Danny Brière PHILADELPHIA	23	12	18	30

FINAL SERIES SCORING

CHICAGO	GP	G	A	PTS	PIM
Patrick Kane	6	3	5	8	2
Duncan Keith	6	1	6	7	0
Patrick Sharp	6	4	2	6	5
Dustin Byfuglien	6	3	3	6	4
Dave Bolland	6	3	2	5	4
Troy Brouwer	6	2	3	5	2
Kris Versteeg	6	2	3	5	6
Marian Hossa	6	1	3	4	4
Andrew Ladd	3	1	2	3	2
Brent Sopel	6	1	2	3	4
Niklas Hjalmarsson	6	0	3	3	0
Jonathan Toews	6	0	3	3	0
Brian Campbell	6	1	1	2	2
Ben Eager	6	1	1	2	12
Tomas Kopecky	6	1	1	2	4
Brent Seabrook	6	1	1	2	6
John Madden	6	0	1	1	0
Nick Boynton	3	0	0	0	2
Adam Burish	3	0	0	0	2
Jordan Hendry	3	0	0	0	0
Antti Niemi	6	0	0	0	0

GOALTENDER	GP	W	L	MIN	GA	SO	AVG
Antti Niemi	6	4	2	369	20	0	3.25

PHILADELPHIA	GP	G	A	PTS	PIM
Danny Brière	6	3	9	12	2
Scott Hartnell	6	5	4	9	10
Ville Leino	6	3	6	9	0
Claude Giroux	6	2	2	4	0
Chris Pronger	6	0	4	4	16
Matt Carle	6	1	2	3	0
Kimmo Timonen	6	1	2	3	2
Simon Gagné	6	2	0	2	0
Arron Asham	6	1	1	2	0
Jeff Carter	6	1	1	2	0
Mike Richards	6	1	1	2	4
James van Riemsdyk	4	1	1	2	0
Lukas Krajicek	6	0	2	2	2
Blair Betts	6	1	0	1	2
Braydon Coburn	6	0	1	1	4
Darroll Powe	6	0	1	1	0
Ryan Parent	1	0	0	0	0
Brian Boucher	2	0	0	0	0
Daniel Carcillo	2	0	0	0	2
Oskars Bartulis	5	0	0	0	0
Ian Laperriere	6	0	0	0	0
Michael Leighton	6	0	0	0	2

GOALTENDERS	GP	W	L	MIN	GA	SO	AVG
Michael Leighton	6	2	2	303	20	0	3.96
Brian Boucher	2	0	2	64	4	0	3.75

Silver and Gold

Six members of the Blackhawks played for their countries at the 2010 Vancouver Winter Olympics: Marian Hossa and Tomas Kopecky represented Slovakia; Patrick Kane was on Team USA; and Jonathan Toews, Duncan Keith and Brent Seabrook competed for Canada. Toews, Keith and Seabrook all won gold, while Kane settled for silver, when Canada beat the U.S. 3–2 in overtime.

STANLEY CUP AND OLYMPIC GOLD IN ONE YEAR

YEAR	PLAYER	COUNTRY	NHL TEAM
2010	Duncan Keith	Canada	Chicago
	Brent Seabrook	Canada	Chicago
	Jonathan Toews	Canada	Chicago
2002	Brendan Shanahan	Canada	Detroit
	Steve Yzerman	Canada	Detroit
1980	Ken Morrow	USA	NY Islanders

Rebuilding a Champion

The Chicago Blackhawks' Stanley Cup title in 2009–10 capped what *Forbes Magazine* called "The Greatest Sports-Business Turnaround Ever." Having missed the playoffs in eight of nine seasons played between 1997–98 and 2006–07, the turnaround began when W. Rockwell "Rocky" Wirtz was named chairman of the team on October 7, 2007, following the passing of his father, William W. "Bill" Wirtz, who had run the team for 41 years. Rocky Wirtz (who had been two years old when his grandfather bought the team in 1954) hired John McDonough as club president on November 20, 2007, and the two quickly modernized a business model that had seemed hopelessly stuck in the 1960s. The Blackhawks season-ticket base grew from 3,400 to over 14,000 in under a year, and by the last home game of the 2010 Stanley Cup final, Chicago had drawn 102 consecutive capacity crowds and led the NHL in attendance for two straight years. Wirtz and McDonough also welcomed back team legends Bobby Hull, Stan Mikita and Tony Esposito, making them club ambassadors along with Denis Savard.

Just as Hull and Mikita had led Chicago on a similar revival and won the team's last Stanley Cup title back in 1961, the Blackhawks of 2009–10 were led on the ice by young stars Patrick Kane (drafted first overall in 2007) and Jonathan Toews (drafted third overall in 2006). After stellar rookie seasons in 2007–08, Kane was rewarded with the Calder Trophy and Toews was named team captain at the age of 21. During the 2009–10 season, Kane, Toews and Tampa Bay's Steven Stamkos were the only three players under the age of 22 to finish among the NHL's top 50 scorers. Duncan Keith won the Norris Trophy as the NHL's best defenseman, and the unheralded goalie combination of Antti Niemi and Cristobal Huet combined for a league-leading 11 shutouts.

The Blackhawks opened the 2009–10 season as one of four NHL teams in Europe, playing a pair of games against the Florida Panthers in Helsinki, Finland. Chicago took three of a possible four points and went on to post a record of 52-22-8, setting team records for wins and points (112) and ending Detroit's eight-season reign of Central Division championships, winning their first division title since 1992–93. Patrick Kane's 88 points (30 goals, 58 assists) ranked ninth in the NHL and were the most by a Chicago player since Jeremy Roenick's 107 in 1993–94. In the playoffs, Toews tied a club record with 29 points (7 goals, 22 assists), and Kane would end Chicago's 49-year championship drought with one of the strangest winning goals in Stanley Cup history.

STANLEY CUP TITLE GAMES DECIDED IN OVERTIME SINCE 1918

YEAR	PLAYER	TEAM	TIME	PERIOD	SCORE	SERIES
2010	Patrick Kane	Chicago	4:06	OT	4–3	4–2
2000	Jason Arnott	New Jersey	8:20	2OT	2–1	4–2
1999	Brett Hull	Dallas	14:51	3OT	3–2	4–2
1996	Uwe Krupp	Colorado	4:31	3OT	1–0	4–0
1980	Bob Nystrom	NY Islanders	7:11	OT	5–4	4–2
1977	Jacques Lemaire	Montreal	4:32	OT	2–1	4–0
1970	Bobby Orr	Boston	0:40	OT	4–3	4–0
1966	Henri Richard	Montreal	2:20	OT	3–2	4–2
1954	Tony Leswick	Detroit	4:20	OT	2–1	4–3
1953	Elmer Lach	Montreal	1:22	OT	1–0	4–1
1951	Bill Barilko	Toronto	2:53	OT	3–2	4–1
1950	Pete Babando	Detroit	8:31	2OT	4–3	4–3
1944	Toe Blake	Montreal	9:12	OT	5–4	4–0
1940	Bryan Hextall	NY Rangers	2:07	OT	3–2	4–2
1934	Mush March	Chicago	10:05	2OT	1–0	3–1
1933	Bill Cook	NY Rangers	7:34	OT	1–0	3–1

Mush March

Kane Was Able

Four minutes into overtime in Game 6 of the Stanley Cup final, Patrick Kane collected the puck along the boards in the Philadelphia zone and tried to shake defenseman Kimmo Timonen. Kane never truly got free, and as he approached the goal line he fired a quick shot at goalie Michael Leighton that seemed to disappear. Kane danced away in celebration, but nobody seemed to be sure what had happened. "I don't think anyone knew it was in the net but me," Kane would say soon after. Replays confirmed that Kane had indeed put the puck past Leighton — only to have it slide out of view under the skirting of the goal frame. The time of the goal was officially 4:06 of the first overtime, though because it took another four seconds until the clock stopped, it was listed as 4:10 in many game reports.

Third Time's the Charm

Early in his career, Marian Hossa earned a reputation as a slick scorer who disappeared come playoff time. Dealt to Pittsburgh late in the 2007–08 season, Hossa collected 12 goals and 14 assists in 20 playoff games that spring, but the Penguins lost the Stanley Cup to Detroit. A few weeks later, Hossa signed with the Red Wings as a free agent and would return to the final, only to lose to his former teammates from Pittsburgh. Hossa signed with Chicago for the 2009–10 season and became the first player in history to reach the Stanley Cup final with three different teams in three straight seasons. This time he finally won.

Pittsburgh Penguins

CONFERENCE QUARTERFINAL	CONFERENCE SEMIFINAL	CONFERENCE FINAL
4 games to 2 over Philadelphia	**4 games to 3 over Washington**	**4 games to 0 over Carolina**

ROSTER

CONN SMYTHE TROPHY EVGENI MALKIN C – PITTSBURGH

Craig Adams

Philippe Boucher

Matt Cooke

Sidney Crosby (captain)

Pascal Dupuis

Mark Eaton

Ruslan Fedotenko

Marc-André Fleury

Mathieu Garon

Hal Gill

Eric Godard

Alex Goligoski

Sergei Gonchar

Bill Guerin

Tyler Kennedy

Chris Kunitz

Kris Letang

Evgeni Malkin

Brooks Orpik

Miroslav Satan

Rob Scuderi

Jordan Staal

Petr Sykora

Maxime Talbot

Mike Zigomanis

Ray Shero (executive vice president/ general manager)

Dan Bylsma (head coach)

Ruslan Fedotenko, Max Talbot, Hal Gill and Evgeni Malkin celebrate a Pittsburgh goal.

FINAL 4 GAMES TO 3

MAY 30	►	Pittsburgh 1 at Detroit 3
MAY 31	►	Pittsburgh 1 at Detroit 3
JUNE 2	►	Detroit 2 at Pittsburgh 4
JUNE 4	►	Detroit 2 at Pittsburgh 4
JUNE 6	►	Pittsburgh 0 at Detroit 5
JUNE 9	►	Detroit 1 at Pittsburgh 2
JUNE 12	►	Pittsburgh 2 at Detroit 1

PLAYOFF SCORING LEADER

Evgeni Malkin	GP	G	A	PTS
PITTSBURGH	24	12	11	23

FINAL SERIES SCORING

PITTSBURGH	GP	G	A	PTS	PIM
Evgeni Malkin	7	2	6	8	29
Maxime Talbot	7	4	2	6	14
Kris Letang	7	1	3	4	0
Tyler Kennedy	7	2	1	3	0
Jordan Staal	7	2	1	3	2
Sidney Crosby	7	1	2	3	2
Ruslan Fedotenko	7	1	2	3	0
Sergei Gonchar	7	1	1	2	2
Chris Kunitz	7	0	2	2	4
Rob Scuderi	7	0	2	2	0
Mark Eaton	7	0	1	1	4
Bill Guerin	7	0	1	1	4
Craig Adams	7	0	0	0	12
Philippe Boucher	1	0	0	0	0
Matt Cooke	7	0	0	0	10
Pascal Dupuis	6	0	0	0	2
Hal Gill	7	0	0	0	2
Brooks Orpik	7	0	0	0	6
Miroslav Satan	6	0	0	0	2
Petr Sykora	1	0	0	0	0

GOALTENDERS	GP	W	L	MIN	GA	SO	AVG
Marc-André Fleury	7	4	3	393	17	0	2.60
Mathieu Garon	1	0	0	24	0	0	0.00

DETROIT	GP	G	A	PTS	PIM
Henrik Zetterberg	7	2	4	6	7
Johan Franzen	7	2	2	4	2
Brian Rafalski	7	1	3	4	0
Jonathan Ericsson	7	2	1	3	4
Marian Hossa	7	0	3	3	2
Jiri Hudler	7	0	3	3	0
Nicklas Lidstrom	7	0	3	3	0
Justin Abdelkader	3	2	0	2	0
Valtteri Filppula	7	2	0	2	2
Brad Stuart	7	2	0	2	2
Darren Helm	7	1	1	2	0
Niklas Kronwall	7	1	1	2	8
Pavel Datsyuk	3	0	2	2	0
Tomas Holmstrom	7	0	2	2	2
Ville Leino	4	0	2	2	0
Daniel Cleary	7	1	0	1	4
Kris Draper	4	1	0	1	0
Chris Osgood	7	0	1	1	0
Mikael Samuelsson	7	0	1	1	2
Brett Lebda	7	0	0	0	12
Kirk Maltby	7	0	0	0	0

GOALTENDER	GP	W	L	MIN	GA	SO	AVG
Chris Osgood	7	3	4	417	13	1	1.87

Scoring Feats

Evgeni Malkin became just the fifth player since the NHL expansion in 1968 to lead the NHL in scoring in the regular season and the playoffs in the same year. Malkin joined Phil Esposito (1968–69, 1971–72), Guy Lafleur (1976–77, 1977–78), Wayne Gretzky (1982–83, 1983–84, 1984–85, 1987–88) and Mario Lemieux (1991–92) on the list. Malkin and Sidney Crosby were the first pair of teammates to top 30 points in the postseason since Brian Leetch and Mark Messier with the New York Rangers in 1994.

March of the Penguins

With no standings on which to base the NHL entry draft following the canceled 2004–05 season, the league turned to a lottery to determine the order of selection. The lottery was weighted to favor struggling teams, and after finishing among the NHL's worst clubs for the three previous seasons, the Pittsburgh Penguins landed the top spot. To no one's surprise, they selected Sidney Crosby with the first pick in the draft.

"Sid the Kid" became the youngest player in NHL history to top 100 points in his rookie season of 2005–06 and became the first teenager in a major professional sport to capture a scoring title when he did so in 2006–07. With Crosby, Evgeni Malkin and Jordan Staal leading the way, the Penguins lineup featured so many talented youngsters it was earning comparisons to the Edmonton Oilers of the 1980s. Pittsburgh was suddenly an NHL powerhouse, reaching the Stanley Cup final in 2007–08 before losing to Detroit in six games. But the Penguins were struggling in 2008–09, and on February 15, 2009, they promoted Dan Bylsma from their Wilkes-Barre/Scranton AHL affiliate to take over as head coach. Pittsburgh was six points out of a playoff spot with 25 games to go, but the team went 18-3-4 under Bylsma to finish the season with 99 points and the fourth-best record in the Eastern Conference. Malkin led the NHL in scoring, with 113 points, while Crosby finished third with 103.

The Penguins opened the playoffs against Philadelphia and eliminated the Flyers in six games, rallying from an early 3–0 deficit in Game 6 to wrap up the series with a 5–3 victory. Next up were the Washington Capitals and a showdown between Crosby and archrival Alex Ovechkin. Washington jumped out to a 2–0 series lead, but Pittsburgh took the next three in a row and went on to win the series in seven. After sweeping Carolina in the Eastern Conference final, Pittsburgh had a chance for revenge against Detroit in the first Stanley Cup rematch since the Oilers had faced the New York Islanders in 1983 and 1984. This time, the Penguins beat the Red Wings in seven.

Sidney Crosby

Rare Clubs

Mario Lemieux, who had won the Stanley Cup as captain of the Penguins in 1991 and 1992, became just the third person to win the Stanley Cup as a player and as a team owner. He joined Frank Patrick, who had won in both roles with the 1915 Vancouver Millionaires, and Frank's brother Lester Patrick, who had won as a player with the Montreal Wanderers in 1906 and 1907 and as owner of the Victoria Cougars in 1925.

Penguins coach Dan Bylsma joined Al MacNeil (Montreal, 1971) as one of only two rookie head coaches to win the Stanley Cup after being hired as a midseason replacement.

Comeback Kids
The Penguins joined the 1942 Maple Leafs and the 1966 and 1971 Montreal Canadiens as the only teams to win the Stanley Cup after falling behind two games to nothing in the final. They were also the first team since Montreal in 1971 to bounce back after losing the first two on the road, and they were the first team in hockey, baseball or basketball to win game seven of a championship series on the road since the 1979 Pittsburgh Pirates.

Captain Kid
At the age of 21 years and 10 months, Sidney Crosby became the youngest captain in NHL history to lead his team to the Stanley Cup.

CONFERENCE QUARTERFINAL
4 games to 2 over Nashville

CONFERENCE SEMIFINAL
4 games to 0 over Colorado

CONFERENCE FINAL
4 games to 2 over Dallas

FINAL 4 GAMES TO 2

MAY 24	►	Pittsburgh 0 at Detroit 4
MAY 26	►	Pittsburgh 0 at Detroit 3
MAY 28	►	Detroit 2 at Pittsburgh 3
MAY 31	►	Detroit 2 at Pittsburgh 1
JUNE 2	►	Pittsburgh 4 at Detroit 3 3X OT
JUNE 4	►	Detroit 3 at Pittsburgh 2

PLAYOFF SCORING LEADERS

	GP	G	A	PTS
Henrik Zetterberg DETROIT	22	13	14	27
Evgeni Malkin PITTSBURGH	20	6	21	27

ROSTER

Chris Chelios
Daniel Cleary
Pavel Datsyuk
Aaron Downey
Dallas Drake
Kris Draper
Valtteri Filppula
Johan Franzen
Dominik Hasek
Darren Helm
Tomas Holmstrom
Jiri Hudler
Tomas Kopecky
Niklas Kronwall
Brett Lebda
Nicklas Lidstrom (captain)
Andreas Lilja
Kirk Maltby
Darren McCarty
Derek Meech
Chris Osgood
Brian Rafalski
Mikael Samuelsson
Brad Stuart
Henrik Zetterberg
Ken Holland (general manager)
Mike Babcock (head coach)

CONN SMYTHE TROPHY HENRIK ZETTERBERG LW – DETROIT

Chris Chelios and Nicklas Lidstrom: an old but reliable tandem.

FINAL SERIES SCORING

DETROIT	GP	G	A	PTS	PIM
Henrik Zetterberg	6	2	4	6	2
Brad Stuart	6	1	4	5	2
Pavel Datsyuk	6	3	1	4	6
Valtteri Filppula	6	2	2	4	0
Brian Rafalski	6	2	2	4	6
Mikael Samuelsson	6	1	3	4	0
Johan Franzen	5	1	2	3	10
Nicklas Lidstrom	6	1	2	3	4
Niklas Kronwall	6	0	3	3	2
Darren Helm	6	1	1	2	2
Tomas Holmstrom	5	1	1	2	6
Daniel Cleary	6	1	0	1	4
Jiri Hudler	6	1	0	1	6
Kirk Maltby	6	0	1	1	6
Dallas Drake	6	0	0	0	6
Kris Draper	6	0	0	0	4
Brett Lebda	6	0	0	0	2
Andreas Lilja	6	0	0	0	6
Darren McCarty	2	0	0	0	0
GOALTENDER	GP	W	L	MIN	GA	SO	AVG
Chris Osgood	6	4	2	409	10	2	1.47

PITTSBURGH	GP	G	A	PTS	PIM
Marian Hossa	6	3	4	7	2
Sidney Crosby	6	2	4	6	4
Evgeni Malkin	6	1	2	3	6
Sergei Gonchar	6	0	3	3	2
Adam Hall	6	2	0	2	2
Maxime Talbot	6	1	1	2	18
Petr Sykora	6	1	0	1	4
Pascal Dupuis	6	0	1	1	2
Ryan Malone	6	0	1	1	8
Gary Roberts	5	0	1	1	16
Hal Gill	6	0	0	0	6
Tyler Kennedy	6	0	0	0	2
Georges Laraque	1	0	0	0	0
Kris Letang	2	0	0	0	2
Brooks Orpik	6	0	0	0	8
Jarkko Ruutu	6	0	0	0	2
Rob Scuderi	6	0	0	0	0
Jordan Staal	6	0	0	0	4
Darryl Sydor	4	0	0	0	2
Ryan Whitney	6	0	0	0	4
GOALTENDER	GP	W	L	MIN	GA	SO	AVG
Marc-André Fleury	6	2	4	407	17	0	2.51

History (Finally) Repeating Itself

Down three games to one in the series and on the road in Detroit, the Penguins stayed alive in game five with a 4–3 victory in triple overtime on a goal by Petr Sykora. Pittsburgh had needed an empty-net goal by Maxim Talbot with 34.3 seconds remaining to force overtime. Talbot's tally marked the first time a team had staved off elimination with an empty-net goal since Pete Kelly scored for Toronto against Detroit all the way back in 1936. Just as they had done against the Maple Leafs that time, the Red Wings bounced back to win the Stanley Cup in the very next game.

Detroit Does It Again

The Detroit Red Wings continued a period of prolonged excellence in 2007–08. Detroit won its seventh straight Central Division title (they would make it eight straight the following season) and won the Presidents' Trophy for the fourth time in six seasons. The Red Wings boasted a league-leading 115 points on a record of 54-21-7 as they topped 50 wins for the third year in a row. The team's 257 goals scored ranked them third in the NHL, while their 184 goals against was best in the league as Chris Osgood and Dominik Hasek shared the Jennings Trophy.

Pavel Datsyuk and Henrik Zetterberg led the Detroit offense as Datsyuk topped the team with 97 points to rank fourth in the NHL. He also won the Lady Byng Trophy as the league's most sportsmanlike player for the third year in a row and won the Selke Trophy as the best defensive forward for the first of three straight seasons. Zetterberg topped the team with 43 goals and ranked sixth in the NHL with 92 points. He also finished third behind Datsyuk in voting for the Selke Trophy. But, as usual, the best defensive player in Detroit was captain Nicklas Lidstrom, who won the Norris Trophy as the league's best defenseman for the third year in a row and sixth time in seven seasons. Lidstrom led all defensemen in scoring, with 70 points, finished second to Datsyuk among the NHL leaders in plus-minus (plus-40) and ranked fourth in average ice time (26:43) at the age of 37.

Detroit opened the playoffs against Nashville and won two games at home before the Predators took two in a row in their arena. Osgood replaced Hasek in goal during Game 4 of the conference quarterfinal and would remain in the nets for the rest of the playoffs. After eliminating Nashville, Colorado and Dallas, Osgood opened the Stanley Cup final against Pittsburgh with two straight shutouts, and the Red Wings went on to beat the Penguins in six games. Lidstrom became the first European-born player to captain his team to the Stanley Cup, while Zetterberg joined him as the second European player to win the Conn Smythe Trophy.

Rare Meeting

The 2008 meeting in the Stanley Cup final between Detroit and Pittsburgh marked the first time the two teams had ever faced each other in the playoffs. The Red Wings and Penguins had not met during the 2007–08 regular season either.

Triple Threat ... Plus One Detroit's Mike Babcock is the only coach in hockey history to win a gold medal at the Olympics (2010), the Stanley Cup (2008) and a World Championship (2004). He also led Canada to a World Junior Championship in 1997.

Mike Babcock

Like a Fine Wine

At the age of 48, Chris Chelios became the oldest player ever to win the Stanley Cup. Chelios, who had first won the Stanley Cup with the Montreal Canadiens back in 1985–86 (and had also won with Detroit in 2001–02), already held the NHL record for most seasons in the playoffs. The 2007–08 season marked his 23rd year in the playoffs, and he would stretch his record to 24 the following spring. Early in the 2008 playoffs, in Game 2 of the conference quarterfinal versus Nashville on April 12, Chelios played in his 248th career playoff game to surpass Patrick Roy as the all-time postseason leader in games played. He would push that mark to 266 in 2009.

Quite The Kick Dubbed "The Mule" by Steve Yzerman because of his size and strength, Johan Franzen really carried the load for the Red Wings throughout the 2008 postseason. Though he missed six of Detroit's 22 playoff games that spring, Franzen still tied Henrik Zetterberg for the postseason lead, with 13 goals. Nine of those goals came during Detroit's sweep of Colorado in the conference semifinal. Franzen set an NHL record for most goals in a four-game series and broke Gordie Howe's team record of eight goals in a single series set in a seven gamer back in 1949. Franzen also had two hat tricks against the Avalanche, tying a franchise record for a single series set by Norm Ullman in 1964.

CONFERENCE QUARTERFINAL	CONFERENCE SEMIFINAL	CONFERENCE FINAL
4 games to 1 over Minnesota	**4 games to 1 over Vancouver**	**4 games to 2 over Detroit**

ROSTER

CONN SMYTHE TROPHY **SCOTT NIEDERMAYER** D – ANAHEIM

- François Beauchemin
- Ilya Bryzgalov
- Ryan Carter
- Joe DiPenta
- Ryan Getzlaf
- Jean-Sébastien Giguère
- Kent Huskins
- Ric Jackman
- Chris Kunitz
- Todd Marchant
- Brad May
- Andy McDonald
- Drew Miller
- Travis Moen
- Joe Motzko
- Rob Niedermayer
- Scott Niedermayer (captain)
- Sean O'Donnell
- Samuel Pahlsson
- George Parros
- Dustin Penner
- Corey Perry
- Chris Pronger
- Teemu Selanne
- Ryan Shannon
- Shawn Thornton
- Brian Burke (executive vice president/general manager)
- Randy Carlyle (head coach)

FINAL 4 GAMES TO 1

MAY 28 ►	Ottawa 2 at Anaheim 3
MAY 30 ►	Ottawa 0 at Anaheim 1
JUNE 2 ►	Anaheim 3 at Ottawa 5
JUNE 4 ►	Anaheim 3 at Ottawa 2
JUNE 6 ►	Ottawa 2 at Anaheim 6

PLAYOFF SCORING LEADERS

	GP	G	A	PTS
Daniel Alfredsson OTTAWA	20	14	8	22
Dany Heatley OTTAWA	20	7	15	22
Jason Spezza OTTAWA	20	7	15	22

FINAL SERIES SCORING

ANAHEIM	GP	G	A	PTS	PIM
Andy McDonald	5	5	2	7	4
Corey Perry	5	2	4	6	10
Ryan Getzlaf	5	2	2	4	8
Travis Moen	5	3	0	3	2
Rob Niedermayer	5	1	2	3	0
Dustin Penner	5	1	2	3	2
Teemu Selanne	5	0	3	3	2
Samuel Pahlsson	5	1	1	2	8
Scott Niedermayer	5	0	2	2	6
François Beauchemin	5	1	0	1	6
Ric Jackman	4	0	1	1	2
Todd Marchant	5	0	1	1	0
Sean O'Donnell	5	0	1	1	2
Chris Pronger	4	0	1	1	4
Ryan Carter	1	0	0	0	0
Joe DiPenta	2	0	0	0	0
Kent Huskins	5	0	0	0	0
Chris Kunitz	2	0	0	0	0
Brad May	5	0	0	0	4
Drew Miller	2	0	0	0	2
Joe Motzko	1	0	0	0	0
Shawn Thornton	4	0	0	0	2

GOALTENDER	GP	W	L	MIN	GA	SO	AVG
Jean-Sébastien Giguère	5	4	1	298	11	1	2.21

OTTAWA	GP	G	A	PTS	PIM
Daniel Alfredsson	5	4	1	5	0
Mike Fisher	5	2	2	4	8
Wade Redden	5	1	1	2	4
Anton Volchenkov	5	1	1	2	6
Chris Kelly	5	0	2	2	0
Andrej Meszaros	5	0	2	2	2
Peter Schaefer	5	0	2	2	4
Jason Spezza	5	0	2	2	4
Dany Heatley	5	1	0	1	2
Dean McAmmond	3	1	0	1	0
Chris Neil	5	1	0	1	6
Mike Comrie	5	0	1	1	2
Joe Corvo	5	0	1	1	0
Patrick Eaves	3	0	1	1	2
Oleg Saprykin	4	0	1	1	0
Christoph Schubert	5	0	1	1	6
Antoine Vermette	5	0	1	1	0
Chris Phillips	5	0	0	0	4
Tom Preissing	5	0	0	0	4

GOALTENDER	GP	W	L	MIN	GA	SO	AVG
Ray Emery	5	1	4	296	16	0	3.24

J.-S. in OT An overtime loss to Vancouver in Game 2 of the Western Conference semifinals snapped Jean-Sébastien Giguère's record overtime shutout streak of 197:52 that dated back through eight games to the 2003 playoffs. After winning four more OT games in the spring of 2007, Giguère improved his record to 12–1 in overtime games. His winning percentage of .923 was the highest in NHL history for any goalie with 10 or more OT decisions.

Coach Carlyle Randy Carlyle was an NHL defenseman for 17 seasons, from 1976 to 1993, playing 1,055 games in the regular season and 69 more in the playoffs without ever winning the Stanley Cup. Carlyle won it in just his second season as an NHL head coach with the Ducks.

Duck Season

Having broken nearly every major club record the year before, the newly christened Anaheim Ducks (as opposed to the Mighty Ducks of Anaheim) enjoyed another record-breaking season in 2006–07. With a mark of 48-20-14, the Ducks set new franchise records for wins and points (110) and won the Pacific Division title for the first time. At age 36, Teemu Selanne led the offense with 48 goals and became the oldest player in NHL history to top 45 in a single season and to reach the 40-goal plateau in back-to-back years. Jean-Sébastien Giguère went 36-10-8 to set a new club record for wins by a goalie, while his 2.26 goals-against average and .918 save percentage ranked among the best in the NHL.

Still, the big story in Anaheim was on defense, where, after signing Scott Niedermayer as a free agent the year before, general manager Brian Burke added Chris Pronger to the blue line in a blockbuster deal with Edmonton. Both Niedermayer (who led all NHL defensemen in scoring, with 69 points) and Pronger would be finalists for the Norris Trophy in 2006–07, finishing second and third respectively behind Detroit's Nicklas Lidstrom.

The 2006–07 season marked the first time in franchise history that the Ducks had reached the playoffs in back-to-back years. They opened against the Minnesota Wild, who were making their first postseason appearance since Anaheim had eliminated them in the 2003 Western Conference final. Ilya Bryzgalov played the first four games in goal while Giguère dealt with a medical complication following the birth of his son, but Giguère was back in time to wrap up the series in Game 5. Anaheim then eliminated Vancouver in five games on a double-overtime goal from Scott Niedermayer. An overtime goal by Selanne in Game 5 against Detroit sparked the Ducks to a six-game victory over the Red Wings in the Western Conference final.

Meanwhile, the Ottawa Senators had lost only three games in the postseason en route to winning the Eastern Conference, but when the Ducks beat them four games to one in the final, Anaheim became the first West Coast team to win the Stanley Cup since the Victoria Cougars (the last non-NHL team to win the Cup) did it in the 1924–25 season.

Jean-Sébastien Giguère

CONFERENCE QUARTERFINAL
4 games to 2 over Montreal

CONFERENCE SEMIFINAL
4 games to 1 over New Jersey

CONFERENCE FINAL
4 games to 3 over Buffalo

CONN SMYTHE TROPHY **CAM WARD** G – CAROLINA

FINAL 4 GAMES TO 3

JUNE 5	►	Edmonton 4 at Carolina 5
JUNE 7	►	Edmonton 0 at Carolina 5
JUNE 10	►	Carolina 1 at Edmonton 2
JUNE 12	►	Carolina 2 at Edmonton 1
JUNE 14	►	Edmonton 4 at Carolina 3 OT
JUNE 17	►	Carolina 0 at Edmonton 4
JUNE 19	►	Edmonton 1 at Carolina 3

PLAYOFF SCORING LEADER

	GP	G	A	PTS
Eric Staal CAROLINA	25	9	19	28

FINAL SERIES SCORING

CAROLINA	GP	G	A	PTS	PIM
Eric Staal	7	2	6	8	4
Cory Stillman	7	2	5	7	4
Mark Recchi	7	2	4	6	2
Ray Whitney	7	3	2	5	10
Frantisek Kaberle	7	2	3	5	2
Matt Cullen	7	0	5	5	6
Justin Williams	7	2	2	4	4
Rod Brind'Amour	7	3	0	3	6
Doug Weight	5	1	2	3	2
Andrew Ladd	7	1	1	2	2
Aaron Ward	7	1	1	2	6
Bret Hedican	7	0	2	2	18
Chad LaRose	3	0	1	1	0
Niclas Wallin	7	0	1	1	4
Craig Adams	7	0	0	0	8
Kevyn Adams	7	0	0	0	2
Mike Commodore	7	0	0	0	6
Oleg Tverdovsky	1	0	0	0	0
Josef Vasicek	3	0	0	0	2
Glen Wesley	7	0	0	0	6

GOALTENDER	GP	W	L	MIN	GA	SO	AVG
Cam Ward	7	4	3	422	16	1	2.27

EDMONTON	GP	G	A	PTS	PIM
Fernando Pisani	7	5	1	6	2
Ales Hemsky	7	2	4	6	2
Jaroslav Spacek	7	0	5	5	8
Chris Pronger	7	1	3	4	8
Raffi Torres	7	1	3	4	4
Shawn Horcoff	7	2	0	2	4
Ryan Smyth	7	2	0	2	6
Michael Peca	7	1	1	2	2
Radek Dvorak	7	0	2	2	4
Steve Staios	7	0	2	2	8
Jarret Stoll	7	0	2	2	4
Dick Tarnstrom	5	0	2	2	6
Ethan Moreau	7	1	0	1	6
Sergei Samsonov	7	1	0	1	2
Matt Greene	7	0	1	1	14
Rem Murray	7	0	1	1	0
Marc-André Bergeron	2	0	0	0	2
Todd Harvey	3	0	0	0	0
Georges Laraque	4	0	0	0	17
Jason Smith	7	0	0	0	6

GOALTENDERS	GP	W	L	MIN	GA	SO	AVG
Dwayne Roloson	1	0	0	54	4	0	4.44
Ty Conklin	1	0	1	6	1	0	10.00
Jussi Markkanen	6	3	3	361	13	1	2.16

ROSTER

Craig Adams
Kevyn Adams
Anton Babchuk
Rod Brind'Amour (captain)
Erik Cole
Mike Commodore
Matt Cullen
Martin Gerber

Bret Hedican
Andrew Hutchinson
Frantisek Kaberle
Andrew Ladd
Chad LaRose
Mark Recchi
Eric Staal
Cory Stillman
Oleg Tverdovsky

Josef Vasicek
Niclas Wallin
Aaron Ward
Cam Ward
Doug Weight
Glen Wesley
Ray Whitney
Justin Williams

Jim Rutherford (president/general manager)
Peter Laviolette (head coach)

Rookies and Veterans

While Cam Ward became a Stanley Cup hero as a rookie, Carolina's victory marked the first championship for veterans Glen Wesley (18th season), Rod Brind'Amour (17th), Doug Weight (15th), Brett Hedican (14th) and Ray Whitney (14th).

Back in Business

The NHL promised changes after the lockout that wiped out the entire 2004–05 season. The new business model, with a salary cap (then set at $39 million), was going to make it possible for every team to compete financially off the ice, but there would be changes on the ice as well. Shootouts would be used in the regular season to settle games that were still tied after overtime so that there would always be a winner. Other rules were tinkered with to increase offense, and the NHL promised that referees would crack down on the obstruction that had been slowing down the game. Offense increased from 5.1 goals per game in 2003–04 to 6.1 in 2005–06, and five players topped 50 goals while seven had 100 points or more. Alex Ovechkin and Sidney Crosby led an impressive crop of rookies, but come the playoffs it was rookie goalie Cam Ward who would make the biggest difference of all.

The Carolina Hurricanes were surprise contenders for top spot in the NHL throughout the 2005–06 season. Though they had been Stanley Cup finalists as recently as 2002, Carolina had missed the playoffs in each of the next two seasons. The team still had nine players left from the 2002 squad, but it was 21-year-old Eric Staal who led the way with a 100-point season and goalie Martin Gerber who set a club record with 38 wins. Carolina battled Ottawa and Buffalo for top spot in the Eastern Conference, finishing second overall with 112 points but easily winning the Southeast Conference by a 20-point margin over Tampa Bay.

Carolina opened the playoffs against Montreal. With Martin Gerber struggling in the first two games, coach Peter Laviolette made the switch to Cam Ward, who would then see the bulk of the action the rest of the way through the postseason. In the final, the Hurricanes faced an Edmonton Oilers team that had barely squeaked into the playoffs but had upset the Presidents' Trophy winning Detroit Red Wings in the first round and then knocked off San Jose and Anaheim. Edmonton fell behind Carolina three games to one but rallied to force a seventh game before the Hurricanes finally won the Cup.

A Different World

The 2006 final between Carolina and Edmonton marked the first time that two former World Hockey Association teams played each other for the Stanley Cup. The Hurricanes had been the Hartford (formerly New England) Whalers when they entered the NHL with the Oilers, Winnipeg Jets and Quebec Nordiques from the WHA in 1979–80.

Penalty Shots Edmonton's Chris Pronger scored the first penalty-shot goal in Stanley Cup final history in Game 1. In Game 5, the Oilers' Fernando Pisani scored the first shorthanded overtime goal in Stanley Cup competition.

The Other Goalie Dwayne Roloson had played every minute in goal for the Oilers throughout the playoffs until he suffered a knee injury late in Game 1 of the Stanley Cup final. It knocked him out for the rest of the series. Jussi Markkanen hadn't played in three months and showed his rust in a 5–0 loss in Game 2 before recovering to help the Oilers push the Hurricanes to seven games.

Easy Come, Easy Go Both the Oilers and the Hurricanes failed to make the playoffs in 2006–07, marking the first time in NHL history that both teams that had played for the Stanley Cup missed the playoffs the very next year.

Cam Ward

Conn Smythe Story

Cam Ward joined Ken Dryden (1971), Patrick Roy (1986) and Ron Hextall (1987) as the fourth rookie goalie in history to win the Conn Smythe Trophy. Ward had been a star in both the Western Hockey League and the American Hockey League, and while his 14-8-2 record in 28 games as a backup to Martin Gerber during the 2005–06 regular season was good, his 3.68 average and .882 save percentage were among the worst in the NHL. But with Gerber battling an undisclosed stomach problem as the playoffs began, Ward got his chance. He won the first seven playoff games he started to tie an NHL mark set by Hall of Famer Tiny Thompson back in 1929 and 1930. Ward played in 23 of Carolina's 25 playoff games and was brilliant in posting a record of 15-8 with a 2.14 goals-against average and a .920 save percentage.

Nine Plus One The nine Carolina players who remained in the lineup from the 2002 team that had reached the final were Craig Adams, Kevyn Adams, Rod Brind'Amour, Erik Cole, Bret Hedican, Josef Vasicek, Niclas Wallin, Glen Wesley and Aaron Ward. Jeff Daniels, who'd been a member of the 2002 team, was a member of the coaching staff in 2006.

2004-05

SEASON NOT PLAYED

CAROL...
PETER KAR...
JASON KARMA...
KEVIN McCA...
SKIP CUNNIN...
CHRIS STEWART...
SHELDON FER...
BERT MARSHA...
ROD BRIND A...
KEVYN ADAMS
MIKE COMMOD...
ANDREW HUTC...
CHAD LA ROSE
JOSEF VASICE...
DOUG WEIGHT

Stanley Cup Trustees

Until the lockout, most hockey fans had been unaware that there were still two trustees in charge of the Stanley Cup. The position had been created back in the beginning, when Lord Stanley designated two men to create the rules that would govern Stanley Cup competition. Those men were Philip Dansken Ross, an Ottawa hockey executive and publisher of the *Ottawa Journal*, and John Sweetland, a medical doctor and sheriff of Carleton County. Ross in particular, and later William Foran, took a lead role in determining the rules that governed which teams were eligible to challenge for the Cup each year.

Over the years, as hockey evolved from an amateur pastime to a professional business, Ross and Foran ensured the Stanley Cup evolved with it. But when the NHL eventually emerged as hockey's top professional league in 1926–27, it seemed to take control of the Cup. Foran tried to accept the occasional outside challenge during the 1930s, but the NHL wanted no part of it. Finally, in 1947 Ross and new trustee Cooper Smeaton formally turned over control of the Cup to the NHL.

However, the NHL was not truly given the trophy outright. It was merely granted the right to determine the rules of the playoff competition. The NHL can return the Stanley Cup to the trustees at any time, and if the NHL should disband or be replaced as the game's top professional organization, control of the Cup would revert back to the trustees.

Locked Out

With the knowledge that the NHL's collective bargaining agreement would expire on September 15, 2004, a lockout by league owners had always been a possibility. A previous lockout 10 years before had wiped out nearly half of the 1994–95 season, and media reports had been speculating about another lockout for more than two years. The warning signs indicated that a new confrontation might be even longer and more drawn out than the last one.

Still, it was easy to ignore the impending deadline during the summer of 2004 as both fans and players prepared for the second World Cup of Hockey. World Cup training camps opened on August 19th, and the tournament stretched until September 14th, when Canada beat Finland in a thrilling one-game final. Just two days later, NHL commissioner Gary Bettman confirmed that the owners were indeed imposing a lockout on the players.

Bettman stated that NHL teams would not play again "until our economic problems have been solved." The NHL owners sought cost certainty; in essence, a league-wide cap on salary spending. The players' association would not accept a cap, instead preferring a "luxury tax" system that applied a surcharge to any team that spent over a set amount.

In December, the players offered a 24 percent rollback on salaries across the board and a modified entry-level salary system. The NHL countered with a revised rollback system but insisted that player salaries be tied to league revenue. With more and more NHL players choosing to play in Europe (some also accepted minor league jobs, though many continued to sit out), the league made a final offer in February. It included a salary cap of $42.5 million per team. It was hoped that a 28- or 30-game season might be salvaged, but when the NHLPA refused the offer, Bettman was forced to announce on February 16, 2005, that the NHL season was canceled.

Just a few days later, speculation that the players might accept a $45 million cap, and that Wayne Gretzky and Mario Lemieux were to take part in new talks, gave hope for a settlement, but there was to be no deal. The NHL became the first major professional sport to lose an entire season to a labor dispute, and the Stanley Cup would not be awarded for the first time since 1919, when the effects of a worldwide flu epidemic forced the cancellation of the final series.

Formal negotiations to end the lockout didn't resume until June and finally wrapped up on July 13th. The players' association ratified the deal on July 21st, with NHL owners approving it the following day. In the end, the players accepted a salary cap, which was pegged at $39 million per team for the 2005–06 season but would be recalculated each year based on a guarantee the players would receive 54 percent of annual NHL revenue.

STANLEY CUP TRUSTEES SINCE 1893

P.D. ROSS	▶ 1893 to 1948
JOHN SWEETLAND	▶ 1893 to 1907
WILLIAM FORAN	▶ 1907 to 1945
COOPER SMEATON	▶ 1946 to 1978
MERVYN "RED" DUTTON	▶ 1950 to 1987
CLARENCE CAMPBELL	▶ 1979 to 1984
WILLARD ESTEY	▶ 1984 to 2002
BRIAN O'NEILL	▶ 1988 to present
IAN "SCOTTY" MORRISON	▶ 2002 to present

P.D. Ross

Free Stanley!

During the lockout, and particularly after the 2004–05 season was canceled, the Hockey Hall of Fame received countless calls from fans offering ways to ensure the Stanley Cup might still be presented. People proposed such things as offering the Stanley Cup along with the Memorial Cup to the junior hockey champion or with the Allan Cup to the Canadian senior amateur champions. There were calls for college teams or the European leagues to get their shot. Adrienne Clarkson, Canada's governor-general at the time (the same job Lord Stanley had held when he donated the trophy) suggested the Cup be awarded to the top women's hockey team.

The NHL, fans argued, didn't really "own" the Stanley Cup. It had originally been donated to recognize the best hockey team in Canada. In Edmonton, a group called "Free Stanley" created a website to seek enough support to return the Stanley Cup to its original challenge cup roots. In Toronto, a couple of pickup hockey players took the NHL to court and actually won concessions that may allow other teams to play for the Cup if a season ever again gets canceled. (They also won a $100,000 donation from the NHL to grassroots hockey organizations in Canada.) However, despite all the hoopla, Stanley Cup trustees Brian O'Neill and Scotty Morrison announced that there would be no outside competition for the Stanley Cup in the spring of 2005.

Tampa Bay Lightning

CONFERENCE QUARTERFINAL
4 games to 1 over NY Islanders

CONFERENCE SEMIFINAL
4 games to 0 over Montreal

CONFERENCE FINAL
4 games to 3 over Philadelphia

ROSTER

CONN SMYTHE TROPHY **BRAD RICHARDS** C – TAMPA BAY

- Dmitry Afanasenkov
- Dave Andreychuk (captain)
- Dan Boyle
- Martin Cibak
- Ben Clymer
- Jassen Cullimore
- Chris Dingman
- Ruslan Fedotenko
- John Grahame
- Nikolai Khabibulin
- Pavel Kubina
- Vincent Lecavalier
- Brad Lukowich
- Fredrik Modin
- Stan Neckar
- Éric Perrin
- Nolan Pratt
- Brad Richards
- André Roy
- Darren Rumble
- Martin St-Louis
- Cory Sarich
- Cory Stillman
- Darryl Sydor
- Tim Taylor
- Jay Feaster (general manager)
- John Tortorella (head coach)

FINAL 4 GAMES TO 3

MAY 25	►	Calgary 4 at Tampa Bay 1
MAY 27	►	Calgary 1 at Tampa Bay 4
MAY 29	►	Tampa Bay 0 at Calgary 3
MAY 31	►	Tampa Bay 1 at Calgary 0
JUNE 3	►	Calgary 3 at Tampa Bay 2 OT
JUNE 5	►	Tampa Bay 3 at Calgary 2 2x OT
JUNE 7	►	Calgary 1 at Tampa Bay 2

PLAYOFF SCORING LEADER

Brad Richards	GP	G	A	PTS
TAMPA BAY	23	12	14	26

FINAL SERIES SCORING

TAMPA BAY	GP	G	A	PTS	PIM
Brad Richards	7	4	5	9	0
Martin St-Louis	7	4	2	6	2
Ruslan Fedotenko	6	3	1	4	4
Dave Andreychuk	7	0	4	4	4
Dan Boyle	7	1	2	3	4
Fredrik Modin	7	1	2	3	4
Vincent Lecavalier	7	0	3	3	9
Martin Cibak	4	0	1	1	0
Jassen Cullimore	7	0	1	1	4
Chris Dingman	7	0	1	1	24
Cory Stillman	6	0	1	1	7
Tim Taylor	7	0	1	1	2
Dmitry Afanasenkov	7	0	0	0	4
Ben Clymer	4	0	0	0	0
Pavel Kubina	6	0	0	0	12
Brad Lukowich	4	0	0	0	4
Nolan Pratt	7	0	0	0	2
André Roy	5	0	0	0	21
Cory Sarich	7	0	0	0	14
GOALTENDER	GP	W	L	MIN	GA	SO	AVG
Nikolai Khabibulin	7	4	3	455	14	1	1.85

CALGARY	GP	G	A	PTS	PIM
Jarome Iginla	7	3	2	5	5
Oleg Saprykin	7	2	1	3	6
Robin Regehr	7	0	3	3	4
Martin Gélinas	7	2	0	2	21
Craig Conroy	7	1	1	2	4
Shean Donovan	5	1	1	2	6
Ville Nieminen	6	1	1	2	17
Marcus Nilson	7	1	1	2	2
Chris Simon	7	1	1	2	21
Stéphane Yelle	7	1	1	2	4
Andrew Ference	7	0	2	2	13
Jordan Leopold	7	0	2	2	2
Chris Clark	7	1	0	1	8
Toni Lydman	3	0	1	1	0
Steve Montador	7	0	1	1	0
Mike Commodore	4	0	0	0	2
Dave Lowry	5	0	0	0	4
Chuck Kobasew	7	0	0	0	16
Krzysztof Oliwa	5	0	0	0	2
Rhett Warrener	7	0	0	0	2
GOALTENDER	GP	W	L	MIN	GA	SO	AVG
Miikka Kiprusoff	7	3	4	454	13	1	1.72

Brad Comes Up Big Of the 12 goals Brad Richards scored in the 2004 playoffs, seven of them were game winners, which broke the previous NHL record of six shared by Joe Sakic (Colorado, 1996) and Joe Nieuwendyk (Dallas, 1999). Tampa Bay was 9–0 in playoff games when Richards scored a goal.

Canadian Content The Calgary Flames were the first Canadian team to reach the Stanley Cup final in 10 years, dating back to the Vancouver Canucks in 1994. Both teams were beaten in seven games. The last Canadian team to win the Stanley Cup was the 1993 Montreal Canadiens.

Lightning Strikes

In their first 10 seasons after entering the NHL in 1992–93, the Tampa Bay Lightning had only made the playoffs once. They had missed the playoffs for six straight seasons when they finally enjoyed a breakthrough season in 2002–03. Vincent Lecavalier and Martin St-Louis tied for the team lead with 33 goals as Tampa Bay topped the Southeast Division with 93 points. The Lightning then rallied from a two-games-to-nothing deficit to beat Washington on a triple overtime goal by St-Louis in Game 6 for the first playoff series victory in franchise history. Tampa Bay was beaten by the eventual Stanley Cup champion New Jersey Devils in round two, but expectations had been raised for 2003–04.

The Lightning not only won the Southeast Division for the second year in a row in 2003–04, they topped the entire Eastern Conference with 106 points. Martin St-Louis led the NHL with 98 points, winning both the Art Ross Trophy and the Hart Trophy as MVP. Vincent Lecavalier led the team with 32 goals and displayed a defensive side to his game that had not been seen before. Brad Richards enjoyed a breakout season with 79 points and just 12 penalty minutes to win the Lady Byng Trophy.

In the playoffs, goalie Nikolai Khabibulin had three shutouts in the opening round as the Lightning downed the New York Islanders in five games. He posted another shutout in Game 1 of a four-game sweep of Montreal in round two. After a seven-game victory against Philadelphia in the Eastern Conference final, Tampa Bay advanced to meet the Calgary Flames for the Stanley Cup.

Led by Jarome Iginla (who tied for the league lead, with 41 goals) and Miikka Kiprusoff (whose 1.69 goals-against average was the NHL's lowest since 1939–40), Calgary was only the sixth seed in the Western Conference playoffs, but the Flames upset Vancouver, Detroit and San Jose to reach the final. Calgary's hot streak continued as they beat Tampa Bay 4–1 in Game 1 and jumped out to a 3–2 series lead. Martin St-Louis scored in double overtime to keep Tampa Bay alive in Game 6. In Game 7, Ruslan Fedotenko scored twice and Khabibulin had a big third period as the Lightning won the Cup with a 2–1 victory.

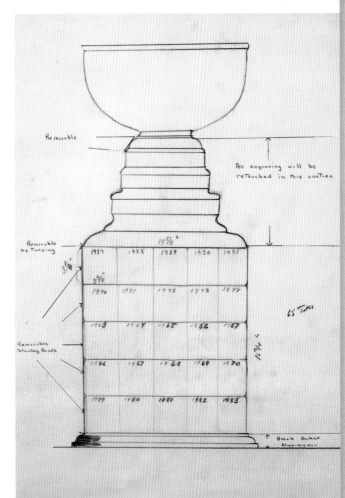

The Band's All Here

Back in 1958, the Stanley Cup was remodeled into the style and shape still in use today. It features a five-banded barrel that makes up the bottom section of the trophy. When all five bands were filled after the Pittsburgh Penguins won the Cup in 1991, the top band (featuring the teams and players that won the Cup from 1928 to 1940) was removed and retired to the Hockey Hall of Fame. The others bands slid up, and a new band was added to the bottom. That band was filled when Tampa Bay won the Cup in 2004.

The Red Mile

The Flames had not reached the playoffs since 1996 and had not won a playoff round since their Stanley Cup victory in 1989. Still, a 9-4-2 stretch over the final 15 games of the 2003–04 regular season had their fans feeling optimistic. During Calgary's first-round upset of Vancouver, fans began to celebrate victories along several blocks of 17th Avenue Southwest, not too far from the Saddledome. When Martin Gélinas scored in overtime to win the series in seven, fans flooded the street in a spontaneous party. As wins piled up against Detroit and San Jose, more and more fans sporting the Flames red colors flocked to the area that was dubbed "the Red Mile." By the time the Flames reached the Stanley Cup final against Tampa Bay, the party along the Red Mile had reached Mardi Gras–like proportions. But even with upward of 50,000 people crowding the area (there were estimates that 100,000 might show up if the Flames won Game 7 against the Lightning), the celebrations along the Red Mile remained remarkably peaceful.

Florida Attractions

Lightning Captain Dave Andreychuk and his family took the Stanley Cup to Disney World — a mere 90 miles or so from Tampa — for a parade down Main Street USA. General Manager Jay Feaster and team PR Director Jay Preble took the Cup to Cape Canaveral to see the space shuttle in preparation for a launch in March 2005.

CONFERENCE QUARTERFINAL	CONFERENCE SEMIFINAL	CONFERENCE FINAL
4 games to 1 over Boston	**4 games to 1 over Tampa Bay**	**4 games to 3 over Ottawa**

ROSTER

CONN SMYTHE TROPHY JEAN-SÉBASTIEN GIGUÈRE G – ANAHEIM

Tommy Albelin

Jiri Bicek

Martin Brodeur

Sergei Brylin

Ken Daneyko

Patrik Elias

Jeff Friesen

Brian Gionta

Scott Gomez

Jamie Langenbrunner

John Madden

Grant Marshall

Jim McKenzie

Scott Niedermayer

Joe Nieuwendyk

Jay Pandolfo

Brian Rafalski

Pascal Rhéaume

Mike Rupp

Corey Schwab

Richard Smehlik

Scott Stevens
(captain)

Turner Stevenson

Oleg Tverdovsky

Colin White

Lou Lamoriello
(CEO/president/
general manager)

Pat Burns
(head coach)

Pat Burns

Pat Burns was a policeman in Montreal and Hull, Quebec, who coached hockey in his spare time until he was hired by Wayne Gretzky in 1984 to coach the junior team Gretzky owned in Hull. In 1988, Burns entered the NHL as coach of the Montreal Canadiens. By the start of the 2002–03 season, he had won 412 games over 12 NHL seasons with Montreal, Toronto and Boston. Burns had won the Jack Adams Award as coach of the year a record three times — but the Devils victory in 2003 marked the first time he had won the Stanley Cup. Sadly, cancer would force Burns to step down as coach after the 2003–04 season and would claim his life in 2010.

FINAL 4 GAMES TO 3

MAY 27 ►	Anaheim 0 at New Jersey 3	
MAY 29 ►	Anaheim 0 at New Jersey 3	
MAY 31 ►	New Jersey 2 at Anaheim 3	OT
JUNE 2 ►	New Jersey 0 at Anaheim 1	OT
JUNE 5 ►	Anaheim 3 at New Jersey 6	
JUNE 7 ►	New Jersey 2 at Anaheim 5	
JUNE 9 ►	Anaheim 0 at New Jersey 3	

PLAYOFF SCORING LEADERS

	GP	G	A	PTS
Jamie Langenbrunner NEW JERSEY	24	11	7	18
Scott Niedermayer NEW JERSEY	24	2	16	18

FINAL SERIES SCORING

NEW JERSEY	GP	G	A	PTS	PIM
Patrik Elias	7	3	4	7	4
Brian Gionta	7	1	5	6	2
Jeff Friesen	7	5	0	5	0
Scott Gomez	7	2	3	5	0
Scott Niedermayer	7	0	5	5	4
Mike Rupp	4	1	3	4	0
Jamie Langenbrunner	7	2	1	3	6
Grant Marshall	7	2	1	3	4
Jay Pandolfo	7	2	1	3	0
Brian Rafalski	7	0	3	3	2
Sergei Brylin	7	0	2	2	2
Scott Stevens	7	0	2	2	2
Oleg Tverdovsky	6	0	2	2	0
Colin White	7	0	2	2	4
Pascal Rhéaume	7	1	0	1	2
John Madden	7	0	1	1	0
Turner Stevenson	3	0	1	1	10
Tommy Albelin	7	0	0	0	0
Jiri Bicek	4	0	0	0	0
Ken Daneyko	1	0	0	0	0
Jim McKenzie	3	0	0	0	4

GOALTENDERS	GP	W	L	MIN	GA	SO	AVG
Martin Brodeur	7	4	3	417	12	3	1.73
Corey Schwab	1	0	0	11	0	0	0.00

ANAHEIM	GP	G	A	PTS	PIM
Petr Sykora	7	2	3	5	4
Paul Kariya	7	1	3	4	2
Steve Rucchin	7	3	0	3	0
Sandis Ozolinsh	7	1	2	3	0
Adam Oates	7	0	3	3	4
Steve Thomas	7	2	0	2	4
Samuel Pahlsson	7	1	1	2	4
Keith Carney	7	0	2	2	6
Rob Niedermayer	7	0	2	2	4
Marc Chouinard	7	1	0	1	0
Ruslan Salei	7	1	0	1	8
Stanislav Chistov	7	0	1	1	2
Jean-Sébastien Giguère	7	0	1	1	0
Niclas Havelid	7	0	1	1	0
Mike Leclerc	7	0	1	1	8
Dan Bylsma	7	0	0	0	2
Jason Krog	7	0	0	0	2
Kurt Sauer	7	0	0	0	2
Vitaly Vishnevski	7	0	0	0	0

GOALTENDER	GP	W	L	MIN	GA	SO	AVG
Jean-Sébastien Giguère	7	3	4	427	19	1	2.67

The Devil You Know

Relying on an all-around team commitment to defense and backed up by the solid goaltending of Martin Brodeur, the New Jersey Devils topped the 100-point plateau for the seventh time in 10 seasons in 2002–03. They won the Atlantic Division title for the fifth time in seven years and were Stanley Cup champions for the third time in nine seasons.

Offensively, Patrik Elias led the Devils in scoring for the fourth straight season, but he had only 57 points. Elias (28), Jeff Friesen (23) and Jamie Langenbrunner (22) were the team's only 20-goal scorers, but with a defense led by captain Scott Stevens and featuring Scott Niedermayer, Brian Rafalski, Ken Daneyko and Colin White, New Jersey tied Philadelphia with a league-low 166 goals against. Brodeur, carrying his usual heavy workload, enjoyed his record-setting fourth 40-win season, topping the league for the fifth year in a row with 41. For the first time in his career, Brodeur was rewarded with the Vezina Trophy.

In the playoffs, New Jersey disposed of both Boston and Tampa Bay in five games before facing the Ottawa Senators in the Eastern Conference final. Ottawa had been the NHL's best team in the regular season with 52 wins and 113 points, and after years of playoff flops they appeared to be at the top of their game. The Senators beat the Devils 3–2 in overtime in Game 1 but then lost three in a row. They staved off elimination with a gritty 3–1 win in Game 5 then evened the series with a 2–1 overtime win in New Jersey. Back in Ottawa for Game 7, the Devils spoiled the party when Jeff Friesen scored with just 2:14 remaining to give New Jersey a 3–2 victory.

The Devils faced the Mighty Ducks of Anaheim for the Stanley Cup in a series that went seven games and marked the first time since 1965 that the home team won every game in the final. Martin Brodeur became just the third goalie in history to post three shutouts in the final, including the deciding game, and he set a new NHL record with seven shutouts in the postseason.

Stevens and Kariya

Perhaps the most memorable moment of the 2003 Stanley Cup final was a thunderous open-ice hit delivered by Devils captain Scott Stevens in Game 6. Stevens caught Ducks star Paul Kariya looking the other way after he'd dished off the puck just outside the New Jersey blue line. He laid out Kariya with what was, essentially, a clean hit at the time (though it would likely be considered targeting the head today). Kariya lay motionless on the ice for a short time before heading for the dressing room. He later returned to the game and scored a goal that helped the Ducks stay alive in the series with a 5–2 victory.

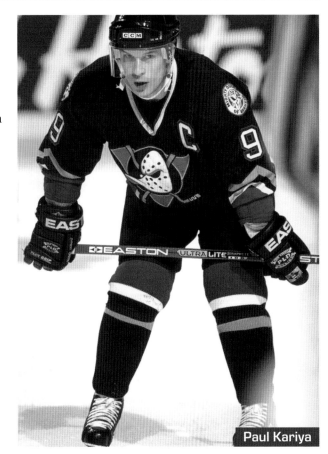

Paul Kariya

Giggy Over Brodeur?

Though his team came up a game short in the end, Jean-Sébastien Giguère enjoyed one of the most remarkable postseason performances of all time in 2003. It began in his very first game, on April 10th, when he led the Ducks to a 2–1 overtime win over Detroit and set a record (later broken by Roberto Luongo) for the most saves in a playoff debut, with 63. After a sweep of Detroit, Giguère stopped 60 of 63 shots against Dallas in a five-overtime game in the opener of the second round, and he sparked the Ducks to a six-game upset of the top-ranked team in the West. Facing the equally surprising Minnesota Wild in the Western Conference final, Giguère posted three straight shutouts to open the series, and he allowed just a single goal in Game 4 as the Ducks ran up another sweep. Even after Anaheim's seven-game loss to New Jersey and Martin Brodeur's record seven playoff shutouts, Giguère's 1.62 goals-against average was the best of the postseason. He became just the fifth player from a losing team to be rewarded with the Conn Smythe Trophy as playoff MVP.

Five of a Kind New Jersey's 2003 championship was the team's third, following victories in 1995 and 2000. Five players were members of all three Devils Stanley Cup teams: Martin Brodeur, Sergei Brylin, Ken Daneyko, Scott Niedermayer and Scott Stevens.

Detroit Red Wings

CONFERENCE QUARTERFINAL	CONFERENCE SEMIFINAL	CONFERENCE FINAL
4 games to 2 over Vancouver	**4 games to 1 over St. Louis**	**4 games to 3 over Colorado**

CONN SMYTHE TROPHY **NICKLAS LIDSTROM** D – DETROIT

FINAL 4 GAMES TO 1

JUNE 4 ▸	Carolina 3 at Detroit 2 OT
JUNE 6 ▸	Carolina 1 at Detroit 3
JUNE 8 ▸	Detroit 3 at Carolina 2 3X OT
JUNE 10 ▸	Detroit 3 at Carolina 0
JUNE 13 ▸	Carolina 1 at Detroit 3

PLAYOFF SCORING LEADER

Peter Forsberg	GP	G	A	PTS
COLORADO	20	9	18	27

FINAL SERIES SCORING

DETROIT	GP	G	A	PTS	PIM
Sergei Fedorov	5	1	4	5	6
Igor Larionov	5	3	1	4	4
Steve Yzerman	5	0	4	4	0
Brendan Shanahan	5	3	0	3	6
Brett Hull	5	2	1	3	2
Nicklas Lidstrom	5	1	2	3	2
Chris Chelios	5	0	3	3	4
Kirk Maltby	5	2	0	2	4
Kris Draper	5	1	1	2	4
Tomas Holmstrom	5	1	1	2	0
Fredrik Olausson	5	0	2	2	2
Boyd Devereaux	5	0	1	1	4
Steve Duchesne	5	0	1	1	8
Jiri Fischer	4	0	1	1	4
Darren McCarty	5	0	1	1	2
Luc Robitaille	5	0	1	1	4
Mathieu Dandenault	5	0	0	0	2
Pavel Datsyuk	5	0	0	0	0
Jiri Slegr	1	0	0	0	2

GOALTENDER	GP	W	L	MIN	GA	SO	AVG
Dominik Hasek	5	4	1	355	7	1	1.18

CAROLINA	GP	G	A	PTS	PIM
Jeff O'Neill	5	3	1	4	2
Ron Francis	5	1	2	3	0
Sean Hill	5	1	1	2	12
Sami Kapanen	5	0	2	2	0
Glen Wesley	5	0	2	2	4
Rod Brind'Amour	5	1	0	1	4
Josef Vasicek	5	1	0	1	4
Aaron Ward	5	1	0	1	4
Martin Glinas	5	0	1	1	4
Kevyn Adams	5	0	0	0	0
Erik Cole	5	0	0	0	10
Jeff Daniels	5	0	0	0	0
Bates Battaglia	5	0	0	0	4
Marek Malik	5	0	0	0	0
Bret Hedican	5	0	0	0	4
Jaroslav Svoboda	5	0	0	0	8
Niclas Wallin	5	0	0	0	2
Tommy Westlund	5	0	0	0	0

GOALTENDER	GP	W	L	MIN	GA	SO	AVG
Arturs Irbe	5	1	4	354	13	0	2.20

ROSTER

Chris Chelios	Tomas Holmstrom	Brendan Shanahan
Mathieu Dandenault	Brett Hull	Jiri Slegr
Pavel Datsyuk	Igor Larionov	Jason Williams
Boyd Devereaux	Manny Legace	Steve Yzerman (captain)
Kris Draper	Nicklas Lidstrom	Ken Holland (general manager)
Steve Duchesne	Kirk Maltby	
Sergei Fedorov	Darren McCarty	Scotty Bowman (head coach)
Jiri Fischer	Fredrik Olausson	
Dominik Hasek	Luc Robitaille	

The Dominator

Already a six-time winner of the Vezina Trophy as the NHL's best goalie (and a two-time winner of the Hart Trophy as MVP), Dominik Hasek added a Stanley Cup to his trophy case in 2002 to go along with the Olympic gold medal he had won in 1998. Hasek and Martin Brodeur are the only goalies to have won both the Stanley Cup and an Olympic gold medal.

Red Wings Reload

Though they had continued to rank among the NHL's best teams since their back-to-back Stanley Cup victories in 1997 and 1998, the Detroit Red Wings had endured three straight early playoff exits. Back-to-back losses to their archrivals from Colorado in 1999 and 2000 were bad enough, but a first-round loss to Los Angeles after a 111-point season in 2000–01 was shocking. Many thought it was time to rebuild, but the Red Wings chose to reload instead.

Through trades and free-agent signings, Detroit added Dominik Hasek, Brett Hull and Luc Robitaille to a lineup that already included aging stars Steve Yzerman, Chris Chelios and Igor Larionov, plus other veterans such as Brendan Shanahan, Sergei Fedorov and Nicklas Lidstrom. Injuries limited Yzerman to just 52 games, but Robitaille, Hull, Fedorov and Shanahan all enjoyed 30-goal seasons. Hasek won a league-leading 41 games as Detroit finished with 51 wins and 116 points to take the Presidents' Trophy for the first time since 1995–96.

Yzerman had seen little action for Detroit after the Olympics, during which he and Shanahan helped Canada win its first gold medal in men's hockey since 1952, but he returned to spark the Red Wings in the playoffs. After losing two straight games to Vancouver to open the postseason (no team in history had ever gone on to win the Stanley Cup after losing their first two playoff games at home, though Boston would do so in 2011), the Red Wings eliminated the Canucks with four straight wins and then downed St. Louis in five. Next up was Colorado, and after falling behind three games to two, the Red Wings rallied to take the bitterly fought series in seven.

In the East, the Carolina Hurricanes emerged as surprise contenders, knocking off New Jersey, Montreal and Toronto in six games apiece. They kept on winning, taking Game 1 of the Stanley Cup final, when Ron Francis scored 58 seconds into overtime for a 3–2 victory. Detroit took Game 2, and gained the series lead when Igor Larionov scored in triple overtime in Game 3. The Red Wings went on to score a five-game victory for their third Stanley Cup title in six years.

By the Dozen

In addition to his nine coaching victories, Scotty Bowman has his name on the Stanley Cup another three times in front office positions with Pittsburgh (1991), Detroit (2008) and Chicago (2010). Still, Bowman's 12 victories are five short of Jean Béliveau, who won the Cup 10 times as a player in Montreal and later got his name engraved seven more times as a member of the Canadiens' front office.

STANLEY CUP COACHING VICTORIES

9	Scotty Bowman, Montreal (1973, 1976, 1977, 1978, 1979), Pittsburgh (1992), Detroit (1997, 1998, 2002)
8	Toe Blake, Montreal (1956, 1957, 1958, 1959, 1960, 1965, 1966, 1968)
5	Hap Day, Toronto (1942, 1945, 1947, 1948, 1949)
4	Dick Irvin, Toronto (1932), Montreal (1944, 1946, 1953) Punch Imlach, Toronto (1962, 1963, 1964, 1967) Al Arbour, New York Islanders (1980, 1981, 1982, 1983) Glen Sather, Edmonton (1984, 1985, 1987, 1988)

Scotty Bowman

Conn Smythe Story

Nicklas Lidstrom entered the NHL in 1991–92 and finished as the runner-up to Pavel Bure for the Calder Trophy as rookie of the year. He would quickly establish himself as one of the best defensemen in the game, but individual awards were slow to follow. It would take until the 2000–01 season before Lidstrom would finally win the Norris Trophy (which he won six times since). In 2002, he became the first European player to win the Conn Smythe Trophy as playoff MVP. Lidstrom was brilliant throughout the playoffs, leading all defensemen with 16 points (five goals, 11 assists) in 23 games and averaging over 31 minutes of ice time per game. He scored the winning goal in Game 2 of the final and was on the ice for 52 minutes during Detroit's key triple-overtime victory in Game 3.

Sweet 16 The 16 years Chris Chelios waited to win the Stanley Cup again after his first victory with Montreal back in 1985–86 was the longest gap ever for an NHL player. For Steve Duchesne, the Cup win was the first of his 16-year career, and he retired after finally becoming a champion. Luc Robitaille was also in his 16th season and celebrated his first Stanley victory. Fredrik Olausson was in his 15th NHL season, but if he had not spent the 2000–01 campaign in Switzerland he would also have been in his 16th year.

Colorado Avalanche

CONFERENCE QUARTERFINAL	CONFERENCE SEMIFINAL	CONFERENCE FINAL
4 games to 0 over Vancouver	**4 games to 3 over Los Angeles**	**4 games to 1 over St. Louis**

ROSTER

CONN SMYTHE TROPHY **PATRICK ROY** G – COLORADO

David Aebischer
Rob Blake
Ray Bourque
Greg de Vries
Chris Dingman
Chris Drury
Adam Foote
Peter Forsberg
Milan Hejduk
Dan Hinote
Jon Klemm
Eric Messier
Bryan Muir
Ville Nieminen
Scott Parker
Shjon Podein
Nolan Pratt
Dave Reid
Steve Reinprecht
Patrick Roy
Joe Sakic (captain)
Martin Skoula
Alex Tanguay
Stéphane Yelle
Pierre Lacroix
(president/general
manager)
Bob Hartley
(head coach)

Mission 16W accomplished! Ray Bourque and Joe Sakic hoist the Cup.

Home and Home

With the New Jersey Devils having been the Colorado Rockies from 1976 to 1982, the 2001 Stanley Cup final was the first time that two teams were playing in a city (Denver) that was the previous home of one team and the current home of the other.

FINAL 4 GAMES TO 3

MAY 26	►	New Jersey 0 at Colorado 5
MAY 29	►	New Jersey 2 at Colorado 1
MAY 31	►	Colorado 3 at New Jersey 1
JUNE 2	►	Colorado 2 at New Jersey 3
JUNE 4	►	New Jersey 4 at Colorado 1
JUNE 7	►	Colorado 4 at New Jersey 0
JUNE 9	►	New Jersey 1 at Colorado 3

PLAYOFF SCORING LEADER

	GP	G	A	PTS
Joe Sakic COLORADO	21	13	13	26

FINAL SERIES SCORING

COLORADO	GP	G	A	PTS	PIM
Joe Sakic	7	4	5	9	2
Alex Tanguay	7	4	3	7	4
Rob Blake	7	2	3	5	4
Chris Drury	7	3	1	4	0
Adam Foote	7	1	3	4	16
Dan Hinote	7	1	3	4	11
Ville Nieminen	7	1	2	3	6
Martin Skoula	7	1	2	3	6
Milan Hejduk	7	0	3	3	0
Ray Bourque	7	1	1	2	2
Steve Reinprecht	7	1	1	2	0
Chris Dingman	7	0	2	2	10
Dave Reid	7	0	2	2	2
Eric Messier	7	0	1	1	6
Shjon Podein	7	0	1	1	6
Greg de Vries	7	0	0	0	6
Jon Klemm	7	0	0	0	2
Stéphane Yelle	7	0	0	0	4
GOALTENDER	GP	W	L	MIN	GA	SO	AVG
Patrick Roy	7	4	3	419	11	2	1.58

NEW JERSEY	GP	G	A	PTS	PIM
Patrik Elias	7	2	3	5	2
Petr Sykora	7	2	2	4	4
Alexander Mogilny	7	1	2	3	4
Brian Rafalski	7	0	3	3	0
Jason Arnott	6	1	1	2	4
Sergei Brylin	7	1	1	2	6
Bob Corkum	6	1	1	2	0
Scott Gomez	7	1	1	2	4
Turner Stevenson	7	1	1	2	6
Bobby Holik	7	0	2	2	6
Scott Niedermayer	7	0	2	2	8
John Madden	7	1	0	1	2
Jay Pandolfo	7	0	1	1	0
Ken Daneyko	7	0	0	0	13
Randy McKay	1	0	0	0	0
Jim McKenzie	1	0	0	0	2
Sergei Nemchinov	7	0	0	0	0
Sean O'Donnell	5	0	0	0	25
Scott Stevens	7	0	0	0	6
Ken Sutton	2	0	0	0	9
Colin White	7	0	0	0	14
GOALTENDER	GP	W	L	MIN	GA	SO	AVG
Martin Brodeur	7	3	4	416	19	0	2.74

Rocky Mountain High

The 2000–01 season was a milestone for three members of the Colorado Avalanche. On October 17, 2000, Patrick Roy recorded the 448th regular-season win of his career with a 4–3 overtime victory over the Washington Capitals and surpassed Terry Sawchuk for top spot on the all-time win list. Roy would go on to win a career-high 40 games in 2000–01 as the Avalanche won the Presidents' Trophy with a franchise record 52 wins and 118 points.

Joe Sakic also had a big year. He scored a career-high 54 goals and ranked second in league scoring to Pittsburgh's Jaromir Jagr with 118 points. Sakic would go on to join Mark Messier, Wayne Gretzky and Bobby Clarke as only the fourth man to captain his team to a Stanley Cup title and win the Hart Trophy in the same season. Sakic earned the MVP honor in his 13th season. No other player in NHL history has captured the award for the first time so late in his career.

Raymond Bourque capped off this season of great accomplishments in Colorado. After nearly 21 full seasons with the Boston Bruins, Bourque had agreed to be traded to the Avalanche late in 1999–2000 in an effort to win the Stanley Cup. He finally won it in the spring of 2001 and announced his retirement shortly thereafter. Bourque's first championship in the final season of his brilliant 22-year career was a fine finish to a campaign in which he had surpassed Paul Coffey as the top-scoring defenseman in NHL history.

Colorado's road to the Cup was not an easy one, despite a first round sweep of the Vancouver Canucks. It took the Avalanche seven games to knock off the surprising Los Angeles Kings in a tough series in which they lost Peter Forsberg to a ruptured spleen. A five-game victory over St. Louis in the Western Conference final set up a Stanley Cup date with the defending champion Devils. New Jersey was the top-ranked team in the Eastern Conference, and this Stanley Cup final marked the first time since 1989 that two number-one seeds would battle for the Cup. As could be expected it was a seesaw affair. After trailing three games to two, Roy kept the Avalanche alive with a 4–0 shutout in Game 6 and Colorado took the series in seven.

Mission 16W

The mission to get Ray Bourque the Stanley Cup had begun in September. It was just after Labor Day, captain Joe Sakic recalled, when "I told him we're going to win, and I wanted him to be the first to lift the Cup." After finishing first overall in the regular season, Mission 16W (for the 16 playoff wins needed to win the Stanley Cup) became Colorado's rallying cry in the postseason. Bourque was often seen wearing the slogan stitched onto a baseball cap. As the mission neared its successful conclusion, Bourque admitted, "I couldn't breathe for the last 30 seconds, and it wasn't because I was tired. I was trying to hold back the tears, the emotion."

True to his word, after Sakic received the Stanley Cup from NHL commissioner Gary Bettman, he immediately handed it off to Bourque. Avalanche coach Bob Hartley said the team held meetings to make sure Mission 16W didn't become a distraction. Even so, he admitted, "In our hearts and in our minds, we were playing for Ray."

Third Time's the Charm

Patrick Roy became the first (and, to date, only) three-time winner of the Conn Smythe Trophy when he was announced as playoff MVP in 2001. Roy had been the youngest Conn Smythe Trophy recipient when he won it as a 20-year-old rookie with Montreal back in 1986. His second win also came with the Canadiens, in 1993.

By the Numbers Ray Bourque had played 1,612 regular-season games plus 214 in the playoffs for a total of 1,826 games in his career by the time he won the Stanley Cup. No one has ever played more games before finally taking the title.

Not Even Born Alex Tanguay was the youngest member of the Avalanche in 2000–01. The second-year forward was just 21 years old. With a birth date of November 21, 1979, Tanguay was not even born when Ray Bourque played his first NHL game with the Boston Bruins, on October 11, 1979.

Super Six Six players who won the 2001 Stanley Cup with Colorado had been members of the team that won the Stanley Cup in 1996: Joe Sakic, Peter Forsberg, Jon Klemm, Stéphane Yelle, Patrick Roy and Adam Foote.

Patrick Roy

CONFERENCE QUARTERFINAL
4 games to 0 over Florida

CONFERENCE SEMIFINAL
4 games to 2 over Toronto

CONFERENCE FINAL
4 games to 3 over Philadelphia

CONN SMYTHE TROPHY **SCOTT STEVENS** D – NEW JERSEY

FINAL　4 GAMES TO 2

MAY 30	▶	Dallas 3 at New Jersey 7
JUNE 1	▶	Dallas 2 at New Jersey 1
JUNE 3	▶	New Jersey 2 at Dallas 1
JUNE 5	▶	New Jersey 3 at Dallas 1
JUNE 8	▶	Dallas 1 at New Jersey 0 3X OT
JUNE 10	▶	New Jersey 2 at Dallas 1 2X OT

PLAYOFF SCORING LEADER

	GP	G	A	PTS
Brett Hull DALLAS	23	11	13	24

FINAL SERIES SCORING

NEW JERSEY	GP	G	A	PTS	PIM
Jason Arnott	6	4	3	7	2
Petr Sykora	6	3	2	5	4
Patrik Elias	6	0	5	5	0
Brian Rafalski	6	1	3	4	4
Sergei Brylin	6	2	1	3	0
Scott Stevens	6	1	2	3	2
Ken Daneyko	6	1	1	2	4
John Madden	6	1	1	2	0
Alexander Mogilny	6	1	1	2	0
Jay Pandolfo	6	0	2	2	0
Scott Niedermayer	6	1	0	1	2
Scott Gomez	6	0	1	1	0
Bobby Holik	6	0	1	1	4
Claude Lemieux	6	0	1	1	4
Vladimir Malakhov	6	0	1	1	4
Randy McKay	6	0	1	1	2
Sergei Nemchinov	6	0	1	1	2
Colin White	6	0	1	1	4

GOALTENDER	GP	W	L	MIN	GA	SO	AVG
Martin Brodeur	6	4	2	434	9	0	1.24

DALLAS	GP	G	A	PTS	PIM
Brett Hull	6	2	2	4	2
Mike Modano	6	1	3	4	0
Jere Lehtinen	6	0	3	3	2
Mike Keane	6	1	1	2	2
Darryl Sydor	6	1	1	2	0
Guy Carbonneau	6	0	2	2	0
Sylvain Côté	6	1	0	1	2
Kirk Muller	6	1	0	1	0
Joe Nieuwendyk	6	1	0	1	0
Jon Sim	6	1	0	1	6
Richard Matvichuk	6	0	1	1	4
Scott Thornton	6	0	1	1	4
Aaron Gavey	1	0	0	0	0
Derian Hatcher	6	0	0	0	6
Jamie Langenbrunner	1	0	0	0	0
Roman Lyashenko	4	0	0	0	0
Dave Manson	6	0	0	0	6
Grant Marshall	3	0	0	0	0
Brenden Morrow	6	0	0	0	4
Blake Sloan	3	0	0	0	2
Sergei Zubov	6	0	0	0	0

GOALTENDERS	GP	W	L	MIN	GA	SO	AVG
Ed Belfour	6	2	4	416	14	1	2.02
Manny Fernandez	1	0	0	17	1	0	3.53

ROSTER

Jason Arnott
Brad Bombardir
Martin Brodeur ▲
Steve Brule
Sergei Brylin
Ken Daneyko
Patrik Elias
Scott Gomez
Bobby Holik

Steve Kelly
Claude Lemieux
John Madden
Vladimir Malakhov
Randy McKay
Alexander Mogilny
Sergei Nemchinov
Scott Niedermayer
Krzysztof Oliwa

Jay Pandolfo
Brian Rafalski
Scott Stevens (captain)
Ken Sutton
Petr Sykora
Chris Terreri
Colin White
Lou Lamoriello (president/general manager)

Larry Robinson (head coach)

Say What?

"Everyone says the first Cup is the most difficult — and it is, until you do it. But I say the second one is more difficult because you are expected to win every year."
— Lou Lamoriello

Dealing with the Devils

For the first time since the Edmonton Oilers defeated the New York Islanders in 1984 did the reigning Stanley Cup–champion return to the final, only to lose. Unfortunately for the 1999 champion Dallas Stars, they were unable to defend their title against a pugnacious crew from New Jersey.

The Devils offense was led by Patrik Elias, who topped the team with 35 goals and 72 points. The team also featured a 20-year-old rookie who was born in Alaska to a Mexican father and Colombian mother. Scott Gomez led all NHL freshmen with 70 points in 1999–2000 and would win the Calder Trophy just a few days after New Jersey won the Stanley Cup. As usual, though, it was goalie Martin Brodeur who was the Devils' biggest star, playing in 72 of the team's 82 games and leading the NHL with 43 wins. Still, New Jersey lost a tight battle with Philadelphia (105 points to 103) for top spot in both the Atlantic Division and the Eastern Conference and had to settle for the fourth seed in the playoffs, behind division leaders Washington and Toronto.

After sweeping the Florida Panthers in the opening round of the playoffs, the Devils eliminated the Maple Leafs in six games to set up a showdown with the Flyers in the Eastern Conference final. Philadelphia jumped out to a 3–1 series lead, but New Jersey rallied to win the series in seven. It was the first time since 1968 that a team had rallied from such a deficit to reach the Stanley Cup final.

Out West, the St. Louis Blues won the Presidents' Trophy for the first time in franchise history, but they were stunned by San Jose in the first round of the playoffs. Dallas defeated San Jose in the second round and then dismissed Colorado for the second straight year to reach the final.

New Jersey won the opener 7–3, but no other game in the series was decided by more than two goals. Dallas staved off elimination with a triple overtime victory in Game 5 only to see the Devils come out on top in Game 6 on a goal by Jason Arnott at 8:20 in double overtime.

Sykora's Sweater

Petr Sykora was knocked out of Game 6 when he took a hard hit from Dallas defenseman Derian Hatcher at 12:08 in the first period. Sykora was watching from his bed at the Baylor University Medical Center when linemate Jason Arnott scored the Cup-winning goal. Coach Larry Robinson wore Sykora's sweater on the ice after the game as a way to make him part of the celebration. Later, Arnott and Patrik Elias took the Stanley Cup to visit Sykora in the hospital.

Best of the Bunch Devils president and GM Lou Lamoriello made the unusual decision to replace coach Robbie Ftorek late in the regular season. Devils assistant coach Larry Robinson (who had spent four seasons as head coach of the Los Angeles Kings after an earlier stint as a Devils assistant) took over behind the bench with just eight games left to play. Robinson had won the Stanley Cup six times as a player in Montreal and once more as a Devils assistant in 1995, but he called the 2000 triumph his sweetest.

Jason Arnott

Arnott in Overtime

With a chance to wrap up the Stanley Cup on home ice in Game 5, New Jersey struggled through 106 minutes and 20 seconds of scoreless hockey. In the end, the Devils were beaten on a Mike Modano goal at 6:21 in triple overtime. (That goal broke the record for the longest 1–0 game in the history of the final, set by Colorado and Florida in 1996.) With the Stars still alive, the teams flew back to Dallas for Game 6, where they traded early second period goals before settling in for another long night.

Late in the first overtime period, Jason Arnott was called for cross-checking the Stars' Blake Sloan. It was the first penalty called since the second period, and the Devils killed it. Arnott made amends midway through the second overtime. After Scott Stevens kept the puck in at the Dallas blue line and threw it into the far corner, Arnott drifted toward the top of the crease to the right of Ed Belfour. He took a clever, no-look backhand pass from Patrik Elias and fired a quick shot past the sliding Dallas goaltender to give the Devils a 2–1 victory.

"A sudden-death goal for the Stanley Cup," said Arnott afterward. "It blows my mind."

CONFERENCE QUARTERFINAL	CONFERENCE SEMIFINAL	CONFERENCE FINAL
4 games to 0 over Edmonton	**4 games to 2 over St. Louis**	**4 games to 3 over Colorado**

ROSTER

CONN SMYTHE TROPHY **JOE NIEUWENDYK** C – DALLAS

Ed Belfour

Guy Carbonneau

Shawn Chambers

Derian Hatcher (captain)

Benoit Hogue

Tony Hrkac

Brett Hull

Mike Keane

Jamie Langenbrunner

Jere Lehtinen

Craig Ludwig

Grant Marshall

Richard Matvichuk

Mike Modano

Joe Nieuwendyk

Derek Plante

Dave Reid

Brent Severyn

Jon Sim

Brian Skrudland

Blake Sloan

Darryl Sydor

Roman Turek

Pat Verbeek

Sergei Zubov

Bob Gainey (vice president, hockey operations/ general manager)

Ken Hitchcock (head coach)

FINAL　4 GAMES TO 2

JUNE 8 ▶	Buffalo 3 at Dallas 2 OT
JUNE 10 ▶	Buffalo 2 at Dallas 4
JUNE 12 ▶	Dallas 2 at Buffalo 1
JUNE 15 ▶	Dallas 1 at Buffalo 2
JUNE 17 ▶	Buffalo 0 at Dallas 2
JUNE 19 ▶	Dallas 2 at Buffalo 1 3X OT

PLAYOFF SCORING LEADER

Peter Forsberg	GP	G	A	PTS
COLORADO	19	8	16	24

FINAL SERIES SCORING

DALLAS	GP	G	A	PTS	PIM
Mike Modano	6	0	7	7	8
Jere Lehtinen	6	2	3	5	0
Brett Hull	5	3	0	3	0
Joe Nieuwendyk	6	2	1	3	9
Jamie Langenbrunner	6	1	2	3	4
Sergei Zubov	6	0	3	3	2
Derian Hatcher	6	1	1	2	10
Craig Ludwig	6	1	1	2	10
Richard Matvichuk	6	0	2	2	6
Dave Reid	6	0	2	2	2
Darryl Sydor	6	1	0	1	8
Pat Verbeek	6	1	0	1	4
Shawn Chambers	6	0	1	1	2
Tony Hrkac	3	0	1	1	2
Mike Keane	6	0	1	1	0
Brian Skrudland	6	0	1	1	8
Guy Carbonneau	6	0	0	0	0
Benoit Hogue	2	0	0	0	2
Jon Sim	2	0	0	0	0
Blake Sloan	6	0	0	0	0

GOALTENDER	GP	W	L	MIN	GA	SO	AVG
Ed Belfour	6	4	2	429	9	1	1.26

BUFFALO	GP	G	A	PTS	PIM
Stu Barnes	6	3	0	3	0
Alexei Zhitnik	6	1	2	3	18
Richard Smehlik	6	0	3	3	2
Wayne Primeau	6	1	1	2	4
Jason Woolley	6	1	1	2	6
Michael Peca	6	1	0	1	2
Geoff Sanderson	6	1	0	1	4
Dixon Ward	6	1	0	1	8
Curtis Brown	6	0	1	1	2
Brian Holzinger	6	0	1	1	9
Joe Juneau	6	0	1	1	0
Miroslav Satan	6	0	1	1	2
Michal Grosek	1	0	0	0	0
Paul Kruse	1	0	0	0	0
Jay McKee	6	0	0	0	2
James Patrick	6	0	0	0	4
Erik Rasmussen	6	0	0	0	2
Rob Ray	1	0	0	0	0
Vaclav Varada	6	0	0	0	6
Rhett Warrener	5	0	0	0	6

GOALTENDER	GP	W	L	MIN	GA	SO	AVG
Dominik Hasek	6	2	4	428	12	0	1.68

Winning Beats Scoring

Brett Hull had only 58 points in 60 games for the Stars when he joined the team for the 1998–99 season. It was the lowest total of his career for any season in which he played at least 60 games. "It was hard for me when I came to Dallas, after being an offensive guy and scoring and scoring," Hull admitted. "Your numbers take a hit. But you can go home in the summer and get a pat on the back from your buddies on how great your season was. Or you can go home and get patted on the back and congratulations for winning the Cup."

The Stars Shine Bright

The 1998–99 regular season began with the NHL realigned into six geographic divisions instead of four. The season ended with the retirement of Wayne Gretzky, who played his last game on April 16, 1999, and left the game as far and away the leading scorer in NHL history. In between, there was a surprising battle between Toronto and Ottawa for top spot in the Northeast Division, as only the New Jersey Devils topped those two teams in the Eastern Conference standings. The best team in the NHL was out West, where the Dallas Stars topped the overall standings with a record of 51-19-12 for 114 points to win the President's Trophy for the second year in a row.

Dallas was defensively solid, with goalies Ed Belfour and Roman Turek winning the Jennings Trophy behind a blue line corps led by Derian Hatcher and Sergei Zubov. Mike Modano led an offense that included Joe Nieuwendyk and Brett Hull, who had just been acquired from St. Louis and was limited to 60 games due to injury. It had been five years since the NHL's best regular-season team had also been its playoff champion, but this year the Stars shone through.

Dallas swept the Edmonton Oilers to open the playoffs and then defeated the St. Louis Blues before taking on the Colorado Avalanche. The Avalanche had knocked off the two-time defending Stanley Cup champions from Detroit in the second round before facing Dallas and forcing the Stars to a seventh game, which the stars won 4–1. The Eastern Conference playoffs saw the Buffalo Sabres upset Ottawa before beating Boston and toppling Toronto to set up a Stanley Cup series with the Stars. The eventual winner of the Conn Smythe Trophy was Dallas' Joe Nieuwendyk, who paced all playoff performers with 11 goals (including six game-winners). Mike Modano's 18 assists were tops in the playoffs, while Ed Belfour provided stellar goaltending, outperforming Buffalo's Dominik Hasek in the Stanley Cup final after besting Colorado's Patrick Roy in the Western Conference final. For the first time since 1994, the final did not end in a sweep, as the series was a seesaw six-game battle. Brett Hull sealed the deal for the Stars after scoring a controversial goal in triple overtime of Game 6 in Buffalo.

Long Time Coming

Jon Sim had played only seven games during the regular season and four in the playoffs for Dallas in 1998–99. Still, Sim got to spend a day with the Stanley Cup in his hometown of New Glasgow, Nova Scotia. It was the Cup's first visit to the small town on Cape Breton Island, and it came some 93 years after the Montreal Wanderers defeated New Glasgow in a Stanley Cup challenge back in 1906.

Keeping the Faith A devout Catholic, Pat Verbeek brought the Stanley Cup to mass. "I figured it would be a regular mass, but little did I know that the Father had spread the word. When I got to the church it was packed and there were lots of kids there. The joy that was on the kids' faces was something that I will never forget."

Pat Verbeek

In the Crease

The clock was approaching 1:30 a.m. and Game 6 was nearing the 15-minute mark of the third overtime period when Jere Lehtinen fired a shot from the faceoff circle to the right of Dominik Hasek. Brett Hull had maneuvered, uncovered, toward the top of the crease and got his stick on the shot. Hasek was flat on the ice to make the save, and Hull proceeded ever so slightly into the blue ice of the crease to get the rebound. He played the puck ahead with his foot, and as his toe edged into the crease again, he slid the puck past Hasek at 14:51 for the Cup-winning goal.

All season long, goals like this had been called back for violation of the NHL's "in the crease" rule. The Sabres and their fans protested, but Dallas had been prepared. Near the end of the season, the NHL had sent out a memo clarifying the rule to say that a player could enter the crease if he already had clear possession of the puck. Stars GM Bob Gainey had repeatedly pointed out that, under league rules, playing a rebound still constituted possession of the puck. For that reason, Hull's goal was good.

Czech It Out Dallas Stars backup goalie Roman Turek was the first player to bring the Stanley Cup to the Czech Republic. More than 10,000 people turned out to see it in Ceska Budejovice.

Detroit Red Wings

CONFERENCE QUARTERFINAL
4 games to 2 over Phoenix

CONFERENCE SEMIFINAL
4 games to 2 over St. Louis

CONFERENCE FINAL
4 games to 2 over Dallas

CONN SMYTHE TROPHY **STEVE YZERMAN** C – DETROIT

FINAL **4 GAMES TO 0**

JUNE 9 ► Washington 1 at Detroit 2

JUNE 11 ► Washington 4 at Detroit 5 OT

JUNE 13 ► Detroit 2 at Washington 1

JUNE 16 ► Detroit 4 at Washington 1

PLAYOFF SCORING LEADER

	GP	G	A	PTS
Steve Yzerman DETROIT	22	6	18	24

FINAL SERIES SCORING

DETROIT	GP	G	A	PTS	PIM
Doug Brown	4	3	2	5	0
Tomas Holmstrom	4	1	4	5	2
Steve Yzerman	4	2	2	4	2
Martin Lapointe	4	2	1	3	6
Sergei Fedorov	4	1	2	3	0
Viacheslav Fetisov	4	0	3	3	2
Nicklas Lidstrom	4	1	1	2	2
Larry Murphy	4	1	1	2	0
Igor Larionov	4	0	2	2	4
Darren McCarty	4	0	2	2	2
Kris Draper	4	1	0	1	2
Joe Kocur	4	1	0	1	4
Anders Eriksson	4	0	1	1	4
Vyacheslav Kozlov	4	0	1	1	0
Bob Rouse	4	0	1	1	2
Brendan Shanahan	4	0	1	1	0
Jamie Macoun	4	0	0	0	0
Kirk Maltby	4	0	0	0	6

GOALTENDER	GP	W	L	MIN	GA	SO	AVG
Chris Osgood	4	4	0	254	7	0	1.65

WASHINGTON	GP	G	A	PTS	PIM
Joe Juneau	4	1	3	4	0
Brian Bellows	4	2	1	3	0
Adam Oates	4	1	2	3	0
Peter Bondra	4	1	1	2	4
Jeff Brown	2	0	2	2	0
Andrei Nikolishin	4	0	2	2	2
Chris Simon	4	1	0	1	6
Richard Zednik	4	1	0	1	4
Sergei Gonchar	4	0	1	1	4
Dale Hunter	4	0	1	1	2
Calle Johansson	4	0	1	1	2
Craig Berube	4	0	0	0	0
Mike Eagles	2	0	0	0	0
Phil Housley	4	0	0	0	2
Ken Klee	2	0	0	0	0
Todd Krygier	2	0	0	0	2
Kelly Miller	3	0	0	0	0
Joe Reekie	4	0	0	0	2
Esa Tikkanen	4	0	0	0	4
Mark Tinordi	4	0	0	0	6
Jeff Toms	1	0	0	0	0

GOALTENDER	GP	W	L	MIN	GA	SO	AVG
Olaf Kolzig	4	0	4	251	13	0	3.11

ROSTER

Doug Brown
Mathieu Dandenault
Kris Draper
Anders Eriksson
Sergei Fedorov
Viacheslav Fetisov
Brent Gilchrist
Kevin Hodson
Tomas Holmstrom

Mike Knuble
Joe Kocur
Vladimir Konstantinov
Vyacheslav Kozlov
Martin Lapointe
Igor Larionov
Nicklas Lidstrom
Jamie Macoun
Kirk Maltby

Darren McCarty
Dmitri Mironov
Larry Murphy
Chris Osgood
Bob Rouse
Brendan Shanahan
Aaron Ward
Steve Yzerman (captain)

Ken Holland
(general manager)
Scotty Bowman
(head coach)

In Tribute

The Red Wings included the names of Vladimir Konstantinov and Sergei Mnatsakanov on the Stanley Cup for the 1997–98 season.

Detroit Does It Again

Dedicating their efforts to teammate Vladimir Konstantinov and team masseur Sergei Mnatsakanov, who had suffered serious brain injuries in a limousine crash following the 1997 championship, the 1997–98 Detroit Red Wings became the first back-to-back Stanley Cup champions since the Pittsburgh Penguins in 1991 and 1992. It was a true team effort in Detroit, as the Red Wings' 250 goals during the regular season was the second-highest total in the NHL despite the fact that no Detroit player ranked among the NHL's top 20 scorers. With Sergei Fedorov missing most of the season in a contract dispute, Steve Yzerman led the team with just 69 points, while Brendan Shanahan's 28 goals was the lowest total to lead the Red Wings in 21 years.

The 1997–98 season marked the first time that the NHL allowed full participation of its players at the Winter Olympics. Many fans expected Canada and the United States to battle for the top spot in Nagano, but instead Dominik Hasek led the Czech Republic to the gold medal. Hasek would lead the NHL with 13 shutouts, winning the Vezina Trophy for the fourth of six times in his career and becoming the only goalie in history to win the Hart Trophy as MVP for a second straight season. In a playoff full of upsets in the Eastern Conference, Hasek led the Buffalo Sabres to the Eastern Conference final, where they were beaten by the Washington Capitals.

Detroit did not have a smooth ride through the playoffs, being forced to six games in each of their Western Conference series en route to the Stanley Cup final. In the Stanley Cup final versus Washington, Detroit took Game 1 by a 2–1 score and then fell behind 4–2 in the latter stages of Game 2. It appeared as though Washington was going to even the series. However, goals by Detroit's Martin Lapointe and Doug Brown sent the game into overtime, where Kris Draper won it for the Wings. Sergei Fedorov scored late in the third period of Game 3 to give Detroit a 2–1 victory and a 3–1 series lead. The Red Wings wrapped up the fourth consecutive sweep of the Stanley Cup final with a 4–1 victory in Game 4.

Osgood as It Gets

Chris Osgood never seemed to get a lot of respect. Though he quickly established himself among the NHL's top goalies after debuting with Detroit in 1993–94, he was relegated to backup duty behind Mike Vernon during the Red Wings' 1997 playoff run. When Vernon was traded during the off-season, Osgood regained the top spot, but the critics were on him once again when he gave up three long goals in the early rounds of the playoffs. With Olaf Kolzig having emerged as a star during the 1997–98 season, goaltending was seen as an advantage for Washington over Detroit in the Stanley Cup final, but Osgood rose to the occasion. He allowed just seven goals during Detroit's four-game sweep and stopped 92 of 99 shots for a .929 save percentage.

An Old Habit Trading away goalies after the Stanley Cup, as they had done with Mike Vernon in 1997, was nothing new for Detroit. After leading the Red Wings to victory in 1950, Harry Lumley was dealt to make room for Terry Sawchuk. Sawchuk had Cup wins in 1952, 1954 and 1955, but he was then traded to open a spot for Glenn Hall.

Chris Osgood

Believe

Vladimir Konstantinov had already been a star with Moscow's Central Red Army and the Soviet national team when he entered the NHL in 1991. He led the NHL with a plus-minus rating of plus-60 in 1995–96 and would be the runner-up to Brian Leetch for the Norris Trophy as the NHL's best defenseman in 1996–97.

On Friday June 13, 1997, six days after the Red Wings had won the Stanley Cup, Konstantinov went home from a team dinner with Viacheslav "Slava" Fetisov and team masseur Sergei Mnatsakanov. The driver of their limousine lost control and hit a tree. Fetisov suffered only minor injuries, but Konstantinov and Mnatsakanov lapsed into comas. Konstantinov emerged five weeks later, but he would never play hockey again. He spent the next year in rehabilitation, struggling to regain his basic motor skills.

During the 1997–98 season, the Red Wings wore a patch on their uniforms with the word "Believe" in English and Russian and the initials VK and SM. Konstantinov's jersey and equipment remained in his locker all season as inspiration. He was in the arena in a private box when Detroit repeated as Stanley Cup champions and was brought onto the ice in a wheelchair after the game, sporting a Red Wings jersey and hat. After captain Steve Yzerman accepted the Stanley Cup from NHL commissioner Gary Bettman, he placed it in Konstantinov's lap while teammates gathered around.

"A year ago, we were told these guys might not live," Yzerman said. Giving Konstantinov the Cup first "was the appropriate thing to do."

CONFERENCE QUARTERFINAL	CONFERENCE SEMIFINAL	CONFERENCE FINAL
4 games to 2 over St. Louis	**4 games to 0 over Anaheim**	**4 games to 2 over Colorado**

CONN SMYTHE TROPHY **MIKE VERNON** G – DETROIT

FINAL 4 GAMES TO 0

MAY 31 ▶	Detroit 4 at Philadelphia 2
JUNE 3 ▶	Detroit 4 at Philadelphia 2
JUNE 5 ▶	Philadelphia 1 at Detroit 6
JUNE 7 ▶	Philadelphia 1 at Detroit 2

PLAYOFF SCORING LEADER

		GP	G	A	PTS
Eric Lindros	PHILADELPHIA	19	12	14	26

FINAL SERIES SCORING

DETROIT	GP	G	A	PTS	PIM
Sergei Fedorov	4	3	3	6	2
Brendan Shanahan	4	3	1	4	0
Steve Yzerman	4	3	1	4	0
Martin Lapointe	4	2	1	3	6
Kirk Maltby	4	2	1	3	2
Darren McCarty	4	1	2	3	4
Larry Murphy	4	0	3	3	0
Joe Kocur	4	1	1	2	2
Viacheslav Fetisov	4	0	2	2	10
Vyacheslav Kozlov	4	0	2	2	0
Nicklas Lidstrom	4	1	0	1	0
Doug Brown	4	0	1	1	2
Kris Draper	4	0	1	1	2
Tomas Sandstrom	4	0	1	1	4
Vladimir Konstantinov	4	0	0	0	2
Igor Larionov	4	0	0	0	4
Bob Rouse	4	0	0	0	0
Aaron Ward	4	0	0	0	0

GOALTENDER	GP	W	L	MIN	GA	SO	AVG
Mike Vernon	4	4	0	240	6	0	1.50

PHILADELPHIA	GP	G	A	PTS	PIM
Rod Brind'Amour	4	3	1	4	0
John LeClair	4	2	1	3	4
Eric Lindros	4	1	2	3	8
Janne Niinimaa	4	0	3	3	0
Eric Desjardins	4	0	2	2	2
Mikael Renberg	4	0	1	1	0
Paul Coffey	2	0	0	0	6
John Druce	4	0	0	0	0
Karl Dykhuis	3	0	0	0	2
Pat Falloon	3	0	0	0	2
Colin Forbes	3	0	0	0	0
Dale Hawerchuk	3	0	0	0	0
Trent Klatt	4	0	0	0	6
Dan Kordic	1	0	0	0	0
Daniel Lacroix	2	0	0	0	2
Joel Otto	4	0	0	0	0
Michel Petit	2	0	0	0	2
Shjon Podein	4	0	0	0	0
Kjell Samuelsson	4	0	0	0	2
Petr Svoboda	1	0	0	0	2
Chris Therien	4	0	0	0	0
Dainius Zubrus	4	0	0	0	0

GOALTENDERS	GP	W	L	MIN	GA	SO	AVG
Ron Hextall	3	0	3	178	12	0	4.04
Garth Snow	1	0	1	58	4	0	4.11

Lucky Charm

Joe Kocur was a member of the New York Rangers when they ended their 54-year Stanley Cup drought in 1994. He then played for the Red Wings when they won their first Stanley Cup in 42 years in 1997.

ROSTER

Doug Brown
Mathieu Dandenault
Kris Draper
Sergei Fedorov
Viacheslav Fetisov
Kevin Hodson
Tomas Holmstrom
Joe Kocur
Vladimir Konstantinov

Vyacheslav Kozlov
Martin Lapointe
Igor Larionov
Nicklas Lidstrom
Kirk Maltby
Darren McCarty
Larry Murphy
Chris Osgood
Jamie Pushor

Bob Rouse
Tomas Sandstrom
Brendan Shanahan
Tim Taylor
Mike Vernon
Aaron Ward
Steve Yzerman (captain)
Jim Devellano (senior vice president)

Ken Holland (assistant general manager)
Scotty Bowman (head coach/director of player personnel)

The First Since 1955

The 1996–97 season marked the 42nd year of the Detroit Red Wings Stanley Cup drought, the longest such drought since the New York Rangers had won the Cup in 1994, ending their 54-year quest to recapture hockey's greatest prize. Detroit had a chance to end their drought in the 1994–95 season, but they were swept by New Jersey in that year's Stanley Cup final.

Following the sweep, the Red Wings set an NHL record in 1995–96 with 62 regular season wins, going 62-13-7 for 131 points (the second-highest total in history behind the 132 of the 1976–77 Montreal Canadiens). Even so, a bitter defeat by the Colorado Avalanche in the Western Conference final convinced coach Scotty Bowman that changes were necessary. Several players were shipped out and among those brought in was Brendan Shanahan, who would be the team's top point-getter during the regular season and top goal-scorer during the playoffs.

Shanahan was just one of many stars to change locations in 1996–97, as Jeremy Roenick, Paul Coffey, Adam Oates, Bill Ranford, Ed Belfour and Doug Gilmour were all traded and Wayne Gretzky signed as a free agent with the New York Rangers. Mario Lemieux staged a farewell tour in Pittsburgh, retiring at season's end at the age of 31. Lemieux won the Art Ross Trophy for a sixth time with 122 points, but defensive hockey continued to dominate the game for the next decade, as terms like "neutral zone trap," "left wing lock" and "obstruction" entered the hockey lexicon.

The Red Wings slipped to 43 wins and 93 points in 1996–97. They had some difficulty against St. Louis in the opening round of the playoffs before sweeping the Mighty Ducks of Anaheim to set up a rematch with Colorado in the Western Conference final. After three close games, Detroit erupted for a 6–0 victory in Game 4 only to be beaten 6–0 in Game 5. Brendan Shanahan then scored an empty-net goal to clinch the series for Detroit with a 3–1 win in Game 6.

Eric Lindros and the Philadelphia Flyers had knocked off Gretzky and the Rangers to reach the Stanley Cup final, but they would only play with a lead for two minutes during the entire series as Detroit swept them to take the title.

Long Wait

Jimmy Devellano's scouting for the New York Islanders had helped them win four straight Stanley Cup titles from 1980 to 1983. He became general manager of the Red Wings in 1982–83 and promised to deliver a Cup to Detroit. "I said we'd get it here," said Devellano, who was now the team's senior vice president. "It took us a long time, but we got it here."

End of an Era In 1996–97, the Boston Bruins missed the playoffs for the first time in 30 seasons, ending what was then the longest consecutive playoff streak ever recorded in the history of North American professional sports. Only the Edmonton Eskimos of the Canadian Football League (34 years, from to 1972 to 2005) have enjoyed a longer streak.

MOST GAMES WON BY A COACH IN THE STANLEY CUP FINALS

36	Scotty Bowman: Montreal (20), Pittsburgh (4), Detroit (12)
34	Toe Blake: Montreal
32	Dick Irvin: Chicago (2), Toronto (9), Montreal (21)
20	Hap Day: Toronto
17	Punch Imlach: Toronto
	Al Arbour: New York Islanders

Toe Blake

Long Season

Seven members of the Detroit Red Wings who won the Stanley Cup in June 1997 had been active since August 1996, when they had gone to training camp for the inaugural World Cup of Hockey. Canada's Steve Yzerman, Russia's Vyacheslav Kozlov, Igor Larionov, Sergei Fedorov and Viacheslav Fetisov and Sweden's Nicklas Lidstrom and Tomas Holmstrom had all participated in the late-summer tournament. Red Wings assistant coach Barry Smith had also worked with the Swedes, while trainer John Wharton had served with the Russians.

Howe About That

The Howe name has been engraved on the Stanley Cup every time the Red Wings have won it. Syd Howe (no relation to Gordie) was the NHL's all-time scoring leader for a brief time in the 1940s and was a member of the Red Wings the first three times they won the Cup, in 1936, 1937 and 1943. Gordie Howe won it in 1950, 1952, 1954 and 1955. There has been no Howe in the lineup for Detroit's Stanley Cup wins since 1997, but Gordie's son Mark Howe has had his name included as part of the team's scouting department.

Winning Isn't Everything, But...

"The majority of this team played in the Stanley Cup final two years ago," said captain Steve Yzerman of Detroit's loss to New Jersey in 1995. "You realize that finishing second means absolutely nothing."

Colorado Avalanche

CONFERENCE QUARTERFINAL
4 games to 2 over Vancouver

CONFERENCE SEMIFINAL
4 games to 2 over Chicago

CONFERENCE FINAL
4 games to 2 over Detroit

CONN SMYTHE TROPHY **JOE SAKIC** C – COLORADO

FINAL 4 GAMES TO 0

JUNE 4	▸ Florida 1 at Colorado 3
JUNE 6	▸ Florida 1 at Colorado 8
JUNE 8	▸ Colorado 3 at Florida 2
JUNE 10	▸ Colorado 1 at Florida 0 3X OT

PLAYOFF SCORING LEADER

	GP	G	A	PTS
Joe Sakic COLORADO	22	18	16	34

FINAL SERIES SCORING

COLORADO	GP	G	A	PTS	PIM
Peter Forsberg	4	3	2	5	0
Joe Sakic	4	1	4	5	2
Adam Deadmarsh	4	0	4	4	4
René Corbet	4	2	1	3	0
Uwe Krupp	4	2	1	3	2
Valeri Kamensky	4	1	2	3	8
Jon Klemm	4	2	0	2	0
Mike Keane	4	1	1	2	0
Scott Young	4	1	1	2	0
Alexei Gusarov	4	0	2	2	2
Sandis Ozolinsh	4	0	2	2	4
Claude Lemieux	2	1	0	1	4
Mike Ricci	4	1	0	1	6
Adam Foote	4	0	1	1	4
Sylvain Lefebvre	4	0	1	1	2
Curtis Leschyshyn	4	0	1	1	4
Dave Hannan	3	0	0	0	0
Warren Rychel	3	0	0	0	19

GOALTENDER	GP	W	L	MIN	GA	SO	AVG
Patrick Roy	4	4	0	285	4	1	0.84

FLORIDA	GP	G	A	PTS	PIM
Ed Jovanovski	4	0	2	2	11
Stu Barnes	4	1	0	1	2
Tom Fitzgerald	4	1	0	1	0
Rob Niedermayer	4	1	0	1	2
Ray Sheppard	4	1	0	1	0
Johan Garpenlov	4	0	1	1	2
Bill Lindsay	4	0	1	1	4
Dave Lowry	4	0	1	1	2
Scott Mellanby	4	0	1	1	4
Martin Straka	4	0	1	1	0
Terry Carkner	4	0	0	0	4
Radek Dvorak	1	0	0	0	0
Mike Hough	4	0	0	0	0
Jody Hull	2	0	0	0	0
Paul Laus	4	0	0	0	2
Gord Murphy	4	0	0	0	0
Brian Skrudland	4	0	0	0	4
Robert Svehla	4	0	0	0	2
Rhett Warrener	3	0	0	0	0
Jason Woolley	2	0	0	0	0

GOALTENDERS	GP	W	L	MIN	GA	SO	AVG
John Vanbiesbrouck	4	0	4	245	11	0	2.69
Mark Fitzpatrick	1	0	0	40	4	0	6.00

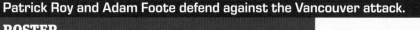

Patrick Roy and Adam Foote defend against the Vancouver attack.

ROSTER

René Corbet
Adam Deadmarsh
Stéphane Fiset
Adam Foote
Peter Forsberg
Alexei Gusarov
Dave Hannan
Valeri Kamensky
Mike Keane
Jon Klemm

Uwe Krupp
Sylvain Lefebvre
Claude Lemieux
Curtis Leschyshyn
Troy Murray
Sandis Ozolinsh
Mike Ricci
Patrick Roy
Warren Rychel
Joe Sakic (captain)

Chris Simon
Craig Wolanin
Stéphane Yelle
Scott Young
Pierre Lacroix (executive vice president/general manager)
Marc Crawford (head coach)

Overseas Adventures

While the German-born Uwe Krupp shared his day with the Stanley Cup with his sled dogs in Colorado, teammate Peter Forsberg became the first player to take the Stanley Cup to Europe when he brought it to his home in Ornskoldsvik, Sweden.

Road to the Stanley Cup

NHL hockey first came to Denver in the summer of 1976, when the Kansas City Scouts became the Colorado Rockies. Unlike most other NHL expansion cities, Denver lacked a long and successful minor league pedigree. There had been only a handful of teams over the years, and most barely lasted more than a season or two—including the Denver Spurs, who survived only a few months during the 1975–76 season of the World Hockey Association. The Rockies fared little better than the others, surviving for six mostly dreadful seasons in Denver before becoming the New Jersey Devils in 1982. The return of NHL hockey to the Rocky Mountain State for the 1995–96 season would be much more successful

In May of 1995, COMSAT Entertainment Group, who owned the Denver Nuggets of the National Basketball Association, purchased the Quebec Nordiques. The NHL approved the sale on June 21, and the team became the Colorado Avalanche. Five straight non-playoff seasons in Quebec, from 1987–88 to 1991–92, had seen the Nordiques load up on talented draft picks such as Joe Sakic, Valery Kamensky and Adam Foote as well as

others who had been traded to obtain the likes of Claude Lemieux, Sandis Ozolinsh and Peter Forsberg. The team that moved to Denver for the 1995–96 season had been one of the NHL's best when it was in Quebec City in 1994–95. The already good club was bolstered with the addition of Patrick Roy on December 6, 1995, after he asked to be traded from Montreal.

Already a 100-point scorer three times in the seven previous seasons, Joe Sakic established a career high with 120 points (51 goals, 69 assists) to finish third in scoring behind Mario Lemieux and Jaromir Jagr of Pittsburgh. A year after winning the Calder Trophy as Rookie of the Year while in Quebec, Peter Forsberg collected 116 points (30 goals, 86 assists) to rank fifth in the NHL. Colorado finished the season with a 47-25-10 record and 104 points, and though they were a long way back of Detroit's record-setting 62 wins and 131 points, the Avalanche knocked off the Red Wings in a vicious Western Conference final before going on to sweep the upstart Florida Panthers to win the Stanley Cup on a goal by Uwe Krupp in triple overtime.

Of Rats and Panthers

The Florida Panthers entered the NHL in 1993–94 and nearly made the playoffs that year after one of the most successful expansion seasons in modern pro sports. Still, no one expected them to reach the Stanley Cup final in their third season. The Panthers were still a typical expansion team, featuring young hopefuls like Rob Niedermayer and Ed Jovanovski along with veteran grinders such as Tom Fitzgerald and Brian Skrudland. Their biggest star was goalie John Vanbiesbrouck. Yet the team had no real identity. This would all change after an incident on October 8, 1995, when Scott Mellanby used his stick to kill a rat in the dressing room at the Miami Arena. That night, Mellanby scored two goals in a 4–3 win over the Calgary Flames, and his teammates kidded him about scoring a "Rat Trick." Soon, Florida fans were throwing rubber rats on the ice whenever anyone on the team scored a goal. It was a craze that gained international attention as the Panthers went deeper and deeper into the playoffs. After the 1995–96 season the NHL instituted a ban on throwing rats on the ice after goals, but in the 2011–12 season, the rats made their way back to the ice during postgame celebrations.

Krupp Wins the Cup

Uwe Krupp was a 10-year NHL veteran in 1995–96. At 6-foot-6 and 235 pounds, he was one of the biggest men in the league and one of just two German-born players. He was a solid defenseman who had scored a career-high 12 goals with the Buffalo Sabres in 1990–91, and he seemed an unlikely candidate to end the longest 1–0 game in the history of the Stanley Cup final. That Krupp was even on the ice at all for the Avalanche was something of a medical miracle. Back on October 6, 1995, in the first game of the season, the big defenseman had suffered a serious knee injury. "The doctors said, 'You've basically blown out anything that there is in your knee,'" Krupp recalled. "My ACL was torn. My MCL was torn. My posterior capsule was blown away. My meniscus was shredded. There wasn't that much left in there." Rehab was supposed to take 10 to 12 months, but working out at home in the snow with his team of sled dogs, Krupp was ready in six. He returned to action on April 6 and played the final five games of the regular season. He played all 22 games for Colorado in the playoffs, notching his improbable marker at 4:31 of the third overtime period in Game 4.

The First... and Only

The 1996 series between the Avalanche and Panthers marked the first time in NHL history that both teams involved were making their first appearance in the final. To date, this is still the only time in league history this has happened.

New Jersey Devils

CONFERENCE QUARTERFINAL
4 games to 1 over Boston

CONFERENCE SEMIFINAL
4 games to 1 over Pittsburgh

CONFERENCE FINAL
4 games to 2 over Philadelphia

CONN SMYTHE TROPHY CLAUDE LEMIEUX RW – NEW JERSEY

FINAL   4 GAMES TO 0

JUNE 17 ►	New Jersey 2 at Detroit 1
JUNE 20 ►	New Jersey 4 at Detroit 2
JUNE 22 ►	Detroit 2 at New Jersey 5
JUNE 24 ►	Detroit 2 at New Jersey 5

PLAYOFF SCORING LEADER

Sergei Fedorov	GP	G	A	PTS
DETROIT	17	7	17	24

FINAL SERIES SCORING

NEW JERSEY	GP	G	A	PTS	PIM
Neal Broten	4	3	3	6	4
John MacLean	4	1	4	5	0
Stéphane Richer	4	2	2	4	0
Scott Niedermayer	4	1	3	4	0
Bill Guerin	4	0	4	4	12
Shawn Chambers	4	2	1	3	0
Bruce Driver	4	1	2	3	0
Claude Lemieux	4	2	0	2	4
Sergei Brylin	3	1	1	2	4
Jim Dowd	1	1	1	2	2
Bobby Holik	4	1	1	2	8
Tommy Albelin	4	0	2	2	2
Tom Chorske	3	0	2	2	0
Scott Stevens	4	0	2	2	4
Randy McKay	4	1	0	1	0
Bob Carpenter	4	0	1	1	2
Brian Rolston	2	0	1	1	0
Ken Daneyko	4	0	0	0	6
Mike Peluso	4	0	0	0	4
Valeri Zelepukin	3	0	0	0	4

GOALTENDER	GP	W	L	MIN	GA	SO	AVG
Martin Brodeur	4	4	0	206	7	0	1.75

DETROIT	GP	G	A	PTS	PIM
Sergei Fedorov	4	3	2	5	0
Doug Brown	4	0	3	3	2
Viacheslav Fetisov	4	0	3	3	0
Dino Ciccarelli	4	1	1	2	6
Paul Coffey	4	1	1	2	0
Nicklas Lidstrom	4	0	2	2	0
Vyacheslav Kozlov	4	1	0	1	0
Steve Yzerman	4	1	0	1	0
Martin Lapointe	2	0	1	1	8
Ray Sheppard	3	0	1	1	0
Shawn Burr	2	0	0	0	0
Kris Draper	4	0	0	0	4
Bob Errey	4	0	0	0	4
Stu Grimson	2	0	0	0	2
Mark Howe	2	0	0	0	0
Vladimir Konstantinov	4	0	0	0	8
Mike Krushelnyski	2	0	0	0	0
Darren McCarty	4	0	0	0	4
Keith Primeau	3	0	0	0	8
Mike Ramsey	2	0	0	0	0
Bob Rouse	4	0	0	0	0
Tim Taylor	2	0	0	0	2

GOALTENDERS	GP	W	L	MIN	GA	SO	AVG
Mike Vernon	4	0	4	240	14	0	4.08
Chris Osgood	1	0	0	32	1	0	1.88

ROSTER

Tommy Albelin
Martin Brodeur
Neal Broten
Sergei Brylin
Bob Carpenter
Shawn Chambers
Tom Chorske
Danton Cole
Ken Daneyko

Kevin Dean
Jim Dowd
Bruce Driver
Bill Guerin
Bobby Holik
Claude Lemieux
John MacLean
Chris McAlpine
Randy McKay

Scott Niedermayer ▲
Mike Peluso
Stéphane Richer
Brian Rolston
Scott Stevens (captain)
Chris Terreri
Valeri Zelepukin

Jacques Lemaire (head coach)
Lou Lamoriello (president/general manager)

Winning When It Matters Most

With a record of 22-18-8 for 52 points in 48 games in 1994–95, New Jersey's regular-season winning percentage of .542 was the lowest for a Stanley Cup champion since Toronto went 32-27-11 for 75 points in 70 games (.536) in 1966–67.

The Devils Get It Done

They had been an NHL laughingstock for years. Whether it was in Kansas City, where the franchise spent its first two seasons, Colorado, where they spent the next six, or New Jersey, where they moved to in 1982–83, the team missed the playoffs for 12 of its first 13 years. They failed to qualify for nine straight seasons, from 1978–79 through 1986–87. In 1983, Wayne Gretzky mocked them as a "Mickey Mouse operation" after a 13–4 Edmonton Oilers romp.

Things finally began to look up for the New Jersey Devils when Lou Lamoriello added the role of general manager to his duties as president before the 1987–88 season. A new era truly dawned on June 28, 1993, when Lamoriello named Jacques Lemaire, a member of eight Stanley Cup–winning Montreal Canadiens teams, as head coach. Former Montreal star Larry Robinson also came on board as assistant coach. Lemaire introduced a defensive system that would become known as the neutral zone trap, and the results were remarkable. The Devils would enjoy their first 100-point season in 1993–94 and push the New York Rangers to double overtime in the seventh game of a thrilling Eastern Conference final. The Devils struggled though a 1994–95 regular season that was shortened to 48 games by a lockout, but they hit their stride in the playoffs. New Jersey upset Boston, Pittsburgh and Philadelphia while losing only four games in three rounds.

Few gave the Devils much of a chance in the Stanley Cup final against a Detroit team that had been the NHL's best during the regular season. The Red Wings were 8–0 at home in the playoffs and had outscored their opponents 30–11 at the Joe Louis Arena. Still, New Jersey took the opener 2–1 on goals by Stéphane Richer and Claude Lemieux and won Game 2 4–2. Back at home in Game 3, the Devils jumped out to a 5–0 lead en route to a 5–2 victory and then wrapped up the series when Neal Broten scored twice in Game 4 to spark another 5–2 win. New Jersey's Claude Lemieux, who scored only six times in the regular season, erupted for 13 goals in the playoffs and won the Conn Smythe Trophy.

Four of a Kind

Four players in NHL history have scored a Stanley Cup–winning goal and coached a team to the Stanley Cup:

PLAYER	COACHED	SCORED
Jacques Lemaire	New Jersey, 1995	Montreal, 1977, 1979
Toe Blake	Montreal, 1956, 1957, 1958, 1959, 1960, 1965, 1966, 1968	Montreal, 1944, 1946
Cy Denneny	Boston, 1941	Ottawa, 1927
Frank Boucher	New York Rangers, 1940	New York Rangers, 1928

Who Cares? Detroit fans didn't give the Devils too much credit as the Stanley Cup final began. When the series opened at the Joe Louis Arena and the New Jersey players were being introduced, a capacity crowd of 19,875 responded to the names by shouting "Who cares?" They would care soon enough. The Red Wings had only lost two games in a row once during the abbreviated 1994–95 season, but the Devils beat them in four straight.

Tough Act to Follow

Nine times in NHL history the Stanley Cup champion has missed the playoffs the following season:

TEAM	CUP YEAR	FINISH NEXT SEASON
Carolina Hurricanes	2006	11th in Eastern Conference
New Jersey Devils	1995	9th in Eastern Conference
Montreal Canadiens	1969	5th in East Division
Toronto Maple Leafs	1967	5th in East Division
Toronto Maple Leafs	1945	5th in overall standings
Chicago Black Hawks	1938	7th in overall standings
Detroit Red Wings	1937	4th in American Division
Toronto St. Patricks	1922	3rd in overall standings
Toronto Arenas	1918	3rd in first- and second-half standings

Locked Out

Similar to the issues that would wipe out the entire 2004–05 season, a battle between the owners and players over a salary cap versus revenue sharing threatened the 1994–95 season. This lockout began on October 1, 1994, and ended on January 13, 1995. A total of 468 games, plus the All-Star Game, were lost to the labor dispute. The 48-game season that was salvaged would stretch from January 20 to May 3. A salary cap for rookies was instituted, and the NHL and the Players' Association agreed to cut back the schedule from the 84 games of the previous two seasons to 82 games in the future.

Road Warriors The Devils were 10–1 away from home in the playoffs in 1995 to set a record for postseason road wins they would match in 2000. (Calgary would also win 10 road games in 2004, as would Los Angeles in 2012.) New Jersey and Los Angeles are the only Stanley Cup champions since the 16-team, four-round playoff format was introduced in 1979–80 to open all of its playoff series on the road. (The Devils also own the record for most postseason victories at home in one season with 12, which they did when they won the Cup in 2003.)

Keepers of the Cup

From the very beginning, it seems, Lord Stanley wanted his Stanley Cup to be seen. It was always intended to go where the people were, despite concerns about whether or not those people could be trusted. Why else would the very first rule handed down from Lord Stanley state: "The winner to give bond for the return of the cup in good order when required by the trustees for the purpose of being handed over to any other team who may in turn win."

Throughout the 1970s, players on the winning team often only saw the Cup when it was being presented on ice or at a parade or team party. That began to change in the 1980s when players on the New York Islanders and Edmonton Oilers got to spend some personal time with the trophy.

According to old newspaper accounts, the bond was for $1,000. In those early days the Stanley Cup was often displayed in the window of the business place of some prominent team backer, such as the Lowry Brothers Pharmacy in Kenora, Ontario, or the Holt Renfrew store in Quebec City.

With only NHL teams playing for the Stanley Cup since 1927, the trophy eventually spent most of its time each year in Montreal. Not because the Montreal Canadiens won it so often, but because the NHL office and the place of business of Carl Petersen, who engraved the names on the trophy, were both in Montreal. When the first Hockey Hall of Fame building opened in Toronto in 1961, the Stanley Cup took up residence there.

Throughout the 1970s, players on the winning team often only saw the Cup when it was being presented on ice or at a parade or team party. That began to change in the 1980s when players on the New York Islanders and Edmonton Oilers got to spend some personal time with the trophy. To celebrate the Stanley Cup's centennial in 1993, every member of the Montreal Canadiens was given his own day to spend with the trophy during the summer. This popular practice was formalized in 1995. Since then the Hockey Hall of Fame has provided the Cup with its own "keeper" to ensure things don't get out of hand.

Since appearing in a MasterCard commercial in 2001, Hockey Hall of Fame vice president and curator Phil Pritchard has become the most famous keeper of the Cup. Sporting a black blazer and his famous white gloves, Pritchard has the honor each year, along with his colleague Craig Campbell, of carrying the Stanley Cup onto the ice for presentation to the NHL champions. A lifelong sports fan, Pritchard admits that he would trade anything to have his role reversed and have the Stanley Cup brought to him instead of him bringing it to each new champion team.

Other keepers of the Cup include Walt Neubrand, Bill Wellman and Howie Borrow, but the workhorse keeper is Mike Bolt. Like the other keepers, Bolt safeguards the Cup during its summers with the champions, but he also escorts it to numerous NHL and charity functions each year. In all, he spends roughly 250 days each year with the Stanley Cup.

Because so many players seem to like to eat out of it—"It's a huge bowl," Bolt acknowledged in a 2011 story by Derek Jory on the Vancouver Canucks' website, "it makes for a great sundae or whatever it may be"—Bolt spends a lot of his time just keeping the Cup clean. "I always make the joke that I'm a professional dishwasher," he said. "My mom is so proud."

He also logs a ton of air miles and has had to wait nervously on a few occasions when the Stanley Cup has missed its connecting flight. For Bolt, the most rewarding flights have been the two he made to bring the Stanley Cup to the troops serving in Afghanistan.

Like Bolt, Walt Neubrand has

react to the Stanley Cup in countries that seldom see NHL hockey was mind-boggling and made me appreciate even more the impact this trophy has on people."

Recalling the 1972 Summit Series he had watched as a boy, Wellman enjoyed hearing the Russian national anthem played when he returned to Russia with Evgeni Malkin in 2009.

Being a keeper of the Stanley Cup means long hours on the road, but none of them are complaining. "Most guys get the Stanley Cup first thing in the morning and have it until late at night," explains Howie Borrow, the Cup's newest keeper. "Eighteen-hour days are part of the routine, but I wouldn't change it for anything!"

Borrow brought the Stanley Cup and the James Norris Memorial Trophy to Slovakia with Zdeno Chara for two very busy days in the summer of 2011, culminating with the big Boston Bruins captain being knighted in a formal ceremony at the medieval Trencin Castle in his hometown.

The keepers of the Stanley Cup have become famous on their own over the years, but none of them really let it go to their head. They know who the real celebrity is.

"It's not about us," Pritchard points out. "It's about the Cup!"

been accompanying the Stanley Cup since 1997. His first assignment that summer was to bring it to Scotty Bowman's home in suburban Buffalo, New York. While keeping the Stanley Cup at the NHL All-Star Game in Tampa, Florida, in 1999, Neubrand met a volunteer from Detroit, Michigan, who would later become his wife. Still, he admits that his favorite trip was taking the Stanley Cup to Rankin Inlet in Nunavut for a hockey tournament.

"People in the area are so passionate about hockey," he told writer Kevin Shea for the final edition of the Hockey Hall of Fame's 2011 Stanley Cup Journal. "Some drove 250 miles by snowmobile to see the Cup."

Bill Wellman has worked at the Hockey Hall of Fame since the new facility opened in Toronto in 1993. He made the occasional trips to events with the Stanley Cup and other NHL trophies, but he did not

Cup keeper Mike Bolt enjoys crepes with Pittsburgh Penguins defenceman Kris Letang in the summer of 2009.

officially become a keeper until 2006, when he took the Cup to Switzerland, Ukraine, Russia, Czech Republic and Sweden.

"I can't begin to tell you how thrilling it was to travel to Europe with the Cup that summer," Wellman told Shea. "To see the way people

New York Rangers

CONFERENCE QUARTERFINAL	CONFERENCE SEMIFINAL	CONFERENCE FINAL
4 games to 0 over NY Islanders	4 games to 1 over Washington	4 games to 3 over New Jersey

ROSTER

Glenn Anderson

Jeff Beukeboom

Greg Gilbert

Adam Graves

Mike Hartman

Glenn Healy

Mike Hudson

Alexander Karpovtsev

Joe Kocur

Alex Kovalev

Nick Kypreos

Steve Larmer

Brian Leetch

Doug Lidster

Kevin Lowe

Craig MacTavish

Stéphane Matteau

Mark Messier (captain)

Sergei Nemchinov

Brian Noonan

Ed Olczyk

Mike Richter

Esa Tikkanen

Jay Wells

Sergei Zubov

Neil Smith (president/general manager)

Mike Keenan (head coach)

CONN SMYTHE TROPHY BRIAN LEETCH D – NEW YORK RANGERS

FINAL 4 GAMES TO 3

MAY 31	►	Vancouver 3 at NY Rangers 2 OT
JUNE 2	►	Vancouver 1 at NY Rangers 3
JUNE 4	►	NY Rangers 5 at Vancouver 1
JUNE 7	►	NY Rangers 4 at Vancouver 2
JUNE 9	►	Vancouver 6 at NY Rangers 3
JUNE 11	►	NY Rangers 1 at Vancouver 4
JUNE 14	►	Vancouver 2 at NY Rangers 3

PLAYOFF SCORING LEADER

	GP	G	A	PTS
Brian Leetch NEW YORK RANGERS	23	11	23	34

FINAL SERIES SCORING

NY RANGERS	GP	G	A	PTS	PIM
Brian Leetch	7	5	6	11	4
Alex Kovalev	7	4	3	7	2
Mark Messier	7	2	5	7	17
Sergei Zubov	6	1	5	6	0
Steve Larmer	7	4	0	4	2
Adam Graves	7	1	3	4	4
Glenn Anderson	7	2	1	3	4
Doug Lidster	7	2	0	2	10
Jeff Beukeboom	7	0	2	2	25
Sergei Nemchinov	7	0	2	2	2
Greg Gilbert	7	0	1	1	2
Craig MacTavish	7	0	1	1	6
Stéphane Matteau	7	0	1	1	6
Brian Noonan	7	0	1	1	0
Esa Tikkanen	7	0	1	1	12
Alexander Karpovtsev	2	0	0	0	0
Joe Kocur	6	0	0	0	2
Nick Kypreos	1	0	0	0	0
Kevin Lowe	6	0	0	0	6
Jay Wells	7	0	0	0	8

GOALTENDER	GP	W	L	MIN	GA	SO	AVG
Mike Richter	7	4	3	439	19	0	2.60

VANCOUVER	GP	G	A	PTS	PIM
Pavel Bure	7	3	5	8	15
Cliff Ronning	7	1	6	7	6
Geoff Courtnall	7	4	1	5	11
Trevor Linden	7	3	2	5	6
Jeff Brown	7	3	1	4	8
Bret Hedican	7	1	3	4	4
Jyrki Lumme	7	0	4	4	6
Greg Adams	7	1	2	3	2
Nathan LaFayette	7	0	3	3	0
Sergio Momesso	7	1	1	2	17
Murray Craven	7	0	2	2	4
Dave Babych	7	1	0	1	2
Martin Gélinas	7	1	0	1	4
Shawn Antoski	7	0	1	1	8
Gerald Diduck	7	0	1	1	6
Brian Glynn	7	0	1	1	0
Tim Hunter	7	0	0	0	18
John McIntyre	7	0	0	0	6

GOALTENDER	GP	W	L	MIN	GA	SO	AVG
Kirk McLean	7	3	4	437	20	0	2.75

Conn Smythe Story

Brian Leetch was on the ice for an amazing 61 of the 81 goals that the Rangers scored during the postseason, including 19 of the team's 22 power-play goals. Leetch routinely played more than 30 minutes per night throughout the playoffs and was rewarded as the first American-born player to win the Conn Smythe Trophy as playoff MVP.

Lots of Experience

Mark Messier, Kevin Lowe, Glenn Anderson, Jeff Beukeboom, Adam Graves, Craig MacTavish and Esa Tikkanen had all won the Stanley Cup at least once with the Edmonton Oilers. Greg Gilbert had won the Stanley Cup with the New York Islanders in 1982 and 1983.

The First Since 1940

The New York Rangers had entered the NHL back in 1926–27. They won their first Stanley Cup title the very next season and were champions twice more by 1940. The team fell on hard times during World War II and would not really recover until the NHL expanded in 1967. Even so, the Stanley Cup continued to elude them. When the New York Islanders emerged as a powerhouse in the early 1980s, their fans would taunt the Rangers with derisive chants of "1940!"

Things began to look up for the Rangers when Brian Leetch won the Calder Trophy in 1988–89. He soon established himself among the NHL's best defensemen. Leetch won the Norris Trophy in 1991–92, which was also the year in which general manager Neil Smith acquired Mark Messier from Edmonton. Messier won the Hart Trophy that season as the Rangers posted the best record in the NHL (50-25-5, 105 points) for the first time in 50 years. The Rangers fell apart and missed the playoffs the following season, but the team made a dramatic turnaround when Mike Keenan took over as coach in 1993–94.

Led by Messier, Leetch, Adam Graves, Sergei Zubov, goalie Mike Richter and other former Oilers, such as Esa Tikkanen, Kevin Lowe and Glenn Anderson, the Rangers established franchise records with 52 wins and 112 points and once again won the Presidents' Trophy. But the Stanley Cup was the ultimate goal, and the Rangers opened the playoffs with a sweep of the Islanders followed by a five-game victory over Washington. The Rangers fell behind New Jersey three games to two in the Eastern Conference final, but they rallied to take the series. Messier scored a hat trick after guaranteeing a victory in Game 6, and Stéphane Matteau scored in double-overtime to win Game 7.

Facing the Vancouver Canucks for the Stanley Cup, the Rangers lost the first game but bounced back to take a 3–1 series lead. With New York already planning the parade before Game 5, Vancouver stayed alive with a 6–3 victory and went on to force a seventh game. The Rangers took an early 2–0 lead in Game 7, went up 3–1 on a second-period goal by Messier and held on during a nail-biting third period for a 3–2 win and the team's first Stanley Cup championship in 54 years.

The Guarantee

Recalling his promise to win Game 6 of the 1994 Eastern Conference final, in 2008 Mark Messier admitted he hadn't really thought it through. "I thought 'what a great idea it would be for the players to wake up the day of the game and find out how much I believed in us,'" he remembered. "My oversight was 14 million other New Yorkers and the New Jersey Devils were going to read the same article. I was so focused in, I thought only the 20 players on our team were going to read that paper."

"We know we have to win," Messier told reporters after the Rangers had lost Game 5 to the Devils. "We can win it. And we are going to win it." Then, with the team trailing 2–0 late in the second period, Messier set up Alex Kovalev for the Rangers' first goal before scoring three of his own in the third period to pull out a 4–2 victory.

From Russia With Love
Alexander Karpovtsev, Alexei Kovalev, Sergei Nemchinov and Sergei Zubov became the first Russian-trained players to have their names engraved on the Stanley Cup.

Mark Messier

Curses!

Like the "Curse of the Bambino" to explain the Boston Red Sox World Series drought of 1918 to 2004 or the "Curse of the Billy Goat" to explain why the Chicago Cubs haven't even won a National League pennant since 1945, there is a curse story behind the New York Rangers' 54-year Stanley Cup drought. In fact, there are two. One story says that Red Dutton, who ran the perennially cash-strapped New York Americans for several seasons, cursed the Rangers when the Americans were forced to drop out of the NHL in 1942. Another story claims the Rangers were cursed by "the hockey gods" when the bank loan to finance Madison Square Garden was paid off during the 1940–41 season and the mortgage papers were burned inside the bowl of the Stanley Cup.

Name Game Because injuries had prevented Ed Olczyk and Mike Hartman from playing the necessary 41 games in the regular season or one game in the final, they were left off the Stanley Cup when the 1994 Rangers had their names engraved on it. They were added later, after the Rangers protested. Since then, the NHL has allowed teams to petition to have players' names included on the Stanley Cup even if they don't meet the standard criteria.

1992–93 Montreal Canadiens

DIVISION SEMIFINAL
4 games to 2 over Quebec

DIVISION FINAL
4 games to 0 over Buffalo

CONFERENCE FINAL
4 games to 1 over NY Islanders

CONN SMYTHE TROPHY **PATRICK ROY** G – MONTREAL

FINAL 4 GAMES TO 1

JUNE 1	► Los Angeles 4 at Montreal 1
JUNE 3	► Los Angeles 2 at Montreal 3 OT
JUNE 5	► Montreal 4 at Los Angeles 3 OT
JUNE 7	► Montreal 3 at Los Angeles 2 OT
JUNE 9	► Los Angeles 1 at Montreal 4

PLAYOFF SCORING LEADER

	GP	G	A	PTS
Wayne Gretzky LOS ANGELES	24	15	25	40

FINAL SERIES SCORING

MONTREAL	GP	G	A	PTS	PIM
Eric Desjardins	5	3	1	4	6
John LeClair	5	2	2	4	0
Kirk Muller	5	2	2	4	6
Vincent Damphousse	5	1	3	4	8
Stéphan Lebeau	5	1	2	3	4
Mike Keane	4	0	3	3	2
Paul DiPietro	5	2	0	2	0
Brian Bellows	5	1	1	2	4
Gilbert Dionne	5	1	1	2	4
Ed Ronan	5	1	1	2	6
Mathieu Schneider	5	1	1	2	8
Lyle Odelein	5	0	2	2	6
Benoit Brunet	5	0	1	1	2
Guy Carbonneau	5	0	1	1	0
Kevin Haller	3	0	1	1	0
Gary Leeman	5	0	1	1	2
Patrice Brisebois	5	0	0	0	8
J.J. Daigneault	5	0	0	0	6
Donald Dufresne	1	0	0	0	0
Sean Hill	1	0	0	0	0
Denis Savard	1	0	0	0	0

GOALTENDER	GP	W	L	MIN	GA	SO	AVG
Patrick Roy	5	4	1	315	11	0	2.10

LOS ANGELES	GP	G	A	PTS	PIM
Wayne Gretzky	5	2	5	7	2
Luc Robitaille	5	3	2	5	4
Tony Granato	5	1	3	4	10
Marty McSorley	5	2	0	2	16
Mike Donnelly	5	1	1	2	0
Dave Taylor	3	1	1	2	6
Tomas Sandstrom	5	0	2	2	4
Pat Conacher	5	1	0	1	2
Jari Kurri	5	1	0	1	2
Rob Blake	5	0	1	1	18
Jimmy Carson	2	0	1	1	0
Mark Hardy	4	0	1	1	4
Alexei Zhitnik	5	0	1	1	4
Charlie Huddy	4	0	0	0	4
Lonnie Loach	1	0	0	0	0
Corey Millen	5	0	0	0	2
Warren Rychel	5	0	0	0	2
Gary Shuchuk	5	0	0	0	0
Darryl Sydor	5	0	0	0	4
Tim Watters	5	0	0	0	4

GOALTENDER	GP	W	L	MIN	GA	SO	AVG
Kelly Hrudey	5	1	4	316	15	0	2.85

ROSTER

Jesse Bélanger
Brian Bellows
Patrice Brisebois
Benoit Brunet
Guy Carbonneau (captain)
J.J. Daigneault
Vincent Damphousse
Eric Desjardins

Gilbert Dionne
Paul DiPietro
Donald Dufresne
Todd Ewen
Kevin Haller
Sean Hill
Mike Keane
Stéphan Lebeau
John LeClair

Gary Leeman
Kirk Muller
Lyle Odelein
André Racicot
Rob Ramage
Mario Roberge
Ed Ronan
Patrick Roy
Denis Savard

Mathieu Schneider
Serge Savard (managing director/ vice president, hockey)
Jacques Demers (head coach)

Staying Focused

"It was a lot easier for me to concentrate and to be focused in the playoffs than it was in the regular season. The outcome of every game was so important."
— Patrick Roy

The NHL celebrated the centennial of the Stanley Cup with a matchup that pitted the greatest franchise in hockey history—the Montreal Canadiens—against arguably the game's greatest player ever, Wayne Gretzky. Gretzky had returned from a serious back injury that sidelined him for the first half of the 1992–93 season to lead the Los Angeles Kings to the final for the first time in team history.

After their surprising Stanley Cup victory in 1986, the Canadiens developed into an outstanding team in the late 1980s, but they had taken a slight step back over the next few years. Despite an Adams Division title in 1991–92, coach Pat Burns resigned to go behind the bench in Toronto and was replaced by Jacques Demers. The Canadiens also traded for Vincent Damphousse and Brian Bellows, who, along with Kirk Muller (who had come on board the year before) would lead the offense in 1992–93. The defense featured Eric Desjardins, Mathieu Schneider, Patrice Brisebois and Lyle Odelein. Patrick Roy handled the bulk of the goaltending duties, but he would struggle during the regular season. Roy would more than make up

for his poor play by going 16-4 with a 2.13 goals-against average during the playoffs.

Montreal played inconsistently as a team during the 1992–93 season, and though they finished the year with a record of 48-30-6 for 102 points, a late-season slump saw them drop to third place in the Adams Division, behind Boston and Quebec. The Canadiens opened the playoffs on the road against the Nordiques. They dropped Game 1 3–2 in overtime and were beaten 4–1 in Game 2, but they rallied to win four in a row, including two in overtime, to set the stage for a remarkable playoff run. The Canadiens next swept the Sabres in four, with overtime wins in the last three games, before beating the Islanders in a five-game series that featured two more overtime victories.

Facing Los Angeles in the Stanley Cup final, Montreal dropped the opener at home before rattling off three straight overtime victories to take command of the series. Back at home for Game 5, Guy Carbonneau kept Wayne Gretzky from firing even a single shot on goal, and the Canadiens wrapped up the series with a 4–1 victory.

Overtime

Of the 85 games played during the 1993 playoffs, a record 28 of them went into overtime. The Montreal Canadiens were involved in 11 overtime games themselves that spring, and, after dropping their first game of the postseason in overtime, they won a remarkable 10 in a row. Montreal's overtime results went like this:

DATE	RESULT	GOAL SCORER	TIME
April 18	Montreal 2 at Quebec 3	Scott Young	16:49
April 22	Quebec 1 at Montreal 2	Vincent Damphousse	10:30
April 26	Montreal 5 at Quebec 4	Kirk Muller	8:17
May 4	Buffalo 3 at Montreal 4	Guy Carbonneau	2:50
May 6	Montreal 4 at Buffalo 3	Gilbert Dionne	8:28
May 8	Montreal 4 at Buffalo3	Kirk Muller	11:37
May 18	NY Islanders 3 at Montreal 4	Stéphan Lebeau	26:21
May 20	Montreal 2 at NY Islanders 1	Guy Carbonneau	12:34
June 3	Los Angeles 2 at Montreal 3	Eric Desjardins	0:51
June 5	Montreal 4 at Los Angeles 3	John LeClair	0:34
June 7	Montreal 3 at Los Angeles 2	John LeClair	14:37

Turning Point

Trailing 1–0 in the series and down 2–1 in Game 2 with just 1:45 remaining, Canadiens coach Jacques Demers took the advice of team trainer Gerard Lefebvre and called for a measurement of Marty McSorley's stick. The stick was deemed illegal, and McSorley was penalized. Eric Desjardins tied the game 32 seconds later and would win it with his third goal of the game, which came just 51 seconds into overtime. Desjardins was the first defenseman in Stanley Cup history to score a hat trick in the final.

Matching the Rocket John LeClair's OT winners in Games 3 and 4 of the 1993 Stanley Cup final made him the first player since Maurice Richard in 1951 to score overtime goals in consecutive playoff games.

Montreal Versus Toronto?

The Maple Leafs made a furious run through the playoffs in 1993, playing 21 games in 42 nights and going the distance in all three rounds they played. If not for a missed call in Game 6 of the Campbell Conference final against Los Angeles, Toronto may well have gone on to play for the Stanley Cup against Montreal. The incident occurred 39 seconds into overtime, when Wayne Gretzky cut Doug Gilmour for eight stitches around his chin. Though the play was clearly accidental, similar stick infractions throughout the season had usually resulted in a five-minute penalty. Gretzky was not penalized, however, and was on the ice to score the game-winning goal 1:02 later. Two nights later, in Game 7, Gretzky scored a hat trick in a 5–4 victory and the Kings eliminated the Maple Leafs, ending the hopes of Canadian hockey fans everywhere for the Leafs and Habs to duke it out for the Cup.

Canadiens and Canadians

With their 24th Stanley Cup title in team history, the Montreal Canadiens had won at least one championship in every decade since winning their first in back in 1916. Since that victory in 1993, no other Canadian team has won the Stanley Cup.

DIVISION SEMIFINAL	DIVISION FINAL	CONFERENCE FINAL
4 games to 3 over Washington	**4 games to 2 over NY Rangers**	**4 games to 0 over Boston**

CONN SMYTHE TROPHY **MARIO LEMIEUX** C – PITTSBURGH

FINAL 4 GAMES TO 0

MAY 26	►	Chicago 4 at Pittsburgh 5
MAY 28	►	Chicago 1 at Pittsburgh 3
MAY 30	►	Pittsburgh 1 at Chicago 0
JUNE 1	►	Pittsburgh 6 at Chicago 5

PLAYOFF SCORING LEADER

	GP	G	A	PTS
Mario Lemieux PITTSBURGH	15	16	18	34

FINAL SERIES SCORING

PITTSBURGH	GP	G	A	PTS	PIM
Rick Tocchet	4	2	6	8	2
Mario Lemieux	4	5	2	7	0
Kevin Stevens	4	2	3	5	0
Ron Francis	4	1	2	3	0
Larry Murphy	4	1	2	3	2
Jim Paek	4	0	3	3	2
Jaromir Jagr	4	2	0	2	2
Shawn McEachern	4	0	2	2	0
Phil Bourque	4	1	0	1	0
Bob Errey	3	1	0	1	0
Troy Loney	4	0	1	1	0
Kjell Samuelsson	4	0	1	1	2
Paul Stanton	4	0	1	1	20
Jock Callander	4	0	0	0	0
Jiri Hrdina	3	0	0	0	0
Dave Michayluk	1	0	0	0	0
Gordie Roberts	4	0	0	0	8
Ulf Samuelsson	4	0	0	0	2
Bryan Trottier	4	0	0	0	2
GOALTENDER	GP	W	L	MIN	GA	SO	AVG
Tom Barrasso	4	4	0	240	10	1	2.50

CHICAGO	GP	G	A	PTS	PIM
Chris Chelios	4	1	4	5	19
Dirk Graham	4	4	0	4	0
Brian Noonan	4	0	3	3	2
Jeremy Roenick	4	2	0	2	0
Brent Sutter	4	1	1	2	0
Greg Gilbert	3	0	2	2	10
Michel Goulet	4	1	0	1	2
Bryan Marchment	4	1	0	1	2
Rod Buskas	3	0	1	1	2
Stu Grimson	2	0	1	1	0
Steve Larmer	4	0	1	1	2
Jocelyn Lemieux	4	0	1	1	0
Stéphane Matteau	4	0	1	1	0
Rob Brown	3	0	0	0	2
Mike Hudson	4	0	0	0	2
Igor Kravchuk	4	0	0	0	0
Frantisek Kucera	4	0	0	0	0
Mike Peluso	3	0	0	0	4
Cam Russell	1	0	0	0	0
Steve Smith	4	0	0	0	4
GOALTENDERS	GP	W	L	MIN	GA	SO	AVG
Ed Belfour	4	0	3	187	11	0	3.53
Dominik Hasek	1	0	1	53	4	0	4.53

ROSTER

Tom Barrasso
Phil Bourque
Jock Callander
Jay Caufield
Jeff Chychrun
Jeff Daniels
Bob Errey
Ron Francis
Jiri Hrdina

Jaromir Jagr
Grant Jennings
Jamie Leach
Mario Lemieux (captain)
Troy Loney
Shawn McEachern
Dave Michayluk
Joe Mullen
Larry Murphy

Mike Needham
Jim Paek
Ken Priestlay
Gordie Roberts
Kjell Samuelsson
Ulf Samuelsson
Paul Stanton
Kevin Stevens
Peter Taglianetti

Rick Tocchet ▲
Bryan Trottier
Ken Wregget
Wendell Young
Craig Patrick (executive vice president/general manager)
Scotty Bowman (director of player development/ coach)
Bob Johnson (head coach)

Early-Round Excitement

A record six of the eight first-round series of the 1992 playoffs required a seventh game to determine a winner. In addition to the Penguins, both Vancouver and Detroit rallied to win after facing deficits of three games to one.

Pittsburgh's Second Straight

The NHL celebrated its 75th season in 1991–92 and the "Original Six" franchises —Montreal, Toronto, Boston, Chicago, Detroit and the New York Rangers—commemorated the occasion by wearing vintage uniforms for select games throughout the year. The Pittsburgh Penguins, who were marking their 25th anniversary as well as their first Stanley Cup championship the year before, had had an eventful summer. The DeBartolo family sold the franchise to a partnership that included Howard Baldwin, Morris Belzberg and Thomas Ruta, and on August 29, 1991, coach Bob Johnson was diagnosed with brain cancer. (He would pass away on November 26th.) Scotty Bowman was the club's director of player development and, though he had not been behind the bench since 1987, was named as Johnson's successor.

With Mario Lemieux back in form after battling back ailments for two years (he would win the scoring title with 131 points despite missing 16 games), Pittsburgh got off to a fast start. A midseason slump would hurt them, but a February deal to acquire Rick Tocchet and Kjell Samuelsson helped them end the season strongly. Still, the Penguins finished only third in the Patrick Division standings.

In the playoffs, Pittsburgh fell behind Washington three games to one in the first round but rallied to take the series in seven. After falling behind the Rangers two games to one, the Penguins won three straight to knock off the Presidents' Trophy winners. Facing Boston in the Wales Conference final, Pittsburgh opened the series with a 4–3 overtime win, and they then posted 5–2, 5–1 and 5–1 victories and found themselves on a seven-game winning streak heading into the Stanley Cup final.

Chicago had won a playoff-record 11 straight games en route to winning the Campbell Conference, and the Blackhawks jumped out to an early 3–0 lead over Pittsburgh in Game 1. Chicago was up 4–1 late in the second, but Pittsburgh rallied to tie the game on a beautiful unassisted goal by Jaromir Jagr at 15:05 of the third and won it 5–4 on a Lemieux goal with just 13 seconds remaining. The Penguins went on to sweep the series, with their four straight victories giving them 11 consecutive wins of their own.

Striking Out

The 1992 Stanley Cup playoffs were jeopardized when NHL players went out on strike on April 1st. By taking action so late in the season, the players felt they had an advantage because the owners made so much of their profits during the playoffs. The strike lasted 10 days, with the players earning modest changes in free agency, an increase in their playoff bonuses and greater control over the use of their likenesses. The season resumed on April 12th and the playoffs began on April 18th.

Conn Smythe Story Despite missing six games after suffering a broken hand during Pittsburgh's second-round series with the Rangers, Mario Lemieux still led all playoff scorers by six points and was rewarded with the Conn Smythe Trophy for the second year in a row. Lemieux and Bernie Parent (Philadelphia, 1974 and 1975) are the only players in history to be named playoff MVP in back-to-back seasons.

Mario Lemieux

Dynasty Derailed

After two straight Stanley Cup championships, the Penguins were better than ever during the 1992–93 season. Just past the midway point, Pittsburgh was first overall in the NHL standings, with 62 points. Mario Lemieux had 39 goals and 65 assists for 104 points and held a 22-point lead over Buffalo's Pat LaFontaine in the scoring race. More importantly, his bad back finally seemed to be a thing of the past.

It was while visiting the doctor for an examination of his back that Lemieux pointed out a lump on this throat. On January 12, 1993, the Penguins announced Lemieux had Hodgkin's disease, a cancer of the lymph nodes. He would be out of the lineup for at least four to six weeks. Radiation treatments lasted from February 1st to March 2nd, when, miraculously, Lemieux made an immediate return to the ice. He had a goal and an assist that night, but Pittsburgh lost 5–4 to Philadelphia.

The Penguins were 11-10-2 in Mario's absence, but they would begin an NHL-record 17-game winning streak on March 9th. Pittsburgh finished the season 56-21-7 for 119 points, setting franchise records for wins and points and winning the Presidents' Trophy. Personally, Lemieux wiped out the 12-point lead LaFontaine had gained in the scoring race and beat him by 12 points (160–148), despite playing just 60 of 84 games.

Pittsburgh began the playoffs with a five-game victory over New Jersey, but the dynasty was derailed in round two. The New York Islanders scored a stunning upset when David Volek beat Tom Barrasso at 5:16 of overtime for a 4–3 victory in Game 7.

DIVISION SEMIFINAL	DIVISION FINAL	CONFERENCE FINAL
4 games to 3 over New Jersey	4 games to 1 over Washington	4 games to 2 over Boston

ROSTER

CONN SMYTHE TROPHY **MARIO LEMIEUX** C – PITTSBURGH

Tom Barrasso
Phil Bourque
Jay Caufield
Paul Coffey
Bob Errey
Ron Francis
Randy Gilhen
Randy Hillier
Jiri Hrdina
Jaromir Jagr
Grant Jennings
Mario Lemieux (captain)
Troy Loney
Joe Mullen
Larry Murphy
Jim Paek
Barry Pederson
Frank Pietrangelo
Mark Recchi
Gordie Roberts
Ulf Samuelsson
Paul Stanton
Kevin Stevens
Peter Taglianetti
Bryan Trottier
Scott Young
Wendell Young
Craig Patrick
(general manager)
Bob Johnson
(head coach)

FINAL 4 GAMES TO 2

MAY 15	►	Minnesota 5 at Pittsburgh 4
MAY 17	►	Minnesota 1 at Pittsburgh 4
MAY 19	►	Pittsburgh 1 at Minnesota 3
MAY 21	►	Pittsburgh 5 at Minnesota 3
MAY 23	►	Minnesota 4 at Pittsburgh 6
MAY 25	►	Pittsburgh 8 at Minnesota 0

PLAYOFF SCORING LEADER

Mario Lemieux	GP	G	A	PTS
PITTSBURGH	23	16	28	44

FINAL SERIES SCORING

PITTSBURGH	GP	G	A	PTS	PIM
Mario Lemieux	5	5	7	12	6
Larry Murphy	6	1	9	10	6
Joe Mullen	6	3	5	8	0
Kevin Stevens	6	4	3	7	27
Ron Francis	6	3	3	6	6
Jaromir Jagr	6	0	5	5	0
Phil Bourque	6	2	2	4	4
Bob Errey	6	2	1	3	8
Mark Recchi	6	2	1	3	8
Ulf Samuelsson	6	2	1	3	12
Bryan Trottier	6	1	2	3	14
Peter Taglianetti	5	0	3	3	8
Scott Young	1	1	1	2	0
Paul Coffey	5	0	2	2	0
Troy Loney	6	1	0	1	26
Jim Paek	5	1	0	1	2
Randy Gilhen	5	0	0	0	12
Jiri Hrdina	2	0	0	0	0
Grant Jennings	2	0	0	0	2
Gordie Roberts	6	0	0	0	23
Paul Stanton	6	0	0	0	8
GOALTENDERS	GP	W	L	MIN	GA	SO	AVG
Tom Barrasso	6	3	2	319	13	1	2.45
Frank Pietrangelo	1	1	0	40	3	0	4.50

MINNESOTA	GP	G	A	PTS	PIM
Dave Gagner	6	4	2	6	14
Neal Broten	6	3	1	4	2
Ulf Dahlen	6	2	2	4	0
Mike Modano	6	2	2	4	6
Brian Propp	6	1	3	4	4
Bobby Smith	6	1	3	4	4
Stew Gavin	6	0	3	3	2
Gaétan Duchesne	6	1	1	2	6
Brian Bellows	6	0	2	2	16
Shawn Chambers	6	0	2	2	6
Marc Bureau	6	1	0	1	8
Chris Dahlquist	6	0	1	1	4
Jim Johnson	6	0	1	1	10
Mark Tinordi	6	0	1	1	15
Perry Berezan	1	0	0	0	0
Shane Churla	5	0	0	0	4
Brian Glynn	6	0	0	0	6
Basil McRae	5	0	0	0	26
Doug Smail	1	0	0	0	0
Neil Wilkinson	6	0	0	0	2
GOALTENDERS	GP	W	L	MIN	GA	SO	AVG
Jon Casey	6	2	3	290	21	0	4.34
Brian Hayward	2	0	1	67	6	0	5.37

Four Before Four players who won the Stanley Cup with Pittsburgh in 1991 had previously won championships with another franchise. Bryan Trottier had won the Cup four times with the New York Islanders (1980, 1981, 1982 and 1983), while Paul Coffey had three wins with the Edmonton Oilers (1984, 1985 and 1987). Joe Mullen and Jiri Hrdina had both won the Cup with Calgary in 1989.

Chumps to Champs The Penguins' Stanley Cup win in 1991 came in only their second playoff appearance in nine years. The Penguins had missed the playoffs for six straight seasons, from 1982–83 through 1987–88, and then missed again in 1989–90.

Lemieux Means "The Best"

The Pittsburgh Penguins flew under the radar for much of the 1990–91 season. While the top teams in the NHL's three other divisions all waged a tight battle for the top spot in the overall standings, Pittsburgh's 88 points (41-33-6) earned the Penguins the Patrick Division title, their first divisional title in franchise history, but it would have placed them no better than third in the Adams, Norris or Smythe Divisions.

Pittsburgh played much of the season without Mario Lemieux, who missed 54 games after back surgery. In his absence, the Penguins developed a balanced attack led by Mark Recchi, Kevin Stevens and Paul Coffey. They also unveiled a promising 18-year-old rookie named Jaromir Jagr. The Penguins were greatly bolstered by Lemieux's late-season return, as well as by the acquisitions of Larry Murphy, Ron Francis and Ulf Samuelsson.

In the playoffs, the Penguins rallied from a three-games-to-two deficit to beat New Jersey in Game 7 of the opening round. They then beat Washington in six games to reach the conference final, where they met the Boston Bruins. Boston had gone to the Stanley Cup final the year before and was the top team in the Wales Conference, with 100 points during the regular season, but Pittsburgh defeated the Bruins in six games to advance to the Cup final.

Minnesota was a surprise winner in the Campbell Conference. The North Stars knocked off the league's top team in Chicago in the opening round and number-two ranked St. Louis in the second before beating the defending Stanley Cup champions from Edmonton. The meeting of Pittsburgh and Minnesota marked the first time that two 1967 expansion teams had faced each other in the final and the first time since 1934 that both clubs vying for the Cup had never won it previously.

The North Stars won Game 1 5–4 and were fighting back from an early 2–0 deficit in Game 2 before Mario Lemieux scored one of the most beautiful goals in hockey history. He sped from end to end, splitting the Minnesota defense and weaving the puck through the skates of Shawn Chambers before dekeing goalie Jon Casey. The Penguins went on to a 4–1 victory. A recurrence of his back problems forced Lemieux out of the lineup for Game 3, but he returned in Game 4 and lead an up-tempo attack that culminated in an 8–0 Stanley Cup victory in Game 6.

Badger Bob

Bob Johnson is an American hockey legend. He became head coach at the University of Wisconsin in 1966 and guided the team for 15 years, winning national championships in 1973, 1977 and 1981. Johnson entered the NHL in 1982 as head coach of the Calgary Flames and spent five seasons with the club, leading Calgary to the Stanley Cup final for the first time in 1986. Johnson then spent three seasons as the head of USA Hockey before Penguins general manager Craig Patrick hired him as the team's new head coach for the 1990–91 season. Johnson's infectious, upbeat attitude (he was known for the slogan "It's a great day for hockey") was just what the talented but cliquey Pittsburgh team needed to finally reach its potential. When the Penguins won, Johnson became the first American-born head coach to lead a team to the Stanley Cup since Bill Stewart with the Chicago Black Hawks in 1938.

Bob Johnson

Three Generations

Pittsburgh Penguins general manager Craig Patrick was the fifth member of his family, and the third generation, to win the Stanley Cup. Craig's grandfather Lester Patrick won the Cup as a player with the Montreal Wanderers in 1906 and 1907, as well as in ownership and/or management with the Victoria Cougars (1925) and New York Rangers (1928, 1933, 1940). Craig's father, Lynn, was a player with the Rangers in 1940, as was his uncle Murray Patrick — who is better known as Muzz. The fourth member of the family to win the Stanley Cup was Lester's brother Frank, who was a player, coach, manager and owner when the Vancouver Millionaires won the Stanley Cup in 1915.

Fleury in OT

One of the most memorable moments of the 1991 playoffs occurred in the very first round. With the Flames facing elimination in Game 6 of their Smythe Division semifinal, Calgary's Theo Fleury pounced on a Mark Messier giveaway in the neutral zone. He outraced everyone to the Oilers net and beat Grant Fuhr to give the Flames a 2–1 overtime victory. Celebrating wildly, Fleury sped back out of the Oilers end with his teammates chasing him. He dropped to his knees near center ice and slid until he crashed into the boards deep in the Flames zone. The Oilers bounced back to win Game 7 in what, to date, remains the last playoff matchup between these two great rivals.

1989–90 Edmonton Oilers

DIVISION SEMIFINAL	DIVISION FINAL	CONFERENCE FINAL
4 games to 3 over Winnipeg	**4 games to 0 over Los Angeles**	**4 games to 2 over Chicago**

ROSTER

CONN SMYTHE TROPHY **BILL RANFORD** G – EDMONTON

Glenn Anderson
Jeff Beukeboom
Dave Brown
Kelly Buchberger
Grant Fuhr
Martin Gélinas
Adam Graves
Randy Gregg
Charlie Huddy
Petr Klima
Jari Kurri
Mark Lamb
Kevin Lowe
Craig MacTavish
Mark Messier (captain)
Craig Muni
Joe Murphy
Bill Ranford
Pokey Reddick
Reijo Ruotsalainen
Craig Simpson
Geoff Smith
Steve Smith
Esa Tikkanen
Glen Sather
(president/general
manager)
John Muckler
(head coach)

FINAL 4 GAMES TO 1

MAY 15	► Edmonton 3 at Boston 2 3X OT
MAY 18	► Edmonton 7 at Boston 2
MAY 20	► Boston 2 at Edmonton 1
MAY 22	► Boston 1 at Edmonton 5
MAY 24	► Edmonton 4 at Boston 1

PLAYOFF SCORING LEADERS

Craig Simpson	GP	G	A	PTS
EDMONTON	22	16	15	31

Mark Messier	GP	G	A	PTS
EDMONTON	22	9	22	31

FINAL SERIES SCORING

EDMONTON	GP	G	A	PTS	PIM
Craig Simpson	5	4	4	8	6
Jari Kurri	5	3	5	8	2
Glenn Anderson	5	4	3	7	6
Esa Tikkanen	5	3	2	5	10
Mark Messier	5	0	5	5	6
Joe Murphy	5	2	2	4	4
Steve Smith	5	1	2	3	13
Mark Lamb	5	0	3	3	2
Adam Graves	5	2	0	2	0
Craig MacTavish	5	0	2	2	2
Reijo Ruotsalainen	5	0	2	2	2
Petr Klima	5	1	0	1	0
Martin Gélinas	5	0	1	1	2
Randy Gregg	5	0	1	1	0
Kelly Buchberger	5	0	0	0	2
Charlie Huddy	5	0	0	0	4
Kevin Lowe	5	0	0	0	0
Craig Muni	5	0	0	0	2

GOALTENDER	GP	W	L	MIN	GA	SO	AVG
Bill Ranford	5	4	1	355	8	0	1.35

BOSTON	GP	G	A	PTS	PIM
Raymond Bourque	5	3	2	5	6
Cam Neely	5	0	4	4	10
Greg Hawgood	5	1	2	3	4
Randy Burridge	5	0	2	2	2
John Byce	3	1	0	1	0
Lyndon Byers	2	1	0	1	0
John Carter	5	1	0	1	19
Greg Johnston	4	1	0	1	4
Bob Sweeney	5	0	1	1	7
Don Sweeney	5	0	1	1	6
Andy Brickley	2	0	0	0	0
Bob Carpenter	5	0	0	0	2
Dave Christian	5	0	0	0	0
Peter Douris	1	0	0	0	0
Garry Galley	5	0	0	0	4
Bobby Gould	4	0	0	0	0
Craig Janney	5	0	0	0	0
Allen Pedersen	5	0	0	0	2
Dave Poulin	2	0	0	0	0
Brian Propp	5	0	0	0	0
Glen Wesley	5	0	0	0	2
Jim Wiemer	2	0	0	0	0

GOALTENDERS	GP	W	L	MIN	GA	SO	AVG
Andy Moog	5	1	4	319	16	0	3.01
Reggie Lemelin	1	0	0	36	4	0	6.67

Déjà Vu During the final in 1988, a power failure at the Boston Garden late in the second period of Game 4 forced the game to be suspended. The lights went out again during the third overtime period of Game 1 in 1990. This time, though, the power came back on and the game was resumed after a 25-minute interruption.

Kurri and Gretzky With a hat trick in Game 2 against Boston, Jari Kurri improved to 92 goals in his postseason career, breaking what was then the playoff record of 89, which he had shared with Wayne Gretzky.

Oilers on Top Again

The 1989–90 season was one of remarkable parity, with a number of teams seen as legitimate threats to win the Stanley Cup. The Boston Bruins, under rookie coach Mike Milbury, were the only team with more than 100 points, finishing with 101 on a record of 46-25-9 to top the defending Cup-champion Calgary Flames by two points in the race for top spot in the regular season.

In their second season since Wayne Gretzky had been traded to Los Angeles, Mark Messier took the Edmonton Oilers under his wing. Messier established a career high with 129 points on 45 goals and 84 assists. After the season, he would edge out Boston's Ray Bourque by two points in voting for the Hart Trophy. With 38 wins and 90 points, Edmonton had the fifth-best record in the NHL, but, even so, few people saw the Oilers as potential Stanley Cup champions. It had been a difficult season. Grant Fuhr missed most of the year with a shoulder injury, leaving Bill Ranford and Pokey Reddick to carry the load in goal. Jimmy Carson, who'd scored 100 points the year before after having been acquired in the Gretzky deal, announced his retirement early in the year. The

Oilers suspended him and then traded him to Detroit in a deal that brought Joe Murphy, Adam Graves and Petr Klima to Edmonton. All three, along with rookie Martin Gélinas, would play a big part in Edmonton's surprising Stanley Cup run.

An injury to Mario Lemieux kept him out of 21 games that season. His absence made it possible for Wayne Gretzky to reclaim the Art Ross Trophy, although his 142 points represented his lowest total since his first NHL season. The Kings struggled to a fourth-place finish in the Smythe Division, but they then upset the Flames in the first round of the playoffs before the Oilers swept them in round two. It was sweet revenge for the Oilers, who had blown a 3–1 series lead to the Kings in the first round the year before. Edmonton then knocked off Chicago to set up a rematch of the 1988 Stanley Cup final against Boston.

Most predicted a close series, but the Oilers' superior speed overcame the Bruins' better defense in five games, as Edmonton won the Cup for the fifth time in seven seasons.

MOST CAREER GOALS IN THE PLAYOFFS

122	Wayne Gretzky, Edmonton, Los Angeles, St. Louis, New York Rangers (208 games)
109	Mark Messier, Edmonton, New York Rangers (236 games)
106	Jari Kurri, Edmonton, Los Angeles, New York Rangers, Anaheim, Colorado (200 games)
103	Brett Hull, Calgary, St. Louis, Dallas, Detroit (202 games)
93	Glenn Anderson, Edmonton, Toronto, New York Rangers, St. Louis (225 games)

MOST CAREER GOALS IN THE FINALS

34	Maurice Richard, Montreal (59 games)
30	Jean Béliveau, Montreal (64 games)
24	Bernie Geoffrion, Montreal (53 games)
21	Henri Richard, Montreal (65 games)
	Yvan Cournoyer, Montreal (50 games)
19	Jacques Lemaire, Montreal (40 games)

Maurice Richard

Longest OT

Game 1 of the 1990 final was a thriller. The Oilers led 2–0 after two periods, only to have the hometown Bruins score twice in the third. Ray Bourque had both goals, his second coming with just 89 seconds left in regulation time.

Boston nearly won the game early in overtime when 55-goal scorer Cam Neely blasted a shot at 1:56 that trickled between the pads of Bill Ranford. The former Bruins goalie managed to reach back and stop the puck with his stick. There were several other good scoring chances in overtime, but the game would not end until nearly 1:30 the next morning. It was then that Petr Klima took a nifty little backhand pass from Jari Kurri at the top of the faceoff circle to the left of the Bruins net and wristed a shot through the legs of former Oilers goalie Andy Moog. The time on the game clock was 15:13 of the third overtime period, making this the longest game in the history of the Stanley Cup final. (The previous record of 53:50 of overtime had been set on April 9, 1931, when Chicago's Cy Wentworth beat George Hainsworth of the Montreal Canadiens.)

For Klima, it was the first time he had even been on the ice during the lengthy overtime session. He had not seen regular action since the first period, as coach John Muckler opted to use only three lines. "I sat for almost three hours," Klima said, "but I was ready and I was fresh."

Bill Ranford faced 52 shots in the game for the Oilers, while Edmonton managed only 31 against Moog. "By the third overtime," Ranford admitted, "I had a headache from concentrating."

Behind the Oilers Dynasty

s coach, general manager and club president, Glen Sather was the architect of the team. But could he have built the Edmonton Oilers without Wayne Gretzky?

Sather wanted his Oilers to play a hybrid style combining the speed and skill of the European game with the power of the North American game.

Gretzky's talents had been hard to recognize in the early days. Those who saw him play as a youngster—and even as a teenage pro in the World Hockey Association and the NHL—were often left wondering how he did it. Unlike past hockey stars, such as Gordie Howe, Maurice Richard, Bobby Hull and Bobby Orr, Gretzky didn't dominate in an obvious way. He was small, scrawny even. He certainly didn't appear fast or durable, and his shot didn't look like much. Yet the puck often seemed to wind up in the net. It was Gretzky's knack for anticipating the play that made him so remarkable, and that was a skill that was difficult to detect. Even when he scored an astounding 92 goals in his third NHL season of 1981–82, it was Gretzky's skill as a playmaker that set him apart.

"Gretzky changed the focus of our play," Montreal Canadiens goalie Ken Dryden would write in 1999. "A passing game made the player without the puck more important than the player with it. He was quicker, more creative and maneuverable. He was the more dangerous one."

But, as Dryden pointed out, "passing required a reason to pass and someone to pass to. Gretzky pushed his teammates to skate, think ahead, create and find open ice in order to be in position to receive one of his on-the-tape passes. Playing this way, they had to become better players, and they did."

Sather wanted a certain kind of athlete. According to the Oilers' chief scout, Barry Fraser, after Edmonton won their first Stanley Cup title in 1984, Sather instructed his people to find him players "who can skate and have character." Sather wanted his Oilers to play a hybrid style combining the speed and skill of the European game with the power of the North American game. Herb Brooks had great success drilling his team of college kids to play that style and won a gold medal for the United States at the 1980 Lake Placid Olympics—but Sather's inspiration had come a year before that.

Back in 1978–79, the Oilers had enjoyed their only truly great season during their seven-year existence in the WHA. They finished first in the regular-season standings and reached the Avco Cup final, only to be swept by the Winnipeg Jets.

"Winnipeg beat us," Fraser recalled, "because Bobby Hull and eight Swedes skated us out of the rink."

Fraser's memory was slightly faulty, in that Hull barely played for the Jets that season and the team's best Swedes—Anders Hedberg and Ulf Nilsson—had already left Winnipeg for the NHL. Even so, it was the success of the Jets in the WHA that was the blueprint Sather's Oilers would take into the NHL.

The team was stripped of most of its talent when it left the WHA. However, Edmonton's scouts led to the selections of Mark Messier, Glenn Anderson, Paul Coffey, Jari Kurri and Grant Fuhr between 1979 and 1981. The team's first selection (21st overall) in the 1979 NHL Entry Draft was Kevin Lowe, who would lead a corps of defensive defensemen, including Charlie Huddy, Randy Gregg and later Steve Smith, proving the Oilers could play a tougher two-way game than most critics thought possible when the Stanley Cup was on the line.

Still, it was offense that defined the Oilers dynasty as Edmonton improved rapidly from 69 points and 16th overall in the 21-team NHL

in their first season, to 74 points and 14th in their second, to 111 points and second place by their third. The Oilers became the first team in NHL history to top 400 goals, with 417 in 1981–82, and would push their record total to 446 by 1983–84. It's difficult to remember now, given all the success that was about to follow, but if the Oilers hadn't won

the Stanley Cup that year, they may well have abandoned Sather's style and gone with a more traditional approach.

"We said before the series, if we didn't win, this team wouldn't be together again," Mark Messier told reporters after receiving the Conn Smythe Trophy as the playoff's Most Valuable Player in 1984. "This is

Wayne Gretzky celebrates with fans in 1987 after helping Edmonton claim their third Cup in four years.

....

a good bunch of guys," he added, "and if we won it, we knew we'd be together for a long time."

Not all of them stayed together, though. Like any team of the

modern era, supporting players came and went. Even stars like Coffey and Gretzky were traded away when money got tight, but the Oilers kept on winning. They made it to five championships in the seven-season stretch from 1983–84 through 1989–90, and Messier, Anderson, Kurri, Fuhr, Lowe, Huddy and Gregg were a part of all of them.

Even without Gretzky on the 1989–90 Stanley Cup team, it's impossible to think back on the Oilers dynasty without acknowledging "The Great One." Yes, the players Sather's scouts found to surround Gretzky turned out to be extremely talented, and yes an improved defense did become key to those championship teams, but it's hard to imagine the Oilers becoming such a dominant team in an era of explosive offense without the greatest offensive player in hockey history. Sadly, it's just as hard to imagine how they could have afforded to keep the team together when salaries exploded in the 1990s and the rest of their stars were dealt away.

So how good might the Oilers have been if they could have kept Gretzky, Coffey, Messier and the others? Gretzky himself has speculated that Edmonton would have won the Stanley Cup four more times.

Calgary Flames

DIVISION SEMIFINAL
4 games to 3 over Vancouver

DIVISION FINAL
4 games to 0 over Los Angeles

CONFERENCE FINAL
4 games to 1 over Chicago

CONN SMYTHE TROPHY **AL MACINNIS** D – CALGARY

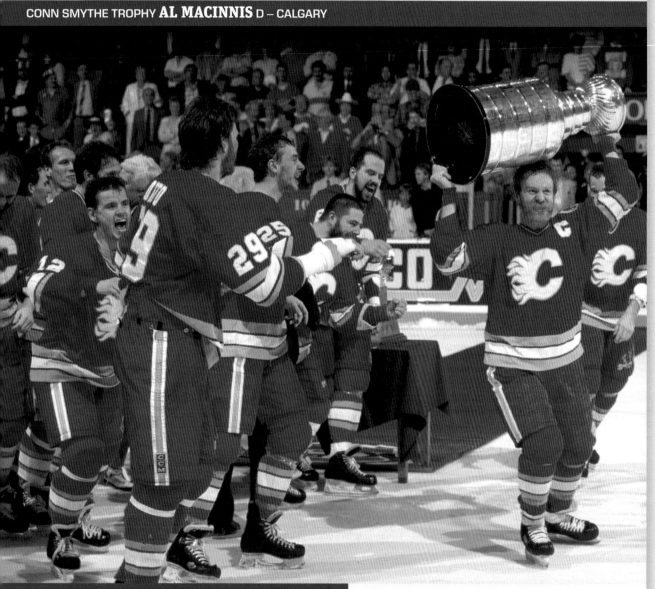

FINAL 4 GAMES TO 2

MAY 14 ►	Montreal 2 at Calgary 3
MAY 17 ►	Montreal 4 at Calgary 2
MAY 19 ►	Calgary 3 at Montreal 4 2X OT
MAY 21 ►	Calgary 4 at Montreal 2
MAY 23 ►	Montreal 2 at Calgary 3
MAY 25 ►	Calgary 4 at Montreal 2

PLAYOFF SCORING LEADER

Al MacInnis	GP	G	A	PTS
CALGARY	22	7	24	31

FINAL SERIES SCORING

CALGARY	GP	G	A	PTS	PIM
Al MacInnis	6	5	4	9	18
Joe Mullen	6	5	3	8	4
Joel Otto	6	2	6	8	4
Doug Gilmour	6	4	3	7	6
Theoren Fleury	6	1	1	2	2
Joe Nieuwendyk	6	1	1	2	2
Colin Patterson	6	1	1	2	16
Tim Hunter	4	0	2	2	6
Jamie Macoun	6	0	2	2	8
Jim Peplinski	4	0	2	2	10
Rob Ramage	6	0	2	2	10
Lanny McDonald	3	1	0	1	2
Mark Hunter	4	0	1	1	12
Hakan Loob	6	0	1	1	0
Brian MacLellan	6	0	1	1	4
Brad McCrimmon	6	0	1	1	6
Dana Murzyn	6	0	1	1	8
Jiri Hrdina	3	0	0	0	0
Ric Nattress	6	0	0	0	12
Gary Roberts	6	0	0	0	8
GOALTENDER	GP	W	L	MIN	GA	SO	AVG
Mike Vernon	6	4	2	397	16	0	2.42

MONTREAL	GP	G	A	PTS	PIM
Chris Chelios	6	1	6	7	10
Bobby Smith	6	3	2	5	20
Mike McPhee	6	1	3	4	4
Claude Lemieux	4	2	1	3	18
Larry Robinson	6	2	1	3	4
Mike Keane	6	1	2	3	4
Mats Naslund	6	1	2	3	4
Brian Skrudland	6	0	3	3	18
Petr Svoboda	6	0	3	3	8
Russ Courtnall	6	2	0	2	12
Stéphane Richer	6	1	1	2	10
Rick Green	6	1	0	1	2
Ryan Walter	6	1	0	1	4
Shayne Corson	6	0	1	1	18
Bob Gainey	6	0	1	1	4
Guy Carbonneau	6	0	0	0	6
Eric Desjardins	6	0	0	0	2
Brent Gilchrist	2	0	0	0	4
Craig Ludwig	6	0	0	0	8
GOALTENDER	GP	W	L	MIN	GA	SO	AVG
Patrick Roy	6	2	4	395	17	0	2.58

ROSTER

Theoren Fleury
Doug Gilmour
Jiri Hrdina
Mark Hunter
Tim Hunter
Hakan Loob
Al MacInnis
Brian MacLellan
Jamie Macoun

Brad McCrimmon
Lanny McDonald
(co-captain)
Joe Mullen
Dana Murzyn
Ric Nattress
Joe Nieuwendyk
Joel Otto
Colin Patterson

Jim Peplinski
(co-captain)
Rob Ramage
Gary Roberts
Gary Suter
Mike Vernon
Rick Wamsley
Cliff Fletcher (president/
general manager)
Terry Crisp (head coach)

Road Warriors

The Montreal Canadiens had never been beaten for the Stanley Cup on home ice before losing to Calgary in 1989. However, the Flames were actually the second visiting team to celebrate a championship at the famed Montreal Forum. Back in 1928, the New York Rangers beat the Montreal Maroons in a five-game series played entirely at the Forum because the circus had taken over Madison Square Garden.

You Can't Touch a Flame When It's Red Hot

It had been something of a fluke when Calgary and Montreal met for the Stanley Cup in 1986. Both teams had finished well back of the league leaders in the regular season, but they had benefited from a playoff filled with upsets. That was not the case when the two teams met again in the spring of 1989. The Flames were the best team in the NHL for the second year in a row, setting franchise records with 54 wins (54-17-9) and 117 points during the season. The Canadiens were second best with a record of 53-18-9 and 115 points.

Calgary's offense was led by Joe Mullen, who had a career high 51 goals and 110 points in 1988–89. Second-year center Joe Nieuwendyk also scored 51 goals for the second straight season. Gary Roberts and the newly acquired Doug Gilmour added two-way grit, as did a rookie named Theo Fleury. Al MacInnis led a talented defensive corps that also featured Jamie Macoun and Brad McCrimmon protecting goalies Mike Vernon and Rick Wamsley.

Despite the big year in Calgary, the biggest story of the 1988–89 season was in Los Angeles. The Kings had acquired Wayne Gretzky from the Oilers on August 9, 1988, and the team suddenly had Hollywood star power. Gretzky scored his first goal for the Kings on his very first shot of the regular season and would rally the Kings to a seven-game defeat of the Oilers in the first round of the playoffs. The Flames struggled against Vancouver in the first round and needed a brilliant save from Mike Vernon in overtime of the seventh game before Jim Peplinski banked in the series-winning goal off Joel Otto's skate. Calgary had little trouble beating Los Angeles and Chicago after that.

Two goals from Al MacInnis and the game-winner by Theo Fleury gave Calgary a 3–2 win over Montreal in the opener of the Stanley Cup final. The Canadiens won Game 2 and then took a 2–1 series lead when a controversial penalty call on Calgary's Mark Hunter in double overtime led to the winning goal in Game 3. However, the Flames bounced back with three straight wins to wrap up the series in six.

The Men in the Nets

The Stanley Cup series between Calgary and Montreal featured a matchup of the two best goalies in the NHL that season. Mike Vernon led the NHL with 37 wins in 1988–89, while Patrick Roy had a league-best 2.49 goals-against average. Shortly after Calgary beat Montreal for the Stanley Cup, Roy beat out Vernon for the Vezina Trophy.

Conn Smythe Story Calgary's Al MacInnis was the Conn Smythe Trophy winner as playoff MVP after becoming the first defenseman in NHL history to top the postseason in scoring. Bobby Orr had tied Phil Esposito with a playoff-best 24 points in 15 games back in 1971–72, but technically Orr finished second in the scoring race because Esposito had nine goals to Orr's five.

Al MacInnis

A Good Year

Calgary's Stanley Cup victory capped off Lanny McDonald's Hall of Fame career in style. After sitting out three games in the final, McDonald returned to the lineup in Game 6 and scored the go-ahead goal to give Calgary a 2–1 lead in a game they would go on to win 4–2. McDonald had also scored his 500th goal during the 1988–89 season and reached the 1,000-point plateau as well. He retired later that summer.

Grey Cup Too Norman Kwong had his name engraved on the Stanley Cup in 1989 as a part owner of the Flames. In his younger days, when he was known as Normie, Kwong had been a star halfback with the Edmonton Eskimos and won the Grey Cup as champions of Canadian football in 1948, 1954, 1955 and 1956. Wayne Gretzky, who won the Stanley Cup four times with the Edmonton Oilers, would later get his name on the Grey Cup as a part owner of the 1991 Toronto Argonauts. Lionel Conacher, who was voted Canada's Athlete of the Half-Century in 1950, won the Grey Cup as a player with the Argos in 1921 and later won the Stanley Cup as a player with the Chicago Black Hawks (1934) and Montreal Maroons (1935). Gerry James, who was a football star with the Winnipeg Blue Bombers while also playing five seasons of professional hockey, almost won both championships in a five-month span. James won the Grey Cup with Winnipeg in November 1959 and then appeared in the Stanley Cup final with the Toronto Maple Leafs in April 1960, but the Leafs lost to the Montreal Canadiens.

The Battle of Alberta

Edmonton quickly got the jump on Calgary in the early years of their NHL rivalry, including a one-sided win in their first playoff matchup in 1983. The Oilers generally came out on top in their regular-season matches as well, but in 1984, Calgary and Edmonton met in a playoff rematch that truly raised the stakes. In a year in which the Oilers would lose only one other game throughout the entire playoffs en route to their first Stanley Cup title, Edmonton nearly squandered a 3–1 series lead against Calgary in the Smythe Division final. They salvaged the series with a 7–4 victory in Game 7.

"This isn't just for Calgary," exclaimed Lanny McDonald after the game. "This is for the oilmen, this is for the old-timers, this is for the kids. To know you've knocked off the Stanley Cup champions. Yeah, it's fabulous."

"Everybody remembers that Calgary series," said Wayne Gretzky after the Oilers defeated the New York Islanders for the Stanley Cup. He added that, before the seventh game against the Flames, "We said in the dressing room, if we win this game, we'll win the Stanley Cup."

"Make sure to say thank you," Edmonton player Kevin Lowe told reporters after the Islanders series. "We owe a lot to Calgary … The Flames were our toughest opponents."

Though Gretzky and Lowe were no doubt genuine in their assessments, their words had to anger Calgary fans. Those fans would get their revenge two years later.

The Oilers finished the 1985–86 season with an NHL-best 119 points on a record of 56-17-7. Gretzky broke his own single-season record with 215 points, and his record-setting 163 assists were not only more than anyone else had points that season, but were more than anyone else had ever scored in NHL history up to that time. The Flames had the second-best record in the Western Conference, but they were still 30 points behind the Oilers that season. Calgary had only one win and one tie in eight games against Edmonton during the regular schedule, but the win was a 9–3 victory on the second-last night of the regular season in a fight-filled game that typified the rivalry.

"One of our guys was in a fight right in front of our bench," remembered Gretzky in 1999, "and Tim Hunter popped him. His nose—you heard it go 'splat.' And the guy on our team, Kevin McClelland, looked to the bench and said: 'Didn't feel a thing.' He kept fighting. Tim Hunter, who was still standing in front of our bench, said, 'That guy is crazy.'"

Edmonton swept the Vancouver Canucks to open the playoffs that year, while Calgary swept the Winnipeg Jets. The Flames stayed on a roll when they opened the Smythe Division final with a 4–1 win over the Oilers in Edmonton. The series seesawed back and forth through six games, with Calgary getting great goaltending from Mike Vernon and timely scoring from Joe Mullen and Lanny McDonald. Game 7 was a seesaw affair of its own, with Calgary taking a 2–0 lead only to see Edmonton tie it up before the end of the second period. Early in the third period, Calgary's Perry Berezan dumped the puck into the Oilers' zone and headed for the bench. Rookie Oilers defenseman Steve Smith, celebrating his 23rd birthday that day, picked up the puck behind the net. Smith's intended cross-ice pass bounced off the leg of goalie Grant Fuhr and into the Edmonton net. The goal at 5:14 held up as the game winner and the Oilers were eliminated.

"This isn't just for Calgary," exclaimed Lanny McDonald after the game. "This is for the oilmen, this is for the old-timers, this is for the kids. To know you've knocked

couldn't recover and went out in four straight.

Gretzky called the overtime goal, "the greatest thrill for me in hockey," adding that, "it's so big because of what it meant to the team."

Just as it was for Edmonton in 1984, winning the Battle of Alberta in 1988 was the key to winning the Stanley Cup.

The rivalry between the cities of Calgary and Edmonton remains strong and still adds a spark to games between the two teams, but, sadly for hockey fans, the Flames and the Oilers have not faced each other in the playoffs since 1991. Despite both teams making appearances in the Stanley Cup final (Calgary in 2004 and Edmonton in 2006), these have been difficult times in Alberta, with both teams missing the playoffs more often than they have made them. However, it looks as though Edmonton is attempting to build a modern version of the dynasty Oilers, as they have benefited from high draft picks, becoming the NHL's best crop of young stars, as players such as Jordan Eberle, Ryan Nugent-Hopkins and Taylor Hall offer hope for the future. Calgary hasn't had the same high draft picks to work with, but will certainly aim to keep pace with their provincial rival.

off the Stanley Cup champions. Yeah, it's fabulous."

Though the Oilers would bounce back to win the Stanley Cup again the very next season, it would take another year for them to exact their revenge on the Flames. Calgary was the first-place team in 1987–88, and Edmonton the underdog,

when the two teams hooked up yet again in the Smythe Division final. The defining moment in this series was a 5–4 Oilers overtime victory in Game 2. Gretzky got the winning goal when he finished off a breakaway while shorthanded by hammering a slap shot over the shoulder of goalie Vernon. Calgary

Wayne Gretzky and Hakan Loob do battle in Calgary during the 1987–88 season.

1987–88 Edmonton Oilers

DIVISION SEMIFINAL
4 games to 1 over Winnipeg

DIVISION FINAL
4 games to 0 over Calgary

CONFERENCE FINAL
4 games to 1 over Detroit

CONN SMYTHE TROPHY WAYNE GRETZKY C – EDMONTON

FINAL   4 GAMES TO 0

MAY 18 ► Boston 1 at Edmonton 2

MAY 20 ► Boston 2 at Edmonton 4

MAY 22 ► Edmonton 6 at Boston 3

MAY 24 ► Edmonton 3 at Boston 3*

MAY 26 ► Boston 3 at Edmonton 6

*Suspended at 16:37 of second period due to power failure.

PLAYOFF SCORING LEADER

Wayne Gretzky	GP	G	A	PTS
EDMONTON	19	12	31	43

FINAL SERIES SCORING
Includes suspended game, May 24, 1988

EDMONTON	GP	G	A	PTS	PIM
Wayne Gretzky	5	3	10	13	0
Esa Tikkanen	5	6	3	9	18
Glenn Anderson	5	3	3	6	4
Jari Kurri	5	1	4	5	4
Craig Simpson	5	3	1	4	10
Steve Smith	5	0	4	4	2
Mike Krushelnyski	5	1	2	3	6
Kevin McClelland	5	1	2	3	26
Mark Messier	5	1	2	3	4
Randy Gregg	5	0	3	3	4
Kevin Lowe	5	0	2	2	4
Craig Muni	5	0	2	2	0
Keith Acton	5	1	0	1	0
Normand Lacombe	5	1	0	1	4
Jeff Beukeboom	4	0	0	0	0
Geoff Courtnall	5	0	0	0	0
Charlie Huddy	1	0	0	0	0
Craig MacTavish	5	0	0	0	2
Marty McSorley	5	0	0	0	4

GOALTENDER	GP	W	L	MIN	GA	SO	AVG
Grant Fuhr	5	4	0	277	12	0	2.60

BOSTON	GP	G	A	PTS	PIM
Ken Linseman	5	2	2	4	6
Glen Wesley	5	2	2	4	0
Cam Neely	5	2	1	3	4
Raymond Bourque	5	0	3	3	6
Steve Kasper	5	2	0	2	2
Randy Burridge	5	1	1	2	2
Bob Joyce	5	1	1	2	0
Moe Lemay	5	1	1	2	6
Craig Janney	5	0	2	2	0
Bob Sweeney	5	0	2	2	2
Greg Hawgood	2	1	0	1	0
Keith Crowder	5	0	1	1	10
Greg Johnston	1	0	1	1	0
Gord Kluzak	5	0	1	1	4
Rick Middleton	5	0	1	1	0
Reed Larson	2	0	0	0	2
Nevin Markwart	1	0	0	0	2
Tom McCarthy	1	0	0	0	0
Jay Miller	3	0	0	0	24
Bill O'Dwyer	5	0	0	0	0
Allen Pedersen	4	0	0	0	6
Willi Plett	2	0	0	0	4
Michael Thelven	4	0	0	0	6

GOALTENDERS	GP	W	L	MIN	GA	SO	AVG
Andy Moog	3	0	2	157	11	0	4.20
Reggie Lemelin	2	0	2	120	8	0	4.00

ROSTER

Keith Acton
Glenn Anderson
Jeff Beukeboom
Geoff Courtnall
Grant Fuhr
Randy Gregg
Wayne Gretzky (captain)
Dave Hannan
Charlie Huddy

Mike Krushelnyski
Jari Kurri
Normand Lacombe
Kevin Lowe
Craig MacTavish
Kevin McClelland
Marty McSorley
Mark Messier
Craig Muni

Bill Ranford
Craig Simpson
Steve Smith
Esa Tikkanen
Glen Sather (general manager/coach)

Photo Opportunity

The tradition of gathering the team together after the final game for an on-ice photo with the Stanley Cup began with the Oilers in 1988. "I knew this was going to be my last year in Edmonton," Gretzky would later recall. "I had too many friends who were telling me that Peter [Pocklington] had been calling around trying to sell me. By the time we hoisted the Cup, I figured that I wasn't going to be an Oiler much longer so I rallied the troops together for a picture on the ice."

Oilers Overcome the Odds

Edmonton's Stanley Cup victory in 1986–87 had marked the team's third title in four seasons. The Oilers had finished first in the Smythe Division standings for six straight seasons since 1981–82 and had topped 100 points during all of those years. They had also been the NHL's top-scoring team for six straight seasons. Those streaks all ended in 1987–88.

Many players had gotten off to an early start for the 1987–88 season, with the fourth Canada Cup tournament beginning late in August. The Canada Cup marked a coming out for Mario Lemieux, who finally seemed to develop the work ethic to go with his immense skills. Playing on a line with Gretzky, Lemieux helped lead Canada to victory in a thrilling final series against the Soviet Union and carried on his brilliant play throughout the NHL season. Aided by former Oiler Paul Coffey, who was traded to Pittsburgh early in the season, Lemieux ended Gretzky's seven-year hold on the Art Ross Trophy as the league's scoring champion.

With Coffey gone and Gretzky missing 16 games due to injuries, Mark Messier had a big year for Edmonton with 111 points. Goalie Grant Fuhr had an even bigger season. With Andy Moog traded to Boston, Fuhr played in 75 of 80 games for the Oilers and led the NHL with 40 wins. Even so, the Oilers "slumped" to 99 points as their rivals in Calgary topped both the Smythe Division and the overall NHL standings with 105 points. When Edmonton met Calgary in the second round of the playoffs, everyone predicted a tight series. Instead, the Oilers won the opener 3–1 then took Game 2 by a 5–4 total on a beautiful Gretzky goal in overtime, and the demoralized Flames fell in four straight.

After Edmonton beat Detroit in five games to win the Campbell Conference title, Boston provided little opposition in the Stanley Cup final. Though the first two games in Edmonton were close and the Bruins battled hard to stay alive at home in Game 4, only a power failure at the Boston Garden that night prevented a sweep. The suspension of that game forced the Oilers to play a fifth game back at home two nights later in order to wrap up the series.

Sweet 16

Edmonton's Grant Fuhr was the first goalie to win 16 games in one playoff year.

MOST POINTS IN THE FINAL, ONE SERIES

13	Wayne Gretzky, Edmonton (3G, 10A in 4 games plus suspended game), 1988
12	Gordie Howe, Detroit, (5G, 7A in 7 games), 1955
	Yvan Cournoyer, Montreal (6G, 6A in 6 games), 1973
	Jacques Lemaire, Montreal (3G, 9A in 6 games), 1973
	Mario Lemieux, Pittsburgh (5G, 7A in 5 games), 1991
	Danny Brière, Philadelphia (3G, 9A in 6 games), 2010

MOST POINTS IN THE FINAL, CAREER

62	Jean Béliveau, Montreal (30G, 32A in 64 games)
53	Wayne Gretzky, Edmonton (16G, 30A in 26 games), Los Angeles (2G, 5A in 5 games); overall (18G, 35A in 31 games)
50	Gordie Howe, Detroit (18G, 32A in 55 games)
47	Henri Richard, Montreal (21G, 26A in 65 games)
46	Maurice Richard, Montreal (34G, 12A in 59 games)
	Bernie Geoffrion, Montreal (24G, 22A in 53 games)

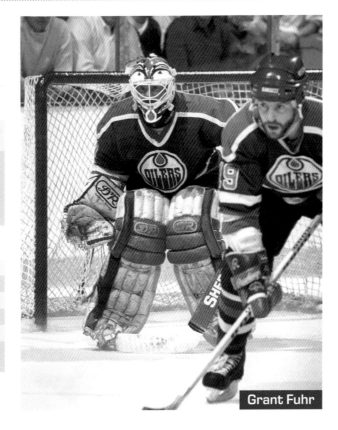

Grant Fuhr

The Night the Lights Went Out

A brief late-afternoon thunderstorm had caused scattered power outages around Boston on May 24, 1988, but the rain had stopped before Game 4 of the Stanley Cup final got started. Still, it was sweltering inside the old Boston Garden that night. The Oilers took an early 2–0 lead, but the Bruins fought back to get ahead on a pair of goals by defenseman Glen Wesley early in the second period. At 16:37 in the second, the red light went on to signify a goal by Craig Simpson that tied the score 3–3. Ten seconds later, the Garden was plunged into darkness. A transformer had blown. Emergency lights went on immediately, but fans were ushered out of the building for their own safety. Power was restored about 35 minutes later, but NHL president John Ziegler said he could not be given any assurance it wouldn't go out again. After consulting with both teams, the game, in accordance with NHL rules, was suspended. Though the statistics would count, the game would not. It would have to be made up in its entirety at the end of the series, if necessary. The Oilers ensured an eighth game would not be necessary by completing the five-game, four-game sweep back home in Edmonton. The blackout marked the first time that an NHL playoff game had not been completed since March 31, 1951, when a semifinal game between the Bruins and Maple Leafs was called after one period of overtime because of a Saturday night curfew necessitated by a Toronto city bylaw that forbade games to be played on Sundays.

1986–87   Edmonton Oilers

DIVISION SEMIFINAL
4 games to 1 over Los Angeles

DIVISION FINAL
4 games to 0 over Winnipeg

CONFERENCE FINAL
4 games to 1 over Detroit

CONN SMYTHE TROPHY RON HEXTALL G – PHILADELPHIA

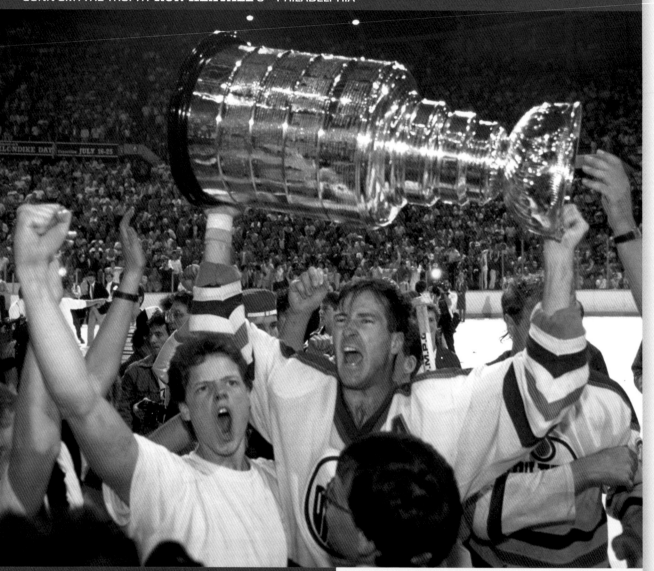

FINAL   4 GAMES TO 3

MAY 17 ►	Philadelphia 2 at Edmonton 4
MAY 20 ►	Philadelphia 2 at Edmonton 3 OT
MAY 22 ►	Edmonton 3 at Philadelphia 5
MAY 24 ►	Edmonton 4 at Philadelphia 1
MAY 26 ►	Philadelphia 4 at Edmonton 3
MAY 28 ►	Edmonton 2 at Philadelphia 3
MAY 31 ►	Philadelphia 1 at Edmonton 3

PLAYOFF SCORING LEADER

	GP	G	A	PTS
Wayne Gretzky EDMONTON	21	5	29	34

FINAL SERIES SCORING

EDMONTON	GP	G	A	PTS	PIM
Wayne Gretzky	7	2	9	11	2
Jari Kurri	7	5	4	9	4
Paul Coffey	7	2	4	6	14
Glenn Anderson	7	4	1	5	14
Mark Messier	7	2	3	5	10
Kevin Lowe	7	2	1	3	4
Randy Gregg	7	1	2	3	0
Mike Krushelnyski	7	1	1	2	6
Charlie Huddy	7	0	2	2	10
Craig MacTavish	7	0	2	2	6
Kevin McClelland	7	1	0	1	4
Marty McSorley	7	1	0	1	10
Dave Hunter	7	0	1	1	4
Craig Muni	5	0	1	1	0
Kent Nilsson	7	0	1	1	0
Jaroslav Pouzar	3	0	1	1	2
Kelly Buchberger	3	0	0	0	5
Reijo Ruotsalainen	7	0	0	0	4
Steve Smith	3	0	0	0	6
Esa Tikkanen	7	0	0	0	6

GOALTENDER	GP	W	L	MIN	GA	SO	AVG
Grant Fuhr	7	4	3	427	17	0	2.39

PHILADELPHIA	GP	G	A	PTS	PIM
Brian Propp	7	4	5	9	0
Pelle Eklund	7	1	7	8	0
Rick Tocchet	7	3	4	7	24
Ron Sutter	7	0	4	4	6
Brad McCrimmon	7	2	1	3	10
Doug Crossman	7	1	2	3	6
Scott Mellanby	7	1	2	3	4
Murray Craven	6	2	0	2	2
Peter Zezel	7	1	1	2	2
Brad Marsh	7	0	2	2	2
Lindsay Carson	6	1	0	1	0
J.J. Daigneault	5	1	0	1	0
Derrick Smith	7	1	0	1	10
Dave Brown	7	0	1	1	11
Mark Howe	7	0	1	1	0
Kjell Samuelsson	7	0	1	1	10
Don Nachbaur	1	0	0	0	0
Dave Poulin	7	0	0	0	8
Ilkka Sinisalo	5	0	0	0	2
Daryl Stanley	4	0	0	0	2
Tim Tookey	1	0	0	0	0

GOALTENDER	GP	W	L	MIN	GA	SO	AVG
Ron Hextall	7	3	4	427	22	0	3.09

ROSTER

Glenn Anderson
Jeff Beukeboom
Kelly Buchberger
Paul Coffey
Grant Fuhr
Randy Gregg
Wayne Gretzky (captain)
Charlie Huddy
Dave Hunter

Mike Krushelnyski
Jari Kurri
Moe Lemay
Kevin Lowe ▲
Craig MacTavish
Kevin McClelland
Marty McSorley
Mark Messier
Andy Moog

Craig Muni
Kent Nilsson
Jaroslav Pouzar
Reijo Ruotsalainen
Steve Smith
Esa Tikkanen
Glen Sather (general manager/coach)

All Is Forgiven

"When we won again in 1987, everyone on the team except Steve Smith kind of collectively knew that I was going to pass the Stanley Cup to him. There was no question that what had happened the year before was devastating to him and his family, but it wasn't his fault we lost and that's the way our guys looked at it. It was just one of those things. And he went on to help with three more Stanley Cups. He became a huge part of that team's core." —Wayne Gretzky

The Oilers Bounce Back

After a brilliant regular season in 1985–86, the Edmonton Oilers had experienced a stunning upset in the second round of the playoffs. Tied 2–2 early in the third period of the seventh game of the Smythe Division final against their arch rivals from Calgary, Steve Smith banked an attempted cross-ice pass off of goalie Grant Fuhr and into his own net. The Flames held on for a 3–2 victory.

"Losing to Calgary in the 1986 playoffs was devastating for everyone," Wayne Gretzky would later recall. "Especially with the way the goal was scored…. [But] I remember saying. 'Hey, sometimes you gotta deal with bumps in the road. We lost and we're all devastated that we lost, but we're healthy, and we gotta start planning today—right now—that we're gonna come back and win next year.' And that's what we did. All of us as a team did that. We bounced right back."

Fueled by their playoff defeat in 1986, the Oilers once again led the regular season standings in 1986–87, though their 106 points were the fewest by a first-place team since 1969–70. Gretzky won the Art Ross Trophy for the seventh consecutive season, with 62 goals and 121 assists, and was later awarded the Hart Trophy as MVP for an eighth year in a row. For the first time in five years, the Oilers didn't reach the 400-goal mark, but their 372 still led the league for the fifth straight season, while the 284 goals they allowed were the fewest since the team entered the NHL in 1979–80. In addition to Gretzky, Jari Kurri and Mark Messier also topped 100 points, ranking second and fourth in the NHL scoring race with 108 and 107 respectively. Andy Moog and Grant Fuhr shared the load in goal, though Fuhr would see the majority of the action once they reached the playoffs.

The Oilers sailed through the postseason with only two losses en route to the Stanley Cup final. There, they met up with the Philadelphia Flyers, who were the only other team in the NHL that season to top 100 points in the standings. The Oilers jumped out to a 3–1 series lead, but they nearly let it slip away before wrapping it up in Game 7. It was the first time since 1971 that the Stanley Cup final had gone the distance.

Conn Smythe Story

Ron Hextall brought an aggressive nature and puckhandling skills rarely seen before in a goaltender when he entered the NHL with the Flyers in 1986–87. He led all NHL goalies with 66 games played and 37 wins that year, and though the Calder Trophy for Rookie of the Year went to Luc Robitaille, Hextall won the Vezina Trophy as the league's top goaltender. In the playoffs he set a record (later tied by Miikka Kiprusoff of Calgary in 2004) for most games played by a goalie in one postseason, with 26, and was rewarded with the Conn Smythe Trophy despite the Flyers' loss to Edmonton in the Stanley Cup final.

Gamesmanship
In an effort to motivate his team, Flyers coach Mike Keenan had the Stanley Cup brought into the Philadelphia dressing room prior to Game 5. He did it again before Game 6, but when Keenan tried to have the Cup brought into the dressing room before Game 7, it could not be found. Keenan was told that the Cup had been delayed in transit, but in actual fact Oilers coach and GM Glen Sather had instructed team trainer Sparky Kulchisky to lock it in the trunk of his car.

Ron Hextall

Comebacks

Not only did the Flyers rally from down three games to one to force a seventh game against the Oilers, they had to rally to win each of the games they won. The Flyers came back from a three-goal deficit to win Game 3, 5–3, and fell behind 2–0 in Games 5 and 6 before pulling out victories. Through the first six games, the Flyers never enjoyed a lead until they scored the game-winning goal. The story was reversed in Game 7, when Philadelphia jumped out to an early 1–0 lead only to see the Oilers rally for a 3–1 victory.

Game 7 and Then Some
In order to cut down on quick upsets, the first round of the playoffs was extended to seven games from a best-of-five in 1986–87. That year's Patrick Division semifinal series between the New York Islanders and Washington Capitals was the only one to go seven—and it went well beyond that! Pat LaFontaine finally scored the winner for the Islanders at 8:47 of the fourth overtime. At the time, it was the fifth-longest game in NHL history. It currently ranks tenth—but it's the longest Game 7 that has ever been played.

Lucky 13
After dropping their first game of the playoffs 5–2 to Los Angeles, Edmonton stormed back with a 13–3 victory in Game 2. The Oilers' 13 goals were nearly as many as the Kings had shots in the game (15) and set an NHL record for the most goals scored by one team in a playoff game.

DIVISION SEMIFINAL	DIVISION FINAL	CONFERENCE FINAL
3 games to 0 over Boston	**4 games to 3 over Hartford**	**4 games to 1 over NY Rangers**

ROSTER

CONN SMYTHE TROPHY **PATRICK ROY** G – MONTREAL

Serge Boisvert

Guy Carbonneau

Chris Chelios

Kjell Dahlin

Lucien DeBlois

Bob Gainey (captain)

Gaston Gingras

Rick Green

John Kordic

Tom Kurvers

Mike Lalor

Claude Lemieux

Craig Ludwig

David Maley

Mike McPhee

Mats Naslund

Chris Nilan

Stéphane Richer

Larry Robinson

Steve Rooney

Patrick Roy

Brian Skrudland

Bobby Smith

Doug Soetaert

Petr Svoboda

Mario Tremblay

Ryan Walter

Serge Savard
(general manager)

Jean Perron (coach)

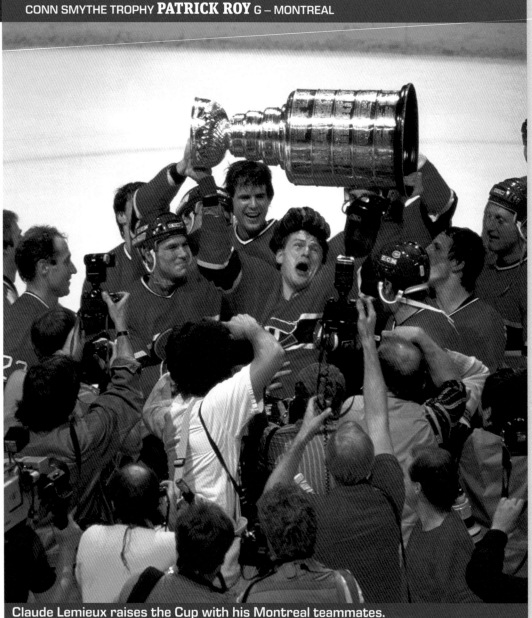

Claude Lemieux raises the Cup with his Montreal teammates.

FINAL 4 GAMES TO 1

MAY 16 ▸	Montreal 2 at Calgary 5
MAY 18 ▸	Montreal 3 at Calgary 2 OT
MAY 20 ▸	Calgary 3 at Montreal 5
MAY 22 ▸	Calgary 0 at Montreal 1
MAY 24 ▸	Montreal 4 at Calgary 3

PLAYOFF SCORING LEADERS

Doug Gilmour	GP	G	A	PTS
ST. LOUIS	19	9	12	21

Bernie Federko	GP	G	A	PTS
ST. LOUIS	19	7	14	21

FINAL SERIES SCORING

MONTREAL	GP	G	A	PTS	PIM
Mats Naslund	5	3	4	7	0
Bobby Smith	5	2	2	4	8
Chris Chelios	5	1	3	4	19
Gaston Gingras	4	2	1	3	0
Claude Lemieux	5	1	2	3	31
David Maley	5	1	2	3	2
Larry Robinson	5	0	3	3	15
Guy Carbonneau	5	0	3	3	23
Brian Skrudland	5	2	0	2	32
Mike Lalor	5	0	2	2	19
Mike McPhee	5	0	2	2	24
Kjell Dahlin	4	1	0	1	0
Bob Gainey	5	1	0	1	2
Rick Green	5	1	0	1	0
Ryan Walter	5	0	1	1	2
Serge Boisvert	2	0	0	0	0
John Kordic	5	0	0	0	15
Craig Ludwig	5	0	0	0	14
Chris Nilan	3	0	0	0	49
Stéphane Richer	1	0	0	0	0
Steve Rooney	1	0	0	0	0
GOALTENDER	GP	W	L	MIN	GA	SO	AVG
Patrick Roy	5	4	1	301	12	1	2.39

CALGARY	GP	G	A	PTS	PIM
Dan Quinn	5	1	4	5	4
Jim Peplinski	5	1	3	4	37
Al MacInnis	5	0	4	4	8
Joe Mullen	4	2	1	3	4
Lanny McDonald	5	2	1	3	6
Joel Otto	5	1	2	3	12
Steve Bozek	4	2	0	2	19
John Tonelli	5	2	0	2	15
Paul Reinhart	5	1	1	2	2
Hakan Loob	5	0	2	2	2
Doug Risebrough	5	1	0	1	12
Paul Baxter	4	0	1	1	17
Nick Fotiu	2	0	1	1	10
Tim Hunter	5	0	1	1	43
Jamie Macoun	5	0	1	1	4
Robin Bartel	4	0	0	0	12
Perry Berezan	2	0	0	0	4
Brian Bradley	1	0	0	0	0
Yves Courteau	1	0	0	0	0
Mike Eaves	2	0	0	0	2
Brett Hull	2	0	0	0	0
Terry Johnson	2	0	0	0	12
Colin Patterson	2	0	0	0	0
Neil Sheehy	5	0	0	0	31
GOALTENDERS	GP	W	L	MIN	GA	SO	AVG
Mike Vernon	5	1	4	260	14	0	3.23
Reggie Lemelin	1	0	0	41	1	0	1.46

St. Patrick

Patrick Roy had to face only 15 shots in Game 4 against Calgary, but each save was crucial in a 1–0 victory that gave the Canadiens a stranglehold on the series. Roy became the first rookie goalie to post a shutout in the Stanley Cup final since 1945, when both Frank McCool (Toronto) and Harry Lumley (Detroit) blanked the opposition in the lowest-scoring seven-game series in Stanley Cup history.

Roy would follow up his Stanley Cup victory of 1986 with another in Montreal in 1993 and two more with Colorado, in 1996 and 2001. He is the only goalie in history to win the Stanley Cup in three different decades.

Canadiens Come Out on Top

The two-time defending Stanley Cup–champion Edmonton Oilers wrapped up their fifth consecutive Smythe Division title in 1985–86. The Oilers also returned to the top spot in the overall standings, with 119 points, and became the inaugural winners of the Presidents' Trophy for finishing in first place. Wayne Gretzky broke his own single-season records with 163 assists and 215 points, but as in his 92-goal, 212-point campaign of 1981–82, regular-season records didn't translate into playoff prosperity. This time, the rival Calgary Flames eliminated the Oilers in a thrilling seven-game Smythe Division final that ended with the Flames winning 3–2 on a goal that the Oilers' Steve Smith put into his own net. Calgary then defeated the Norris Division–champion St. Louis Blues in seven games to reach the Stanley Cup final.

There were also upsets in the Wales Conference, particularly in the Patrick Division, where the fourth-place Rangers, with their 78 points, stunned the 110-point Flyers, while the 90-point Islanders knocked off the 107-point Capitals. In the Adams Division, fourth-place Hartford knocked off first-place Quebec. The early elimination of the top three teams in the conference helped clear the way for the Montreal Canadiens.

The Canadiens were led by Mats Naslund, whose 110 points made him the first Montreal player to crack the top-10 in scoring since Guy Lafleur in 1980. The team also featured a number of rookies who had been members of Montreal's Sherbrooke farm team when they had won the Calder Cup as champions of the American Hockey League the year before. Among those were goalie Patrick Roy, defenseman Gaston Gingras and forwards Brian Skrudland and Stéphane Richer. Claude Lemieux played only 10 games for the Canadiens during the 1985–86 season, spending most of that season in Sherbrooke, but he would play all 20 games for Montreal in the playoffs and lead the team with 10 goals. Roy was even more impressive, playing every minute in goal for the Canadiens throughout the postseason, winning 15 games with a 1.92 goals-against average and establishing himself as a future superstar.

The Canadiens opened the Stanley Cup final with a 5–2 loss in Calgary, but they rallied to win the next four in a row.

STANLEY CUP WINS WITH THREE OR MORE TEAMS

TEAMS	PLAYER (TOTAL WINS)	TEAM AND YEAR
4	Jack Marshall (6)	Winnipeg Victorias 1901; Montreal AAA 1902, 1903; Montreal Wanderers 1907, 1910; Toronto 1914
3	Hap Holmes (4)	Toronto 1914, 1918; Seattle 1917; Victoria 1925
3	Frank Foyston (3)	Toronto 1914; Seattle 1917; Victoria 1925
3	Jack Walker (3)	Toronto 1914; Seattle 1917; Victoria 1925
3	Gord Pettinger (4)	New York Rangers 1933; Detroit 1936, 1937; Boston 1939
3	Al Arbour (4)	Detroit 1954; Chicago 1961; Toronto 1962, 1964
3	Larry Hillman (6)	Detroit 1955; Toronto 1962, 1963, 1964, 1967; Montreal 1969
3	Claude Lemieux (4)	Montreal 1986; New Jersey 1995, 2000; Colorado 1996
3	Joe Nieuwendyk (3)	Calgary 1989; Dallas 1999; New Jersey 2003
3	Mike Keane (3)	Montreal 1993; Colorado 1996; Dallas 1999

Joe Nieuwendyk

Championship Record

The Canadiens' Stanley Cup title in 1986 marked the 23rd championship in the club's history (22 since entering the NHL, plus their first back in 1916). At the time, the victory set a record for professional sports teams in North America, breaking a tie with the New York Yankees, who had won the World Series 22 times.

Shortest Overtime

After dropping the first game of the final to Calgary, the Canadiens drew even with a 3–2 victory in Game 2. Montreal won the game just nine seconds into overtime, when Mike McPhee faked a shot on goal and instead sent a pass to Brian Skrudland, who redirected the puck past Flames goalie Mike Vernon. It is the shortest overtime game in NHL history.

Canada's Cup The 1986 matchup between Montreal and Calgary marked the first all-Canadian Stanley Cup final since 1967, when the Canadiens lost to the Toronto Maple Leafs.

DIVISION SEMIFINAL	DIVISION FINAL	CONFERENCE FINAL
3 games to 0 over Los Angeles	**4 games to 0 over Winnipeg**	**4 games to 2 over Chicago**

ROSTER

CONN SMYTHE TROPHY **WAYNE GRETZKY** C – EDMONTON

Glenn Anderson

Billy Carroll

Paul Coffey

Lee Fogolin Jr.

Grant Fuhr

Randy Gregg

Wayne Gretzky
(captain)

Charlie Huddy

Pat Hughes

Dave Hunter

Don Jackson

Mike Krushelnyski

Jari Kurri

Willy Lindstrom

Kevin Lowe

Dave Lumley

Kevin McClelland

Larry Melnyk

Mark Messier

Andy Moog

Mark Napier

Jaroslav Pouzar

Dave Semenko

Esa Tikkanen

Glen Sather
(general manager/
coach)

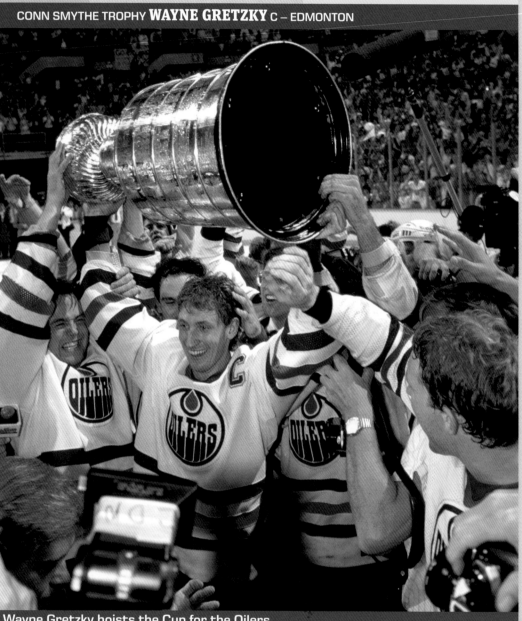

Wayne Gretzky hoists the Cup for the Oilers.

FINAL 4 GAMES TO 1

MAY 21 ▸	Edmonton 1 at Philadelphia 4	
MAY 23 ▸	Edmonton 3 at Philadelphia 1	
MAY 25 ▸	Philadelphia 3 at Edmonton 4	
MAY 28 ▸	Philadelphia 3 at Edmonton 5	
MAY 30 ▸	Philadelphia 3 at Edmonton 8	

PLAYOFF SCORING LEADER

	GP	G	A	PTS
Wayne Gretzky EDMONTON	18	17	30	47

FINAL SERIES SCORING

EDMONTON	GP	G	A	PTS	PIM
Wayne Gretzky	5	7	4	11	0
Paul Coffey	5	3	8	11	6
Jari Kurri	5	1	6	7	0
Mark Messier	5	2	4	6	6
Charlie Huddy	5	1	5	6	6
Mike Krushelnyski	5	2	2	4	4
Willy Lindstrom	5	3	0	3	2
Glenn Anderson	5	1	1	2	12
Dave Hunter	5	1	0	1	25
Randy Gregg	4	0	1	1	2
Kevin McClelland	5	0	1	1	41
Billy Carroll	2	0	0	0	0
Lee Fogolin Jr.	5	0	0	0	8
Pat Hughes	4	0	0	0	2
Don Jackson	5	0	0	0	35
Kevin Lowe	5	0	0	0	4
Dave Lumley	1	0	0	0	2
Larry Melnyk	1	0	0	0	0
Mark Napier	5	0	0	0	0
Jaroslav Pouzar	1	0	0	0	0
Dave Semenko	4	0	0	0	14
Esa Tikkanen	3	0	0	0	4
GOALTENDER	**GP**	**W**	**L**	**MIN**	**GA**	**SO**	**AVG**
Grant Fuhr	5	4	1	300	13	0	2.60

PHILADELPHIA	GP	G	A	PTS	PIM
Derrick Smith	5	1	4	5	0
Dave Poulin	5	1	3	4	4
Rich Sutter	3	3	0	3	4
Tim Kerr	3	2	1	3	9
Brian Propp	5	2	1	3	0
Murray Craven	5	1	2	3	4
Ron Sutter	5	1	2	3	6
Todd Bergen	4	1	1	2	0
Mark Howe	5	1	1	2	0
Lindsay Carson	3	0	2	2	2
Doug Crossman	5	0	2	2	12
Rick Tocchet	5	0	2	2	14
Ilkka Sinisalo	5	1	0	1	0
Brad Marsh	5	0	1	1	43
Peter Zezel	5	0	1	1	4
Ray Allison	1	0	0	0	2
Dave Brown	1	0	0	0	19
Miroslav Dvorak	5	0	0	0	2
Thomas Eriksson	4	0	0	0	0
Len Hachborn	1	0	0	0	0
Ed Hospodar	5	0	0	0	34
Joe Paterson	5	0	0	0	19
GOALTENDERS	**GP**	**W**	**L**	**MIN**	**GA**	**SO**	**AVG**
Pelle Lindbergh	4	1	3	185	11	0	3.57
Bob Froese	3	0	1	115	9	0	4.70

Seven and Eleven

Wayne Gretzky's seven goals, in the final against Philadelphia tied the modern-era record shared by Mike Bossy (in four games versus Vancouver in 1982) and Jean Béliveau (in five games versus Detroit in 1956). The 11 points both Gretzky and Paul Coffey had in 1985 broke the record of 10 in a five-game series, last accomplished by Béliveau back in 1956.

MOST POINTS IN ONE PLAYOFF YEAR

47	Wayne Gretzky, Edmonton, 1985	17 goals, 30 assists in 18 games
44	Mario Lemieux, Pittsburgh, 1991	16 goals, 28 assists in 23 games
43	Wayne Gretzky, Edmonton, 1988	12 goals, 31 assists in 19 games
40	Wayne Gretzky, Los Angeles, 1993	15 goals, 25 assists in 24 games
38	Wayne Gretzky, Edmonton, 1983	12 goals, 26 assists in 16 games

Edmonton Again

Having won the Stanley Cup for the first time the year before, the Edmonton Oilers showed no signs of letting up in 1984–85. Wayne Gretzky topped the 200-point plateau for the second straight season, and the third time in four years, with 73 goals and 135 assists for 208 points. Linemate Jari Kurri's 71 goals and 135 points trailed only Gretzky in the league scoring race, while defenseman Paul Coffey enjoyed his second straight 100-point season and finished fifth in the scoring race, with 121 points. The Oilers were the top team in both the Smythe Division and the Campbell Conference for the fourth year in a row, but after leading the NHL's overall standings for the first time in 1983–84, their 109 points in 1984–85 were second best behind the Philadelphia Flyers.

Former Flyer captain Bobby Clarke was now the general manager in Philadelphia, and new coach Mike Keenan got 53 wins and 113 points from the team. Tim Kerr led the Flyers offense with 54 goals, but it was a tight defense, led by Mark Howe and Vezina Trophy–winning goalie Pelle Lindbergh, that was key to Philadelphia's success. The Flyers outdistanced the Washington Capitals for top spot in the Patrick Division, while the New York Islanders slipped to third place. In the playoffs, the Islanders upset Washington but suffered their earliest postseason defeat since 1979, when they lost to Philadelphia in the second round. The Flyers then beat the Quebec Nordiques to reach the Stanley Cup final, where they would face the Oilers.

Edmonton had been at its offensive best throughout the playoffs. They eliminated Smythe Division rivals Los Angeles and Winnipeg in the first two rounds without losing a single game. Facing Chicago for the Campbell Conference crown, the Oilers set an NHL playoff record with 44 goals (the Blackhawks added 25 of their own for a combined record of 69) and won the series in six games. Wayne Gretzky's 18 points (four goals, 14 assists) were the most ever for a six-game series, while Jari Kurri's 12 goals were the most in a playoff series of any length. Pelle Lindbergh and the Flyers shutdown the high-flying Oilers for a 4–1 victory in Game 1 of the Stanley Cup final, but Edmonton stormed back with 20 goals over the next four games as they wrapped up the series in five.

MOST GOALS IN ONE PLAYOFF YEAR

19	Reggie Leach, Philadelphia, 1976	16 games
	Jari Kurri, Edmonton, 1985	18 games
18	Joe Sakic, Colorado, 1996	22 games
17	Newsy Lalonde, Montreal, 1919	10 games
	Mike Bossy, New York Islanders, 1981	18 games
	Steve Payne, Minnesota, 1981	19 games
	Mike Bossy, New York Islanders, 1982	19 games
	Mike Bossy, New York Islanders, 1983	19 games
	Wayne Gretzky, Edmonton, 1985	18 games
	Kevin Stevens, Pittsburgh, 1991	24 games

MOST ASSISTS IN ONE PLAYOFF YEAR

31	Wayne Gretzky, Edmonton, 1988	19 games
30	Wayne Gretzky, Edmonton, 1985	18 games
29	Wayne Gretzky, Edmonton, 1987	21 games
28	Mario Lemieux, Pittsburgh, 1991	23 games
26	Wayne Gretzky, Edmonton, 1983	16 games

Pelle Lindbergh

Pelle Lindbergh

Pelle Lindbergh was a star in his native Sweden, earning the top job on the national team by the age of 20 and helping his country win a bronze medal at the 1980 Lake Placid Winter Olympics. He would go on to become the first European goaltender to star in the NHL.

Lindbergh had grown up idolizing Bernie Parent of the Philadelphia Flyers, and he was selected by Philadelphia in the second round of the 1979 NHL draft. Lindbergh had a big season in 1980–81 with Philadelphia's American Hockey League affiliate out of Maine, and he made his NHL debut in 1981–82. He became an NHL regular in 1982–83, playing in the All-Star Game and being named to the All-Rookie Team. By the 1984–85 season, he was the best goalie in the NHL.

Tragically, Lindbergh crashed his car after a night of partying early on the morning of November 10, 1985. He was declared brain dead by doctors and taken of life support two days later, when his parents gave permission for his organs to be donated for transplants. The Flyers held a lengthy memorial for Lindbergh before their game on November 14. The opponent that night was the Edmonton Oilers, and the Flyers beat them 5–3.

The night's most stirring moment came when Mark Howe scored the game's first goal late in the first period and Lindbergh's father, Sigge, leaped to his feet. "Just seeing his face," said the Flyers' Brad Marsh, "made us feel better."

Edmonton Oilers

DIVISION SEMIFINAL
3 games to 0 over Winnipeg

DIVISION FINAL
4 games to 3 over Calgary

CONFERENCE FINAL
4 games to 0 over Minnesota

FINAL 4 GAMES TO 1

MAY 10	► Edmonton 1 at New York Islanders 0
MAY 12	► Edmonton 1 at New York Islanders 6
MAY 15	► New York Islanders 2 at Edmonton 7
MAY 17	► New York Islanders 2 at Edmonton 7
MAY 19	► New York Islanders 2 at Edmonton 5

PLAYOFF SCORING LEADER

Wayne Gretzky	GP	G	A	PTS
EDMONTON	19	13	22	35

ROSTER

Glenn Anderson
Paul Coffey
Pat Conacher
Lee Fogolin Jr.
Grant Fuhr
Randy Gregg
Wayne Gretzky (captain)
Charlie Huddy
Pat Hughes
Dave Hunter
Don Jackson
Jari Kurri
Willy Lindstrom
Ken Linseman
Kevin Lowe
Dave Lumley
Kevin McClelland
Mark Messier
Andy Moog
Jaroslav Pouzar
Dave Semenko
Glen Sather (general manager/ coach)

CONN SMYTHE TROPHY MARK MESSIER C – EDMONTON

Dave Semenko, Kevin McClelland and Glenn Anderson count down the seconds to Edmonton's first Cup.

FINAL SERIES SCORING

EDMONTON	GP	G	A	PTS	PIM
Wayne Gretzky	5	4	3	7	4
Jari Kurri	5	1	5	6	2
Mark Messier	5	3	1	4	7
Paul Coffey	5	2	2	4	0
Kevin McClelland	5	2	2	4	16
Glenn Anderson	5	1	3	4	8
Willy Lindstrom	5	2	1	3	0
Dave Semenko	5	1	2	3	4
Charlie Huddy	5	0	3	3	4
Pat Hughes	5	0	3	3	4
Ken Linseman	5	1	1	2	26
Dave Lumley	5	1	1	2	17
Pat Conacher	2	1	0	1	0
Randy Gregg	5	1	0	1	2
Kevin Lowe	5	1	0	1	4
Lee Fogolin Jr.	5	0	1	1	6
Dave Hunter	3	0	1	1	6
Don Jackson	5	0	0	0	13
Jaroslav Pouzar	5	0	0	0	6

GOALTENDERS	GP	W	L	MIN	GA	SO	AVG
Andy Moog	3	2	0	128	4	0	1.88
Grant Fuhr	3	2	1	172	8	1	2.79

NY ISLANDERS	GP	G	A	PTS	PIM
Clark Gillies	5	5	3	8	0
Bryan Trottier	5	2	2	4	2
Pat Flatley	5	1	3	4	8
Pat LaFontaine	5	2	1	3	0
Brent Sutter	5	1	2	3	6
Mike Bossy	5	0	3	3	0
Greg Gilbert	5	1	1	2	26
Paul Boutilier	5	0	2	2	0
Stefan Persson	4	0	2	2	2
Anders Kallur	5	0	1	1	0
Ken Morrow	5	0	1	1	4
Denis Potvin	5	0	1	1	6
Billy Carroll	1	0	0	0	0
Gord Dineen	3	0	0	0	24
Butch Goring	5	0	0	0	0
Mats Hallin	2	0	0	0	0
Tomas Jonsson	5	0	0	0	8
Dave Langevin	2	0	0	0	5
Bob Nystrom	2	0	0	0	4
Duane Sutter	5	0	0	0	26
John Tonelli	5	0	0	0	4

GOALTENDERS	GP	W	L	MIN	GA	SO	AVG
Billy Smith	5	1	3	245	17	0	4.16
Roland Melanson	3	0	1	55	3	0	3.27

Win or Else

"We were winning a lot of hockey games with this system, but we hadn't won a Stanley Cup yet. The thinking was that we had to win it in 1983–84 or the club would be dismantled and a new approach would be tried."
— Kevin Lowe

City of Champions

The Edmonton Eskimos won the Grey Cup as champions of the Canadian Football League five years in a row from 1978 through 1982. They won it again in 1987. The Edmonton Oilers won the Stanley Cup five times in seven years from 1984 through 1990.

Edmonton Ends the Islanders' Reign

The Edmonton Oilers were young and cocky heading into the Stanley Cup final against the New York Islanders in 1983. In just their fourth NHL season, the Oilers had already rewritten the NHL record book and seemed to feel the Stanley Cup was theirs by right. But it wouldn't be just yet.

Leaving the Nassau County Coliseum after the Islanders swept them for the 1982–83 Cup, Wayne Gretzky and Kevin Lowe walked past the home team's dressing room. Gretzky expected to see the Islanders celebrating. Instead what he saw was an exhausted team attending to their injuries. Lowe turned to Gretzky and said, "That's why they won and we didn't. They gave it all they had."

In 1983–84 the Oilers certainly gave it all they had. They set an all-time NHL record with 446 goals, won a franchise-best 57 games and led the NHL with 119 points. Gretzky had 87 goals and 118 assists for 205 points. Paul Coffey, Jari Kurri and Mark Messier each topped 100 points, with Kurri (52) and Glenn Anderson (54) making the Oilers the first team in history to boast three 50-goal scorers. In the playoffs, the Oilers sandwiched a pair of easy wins around a tough seven-game series with Calgary to reach the Stanley Cup final once again.

The Islanders had showed every indication in the regular season that they were a legitimate threat to equal the Montreal Canadiens' record of five consecutive Stanley Cup championships. Mike Bossy and Bryan Trottier were still among the NHL's elite offensive performers, Denis Potvin was still an All-Star on defense and the goaltending of Billy Smith, backed up by Roland Melanson and Kelly Hrudey, was still among the toughest to score on. The Islanders 50 wins and 104 points made them the top team in the Wales Conference, but the playoffs were a grind and the Islanders were a wounded team when they reached the final.

The Oilers proved in Game 1 that they weren't just an offensive juggernaut by playing hard defense and defeating the Islanders 1–0. It was the Islanders' first loss in nine games of Cup-final play dating back to 1981; the loss also ended New York's 10-game winning streak against the Oilers. The defending champions rebounded for a 6–1 victory in Game 2, but it was all Oilers after that as Edmonton won the Stanley Cup in five games.

Streaks Snapped

MULTIPLE CUP-WINNING NHL TEAMS AND THE TEAMS THAT SNAPPED THEIR STREAKS

TEAM	STREAK	DEFEATED BY	NEW CHAMPION
Montreal Canadiens	(5) 1956 to 1960	Chicago (semifinals)	Chicago Black Hawks
New York Islanders	(4) 1980 to 1983	Edmonton (final)	Edmonton Oilers
Montreal Canadiens	(4) 1976 to 1979	Minnesota (quarterfinals)	New York Islanders
Toronto Maple Leafs	(3) 1947 to 1949	Detroit (semifinals)	Detroit Red Wings
Toronto Maple Leafs	(3) 1962 to 1964	Montreal (semifinals)	Montreal Canadiens
Ottawa Senators	(2) 1920, 1921	Toronto (NHL final)	Toronto St. Pats
Montreal Canadiens	(2) 1930, 1931	New York Rangers (semifinals)	Toronto Maple Leafs
Detroit Red Wings	(2) 1936, 1937	missed playoffs	Chicago Black Hawks
Detroit Red Wings	(2) 1954, 1955	Montreal (final)	Montreal Canadiens
Montreal Canadiens	(2) 1965, 1966	Toronto (final)	Toronto Maple Leafs
Montreal Canadiens	(2) 1968, 1969	missed playoffs	Boston Bruins
Philadelphia Flyers	(2) 1974, 1975	Montreal (final)	Montreal Canadiens
Edmonton Oilers	(2) 1984, 1985	Calgary (division final)	Montreal Canadiens
Edmonton Oilers	(2) 1987, 1988	Los Angeles (division semifinal)	Calgary Flames
Pittsburgh Penguins	(2) 1991, 1992	New York Islanders (division final)	Montreal Canadiens
Detroit Red Wings	(2) 1997, 1998	Colorado (conference semifinal)	Dallas Stars

Beating the Best

"The first thing that sticks out in my mind from that first Stanley Cup was the team that we beat. The Islanders were such a great team and they were great champions. They had a never-say-die attitude and playing against them, you could never trust any lead you had. In the deciding game, we were up 4–0 after two periods, and they changed their game for the third period. All of a sudden, they score two quick goals and I remember Kevin [Lowe] looking at me on the bench and saying, 'Holy s---.'"
— Lee Fogolin

Great Teams

"I felt no shame turning the Cup over to them. I'm damn proud. Several [players] talked about idolizing us as we shook hands. One great team turned the Cup over to a team that was great all year. They deserve it."
— Denis Potvin

Bye Bye Billy Billy Smith was one of the top clutch goaltenders in the NHL and a key component in the Islanders' Stanley Cup dynasty. He was also well known for using his stick to punish opponents who crowded his crease. Smith drew the ire of Oilers fans during the 1983 final for slashing Glenn Anderson in Game 1 and for calling Wayne Gretzky a crybaby after an incident in Game 2. Following the Oilers victory in 1984, a couple of fans were seen on the streets of Edmonton with a full-sized coffin bearing a likeness of the Islanders goalie. On it were the letters RIP and the message "Bye Bye Billy."

What's in a Name?

The original Stanley Cup, as presented for the first time back in 1893, featured a silver bowl (purchased in London at Lord Stanley's request) mounted on an ebony base. The base was fitted with its own band of silver encircling it. This extra ring of silver was not merely for decoration, it was there so that each winning team could have their club name engraved on it along with the year they had won (at the team's own expense!). Over the years, as more bands were added, the Cup began to grow. In 1907 the Montreal Wanderers became the first team to engrave the names of both their winning players and their club executives onto the Stanley Cup. Since 1924 every winning team has followed suit.

Although the word "engraved" is always used to describe how the names get put on the Stanley Cup, the truth is that they're actually stamped on.

In the early days of the Stanley Cup there wasn't much need for rules about who could get their name on the trophy. Teams had fewer players on their roster and much smaller staffs. Even into the 1930s and 1940s there was plenty of room for the Toronto Maple Leafs to engrave the names of team owner Conn Smythe's sons, Stafford and Hugh Smythe, onto the Stanley Cup as team mascots. Players often got their names on the Cup even if they'd only played a handful of games with the team.

But then in 1976 Don Awrey had his name left off of the Cup—despite playing 72 games for the Montreal Canadiens that season—because he did not play a single game during the playoffs. John Van Boxmeer, who played 46 games for Montreal that season, had his name omitted for the same reason. Shortly thereafter, the NHL instituted a rule that anyone who played at least half the games during the regular season—provided they were still on the roster at the end of the year—or even one game during the Stanley Cup final would get their name on the trophy. (Neither Awrey nor Van Boxmeer have been added retroactively, though Awrey's name is on the Cup as a member of the Boston Bruins in 1970 and 1972.)

These days a total of 53 names can be engraved on the Stanley Cup for each winning team. During the summer, the champions submit a list of names to the NHL commissioner for approval. Since 1994, when the New York Rangers lobbied to have the names of Ed Olczyk and Mike Hartman added to the Stanley Cup, the NHL has allowed players who fall short of the criteria to get their name on the Cup if they are judged to have made a significant contribution to the team. Teams also engrave the names of as many coaches and front office personnel as they have room for on the Stanley Cup.

Although the word "engraved" is always used to describe how the names get put on the Stanley Cup, the truth is that they're actually stamped on. Special hammers of different weights are used to strike against a letter punch to sink each letter. Given that each name on the Stanley Cup has to be written one letter at a time using a tiny letter punch, it's not surprising

EDMONTON OILERS 1983-84
PETER POCKLINGTON OWNER ~~XXXX XXXXXXXXX~~
GLEN SATHER G.M. & COACH
BRUCE MACGREGOR ASST. G.M.
JOHN MUCKLER   TED GREEN ASST. COACHES
BARRY FRASER DIR. P.P.& C. SCOUT

W. GRETZKY CAPT. G. ANDERSON P. COFFEY
P. CONACHER L. FOGOLIN G. FUHR R. GREGG
C. HUDDY P. HUGHES D. HUNTER D. JACKSON
J. KURRI W. LINDSTROM K. LINSEMAN K. LOWE
D. LUMLEY K. MCCLELLAND M. MESSIER A. MOOG
J. POUZAR D. SEMENKO
P. MILLAR ATHLETIC THERAPIST B. STAFFORD TR.
L. KULCHISKY ASST. TR.

the occasional spelling mistake gets made. Hockey Hall of Famer Alex Delvecchio is on the Cup as Alex Belvecchio for 1951–52, while the team names Toronto Maple Leaes (1962–63), Bqstqn Bruins (1971–72) and New York Ilanders (1980–81) also appear on the trophy. In recent years, Adam Deadmarsh, Manny Legace, Eric Staal and Kris Versteeg had spelling mistakes made in their names, but these were later corrected.

Easily the most unique case in the history of Stanley Cup names is that of Basil Pocklington. His name was added to the Stanley Cup list in 1983–84 by his son Peter, the owner of the Edmonton Oilers. When the NHL learned that Basil Pocklington (who had no actual involvement with the team whatsoever) had been engraved on the Stanley Cup, they demanded that his name be crossed out. This was done by stamping a row of Xs over the original letters in Pocklington's name. But the story doesn't end there. In 1993, the entire band of silver that held the names of the 1983–84 Oilers had to be replaced. When all the names of the 13 teams that filled that row were re-engraved, Basil Pocklington was omitted. However, the name was later added and crossed out again because the row of Xs had become a part of Stanley Cup lore.

DIVISION SEMIFINAL	DIVISION FINAL	CONFERENCE FINAL
3 games to 1 over Washington	**4 games to 2 over NY Rangers**	**4 games to 2 over Boston**

ROSTER

CONN SMYTHE TROPHY **BILLY SMITH** G – NEW YORK ISLANDERS

Mike Bossy
Bob Bourne
Paul Boutilier
Billy Carroll
Greg Gilbert
Clark Gillies
Butch Goring
Mats Hallin
Tomas Jonsson
Anders Kallur
Gord Lane
Dave Langevin
Mike McEwen
Roland Melanson
Wayne Merrick
Ken Morrow
Bob Nystrom
Stefan Persson
Denis Potvin (captain)
Billy Smith
Brent Sutter
Duane Sutter
John Tonelli
Bryan Trottier
Bill Torrey
(president/
general manager)
Al Arbour (coach)

FINAL   4 GAMES TO 0

MAY 10 ►	New York Islanders 2 at Edmonton 0	
MAY 12 ►	New York Islanders 6 at Edmonton 3	
MAY 14 ►	Edmonton 1 at New York Islanders 5	
MAY 17 ►	Edmonton 2 at New York Islanders 4	

PLAYOFF SCORING LEADER

Wayne Gretzky	GP	G	A	PTS
EDMONTON	16	12	26	38

FINAL SERIES SCORING

NY ISLANDERS	GP	G	A	PTS	PIM
Duane Sutter	4	2	5	7	0
Ken Morrow	4	3	2	5	2
Brent Sutter	4	3	2	5	10
Mike Bossy	3	2	2	4	0
Bob Bourne	4	2	2	4	6
Bryan Trottier	4	1	3	4	4
Denis Potvin	4	0	3	3	4
Tomas Jonsson	4	1	1	2	8
Anders Kallur	4	1	1	2	4
Bob Nystrom	4	1	1	2	2
Stefan Persson	4	0	2	2	4
John Tonelli	4	1	0	1	0
Clark Gillies	4	0	1	1	6
Dave Langevin	4	0	1	1	0
Billy Carroll	4	0	0	0	0
Greg Gilbert	1	0	0	0	0
Butch Goring	4	0	0	0	0
Gord Lane	4	0	0	0	2
Wayne Merrick	4	0	0	0	0

GOALTENDER	GP	W	L	MIN	GA	SO	AVG
Billy Smith	4	4	0	240	6	1	1.50

EDMONTON	GP	G	A	PTS	PIM
Wayne Gretzky	4	0	4	4	0
Jari Kurri	4	3	0	3	2
Glenn Anderson	4	1	1	2	11
Lee Fogolin Jr.	4	0	2	2	0
Mark Messier	4	1	0	1	2
Dave Semenko	4	1	0	1	0
Paul Coffey	4	0	1	1	4
Charlie Huddy	4	0	1	1	0
Tom Roulston	4	0	1	1	0
Ray Cote	4	0	0	0	0
Randy Gregg	4	0	0	0	0
Pat Hughes	4	0	0	0	2
Dave Hunter	4	0	0	0	8
Don Jackson	4	0	0	0	4
Willy Lindstrom	4	0	0	0	0
Ken Linseman	4	0	0	0	4
Kevin Lowe	4	0	0	0	2
Dave Lumley	4	0	0	0	9

GOALTENDER	GP	W	L	MIN	GA	SO	AVG
Andy Moog	4	0	4	240	15	0	3.75

Changing of the Guard

"I was talking to my wife, and I told her that the Oilers were going to win a Stanley Cup very soon. Maybe next year or maybe the year after that. I just hope it's not against us when they do it."

— Bob Bourne, New York Islanders

End of the Line

No team in North American professional sports has won four straight championships since the New York Islanders. Only the Chicago Bulls (1991 to 1993 and 1996 to 1998) and New York Yankees (1998 to 2000) have managed three straight.

Four Straight

The New York Islanders were three-time defending Stanley Cup champions entering the 1982–83 season, but their three lengthy postseason runs were starting to wear them out. "We already had been through a lot of playoff action," Bob Bourne later admitted, "and it was taking its toll on us, mentally and physically."

The Islanders started the season slowly, and though they came on strong later they failed to top the 100-point plateau for only the second time in eight years. Captain Denis Potvin missed significant playing time for the third time in four seasons, and his 66 points in 69 games marked the first time that the star defenseman had averaged less than a point a game since the 1974–75 season. Bryan Trottier played all 80 games, but his 89 points marked the first time he'd failed to top 100 since 1976–77. Mike Bossy continued to put up big numbers, with 60 goals and 118 points. Still, it was a tight defense featuring Potvin, Stefan Persson, Ken Morrow and Dave Langevin in front of goalies Billy Smith and Roland Melanson that led the team as the Islanders surrendered a league-low 226 goals. Even so, their 96 points on a record of 42-26-12 left them 10 back of the Philadelphia Flyers in the Patrick Division standings.

In the playoffs, Philadelphia lost to the New York Rangers in the first round, while the Islanders were peaking at the right time. They beat the Washington Capitals and then the Rangers to win the Patrick Division title and set up a Wales Conference showdown with Boston. The Bruins had been the NHL's best team in the regular season, with 110 points, but they fell to the Islanders in six games. Mike Bossy scored the game-winning goal in all four Islanders victories, though the games were all pretty one-sided.

Facing the Islanders in the Stanley Cup final were the high-flying Edmonton Oilers. Led by Wayne Gretzky, the Oilers had become a record-setting offensive power in just their fourth NHL season, and yet the Islanders shut them down almost completely. The Oilers were held to just six goals in the final as the Islanders beat them in four straight to win their fourth consecutive Stanley Cup title.

The Drive for Five

The Islanders would come up short in their effort to match the Montreal Canadiens of 1956 to 1960 with five straight Stanley Cup titles, but in reaching the final again in 1984, the Islanders did set a record that appears unlikely to be matched. They won 19 straight playoff series over a span of five seasons.

Sweet 16 There were 16 players who played on all four Islanders Stanley Cup teams: Mike Bossy, Bob Bourne, Clark Gillies, Butch Goring, Anders Kallur, Gord Lane, Dave Langevin, Wayne Merrick, Ken Morrow, Bob Nystrom, Stefan Persson, Denis Potvin, Billy Smith, Duane Sutter, John Tonelli and Bryan Trottier.

Battlin' Billy Billy Smith shared the net with Glenn "Chico" Resch and Roland Melanson during the Islanders' dynasty years, but there was no question about who was number one when it came time for the playoffs. The Islanders won 60 games against just 18 losses en route to their four straight Stanley Cup titles. Smith posted a record of 57-13 during that stretch.

Oh for Four When the Islanders held Wayne Gretzky goalless during the 1983 final, it marked the only time all season that he had gone four straight games without scoring a goal.

Billy Smith

Behind the Islanders Dynasty

The first major expansion of the NHL from six to 12 teams in 1967–68 was deemed such a success that two more teams were added for the 1970–71 season. Future expansion seemed inevitable, but it wasn't thought that the NHL would add any more teams until 1974. However, with the announcement in 1971 that the rival World Hockey Association planned to launch in 1972–73, the NHL took prompt action to beat them into a couple of new markets. Two new teams—the Atlanta Flames and the New York Islanders (based in suburban Long Island)—were added to the NHL in 1972.

Many teams had overlooked Bossy in the draft, fearing he lacked toughness, but the Islanders were thrilled to get him with the 15th pick in 1977.

From the beginning, Islanders general manager Bill Torrey planned to build his team around youth.

"Let's be realistic, I don't think anybody expects us to be contending right away," admitted Torrey after taking the job on February 15, 1972.

Torrey would emphasize younger players in the Expansion Draft, like 22-year-old goalie Billy Smith. (Veteran Ed Westfall, at 32 years old, was an exception.) He would then build the team through the NHL Amateur Draft. Torrey knew his young team would struggle, but he had not expected the woeful 12-60-6 season in 1972–73 that set new modern records for least wins and most losses in a single season.

"Hapless was the word," Torrey told author Stan Fischler. "The Rangers play the hapless Islanders tonight. The Bruins get a breather against the hapless Islanders …

Cripes, I though hapless was the only word in the English language."

But the upside of a hapless season was the opportunity to select Denis Potvin with the first choice in the 1973 NHL Draft. Sam Pollock, general manager of the Montreal Canadiens, made several offers to lure the top pick away from Torrey, but the Islanders' GM stuck with his plan. Another key move came a month after the draft when Torrey hired Al Arbour as the team's new head coach. Originally hired for his defensive prowess, Arbour would evolve his approach to the game when the team began to accumulate more offensive stars. In the meantime, Potvin became the foundation around which Torrey and Arbour built the Islanders. The NHL Draft was where the team would continue to find its talent.

Clark Gillies was the team's first pick (fourth overall) in 1974. As important as Gillies would become to the Islanders, the team's second-round pick was key: Bryan Trottier was just 17 years old when he was drafted, but after one more year in junior hockey he set a rookie scoring record with 95 points in 1975–76, and he joined Potvin as the Islanders' second Calder Memorial Trophy winner. Two years later, Mike Bossy became the third after scoring 53 goals in his debut season. Many teams had overlooked Bossy in the draft, fearing he lacked toughness, but the Islanders were thrilled to get him with the 15th pick in 1977. Among other key players to the future dynasty selected in the draft were brothers Duane and Brent Sutter, John Tonelli, Stefan Persson, Dave Langevin and Tomas Jonsson.

Based on wins and losses, the Islanders' second season in 1973–74 showed only modest improvement over the first, though Arbour's defensive philosophy saw them cut their goals against from 347 to 247. The big breakthrough came a year later when the Islanders improved to 88 points in 1974–75. They didn't just make the playoffs, they eliminated the rival New York Rangers in the preliminary round, and then became the first team since the

late-season acquisition of Butch Goring from the Los Angeles Kings gave the team a lift heading into the playoffs.

"With Butchie at center," Potvin later recalled, "there was a sense of hope we didn't have before."

The revitalized Islanders went all the way to the final, beating Philadelphia on Bob Nystrom's overtime goal in Game 6 to win the Stanley Cup. It had taken the Islanders just eight years to win hockey's ultimate prize—and they would win it four years in a row.

After the Islanders defeated the Edmonton Oilers for their fourth straight title in 1983, the two teams hooked up again in 1984. This time, the young challengers proved too much for the aging champions, and the Islanders were denied a record-tying fifth straight Stanley Cup title.

"This is the worst disappointment I've every felt," Bossy admitted after the loss to the Oilers. "I always thought that we could overcome whatever setbacks we faced. It's a crushing feeling."

"Maybe when I'm old with a grey beard, smoking a pipe in a rocking chair, I'll think about our place in history," said coach Al Arbour. "Right now all I can think about is the loss. In the end, we just ran out of gas."

1942 Toronto Maple Leafs to rally from a three-games-to-nothing deficit when they beat the Pittsburgh Penguins in seven games in the quarterfinal. They nearly did the same against the Stanley Cup champion Philadelphia Flyers before falling in seven in the semifinals.

With Potvin, Trottier, Bossy and Smith leading the way, the Islanders challenged the Montreal Canadiens, Boston Bruins, Buffalo Sabres and the Flyers for the top spot in hockey over the next four years. But good as they were in the regular season, the Islanders were gaining a reputation as a team that couldn't go all the way. In 1977–78 they finished third overall with 111 points, but were eliminated in the quarterfinals by an overtime goal from Lanny McDonald in a tough seven-game series with Toronto. A year later, the Islanders topped the NHL with 116

Denis Potvin shares the Stanley Cup with his teammates in 1980. It was the first of four straight Cup victories for the Islanders.

points, but were knocked off in the semifinals by the red-hot goaltending of the Rangers' John Davidson.

The Islanders slipped a bit in the standings when they dipped to 91 points in 1979–80, but Torrey's

DIVISION SEMIFINAL	DIVISION FINAL	CONFERENCE FINAL
3 games to 2 over Pittsburgh	**4 games to 2 over NY Rangers**	**4 games to 0 over Quebec**

ROSTER

CONN SMYTHE TROPHY **MIKE BOSSY** RW – NEW YORK ISLANDERS

- Mike Bossy
- Bob Bourne
- Billy Carroll
- Greg Gilbert
- Clark Gillies
- Butch Goring
- Tomas Jonsson
- Anders Kallur
- Gord Lane
- Dave Langevin
- Hector Marini
- Mike McEwen
- Roland Melanson
- Wayne Merrick
- Ken Morrow
- Bob Nystrom
- Stefan Persson
- Denis Potvin (captain)
- Billy Smith
- Brent Sutter
- Duane Sutter
- John Tonelli
- Bryan Trottier
- Bill Torrey (president/ general manager)
- Al Arbour (coach)

FINAL 4 GAMES TO 0

MAY 8	▶	Vancouver 5 at NY Islanders 6 OT
MAY 11	▶	Vancouver 4 at NY Islanders 6
MAY 13	▶	NY Islanders 3 at Vancouver 0
MAY 16	▶	NY Islanders 3 at Vancouver 1

PLAYOFF SCORING LEADER

Bryan Trottier	GP	G	A	PTS
NEW YORK ISLANDERS	19	6	23	29

FINAL SERIES SCORING

NY ISLANDERS	GP	G	A	PTS	PIM
Denis Potvin	4	2	7	9	4
Mike Bossy	4	7	1	8	0
Bryan Trottier	4	1	6	7	10
Stefan Persson	4	0	5	5	4
Clark Gillies	4	2	1	3	8
Butch Goring	4	1	2	3	2
Bob Nystrom	4	2	0	2	21
Bob Bourne	4	1	1	2	17
Billy Carroll	4	1	1	2	2
Brent Sutter	4	0	2	2	0
John Tonelli	4	0	2	2	4
Duane Sutter	4	1	0	1	32
Tomas Jonsson	2	0	1	1	2
Wayne Merrick	4	0	1	1	0
Gord Lane	4	0	0	0	22
Dave Langevin	4	0	0	0	2
Anders Kallur	4	0	0	0	0
Mike McEwen	2	0	0	0	0
Ken Morrow	4	0	0	0	0
GOALTENDER	GP	W	L	MIN	GA	SO	AVG
Billy Smith	4	4	0	260	10	1	2.31

VANCOUVER	GP	G	A	PTS	PIM
Thomas Gradin	4	3	2	5	2
Lars Molin	4	0	4	4	0
Gerry Minor	4	1	2	3	0
Curt Fraser	4	0	3	3	28
Tiger Williams	4	0	3	3	14
Ivan Boldirev	4	2	0	2	2
Stan Smyl	4	2	0	2	19
Lars Lindgren	4	1	0	1	2
Jim Nill	3	1	0	1	6
Colin Campbell	4	0	1	1	26
Doug Halward	4	0	1	1	4
Per-Olov Brasar	1	0	0	0	0
Neil Belland	4	0	0	0	4
Garth Butcher	1	0	0	0	0
Marc Crawford	3	0	0	0	0
Ron Delorme	4	0	0	0	4
Anders Eldebrink	3	0	0	0	2
Ivan Hlinka	2	0	0	0	0
Gary Lupul	2	0	0	0	0
Blair MacDonald	1	0	0	0	0
Darcy Rota	4	0	0	0	19
Harold Snepsts	4	0	0	0	16
GOALTENDER	GP	W	L	MIN	GA	SO	AVG
Richard Brodeur	4	0	4	260	17	0	3.92

Other Records Bryan Trottier's 23 assists during the 1982 playoffs were an NHL record at the time. Denis Potvin's nine points in the final remain the most ever by a defenseman in a four-game series. Mike Bossy's seven goals also remain a record for a four-game final.

Long Time Coming The Canucks were the first Vancouver team to reach the Stanley Cup final since the 1922 Vancouver Millionaires. They were the first West Coast team to play for the Stanley Cup since the NHL's Montreal Maroons defeated the Western Hockey League's Victoria Cougars in 1926.

Third Time's the Charm

The NHL was realigned in 1981–82, with the Adams, Patrick, Norris and Smythe Divisions being reorganized on geographic lines and the league giving new emphasis to division play in both the regular season and the playoffs. From this year until 1992–93, the playoffs would feature a semifinal and final within each division, leading up to a conference final in both the Prince of Wales and Clarence Campbell Conferences that would determine the two Stanley Cup finalists.

The big story of the 1981–82 season was the emergence of the Edmonton Oilers as a true powerhouse. Wayne Gretzky led the way with an astounding 92 goals and 120 assists for 212 points, shattering Phil Esposito's record of 76 goals in a single season after having scored 50 in just 39 games only one year after the Islanders' Mike Bossy had become the first player since Maurice Richard in 1944–45 to score 50 goals in 50 games. The Oilers had the best record in the Campbell Conference, with a mark of 48-17-15 for 111 points, but were shocked in the first round of the playoffs by the Los Angeles Kings in a stunning upset dubbed "The Miracle on Manchester." It was a playoff year marked by upsets in both conferences, with the Patrick Division being the only one to hold form, with the New York Islanders advancing all the way to the Stanley Cup final en route to their third straight championship.

The Islanders had their best season in franchise history in 1981–82, posting a record of 54-16-10 to lead the NHL's overall standings with 118 points. Mike Bossy's 64 goals and 147 points were topped only by Gretzky's record-setting totals. Bryan Trottier finished fifth in scoring with 129 points, while Billy Smith won the Vezina Trophy as the NHL's best goalie. Facing Vancouver in the final, the Islanders had their biggest test in Game 1. Trailing 5–4 late in the third, Bossy tied things for the Islanders with five minutes to go and then won it with two seconds left in the first overtime period. The brilliant goaltending of Vancouver's Richard Brodeur kept each game close, but the Islanders still swept the series to become the first (and only) American-based team to win the Stanley Cup three years in a row.

Towel Power

The Canucks reached the Stanley Cup final by downing the Black Hawks rather easily in the Campbell Conference final, defeating Chicago in five games. There was one thing, however, that made the series memorable. Late in the third period of Game 2, Denis Savard scored to give Chicago a 4–1 lead while Vancouver's Harold Snepsts was in the penalty box. The Canucks had not been happy with the refereeing of Bob Myers, and coach Roger Neilson waved a white towel from the end of a hockey stick in mock surrender. Several players joined in. While Black Hawks coach and GM Bob Pulford thought the gesture showed "a complete lack of class," the move is still celebrated in Vancouver, where a statue of Neilson holding a towel on a stick stands outside the Rogers Arena.

Harold Snepsts

Almost Over

The Islanders dynasty nearly died among the many upsets in the opening round of the 1982 playoffs. Down 3–1 to Pittsburgh late in the third period of the decisive fifth game of their Patrick Division semifinal, the Islanders got a goal from Mike McEwen at 14:33. John Tonelli then tied the game with 2:31 remaining and won it with his second goal at 6:19 of overtime. "When you're down 3–1 in the third period," Tonelli said after the game, "all you can think about is that it could be a long summer."

Who's the Boss? Mike Bossy scored 50 goals or more for a record nine consecutive seasons, missing only in his final season of 1986–87, when the back injury that would end his career limited him to 38 goals in 63 games played. With 573 goals in just 752 games in his career, Bossy averaged better than three goals for every four games he played in the NHL. His goals-per-game average of .762 is the best in history for anyone who has scored more than 200 career goals. Bossy was the NHL's top playoff-goal scorer for three years in a row, from 1981 to 1983, with 17 goals in each of those years. He is credited with the Stanley Cup–winning goal in 1982 and 1983, making him and Jack Darragh (Ottawa, 1920 and 1921) the only NHL players to achieve the feat.

PRELIMINARY ROUND
3 games to 0 over Toronto

QUARTERFINALS
4 games to 2 over Edmonton

SEMIFINALS
4 games to 0 over NY Rangers

ROSTER

CONN SMYTHE TROPHY **BUTCH GORING** C – NEW YORK ISLANDERS

Mike Bossy
Bob Bourne
Billy Carroll
Clark Gillies
Butch Goring
Garry Howatt
Anders Kallur
Gord Lane
Dave Langevin
Bob Lorimer
Hector Marini
Mike McEwen
Roland Melanson
Wayne Merrick
Ken Morrow
Bob Nystrom
Stefan Persson
Denis Potvin (captain)
Jean Potvin
Billy Smith
Duane Sutter
John Tonelli
Bryan Trottier
Bill Torrey (president/general manager)
Al Arbour (coach)

FINAL　4 GAMES TO 1

MAY 12	▸	Minnesota 3 at NY Islanders 6
MAY 14	▸	Minnesota 3 at NY Islanders 6
MAY 17	▸	NY Islanders 7 at Minnesota 5
MAY 19	▸	NY Islanders 2 at Minnesota 4
MAY 21	▸	Minnesota 1 at NY Islanders 5

PLAYOFF SCORING LEADER

	GP	G	A	PTS
Mike Bossy NEW YORK ISLANDERS	18	17	18	35

FINAL SERIES SCORING

NY ISLANDERS	GP	G	A	PTS	PIM
Mike Bossy	5	4	4	8	0
Wayne Merrick	5	3	5	8	0
Butch Goring	5	5	2	7	0
Bryan Trottier	5	2	5	7	14
Denis Potvin	5	2	4	6	8
John Tonelli	5	0	5	5	8
Anders Kallur	5	2	2	4	4
Bob Nystrom	5	2	2	4	10
Billy Carroll	5	1	3	4	0
Mike McEwen	5	2	1	3	2
Bob Bourne	5	1	2	3	12
Clark Gillies	5	0	3	3	8
Dave Langevin	5	0	2	2	10
Gord Lane	5	1	0	1	18
Ken Morrow	5	1	0	1	2
Duane Sutter	5	0	1	1	0
Bob Lorimer	5	0	0	0	9

GOALTENDER	GP	W	L	MIN	GA	SO	AVG
Billy Smith	5	4	1	300	16	0	3.20

MINNESOTA	GP	G	A	PTS	PIM
Steve Payne	5	5	2	7	2
Dino Ciccarelli	5	3	2	5	19
Bobby Smith	5	2	3	5	2
Craig Hartsburg	5	1	4	5	2
Steve Christoff	5	2	2	4	0
Al MacAdam	5	1	3	4	2
Brad Maxwell	4	0	4	4	9
Tom McCarthy	3	0	3	3	2
Tim Young	2	0	3	3	0
Kent-Erik Andersson	5	1	0	1	0
Brad Palmer	5	1	0	1	4
Neal Broten	5	0	1	1	2
Gordie Roberts	5	0	1	1	2
Greg Smith	5	0	1	1	6
Fred Barrett	3	0	0	0	6
Jack Carlson	2	0	0	0	0
Curt Giles	5	0	0	0	2
Kevin Maxwell	2	0	0	0	4
Mike Polich	3	0	0	0	0
Paul Shmyr	2	0	0	0	2
Ken Solheim	1	0	0	0	0
Tom Younghans	3	0	0	0	4

GOALTENDERS	GP	W	L	MIN	GA	SO	AVG
Don Beaupre	3	1	2	180	13	0	4.33
Gilles Meloche	2	0	2	120	12	0	6.00

Scoring Streaks

Though Butch Goring won the Conn Smythe Trophy for his two-way excellence throughout the playoffs and Mike Bossy set a new record for playoff scoring, Bryan Trottier had a pretty impressive run himself. Trottier had 11 goals and 18 assists and picked up at least one point in each of the Islanders 18 playoff games, setting a record for the longest scoring streak in one playoff year. Including the last seven games of the 1980 playoffs and the first two games of 1982, Trottier's 27-game streak over three playoff years is also an NHL record.

The Islanders Again

After winning their first Stanley Cup title in 1979–80, the New York Islanders were the NHL's best team during the 1980–81 regular season. The Islanders could play it tough if teams wanted to mix it up, but they possessed plenty of skill and finesse as well. "We were very adjustable," coach Al Arbour would later say, "and we were always changing."

Mike Bossy, who had "slumped" to 51 goals in 1979–80 after leading the NHL with 69 the year before, quietly set a new goal for himself in 1980–81. He wanted to match Maurice Richard by scoring 50 goals in 50 games, as the Rocket had done back in 1944–45. Bossy managed to maintain his goal-a-game pace, but so did Charlie Simmer of the Los Angeles Kings. Simmer fell one goal short with 49 through 50 games, while Bossy matched the mark with a pair of goals in the third period of his 50th game later that evening. After matching the Rocket, the pressure was on for Bossy to match Phil Esposito's single-season record of 76 goals, but Bossy fell short, ending with a league-leading 68. Heating up again in the playoffs, Bossy would lead all scorers with 17 goals, 18 assists and 35 points in just 18 games. Bossy's 35 points were a postseason record at the time, and his nine power-play goals in the playoffs have been matched only by Boston's Cam Neely, in 1991.

After finishing atop the NHL's regular-season standings with a record of 48-18-4 for 110 points, the Islanders breezed past Toronto to open the playoffs before knocking off the upstart Edmonton Oilers. Next up was the New York Rangers, whom the Islanders swept by with scores of 5–2, 7–3, 5–1 and 5–2.

In the Campbell Conference, the Minnesota North Stars upset Boston, Buffalo and Calgary to reach the final. Craig Hartsburg and Curt Giles anchored the Minnesota defense, while Bobby Smith and Steve Payne led the offense along with Dino Ciccarelli, who set rookie playoff records with 14 goals and 21 points. The North Stars, behind 3–0 in the series, stayed alive against the Islanders with a win in Game 4, but two early goals from Butch Goring in Game 5 sparked a 5–1 victory for the Islanders and a second straight Stanley Cup.

Here We Go Oilers

After upsetting the Canadiens in the preliminary round, the Oilers pushed the Islanders to six games in their quarterfinal series. The most memorable moments of the series occurred during the final moments of Edmonton's 4–3 win in Game 5 as the players all chanted "Here we go Oilers, here we go!" on the bench.

"It just felt right," said Paul Coffey, who admitted that Mark Messier had started it. "We don't know how to be goodie-goodies yet. We're a young team. We don't know how to sit and take it all in stride."

MOST POINTS BY A DEFENSEMAN IN ONE PLAYOFF YEAR

37	Paul Coffey, Edmonton, 1985	12 goals and 25 assists in 18 games
34	Brian Leetch, New York Rangers, 1994	11 goals and 23 assists in 23 games
31	Al MacInnis, Calgary, 1989	7 goals and 24 assists in 22 games
25	Denis Potvin, New York Islanders, 1981	8 goals and 17 assists in 18 games
	Raymond Bourque, Boston, 1991	7 goals and 18 assists in 19 games

Mike Bossy

On a Roll

The Islanders finished the 1980–81 regular season with only two losses (and four ties) in their last 20 games. "Other teams aren't going to beat us," said Bob Nystrom before the playoffs. "If we lose, we'll beat ourselves. I really feel that if we play up to our potential, we'll win."

One-Sided Win As the NHL's top team, with a record of 48-18-4 for 110 points, in 1980–81, the Islanders opened the playoffs against the 16th seeded Toronto Maple Leafs. The series was as one-sided as most people expected, with the Islanders scoring 9–2, 5–1 and 6–1 victories to outscore Toronto 20 to 4 in the best-of-five series. The only team ever to score more goals in a three-game NHL playoff series was the Chicago Blackhawks, who outscored the Detroit Red Wings 23 to 8 in their 1985 Norris Division Semifinal series.

In His Back Pocket

Despite Wayne Gretzky's record-breaking 109 assists and 164 points in 1980–81, few gave the 14th overall Edmonton Oilers much of a chance in their opening-round series against the third-ranked Montreal Canadiens. "[Guy] Lafleur will put Gretzky in his back pocket," predicted Canadiens goalie Richard Sevigny. Instead, Gretzky picked up five assists in a series-opening 6–3 victory that sparked the Oilers to a stunning three-game sweep.

PRELIMINARY ROUND	QUARTERFINALS	SEMIFINALS
3 games to 1 over Los Angeles	**4 games to 1 over Boston**	**4 games to 2 over Buffalo**

ROSTER

- Mike Bossy
- Bob Bourne
- Clark Gillies
- Butch Goring
- Lorne Henning
- Garry Howatt
- Anders Kallur
- Gord Lane
- Dave Langevin
- Bob Lorimer
- Alex McKendry
- Wayne Merrick
- Ken Morrow
- Bob Nystrom
- Stefan Persson
- Denis Potvin (captain)
- Jean Potvin
- Glenn Resch
- Billy Smith
- Duane Sutter
- Steve Tambellini
- John Tonelli
- Bryan Trottier
- Bill Torrey (president/general manager)
- Al Arbour (coach)

CONN SMYTHE TROPHY BRYAN TROTTIER C – NEW YORK ISLANDERS

The Islanders mob Bob Nystrom after his Stanley Cup–winning overtime goal.

Just Like the Real Thing

"My brother and I used to play for the Stanley Cup in our basement. There used to be an old ashtray down there. It was about three feet high and silver-topped, and to me it was just like the Stanley Cup. I used to carry it around the room. I was amazed to see how much it resembled the real Stanley Cup."

— John Tonelli, reminiscing with Brian McFarlane in 1986

FINAL 4 GAMES TO 2

MAY 13	▶	NY Islanders 4 at Philadelphia 3 OT
MAY 15	▶	NY Islanders 3 at Philadelphia 8
MAY 17	▶	Philadelphia 2 at NY Islanders 6
MAY 19	▶	Philadelphia 2 at NY Islanders 5
MAY 22	▶	NY Islanders 3 at Philadelphia 6
MAY 24	▶	Philadelphia 4 at NY Islanders 5 OT

PLAYOFF SCORING LEADER

	GP	G	A	PTS
Bryan Trottier NEW YORK ISLANDERS	21	12	17	29

FINAL SERIES SCORING

NY ISLANDERS	GP	G	A	PTS	PIM
Mike Bossy	6	4	7	11	4
Denis Potvin	6	5	4	9	6
Bryan Trottier	6	4	4	8	0
Clark Gillies	6	2	6	8	13
Stefan Persson	6	3	4	7	10
Butch Goring	6	3	3	6	0
Bob Nystrom	6	3	1	4	30
Duane Sutter	6	1	3	4	28
Bob Bourne	6	0	4	4	2
John Tonelli	6	0	3	3	4
Lorne Henning	6	1	1	2	0
Garry Howatt	6	0	1	1	21
Gord Lane	6	0	0	0	28
Dave Langevin	6	0	0	0	9
Bob Lorimer	6	0	0	0	6
Wayne Merrick	6	0	0	0	0
Ken Morrow	6	0	0	0	6

GOALTENDERS	GP	W	L	MIN	GA	SO	AVG
Billy Smith	6	4	2	351	23	0	3.93
Glenn Resch	1	0	0	20	2	0	6.00

PHILADELPHIA	GP	G	A	PTS	PIM
Paul Holmgren	5	4	4	8	15
Ken Linseman	6	1	7	8	16
Bobby Clarke	6	4	3	7	2
Rick MacLeish	6	3	3	6	2
Brian Propp	6	3	3	6	4
Reggie Leach	6	1	4	5	0
Bill Barber	6	1	4	5	9
Mel Bridgman	6	1	3	4	53
Bob Dailey	6	1	3	4	4
Behn Wilson	6	0	4	4	28
Mike Busniuk	6	2	1	3	7
John Paddock	2	2	0	2	0
Tom Gorence	5	1	1	2	16
Bob Kelly	6	1	0	1	9
André Dupont	6	0	1	1	14
Jimmy Watson	5	0	1	1	9
Norm Barnes	1	0	0	0	4
Al Hill	6	0	0	0	2
Jack McIllhargey	6	0	0	0	25

GOALTENDERS	GP	W	L	MIN	GA	SO	AVG
Pete Peeters	5	2	3	311	20	0	3.86
Phil Myre	1	0	1	60	6	0	6.00

Islanders Cap a Season of Change

By the end of the 1970s, the New York Islanders had gone from a hapless expansion team to an elite NHL club—with a reputation for choking in the playoffs. Bryan Trottier, Mike Bossy and Denis Potvin had all become big stars. The Islanders posted 100-point seasons four years in a row, from 1975–76 through 1978–79, but they could never get past the semifinals in the playoffs. The team seemed to take a small step back in 1979–80, slipping to 91 points in the standings after topping the NHL with 116 the year before. But the playoffs would tell a different story.

A year after the merger of the Cleveland Barons and the Minnesota North Stars reduced the NHL to 17 teams, the league's ranks grew to 21 in 1979–80, when it absorbed the four survivors of the World Hockey Association: the Edmonton Oilers, Winnipeg Jets, Quebec Nordiques and Hartford (formerly New England) Whalers. Aging stars Bobby Hull, Dave Keon and Gordie Howe all returned to the NHL, and there was an influx of young WHA talent that included Mike Gartner, Rick Vaive, Michel Goulet, Mark Messier and, of course, Wayne Gretzky. Gretzky

had finished third in the WHA in scoring as a 17-year-old in 1978–79. His critics doubted that he was ready to succeed in the NHL, but Gretzky tied Marcel Dionne for the league lead with 137 points. (The Art Ross Trophy went to Dionne because his 53 goals were two more than Gretzky's 51.)

The Montreal Canadiens had won four straight Stanley Cup titles entering the 1979–80 season, but the team had experienced a few key changes. Goalie Ken Dryden had retired, and coach Scotty Bowman had left to run the Buffalo Sabres. The team still finished the regular season with 107 points, but the dream of a fifth straight Stanley Cup ended in the quarterfinals with a loss to Minnesota. The Philadelphia Flyers were the NHL's best team during the regular season, posting a pro sports record 35-game unbeaten streak (25 wins, 10 ties) between October 14th and January 6th and finishing the year 48-12-20 for 116 points. After easy playoff wins over the Oilers, Rangers and North Stars, the Flyers faced the Islanders for the Stanley Cup. The series went six, with the Islanders winning the Cup on an overtime goal by Bob Nystrom.

Unsung Hero

Ken Morrow was the first player in hockey history to win an Olympic gold medal and the Stanley Cup in the same season. Morrow won Olympic gold with the "Miracle on Ice" United States team at the 1980 Lake Placid Olympics in February before joining the Islanders and winning the Stanley Cup in May. Drafted by the Islanders back in 1976, Morrow became the first All-American player ever at Bowling Green State University and the Central Collegiate Hockey Association player of the year in 1978–79. He won the Cup four times with the Islanders and was inducted into the United States Hockey Hall of Fame in 1995.

From Worst to First The Islanders were the second post-1967 NHL expansion team (after the Flyers in 1974 and 1975) to win the Stanley Cup, taking their first title in just their eighth season. Four members of the Cup-winning team had been with the club since the very beginning, struggling through the woeful 12-60-6 season in 1972–73 that was among the worst in NHL history. Lorne Henning, Bob Nystrom and Garry Howatt had all been selected in the 1972 NHL draft, while goalie Billy Smith was acquired in the expansion draft.

Ken Morrow

Nystrom's OT Winner

Bob Nystrom was born in Sweden but grew up playing junior hockey in Canada. The Islanders selected him in the third round (33rd overall) in their first NHL draft upon entering the league in 1972.

A tough, physical player whose hustle made up for any lack of natural talent, Nystrom was a consistent 20-goal scorer during the first 10 years of his career. He seemed to have a knack for raising his game in the playoffs, scoring four overtime goals between 1978 and 1980, which trailed only Maurice Richard on the NHL playoff list at that time. The biggest goal he ever scored was the Stanley Cup winner in overtime in Game 6 of the final against Philadelphia.

The play that led to the Cup-winning goal began deep in the Flyers zone, when Nystrom hammered Philadelphia's Bob Dailey in the corner. Though the Flyers managed to clear the zone, they never regained control of the puck. The Islanders' Stefan Persson corralled it just outside the Philadelphia blue line and played it to Lorne Henning, who retreated toward the Islanders end before turning and making a crisp cross-ice pass to John Tonelli at the red line. Tonelli maneuvered around a tired-looking Dailey and into the Flyers zone, creating a two-on-one with Nystrom against Philadelphia's André Dupont. Dupont moved to check Tonelli and left Nystrom alone to dart for the net. Tonelli spun to his forehand and fired a pass to the streaking Nystrom, who took it in stride on his backhand and chipped the puck over a sprawling Pete Peeters. Time of the goal was a lucky 7:11.

Montreal Canadiens

ROSTER

CONN SMYTHE TROPHY **BOB GAINEY** LW – MONTREAL

Rick Chartraw

Cam Connor

Yvan Cournoyer
(captain)

Ken Dryden

Brian Engblom

Bob Gainey

Réjean Houle

Pat Hughes

Doug Jarvis

Guy Lafleur

Yvon Lambert

Rod Langway

Guy Lapointe

Michel Larocque

Pierre Larouche

Jacques Lemaire

Gilles Lupien

Pierre Mondou

Mark Napier

Doug Risebrough

Larry Robinson

Serge Savard

Richard Sevigny

Steve Shutt

Mario Tremblay

Sam Pollock
(director)

Scotty Bowman
(coach)

FINAL 4 GAMES TO 1

MAY 13	▶	NY Rangers 4 at Montreal 1
MAY 15	▶	NY Rangers 2 at Montreal 6
MAY 17	▶	Montreal 4 at NY Rangers 1
MAY 19	▶	Montreal 4 at NY Rangers 3 OT
MAY 21	▶	NY Rangers 1 at Montreal 4

PLAYOFF SCORING LEADERS

Jacques Lemaire	GP	G	A	PTS
MONTREAL	16	11	12	23

Guy Lafleur	GP	G	A	PTS
MONTREAL	16	10	13	23

FINAL SERIES SCORING

MONTREAL	GP	G	A	PTS	PIM
Jacques Lemaire	5	4	3	7	2
Yvon Lambert	5	2	4	6	4
Steve Shutt	5	2	4	6	2
Bob Gainey	5	3	2	5	6
Réjean Houle	5	1	4	5	2
Guy Lafleur	5	2	1	3	0
Doug Risebrough	5	1	2	3	12
Serge Savard	5	1	2	3	2
Rick Chartraw	5	1	1	2	12
Mario Tremblay	5	1	1	2	4
Doug Jarvis	5	0	2	2	2
Mark Napier	5	1	0	1	2
Larry Robinson	5	0	1	1	0
Brian Engblom	5	0	0	0	0
Rod Langway	5	0	0	0	12
Pierre Larouche	1	0	0	0	0
Gilles Lupien	4	0	0	0	2
Pierre Mondou	5	0	0	0	2

GOALTENDERS	GP	W	L	MIN	GA	SO	AVG
Ken Dryden	5	4	1	287	11	0	2.30
Michel Larocque	1	0	0	20	0	0	0.00

NY RANGERS	GP	G	A	PTS	PIM
Phil Esposito	5	2	1	3	10
Anders Hedberg	5	1	2	3	2
Pat Hickey	5	1	2	3	0
Dave Maloney	5	1	2	3	10
Ron Duguay	5	2	0	2	4
Don Murdoch	5	1	1	2	2
Steve Vickers	5	1	1	2	0
Mike McEwen	5	0	2	2	4
Ron Greschner	5	1	0	1	8
Carol Vadnais	5	1	0	1	0
Don Maloney	5	0	1	1	6
Bobby Sheehan	5	0	1	1	0
Walt Tkaczuk	5	0	1	1	4
Lucien DeBlois	2	0	0	0	0
Dave Farrish	1	0	0	0	0
Eddie Johnstone	5	0	0	0	2
Mario Marois	5	0	0	0	4
Ulf Nilsson	2	0	0	0	2
Pierre Plante	5	0	0	0	0

GOALTENDER	GP	W	L	MIN	GA	SO	AVG
John Davidson	5	1	4	307	19	0	3.17

Playoff Formats

The 1978–79 season marked the end of a playoff format that had essentially been in place since the NHL grew to 18 teams in 1974–75. From 1974–75 to 1976–77, the regular-season champions of the league's four divisions received a bye into the quarterfinals, and the eight teams that finished second and third in each division were pooled together in a best-of-three preliminary round to determine the other four quarterfinalists. The format was altered slightly for 1977–78 and 1978–79, and the preliminary round comprised the four teams that finished second in each division along with the teams with the next four best records, regardless of the division to which they belonged.

... And Still Champions

After three straight Stanley Cup wins that capped off three of the greatest seasons in NHL history, the Montreal Canadiens were not the NHL's best team in 1978–79. They were certainly good, topping the NHL with 52 wins (52-17-11) and surrendering the fewest goals against for the fourth straight season, but their 115 points had them one back of the New York Islanders, who led the overall standings with 116 points. The Islanders were the NHL's top-scoring team, with 358 goals, as Bryan Trottier ended Guy Lafleur's three-year hold on the Art Ross Trophy as the league's leading scorer, with 134 points. Islander sniper Mike Bossy led the league with 69 goals, but, the Islanders came up short in the playoffs, losing to the rival New York Rangers in the semifinals.

With 91 points during the regular season, the Rangers had the NHL's fifth-best record but had still finished 25 points behind the Islanders. Phil Esposito was the team's top scorer and led them past Los Angeles in the preliminary round of the playoffs and Philadelphia in the quarterfinals, but it was the superb goaltending of John Davidson that sparked the six-game upset of the Islanders in the semifinals.

The Canadiens opened the playoffs with a sweep of Toronto in the quarterfinals, though it took a double-overtime victory in Game 3 and another overtime win in Game 4 to complete it. Their semifinal series with the Bruins was a classic. The two teams had met for the Stanley Cup in 1977 and 1978, but this series was the best. The Canadiens won their first three games at the Forum rather easily, but the Bruins had kept pace with home wins of their own, forcing a pivotal seventh game for the right to face the New York Rangers for the Cup. With the Islanders surprise elimination at the hands of the Rangers, many argued that the Montreal–Boston Game 7 would be the true Stanley Cup final. The game did not disappoint, with Guy Lafleur tying the score late in the third period before Yvon Lambert won it in overtime.

In the final, the Rangers jumped on the Canadiens for a 4–1 win in Game 1 and took an early 2–0 lead in Game 2 before Montreal stormed back for a 6–2 victory. The Canadiens went on to take the series in five. Bob Gainey's goal midway through the second period sealed the Rangers' fate and solidified the selection of the defensive specialist for the Conn Smythe Trophy as playoff MVP.

A Tale of Two Goalies

Michel "Bunny" Larocque saw plenty of action as Ken Dryden's backup during the regular season in the late 1970s, but it was always Dryden who carried the load in the playoffs. When coach Scotty Bowman pulled Dryden after two periods in Game 1 of the Stanley Cup final, it marked Larocque's first playoff appearance since 1974. Bowman planned to start Larocque in Game 2, but when he was injured in the pre-game warmup, Dryden returned to the net and remained there for the rest of the series.

Four for Four There were 15 players who played on all four Canadiens Stanley Cup teams from 1976 to 1979: Rick Chartraw, Yvan Cournoyer, Ken Dryden, Bob Gainey, Doug Jarvis, Guy Lafleur, Yvon Lambert, Guy Lapointe, Michel Larocque, Jacques Lemaire, Doug Risebrough, Larry Robinson, Serge Savard, Steve Shutt and Mario Tremblay.

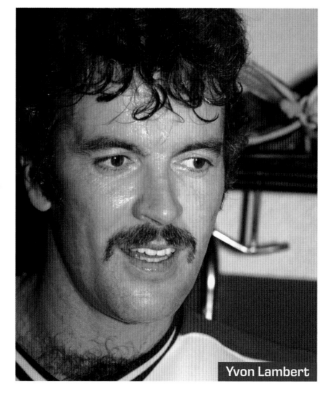

Yvon Lambert

Flower Power

Guy Lafleur had 52 goals and 129 points in 1978–79. After having won three straight scoring titles, those totals had him slip to third place in both categories, but there was still no question who the Canadiens' most dangerous player was. Preparing to face Montreal before the semifinals, Boston coach Don Cherry predicted good things for his Bruins "if we can just control that damned Lafleur."

Though the Bruins didn't really control Lafleur, they still managed to push the Canadiens to a seventh game, where they took a 3–1 lead after two periods. "If we didn't go out and work our butts off," Larry Robinson told reporters afterward, "it was going to be an early summer." No one worked harder than Lafleur, who barely sat on the bench at all during the third period. He set up Mark Napier at 6:10 and then set up Guy Lapointe to tie the score two minutes later (after a questionable penalty to Dick Redmond that prompted a sarcastic bow from Cherry). The Bruins went ahead 4–3 with just 3:59 to play, but then, in an effort to keep Lafleur covered, Boston took a penalty for too many men on the ice with 2:34 remaining. The Bruins killed off the first minute of the Montreal power play and fired the puck deep into the Canadiens' end, but Lafleur carried the puck out of the zone. He fired a long pass to Jacques Lemaire, raced up the ice to take a drop pass and then blasted a slap shot low along the ice past Gilles Gilbert with 1:14 to go. Yvon Lambert would win the game for Montreal at 9:33 in overtime.

A Dynasty by the Numbers

Going strictly by the numbers, it's hard to argue against the Montreal Canadiens of 1975–76 through 1978–79 being the greatest hockey team of all time. During those four years, the Canadiens played 320 games in the regular season. Their combined record was 229 wins against only 46 losses with 45 ties. Putting it another way, the Canadiens garnered 503 of a possible 640 points during those four seasons, for a winning percentage of .786 and a yearly average of nearly 126 points per season.

> "It wasn't their offense that was their strongest point. It was their checking ability. They may have a bunch of superstars on that team, but they don't play like individuals. They're the best checking team in the National Hockey League and that's why they're so good."
>
> — Harry Sinden,
>   general manager,
>   Boston Bruins

Montreal was even more dominant in the playoffs. The Canadiens played 58 playoff games during this stretch and won 48 of them for a percentage of .828. Of the 12 playoff series it took to win four straight Stanley Cup titles, the Canadiens were only pushed to a seventh game once, in the thrilling 1979 semifinal series against the Boston Bruins. They went as far as six games on only two occasions, and they won six of their 12 playoff series in four-game sweeps. The Canadiens were at their very best in the Stanley Cup final, where they recorded two of those six sweeps (over the Philadelphia Flyers in 1976 and over Boston in 1977), and posted a record of 16–3 for an .842 winning percentage.

Of the 15 Canadiens players who were members of all four Stanley Cup–winning teams between 1976 and 1979, Ken Dryden, Bob Gainey, Guy Lafleur, Guy Lapointe, Jacques Lemaire, Larry Robinson, Serge Savard and Steve Shutt would later be elected to the Hockey Hall of Fame. (Yvan Cournoyer brings the count to nine future Hall of Famers, although he missed the majority of the 1978–79 season, as well as large chunks of the previous three years, due to injuries.)

Dryden, Lafleur, Lapointe, Robinson, Savard and Shutt combined for 16 NHL All-Star selections (12 to the First All-Star Team—including four each for Dryden and Lafleur—plus four to the Second All-Star Team), while Lafleur, Dryden (along with backup goalie Michel "Bunny" Larocque), Robinson, Savard and Bob Gainey won a total of 16 major NHL trophies. In addition to winning the Art Ross Trophy three times, the Hart Memorial Trophy twice and the Conn Smythe Trophy once, Lafleur also won the NHL Players' Association's Lester B. Pearson

Award (now known as the Ted Lindsay Award) in 1976, 1977 and 1978 to bring the total trophy haul to 19.

But for all their star players, it was the overall balance of the Canadiens that made the team so great. Players like Yvon Lambert, Mario Tremblay, Doug Jarvis and Doug Risebrough were just as important to the Montreal dynasty for the toughness and checking skills they brought to the team.

"I kept telling our guys and everybody else that it didn't matter how many 40, 50 and 60-goal scorers the Canadiens had," said Bruins general manager Harry Sinden after Montreal swept Boston in the final in 1978. "It wasn't their offense that was their strongest point. It was their checking ability. They may have a bunch of superstars on that team, but they don't play like individuals. They're the best checking team in the National Hockey League and that's why they're so good."

After the same series, Dryden told reporters: "The essence of this team is hard work. Lafleur and Steve Shutt and the defensemen add the flavor to it, but the basic reason we do so well is the effort everybody gives."

With a team as tough, talented and dominant as the Canadiens,

the biggest test was often just trying to keep the players motivated throughout the entire season. Coach Scotty Bowman had a unique way of handling that challenge.

"They key guy on our team was Scotty," Shutt told Dick Irvin Jr. for his 1991 book *The Habs: An Oral History of the Montreal Canadiens, 1940–1980*. "He realized that the only team that could beat our team was ourselves. We had such a good team that petty little grievances could develop that might bring the team down. So what Scotty did, he

made himself the focal point. The thing that we had in common was that everybody hated Scotty... You know, Scotty is basically a very shy person, but he figured he had to be the front man if he was going to keep the team together."

Hockey writer Al Strachan had a similar recollection of Bowman's dictatorial style behind the Canadiens' bench. "The players hated Scotty 364 days a year," Strachan once said. "On the other day, they cashed their Stanley Cup cheques."

Ken Dryden looks intently at the action in front of him while Guy Lapointe and Bryan Trottier fight for a loose puck.

....

But, of course, the one number where the Canadiens of the late 1970s fall slightly short in the comparison of greatest teams is the number four, instead of five. In their efforts to match the five straight Stanley Cup victories of the Montreal Canadiens of 1955–56 to 1959–60, this Canadiens squad came up short.

Scotty Bowman left Montreal after the 1978–79 season to become coach and general manager of the Buffalo Sabres, and the Canadiens also lost Dryden, Lemaire and Cournoyer to retirement that year. Injuries would also take their toll in 1979–80, as new captain Serge Savard was limited to just 46 games and Lapointe played just 45.

Pierre Larouche boosted the offense with 50 goals and Lafleur also netted 50, while Shutt scored 47 as the Canadiens nearly became the first team in NHL history to boast three 50-goal scorers in one season. Montreal's 328 goals led the league in 1979–80, but the three-man goaltending crew of Larocque, Denis Herron and Richard Sevigny (who would combine to share the Vezina Trophy the following season) couldn't quite fill Dryden's shoes this season.

Montreal's record of 47-20-13 was good for 107 points, a Norris Division title and the third-best record in the newly expanded 21-team NHL. However, after a three-game sweep of the Hartford Whalers in the preliminary round, the quest for a fifth straight Stanley Cup ended with a seven-game loss to the Minnesota North Stars in the quarterfinals.

Montreal Canadiens

QUARTERFINALS
4 games to 1 over Detroit

SEMIFINALS
4 games to 0 over Toronto

CONN SMYTHE TROPHY LARRY ROBINSON D – MONTREAL

Larry Robinson clears Wayne Cashman out of harm's way.

ROSTER

Pierre Bouchard	Yvon Lambert	Larry Robinson
Rick Chartraw	Guy Lapointe	Serge Savard
Yvan Cournoyer (captain)	Michel Larocque	Steve Shutt
Ken Dryden	Pierre Larouche	Mario Tremblay
Brian Engblom	Jacques Lemaire	Murray Wilson
Bob Gainey	Gilles Lupien	Sam Pollock (vice president/ general manager)
Réjean Houle	Pierre Mondou	
Doug Jarvis	Bill Nyrop	Scotty Bowman (coach)
Guy Lafleur	Doug Risebrough	

A Worthy Winner

"Larry Robinson killed us single-handedly. I repeat. He was the guy who killed us. Nobody ever deserved the Conn Smythe Trophy more than that guy."
—Boston's Don Marcotte

FINAL **4 GAMES TO 2**

MAY 13 ►	Boston 1 at Montreal 4
MAY 16 ►	Boston 2 at Montreal 3 OT
MAY 18 ►	Montreal 0 at Boston 4
MAY 21 ►	Montreal 3 at Boston 4 OT
MAY 23 ►	Boston 1 at Montreal 4
MAY 25 ►	Montreal 4 at Boston 1

PLAYOFF SCORING LEADERS

Guy Lafleur	GP	G	A	PTS
MONTREAL	15	10	11	21

Larry Robinson	GP	G	A	PTS
MONTREAL	15	4	17	21

FINAL SERIES SCORING

MONTREAL	GP	G	A	PTS	PIM
Larry Robinson	6	2	4	6	4
Guy Lafleur	6	3	2	5	8
Steve Shutt	6	3	1	4	2
Pierre Mondou	6	1	3	4	4
Mario Tremblay	3	2	1	3	14
Yvan Cournoyer	6	1	2	3	6
Yvon Lambert	6	1	2	3	2
Jacques Lemaire	6	1	2	3	6
Doug Jarvis	6	0	3	3	10
Serge Savard	6	0	3	3	4
Bob Gainey	6	1	1	2	10
Réjean Houle	6	1	1	2	4
Guy Lapointe	6	0	2	2	5
Bill Nyrop	5	0	2	2	6
Pierre Larouche	2	1	0	1	0
Doug Risebrough	6	1	0	1	7
Pierre Bouchard	4	0	0	0	5
Rick Chartraw	3	0	0	0	0
Brian Engblom	1	0	0	0	0
Gilles Lupien	2	0	0	0	17

GOALTENDER	GP	W	L	MIN	GA	SO	AVG
Ken Dryden	6	4	2	379	13	0	2.06

BOSTON	GP	G	A	PTS	PIM
Brad Park	6	4	1	5	8
Peter McNab	6	2	3	5	2
Gregg Sheppard	6	1	3	4	2
Don Marcotte	6	1	2	3	4
Terry O'Reilly	6	1	2	3	16
Bobby Schmautz	6	1	2	3	11
Mike Milbury	6	0	3	3	10
Jean Ratelle	6	0	3	3	0
Wayne Cashman	6	0	2	2	2
Gary Doak	6	1	0	1	4
Rick Middleton	6	1	0	1	0
Rick Smith	6	1	0	1	10
Bob Miller	6	0	1	1	9
Stan Jonathan	6	0	0	0	20
Dennis O'Brien	5	0	0	0	6
Al Sims	3	0	0	0	0
John Wensink	6	0	0	0	24

GOALTENDERS	GP	W	L	MIN	GA	SO	AVG
Gerry Cheevers	6	2	4	359	18	1	3.01
Ron Grahame	1	0	0	20	0	0	0.00

Beating Boston Again

It was another spectacular season for the Montreal Canadiens in 1977–78. They followed up their record-setting 60-win season of the year before with 59 more victories, going 59-10-11 and posting 129 points. Guy Lafleur led the NHL with 60 goals and 132 points, winning the Art Ross Trophy as scoring leader for the third year in a row and the Hart Trophy as MVP for the second straight season. Once again the Canadiens were the league's top-scoring team, with 359 goals. Goalies Ken Dryden and Michel Larocque shared the Vezina Trophy for the second of three years in a row (Dryden had won it alone in 1975–76), surrendering a league-low 187 goals. The defense was led by "The Big Three" of Larry Robinson, Serge Savard and Guy Lapointe, but the forwards played a strong two-way game led by Bob Gainey, who won the newly created Selke Trophy as the NHL's best defensive forward—he would go on to win it four years in a row.

The Boston Bruins were the second-best team in the NHL during the regular season, collecting 113 points on a record of 51-18-11 and finishing third in the league, with 333 goals. Don Cherry's hard-working "Lunch Bucket" brigade didn't have the star power to match Montreal. They had talented players in Jean Ratelle, Brad Park and Rick Middleton and a 40-goal scorer in Peter McNab, but it was Terry O'Reilly (who led the team with 91 points despite 211 penalty minutes) who epitomized the Bruins and their abrasive style. Both Boston and Montreal needed just nine games to get through two rounds of the playoffs and advance to the final, with the Bruins sweeping Chicago in the opening round before beating Philadelphia in five to set up a Stanley Cup rematch with the Canadiens.

Montreal had swept Boston to win the Cup in 1977 and opened the 1978 final with two more wins, the second coming on a Guy Lafleur goal at 13:09 of overtime. Boston finally got a win in Game 3 and overcame the disappointment of Lafleur tying Game 4 in the final seconds with Bobby Schmautz's overtime winner. But those two wins were as close to the Cup as Boston would get, as the Canadiens won the next two games 4–1 to take their third straight championship.

MOST CONSECUTIVE VICTORIES IN THE STANLEY CUP FINAL

10	MONTREAL CANADIENS

Streak began May 9, 1976, at Montreal with a 4–3 win over Philadelphia in Game 1 and ended May 18, 1978, at Boston with a 4–0 loss in Game 3. Included in the streak were four wins versus Philadelphia in 1976, four versus Boston in 1977 and two versus Boston in 1978.

9	TORONTO MAPLE LEAFS

Streak began April 19, 1947, at Toronto with a 2–1 win over Montreal in Game 6 and ended when the team failed to advance to the 1950 final. Included in the streak were one win versus Montreal in 1947, four versus Detroit in 1948 and four versus Detroit in 1949.

	NEW YORK ISLANDERS

Streak began May 21, 1981, at New York with a 5–1 win over Minnesota in Game 5 and ended May 10, 1984, at New York with a 1–0 loss to Edmonton in Game 1. Included in the streak were one win versus Minnesota in 1981, four versus Vancouver in 1982 and 4 versus Edmonton in 1983.

Guy Lafleur and his father

Guy's Getaway

Guy Lafleur, Yvon Lambert, Steve Shutt and Michel Larocque of the Canadiens, Denis Potvin, Clark Gillies and Gerry Hart of the New York Islanders and Rangers general manager John Ferguson (a former Canadiens star) were guests of the Canadian Society of New York at the Waldorf-Astoria Hotel on May 30, 1978. It was there that Lafleur told the story of how he had stolen the Stanley Cup a few days earlier and taken it to his hometown of Thurso, Quebec.

The plot was hatched after a visit to Toe Blake's tavern. "Every time we win the Stanley Cup, we're there and we have a lot of fun," Lafleur said. "It's a day when all the guys get together and go out. It's tough on the wives, but it's nice for us."

After Toe Blake's, the celebrating players stopped at the tavern of another former Montreal star, Henri Richard. Canadiens publicity director Claude Mouton had brought the Cup along, and Lafleur told a friend (who was not a player), "I'm going to get Mouton's keys and have some keys made and I'm going to steal the Cup from him and I'm going to keep it for a few days."

After the visit to Richard's, "one of my friends got into Mouton's trunk and put the Cup in my car and I drove it home."

Lafleur left the Cup on the grass outside his parents' house. After assuring his father that it was real, "he got on the phone and phoned all his friends. Thurso is a small town with just about 4,000 people, and I think we had 5,000 there. They really enjoyed it, and I know those guys, they never had a chance to see the Cup. I was proud."

Montreal Canadiens

CONN SMYTHE TROPHY **GUY LAFLEUR** RW – MONTREAL

FINAL 4 GAMES TO 0

MAY 7	▸	Boston 3 at Montreal 7
MAY 10	▸	Boston 0 at Montreal 3
MAY 12	▸	Montreal 4 at Boston 2
MAY 14	▸	Montreal 2 at Boston 1 OT

PLAYOFF SCORING LEADER

	GP	G	A	PTS
Guy Lafleur MONTREAL	14	9	17	26

FINAL SERIES SCORING

MONTREAL	GP	G	A	PTS	PIM
Guy Lafleur	4	2	7	9	4
Jacques Lemaire	4	4	2	6	2
Steve Shutt	4	2	3	5	0
Yvon Lambert	4	2	2	4	6
Pete Mahovlich	4	1	3	4	4
Guy Lapointe	4	0	4	4	0
Doug Risebrough	2	2	1	3	2
Larry Robinson	4	0	3	3	6
Mario Tremblay	4	2	0	2	5
Serge Savard	4	0	2	2	0
Rick Chartraw	4	1	0	1	4
Pierre Bouchard	4	0	1	1	6
Doug Jarvis	4	0	1	1	0
Murray Wilson	4	0	1	1	6
Bob Gainey	4	0	0	0	12
Pierre Mondou	2	0	0	0	0
Bill Nyrop	1	0	0	0	0
Mike Polich	1	0	0	0	0
Jimmy Roberts	4	0	0	0	4

GOALTENDER	GP	W	L	MIN	GA	SO	AVG
Ken Dryden	4	4	0	245	6	1	1.47

BOSTON	GP	G	A	PTS	PIM
Brad Park	4	1	4	5	2
Bobby Schmautz	4	2	0	2	0
Rick Middleton	4	0	2	2	0
Peter McNab	4	1	0	1	2
Terry O'Reilly	4	1	0	1	8
Gregg Sheppard	4	1	0	1	6
Wayne Cashman	4	0	1	1	13
Jean Ratelle	4	0	1	1	0
Earl Anderson	2	0	0	0	0
John Bucyk	2	0	0	0	0
Gary Doak	4	0	0	0	4
Darryl Edestrand	2	0	0	0	0
Dave Forbes	4	0	0	0	0
Matti Hagman	1	0	0	0	0
Mike Milbury	3	0	0	0	20
Stan Jonathan	4	0	0	0	4
Don Marcotte	4	0	0	0	4
Al Sims	2	0	0	0	0
Rick Smith	4	0	0	0	6
John Wensink	3	0	0	0	4

GOALTENDER	GP	W	L	MIN	GA	SO	AVG
Gerry Cheevers	4	0	4	245	16	0	3.92

ROSTER

Pierre Bouchard	Yvon Lambert	Mike Polich	Sam Pollock (vice president/ general manager)
Rick Chartraw	Guy Lapointe	Doug Risebrough	
Yvan Cournoyer (captain)	Michel Larocque	Jimmy Roberts	Scotty Bowman (coach)
Ken Dryden	Pierre Larouche	Larry Robinson	
Brian Engblom	Jacques Lemaire	Serge Savard	
Bob Gainey	Gilles Lupien	Steve Shutt	
Réjean Houle	Pete Mahovlich	Mario Tremblay	
Doug Jarvis	Pierre Mondou	Murray Wilson	
Guy Lafleur ▲	Bill Nyrop		

Great in Any Era

"This is a great team, and with the assets it has it would be considered great in any age. No one can compare teams of different eras, but this would be a great team even if it was playing in a six-team league like the other great Canadiens teams."

— Pete Mahovlich

60 Wins and the Stanley Cup

Having established NHL records for wins (58) and points (127) in 1975–76 and knocking off the defending-champion Philadelphia Flyers to win the Stanley Cup, the Montreal Canadiens had set the bar high. That they were able to surpass that brilliant performance by going 60-8-12 for 132 points in 1976–77 was a mark of just how truly remarkable this team was. The home crowd had plenty to cheer for, as the Canadiens lost just once on home ice, going 33-1-6 at the Forum. They were the NHL's top-scoring team, with 387 goals for, and the best defensive club, with just 171 against.

Guy Lafleur won his second straight scoring title with 136 points and also won the Hart Trophy as MVP. Scotty Bowman won the Jack Adams Award as coach of the year. Steve Shutt led the NHL with 60 goals (setting a club record Lafleur would tie the following season), Larry Robinson won the Norris Trophy as best defenseman and Ken Dryden and Michel "Bunny" Larocque shared the Vezina Trophy. Lafleur, Shutt, Robinson and Dryden were all named First Team All-Stars.

Jacques Lemaire's 75 points while centering Shutt and Lafleur tended to be forgotten alongside his illustrious linemates, but his play was a key to the Canadiens' success. So was the continued development of young grinders such as Mario Tremblay and Doug Jarvis, whose improvement helped to lessen the impact when captain Yvan Cournoyer missed 20 games and all of the playoffs after undergoing back surgery.

The Flyers had another good season this year, going 48-16-16 for 112 points, but their chance to avenge their loss to the Canadiens ended when the Bruins eliminated them in the semifinals. Boston had 106 points during the regular season, and though they were pushed to six games by Los Angeles in the quarterfinals, they swept the Flyers in four close games to reach the Stanley Cup final against Montreal.

The Canadiens pumped two quick goals past Gerry Cheevers in Game 1, and though they led only 4–3 entering the third period, two quick goals to start that frame helped to secure a 7–3 victory. The Bruins were tighter defensively in Game 2 but could muster no offense in a 3–0 Canadiens victory. After a 4–2 loss in Game 3, the Bruins played their best hockey of the series in Game 4 but were beaten 2–1 when Jacques Lemaire scored the Cup-winning goal at 4:32 of overtime.

By the Numbers

Counting regular-season and playoff games in 1976–77, the Canadiens played 94 times. They had 72 wins and only 10 losses. Three of those losses came against the Bruins during their five meetings in the regular season, including Montreal's only loss on home ice, on October 30, 1976.

Better, But... "I'll tell you one thing," Don Cherry said after the Canadiens swept the Bruins in 1977, "Montreal can't get any better, but we can." Boston was better in 1977–78 but still wouldn't be good enough to beat Montreal in their Stanley Cup rematch.

Jacques Lemaire

It was obvious even from the pregame skate that Jacques Lemaire was ready for a big performance. "I really felt good," he said afterward. "The guys noticed it too, because after the warmup they all said, 'Shoot that puck — you look good.'"

But Lemaire and the Canadiens came out slowly in Game 4. They fired only four shots at Bruins goalie Gerry Cheevers in the first period and were down 1–0. However, Boston's lead survived less than two minutes of the second period, as Lafleur set up Lemaire, who whipped a wrist shot over Cheevers' glove and under the crossbar at 1:34. The game remained tight from then on, with both sides hitting hard and the goalies playing great. The score was still 1–1 at the end of regulation, but the Canadiens sensed the Bruins were tiring. Scotty Bowman instructed his team to go right at the Bruins in overtime.

The Canadiens put on the pressure, and as the game approached 4:30 of overtime, Guy Lafleur carried the puck out of the corner to the left of Cheevers. He spotted Lemaire open out front and slid him a pass. Lemaire simply tapped the puck past Cheevers on the far side for the Stanley Cup–winning goal.

"It couldn't happen to a nicer guy," Larry Robinson said. "All year long, Guy Lafleur and Steve Shutt got the publicity, and although they deserve it, Lemaire should have gotten a lot too."

When asked about finally upstaging his famous teammates, Lemaire smiled as he said, "It's a mistake."

The Game I'll Never Forget

STEVE SHUTT • L.WING

"It took me two years to learn how to play the game the way the Canadiens wanted me to."

Hockey Digest: April 1983
By Steve Shutt, as told to George Vass

My first couple of years with the Montreal Canadiens were among the most frustrating of my life. I wanted to be a regular, but I wasn't. It seems I spent most of my time not even suited up, or when I was, sitting on the bench.

I guess I had a pretty good opinion of myself when I first joined the Canadiens in 1972. I had scored 70 goals in my last year as a junior and 63 the year before. People had been talking about me, and I was a big star with the Toronto Marlboros. The way I looked at it, there was no reason I couldn't step into the NHL and do the same thing… Score a lot of goals right from the start.

When I first got to the Canadiens' camp and counted the left wings—Frank Mahovlich, Murray Wilson, Marc Tardif and Chuck Lefley—I began to have my first doubts about where I was supposed to fit in. These were all solid players, and here I was, a kid fresh from the juniors, hoping to break in.

It took a lot longer than I expected. Maybe I was a little too cocky as a kid. That sort of drained out of me as I spent more games the first two years watching from the press box than I did playing. We won the Stanley Cup my first year, but I wasn't even dressed for the final game. I didn't feel I had contributed anything.

Later on I realized I didn't know a lot of the little things it took to play in the NHL, especially about the defensive side of the game. It was something I hadn't taken enough time to learn as a junior, something that could only come from making adjustments, from the experience of playing in the NHL.

It took me two years to learn how to play the game the way the Canadiens wanted me to. I played in spots, scored eight goals the first year, 15 the next. I got to wondering whether I could even play the game, whether I could skate hard enough and learn all the little things NHL regulars knew.

The frustration was tremendous. I suppose now that I would agree that the Canadiens were right in taking their time breaking me into the lineup, but I sure didn't think so at the time.

My chance to be a regular in the lineup finally came in my third year. When Frank Mahovlich and Tardif left, they had to play me. My third year I got a lot more ice time, and I scored 30 goals. The next year things really began to fall into place. The odd thing about it was that things began to pick up just when they looked at their worst. We weren't going too well early in the 1975–76 season, and coach Scotty Bowman threatened to bench me. Then he changed his mind and put me on a line with Pete Mahovlich and Yvan Cournoyer. We got hot right away. I think we scored something like 19 goals in the next eight games, and I got eight of them. From then on things went really well. I put up 45 goals, and we went on to win the Stanley Cup, the first of four in a row.

The goals began to come regularly and I built up my confidence, which is the key to success in everything. When you haven't got it you're in trouble. It's difficult to get back on track again.

But I was on track now, and more or less to stay. Not all my goals were pretty. Some people called me a garbage collector, as if scoring goals the way I did it was easy. But I always worked hard, and I was always there for the rebound, the chance. I made a point of being in the right place at the right time, and I was fortunate in having the right linemates.

Take the 1976–77 season, when I scored 60 goals, playing mostly with Pete Mahovlich and Guy Lafleur. We

April 23, 1977
Game 1, Stanley Cup semifinals · Montreal Forum, Montreal

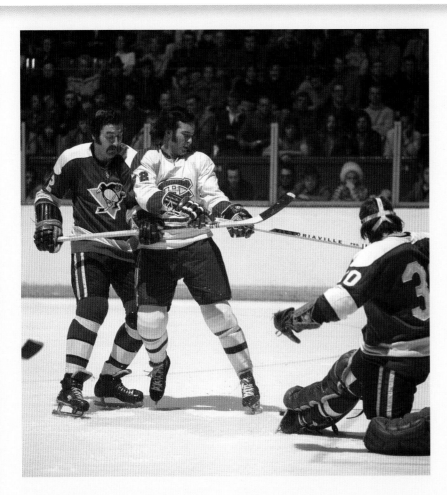

Steve Shutt, in front of the net, tracking a rebound against the Pittsburgh Penguins.

fit together well. I can't puckhandle through a team like Pete Mahovlich or skate circles around everybody like Lafleur, but with those two out there, a lot of people didn't even notice me, and I tried to always be in the right spot for the rebound or the loose puck. I had the anticipation. There is a knack you need to have for tracking rebounds, and I've been fortunate enough to have it.

In 1976–77 we lost only eight games all season, and we went into the playoffs with a head of

steam. The final game, when we beat the Boston Bruins in overtime on Jacques Lemaire's goal, was memorable, and while I've scored in several playoff games, the most memorable game that season came in the semifinal against the New York Islanders. The Islanders were a talented club that was just beginning to come on that year. It took

us six games to beat them, and I'll never forget the first game of the series, April 23, 1977.

The Islanders were hot coming into the series. They'd won six straight in the playoffs, taking two from Chicago in the opening round then four straight from Buffalo. So far, everything had been falling into place for them, and they came out strong and took a 3–1 lead from us in the first period—not something many clubs could do in the Montreal Forum. The odd thing about it was that Billy Harris, who had been a good friend of mine as a junior, scored all the goals for the Islanders.

All of a sudden we started to turn the game around. First Murray Wilson tipped in a shot from the point by Serge Savard to make it 3–2, still early in the second period. Then, just a couple of minutes into the third period, Lafleur tied the game at 3–3.

It must have been a couple of minutes later that I got what was to be the winning goal, when Lemaire set me up and I beat Islanders goalie Billy Smith with a wrist shot. We held on to win the game 4–3.

There have been a lot of other games memorable in their own way, especially those that clinched the Stanley Cup, but for me that's one of the best because it was one of the first in which I really felt I had contributed.

Montreal 4, NY Islanders 3

FIRST PERIOD

1 ▸ Harris (Trottier, Gillies), New York Islanders, 8:39 PP

2 ▸ Mahovlich (Houle, Wilson), Montreal, 12:14

3 ▸ Harris (Lewis, Trottier), New York Islanders, 12:56

PENALTIES: Hart, New York Islanders (holding), 3:31; Lemaire, Montreal (hooking), 7:25

SECOND PERIOD

4 ▸ Harris (Gillies, Hart), New York Islanders, 0:49

5 ▸ Wilson (Savard), Montreal, 9:40

PENALTIES: Marshall, New York Islanders (interference), 12:15; Smith, New York Islanders (slashing), 12:48; Robinson, Montreal (interference), 12:48

THIRD PERIOD

6 ▸ Lafleur (Lapointe, Lemaire), Montreal 2:25

7 ▸ Shutt (Lemaire), Montreal 4:07

NO PENALTIES

SHOTS ON GOAL

	1	2	3	TOTAL
Montreal	15	9	14	38
NY Islanders	8	6	5	19

GOALIES: Dryden, Montreal; Smith, New York Islanders

REFEREE: Brian Lewis

LINESMEN: Matt Pavelich, Willard Norris

Montreal Canadiens

QUARTERFINALS
4 games to 0 over Chicago

SEMIFINALS
4 games to 1 over New York Islanders

CONN SMYTHE TROPHY **REGGIE LEACH** RW – PHILADELPHIA

FINAL **4 GAMES TO 0**

MAY 9	▶	Philadelphia 3 at Montreal 4
MAY 11	▶	Philadelphia 1 at Montreal 2
MAY 13	▶	Montreal 3 at Philadelphia 2
MAY 16	▶	Montreal 5 at Philadelphia 3

PLAYOFF SCORING LEADER

Reggie Leach	GP	G	A	PTS
PHILADELPHIA	16	19	5	24

FINAL SERIES SCORING

MONTREAL	GP	G	A	PTS	PIM
Guy Lafleur	4	2	5	7	2
Steve Shutt	4	3	3	6	0
Pete Mahovlich	4	1	4	5	4
Pierre Bouchard	4	2	0	2	2
Jacques Lemaire	4	2	0	2	2
Yvan Cournoyer	4	1	1	2	0
Larry Robinson	4	1	1	2	4
Doug Risebrough	4	0	2	2	2
Guy Lapointe	4	1	0	1	8
Jimmy Roberts	4	1	0	1	0
Bob Gainey	4	0	1	1	12
Bill Nyrop	4	0	1	1	2
Murray Wilson	3	0	1	1	0
Rick Chartraw	2	0	0	0	0
Doug Jarvis	4	0	0	0	0
Yvon Lambert	3	0	0	0	4
Mario Tremblay	2	0	0	0	7
Serge Savard	4	0	0	0	2
GOALTENDER	GP	W	L	MIN	GA	SO	AVG
Ken Dryden	4	4	0	240	9	0	2.25

PHILADELPHIA	GP	G	A	PTS	PIM
Reggie Leach	4	4	0	4	0
Tom Bladon	4	0	3	3	2
Bobby Clarke	4	0	3	3	4
Bill Barber	4	1	1	2	6
André Dupont	4	1	1	2	7
Larry Goodenough	4	1	1	2	2
Mel Bridgman	4	0	2	2	4
Ross Lonsberry	4	1	0	1	0
Dave Schultz	4	1	0	1	10
Gary Dornhoefer	4	0	1	1	6
Jack McIlhargey	4	0	1	1	4
Terry Crisp	1	0	0	0	0
Bob Kelly	4	0	0	0	2
Orest Kindrachuk	4	0	0	0	0
Terry Murray	2	0	0	0	0
Don Saleski	4	0	0	0	4
Jimmy Watson	4	0	0	0	4
Joe Watson	4	0	0	0	2
GOALTENDER	GP	W	L	MIN	GA	SO	AVG
Wayne Stephenson	4	0	4	240	14	0	3.50

Serge Savard and Yvan Cournoyer salute fans during the Stanley Cup parade.

ROSTER

Pierre Bouchard
Rick Chartraw
Yvan Cournoyer (captain)
Ken Dryden
Bob Gainey
Doug Jarvis
Guy Lafleur
Yvon Lambert

Guy Lapointe
Michel Larocque
Jacques Lemaire
Pete Mahovlich
Bill Nyrop
Doug Risebrough
Jimmy Roberts
Larry Robinson
Serge Savard

Steve Shutt
Mario Tremblay
Murray Wilson
Sam Pollock (vice president/ general manager)
Scotty Bowman (coach)

Five for Five

Reggie Leach was one of two players to score five goals in one game during the 1976 playoffs. Darryl Sittler scored five for the Maple Leafs against Leach's Flyers in an 8–5 Toronto win on April 22. Leach and Sittler tied the NHL record for goals in a playoff game first set by Newsy Lalonde of the Montreal Canadiens on March 1, 1919, and equaled by Maurice Richard on March 23, 1944. The only other player to score five goals in one NHL playoff game is Mario Lemieux, on April 25, 1989.

Good vs Evil — Hockey Style

"There was a great sense of quest that season," Ken Dryden said of 1975–76 in his classic book *The Game*, first published in 1983. The quest was not just to bring the Stanley Cup back to Montreal but also to end the championship reign of the Philadelphia Flyers, who had won two straight titles through their tactics of violence and intimidation.

The Flyers had another outstanding season in 1975–76 and set a club record with 118 points (51-13-16). Philadelphia led the NHL with 348 goals, including a league-best 61 from Reggie Leach. Bobby Clarke was tops with 89 assists and won the Hart Trophy as MVP for the second year in a row. However, it was the Canadiens who topped the NHL's overall standings by setting new league records (which they would soon break), with 58 wins (58-11-11) and 127 points. Leading the way was Guy Lafleur, who won his first of three straight scoring titles with 125 points on 56 goals and 69 assists. Dryden also had a big year in goal for the Canadiens. He led the NHL with a career-best 42 wins, eight shutouts and a 2.03 goals-against average to win the Vezina Trophy as Montreal allowed the fewest goals against, with 174.

Flyers goalie Bernie Parent missed most of the season with a neck injury and did not play well in the playoffs. After Parent struggled in a seven-game quarterfinal series with Toronto and lost Game 1 to Boston in the semifinals, coach Fred Shero switched to Wayne Stephenson. Stephenson sparked the Flyers to four straight wins and their third straight trip to the Stanley Cup final.

The matchup of Montreal and Philadelphia was billed as a clash of hockey philosophies. "This series can be seen as a test of the kind of slick hockey that purists called traditional against the currently popular rough-edged variety of play," wrote Robin Herman of the New York Times News Service. "The teams both carry weighty reputations that will outlast their performances in one particular playoff series."

The Flyers got off to a quick start when Reggie Leach scored just 21 seconds into Game 1, but a late goal from Guy Lapointe with 1:22 remaining gave Montreal a 4–3 victory. After two more one-goal victories, Leach gave the Flyers another early lead in Game 4, but a late goal from Guy Lafleur with 5:42 remaining and another from Pete Mahovlich 58 seconds later gave the Canadiens a 5–3 victory and a Stanley Cup sweep.

Conn Smythe Story

Four goaltenders have been named playoff MVP despite playing for a team that did not win the Stanley Cup. The only position player to win the Conn Smythe Trophy on a losing team was Reggie Leach of the Flyers in 1976.

Leach had played junior hockey with Bobby Clarke in Flin Flon, Manitoba. After beginning his NHL career with the Boston Bruins and California Golden Seals, Leach was acquired by the Flyers a week after their first Stanley Cup victory, in 1974. After helping them repeat as champions in 1975, Leach ended Phil Esposito's run of six-straight seasons as the NHL's leading goal scorer in 1975–76, when he scored 61 times. Leach added 19 goals in the postseason to set a playoff record (later equaled by Jari Kurri in 1985), including five in one game against the Boston Bruins, on May 6, 1976.

Lafleur Kidnap Plot

Twelve days after the Canadiens won the Stanley Cup, Montreal's *La Presse* newspaper revealed that Guy Lafleur had played the entire playoffs knowing that there was a plot to kidnap him and hold him for ransom. Montreal police apparently learned of the plot while investigating an armored car robbery that took place on March 30th. The NHL, the Canadiens and Lafleur were advised of the plot. Montreal police kept Lafleur under close surveillance.

Stanley Cup in September

On September 20, 1975, the Canadiens hosted the Flyers in a preseason game, and Philadelphia was already looking to set the tone for the season. Dave Schultz, who was the baddest of the Flyers' "Broad Street Bullies," was coming off a season where he had collected an NHL-record 472 penalty minutes, crosschecked Canadiens captain Yvan Cournoyer hard across the back.

Rough stuff and intimidation were the biggest part of Schultz' game. But Doug Risebrough didn't back down, and his fight with Schultz set the stage for a bigger brawl the following night.

Playing a return match in Philadelphia, the Canadiens stocked their lineup with the toughest players in their system. Players like Pierre Bouchard, Rick Chartraw, Glen Gouldup and Sean Shanahan all saw action. Tempers were on edge all night as the Canadiens took a 6–2 lead, and the situation finally exploded with 1:35 remaining, when Risebrough picked a fight with Flyers captain Bobby Clarke. The incident sparked a bench-clearing brawl that lasted more than 10 minutes.

The message from the Canadiens was clear: we'd prefer to beat you with our skill, but you can no longer intimidate us with your tactics. "If we could eliminate the Flyers' physical edge," Robinson would later write in his autobiography, "our superior hockey skills would allow us to beat them."

"We won the Stanley Cup that night," Steve Shutt would tell authors Chrys Goyens and Allan Turowetz. "It just wasn't official until next May."

The Game I'll Never Forget

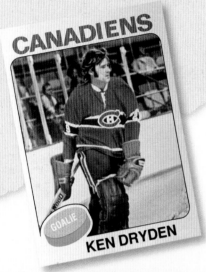

CANADIENS

KEN DRYDEN

GOALIE

" Everybody was more pumped up for this game than any that I can recall. Perhaps the extravaganza had the opposite effect of what the Flyers management intended, though it certainly excited their players. But it also pumped up ours."

Hockey Digest: April 1979
By Ken Dryden, as told to George Vass

Something that I've thought about from time to time is that there are very, very few saves that I can remember. Over the time I've played, I can remember five or six saves, that's all.

I remember games, and I can remember goals. I retain a sort of feeling of winning and losing games, feelings that come from those wins and losses. The saves I remember are very, very few. But I can remember an awful lot of goals that have been scored. I can perhaps tell you scores of games long afterward, even years, and goals that were scored, but the rest is gone.

When I think about my most memorable games, I would choose three. One of them would be the final game of the Stanley Cup playoffs against the Black Hawks in 1971, a game we won 3–2 in Chicago Stadium.

Another game would be the eighth game in Moscow in 1972, in which we defeated the Russians to take the series against them after being shocked by their skill in the beginning.

The third game that is memorable is the third game of the final series against the Philadelphia Flyers in 1976. It wasn't made memorable for me so much by the outcome, by the way it was played or anything that took place during the game itself, but by the general atmosphere.

It think the part that made that game, and even that final Stanley Cup series, so different was that we had gone two years without winning the Cup while the Flyers had won it, that we had won the first two games of that series at Montreal and that it was almost required for Philadelphia to win this game if it was to retain hopes of another Cup. All these factors combined to heighten the emotional atmosphere leading up to the game itself.

When we got to Philadelphia for Game 3 on Thursday, May 13, 1976, the Flyers management kind of pulled out all the stops, put on one of the extravaganzas. What I mean by "extravaganzas" is the atmosphere they built up before the game was to start.

They turned the lights down, put the spotlights on and brought in Kate Smith to sing "God Bless America," so it was a very special start to a game. All the parts of the extravaganza were to be expected, and the only thing that wasn't certain was whether Kate would be there or not. The expectation was that she would be, but nobody knew. But all the other parts of the extravaganza were enough to get one very excited.

Then, at the last moment, as they were saying "Now Kate Smith will sing 'God Bless America,'" the place just went crazy. As the place went crazy, those in the place, including the players, got rather excited.

What I remember most about that is that instead of what usually happens after the national anthem is sung, with the teams lined up on the blue lines, the reaction this time was quite different.

Usually, after the anthem is sung, most of the players start skating around the net until the referee blows the whistle and then tap the goalie on the pads and line up for the start of the game.

This time, when Kate finished singing everybody just took off. Everybody was so hyped up by the atmosphere in the arena that they were all skating around like Keith Magnuson of the Black Hawks skates when he comes out on the ice for the start of a period. Then when the players came back to me, instead of the usual perfunctory taps on the pads they whacked me hard—I needed the pads to save my legs from the sticks.

May 13, 1976
Game 3, Stanley Cup final · The Spectrum, Philadelphia

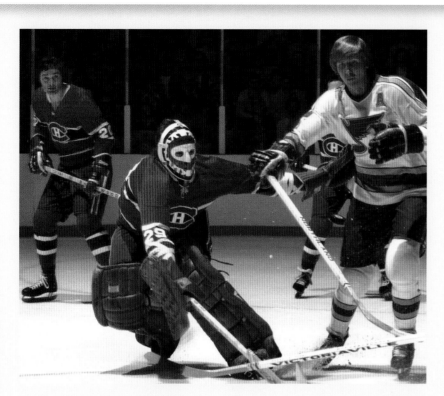

Ken Dryden in action in the mid-1970s.

Everybody was more pumped up for this game than any that I can recall. Perhaps the extravaganza had the opposite effect of what the Flyers management intended, though it certainly excited their players. But it also pumped up ours.

As for the game itself, it was like the rest of the series, a very hard-earned victory. Looking back, people will think that since we won that final series in four games that it was easy, but they couldn't be more wrong. The Flyers played well and they were a good team. We just played better, and that year we were an outstanding team.

As I've said, I do not really recollect saves. In fact, I don't believe there were many outstanding ones for me in that game, my defense protected me so well.

I do vaguely recall the course of the game. I believe we scored first [Steve Shutt early in the first period] and that Reggie Leach scored twice for the Flyers before we tied the game 2–2 [Shutt again] in the second period. Leach, of course, had a remarkable playoff record that year, scoring 19 goals in 16 games. He played on a line with center Bobby Clarke and left wing Bill Barber.

Our tactics included wearing down Clarke by double-shifting men against him throughout the series. Clarke clearly was the key player of the Flyers, and though it was impossible to keep him or his linemates Barber and Leach from scoring some goals, at least you could diminish their opportunities.

Our players did an extremely good job of controlling the pace of the game and of keeping the Flyers' scoring opportunities to a minimum. I faced only 22 shots, and of those only 13 in the last two periods.

The game was still tied 2–2 midway in the third period when we scored what was to be the winning goal. Rick Chartraw and Pierre Bouchard combined to score it.

Chartraw had the Flyers' Dave Schultz tied up in front of Wayne Stephenson, the goaltender, when Bouchard fired a 45-foot shot. Stephenson undoubtedly was screened and never saw the puck go into the net.

We won the game 3–2 and two nights later defeated the Flyers again to sweep the final series in four games. The sweep made it seem that the series had been easy, but it really wasn't. We had to sip our champagne sitting down.

However, rather than the game itself, what made it most memorable for me, as I've said, was the atmosphere before it started. I've never experienced anything quite like it, nothing that could compare with that extravaganza.

Montreal 3, Philadelphia 2

FIRST PERIOD

1 ▸ Shutt (Lafleur), Montreal, 3:17 PP

2 ▸ Leach (Clarke, Goodenough), Philadelphia, 8:40 PP

3 ▸ Leach (unassisted), Philadelphia, 18:14

PENALTIES: Barber, Philadelphia (elbowing), 1:52; Risebrough, Montreal (high-sticking), 8:02; Gainey, Montreal (elbowing), 9:18; Bridgman, Philadelphia (hooking), 15:45; Dornhoefer, Philadelphia (elbowing), 19:59

SECOND PERIOD

4 ▸ Shutt (Lafleur, Mahovlich), Montreal 1:09 PP

PENALTIES: Nyrop, Montreal (interference), 2:38; McIlhargey, Philadelphia (tripping), 5:47; Robinson, Montreal (roughing), 9:57; Gainey, Montreal (roughing), 9:57; McIlhargey, Philadelphia (roughing), 9:57; Kelly, Philadelphia (roughing), 9:57

THIRD PERIOD

5 ▸ Bouchard (Wilson), Montreal 9:16

NO PENALTIES

SHOTS ON GOAL

	1	2	3	TOTAL
Montreal	5	13	7	25
Philadelphia	9	6	7	22

GOALIES: Dryden, Montreal; Stephenson, Philadelphia

REFEREE: Wally Harris

LINESMEN: John D'Amico, Matt Pavelich

QUARTERFINALS
4 games to 0 over Toronto

SEMIFINALS
4 games to 3 over New York Islanders

FINAL　4 GAMES TO 2

MAY 15	▶	Buffalo 1 at Philadelphia 4
MAY 18	▶	Buffalo 1 at Philadelphia 2
MAY 20	▶	Philadelphia 4 at Buffalo 5 OT
MAY 22	▶	Philadelphia 2 at Buffalo 4
MAY 25	▶	Buffalo 1 at Philadelphia 5
MAY 27	▶	Philadelphia 2 at Buffalo 0

ROSTER

Bill Barber
Tom Bladon
Bobby Clarke (captain)
Bill Clement
Terry Crisp
Gary Dornhoefer
André Dupont
Larry Goodenough
Ted Harris
Bob Kelly
Orest Kindrachuk
Reggie Leach
Ross Lonsberry
Rick MacLeish
Bernie Parent
Don Saleski
Dave Schultz
Wayne Stephenson
Bobby Taylor
Ed Van Impe
Jimmy Watson
Joe Watson
Keith Allen
(vice president/
general manager)
Fred Shero (coach)

CONN SMYTHE TROPHY **BERNIE PARENT** G – PHILADELPHIA

PLAYOFF SCORING LEADER

Rick MacLeish		GP	G	A	PTS
PHILADELPHIA		17	11	9	20

FINAL SERIES SCORING

PHILADELPHIA	GP	G	A	PTS	PIM
Bill Barber	6	2	4	6	0
Bobby Clarke	6	2	3	5	2
Reggie Leach	6	3	1	4	0
Bob Kelly	5	2	2	4	7
Rick MacLeish	6	1	3	4	2
Terry Crisp	4	0	4	4	0
Ross Lonsberry	6	2	1	3	2
Gary Dornhoefer	6	2	0	2	14
Dave Schultz	6	2	0	2	13
Don Saleski	6	1	1	2	8
Larry Goodenough	2	0	2	2	2
Ted Harris	6	0	2	2	2
Ed Van Impe	6	0	2	2	8
Orest Kindrachuk	5	0	2	2	2
Jimmy Watson	6	0	2	2	0
Bill Clement	5	1	0	1	2
André Dupont	6	1	0	1	10
Tom Bladon	4	0	1	1	8
Joe Watson	6	0	0	0	2
GOALTENDER	GP	W	L	MIN	GA	SO	AVG
Bernie Parent	6	4	2	378	20	1	3.17

BUFFALO	GP	G	A	PTS	PIM
Rick Martin	6	2	4	6	6
Don Luce	6	2	3	5	12
Danny Gare	6	2	1	3	4
Jerry Korab	6	2	1	3	6
Jim Lorentz	6	1	2	3	2
René Robert	6	1	2	3	6
Gilbert Perreault	6	1	1	2	6
Craig Ramsay	6	0	2	2	0
Jim Schoenfeld	6	0	2	2	11
Bill Hajt	6	1	0	1	2
Rick Dudley	4	0	1	1	9
Jocelyn Guevremont	6	0	1	1	8
Brian Spencer	6	0	1	1	4
Larry Carrière	6	0	0	0	4
Lee Fogolin Jr.	4	0	0	0	0
Peter McNab	6	0	0	0	0
Fred Stanfield	6	0	0	0	0
GOALTENDERS	GP	W	L	MIN	GA	SO	AVG
Roger Crozier	2	1	1	118	3	0	1.53
Gerry Desjardins	5	1	3	260	16	0	3.69

Batmen Fog inside the Memorial Auditorium was not the only unusual aspect of Game 3. In the first period, a bat swooped low over the ice as the teams were lined up for a faceoff. Buffalo's Jim Lorentz raised his stick and smacked the bat to the ice, dead. Philadelphia's Rick MacLeish picked it up and tossed it into the penalty box.

No Fluke

"Last year, we were in the clouds when we won. This year it was different. We knew what we were doing. We proved to ourselves that it was no fluke that we are the champs."
— Bernie Parent

Back to Back for the Bullies

The Philadelphia Flyers shed their reputation as an expansion team with bad luck and became "The Broad Street Bullies" at training camp in 1972. Bob Kelly, who'd been with the team for two years, was instructed to start hitting. Dave Schultz was given a spot in the lineup, as was Don Saleski. Suddenly, there was a lot more room on the ice for goal scorers Bobby Clarke, Bill Barber and Rick MacLeish. The 1972–73 Flyers posted the first winning season in the six-year history of the franchise with a record of 37-30-11. The return of Bernie Parent in 1973–74 gave Philadelphia the best goalie in the NHL and increased the Flyers' confidence in their ability to compete while playing shorthanded. The result was a regular-season mark of 50-16-12 for 112 points and a Stanley Cup championship.

Though critics decried the Flyers' violent tactics, there was no doubt that the team was successful. The 1974–75 Flyers won 51 games (51-18-11) and had 113 points to finish atop the NHL standings. The team also topped their record 1,750 regular-season penalty minutes (posted in 1973–74) with 1,953. Clarke finished with 116 points (29 goals, 87 assists) and won the Hart Trophy for the second time. The Flyers swept Toronto to open the playoffs but then ran into trouble with the New York Islanders. The Islanders had bounced back from a three-games-to-nothing deficit to defeat Pittsburgh in the quarterfinals and nearly did the same thing against Philadelphia. This time, though, a hat trick from Rick MacLeish gave the Flyers a 4–1 victory in the seventh game and a return trip to the Stanley Cup final.

This year the Flyers faced the Buffalo Sabres, who had reached the final in just their fifth season. This series marked the first time that two expansion teams met for the Stanley Cup. Buffalo was led by their "French Connection" line of Gilbert Perreault, Rick Martin and René Robert and had also had 113 points in 1974–75 (as had the Montreal Canadiens, whom the Sabres beat in the semifinals). Buffalo gave Philadelphia a good battle, but the Flyers prevailed in six games.

Conn Smythe Story

Bernie Parent was a native of Montreal who grew up watching Jacques Plante play goal for the Canadiens on television. He would later play with Plante on the Toronto Maple Leafs, and their time together would help Parent develop into one of the great goaltenders in the NHL. Parent set an NHL record with 47 victories for the Flyers in 1973–74 and shared the Vezina Trophy with Chicago's Tony Esposito after leading the NHL with 12 shutouts and a 1.89 goals-against average. In 1974–75, Parent won the Vezina Trophy outright after recording 44 wins, 12 shutouts and a 2.03 average. He was brilliant in the playoffs as well, capping off Stanley Cup wins with shutouts in the final game in both 1974 and 1975. Parent had a 1.89 playoff goals-against average in 1975 and became the first player to win the Conn Smythe Trophy in back-to-back years, a feat matched only by Mario Lemieux, in 1991 and 1992.

Rick MacLeish

Game 3 of the final, on May 20, 1975, marked the latest date that a Stanley Cup game had ever been played at that point in history. The weather that day in Buffalo was unseasonably warm and humid. With a full house of 15,863 jamming the Memorial Auditorium and vocally supporting the Sabres as they tried to climb back into the series after two losses in Philadelphia, the heat and humidity inside the rink was rising as well. With no air conditioning, the temperature at ice level had climbed to 87ºF (many reports say above 90) by the third period. "It felt like a hundred," said Sabres defenseman Jerry Korab.

A fog rose over the ice that became so thick it was difficult to follow the puck. Play had to be halted 12 times in the game's latter stages. The players were instructed to skate around the ice in circles in an effort to disperse the fog. Arena workers waved white bed sheets to try to break up the clouds. Nothing really worked, and the fog was still a problem as the game went into overtime. It played a part in the Sabres' winning goal at 18:29.

The play began when Rick Martin cleared the Sabres' zone and got the puck to Gilbert Perreault. "I heard René (Robert) yelling," Perreault said, "and passed the red line and fired it into the corner, hoping he'd get it." Robert did get it. He fired the puck at Bernie Parent from a bad angle, and his shot wound up in the net. Asked if the fog had affected him, Parent admitted it had. "Yes," he said, "to this degree. I didn't pick up Perreault's shot as quickly as Robert did."

QUARTERFINALS
4 games to 0 over Atlanta

SEMIFINALS
4 games to 3 over New York Rangers

MAY 7	►	Philadelphia 2 at Boston 3
MAY 9	►	Philadelphia 3 at Boston 2 OT
MAY 12	►	Boston 1 at Philadelphia 4
MAY 14	►	Boston 2 at Philadelphia 4
MAY 16	►	Philadelphia 1 at Boston 5
MAY 19	►	Boston 0 at Philadelphia 1

ROSTER

Barry Ashbee
Bill Barber
Tom Bladon
Bobby Clarke (captain)
Bill Clement
Bruce Cowick
Terry Crisp
Gary Dornhoefer
André Dupont
Bill Flett
Bob Kelly
Orest Kindrachuk
Ross Lonsberry
Rick MacLeish
Simon Nolet
Bernie Parent
Don Saleski
Dave Schultz
Bobby Taylor
Ed Van Impe
Jimmy Watson
Joe Watson
Keith Allen (vice president/general manager)
Fred Shero (coach)

CONN SMYTHE TROPHY BERNIE PARENT G – PHILADELPHIA

PLAYOFF SCORING LEADER

	GP	G	A	PTS
Rick MacLeish PHILADELPHIA	17	13	9	22

FINAL SERIES SCORING

PHILADELPHIA	GP	G	A	PTS	PIM
Bobby Clarke	6	3	3	6	14
Rick MacLeish	6	2	3	5	4
André Dupont	6	2	1	3	33
Dave Schultz	6	1	2	3	38
Bill Flett	6	0	3	3	4
Don Saleski	6	0	3	3	6
Orest Kindrachuk	6	2	0	2	11
Bill Barber	6	1	1	2	2
Tom Bladon	6	1	1	2	21
Terry Crisp	6	1	1	2	2
Ross Lonsberry	6	1	1	2	2
Ed Van Impe	6	0	2	2	13
Joe Watson	6	0	2	2	16
Bill Clement	3	1	0	1	2
Simon Nolet	6	0	1	1	0
Jimmy Watson	6	0	1	1	30
Bruce Cowick	6	0	0	0	7
Gary Dornhoefer	3	0	0	0	0

GOALTENDER	GP	W	L	MIN	GA	SO	AVG
Bernie Parent	6	4	2	372	13	1	2.10

BOSTON	GP	G	A	PTS	PIM
Bobby Orr	6	3	4	7	8
Gregg Sheppard	6	2	3	5	2
Ken Hodge	6	1	4	5	6
Wayne Cashman	6	2	2	4	41
John Bucyk	6	1	3	4	2
Phil Esposito	6	2	1	3	10
Carol Vadnais	6	0	3	3	22
André Savard	6	1	1	2	20
Dallas Smith	6	0	2	2	8
Don Marcotte	6	1	0	1	2
Dave Forbes	6	0	1	1	2
Terry O'Reilly	6	0	1	1	25
Darryl Edestrand	6	0	0	0	2
Rich Leduc	5	0	0	0	9
Bobby Schmautz	6	0	0	0	18
Al Sims	6	0	0	0	4

GOALTENDER	GP	W	L	MIN	GA	SO	AVG
Gilles Gilbert	6	2	4	372	15	0	2.42

Shero-isms

"When you have bacon and eggs for breakfast, the chicken makes a contribution but the pig makes a commitment."

"Success is not the result of spontaneous combustion. You must first set yourself on fire."

"Win together now and we'll talk together forever."
— Fred Shero's message to the Flyers on the blackboard in the dressing room before Game 6

First for the Flyers

After posting their first winning season, 1972–73, the Philadelphia Flyers emerged as both a new, and new-fangled, NHL power in 1973–74. Known as "The Broad Street Bullies," the Flyers won by intimidation as much as they did by talent.

Philadelphia featured an offense led by captain Bobby Clarke, Bill Barber and Rick MacLeish. The defense included Tom Bladon, André "Moose" Dupont, Ed Van Impe and brothers Joe and Jimmy Watson. The Flyers also had the prototypical enforcer in Dave Schultz, whose reputation as a fighter kept opponents from getting too rough with the team's stars and emboldened other Flyers to play the violent style that coach Fred Shero espoused.

Shero had turned down a chance to go pro as a boxer to pursue a career in hockey after World War II. He played three seasons in the NHL with the New York Rangers, but he spent most of his career in the minors, where he got into coaching. Hired by the Flyers in 1971, his fondness for the hitting game—along with his penchant for unique drills and unusual sayings—helped to build the toughest team in hockey.

The Flyers recorded a 50-16-12 mark to lead the West Division with 112 points, just one point behind the East Division's Boston Bruins, for top spot overall. Boston's Phil Esposito, Bobby Orr, Ken Hodge and Wayne Cashman finished first, second, third and fourth in the NHL scoring race, with the Flyers' Clarke placing fifth. In the playoffs, the Bruins knocked off Toronto and Chicago to reach the Stanley Cup final. The Flyers swept the Atlanta Flames and then beat up the New York Rangers in a tough seven-game series to become the first NHL expansion team to defeat an Original Six club in the playoffs.

Boston won Game 1 of the final 3–2 on a late goal by Bobby Orr, but the Flyers became the first expansion team to win a game in the Stanley Cup final when Clarke scored in overtime for a 3–2 Philadelphia win in Game 2. By Game 6, with Kate Smith belting out "God Bless America," Philadelphia became the NHL's first expansion champion, with a 1–0 victory. Rick MacLeish had the game's only goal, when he tipped in a Moose Dupont shot on a power play at 14:48 of the first period. Bernie Parent's shutout sealed his selection as Conn Smythe Trophy winner.

Barry Ashbee

Barry Ashbee was a career minor leaguer who'd played just 14 games in the NHL before he joined the Flyers as a 31-year-old in 1971–72. Like many Philadelphia players of his era, what Ashby lacked in skill he made up for with hustle and desire. He earned a spot on the NHL Second All-Star Team for the 1973–74 season. Sadly, Ashby's career came to a premature end when a shot from New York defenseman Dale Rolfe deflected and hit Ashbee just below the right eyebrow in Game 4 of the Flyers' 1974 semifinal series against the Rangers. A year later, he became an assistant coach with the team, and the Flyers created the Barry Ashbee Trophy for the team's outstanding defenseman. Ashbee was still coaching with the team when he was diagnosed with leukemia. He died on May 12, 1977.

Strange Strategy
Fred Shero's strategy to contain Bobby Orr was to let him have the puck as much as possible to try to tire him out. Did the strategy work? Orr was the leading scorer during the final, but Philadelphia won the series.

Barry Ashbee

God Bless Kate Smith

Kate Smith's rendition of Irving Berlin's "God Bless America" was played instead of "The Star-Spangled Banner" at a Flyers game for the first time on December 11, 1969. The Flyers beat the Toronto Maple Leafs 6–3 that night. After a loss in their next home game and three losses and a tie in a four-game road trip, "God Bless America" was played once again on December 21st and Philadelphia beat Pittsburgh 4–0.

Over the next few years, the Kate Smith recording would be brought out from time to time for big games, and the Flyers would almost never lose. Strange as it seems, the old-time radio star became a lucky charm for the toughest team in hockey. Ms. Smith made her first live appearance to sing at the Spectrum on the opening night of the 1973–74 season. Her recorded version was played seven more times that season, including Game 4 of the Stanley Cup final. The Flyers won every time, running their record to 36-3-1 when "God Bless America" was played. She returned to close out the season in style, appearing live again before Game 6 of the final.

Turning It Around
Entering the Stanley Cup final, the Flyers had not won a game at the Boston Garden since making their first visit there in 1967. Philadelphia's victory in Game 2 ended that slide and marked only the fifth time in 40 games that the Flyers had ever beaten the Bruins.

Montreal Canadiens

ROSTER

Pierre Bouchard
Yvan Cournoyer
Ken Dryden
Réjean Houle
Guy Lafleur
Jacques Laperrière
Guy Lapointe
Claude Larose
Chuck Lefley
Jacques Lemaire
Frank Mahovlich
Pete Mahovlich
Bob Murdoch
Michel Plasse
Henri Richard
(captain)
Jimmy Roberts
Larry Robinson
Serge Savard
Steve Shutt
Marc Tardif
Murray Wilson
Sam Pollock
(vice president/
general manager)
Scotty Bowman
(coach)

CONN SMYTHE TROPHY **YVAN COURNOYER** RW – MONTREAL

FINAL   4 GAMES TO 2

APR. 29	▶	Chicago 3 at Montreal 8
MAY 1	▶	Chicago 1 at Montreal 4
MAY 3	▶	Montreal 4 at Chicago 7
MAY 6	▶	Montreal 4 at Chicago 0
MAY 8	▶	Chicago 8 at Montreal 7
MAY 10	▶	Montreal 6 at Chicago 4

PLAYOFF SCORING LEADER

Yvan Cournoyer	GP	G	A	PTS
MONTREAL	17	15	10	25

FINAL SERIES SCORING

MONTREAL	GP	G	A	PTS	PIM
Yvan Cournoyer	6	6	6	12	0
Jacques Lemaire	6	3	9	12	0
Frank Mahovlich	6	5	6	11	0
Pete Mahovlich	6	3	5	8	12
Claude Larose	6	3	4	7	2
Chuck Lefley	6	3	3	6	2
Marc Tardif	6	3	3	6	4
Guy Lapointe	6	1	3	4	8
Henri Richard	6	2	1	3	0
Réjean Houle	6	1	2	3	0
Jacques Laperrière	2	1	1	2	0
Guy Lafleur	6	0	2	2	0
Larry Robinson	6	0	2	2	2
Murray Wilson	6	0	2	2	2
Pierre Bouchard	6	1	0	1	4
Serge Savard	6	1	0	1	6
Bob Murdoch	4	0	0	0	2
Jimmy Roberts	6	0	0	0	6
GOALTENDER	GP	W	L	MIN	GA	SO	AVG
Ken Dryden	6	4	2	360	21	1	3.50

CHICAGO	GP	G	A	PTS	PIM
Stan Mikita	5	3	5	8	0
Pat Stapleton	6	0	8	8	4
Dennis Hull	6	3	4	7	4
Pit Martin	6	5	0	5	4
Jim Pappin	6	3	2	5	10
Ralph Backstrom	6	1	3	4	0
Bill White	6	1	3	4	2
Cliff Koroll	6	1	2	3	2
Dave Kryskow	3	2	0	2	0
Lou Angotti	6	1	1	2	0
Len Frig	4	1	1	2	0
John Marks	6	1	1	2	2
Chico Maki	6	0	2	2	0
J.P. Bordeleau	6	1	0	1	4
Doug Jarrett	6	0	1	1	0
Dick Redmond	4	0	1	1	0
Phil Russell	6	0	1	1	16
Jerry Korab	5	0	0	0	6
GOALTENDERS	GP	W	L	MIN	GA	SO	AVG
Tony Esposito	6	2	4	355	32	0	5.41
Gary Smith	1	0	0	5	0	0	0.00

No TV Coverage

NHL president Clarence Campbell announced during the 1973 Stanley Cup final that television cameras would not be allowed in the winning team's dressing room after the series. Campbell said that scenes inside the victor's dressing room did little more than "glorify alcohol, the number-one poison in the country." He added that, "as long as I'm president, I'm not going to condone anything that downgrades the image of hockey."

Canadiens a Constant in World of Change

There were big changes in the hockey world in 1972. The NHL faced its first major professional rival since the fall of the old Western Hockey League in 1926 with the launch of the World Hockey Association. The NHL responded to the WHA threat by adding the Atlanta Flames and the New York Islanders as the league expanded to 16 teams.

Before either league began its 1972–73 schedule, hockey fans focused their attention on an eight-game series pitting an all-NHL Team Canada against the Soviet Union's national team. Canadian fans had always been confident that their best NHL pros could defeat the perennial world amateur champions. The series, however, went right down to the wire, with Paul Henderson's goal with 34 seconds remaining in the final game giving Canada a victory. Ken Dryden and Tony Esposito had shared goaltending duties for Team Canada during the series in September. At season's end, they faced each other for the Stanley Cup in a rematch of 1971.

Phil Esposito won his third of four straight scoring titles, and Bobby Orr recovered from off-season knee surgery to enjoy another 100-point season, but Boston's league-leading 330 goals were only one more than Montreal's 329. Jacques Lemaire (44) and Yvan Cournoyer (40) were the Canadiens' top goal-scorers, while Lemaire (95) and Frank Mahovlich (93) led the team in points. Defense was the key, however, as rookie Larry Robinson joined a blue line corps that already featured veteran Jacques Laperrière as well as Serge Savard and Guy Lapointe. With 184 goals against, the Canadiens were the only NHL team to surrender fewer than 200 as Ken Dryden won the Vezina Trophy for the first time.

The Stanley Cup final between Montreal and Chicago was expected to be a defensive battle. It wasn't. Both Yvan Cournoyer and Jacques Lemaire collected 12 points to tie Gordie Howe's 1955 record for scoring in the finals. Montreal's 33 goals and the two team's combined total of 56 made 1973 the highest-scoring final in NHL history, and Chicago's 8–7 victory in Game 5 was (and still remains) the highest-scoring Stanley Cup game since the NHL began playing for the trophy in 1918. Cournoyer, who scored the Cup-winner when he broke a 4–4 tie in the third period of Game 6, set a new playoff record with 15 goals, and Henri Richard won the Stanley Cup for the 11th time.

Champions of the World

On May 6, 1973, the New England Whalers defeated the Winnipeg Jets 9–6 for a four-games-to-one victory to claim the Avco Cup as the first championships of the World Hockey Association. Immediately after the game, Whalers president Howard Baldwin issued a challenge for the Stanley Cup. He suggested a one-game playoff, on neutral ice, with the proceeds to go to charity. "This challenge is meant in no disrespect to (Montreal or Chicago) or the National Hockey League," Baldwin said. "This is a challenge intended only to restore the people their right to see a true champion decided in this, the world's fastest sport."

Two weeks later came word of a proposed new European Professional Hockey League with teams in Sweden, Finland, England and Germany. Organizers hoped their champion might face teams from the Soviet Union and Czechoslovakia for the right to challenge the NHL's Stanley Cup champions. Neither this, nor the WHA challenge, ever took place.

MOST CAREER STANLEY CUP WINS

11	Henri Richard	Montreal (1956, 1957, 1958, 1959, 1960, 1965, 1966, 1968, 1969, 1971, 1973)
10	Jean Béliveau	Montreal (1956, 1957, 1958, 1959, 1960, 1965, 1966, 1968, 1969, 1971)
	Yvan Cournoyer	Montreal (1965, 1966, 1968, 1969, 1971, 1973, 1976, 1977, 1978, 1979)
9	Claude Provost	Montreal (1956, 1957, 1958, 1959, 1960, 1965, 1966, 1968, 1969)
8	Red Kelly	Detroit (1950, 1952, 1954, 1955) Toronto (1962, 1963, 1964, 1967)
	Maurice Richard	Montreal (1944, 1946, 1953, 1956, 1957, 1958, 1959, 1960)
	Jacques Lemaire	Montreal (1968, 1969, 1971, 1973, 1976, 1977, 1978, 1979)
	Serge Savard	Montreal (1968, 1969, 1971, 1973, 1976, 1977, 1978, 1979)
7	Jean-Guy Talbot	Montreal (1956, 1957, 1958, 1959, 1960, 1965, 1966)

ALL IN THE FAMILY

1973 Scotty Bowman's wife, Suella, was eight months pregnant during the 1973 Stanley Cup final. Bowman promised that if the Canadiens won, he'd name the child after the Stanley Cup. On June 28, 1973, Suella gave birth to an 8-pound, 15-ounce baby boy whom the Bowman's named Stanley. In 2010, Stan Bowman would get his name on the Stanley Cup as general manager of the Chicago Blackhawks.

ALL IN THE FAMILY

1916 On March 30, 1916, the Montreal Canadiens beat the Portland Rosebuds 2–1 to win the Stanley Cup for the first time in team history. According to stories, the wife of Canadiens goalie Georges Vezina gave birth to a baby boy that same night and Vezina told Canadiens owner George Kennedy he would name the boy Marcel Stanley Vezina in honor of the team's victory.

In actual fact, the boy was born on March 31, 1916. His given name was Joseph Louis Marcel Vezina, though Marcel Stanley was something of a family nickname.

ALL IN THE FAMILY

1905 Harry "Rat" Westwick was a star for the Ottawa Silver Seven during their Stanley Cup reign from 1903 to 1906. On January 19, 1905 — three days after Ottawa routed Dawson City in their famous challenge — Westwick's wife gave birth to a son. The boy was named Thomas Stanley after his grandfather and the Stanley Cup. Westwick later scratched his son's name and the date (Feb. 23, 1905) into the Stanley Cup bowl.

QUARTERFINALS
4 games to 1 over Toronto

SEMIFINALS
4 games to 0 over St. Louis

FINAL   4 GAMES TO 2

APR. 30	▶	New York Rangers 5 at Boston 6
MAY 2	▶	New York Rangers 1 at Boston 2
MAY 4	▶	Boston 2 at New York Rangers 5
MAY 7	▶	Boston 3 at New York Rangers 2
MAY 9	▶	New York Rangers 3 at Boston 2
MAY 11	▶	Boston 3 at New York Rangers 0

ROSTER

Don Awrey
Garnet Bailey
John Bucyk
Wayne Cashman
Gerry Cheevers
Phil Esposito
Ted Green
Ken Hodge
Eddie Johnston
Don Marcotte
John McKenzie
Bobby Orr
Derek Sanderson
Dallas Smith
Fred Stanfield
Carol Vadnais
Mike Walton
Ed Westfall
Milt Schmidt (general manager)
Tom Johnson (coach)

CONN SMYTHE TROPHY **BOBBY ORR** D – BOSTON

PLAYOFF SCORING LEADERS

	GP	G	A	PTS
Phil Esposito BOSTON	15	9	15	24
Bobby Orr BOSTON	15	5	19	24

FINAL SERIES SCORING

BOSTON	GP	G	A	PTS	PIM
Ken Hodge	6	5	3	8	19
Bobby Orr	6	4	4	8	17
Phil Esposito	6	0	8	8	14
Mike Walton	6	1	4	5	6
Wayne Cashman	6	3	1	4	15
John Bucyk	6	1	2	3	2
Fred Stanfield	6	1	2	3	0
John McKenzie	6	0	2	2	25
Ed Westfall	6	0	2	2	10
Garnet Bailey	6	1	0	1	14
Don Marcotte	5	1	0	1	6
Derek Sanderson	6	1	0	1	26
Dallas Smith	6	0	1	1	10
Carol Vadnais	6	0	1	1	13
Don Awrey	6	0	0	0	21
Ted Green	4	0	0	0	0

GOALTENDERS	GP	W	L	MIN	GA	SO	AVG
Eddie Johnston	3	2	1	180	6	0	2.00
Gerry Cheevers	3	2	1	180	10	1	3.33

NY RANGERS	GP	G	A	PTS	PIM
Rod Gilbert	6	4	3	7	11
Brad Park	6	2	4	6	11
Ted Irvine	6	1	4	5	10
Bobby Rousseau	6	2	2	4	5
Vic Hadfield	6	1	3	4	16
Pete Stemkowski	6	1	3	4	8
Bruce MacGregor	6	1	2	3	2
Walt Tkaczuk	6	1	2	3	17
Dale Rolfe	6	2	0	2	10
Rod Seiling	6	1	1	2	6
Bill Fairbairn	6	0	2	2	0
Jim Neilson	3	0	1	1	2
Jean Ratelle	6	0	1	1	0
Gene Carr	6	0	0	0	9
Ab DeMarco Jr.	1	0	0	0	0
Gary Doak	5	0	0	0	34
Jim Dorey	1	0	0	0	0
Phil Goyette	3	0	0	0	0
Glen Sather	6	0	0	0	11
Ron Stewart	1	0	0	0	0

GOALTENDERS	GP	W	L	MIN	GA	SO	AVG
Gilles Villemure	3	1	2	180	7	0	2.33
Ed Giacomin	3	1	2	180	11	0	3.67

Beating the Blues In Boston's semifinal sweep of St. Louis, they outscored the Blues 6–1, 10–2, 7–2 and 5–3. The 28 goals the Bruins scored are the most ever in a four-game playoff series.

Top Dogs The 1972 Stanley Cup final marked the first time since 1960 that the top two teams in the NHL's overall standings met to decide the championship.

Boston Back on Top

After their record-breaking performance the year before had ended in playoff disappointment, the Boston Bruins were back on top in 1971–72 with a record of 54-13-11 for 119 points. Phil Esposito led the NHL in scoring for the second straight year, with 66 goals and 133 points, while Bobby Orr had 37 goals and 80 assists for 117 points to finish second, again. Orr also won the Norris Trophy as best defenseman for a record-breaking fifth straight season and became the first player to win the Hart Trophy as MVP three years in a row.

Like the Bruins, the New York Rangers had struggled for years during the Original Six era before reemerging as a top team after NHL expansion. The Rangers' resurgence was led by forwards Jean Ratelle, Vic Hadfield and Rod Gilbert, who became known as the GAG line (which stood for Goal-a-Game). The high-scoring trio finished third, fourth and fifth in scoring behind Orr and Esposito in 1972–73, and the Rangers finished second overall in the NHL standings behind the Bruins for the second straight season with 109 points. Hadfield was the first Ranger to score 50 goals this season, and Ratelle set a club record with 109 points in just 63 games. He was battling Esposito for the scoring lead until breaking a bone above his right ankle on March 1st. Ratelle missed two months before returning to action for the Stanley Cup final.

The Rangers took an early lead in Game 1 against Boston only to see the Bruins storm back with five straight goals, including a hat trick from Ken Hodge. However, it took a late goal by Garnet "Ace" Bailey to give the Bruins a 6–5 victory. After a defensive battle in Game 2, Brad Park and Rod Gilbert each scored twice to give the Rangers a 5–2 victory at home in Game 3. Bobby Orr scored twice and set up Don Marcotte for the winning goal in Game 4. The Bruins had a chance to wrap up the series on home ice in Game 5, but the Rangers stayed alive. Game 6 was another defensive struggle. Bobby Orr scored in the first period, and Gerry Cheevers made the lead hold up until Wayne Cashman scored twice in the third for a 3–0 victory that gave the Bruins their second Stanley Cup championship in three years.

Conn Smythe Story

Bobby Orr was an overwhelming choice for the Conn Smythe Trophy, making him the first two-time winner of the playoff MVP award. "You want to know what turned this game around?" asked Rangers star Vic Hadfield after Boston wrapped up the series, "The same thing that turned the whole thing around — Bobby Orr. The two clubs were even in faceoffs, even in power plays, even in penalty killing, even in everything — expect they had Orr."

"That Orr," agreed Brad Park, who would finish second to the Boston defenseman in Norris Trophy voting for the third straight year, "He's fantastic, just terrific."

Bobby Orr

Format Change

The playoffs were modified in 1972 so that the first-placed team in each division would face the fourth-placed team in the quarterfinals. This replaced the old system, which had pitted one against three and two against four since 1943. The reason for the change was to increase the competitive advantage for teams that finished atop their division.

All-American The 1972 Stanley Cup final marked the second time the Rangers and Bruins had played for the championship. Their series back in 1929 had marked the first time that two American teams had competed for what had once been the hockey championship of Canada. The Bruins won that best-of-three series in a two-game sweep.

Future Success Assured

The Montreal Canadiens made two moves prior to the 1971–72 season that would ensure the success of the franchise for the rest of the decade. Having already acquired the California Seals first draft choice one year earlier, the Canadiens used what turned out to be the number-one pick overall to select Guy Lafleur from the Quebec Remparts on June 10, 1971. That same day, the Canadiens hired Scotty Bowman as their new head coach. Bowman had spent a long apprenticeship in the Canadiens system before spending the previous four seasons with the St. Louis Blues as coach and/or general manager.

The Game I'll Never Forget

BRUINS

PHIL ESPOSITO — CENTER

66 **There wasn't any champagne that night. We had to settle for beer. But it tasted just as good. Anytime you win, it's sweet."**

Hockey Digest: February 1974
By Phil Esposito, as told to George Vass

It's really tough to pick one game out of so many hundred and say that's the one I'll never forget. Milestone games rank as some of my most memorable, like the game I scored my 59th goal of the season to break Bobby Hull's single-season scoring record of 58, or the game later the same year in which I scored goal number 76.

Then there's the first time I was on a Stanley Cup winner, when we beat St. Louis in 1970 to take it all. I could never forget the first time I drank out of the Cup, and I'll never have that moment again—but it's still sweet every time you win.

The Boston team we had in 1970, we figured we'd beat St. Louis. It would have been a great upset if we hadn't. It was only the third year of expansion, and the way the league was aligned at the time, all the power was in the Eastern Division. We'd beaten two tougher teams in New York and Chicago before we defeated St. Louis for the Cup, although they gave us a fight in Game 4, sending it to overtime before we did win. That was far different than the final we had in 1972—the series for the Cup against

the Rangers was much tougher.

The sixth game of the Stanley Cup final, on May 11, 1972, in New York is the game I'll never forget. How could I?

We had won three of the first four games of the series and were primed to win the Cup in Boston in Game 5, but we lost that game. I can laugh about it now, although it didn't seem funny at the time. When we were playing the fifth game the champagne was ready. Everybody assumed we'd beat the Rangers on our ice. It didn't work out that way. Bobby Rousseau scored a couple of goals for the Rangers, and they took it 3–2 to take the series back to New York for Game 6.

The organizers had to cancel the reception at Boston City Hall planned for the next day, and all the instructions on how the Stanley Cup was to be presented had to be put on ice.

We were going to have to wait, but not too long. When we took the ice in Madison Square Garden two days later, on Thursday, May 11, we were confident. The Garden fans greeted us in their usual way, but we'd heard it all before. They

couldn't be any tougher than in 1971, when they'd hung up signs like "Pig Face McKenzie" making fun of John "Pie Face" McKenzie. There is such a strong rivalry between the Bruins and the Rangers. A lot of it went back to the opening round of the 1970 playoffs, when we beat them, and it was still strong in 1972.

The Rangers started Gilles Villemure in goal. Gerry Cheevers worked for us. They both were good, but Cheevers wasn't going to be beaten this time out. He was all around the cage, but he didn't have to work as hard as Villemure. We put the pressure on the Rangers.

Bobby Orr got the first goal for us, somewhere around the middle of the first period. He'd gone into the game with his knee heavily taped. That knee had been bothering him quite a while, and he had surgery on it later. But you could hardly tell from the way he played, the trouble he was having with that knee. He made some kind of move around Bruce MacGregor and put a wrist shot past Villemure from about 30 feet out to give us a 1–0 lead early in the first period.

That goal had to stand up the rest of that period and right through the end of second period, too.

We were leading 1–0, and it was still anybody's game early in the third period when we had a faceoff near Villemure. I squared off against Walt Tkaczuk, the strong Rangers center.

May 11, 1972
Game 6, Stanley Cup final · Madison Square Garden, New York

Rangers coach Emile Francis tried to send out Pete Stemkowski in place of Tkaczuk, whom I'd been beating, but the referee waved him back to the bench. While they were arguing I skated over to Orr and told him I'd try to get the puck back to him.

I beat Tkaczuk on the drop and

Phil Esposito in action in the early 1970s.

laid the puck right on Orr's stick. He shot from the point, and Wayne Cashman got in front of the net just in the right spot and deflected the shot past Villemure to give us a 2–0 lead.

We weren't home free yet. You couldn't be sure with the Rangers pressing like they were, and there was still 14 minutes to play.

But with just a couple of minutes left in the game we broke their backs. I got a semi-breakaway and spotted Kenny Hodge. I passed the puck to him, and he got it over to Cashman, who dumped it between Villemure's legs.

That made it 3–0 with less than two minutes to play. For the first time in the game I was sure we'd win.

We did, 3–0. After the final buzzer went off, NHL president Clarence Campbell presented Johnny Bucyk, our captain, with the Cup and we got off the ice in a hurry. Those Ranger fans had pretty good aim, and they were zeroing in on us.

We'd won the Cup and finished first. It was our second Cup in three years, and not many players get a chance to be on one winner, let alone two. To beat New York twice at Madison Square Garden was something special, too.

There wasn't any champagne that night. We had to settle for beer. But it tasted just as good. Anytime you win, it's sweet.

Boston 3, New York Rangers 0

FIRST PERIOD

1 ▸ Orr (Hodge, Bucyk), Boston, 11:18 PP

PENALTIES: McKenzie, Boston (slashing), 2:32; Irvine, NY Rangers (slashing), 5:44; Hodge, Boston (tripping), 7:07; Tkaczuk, NY Rangers (hooking), 10:25; Hodge (high-sticking, fighting), Boston, 13:06; Hadfield, NY Rangers (high-sticking, fighting), 13:06; Cashman, Boston (charging), 14:46; Orr, Boston (misconduct), 14:46; Doak (high-sticking), NY Rangers 14:46

SECOND PERIOD

NO SCORING

PENALTIES: Vadnais, Boston (holding), 3:45; Hadfield, NY Rangers (roughing), 3:45; Sanderson, Boston (kneeing, fighting), 4:33; Marcotte, Boston (boarding), 4:33; Gilbert, NY Rangers (fighting), 4:33; Carr, NY Rangers (tripping), 9:16; Cashman, Boston (high-sticking), 12:05; Doak, NY Rangers (high-sticking), 12:05; Cashman, Boston (fighting), 16:01; Tkaczuk, NY Rangers (fighting), 16:01

THIRD PERIOD

2 ▸ Cashman (Esposito, Orr), Boston, 5:10 PP

3 ▸ Cashman (Hodge, Esposito), Boston 18:11

PENALTIES: Rolfe, NY Rangers (holding), 3:20; D. Smith, Boston (tripping), 10:36

SHOTS ON GOAL

	1	2	3	TOTAL
Boston	9	11	13	33
NY Rangers	8	9	10	27

GOALIES: Cheevers, Boston; Villemure, NY Rangers

REFEREE: Art Skov

LINESMEN: Matt Pavelich, Neil Armstrong

Montreal Canadiens

CONN SMYTHE TROPHY **KEN DRYDEN** G – MONTREAL

FINAL 4 GAMES TO 3

MAY 4	▶	Montreal 1 at Chicago 2 OT
MAY 6	▶	Montreal 3 at Chicago 5
MAY 9	▶	Chicago 2 at Montreal 4
MAY 11	▶	Chicago 2 at Montreal 5
MAY 13	▶	Montreal 0 at Chicago 2
MAY 16	▶	Chicago 3 at Montreal 4
MAY 18	▶	Montreal 3 at Chicago 2

PLAYOFF SCORING LEADER

Frank Mahovlich	GP	G	A	PTS
MONTREAL	20	14	13	27

FINAL SERIES SCORING

MONTREAL	GP	G	A	PTS	PIM
Frank Mahovlich	7	4	4	8	4
Pete Mahovlich	7	5	2	7	16
Yvan Cournoyer	7	4	2	6	6
Jacques Lemaire	7	3	1	4	11
Jean Béliveau	7	1	3	4	6
Henri Richard	7	2	1	3	2
Guy Lapointe	7	1	2	3	19
Réjean Houle	7	0	3	3	10
Jacques Laperrière	7	0	3	3	2
J.C. Tremblay	7	0	3	3	7
Terry Harper	7	0	2	2	10
John Ferguson	6	0	1	1	8
Pierre Bouchard	3	0	0	0	2
Claude Larose	2	0	0	0	0
Bob Murdoch	2	0	0	0	0
Phil Roberto	5	0	0	0	12
Leon Rochefort	6	0	0	0	6
Marc Tardif	7	0	0	0	19

GOALTENDER	GP	W	L	MIN	GA	SO	AVG
Ken Dryden	7	4	3	441	18	0	2.45

CHICAGO	GP	G	A	PTS	PIM
Bobby Hull	7	3	6	9	8
Jim Pappin	7	4	2	6	8
Cliff Koroll	7	2	3	5	4
Stan Mikita	7	1	4	5	6
Dennis Hull	7	3	1	4	2
Lou Angotti	7	2	2	4	9
Chico Maki	7	2	1	3	4
Danny O'Shea	7	1	1	2	12
Pit Martin	6	0	2	2	4
Pat Stapleton	7	0	2	2	0
Bill White	7	0	2	2	10
Rick Foley	4	0	1	1	4
Doug Jarrett	7	0	1	1	2
Jerry Korab	2	0	0	0	14
Keith Magnuson	7	0	0	0	36
Dan Maloney	2	0	0	0	4
Eric Nesterenko	7	0	0	0	8
Gerry Pinder	5	0	0	0	2
Paul Shmyr	3	0	0	0	17

GOALTENDER	GP	W	L	MIN	GA	SO	AVG
Tony Esposito	7	3	4	441	20	1	2.72

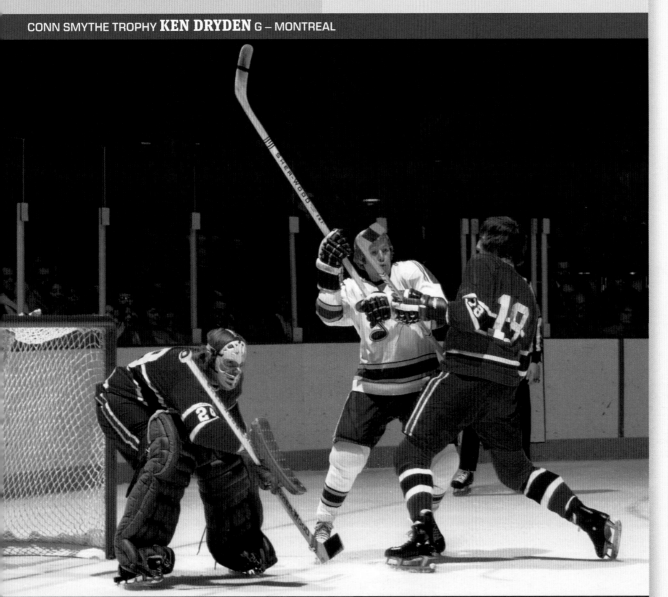

Serge Savard clears the way for Ken Dryden.

ROSTER

Jean Béliveau (captain)
Pierre Bouchard
Yvan Cournoyer
Ken Dryden
John Ferguson
Terry Harper
Réjean Houle
Jacques Laperrière
Guy Lapointe

Claude Larose
Chuck Lefley
Jacques Lemaire
Frank Mahovlich
Pete Mahovlich
Bob Murdoch
Henri Richard
Phil Roberto
Leon Rochefort

Bobby Sheehan
Marc Tardif
J.C. Tremblay
Rogie Vachon
Sam Pollock (vice president/general manager)
Al MacNeil (coach)

Coaching Carousel

Al MacNeil replaced Claude Ruel behind the Canadiens bench on December 3, 1970, but winning the Stanley Cup as a rookie head coach didn't save MacNeil's job. After the season, Montreal hired Scotty Bowman as its new coach. MacNeil took over as coach and GM of Montreal's Nova Scotia Voyageurs farm club.

Montreal's Miracle Cup

The Boston Bruins followed up their Stanley Cup victory in 1970 with a record-breaking season in 1970–71. Their 57 wins, 121 points and 399 goals all established new NHL highs. Phil Esposito set new records with 76 goals and 152 points, while Bobby Orr established a new mark with 102 assists. Esposito, Orr, John Bucyk and Ken Hodge finished first, second, third and fourth in the NHL scoring race and were the only players in the league to top 100 points. Espo and Bucyk became the first teammates to top 50 goals in a single season. But Boston's apparent dynasty-in-the-making was denied when the Bruins couldn't get past Montreal in the first round of the playoffs.

Montreal, after having missed the playoffs for the first time in 22 years in 1969–70, didn't just return to the postseason and spoil the Bruins party, they won the Stanley Cup. Ken Dryden, who had not even played enough games in the regular season to qualify as a rookie, was Montreal's playoff hero, but he was not the only newcomer to make an impression. Guy Lapointe, Réjean Houle and Pete Mahovlich all played their first full seasons with the Canadiens and made important contributions, as did Pete's brother Frank, who came over from Detroit in a midseason trade. Younger veterans such as Yvan Cournoyer, Jacques Lemaire, and J.C. Tremblay all had good years too. Still, it was Jean Béliveau, playing his 20th and final season, who led the team in scoring, and Henri Richard, rebounding from an off year and a feud with new coach Al MacNeil, who was the ultimate Stanley Cup hero.

Facing the Black Hawks in the Stanley Cup final, the Canadiens lost the first two games in Chicago. Frank Mahovlich then scored twice in Montreal's 4–2 victory at home in Game 3, while Cournoyer had two in a 5–2 victory in Game 4. After dropping Game 5, the Canadiens stayed alive with another home victory in Game 6, when the Mahovlich brothers figured in all four goals in a 4–3 victory. Game 7 in Chicago saw Montreal fall behind 2–0, but goals by Jacques Lemaire and Henri Richard evened the score after two periods. Richard scored again at 2:34 into the third period, and the goal stood up as the series winner.

"The Stanley Cup," said Jean Béliveau afterward, "always should be in Montreal."

Stanley Before Calder

While Ken Dryden is the only player to win the Conn Smythe Trophy before he officially qualified as an NHL rookie, he is not the only player to win the Stanley Cup one year and the Calder Trophy the next. In 1967–68, Danny Grant played 22 games with the Montreal Canadiens, 10 more in the playoffs and got his name on the Stanley Cup. That June, he was traded to the Minnesota North Stars. He spent his first full season in the NHL and was named Rookie of the Year in 1968–69. Tony Esposito played 13 games in goal for Montreal during the 1968–69 season and none in the playoffs, but he still got his named engraved on the Cup when the Canadiens repeated as champions. He was claimed by Chicago in the intra-league draft in June 1969 and won the Calder Trophy after his first full NHL season of 1969–70. Twenty years earlier, Terry Sawchuk had played seven games for Detroit in 1949–50 but did not get his name engraved on the Stanley Cup when the Red Wings had won it. Even so, he took over as the team's top goalie in 1950–51 and won the Calder as Rookie of the Year.

More Changes

The NHL added two new teams for the 1970–71 season, growing to 14. To improve the league's competitive balance, both the Buffalo Sabres and the Vancouver Canucks were placed in the East Division, while the Chicago Black Hawks moved out West. The regular season was expanded from 76 to 78 games and featured a balanced schedule. The playoff structure, which had ensured that an expansion club would meet an Original Six team in the Stanley Cup final the past three seasons, was also altered. After playing the quarterfinals along divisional lines, the winners would cross over to face a club from the other division in the semifinals. This meant that two teams from the same division could wind up facing each other for the Stanley Cup, as was the case in 1972.

The Big M A four-time Stanley Cup winner with Toronto in the 1960s, Frank Mahovlich played arguably the best hockey of his career with Montreal during the playoffs in 1971. His 14 postseason goals established a modern NHL record at the time, and his 27 points tied the mark Phil Esposito had set one year before.

Conn Smythe Story

The Montreal Canadiens waited a long time for Ken Dryden. Dryden was originally selected by the Boston Bruins 14th overall among the 24 players who were taken in the 1964 NHL amateur draft. Guy Allen was the player Boston really wanted, but Montreal had chosen him with the 12th pick. In a trade shortly after the draft, Dryden became the property of the Canadiens.

NHL teams were already aware of Dryden's plans to attend Cornell, and he starred at the American university from 1966 through 1969. Still, he surprised the Canadiens when he signed a three-year contract with the Canadian national team after graduation, feeling it would be a better way for him to combine hockey with law school. When Canada withdrew from international hockey in 1970, Dryden finally signed with the Canadiens. He spent the majority of the 1970–71 season in the American Hockey League before getting called up on March 7, 1971. He made his debut one week later, beating Pittsburgh 5–1. Dryden played in six games, winning them all and allowing just nine goals for a 1.67 average. And then, coach Al MacNeil started Dryden against Boston in the playoffs.

Dryden was brilliant against the Bruins, frustrating their high scorers and leading the Canadiens to a stunning upset. Dryden played all 20 games in goal for the Canadiens during their surprising march to the Stanley Cup. He was the first player to win the Conn Smythe Trophy in a vote by hockey writers, as the NHL governors had previously determined the winner.

Montreal versus Boston

The rivalry between the Montreal Canadiens and the Detroit Red Wings in the 1950s was intense, and the rivalry between the cities of Montreal and Toronto will always spice up any game between those two teams. But for sheer intensity year in and year out, decade after decade, the rivalry between the Montreal Canadiens and the Boston Bruins has very few to match it anywhere in sports.

Two of the greatest moments in the long rivalry between Boston and Montreal occurred when the teams faced each other in the semifinals.

The Bruins and the Canadiens have met more times in regular-season and playoff games combined than any two teams in NHL history. Though the results have historically favored Montreal (Boston suffered through 18 straight playoff defeats from 1946 through 1987), the rivalry has produced some of the biggest moments in hockey history.

The "Flying Frenchmen" were already famed among hockey fans everywhere when the Bruins entered the NHL in 1924–25. Montreal was the defending Stanley Cup champion that year while Boston was a sad-sack expansion team, but the Bruins improved quickly. They won the Stanley Cup for the first time in 1928–29 and were brilliant throughout the 1929–30 season. With forward passing fully opening the game up and modern offside rules introduced, the Bruins rewrote the NHL record book that season. The team was an astounding 38-5-1 for 77 points during the 44-game regular season and had an .875 winning percentage that has never been matched.

In fact, the Bruins went the entire season without ever losing two games in a row—until they met the Canadiens in the Stanley Cup final. Howie Morenz and company swept the Bruins in a best-of-three series that was considered such a shocking upset that the NHL went back to a best-of-five format the following year. The 1930 Stanley Cup final marked the first of seven championship matches between Boston and Montreal, with the Canadiens beating the Bruins six more times, in 1946, 1953, 1957, 1958, 1977 and 1978.

Two of the greatest moments in the long rivalry between Boston and Montreal occurred when the teams faced each other in the semifinals. The first was on April 8, 1952, when the teams met in a seventh game for the very first time. Maurice Richard had been cut for six stitches late in the second period and spent most of the third period on the bench. He finally returned to action late in a 1–1 game and capped a brilliant individual rush that he'd begun behind his own blue line by scoring the go-ahead goal with 3:41 remaining.

A picture taken after the game of Bruins goalie Sugar Jim Henry all but bowing before the bloodied Rocket as he shakes his hand is one of the game's most iconic photographs. In today's NHL, it is unlikely Richard would have returned to action, as there can be little doubt he had suffered a concussion. The Rocket, who reportedly burst into tears in the dressing room after the game, was sitting quietly with his head in his hands, his teammates running happily around the dressing room, when the reporters got to him.

"My legs were all right," he told them. "But I was dizzy. I heard the crowd yell," he said of the goal, "but by that time I was too dizzy even to see."

"He told me he was all right," said coach Dick Irvin of Richard's return to the bench from the Montreal Forum clinic. "But he wasn't just then. He didn't even know the score of the game."

Bruins' goaltender Gerry Cheevers in a 3–1 Boston victory in Game 1. The Bruins roared out to a 5–1 lead in Game 2, but Montreal bounced back for a 7–5 victory that turned the series around. With the young Canadiens goalie gaining confidence with every game, Montreal went on to take the series in seven.

"That's one dynasty that didn't last very long," remarked Canadiens tough guy John Ferguson sarcastically.

Dryden has admitted to a disconnected feeling during his late-season NHL debut, as if, "If these are the real Montreal Canadiens, then why am I here?" It all became real to him when a huge crowd showed up at the Montreal-Dorval International Airport to welcome the team home from Game 7 in Boston.

After three more Montreal playoff victories in the 1970s, the NHL's new divisional playoff format in the 1980s saw the Canadiens face the Bruins in the playoffs for nine straight springs beginning in 1984. Boston finally began to take the upper hand in the playoff rivalry during the 1990s, and in 2011 the Bruins opened their surprising run to the Stanley Cup by rallying to beat Montreal in seven after dropping the first two games of the series at home.

Twenty-seven years later, on May 10, 1979, Guy Lafleur created another magic moment for a new generation of fans when his brilliant goal with just 1:14 remaining sent Game 7 of the semifinals into overtime, where the Canadiens downed the Bruins once again. But of all the great moments in the long rivalry between the two teams, there is little to match Montreal's stunning upset of Boston in the 1971 quarter-finals. After their Stanley Cup win

in 1970, Bruins coach Harry Sinden predicted a bright future for his team.

"They'll be better," Sinden said. "I'll say it now, we're going to be a power in this league."

And much like the 1929–30 Boston team, the Bruins did follow up their Stanley Cup victory with a spectacular season… Only to run into the Canadiens again.

Boston's 121 points in 1970–71 were 24 more than Montreal, and

Jacques Lemaire and Jean Ratelle face off during the 1978–79 semifinals.

....

their 399 goals were more than 100 better than the Canadiens' second-best NHL total of 291. The Bruins' Bobby Orr and Phil Esposito were the biggest stars in hockey, and Montreal's decision to start rookie Ken Dryden in net didn't really seem like it would make much difference, even when he outperformed

QUARTERFINALS
4 games to 2 over New York Rangers

SEMIFINALS
4 games to 0 over Chicago

ROSTER

CONN SMYTHE TROPHY **BOBBY ORR** D – BOSTON

John Adams
Don Awrey
Garnet Bailey
Ivan Boldirev
John Bucyk
Wayne Carleton
Wayne Cashman
Gerry Cheevers
Gary Doak
Phil Esposito
Ted Green
Ken Hodge
Eddie Johnston
Bill Lesuk
Jim Lorentz
Don Marcotte
John McKenzie
Ron Murphy
Bobby Orr
Derek Sanderson
Danny Schock
Dallas Smith
Rick Smith
Bill Speer
Fred Stanfield
Ed Westfall
Milt Schmidt
(general manager)
Harry Sinden (coach)

FINAL 4 GAMES TO 0

MAY 3	Boston 6 at St. Louis 1
MAY 5	Boston 6 at St. Louis 2
MAY 7	St. Louis 1 at Boston 4
MAY 10	St. Louis 3 at Boston 4 OT

PLAYOFF SCORING LEADER

	GP	G	A	PTS
Phil Esposito PHILADELPHIA	14	13	14	27

FINAL SERIES SCORING

BOSTON	GP	G	A	PTS	PIM
Phil Esposito	4	2	6	8	4
John Bucyk	4	6	0	6	0
Derek Sanderson	4	3	3	6	8
John McKenzie	4	1	4	5	14
Bobby Orr	4	1	4	5	6
Rick Smith	4	1	3	4	2
Fred Stanfield	4	1	3	4	4
Ed Westfall	4	2	1	3	0
Ken Hodge	4	0	3	3	2
Wayne Cashman	4	2	0	2	8
Wayne Carleton	4	1	1	2	0
Don Awrey	4	0	1	1	12
Dallas Smith	4	0	1	1	6
Gary Doak	4	0	0	0	2
Bill Lesuk	2	0	0	0	0
Jim Lorentz	4	0	0	0	0
Don Marcotte	4	0	0	0	0
Bill Speer	1	0	0	0	0
GOALTENDER	GP	W	L	MIN	GA	SO	AVG
Gerry Cheevers	4	4	0	241	7	0	1.74

ST. LOUIS	GP	G	A	PTS	PIM
Frank St. Marseille	4	2	1	3	2
Jimmy Roberts	4	1	1	2	4
Phil Goyette	4	0	2	2	2
Red Berenson	4	1	0	1	4
Terry Gray	4	1	0	1	0
Larry Keenan	4	1	0	1	0
Gary Sabourin	4	1	0	1	0
Tim Ecclestone	4	0	1	1	6
Bill McCreary	3	0	1	1	0
Ab McDonald	4	0	1	1	0
Noel Picard	4	0	1	1	14
Bob Plager	4	0	1	1	6
Ron Anderson	1	0	0	0	2
Al Arbour	2	0	0	0	0
André Boudrias	3	0	0	0	2
Terry Crisp	4	0	0	0	0
Norm Dennis	1	0	0	0	2
Ray Fortin	3	0	0	0	6
Barclay Plager	1	0	0	0	0
Bill Plager	2	0	0	0	0
Jean-Guy Talbot	4	0	0	0	0
GOALTENDERS	GP	W	L	MIN	GA	SO	AVG
Jacques Plante	1	0	0	24	1	0	2.50
Glenn Hall	2	0	2	121	8	0	3.97
Ernie Wakely	2	0	2	96	11	0	6.87

Woe Canada With both Montreal and Toronto missing the playoffs this year, the 1969–70 season marks the only time in NHL history that no Canadian team was represented.

Perfect 10 The Bruins capped their run through the playoffs with 10 straight victories, an NHL record at the time.

First Time Not one player on the 1969–70 Boston Bruins had ever won the Stanley Cup before.

The Chief The Bruins didn't have a captain from 1967–68 through 1972–73. When they won the Stanley Cup in 1970 (and in 1972), NHL president Clarence Campbell presented the trophy to John Bucyk, the team's longest-serving player. Bucyk had been with the Bruins since 1957.

Boston Breakthrough

The Boston Bruins missed the playoffs eight years in a row, from 1960 through 1967, but the bad times had begun to end when Bobby Orr joined the team in 1966. The Bruins got another big boost just before expansion in 1967, when they landed Phil Esposito, Ken Hodge and Fred Stanfield in a one-sided swap with Chicago. With Derek Sanderson and Wayne Cashman soon added to a mix that already included veterans John Bucyk, Ted Green, Eddie Johnston and Gerry Cheevers, the Bruins were ready for a breakthrough. They battled Montreal for top spot in the standings in 1968–69, as Phil Esposito became the first player in NHL history to top 100 points.

In 1969–70, Bobby Orr became the first (and only) defenseman to win a scoring title, when he finished the year with 120 points. The Bruins had a record of 40-17-19 for 99 points and finished second overall behind the Chicago Black Hawks, who also had 99 points but an NHL-best 45 wins. The East Division standings were incredibly tight, with five of the six teams finishing within seven points of each other and Montreal missing the playoffs for the first time in 22 years, despite a 92-point season that was better than any of the teams in the West Division.

In the playoffs, the Bruins and Rangers hooked up in the quarterfinals. Like the Bruins, the Rangers were finally improving after years of poor play. The two teams genuinely disliked one another, and they set a playoff record with 375 penalty minutes in their six-game series. After beating the Rangers, Boston faced Chicago in a highly anticipated semifinal that matched Bobby Orr against Bobby Hull and Phil Esposito against his brother Tony, who had 15 shutouts during the season. The series proved to be a dud, however, with Ed Westfall shutting down Hull almost completely in a four-game sweep.

St. Louis had downed Minnesota and Pittsburgh in six games each, and, because they had won the West Division, the Blues had home ice advantage against the Bruins in the Stanley Cup final. It made little difference, as Boston won two lopsided games in St. Louis. The Blues were at their best in Game 4 at Boston, but the Bruins won the Stanley Cup for the first time since 1941 when Bobby Orr scored just 40 seconds into overtime to compete a series sweep.

Ted Green

Ted Green got his name on the Stanley Cup with Boston in 1970 and a share of the team's championship bonus even though he didn't play a single game during the 1969–70 regular season and playoffs. Green had been a mainstay on the Bruins defense since 1961–62, but he missed the entire 1969–70 season (and nearly lost his life) after suffering a compound skull fracture in a preseason stick-swinging duel with Wayne Maki of St. Louis. Green returned to the Bruins the following season, won the Stanley Cup with Boston in 1972 and continued plying his trade in the rival World Hockey Association until 1979.

Scoring Records
Phil Esposito's 27 points shattered the previous NHL playoff record of 21, set by Stan Mikita in 1962. His 13 goals broke the modern record of 12 shared by Jean Béliveau (1955) and Maurice Richard (1944). Of course, Espo had the advantage of one more playoff round than the previous record holders.

Ted Green

Singing the Blues

When the NHL expanded in 1967, the Philadelphia Flyers, Los Angeles Kings, St. Louis Blues, Pittsburgh Penguins, Minnesota North Stars and Oakland Seals were all placed in the newly created West Division. The so-called "Original Six" all played in the East. They would play an interlocking schedule, and, as a way to ensure interest in the six new cities, the playoffs were set up so that for the first three seasons the quarterfinals and semifinals would all take place within each division, guaranteeing that an expansion team would get to play for the Stanley Cup. In each of those first three seasons, the St. Louis Blues reached the final.

The Blues were built by Lynn Patrick and Scotty Bowman, and Bowman used his ties as a minor league executive with the Montreal Canadiens to put the Blues together. Red Berenson was a former Canadiens farmhand who quickly became the offensive leader in St. Louis, but the Blues employed former Canadiens legends Dickie Moore and Doug Harvey to give the first-year team a boost. Goalie Glenn Hall was the key to a disciplined defensive system, and he would share the net with Canadiens legend Jacques Plante in 1968–69 and 1969–70.

Being the best of the expansion lot didn't mean much in those days, as the Canadiens swept St. Louis in the 1968 and 1969 Stanley Cup finals. Though Glenn Hall bravely told the press, "They don't scare us," before the 1970 series against Boston, the Bruins also swept the Blues, leaving St. Louis with a record of 0–12 in Stanley Cup games, which they maintain to this day.

He Shoots, He Soars!

The photograph taken by Ray Lussier of the *Boston Herald* is one of the most famous in hockey history. It captures the Boston Bruins' Bobby Orr in mid-flight the instant after he slipped the puck past St. Louis Blues goaltender Glenn Hall and was sent flying by Blues defenseman Noel Picard. The expression on Orr's face is that of sheer joy. In the background, the Boston Garden explodes in celebration.

After four brilliant seasons with the Oshawa Generals, Orr was universally hailed as the finest young prospect in hockey.

May 10, 1970, was a hot one in Boston, and the game that day was easily the best of a one-sided series. Boston got on the scoreboard first, but St. Louis tied the game with just 43 seconds remaining in the opening frame. The Blues went on top early in the second period, and after Phil Esposito tied the game, St. Louis took the lead again just 19 seconds into the third period. This time, it looked like the lead might hold up—until John Bucyk got Boston even with 6:32 remaining. The score remained tied at three when regulation time ran out. It didn't stay tied for long.

The Blues won the opening faceoff in overtime, but did little in the 10 seconds or so before Boston went on the attack. With the Blues desperate to clear their zone, Orr pinched in from the blue line and snagged the puck along the boards near the faceoff circle to the left of the St. Louis net. He fired a pass to Derek Sanderson, who was down low behind the goal, and then Orr slipped out front. Sanderson fed him a return pass and Orr had little to do but tap it in at the 40-second mark before Picard sent him flying. It had been 29 years since Boston's last Stanley Cup victory, and there could have been no more fitting end to those years of frustration than to have Orr score the winning goal.

Back in the early days of the Bruins, Eddie Shore had been the team's big star. The Bruins had yet to make the playoffs before Shore arrived in Boston for the team's third season of 1926–27. They would miss the playoffs only once over the next 12 years, finish in first place in the league or their division on 10 occasions and win the Stanley Cup in 1929, 1939 and 1941. But the team would struggle throughout the 1940s and '50s, and hit rock bottom during the 1960s. Boston finished dead last in the six-team NHL for five straight seasons from 1960–61 through 1964–65. It was during the 1960–61 season that Boston's Wren Blair first saw the Bruins' next Eddie Shore. Bobby Orr was just 12 years old at the time.

The Bruins were not alone in their discovery of this young hockey phenom. The Detroit Red Wings already knew about him and a Montreal Canadiens scout named Scotty Bowman had seen him play

the Bruins they wanted a two-year deal worth $100,000. Negotiations between the Bruins and Eagleson lasted all summer, and though details have never been released it's thought that the deal he worked out for Orr paid him $40,000 per year for two years—which was more money than Jean Béliveau, Bobby Hull or Gordie Howe were being paid to play hockey at that time.

Though knee injuries would hamper him in his first two seasons (and later bring an early end to his brilliant career), Orr quickly became the most exciting player in hockey. During the week leading up to his Stanley Cup–winning goal in 1970, Orr was presented with the Art Ross Trophy as the NHL scoring leader, the James Norris Memorial Trophy (for the third of eight straight years) as the league's best defenseman and the Hart Memorial Trophy (for the first of three straight years) as the NHL's Most Valuable Player. A day after winning the Stanley Cup, it was announced—to no one's surprise—that he had also won the Conn Smythe Trophy as playoff MVP.

"The Stanley Cup is the only trophy I ever wanted," Orr told reporters after his overtime goal. "I never even thought about any of these individual awards."

too. Soon the Toronto Maple Leafs would be made aware of the prodigy from Parry Sound, Ontario. Those teams were all interested, but they weren't prepared to invest a lot of time in a 12-year-old boy. But Blair was. Blair spent two years wooing Orr's parents, and when Bobby was 14 he joined the Bruins' junior farm club in Oshawa, Ontario. After four brilliant seasons with the Oshawa

Generals, Orr was universally hailed as the finest young prospect in hockey—and the Bruins couldn't wait to sign the 18-year-old to his first professional contract. They offered him the standard rookie salary of $7,000 and $8,000 for his first two seasons, plus a signing bonus of $5,000.

Orr refused to sign. Alan Eagleson, the lawyer Orr's family had hired to represent him, told

Bobby Orr sails through the air (with some assistance from Noel Picard) after scoring the Bruins' Stanley Cup–winning goal on May 10, 1970.

QUARTERFINALS
4 games to 0 over New York Rangers

SEMIFINALS
4 games to 2 over Boston

ROSTER

- Ralph Backstrom
- Jean Béliveau (captain)
- Christian Bordeleau
- Yvan Cournoyer
- Dick Duff
- Tony Esposito
- John Ferguson
- Terry Harper
- Ted Harris
- Larry Hillman
- Jacques Laperrière
- Jacques Lemaire
- Claude Provost
- Mickey Redmond
- Henri Richard
- Bobby Rousseau
- Serge Savard
- Gilles Tremblay
- J.C. Tremblay
- Rogie Vachon
- Gump Worsley
- Sam Pollock (vice president/ general manager)
- Claude Ruel (coach)

CONN SMYTHE TROPHY SERGE SAVARD D – MONTREAL

FINAL **4 GAMES TO 0**

APR. 27	►	St. Louis 1 at Montreal 3
APR. 29	►	St. Louis 1 at Montreal 3
MAY 1	►	Montreal 4 at St. Louis 0
MAY 4	►	Montreal 2 at St. Louis 1

PLAYOFF SCORING LEADER

	GP	G	A	PTS
Phil Esposito BOSTON	10	8	10	18

FINAL SERIES SCORING

MONTREAL	GP	G	A	PTS	PIM
Dick Duff	4	4	2	6	2
Jean Béliveau	4	0	5	5	4
Yvan Cournoyer	4	1	3	4	0
John Ferguson	4	2	0	2	20
Ralph Backstrom	4	1	1	2	4
Serge Savard	4	1	1	2	8
J.C. Tremblay	4	0	2	2	6
Ted Harris	4	1	0	1	6
Jacques Lemaire	4	1	0	1	4
Bobby Rousseau	4	1	0	1	2
Claude Provost	3	0	1	1	0
Mickey Redmond	4	0	1	1	0
Henri Richard	4	0	1	1	2
Christian Bordeleau	3	0	0	0	0
Terry Harper	4	0	0	0	4
Jacques Laperrière	4	0	0	0	22

GOALTENDER	GP	W	L	MIN	GA	SO	AVG
Rogie Vachon	4	4	0	240	3	1	0.75

ST. LOUIS	GP	G	A	PTS	PIM
Frank St. Marseille	4	1	1	2	2
Terry Gray	3	1	0	1	8
Larry Keenan	4	1	0	1	8
Terry Crisp	4	0	1	1	2
Bill McCreary	4	0	1	1	4
Noel Picard	4	0	1	1	8
Barclay Plager	4	0	1	1	0
Jimmy Roberts	4	0	1	1	4
Al Arbour	4	0	0	0	4
Red Berenson	4	0	0	0	4
Craig Cameron	2	0	0	0	0
Tim Ecclestone	4	0	0	0	10
Camille Henry	2	0	0	0	0
Ab McDonald	4	0	0	0	4
Bill Plager	3	0	0	0	4
Bob Plager	2	0	0	0	2
Ron Schock	4	0	0	0	2
Jean-Guy Talbot	4	0	0	0	2
Gary Sabourin	4	0	0	0	4

GOALTENDERS	GP	W	L	MIN	GA	SO	AVG
Glenn Hall	2	0	2	120	5	0	2.50
Jacques Plante	2	0	2	120	6	0	3.00

Working Overtime

After the Canadiens had edged out the Bruins by just three points (103–100) for top spot in the NHL standings during the regular season, Montreal and Boston went at it again in the East Division semifinal. Again it was tight, with Montreal needing overtime goals from Ralph Backstrom and Mickey Redmond to take the first two games. The Bruins battled back to even the series, but they would lose it in six when Jean Béliveau scored in double overtime to give Montreal a four-games-to-two victory. It was the only overtime goal Béliveau ever scored.

New Coach, Old Champions

The Montreal Canadiens had a new coach for the 1968–69 season. After winning the Stanley Cup for the eighth time in 13 years, Toe Blake had stepped down. "The tension is just too much," Blake explained. "It gets tougher every year." Former players Butch Bouchard and, in particular, Floyd Curry were thought to be in line for the job. Instead, the Canadiens hired Claude Ruel. Only 29 years old, Ruel was the youngest coach in NHL history. He had gone behind the bench at age 19, shortly after losing the sight in his left eye in a junior game, and he had been the Canadiens head scout since 1964.

Playing in the newly renovated Montreal Forum, Ruel's Canadiens set club records with 46 wins and 103 points (though the newly expanded 76-game season obviously helped). Yvan Cournoyer established himself as a star with a team-best 43 goals and 44 assists, while the ageless Jean Béliveau contributed 82 points. Still, the biggest stories of the season were in Boston, where Phil Esposito smashed scoring records with 126 points, and in Chicago, where Bobby Hull had held out for a $100,000 contract and broke his own league record with 58 goals. The Black Hawks failed to make the playoffs, but the Bruins were a close second behind Montreal in the East Division standings. Boston swept Toronto in the quarterfinals before falling to Montreal in a tight six-game semifinal.

For the second year in a row, St. Louis proved to be the best team in the West. The Blues had enticed Jacques Plante out of retirement to join Glenn Hall in goal, and the two veterans combined for 13 shutouts and shared the Vezina Trophy by backstopping the league's best defense. Red Berenson led the team with 82 points and was the only player in the West Division to finish among the top 10 in scoring.

The Blues hoped to beat the Canadiens with a physical game, but tough guy John Ferguson ensured that Montreal wouldn't be intimidated. After three straight Canadiens victories, Game 4 was the roughest of the series. St. Louis led 1–0 after two periods, but Ted Harris scored for Montreal just 43 seconds into the third. Ferguson scored two minutes later. "It's great that Fergy could get the winning goal," said Claude Ruel. "He's been fighting for us. He's a leader."

ROOKIE NHL COACHES WHO WON THE STANLEY CUP

DICK CARROLL, TORONTO ARENAS	► 1917–18
PETE GREEN, OTTAWA SENATORS	► 1919–20
GEORGE O'DONOGHUE, TORONTO ST. PATS	► 1921–22
DAVE GILL, OTTAWA SENATORS	► 1926–27
CY DENNENY, BOSTON BRUINS	► 1928–29
BILL STEWART, CHICAGO BLACK HAWKS	► 1937–38
FRANK BOUCHER, NEW YORK RANGERS	► 1939–40
JOE PRIMEAU, TORONTO MAPLE LEAFS	► 1950–51
JIMMY SKINNER, DETROIT RED WINGS	► 1954–55
TOE BLAKE, MONTREAL CANADIENS	► 1955–56
CLAUDE RUEL, MONTREAL CANADIENS	► 1968–69
AL MACNEIL, MONTREAL CANADIENS	► 1970–71
JEAN PERRON, MONTREAL CANADIENS	► 1985–86
DAN BYLSMA, PITTSBURGH PENGUINS	► 2008–09

Claude Ruel

The Conn Smythe Story

Serge Savard of the Montreal Canadiens became the first defenseman to win the Conn Smythe Trophy. The announcement, which was made two days after Montreal won the Stanley Cup, was somewhat of a surprise. Many had figured the playoff MVP award would go to Rogie Vachon, who took over in goal when Gump Worsley was injured during the semifinal series with Boston. Others considered for the honor were Dick Duff (the top scorer during the final) and Jean Béliveau.

Savard was, however, a worthy recipient. He had 10 points in 14 playoff games, and his four goals were one short of the NHL record for defensemen at the time, which was shared by Earl Seibert (Chicago, 1938) and Red Kelly (Detroit, 1955). He was also solid defensively, particularly when killing penalties, as Montreal allowed just two power-play goals throughout the playoffs.

Cup Bookends Claude Provost, a 15-year veteran of the Montreal Canadiens, and Cooney Weiland, who played 11 years for Boston, Detroit and Ottawa, are the only players to spend at least a decade in the NHL and win the Stanley Cup in both their first and last seasons in the league. Provost won his first as a rookie in 1955–56 and his last in 1968–69 — and seven more in between! Weiland began his career with a first Cup win in Boston in 1928–29 and ended it with a second in Boston in 1938–39.

Montreal's Forgotten Dynasty

After winning the Stanley Cup five straight times to close out the 1950s, the Montreal Canadiens went into decline. True they still topped the NHL standings in 1960–61 and 1961–62, but they fell to third place in the three-team league the following season and were knocked out of the playoffs in the first round for the third straight season. For the Canadiens of this era, that type of performance was unacceptable.

> "He's a little awkward," Blake admitted to reporters, "but he digs hard and can really shoot. He could be just the man we need."

General manager Frank Selke, who had guided the club since 1946, felt his team had gotten soft. They needed someone with a little more muscle to stop other teams from taking liberties with their stars.

It was apparently former Canadiens player Floyd Curry, who was then coaching the Quebec Aces of the American Hockey League, who tipped the Canadiens to John Ferguson of the Cleveland Barons. As the story goes, Canadiens coach Toe Blake was dispatched to Cleveland to watch the team practice, where he saw Ferguson fire a puck at a teammate in anger because he was loafing. This was exactly the kind of attitude the Canadiens were looking for. They acquired Ferguson's rights from Cleveland after the 1962–63 season and brought him to training camp in September 1963.

"He's a little awkward," Blake admitted to reporters, "but he digs hard and can really shoot. He could be just the man we need."

Ferguson had improved from 13 to 20 to 38 goals during his three years in Cleveland, but he had accumulated 451 penalty minutes in that time. Blake advised him to cut down.

"He didn't tell me to curb my temper or stay out of scraps," Ferguson insisted. "He just told me to cut down a little bit."

In his very first regular-season game with the Canadiens, Ferguson picked a fight with Boston Bruins tough guy Ted Green just 12 seconds after the opening faceoff. He also picked up two goals and an assist. He was, indeed, the man the Canadiens had needed.

Ferguson would play only eight seasons in the NHL, but he helped the Canadiens win the Stanley Cup five times. Jean Béliveau has called him "the most formidable player of the decade, if not in the Canadiens' history." Ferguson protected his teammates on the ice, but he was no mere goon. True, he finished among the top 10 in the NHL in penalty minutes seven times in eight seasons, but he never had more than 185 minutes. He also finished among Montreal's top 10 scorers every season he played and scored a career-high 29 goals in 1968–69. Ferguson refused to fraternize with players from other teams even during the off-season, and winning was always his top priority.

"You would not dare to give less than your best if you wore the same shirt as John Ferguson," Béliveau has said.

But of course Ferguson didn't win all those Stanley Cups on his own. In addition to him and Béliveau there were 11 other players who were members of all four Montreal Stanley Cup teams in the 1960s. They were Ralph Backstrom, Yvan Cournoyer, Dick Duff, Terry Harper, Ted Harris, Jacques Laperrière, Claude Provost, Henri Richard, Bobby Rousseau, J.C. Tremblay and Gump Worsley.

Longtime player personnel director Sam Pollock succeeded Frank Selke as general manager after the 1963–64 season. Pollock is best remembered for building the team that would dominate the 1970s, but he was also the key man behind the 1960s squad and would always have a fondness for Montreal's so-called forgotten dynasty. Even so, Pollock

tinkered with his lineup regularly. Players like Jean-Guy Talbot, Leon Rochefort, Charlie Hodge and Dave Balon helped win the Cup in 1965 and 1966, but they were all moved out to make room for newcomers such as Rogie Vachon, Serge Savard, Guy Lapointe and Jacques Lemaire. Pollock's maneuvering ensured that the Canadiens were just as strong after the NHL expansion in 1967 as they had been before it.

"We had a good team in those years, really good," Gump Worsley told Dick Irvin Jr. for his book *The Habs: An Oral History of the Montreal Canadiens, 1940–1980*. "They don't talk about that team of the Sixties because we didn't win four in a row, or five in a row. We won two, then lost to Toronto [in 1967], then won two more."

Many of the Canadiens truly believed the 1960s team should have won five Cups in a row. Béliveau certainly did.

"We had no business losing in '67 to Toronto," he told Irvin Jr. "Terry Sawchuk was the [only] reason." Béliveau recalled a particular save Sawchuk made in Game 6 as the turning point. "I always had the feeling that if I scored on that play, if he doesn't make that tremendous save, it very easily could have been another five Stanley Cups in a row."

John Ferguson, the final piece of the Canadiens' puzzle, in action in the late 1960s.

QUARTERFINALS
4 games to 0 over Boston

SEMIFINALS
4 games to 1 over Chicago

CONN SMYTHE TROPHY **GLENN HALL** G – ST. LOUIS

ROSTER

Ralph Backstrom	Claude Larose	Rogie Vachon
Jean Béliveau (captain)	Jacques Lemaire	Carol Vadnais
Yvan Cournoyer	Claude Provost	Ernie Wakely
Dick Duff	Mickey Redmond	Gump Worsley
John Ferguson	Henri Richard	Sam Pollock (vice president/general manager)
Danny Grant	Bobby Rousseau	
Terry Harper	Serge Savard	Toe Blake (coach)
Ted Harris	Gilles Tremblay	
Jacques Laperrière	J.C. Tremblay	

FINAL   4 GAMES TO 0

MAY 5	▶	Montreal 3 at St. Louis 2 OT
MAY 7	▶	Montreal 1 at St. Louis 0
MAY 9	▶	St. Louis 3 at Montreal 4 OT
MAY 11	▶	St. Louis 2 at Montreal 3

PLAYOFF SCORING LEADER

	GP	G	A	PTS
Bill Goldsworthy MINNESOTA	14	8	7	15

FINAL SERIES SCORING

MONTREAL	GP	G	A	PTS	PIM
Yvan Cournoyer	4	2	2	4	2
Henri Richard	4	2	1	3	0
John Ferguson	4	0	3	3	4
Serge Savard	4	2	0	2	0
Ralph Backstrom	4	1	1	2	0
Dick Duff	4	1	1	2	2
Jacques Lemaire	4	1	1	2	4
J.C. Tremblay	4	1	1	2	0
Bobby Rousseau	4	1	0	1	6
Ted Harris	4	0	1	1	6
Claude Larose	4	0	1	1	0
Claude Provost	4	0	1	1	2
Jean Béliveau	1	0	0	0	0
Danny Grant	4	0	0	0	0
Terry Harper	4	0	0	0	4
Jacques Laperrière	4	0	0	0	6
Mickey Redmond	2	0	0	0	0
Carol Vadnais	1	0	0	0	2

GOALTENDER	GP	W	L	MIN	GA	SO	AVG
Gump Worsley	4	4	0	243	7	1	1.73

ST. LOUIS	GP	G	A	PTS	PIM
Red Berenson	4	2	1	3	7
Barclay Plager	4	1	1	2	6
Frank St. Marseille	4	1	1	2	0
Craig Cameron	1	1	0	1	0
Dickie Moore	4	1	0	1	4
Gary Sabourin	4	1	0	1	2
Al Arbour	4	0	1	1	0
Tim Ecclestone	4	0	1	1	2
Doug Harvey	2	0	1	1	4
Noel Picard	4	0	1	1	6
Jean-Guy Talbot	4	0	1	1	4
Gary Veneruzzo	3	0	1	1	0
Terry Crisp	4	0	0	0	0
Larry Keenan	4	0	0	0	0
Bill McCreary	3	0	0	0	0
Gerry Melnyk	3	0	0	0	0
Bob Plager	4	0	0	0	20
Jimmy Roberts	4	0	0	0	2
Ron Schock	4	0	0	0	0

GOALTENDER	GP	W	L	MIN	GA	SO	AVG
Glenn Hall	4	0	4	243	11	0	2.72

Tough Act to Follow

"You could fill the job but you can't replace Toe, not with 15 guys. It's a tough act to follow. Yeah, like trying to sing after Sinatra. Only that's a one-nighter. You'd have to follow Blake all year." —Gump Worsley

Back on Top in a 12-Team League

Official acceptance for new franchises in Los Angeles, San Francisco (Oakland), St. Louis, Pittsburgh, Philadelphia and Minneapolis–St. Paul had been granted on February 8, 1966. On June 6, 1967, an expansion draft was held. The new NHL season opened on October 11, 1967, with 10 of the 12 teams in action. The last time there had been five games on the schedule in a single night was on January 8, 1931.

Sam Pollock had helped to draw up the rules for expansion, and though the Canadiens lost many players and prospects, Pollock had retained his core players. He would also begin to incorporate key rookies such as Jacques Lemaire and Serge Savard from his deep farm system. Even so, the Canadiens were slow to get started.

On Christmas Day 1967, Montreal sat last in the East Division with a record of 12-14-7. However, the Canadiens went 22-1-2 from December 27, 1967, through February 22, 1968, to pull comfortably into first place. Rogie Vachon allowed just 15 goals in the 21 games he played during that stretch, and Jean Béliveau led the offense with 13 goals and 34 points in 23 games. On March 2, 1968, Béliveau joined Gordie Howe as the only players (at that point in NHL history) to reach 1,000-points.

A strong finish by the New York Rangers made them a close second behind Montreal in the East Division, with Chicago and Boston finishing third and fourth. The defending Stanley Cup champions from Toronto were fifth and missed the playoffs, as did Detroit, who finished a distant sixth. Montreal made easy work of Boston in the quarterfinals. Chicago upset the Rangers, but the Canadiens beat the Black Hawks 9–2 to open the semifinals and weren't seriously threatened after that. Out West, the Flyers finished the regular season in first place, but Philadelphia lost to St. Louis in seven games in the quarterfinals. The Blues then beat the Minnesota North Stars in seven and would face the Canadiens for the Stanley Cup.

Montreal beat St. Louis in four straight games, but the final was still closer than people had expected. Every game was decided by just one goal. Jacques Lemaire and Bobby Rousseau scored overtime goals to win Games 1 and 3, while Serge Savard had the lone tally in a 1–0 victory in Game 2. St. Louis took a 2–1 lead into the third period of Game 4 before Henri Richard and J.C. Tremblay scored to wrap up the series.

Going Out Like He Came In

Toe Blake had hinted at it on television before making it clear in the dressing room following Montreal's Game 4 victory over St. Louis: he was retiring as coach of the Canadiens, choosing to go out as a champion. He had also come in like one, winning the Stanley Cup in his first season behind the bench back in 1955–56 — and on six other occasions as well! Blake's eight titles in his 13 years behind the bench with Montreal are topped only by Scotty Bowman, who won nine times with three different teams in his 30-year career. Blake also won the Cup as a part-time player with the Montreal Maroons in his rookie season of 1933–34 and won it twice more as a star with the Montreal Canadiens in the 1940s.

Heart of the Team

"Toe Blake hated so much to lose that he made us the same way. He was the heart of this team, and I'm happy he was able to quit after we won everything." — J.C. Tremblay

Friends Turned Foe

"I hardly expected to beat the Canadiens for the Cup," admitted former Montreal star defenseman Doug Harvey after the series, "but I felt sure we'd win at least one game."

"It's just as tough to lose wearing a St. Louis sweater as when I wore one with the Canadiens," said Dickie Moore.

Memorial Observance Numerous games in several sports were postponed in the days following the assassination of civil rights leader Martin Luther King Jr. on April 4, 1968. Major League Baseball delayed opening day in several cities, and the NHL quarterfinal playoff games in New York, St. Louis and Minneapolis–St. Paul were all rescheduled.

The Conn Smythe Story

No one doubted that the St. Louis Blues wouldn't have gone as far as they did in the playoffs without Glenn Hall. He played in all 18 of their postseason games. Eight of those games went into overtime, including four against Minnesota in the semifinals. Game 7 of that series went into double overtime, and though the North Stars carried the play for most of the night, Hall made 44 saves in a 2–1 victory. He was brilliant throughout the Stanley Cup final against Montreal. The Blues were outshot 36–19 in their 1–0 loss in Game 2 and 46–15 in their 4–3 overtime loss in Game 3. Still, not everyone was happy when Hall became the second player from a losing team to win the Conn Smythe Trophy in the four-year history of the award.

Hall had eight wins and 10 losses in the playoffs. He allowed 45 goals for an average of 2.43. Gump Worsley, on the other hand, played in only 12 games but had a record of 11–0. He allowed just 21 goals for a 1.88 average.

"It looks like Gump is getting the shaft," an unnamed Canadiens teammate complained, "because we went through the playoffs in only 13 games. But we couldn't have done it if he hadn't played so well, especially against Boston and Chicago."

"Who could have played better?" wondered coach Toe Blake. "After all, we won the Cup so Gump should be the logical choice."

Montreal's Claude Provost, Jacques Laperrière, Terry Harper and Jacques Lemaire were also seen as potential winners of the playoff MVP award, as was former Canadien Dickie Moore.

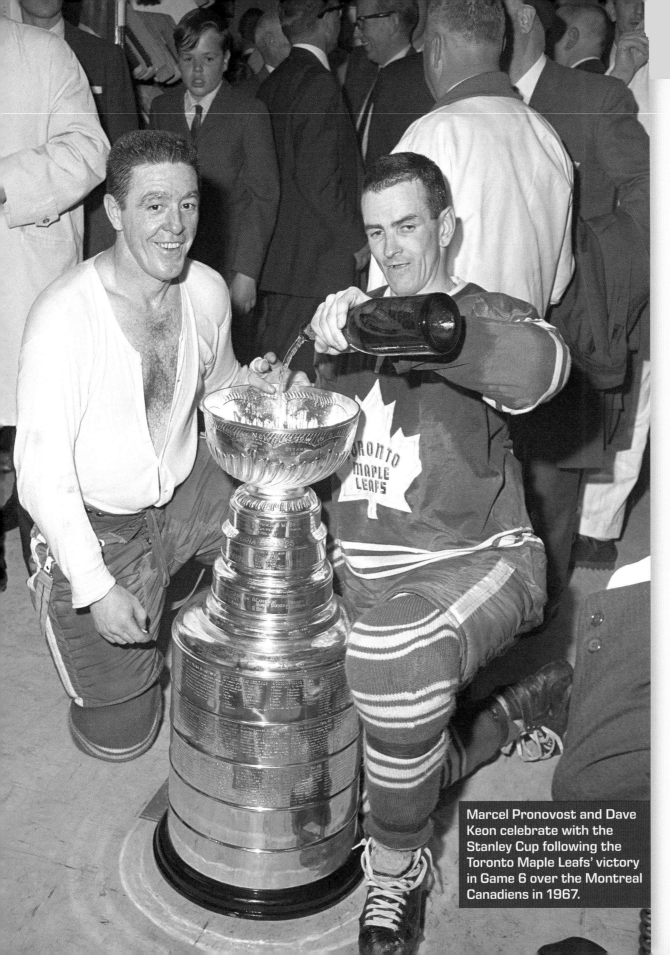

Marcel Pronovost and Dave Keon celebrate with the Stanley Cup following the Toronto Maple Leafs' victory in Game 6 over the Montreal Canadiens in 1967.

Season Lengths

50 GAMES	▶	1942–43 through 1945–46 (four seasons)
60 GAMES	▶	1946–47 through 1948–49 (three seasons)
70 GAMES	▶	1949–50 through 1966–67 (18 seasons)

Stanley Cup Wins by Original Six Teams

10	▶	Montreal Canadiens
9	▶	Toronto Maple Leafs
5	▶	Detroit Red Wings
1	▶	Chicago Black Hawks
0	▶	Boston Bruins, New York Rangers

The Original Six: 1942–43 to 1966–67

After the heady optimism of the Roaring Twenties had seen the NHL grow to 10 teams, the bleak years of the Great Depression saw franchises begin to fall by the wayside. The threat and then outbreak of World War II erased other struggling franchises, and by the 1942–43 season, the NHL was left with just six teams: the Boston Bruins, Chicago Black Hawks, Detroit Red Wings, Montreal Canadiens, New York Rangers and Toronto Maple Leafs.

If the 1920s were the "Golden Age of Sports," then for many, the Original Six era was the "Golden Age of Hockey." Seventy-game schedules meant that each of the teams faced the other five clubs 14 times during the regular season, breeding a familiarity — and a contempt — that is impossible to imagine today. Fraternization among players was rare, and the fear for all but the biggest stars of being sent to the minors — or, worse, back to the farming or mining town they came from — was always there. It made for fierce rivalries and intensely loyal fans. And yet the teams themselves were anything but even. While Montreal, Toronto and Detroit dominated Stanley Cup competition with some of the greatest dynasties the game has ever seen, New York, Boston and Chicago struggled almost every season. The Black Hawks were hurting so badly in the early 1950s that they nearly went out of business. The Rangers missed the playoffs 18 times in 25 years, while the Bruins failed to qualify for eight straight seasons, from 1959–60 through 1966–67.

It's easy to look back now at the period of NHL history from 1942–43 through 1966–67 as one singular era of leather skates, wooden sticks and helmet-less players in brush cuts or Brylcreem. Only about 100 players had steady jobs during this era, and the men who starred during the 25 years from 1942 to 1967 are still remembered today with awe and affection. But despite a great deal of same-ness, the game changed a lot. The introduction of the center ice red line in 1943–44 helped open up offensive play and led to the "firewagon hockey" of the great Montreal teams of this era. The slap shots and curved sticks of the 1950s and '60s further opened up the game, and in response, goaltenders who had always played the game bare-faced began to wear masks. The face of hockey was definitely changing.

SEMIFINALS
4 games to 2 over Chicago

CONN SMYTHE TROPHY **DAVE KEON** C – TORONTO

FINAL **4 GAMES TO 2**

APR. 20 ▶	Toronto 2 at Montreal 6	
APR. 22 ▶	Toronto 3 at Montreal 0	
APR. 25 ▶	Montreal 2 at Toronto 3 2x OT	
APR. 27 ▶	Montreal 6 at Toronto 2	
APR. 29 ▶	Toronto 4 at Montreal 1	
MAY 2 ▶	Montreal 1 at Toronto 3	

PLAYOFF SCORING LEADER

Jim Pappin	GP	G	A	PTS
TORONTO	12	7	8	15

FINAL SERIES SCORING

TORONTO	GP	G	A	PTS	PIM
Jim Pappin	6	4	4	8	6
Bob Pulford	6	1	6	7	0
Pete Stemkowski	6	2	4	6	4
Tim Horton	6	2	3	5	8
Mike Walton	6	2	1	3	0
Red Kelly	6	0	3	3	2
Brian Conacher	6	1	1	2	19
Ron Ellis	6	1	1	2	4
Larry Hillman	6	1	1	2	0
Dave Keon	6	1	1	2	0
Frank Mahovlich	6	0	2	2	8
George Armstrong	6	1	0	1	4
Marcel Pronovost	6	1	0	1	4
Allan Stanley	6	0	1	1	6
Bob Baun	5	0	0	0	2
Aut Erickson	1	0	0	0	2
Milan Marcetta	2	0	0	0	0
Eddie Shack	4	0	0	0	8
GOALTENDERS	GP	W	L	MIN	GA	SO	AVG
Johnny Bower	3	2	0	163	3	1	1.10
Terry Sawchuk	4	2	2	225	12	0	3.20

MONTREAL	GP	G	A	PTS	PIM
Henri Richard	6	4	3	7	0
Jean Béliveau	6	4	2	6	10
Yvan Cournoyer	6	2	2	4	4
Bobby Rousseau	6	0	4	4	2
Dick Duff	6	1	2	3	4
Ralph Backstrom	6	2	0	2	2
John Ferguson	6	1	1	2	16
Leon Rochefort	6	1	1	2	2
Dave Balon	5	0	2	2	2
J.C. Tremblay	6	0	2	2	0
Jimmy Roberts	3	1	0	1	0
Ted Harris	6	0	1	1	12
Claude Larose	6	0	1	1	15
Gilles Tremblay	6	0	1	1	0
Terry Harper	6	0	0	0	6
Jacques Laperrière	6	0	0	0	2
Claude Provost	4	0	0	0	0
Jean-Guy Talbot	6	0	0	0	0
GOALTENDERS	GP	W	L	MIN	GA	SO	AVG
Rogie Vachon	5	2	3	308	14	0	2.73
Gump Worsley	2	0	1	80	2	0	1.50

ROSTER

George Armstrong (captain)

Bob Baun

Johnny Bower

Brian Conacher

Ron Ellis

Aut Erickson

Larry Hillman

Tim Horton

Larry Jeffrey

Red Kelly

Dave Keon

Frank Mahovlich

Milan Marcetta

Jim Pappin

Marcel Pronovost

Bob Pulford

Terry Sawchuk

Eddie Shack

Allan Stanley

Pete Stemkowski

Mike Walton

Punch Imlach (general manager/coach)

Beating the Odds

"They didn't pick us to win. They said Chicago had too much scoring power and Montreal had too much skating power. But they forgot our ability to work and our desire to win."

—Maple Leafs captain George Armstrong

End of an Era

With the NHL set to expand, the 1966–67 season brought an end to the six-team era that had begun in 1942–43. And with Canada celebrating the 100th anniversary of its confederation, there could be no more fitting way to mark both occasions than with a Stanley Cup matchup between Toronto and Montreal.

The story of the regular season was the Chicago Black Hawks, who finished atop the NHL standings for the first time in franchise history. Bobby Hull led the NHL with 52 goals, while Stan Mikita set a new league record with 62 assists and tied Hull's one-year-old mark with 97 points. In addition to the Art Ross Trophy, Mikita would also win the Hart Trophy as MVP and the Lady Byng Trophy for sportsmanship, making him the first player in league history to capture three major awards in one season. The Black Hawks also boasted the league's best defense, and Chicago's 94 points, on a record of 41-17-12, were 17 more than second-place Montreal. Most experts expected them to make easy work of Toronto in the semifinals.

The Maple Leafs had struggled during the regular season. A 10-game losing streak at the midway point of the schedule nearly cost them a playoff spot, but the team recovered with a 7-2-1 record during a 10-game stint in which King Clancy replaced a hospitalized Punch Imlach behind the bench. Leaf veterans Red Kelly, Frank Mahovlich, Dave Keon and Allan Stanley all missed some time due to injuries, though Tim Horton and George Armstrong both played the full 70 games. Younger players such as Ron Ellis, Pete Stemkowski and Jim Pappin were also important. In the playoffs, veteran Leafs goalies Terry Sawchuk and Johnny Bower would make the difference.

Sawchuk was spectacular as Toronto upset Chicago in six games during the semifinals. When he faltered in Game 1 of the final against Montreal, Imlach went to Bower, who responded with 31 saves in a 3–0 shutout that turned the series around. Game 3 went into overtime, and Bower made 60 saves before Bob Pulford scored at 8:26 of the second extra session to give Toronto a 3–2 win. Bower was hurt in the warm-up before Game 4, and the Leafs had to switch back to Sawchuk. He struggled in another lopsided loss, but he closed the door on the Canadiens in Games 5 and 6 as the Maple Leafs won the Stanley Cup.

Rookie Goalie

Rogie Vachon was called up to the Canadiens from the minors late in the 1966–67 season. Though he had not been good enough to make the Junior Canadiens a few years before, Vachon got on a roll. In the playoffs, he led Montreal to a sweep of the Rangers in the semifinals and then announced he'd be glad to face the Maple Leafs instead of the Black Hawks. Leafs boss Punch Imlach was not amused. "Tell that cocky Junior B goalkeeper that he won't be facing New York Rangers peashooters when the Leafs open up on him." Imlach added that there was no way the Canadiens could beat the Leafs with a kid in goal.

Though Vachon played well in the series, there are some who say that Toe Blake only stuck with him to prove Imlach wrong. When Blake finally pulled Vachon in the third period of Game 5 and went with Gump Worsley in Game 6, it was too late.

Expo 67

As part of Canada's centennial celebration, the city of Montreal hosted a world's fair. When Montreal won the Stanley Cup in 1966, Toe Blake promised Mayor Jean Drapeau that the Canadiens would win it again the next year and that the Cup would go on display at the Quebec Pavilion at Expo 67. Toronto's win upset those plans, though the Stanley Cup did still go on display from June 16th to July 16th—only it was at the Ontario Pavilion.

Wanna Bet Canadian Prime Minister Lester Pearson (a Maple Leafs fan from Toronto) won a $1 bet on the Stanley Cup with Quebec Premier Daniel Johnson, but he only collected a quarter. "Twenty-five cents out of the dollar is more than one normally expects the federal government to get from any province," quipped Pearson.

Veteran Presence

With expansion coming, Maple Leafs veterans rallied around their last chance to win together in 1967. Nursing a 2–1 lead in the dying moments of Game 6, Punch Imlach sent out some of his oldest players to take care of business.

With 55 seconds to go, 37-year-old defenseman Tim Horton lined up in front of 37-year-old goalie Terry Sawchuk, and 41-year-old Allan Stanley beat Jean Béliveau on the faceoff. The puck went to 39-year-old Red Kelly, who fed a short pass to Bob Pulford. The relatively youthful 31-year-old carried the puck across the blue line and dished it off to George Armstrong near center. The 36-year-old Leafs captain took a few strides and fired a long shot into an open net for the Stanley Cup–clinching goal.

Playoff Format

Though the regular season would quickly grow from 50 games in 1942–43 to 60 in 1946–47 to 70 in 1949–50, the playoff format remained the same throughout the entire six-team era. The first four teams qualified for the playoffs every season from 1942–43 through 1966–67. The first-place team met the third-place team in one semifinal series, while the second-place team met the fourth-place team in the other. The winner of the two semifinal series advanced to face each other in the Stanley Cup final.

Toronto and Montreal

The rivalry between Canada's two largest cities is as old as the country itself. Older, in fact, as it dates back to the days when the Province of Canada was still a British colony. It may well have begun when the capital city was moved from Montreal to Toronto after the burning of Parliament in 1849. Or perhaps it dates all the way back to 1759, when the British conquered Quebec on the Plains of Abraham.

> **"We feel we are representing French Canada when we play hockey."**
>
> — Jean Béliveau

The French-English rivalry has always been a part of the friction between Montreal and Toronto. Religion has also played its part, with Quebec being predominantly Catholic and Ontario predominantly Protestant. The stereotype of Toronto's Protestant work ethic versus Montreal's French *joie de vivre* is still a big factor in the rivalry that the citizens of the two cities maintain with each other. While the rivalry has involved everything from the location of corporate headquarters of big businesses to which city has the better bagels, it's felt most keenly in sports—and in hockey in particular.

"We feel we are representing French Canada when we play hockey," the Montreal Canadiens' Jean Béliveau told Toronto reporters during the 1967 Stanley Cup final.

The rivalry between the Toronto Maple Leafs and the Montreal Canadiens is the oldest in the NHL. Both cities were there when the league began in 1917, though there were a couple of different names before Toronto became the Maple Leafs in 1927. But in the early days of the NHL, both cities had a more important rivalry with Ottawa—who had the best team in the league—than they had with each other. And both the Leafs and Canadiens had a much bigger rivalry with the Montreal Maroons for most of the 1930s. The rivalry between the Leafs and the Canadiens didn't truly begin until the 1940s.

By the 1939–40 season the Great Depression had already claimed the Maroons. The Canadiens, who finished last in the seven-team NHL with a record of 10-33-5, were not guaranteed to survive either. Then on April 17, 1940, word came that Maple Leafs coach Dick Irvin had signed a two-year contract to take over in Montreal. In Irvin's nine seasons in Toronto, the Maple Leafs had never missed the playoffs. They'd won the Stanley Cup in 1932 and reached the final on six other occasions. In fact, the New York Rangers had beaten Toronto for the Stanley Cup just four days before Irvin signed a contract with Montreal. Maple Leafs owner Conn Smythe admitted he was sorry to lose his coach, and he let slip that the move was more or less a matter of charity.

"We hate to see Irvin go," the Leafs boss told reporters, "but we felt that the sorry condition in which the Canadiens had found themselves wasn't doing any team in the league any good."

Under Irvin, the Canadiens won the Stanley Cup in 1944 and 1946. Toronto won it in 1942 and 1945. Still, there wasn't really much of a rivalry between the two teams until another Maple Leafs front office member left for Montreal in the summer of 1946. Frank Selke did not leave Toronto on the same good terms that Irvin had.

Selke had been working quietly behind the scenes in Toronto since 1929. He was instrumental in building the farm system that had kept Toronto loaded with talent during the 1930s, but Smythe was not happy with the way Selke and others ran the team in his absence while serving in the military during World War II. Despite the team's

A typical Toronto-Montreal brouhaha.

Stanley Cup victories over Toronto in 1959 and 1960.

Montreal and the Detroit Red Wings were the big rivals of the 1950s, but by the mid-1960s it was the Leafs and the Canadiens who took center stage once again. The two teams faced each other in the semifinals for four straight seasons, with Toronto winning in 1963 and 1964 en route to winning the Stanley Cup. The Canadiens knocked off the Maple Leafs in 1965 and 1966 before going on to Stanley Cup victories of their own. In 1967 the two teams met in the final once again. Twenty years earlier, it had been a young Toronto team that had surprised Montreal. This time, it was a veteran club that pulled off the upset.

Today, fans of the Montreal Canadiens are dealing with the longest Stanley Cup drought in franchise history. Their team has not won it since 1993. And Toronto hasn't celebrated with the Cup since the Maple Leafs' victory in 1967. Nowadays, the rivalry is as much about nostalgia and which city is really the center of the hockey universe as it is about who has the better team. And yet, there's still a certain something in the air whenever Toronto and Montreal meet, particularly on a Saturday night.

continued success, the relationship between Smythe and Selke was permanently soured.

Selke left quietly when he resigned in May 1946. "I've boosted the organization to the skies," he said, "and I have no wish now to throw any [darts]. Of what use would it be to try to hurt people with whom you have worked so long?"

Even so, there was clearly bad blood between Selke and Smythe. It would carry over to their two teams,

and the Montreal-Toronto rivalry was truly born when the Canadiens faced the Maple Leafs in the Stanley Cup final for the first time in 1947.

Montreal was favored over the rebuilding Toronto team, but the Maple Leafs took the 1947 series in six games. Game 2 was key, when Maurice "Rocket" Richard retaliated against the overzealous checking efforts of Vic Lynn and Bill Ezinicki. The Rocket was suspended from Game 3, and Selke refused to let any

Toronto media into the Montreal dressing room after the Leafs defeated the Canadiens. Richard was not the same player when he returned to action in Game 4, and the series turned in Toronto's favor. The Leafs would repeat as Stanley Cup champions in 1948 and 1949 and beat the Canadiens in the final again in 1951. Montreal would get its revenge with

The Game I'll Never Forget

> **If you play the game the way you're supposed to — skate, check and do your job defensively — the opportunities will present themselves and the goals will come.**

Hockey Digest: February 1983
By Dave Keon, as told to George Vass

I was never good at talking about myself. I always figured that if you played the game, worked hard and did your job, your actions would speak for themselves. Hockey is a team game. You have 18 guys and if they play together, you're going to have some success.

I was fortunate enough to be a player a long time, 22 seasons to be exact: the first 15 with the Toronto Maple Leafs then seven more with various clubs, finishing with the Hartford Whalers. When I look back over that period of time it makes me wonder how I lasted that long. For me, I always thought that as long as I could help a team, I could play.

I never put as much emphasis on goal scoring as some people did, though I scored close to 500 pro goals. If you play the game the way you're supposed to—skate, check and do your job defensively—the opportunities will present themselves and the goals will come. That's the way I tried to play, particularly in Toronto when Punch Imlach was coaching the Leafs.

We had some goal-scorers on the Maple Leafs in the 1960s, but mostly we were a hard-working, checking team with a lot of veteran players who knew how to play the game. The game Imlach preached was a strong, aggressive checking game at both ends of the rink. It was backed by good goaltending and the patience to wait for the breaks. If you didn't play that style of game, Imlach wasn't afraid to let you know.

I was always covering the opposing team's best centerman; in my first eight or nine years in the NHL, I figured the only centers in the league were Norn Ullman, Alex Delvecchio, Stan Mikita, Jean Béliveau and Henri Richard. When they were on the ice, I was on the ice. When you're up against players of that caliber, you are out on the ice primarily to check. I always felt I'd done my job if I kept my assignment from scoring. For me, scoring a goal was not a measure of success. I did get my share of goals, better than 20 a season. A lot of them came when somebody on the other team would make a mistake and I'd get an opportunity. A goal like that would be an accident, but then that's often the result of good forechecking.

It's difficult to remember all the high spots of a long career, much less the details of a particular game. There were quite a few, of course. That stands to reason when you've played on four teams that won the Stanley Cup, like I did with Toronto. If I had to put my finger on a particular year, it might be 1967, when we won our fourth Cup in six years. That win was the most gratifying because not many people expected us to do it. The Chicago Black Hawks and the Montreal Canadiens were the teams that looked to have the upper hand in the 1966–67 season. Chicago finished first in the league, and some thought they were the best team ever, with players like Mikita, Bobby Hull, Glenn Hall, Pierre Pilote and others. The Canadiens, as usual, had a fine team.

When we met Chicago in the first round of the playoffs, not many people gave us —or our veteran core of Tim Horton, Red Kelly, George Armstrong, Allan Stanley, Johnny Bower and Terry Sawchuk—a chance. Well, we sure surprised them. I remember the fifth game in particular, the one that Bower started in goal. He looked shaky, and early in the second period Imlach brought in Sawchuk. He hadn't been in the game more than a few minutes when Hull let go with a slapshot that hit him in the shoulder then glanced up and hit his mask. Sawchuk went down as if he had been knocked out. But he just shook

May 2, 1967
Game 6, Stanley Cup final · Maple Leaf Gardens, Toronto

Hard-nosed, two-way center Dave Keon catching a breather before his next shift.

it off, got up and he must have made 40 saves the rest of the game to lead us to the win. Then we won the sixth game to knock them out of the playoffs.

That put us into the final against Montreal, who had eliminated the New York Rangers. They slaughtered us 6–2 in the first game, and everybody started to write us off. But we came back in the second game to win 3–0, Bower playing one of his best games in goal. We won the third game, Montreal the fourth and then we beat them in the fifth to take a 3–2 lead in the series. I got my only goal of the final in that game, but my job was mainly penalty killing and checking—stopping Béliveau and Henri Richard—and if I could do that, I'd done my job.

Our win brought us to the sixth game, May 2, 1967, in Toronto, easily the most memorable game I played in the most memorable series I've played in.

You couldn't ask for a better finish for the Stanley Cup. Gump Worsley started in goal for Montreal, Sawchuk for us. Nobody could get anything past them the first period. In the second period, we got a couple of goals by Ron Ellis and Jim Pappin, and the Canadiens cut our lead 2–1 in the third period.

It stayed that way to the final minute of play, when the Canadiens pulled Worsley. Imlach put our veterans on the ice—Horton, Stanley, Kelly, Armstrong and Bob Pulford in front of Sawchuk. Not a man under 30. And they did the job. On the faceoff, Stanley shoved Béliveau off the puck, Kelly picked it up and passed to Armstrong, who put it into the empty net.

We won 3–1 and took the Cup. It was the fourth Stanley Cup winner I'd been part of, but in many ways it was the most satisfying, not because I'd scored so many goals but because I'd done the job I had been asked to do.

Afterward, I was given the Conn Smythe Trophy as the outstanding player in the playoffs. I thought there were other guys who might have won the Smythe instead of me. The big thing was winning the Stanley Cup, and it took 18 players to do it.

Toronto 3, Montreal 1

FIRST PERIOD

NO SCORING

PENALTIES: Conacher, Toronto (interference), 2:30; Backstrom, Montreal (holding), 5:16; Béliveau, Montreal (cross-checking), 10:21; Conacher, Toronto (interference), 13:25; Ferguson, Montreal (elbowing), 18:50

SECOND PERIOD

1 ▶ Ellis (Kelly, Stanley), Toronto 6:25

2 ▶ Pappin (Stemkowski, Pulford), Toronto 19:24

PENALTIES: Harper, Montreal (holding), 3:05; Stemkowski, Toronto (cross-checking), 7:14; Stanley, Toronto (hooking), 13:23

THIRD PERIOD

3 ▶ Duff (Harris), Montreal, 5:28

4 ▶ Armstrong (Pulford, Kelly), Toronto, 19:13 EN

PENALTY: Pappin, Toronto (slashing), 11:46

SHOTS ON GOAL

	1	2	3	TOTAL
Toronto	11	16	9	36
Montreal	17	14	10	41

GOALIES: Sawchuk, Toronto; Worsley, Montreal

REFEREE: John Ashley

LINESMEN: Matt Pavelich, B. Castleman

SEMIFINALS
4 games to 0 over Toronto

ROSTER

CONN SMYTHE TROPHY **ROGER CROZIER** G – DETROIT

Ralph Backstrom

Dave Balon

Jean Béliveau
(captain)

Yvan Cournoyer

Dick Duff

John Ferguson

Terry Harper

Ted Harris

Charlie Hodge

Jacques Laperrière

Claude Larose

Noel Price

Claude Provost

Henri Richard

Jimmy Roberts

Leon Rochefort

Bobby Rousseau

Jean-Guy Talbot

Gilles Tremblay

J.C. Tremblay

Gump Worsley

Sam Pollock
(general manager)

Toe Blake (coach)

FINAL   4 GAMES TO 2

APR. 24	▶	Detroit 3 at Montreal 2
APR. 26	▶	Detroit 5 at Montreal 2
APR. 28	▶	Montreal 4 at Detroit 2
MAY 1	▶	Montreal 2 at Detroit 1
MAY 3	▶	Detroit 1 at Montreal 5
MAY 5	▶	Montreal 3 at Detroit 2 OT

PLAYOFF SCORING LEADER

Norm Ullman	GP	G	A	PTS
DETROIT	12	6	9	15

FINAL SERIES SCORING

MONTREAL	GP	G	A	PTS	PIM
J.C. Tremblay	6	1	5	6	0
Jean Béliveau	6	3	2	5	0
Henri Richard	6	1	4	5	2
Ralph Backstrom	6	2	2	4	2
Dave Balon	6	2	2	4	16
Gilles Tremblay	6	2	2	4	0
Dick Duff	6	1	3	4	2
Yvan Cournoyer	6	2	1	3	0
Terry Harper	6	1	2	3	4
Bobby Rousseau	6	1	2	3	4
Claude Provost	6	1	1	2	2
Leon Rochefort	4	1	1	2	4
Noel Price	1	0	1	1	0
Jimmy Roberts	6	0	1	1	10
Jean-Guy Talbot	6	0	1	1	8
John Ferguson	6	0	0	0	8
Ted Harris	6	0	0	0	4
Claude Larose	2	0	0	0	0

GOALTENDER	GP	W	L	MIN	GA	SO	AVG
Gump Worsley	6	4	2	362	14	0	2.32

DETROIT	GP	G	A	PTS	PIM
Norm Ullman	6	4	2	6	6
Floyd Smith	6	3	1	4	0
Andy Bathgate	6	1	3	4	4
Paul Henderson	6	1	3	4	4
Ab McDonald	4	1	2	3	2
Alex Delvecchio	6	0	3	3	0
Bill Gadsby	6	1	1	2	2
Gordie Howe	6	1	1	2	6
Bruce MacGregor	6	1	1	2	2
Dean Prentice	6	1	1	2	2
Bert Marshall	6	0	2	2	8
Gary Bergman	6	0	1	1	4
Leo Boivin	6	0	0	0	6
Val Fonteyne	6	0	0	0	0
Warren Godfrey	1	0	0	0	0
Murray Hall	1	0	0	0	0
Parker MacDonald	6	0	0	0	2
Irv Spencer	1	0	0	0	0
Bob Wall	4	0	0	0	2
Bryan Watson	6	0	0	0	12

GOALTENDERS	GP	W	L	MIN	GA	SO	AVG
Roger Crozier	6	2	3	308	16	0	3.12
Hank Bassen	1	0	1	54	2	0	2.22

Two Isn't Four

The Red Wings were just the second team in history to lose the Stanley Cup after winning the first two games in the final. The first was the 1942 Red Wings, who lost four straight after taking a three-games-to-nothing lead over the Toronto Maple Leafs. The Canadiens had suffered a similar fate in the semifinals in 1962, losing four straight to Chicago after winning the first two games. The Red Wings had also won four in a row after losing two straight to the Black Hawks in the 1963 semifinals.

Canadiens Clip Red Wings

The Montreal Canadiens had won the Stanley Cup the year before, and they entered the 1965–66 season with their lineup virtually intact. The Detroit Red Wings were coming off a first-place finish in the 1964–65 regular season, but they had suffered a first-round loss to Chicago in the playoffs. The Red Wings shook up their roster with an eight-player trade that saw veteran defenseman Marcel Pronovost go to Toronto and Andy Bathgate sent to Detroit. The Red Wings, Canadiens and Chicago Black Hawks were in a tight battle for first place during the first half of the 1965–66 season, but Montreal pulled away to come out on top while Detroit slipped into fourth.

Chicago finished second behind a big year from Bobby Hull. Hull became the first player in NHL history to score more than 50 goals in a single season, setting new records with 54 goals and 97 points. The Black Hawks met the Red Wings in the semifinals for the third year in a row. The powerful Chicago team had won 11 of 14 games against Detroit during the season and was expected to make easy work of the injury-riddled Red Wings. However, a stunning 7–0 victory in Game 2 sparked Detroit to a six-game victory and a spot in the Stanley Cup final.

Montreal didn't have a scorer to match Bobby Hull, but Bobby Rousseau and Jean Béliveau both tied Stan Mikita for the league lead with 48 assists. Defensively, Jacques Laperrière won the Norris Trophy and Gump Worsley and Charlie Hodge shared the Vezina Trophy as the Canadiens allowed the fewest goals in the NHL. Facing Toronto in the semifinals, coach Toe Blake thought Montreal was lucky to emerge with a 4–3 win on a late goal by Béliveau in Game 1. The Canadiens went on to sweep the series.

Detroit goalie Roger Crozier was a standout in the first two games of the final, and the Red Wings took both games from the Canadiens right in Montreal. The Canadiens bounced back with a win in Game 3 and then took Game 4 as well after Crozier hurt his knee in the early going. Crozier returned to action in Game 5, but he played poorly and Detroit lost 5–1. The Red Wings goalie was back in form for Game 6, but the Canadiens won the game and the Stanley Cup with a 3–2 victory when Henri Richard scored at 2:20 of overtime.

Conn Smythe Story

Roger Crozier made his debut with the Detroit Red Wings in 1963–64 when he played 15 games for the injured Terry Sawchuk. Crozier replaced the future Hall of Famer in 1964–65 and played in all 70 games, making him the last goalie in NHL history to play in every game on the schedule. He won the Calder Trophy as rookie of the year and earned a selection to the First All-Star Team. Pancreatitis kept him out of action at the beginning of the following year, but he still played 64 games and led the Red Wings to the Stanley Cup final. Crozier was sitting in the dressing room, still stewing over Henri Richard's Cup-winning goal, when he was told he'd won the Conn Smythe Trophy. He had to hustle into his street clothes to accept the trophy. Being named MVP of the playoffs also included a $1,000 bonus and a gold-colored Ford Mustang.

Didn't Matter

Superstitious coach Toe Blake wasn't happy that the Stanley Cup traveled from Montreal to Detroit before game six on the same train as the Canadiens.

STANLEY CUP WINS IN THE SIX-TEAM ERA (1942–43 TO 1966–67)

10	Montreal (1944, 1946, 1953, 1956, 1957, 1958, 1959, 1960, 1965, 1966)
9	Toronto (1945, 1947, 1948, 1949, 1951, 1962, 1963, 1964, 1967)
5	Detroit (1943, 1950, 1952, 1954, 1955)
1	Chicago (1961)
0	Boston
0	New York

Overtime Winner

Though Detroit was outplaying Montreal on home ice in Game 6, the Red Wings were forced to rally just to send the game into overtime. A first-period goal by Jean Béliveau and a second-period tally by Leon Rochefort had the Canadiens up 2–0 at the midway point of the game. Norm Ullman finally got Detroit on the scoreboard at 11:55 of the second period, and Floyd Smith tied it at 10:30 of the third.

Both teams had great chances in the final minutes. Gump Worsley made great saves on Dean Prentice and Bryan Watson, and he made the best save of the night when he did the splits to stop Gordie Howe. Jean Béliveau had two close calls for the Canadiens, but the score remained 2–2 at the end of regulation.

As overtime moved past the 2-minute mark, Henri Richard got the puck at his own blue line and carried it into the Detroit end. He passed to Dave Balon, who then made a quick return pass to Richard. Although Richard was hauled down before he could shoot, somehow the puck wound up in the Detroit net. Roger Crozier insisted Richard had swiped it in with his glove, but referee Frank Udvari ruled it a goal.

Though it looked like Richard had directed the puck with his forearm, he claimed there was nothing illegal about the play. "I tried to swing my stick at the puck... Their defenseman tripped me [and] it hit my leg and bounced ahead of me into the goal."

"I don't know what the Red Wings are complaining about," added Balon. "A goal doesn't have to be pretty. All the puck has to do is go into the net."

SEMIFINALS
4 games to 2 over Toronto

CONN SMYTHE TROPHY **JEAN BÉLIVEAU** C – MONTREAL

Ralph Backstrom
Dave Balon
Jean Béliveau (captain)
Red Berenson
Yvan Cournoyer
Dick Duff
John Ferguson
Jean Gauthier
Terry Harper
Ted Harris
Charlie Hodge
Jacques Laperrière
Claude Larose
Garry Peters
Noel Picard
Claude Provost
Henri Richard
Jimmy Roberts
Bobby Rousseau
Jean-Guy Talbot
Gilles Tremblay
J.C. Tremblay
Ernie Wakely
Bryan Watson
Gump Worsley
Sam Pollock
(general manager)
Toe Blake (coach)

FINAL 4 GAMES TO 3

APR. 17 ▶	Chicago 2 at Montreal 3
APR. 20 ▶	Chicago 0 at Montreal 2
APR. 22 ▶	Montreal 1 at Chicago 3
APR. 25 ▶	Montreal 1 at Chicago 5
APR. 27 ▶	Chicago 0 at Montreal 6
APR. 29 ▶	Montreal 1 at Chicago 2
MAY 1 ▶	Chicago 0 at Montreal 4

PLAYOFF SCORING LEADER

	GP	G	A	PTS
Bobby Hull CHICAGO	14	10	7	17

FINAL SERIES SCORING

MONTREAL	GP	G	A	PTS	PIM
Jean Béliveau	7	5	5	10	18
Dick Duff	7	3	5	8	5
Bobby Rousseau	7	1	5	6	4
J.C. Tremblay	7	1	5	6	14
Henri Richard	7	3	0	3	20
John Ferguson	7	2	1	3	13
Ted Harris	7	0	3	3	34
Yvan Cournoyer	7	2	0	2	0
Ralph Backstrom	7	1	1	2	4
Claude Provost	7	0	2	2	12
Red Berenson	7	0	1	1	2
Noel Picard	3	0	1	1	0
Dave Balon	5	0	0	0	0
Jean Gauthier	2	0	0	0	4
Terry Harper	7	0	0	0	19
Claude Larose	7	0	0	0	4
Jimmy Roberts	7	0	0	0	14
Jean-Guy Talbot	7	0	0	0	18

GOALTENDERS	GP	W	L	MIN	GA	SO	AVG
Gump Worsley	4	3	1	240	5	2	1.25
Charlie Hodge	3	1	2	180	7	1	2.33

CHICAGO	GP	G	A	PTS	PIM
Bobby Hull	7	2	2	4	10
Chico Maki	7	1	3	4	8
Stan Mikita	7	0	3	3	35
Pierre Pilote	5	0	3	3	14
Phil Esposito	7	1	1	2	8
Doug Mohns	7	1	1	2	15
Matt Ravlich	7	1	1	2	8
Fred Stanfield	7	1	1	2	0
Moose Vasko	7	1	1	2	12
Bill Hay	7	1	0	1	0
Camille Henry	7	1	0	1	2
Doug Jarrett	7	1	0	1	10
Kenny Wharram	5	1	0	1	2
Dennis Hull	1	0	0	0	0
Al MacNeil	7	0	0	0	12
John McKenzie	4	0	0	0	0
Gerry Melnyk	6	0	0	0	0
Eric Nesterenko	7	0	0	0	6

GOALTENDERS	GP	W	L	MIN	GA	SO	AVG
Glenn Hall	7	3	4	400	15	0	2.25
Denis DeJordy	1	0	0	20	3	0	9.00

Toe on Top

Toe Blake's sixth Stanley Cup victory broke the record of most wins by a coach, which he had previously shared with Toronto's Hap Day. "There's more satisfaction in winning this one than any of the others," Blake said.

Jean Béliveau agreed. "There's more satisfaction," said Béliveau, who had also won his sixth Cup, but his first as team captain, "because no one in this room [meaning the sportswriters] thought we would win."

Back on Top

On May 14, 1964, Frank Selke retired after 18 seasons as general manager of the Montreal Canadiens. Selke was the architect of the greatest dynasty in hockey history, having built the team that won the Stanley Cup five years in a row, from 1956 to 1960. "He has had probably the most successful individual career in the history of hockey," said Canadiens owner Senator Hartland Monahan, who also stepped down as president of the team that day in favor of his nephew, J. David Molson. Sam Pollock succeeded Selke, and though he made only minor moves that summer, he would quickly restore the Canadiens to Stanley Cup glory.

The departure of Bernie Geoffrion was the only significant loss to the Canadiens' roster, but Pollock began to integrate several new faces from the farm system into the lineup. Ted Harris and Jimmy Roberts joined a strong defense led by Jacques Laperrière, Jean-Guy Talbot, J.C. Tremblay and Terry Harper. Claude Larose added grit and 21 goals to the offense. Dick Duff added muscle when acquired in a trade, and Yvan Cournoyer was brought along slowly. Still, it was veterans Jean Béliveau and Henri Richard who had the Canadiens off to a flying start before injuries saw the team slump to a second-place finish in the regular-season standings.

The top team in the NHL this season was the Detroit Red Wings, who had not finished first since 1956–57. Ted Lindsay came back from a four-year retirement, but it was the play of young goalie Roger Crozier, as well as the offensive power of Gordie Howe, Alex Delvecchio and Norm Ullman, that fueled the Red Wings' resurgence. Ullman led the NHL with 42 goals, and his 83 points trailed only Stan Mikita's 87. Mikita and the Chicago Black Hawks fought Montreal and Detroit in a three-way battle for first place, but they had to settle for third. A string of injuries saw Toronto fall into fourth place. The Maple Leafs' reign as three-time Stanley Cup champions then came to an end when the Canadiens beat them in the semifinals. Claude Provost scored the series winner at 16:33 of overtime in Game 6.

Chicago knocked off Detroit in seven games, reversing the results of the previous year, but the Canadiens beat the Black Hawks in a tough seven-game series to win the Stanley Cup for the first time since their five-year dynasty had come to an end.

Conn Smythe Story

Maple Leaf Gardens Limited presented the Conn Smythe Trophy to the NHL in the summer of 1964 in honor of the longtime coach, general manager, president and owner-governor of the Toronto Maple Leafs. Unlike similar trophies in other sports, the Conn Smythe Trophy is based on performance in the entire playoffs, not just the championship round. The award was presented for the first time in 1965 and was won by Jean Béliveau. Béliveau's eight goals and 16 points in 13 playoff games trailed only Chicago's Bobby Hull. Against the Black Hawks in the final, Béliveau was the leading scorer, with 10 points. He also scored the game-winning goal in three Montreal victories and set up the game winner in the team's other win.

Long Memories

Many fans booed NHL president Clarence Campbell when he presented the Stanley Cup and the Conn Smythe Trophy to Jean Béliveau. "Some fans," wrote Pat Curran in the *Montreal Gazette*, "still haven't forgotten the incidents of 1955, when Campbell suspended Maurice Richard for the last three games of the season and the playoffs after the Rocket had punched a linesman at Boston."

PLAYOFF APPEARANCES IN THE SIX-TEAM ERA (1942–43 TO 1966–67)

MONTREAL	▸ 24		BOSTON	▸ 14
DETROIT	▸ 22		CHICAGO	▸ 12
TORONTO	▸ 21		NEW YORK	▸ 7

The Final

Charlie Hodge had seen the bulk of the action in goal for the Canadiens during the 1964–65 season, but when he was hurt in Game 2 of the semifinals, Montreal turned to Gump Worsley. Worsley was a 12-year NHL veteran who had spent his first 10 seasons with the weak New York Rangers. When Toe Blake selected him to start against Chicago, it marked his first appearance in the Stanley Cup finals.

Worsley played well as Montreal won the first two games at home, but he only had to make 18 saves in a 2–0 shutout in Game 2. The Black Hawks had played the first two games without Pierre Pilote and Kenny Wharram, but they returned when the series shifted to Chicago, and the results were a lot different. When Worsley was hurt in the warm-up before Game 4, a rusty Hodge had to take over, and he gave up a couple of soft goals in a 5–1 Chicago victory that included 15 penalties called against Montreal. Hodge was much better behind a solid defense back in Montreal, and the Canadiens got four power-play goals in a 6–0 victory. Jean Béliveau had two goals and two assists. Once again Chicago evened the series at home, and the teams returned to Montreal for Game 7.

Blake went back to Worsley for the finale, figuring "he might not be as nervous as Charlie." But there was little reason for nerves. Béliveau scored just 14 seconds into the game and then set up Dick Duff at 5:03. Worsley made some big saves while it was 2–0, but two more goals before the first period ended led to a 4–0 victory.

The Game I'll Never Forget

LORNE WORSLEY / GOALIE MONTREAL CANADIENS

> **Just a couple of days earlier I couldn't even walk stairs, and here I was getting ready to play the seventh game of the Stanley Cup final with everything on the line.**

Hockey Digest: March 1973
By Gump Worsley, as told to George Vass

When I played with the New York Rangers we made the Stanley Cup playoffs a few times in the dozen years I was there, but we never made it to the final. Even when we finished the regular season in second place we would get beat in the first round of the playoffs by the fourth-place team.

In 1963 the Rangers traded me to Montreal, and I began to think that it was my chance to get into the final and play for the Stanley Cup. When you're with a club like Montreal you always know the chances of winning the Stanley Cup are good. It took quite a bit of time for me, though. I even played games at Quebec of the American League before I got my chance in the Stanley Cup final, in 1964–65.

That season we beat Toronto in the first round to set up the final against Chicago. The series was just one of those where each team won the games on its own ice until a seventh game was forced.

I was going pretty good in the series until I got hurt. I had shut out Chicago in Game 2, and that's when I was injured. Stan Mikita ran into me, and I twisted my knee. It was bad and I thought I was through for the series.

Heading into Game 7 at the Forum on Saturday, May 1, 1965, I'd skated a little during practice on the Friday but hadn't thought too much about it. Fact is, I didn't even expect to suit up for the game. I was sure coach Toe Blake would use Charlie Hodge. He even had an extra goalie to suit up and take my place on the bench.

I was sitting in a restaurant having coffee with my wife the afternoon before the game when one of our trainers came in and walked up to me.

"Gump, Blake says he wants you to play tonight," he told me.

"You must be kidding," I said. "I've only been on skates once since I got hurt."

"No, Blake said to find you and tell you he wants you to play tonight."

Well, Blake had asked me how I felt after practice and I had said "Pretty good," because I did feel good. He thought if I felt that way it was all right to play me.

Later he told people, "He practiced Friday and looked hot so I decided to take a chance on him. I figured Gump would be less nervous under pressure than Charlie Hodge."

I can tell you I was nervous enough. Just a couple of days earlier I couldn't even walk stairs, and here I was getting ready to play the seventh game of the Stanley Cup final with everything on the line.

Luckily, I didn't have all that much time to think about it. Blake hadn't told me he was going to use me until just a few hours before the game. It didn't really hit me until I started getting my pads on.

I calmed down in a hurry once the game began because we got a big break and that took a little of the pressure off me—although with guys like Bobby Hull, Mikita, Kenny Wharram and Doug Mohns coming at you, you could never really relax against Chicago. Right at the beginning, the puck skipped from the center zone over Chicago defenseman Pierre Pilote's stick toward their net. Dick Duff charged in for us and was the first to get to the puck. He passed it to Jean Béliveau, coming in onto the left of Chicago goalie Glenn Hall, and Béliveau let one go and beat Hall just 14 seconds into the game.

Something like that always takes the sting out of the other team, and it must have had an effect on Chicago because they began to play a little down. Whatever it was, we

May 1, 1965
Game 7, Stanley Cup final · Montreal Forum, Montreal

Gump Worsley, far out from his net to cut down the shooter's angle, watches the puck sail wide.

got three more goals in the first period from Duff, Yvan Cournoyer and Henri Richard. We went to the dressing room with a 4–0 lead.

Chicago couldn't get untangled the rest of the game, and there was no way our guys were going to let them score. My game was a little easier than it might have been.

I can only remember one big save I needed to make. It was early in the game, when we were up 1–0. All of a sudden I looked up and I saw Chicago's Camille Henry standing in front of me with the puck right

in front of the net. It wasn't an easy situation, no matter who was there, but Henry was tougher in front than most. I played with him in New York and knew how accurate and deadly he was at short range. He got the shot off and I stopped it with my shoulder. Must have popped over the net. I don't know whether it helped me a bit having played with him or not, or whether I was just lucky, but that was the big save. In a Cup game a chance in front like that is a big opportunity. Those games are played tight, and one goal can do it.

As it turned out, our first goal was all we needed to win. Chicago had a hard time getting the puck into our end, and in the third period, with five minutes to go, there was no way they could get near me. We had five guys back, dumping the puck into center ice, more or less playing for me and the shutout—my second in that series.

The last five minutes of the game in the Forum you couldn't even hear yourself think, everybody singing and yelling. When the game finally ended, my teammates lifted both me and Toe Blake on their shoulders and carried us around the ice.

Like I said, with the way our guys played I didn't have to make that many big saves, but winning that first Stanley Cup after 13 years of playing hockey has to be the biggest thrill I've ever had.

Montreal 4, Chicago 0

FIRST PERIOD

1 ▸ Béliveau (Duff, Rousseau), Montreal, 0:14

2 ▸ Duff (Béliveau, Rousseau), Montreal, 5:03

3 ▸ Cournoyer (Duff, Rousseau), Montreal, 16:29

4 ▸ Richard (Harris), Montreal, 18:45 PP

PENALTIES: Harris, Montreal (holding), 7:55; Pilote, Chicago (hooking), 16:08; Esposito, Chicago (hooking), 18:00; Harris, Montreal (elbowing, misconduct), 19:56

SECOND PERIOD

NO SCORING

PENALTIES: Nesterenko, Chicago (hooking), 7:11; Jarrett, Chicago (charging), 17:42

THIRD PERIOD

NO SCORING

PENALTIES: Vasko, Chicago (high-sticking), 4:03; Richard, Montreal (slashing), 4:03; Mikita, Chicago (slashing), 6:16; Mohns, Chicago (holding), 9:16; Provost, Montreal (hooking), 14:23; Béliveau, Montreal (tripping), 17:39; Henry, Chicago (high-sticking), 18:30; Provost, Montreal (hooking), 19:27

SHOTS ON GOAL

	1	2	3	TOTAL
Montreal	15	12	8	35
Chicago	9	6	5	20

GOALIES: Worsley, Montreal; Hall, Chicago

REFEREE: John Ashley

LINESMEN: Matt Pavelich, John D'Amico

Toronto Maple Leafs

SEMIFINALS
4 games to 3 over Montreal

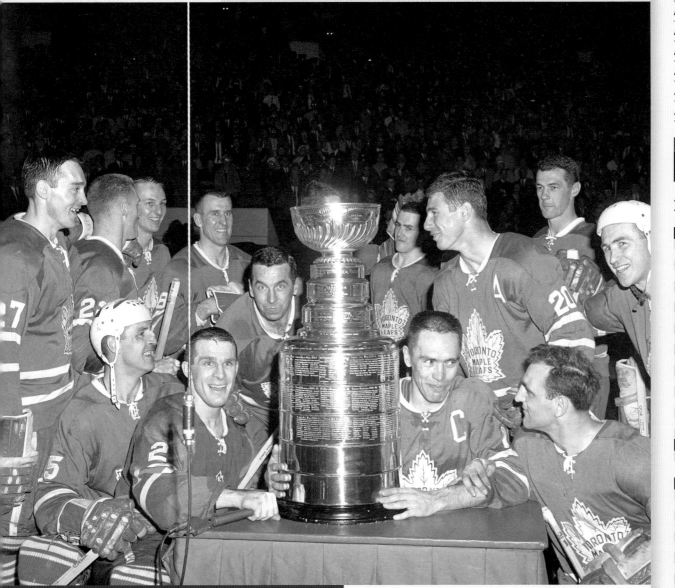

APR. 11	▶	Detroit 2 at Toronto 3
APR. 14	▶	Detroit 4 at Toronto 3 OT
APR. 16	▶	Toronto 3 at Detroit 4
APR. 18	▶	Toronto 4 at Detroit 2
APR. 21	▶	Detroit 2 at Toronto 1
APR. 23	▶	Toronto 4 at Detroit 3 OT
APR. 25	▶	Detroit 0 at Toronto 4

PLAYOFF SCORING LEADER

	GP	G	A	PTS
Gordie Howe DETROIT	14	9	10	19

FINAL SERIES SCORING

TORONTO	GP	G	A	PTS	PIM
Frank Mahovlich	7	1	7	8	0
George Armstrong	7	4	3	7	10
Red Kelly	7	2	4	6	2
Don McKenney	5	1	5	6	0
Dave Keon	7	4	1	5	0
Andy Bathgate	7	3	2	5	12
Bob Pulford	7	3	2	5	10
Allan Stanley	7	1	3	4	12
Bob Baun	7	1	2	3	16
Ron Stewart	7	0	3	3	2
Billy Harris	7	1	1	2	4
Tim Horton	7	0	2	2	12
Gerry Ehman	7	1	0	1	2
Carl Brewer	5	0	1	1	10
Al Arbour	1	0	0	0	0
Larry Hillman	6	0	0	0	2
Ed Litzenberger	1	0	0	0	10
Jim Pappin	7	0	0	0	0
Eddie Shack	7	0	0	0	4

GOALTENDER	GP	W	L	MIN	GA	SO	AVG
Johnny Bower	7	4	3	430	17	1	2.37

DETROIT	GP	G	A	PTS	PIM
Gordie Howe	7	4	4	8	8
Alex Delvecchio	7	1	4	5	0
Norm Ullman	7	1	3	4	2
Floyd Smith	7	3	0	3	0
Bruce MacGregor	7	3	0	3	4
Eddie Joyal	7	2	1	3	6
Larry Jeffrey	7	1	2	3	4
Pit Martin	7	1	2	3	10
Doug Barkley	7	0	3	3	8
Bill Gadsby	7	0	2	2	14
André Pronovost	7	0	2	2	8
Paul Henderson	7	1	0	1	4
Parker MacDonald	7	0	1	1	0
John MacMillan	4	0	1	1	2
Bob Dillabough	1	0	0	0	0
Alex Faulkner	1	0	0	0	0
Albert Langlois	7	0	0	0	8
Marcel Pronovost	7	0	0	0	8
Irv Spencer	7	0	0	0	0

GOALTENDER	GP	W	L	MIN	GA	SO	AVG
Terry Sawchuk	7	3	4	430	22	0	3.07

ROSTER

Al Arbour

George Armstrong (captain)

Andy Bathgate

Bob Baun

Johnny Bower

Carl Brewer

Gerry Ehman

Billy Harris

Larry Hillman

Tim Horton

Red Kelly

Dave Keon

Ed Litzenberger

Frank Mahovlich

Don McKenney

Jim Pappin

Bob Pulford

Eddie Shack

Don Simmons

Allan Stanley

Ron Stewart

Punch Imlach (coach/ general manager)

Record-Setting Red Wings

Detroit players reached two major NHL milestones during the 1963–64 season. First, Gordie Howe surpassed Maurice Richard as the NHL's all-time leader with his 545th career goal on November 10, 1963. Second, Terry Sawchuk became the league leader in shutouts when the 95th of his career, on January 18, 1964, moved him past George Hainsworth.

Three the Hard Way

The Toronto Maple Leafs won the Stanley Cup for the third straight season in 1963–64, but the route to this year's championship was considerably tougher than the second one. The Maple Leafs started the year with very few changes to their lineup, but it took a late trade to salvage the season.

After three straight early playoff exits, the Montreal Canadiens made most of their big moves in the off-season. The biggest was a multi-player deal that sent Jacques Plante, Phil Goyette and Don Marshall to New York for Gump Worsley, Dave Balon, Leon Rochefort and Len Ronson. The reconfigured Canadiens returned to first place in the NHL standings (36-21-13 with 85 points) in a tight battle with Chicago (36-22-12 with 84 points). The Black Hawks were led by Stan Mikita and Bobby Hull, who finished first and second in the league in both goals and points.

The Maple Leafs, meanwhile, were struggling. Johnny Bower was solid in goal (his 2.11 average would lead the league), but the offense was sputtering. The team was in danger of falling out of a playoff position when Punch Imlach sent Dick Duff, Bob Nevin, Rod Seiling, Arnie Brown and Bill Collins to New York for Andy Bathgate and Don McKenney just prior to a game with the Rangers on February 22, 1964. The Leafs went 9-4-2 in their final 15 games, including five wins and a tie in their last six games, to climb comfortably into third place.

Frank Mahovlich had slumped all season, but he came to life in the playoffs against Montreal. Mahovlich scored the winning goal in a 2–1 victory in Game 2 and had two goals and three assists in a 5–3 win in Game 4. Johnny Bower and Dave Keon became the heroes after Montreal won Game 5. Bower earned a 3–0 shutout in Game 6 and made 38 saves in Game 7. Keon scored a hat trick in the 3–1 victory.

Detroit had upset Chicago to set up a rematch with Toronto for the Stanley Cup. A late goal by Bob Pulford gave the Maple Leafs a 3–2 win in Game 1, but the Red Wings took three of the next four games. Toronto stayed alive in Game 6 when Bob Baun scored the overtime winner while playing with a fibula that was fractured just above the ankle. The Maple Leafs then took the Stanley Cup with a 4–0 win in Game 7.

Game Seven

With both Bob Baun and Red Kelly in the lineup despite serious injuries suffered in Game 6, an inspired Toronto team came out strong for Game 7 at Maple Leaf Gardens. Andy Bathgate put Toronto on top early when he scored at 3:04 of the first period. With Johnny Bower stopping everything Detroit fired at him, only the equally fine play of Terry Sawchuk kept Detroit close after that. Dave Keon finally got the next goal at 4:26 of the third period, and when Kelly scored 87 seconds later, the game was all but over. Frank Mahovlich set up George Armstrong for the final goal at 15:26.

Seven × Three The 1964 playoffs marked the only time in the six-team era in which each of the three series went the full seven games.

Walking Wounded

In addition to Bob Baun and Red Kelly, George Armstrong and Carl Brewer were also injected with painkillers prior to Game 7. Brewer had torn rib cartilage and Armstrong had a bad shoulder. Kelly had strained ligaments in his left knee, and both he and Baun took shots of novocaine before the game and after the first and second periods. After the game, Kelly collapsed on the way to the shower and had to be rushed to the hospital.

Kelly's Kid In later years, Red Kelly would recall Leafs co-owner Harold Ballard bringing the Cup and a couple of bottles of champagne to his house. He has joked about his infant son doing what babies do while posing for pictures inside the Stanley Cup bowl and how he and his family laugh every time they see a player drinking from the Stanley Cup. At the time, though, when he returned to his job as a member of Parliament in Ottawa a few days after the Leafs' victory, Kelly told reporters that he had missed all the celebrations and had not yet drank even one drop of champagne.

19:58... Or So

Because both semifinals had gone seven games, the Maple Leafs and Red Wings had only one day off before starting the Stanley Cup final. Game 1 was sluggish, with both teams seeming more concerned with stopping the other than scoring themselves. Tied 2–2 late in the third, the game seemed destined for overtime until Toronto's Allan Stanley took a penalty at 19:18. The Red Wings had the pressure on, but Bob Pulford managed to pull away for a shorthanded goal that gave Toronto a 3–2 victory. Officially, the time of the winning goal was 19:58, although accounts of the game indicate that the excited timekeeper was a little bit slow in stopping the clock and that the goal was likely scored about three seconds earlier.

Other Tight Finishes

The Red Wings outplayed Toronto in Game 2, but when Toronto's Gerry Ehman scored with just 43 seconds left in regulation, Detroit was forced to go into overtime. The Red Wings' Larry Jeffrey scored at 7:42 for a 4–3 victory. Back home in Game 3, Detroit jumped out to a 3–0 lead but saw Toronto rally to tie it when Don McKenney scored at 18:47 of the third. However, Alex Delvecchio tapped in a setup from Gordie Howe with just 17 seconds left to give the Red Wings a second straight 4–3 victory.

Bob Baun's Broken Ankle

The 1963–64 Toronto Maple Leafs boasted 10 future Hockey Hall of Famers in their lineup. Eleven if you count Al Arbour, who played just a handful of games for the Leafs that season and would be inducted as a builder after a brilliant coaching career with the New York Islanders. There were plenty of players more likely to score a big goal than the stocky little defenseman known best for his bodychecks, but Bob Baun didn't just emerge as a goal-scoring hero, he became a hockey legend. Leaving the game on a stretcher late in the third period, Baun returned to keep Toronto's hopes alive by scoring the winning goal in overtime in Game 6 of the 1964 Stanley Cup final.

Baun lined up against Howe, lost the draw, felt his ankle crack and dropped to the ice.

As it says in his biography on the Hockey Hall of Fame's NHL Player Search website, with the exception of 1972 Team Canada hero Paul Henderson, there is perhaps no other professional hockey player who has become as well known for his exploits in just a single game as Bob Baun.

Baun played 17 years in the NHL. In his 964 regular-season games he scored just 37 goals. He added only three more in his 96 career playoff games. After scoring his big goal on April 23, 1964, he would not score again until February 1, 1967. But if Baun wasn't known for scoring goals, he did have a knack for winning championships.

A native of Lanigan, Saskatchewan, Baun became a part of the Maple Leafs system when he was brought to Toronto as a 16-year-old in 1952. He began the 1952–53 season playing minor midget hockey in the city, but quickly progressed to the Junior B Weston Dukes and then to the Junior A Toronto Marlboros. With the Marlboros, Baun won the Memorial Cup in 1955 and 1956. His teammates included Bob Pulford, Bob Nevin and Billy Harris, all of whom would go on to the win the Stanley Cup with the Maple Leafs several times in the 1960s. Baun appeared at his first NHL training camp in the fall of 1956. He split the 1956–57 season between Toronto and the Rochester Americans of the American Hockey League, but was in the NHL to stay by 1957–58. With his physical style of play, the 5-foot-9, 175-pound Baun suffered more than his share of injuries, though size had little to do with the ankle injury that felled him in Game 6.

After scoring four times in 52 games during the 1963–64 season, Baun had already scored one big goal in the playoffs. He beat the Montreal Canadiens' Charlie Hodge on a breakaway late in the second period to give Toronto a 2–0 lead en route to the 3–0 victory that kept the Maple Leafs alive in Game 6 of the semifinals. For Baun it was his first playoff goal in 25 games dating back to the spring of 1960, but when Toronto needed another win to stay alive again in Game 6 of the final against the Detroit Red Wings, Baun came up with an even bigger goal.

The events surrounding Baun's injury late in the third period of the big game are a bit confusing. Even at the time reporters couldn't seem to get straight whether it was Gordie Howe or Alex Delvecchio who had fired the puck that hurt him. But whoever it was, Baun stayed on the ice a little bit longer. In this era, the Maple Leafs occasionally used defensemen to take key faceoffs, feeling it was sometimes more important to tie up the opposing center than it was to get the puck. Baun lined up against Howe, lost the draw, felt his ankle crack and dropped to the ice. He struggled

back to his feet, but was down again when the puck was shot over the glass about six seconds later. Teammates quickly gathered around as trainer Bob Haggert arrived. The pain was apparent on Baun's face when he was carried off the ice on a stretcher. Again, the details are fuzzy, as newspapers reported the time as both 13:14 and 13:46.

Though fairly certain he had broken a bone, Baun asked for his ankle to be frozen. His ankle was injected with Carbocaine and wrapped heavily in tape, and he went back to the bench before the third period ended. The score was tied 3–3, and the game soon went into overtime. Early in the extra session, Baun pinched in at the Detroit blue line. He cut off a clearing attempt and slapped the puck toward the net all in one motion. His wobbly shot struck the stick of Detroit defenseman Bill Gadsby and bounced past Detroit goaltender Terry Sawchuk.

The time was 1:43 and the Maple Leafs were still alive.

When the anesthetic wore off after the game, Baun was unable to walk on his own. He skipped practice the next day (Friday), but refused to have his ankle x-rayed and vowed he'd be in the lineup for Game 7 on Saturday night. After the Maple Leafs won the Cup, Baun finally went for x-rays on the morning of Monday, April 27, four days after the injury. They revealed that

Bob Baun battles for position in front of the Toronto goal.

he had suffered a hairline fracture of the fibula. That afternoon Baun made the injury worse when he slipped and fell while stepping into a convertible that was supposed to take him to the festivities at Toronto City Hall. Baun had to skip the Stanley Cup parade, but hockey fans would never forget the hero of the 1964 Stanley Cup final.

SEMIFINALS
4 games to 1 over Montreal

FINAL **4 GAMES TO 1**

APR. 9	▶	Detroit 2 at Toronto 4
APR. 11	▶	Detroit 2 at Toronto 4
APR. 14	▶	Toronto 2 at Detroit 3
APR. 16	▶	Toronto 4 at Detroit 2
APR. 18	▶	Detroit 1 at Toronto 3

ROSTER

George Armstrong (captain)

Bob Baun

Johnny Bower

Carl Brewer

Kent Douglas

Dick Duff

Billy Harris

Larry Hillman

Tim Horton

Red Kelly

Dave Keon

Ed Litzenberger

John MacMillan

Frank Mahovlich

Bob Nevin

Bob Pulford

Eddie Shack

Don Simmons

Allan Stanley

Ron Stewart

Punch Imlach (coach/general manager)

Punch Imlach and George Armstrong get ready to drink from the Stanley Cup.

PLAYOFF SCORING LEADERS

	GP	G	A	PTS
Gordie Howe DETROIT	11	7	9	16
Norm Ullman DETROIT	11	4	12	16

FINAL SERIES SCORING

TORONTO	GP	G	A	PTS	PIM
Dave Keon	5	4	2	6	0
Red Kelly	5	2	2	4	2
Tim Horton	5	1	3	4	4
Allan Stanley	5	0	4	4	4
Bob Nevin	5	3	0	3	0
Dick Duff	5	2	1	3	2
George Armstrong	5	1	2	3	0
Ed Litzenberger	5	1	2	3	4
Bob Pulford	5	0	3	3	8
Ron Stewart	5	2	0	2	2
Eddie Shack	5	1	1	2	4
Bob Baun	5	0	1	1	6
Carl Brewer	5	0	1	1	4
Kent Douglas	5	0	1	1	2
Billy Harris	5	0	1	1	0
Frank Mahovlich	4	0	1	1	4
John MacMillan	1	0	0	0	0

GOALTENDER	GP	W	L	MIN	GA	SO	AVG
Johnny Bower	5	4	1	300	10	0	2.00

DETROIT	GP	G	A	PTS	PIM
Gordie Howe	5	3	3	6	8
Marcel Pronovost	5	0	4	4	0
Norm Ullman	5	0	4	4	2
Larry Jeffrey	5	2	1	3	4
Alex Delvecchio	5	1	2	3	0
Alex Faulkner	5	2	0	2	2
Floyd Smith	5	0	2	2	4
Eddie Joyal	5	1	0	1	0
Vic Stasiuk	4	1	0	1	0
Parker MacDonald	5	0	1	1	2
Bruce MacGregor	5	0	1	1	2
André Pronovost	5	0	1	1	0
Doug Barkley	5	0	0	0	6
Bob Dillabough	1	0	0	0	0
Val Fonteyne	5	0	0	0	0
Bill Gadsby	5	0	0	0	12
Pete Goegan	5	0	0	0	2
Gerry Odrowski	2	0	0	0	2
Howie Young	2	0	0	0	0

GOALTENDER	GP	W	L	MIN	GA	SO	AVG
Terry Sawchuk	5	1	4	300	17	0	3.40

Semifinal History

Toronto and Detroit had last met for the Stanley Cup in 1949, but in the 12 years in between, they had met in the semifinals seven times. The Red Wings had come out on top in 1950, 1952, 1954, 1955, 1956 and 1961, with the Maple Leafs winning only in 1960.

Unlikely Hero

"I was trying to get the hell out of the way. It hit my stick and went in."
—Eddie Shack on scoring the Stanley Cup–winning goal.

Two Straight for Toronto

Only five points separated the top four teams in the final standings in 1962–63, making this the tightest season-long race in the history of the six-team era. The Maple Leafs finished in first place for the first time since 1947–48, with a record of 35-23-12 for 82 points. The Black Hawks were just one point behind, followed by the Canadiens with 79 and the Red Wings with 77. The Rangers and Bruins were hopelessly out of playoff contention with 56 and 45 points respectively.

Having won the Stanley Cup the year before, the Maple Leafs kept their lineup virtually intact. The departure of Bert Olmstead meant more playing time for Eddie Shack, and the only significant addition to the roster was defenseman Kent Douglas, who would win the Calder Trophy as Rookie of the Year. Toronto had also had trouble signing Frank Mahovlich, and they were offered $1 million for his services by Black Hawks owner Jim Norris. Stafford Smythe admitted that the team was tempted, but he and co-owners John Bassett and Harold Ballard officially declined the offer. Mahovlich, who was coming off a big year, was even better in 1962–63, finishing third in the NHL with 36 goals and fourth in the league with 73 points. For the second straight year, Dave Keon picked up only a single penalty during the regular season and won the Lady Byng Trophy. Don Simmons (who shared goaltending duties with Johnny Bower) led the league with a goals-against average of 2.46.

After five straight seasons atop the NHL standings, injuries plagued Montreal throughout the 1962–63 campaign. Twenty-three ties in 70 games kept them close in the standings, and although the Canadiens were only three points back of first-place Toronto, even Toe Blake admitted before the semifinals that, "unless we improve considerably, we'll lose the series in four games." After dropping three straight, the Canadiens did manage to win one game, but they lost to Toronto in five. Johnny Bower posted a pair of shutouts, and the Leafs allowed just six goals in the series.

Detroit upset Chicago in the other semifinal and faced Toronto for the Stanley Cup. The Red Wings held a slight advantage of 7-6-1 in their 14 meetings during the regular season, but Toronto was the better team in the final. The games were all close, but the Maple Leafs took the series in five games.

Double Your Pleasure

Five different Maple Leafs enjoyed two-goal games in Toronto's four victories over Detroit. Bob Nevin and Dick Duff both scored two in the 4–2 victory in Game 1. Ron Stewart scored twice in the 4–2 win in Game 2, and Red Kelly had a pair of goals in the 4–2 win in Game 4. Dave Keon scored two in the 3–1 victory that wrapped up the series in Game 5. Duff's goals in Game 1 came at 0:49 and 1:08 of the first period, making them the two fastest goals from the start of a game in NHL playoff history.

LONGEST CAREERS WITHOUT CUPS

SEASONS	GAMES*	NAME	FINALS APPEARANCES
22	1,484	Doug Mohns	1957 and 1958 (Boston), 1965 (Chicago)
22	1,432	Dean Prentice	1966 (Detroit)
21	1,590	Phil Housley	1998 (Washington)
21	1,567	Scott Mellanby	1987 (Philadelphia), 1996 (Florida)
21	1,486	Luke Richardson	none
21	1,449	Harry Howell	none°
20	1,517	Jeremy Roenick	1992 (Chicago)
20	1,516	Norm Ullman	1963, 1964 and 1966 Detroit)
20	1,454	Teppo Numminen	none
20	1,315	Bill Gadsby	1963, 1964 and 1966 (Detroit)
19	1,593	Dale Hunter	1998 (Washington)
19	1,544	Mike Gartner	none
19	1,506	Trevor Linden	Vancouver (1994)
19	1,500	Adam Oates	Washington (1998), Anaheim (2003)
19	1,490	Roman Hamrlik	none

*Regular season and playoffs combined
°Won as a scout with Edmonton in 1990

Shorthanded Goals

Dave Keon's two goals in Game 5 were both scored while the Leafs were killing a penalty, making Keon the first player in NHL history to score two shorthanded goals in one playoff game. Since then, 10 other players have matched this feat (including Wayne Gretzky, twice), although no one but Keon has ever managed it during the Stanley Cup finals. Keon's second was a 180-footer into an open net that made it 3–1 for the Leafs, clinching the Stanley Cup for Toronto.

Red Wings Rebound

Detroit had missed the playoffs in 1961–62, which led to the resignation of Jack Adams after 35 years with the club. Sid Abel added Adams' GM job to his coaching portfolio for the 1962–63 season, and it was his former Production Line-mate Gordie Howe who led Detroit back into the playoffs. Howe led the NHL with 38 goals and 86 points, earning not only the Art Ross Trophy as scoring champion but the Hart Trophy as NHL MVP. (It was the sixth, and final, time he'd receive these honors, which was a record in his day.) Still, Chicago was favored to defeat Detroit in the playoffs, but after the Black Hawks opened the series with two wins the Red Wings took the next four in a row.

SEMIFINALS
4 games to 2 over New York Rangers

FINAL 4 GAMES TO 2

APR. 10 ►	Chicago 1 at Toronto 4
APR. 12 ►	Chicago 2 at Toronto 3
APR. 15 ►	Toronto 0 at Chicago 3
APR. 17 ►	Toronto 1 at Chicago 4
APR. 19 ►	Chicago 4 at Toronto 8
APR. 22 ►	Toronto 2 at Chicago 1

PLAYOFF SCORING LEADER

	GP	G	A	PTS
Stan Mikita CHICAGO	12	6	15	21

FINAL SERIES SCORING

TORONTO	GP	G	A	PTS	PIM
Frank Mahovlich	6	4	3	7	21
George Armstrong	6	3	4	7	0
Tim Horton	6	1	6	7	12
Dick Duff	6	1	4	5	16
Ron Stewart	6	0	5	5	2
Bob Pulford	6	3	0	3	14
Billy Harris	6	2	1	3	0
Dave Keon	6	2	1	3	0
Red Kelly	6	1	2	3	0
Bob Baun	6	0	3	3	15
Bob Nevin	6	1	1	2	4
Carl Brewer	6	0	1	1	18
Bert Olmstead	4	0	1	1	0
Allan Stanley	6	0	1	1	2
Al Arbour	2	0	0	0	0
Ed Litzenberger	4	0	0	0	2
Eddie Shack	5	0	0	0	12

GOALTENDERS	GP	W	L	MIN	GA	SO	AVG
Johnny Bower	4	2	1	195	7	0	2.15
Don Simmons	3	2	1	165	8	0	2.91

CHICAGO	GP	G	A	PTS	PIM
Bobby Hull	6	4	4	8	6
Stan Mikita	6	3	5	8	15
Ab McDonald	6	3	2	5	0
Bill Hay	6	0	4	4	4
Eric Nesterenko	6	0	4	4	14
Pierre Pilote	6	0	4	4	6
Reggie Fleming	6	2	0	2	18
Murray Balfour	6	1	1	2	11
Bronco Horvath	6	1	1	2	2
Bob Turner	6	1	0	1	0
Dollard St. Laurent	6	0	1	1	8
Kenny Wharram	6	0	1	1	4
Jack Evans	6	0	0	0	12
Merv Kuryluk	2	0	0	0	0
Gerry Melnyk	5	0	0	0	2
Moose Vasko	6	0	0	0	0

GOALTENDER	GP	W	L	MIN	GA	SO	AVG
Glenn Hall	6	2	4	360	18	1	3.00

Deal Was No Dog

A shoulder injury kept Bert Olmstead out for the latter part of the regular season and the first round of the playoffs, but his intensity and team-first attitude during his four seasons in Toronto are always credited as a big part of Toronto's Stanley Cup championship in 1962. Olmstead was acquired from Montreal for the waiver price of $15,000 in the summer of 1958, but it cost Toronto a little bit extra too. "When we tried to deal for Olmstead," Stafford Smythe recalled after the 1962 victory, "Frank Selke said he'd make the deal only if I bought his boxer puppy from him. So, to get Olmstead I had to take the dog too." Smythe kept the dog and named him Duke. "It's been a good deal all around," he said.

Toronto Takes It

Heading into the 1961–62 season, three of the NHL's six teams felt they had a legitimate shot at the Stanley Cup. With young stars Bobby Hull and Stan Mikita leading the offense in front of defenseman Pierre Pilote and goalie Glenn Hall, the defending-champion Chicago Black Hawks were a solid contender. Hull became just the third player in NHL history (along with Maurice Richard and Bernie Geoffrion) to score 50 goals—which was 17 better than anyone else that season—but the Black Hawks finished third in the standings with 75 points.

The Montreal Canadiens run of five straight Stanley Cup championships had ended the previous spring when Chicago eliminated them in the semifinals, but the Canadiens stuck with their veteran lineup. The only major change saw them trade Doug Harvey to the Rangers, where the star defenseman would become a playing coach. Jacques Plante's brilliant play in goal earned him both the Vezina and Hart Trophies as he led Montreal to first place with 98 points on a record of 42-14-14.

Toronto's strong 1960–61 season had ended with a shocking playoff loss to Detroit, but Punch Imlach believed he had the team to beat in 1961–62. Injuries to several key players, including Red Kelly and Johnny Bower, kept the Maple Leafs well back of the Canadiens, but Frank Mahovlich, Dave Keon and George Armstrong all had big years, and Toronto finished comfortably in second place with 85 points.

The New York Rangers had finished fourth to make the playoffs for the first time since 1958, but Toronto was expected to make easy work of them in the semifinals. The Maple Leafs opened the series with two wins at home, but the Rangers bounced back with two wins in New York before Toronto took the lead again with a Red Kelly goal for a 3–2 win in double overtime in Game 5. Game 6 was also in Toronto, where the Rangers had not won in 16 games, dating back to 1960. The Leafs romped to a 7–1 victory and advanced to the final.

Chicago had lost their first two games to Montreal in their semifinal, but they won the next four in a row and would take on Toronto for the Stanley Cup. An injury to Johnny Bower early in Game 4 forced the Leafs to switch to Don Simmons in goal, and he led Toronto to victory in six.

Rare Doubles
PLAYERS WITH BACK-TO-BACK CUP WINS WITH TWO DIFFERENT TEAMS

PLAYER	TEAM 1	TEAM 2
Jack Marshall	Winnipeg Victorias, 1901	Montreal AAA, 1902
Alf Smith	Ottawa Silver Seven, 1906*	Kenora Thistles, 1907*
Harry Westwick	Ottawa Silver Seven, 1906*	Kenora Thistles, 1907*
Tom Hooper	Kenora Thistles, 1907*	Montreal Wanderers, 1908
Art Ross	Kenora Thistles, 1907*	Montreal Wanderers, 1908
Bruce Stuart	Montreal Wanderers, 1908	Ottawa Senators, 1909
Harry Holmes	Seattle Metropolitans, 1917	Toronto Arenas, 1918
Eddie Gerard	Ottawa Senators, 1921	Toronto St. Pats, 1922
Eddie Gerard	Toronto St. Pats, 1922	Ottawa Senators, 1923
Lionel Conacher	Chicago Black Hawks, 1934	Montreal Maroons, 1935
Ab McDonald	Montreal Canadiens, 1960	Chicago Black Hawks, 1961
Al Arbour	Chicago Black Hawks, 1961	Toronto Maple Leafs, 1962
Ed Litzenberger	Chicago Black Hawks, 1961	Toronto Maple Leafs, 1962
Claude Lemieux	New Jersey Devils, 1995	Colorado Avalanche, 1996

*Challenge-Era team won the Stanley Cup, but did not finish season as Stanley Cup champion.

Ed Litzenberger

Toronto Maple Leafs

11 Years Later

Toronto's Stanley Cup win in 1962 was their first in 11 years, dating back to 1951, when Bill Barilko had scored the winning goal before disappearing on a fishing trip later that summer. On June 6, 1962, the wreckage of the plane Barilko had crashed in was finally found in a heavily forested area north of Cochrane, Ontario.

Simmons Steps In

Don Simmons was so unhappy when the Boston Bruins sent him to the minors in November 1960, he decided to quit rather than report to Providence. He eventually changed his mind, but he later refused to report to Rochester when Toronto acquired him in January 1961.

Punch Imlach convinced Simmons to attend training camp with the Maple Leafs in the fall of 1961. He even convinced him to play the 1961–62 season in Rochester. Simmons made a few appearances in Toronto when Johnny Bower was hurt, and he was with the Maple Leafs for the playoffs. He got his chance in the Stanley Cup final when Bower pulled a leg muscle late in the first period of Game 4. Unfortunately, Simmons let in the first Chicago shot he faced in a 4–1 Black Hawks victory. He was shaky again in an 8–4 Toronto win in Game 5.

The Leafs played much better in a tense sixth game. Bobby Hull broke a scoreless tie at 8:56 of the third period, but the Leafs were able to regroup during a 10-minute delay to clear the Chicago Stadium ice of debris. Goals from Bob Nevin at 10:29 and Dick Duff at 14:14 gave Simmons and Toronto a 2–1 victory.

Punch Imlach and the Leafs

The beginning of the Toronto Maple Leafs' Stanley Cup dynasty of the 1960s can be traced to July 10, 1958. On that Thursday evening, the long-rumored appointment of George "Punch" Imlach to the position of assistant general manager was announced.

Imlach demanded loyalty, though he had a strange way of showing it himself.

Imlach had been a pretty good hockey player growing up in Toronto, but he had made his reputation with the Quebec Aces of the Quebec Senior Hockey League, where he served as a player, coach, general manager and part owner from 1945 through 1956. He returned to his hometown in 1958 with a two-year contract to commence on August 1st. At the time, Francis "King" Clancy was already the team's assistant general manager, but Clancy was to focus on public relations while Imlach was put in charge of rebuilding the farm system.

The Maple Leafs had two assistant GMs on their payroll, but as the *Toronto Star* seemed to delight in pointing out, they didn't actually have a general manager. Instead, a committee of seven men headed up by chairman Stafford Smythe, the son of team owner Conn Smythe, had run the team for the past year. The results had been a last-place finish in 1957–58 and a second straight season out of the playoffs. Imlach wasn't worried.

"I came here with my eyes wide open," he told the *Star*'s Red Burnett in mid-August. "This is going to be a tough uphill struggle, but we'll make it. I wouldn't be at this desk if I wasn't positive of this fact. We'll grab any players we think will help the big team or the minor pro clubs."

Very soon Imlach would be given much more say on how to improve the big team. With the Leafs still in last place five weeks into the 1958–59 season, Stafford Smythe and his committee decided to put Imlach in charge. A week after taking over as general manager on November 21, 1958, the team had a record of 5-12-3 and Imlach fired coach Billy Reay. He named himself the new coach and named Bert Olmstead as a player-coach. Olmstead was responsible for running practices and maintaining discipline in the dressing room, while Imlach ran the team during games.

Despite the Leafs' struggles, Imlach had handed himself a pretty good team. George Armstrong and Tim Horton were already on board, and the farm system had recently produced Frank Mahovlich, Bob Pulford, Dick Duff, Billy Harris, Carl Brewer and Bob Baun. (Dave Keon would arrive for the 1960–61 season.) Olmstead, Allan Stanley and Johnny Bower (whom Imlach had signed to a Leafs contract shortly after commencing his job in August) had all been acquired by Stafford Smythe's committee, and would play a big role as Imlach built the team into a Stanley Cup contender.

At first, however, the Leafs continued to struggle. Still seven points out of a playoff spot with just five games to go in the 1958–59 season, the Leafs won all five to overhaul the slumping New York Rangers for fourth place. Once in the playoffs, they upset the Boston Bruins to reach the final, but were no match for the Montreal Canadiens who won the Stanley Cup for the fourth straight year. Montreal would make it five in a row in 1960 by downing Imlach's Leafs in the final once again.

Imlach's masterstroke of the 1959–60 season had been to step in and acquire veteran defenseman Red Kelly when he refused a trade from the Detroit Red Wings to New York. He then converted Kelly to center and put him on a line with Mahovlich. The move revitalized the Leafs' slumping left-winger

TORONTO MAPLE LEAFS

THE PRICE OF SUCCESS IS HARD WORK

and turned him into one of the league's top scorers over the next few seasons—though Mahovlich would never really be comfortable under Imlach's dictatorial style. In truth, Imlach was a stubborn man with a pretty high opinion of his own hockey genius, and his bullying ways were difficult for many of his players to take. Like him or not, Imlach certainly drove the players to succeed. The proof was there in the Stanley Cup victories of 1962, 1963, 1964 and 1967.

Imlach demanded loyalty, and though he had a strange way of showing it himself, he did tend to stick with the core of the club that won for him. George Armstrong, Bob Baun, Johnny Bower, Carl Brewer, Billy Harris, Larry Hillman, Tim Horton, Red Kelly, Dave Keon, Frank Mahovlich, Bob Pulford, Eddie Shack, Don Simmons, Allan Stanley and Ron Stewart were all a part of the team that won three Cups in a row. Of that group of 15, only Brewer, Harris, Simmons and

Punch Imlach in a rare moment of respite after winning the Stanley Cup in 1967.

Stewart were gone from the team when they won the Cup again in 1967.

Hard as it might be for current Maple Leafs fans to believe, four Stanley Cup wins in six seasons made winning seem routine in Toronto. When the Leafs won the Cup in 1962, a crowd of 3,000 people showed up at the airport at 3 a.m. to welcome the team home from Chicago, and more than 100,000 people lined the downtown streets at noon a few days later for a civic reception. The crowd dropped to 60,000 the following year. With rainy weather and the time of the parade changed to late afternoon in 1964, some estimates placed the crowd that year at 30,000, but others pegged it as low as 8,000. The crowd in 1967 was thought to have been between 20,000 and 25,000.

Toronto mayor William Dennison was the fourth different chief magistrate to welcome the team at Toronto City Hall since 1962. "Such receptions have become a tradition," the mayor said, "and we are proud to honor this team."

If the Toronto fans had known how long they'd wait for the chance to honor another Stanley Cup champion, perhaps a few more of them would have shown up!

The Game I'll Never Forget

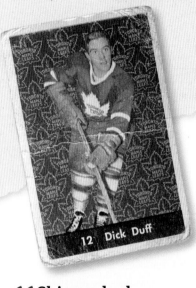

12 Dick Duff

> **Chicago had a reputation as a rough team. They'd slowed Montreal down with heavy checking, and some people figured they'd do the same to us. That was a challenge to our pride.**

Hockey Digest: June 1980
By Dick Duff, as told to George Vass

Different players have different places they remember; places where they have good games on the road. I had some good nights in Detroit when I was playing for the Toronto Maple Leafs and the Montreal Canadiens, but I had some of my best in Chicago.

In the late 1950s and the 1960s the Chicago Stadium was always an exciting place to play. They had some great teams in Chicago those days, with Stan Mikita, Bobby Hull and Glen Hall coming on the scene. We always knew we had our hands full because the Chicago Black Hawks were an explosive team.

Hockey in those days was pretty rough and always very competitive, which added to the excitement. In the six-team NHL we played each other 14 times a season, and feelings built up a little more and carried over more than they do today with the teams playing each other less often.

The Leafs were a team that was coming on in the late 1950s and early 1960s, after Punch Imlach took over in 1958–59. Detroit and Montreal had had things pretty much their own way in Stanley Cup play during the 1950s, but there was a feeling things were changing in the '60s, a feeling that Toronto and Chicago were improving.

The Toronto team Imlach took over in 1958–59 was mostly young guys—Bob Pulford, George Armstrong, myself—then he got Bert Olmstead from the Canadiens. He got Allan Stanley, Johnny Bower, a few young guys to work in with the veterans, and we just kind of picked it up.

We felt that we were one of the good teams. Even when we lost in the 1960–61 semifinals we knew we had the right blend to do it.

In 1961–62 we finished second to the Canadiens in the regular season, for the second season in a row, but went into the playoffs feeling good about our chances. We put the New York Rangers out in the semifinals while Chicago was beating Montreal.

Chicago had won the Cup in '61, and I guess you'd have to say that being the defending Stanley Cup champions gave them an advantage in the final: if you've won before, it's the edge you have knowing you can do it.

We weren't quite healthy going into the 1962 Stanley Cup final against the Hawks. Olmstead had been out with a broken shoulder for more than a month. I'd been hurt, too, and had missed 19 games, but I was coming around.

Chicago had a reputation as a rough team. They'd slowed Montreal down with heavy checking, and some people figured they'd do the same to us. That was a challenge to our pride. We won the first two games in Toronto, and it cost us. Pulford tore the ligaments in his shoulder the first game of the series and had to play hurting.

Chicago won Games 3 and 4 on home ice, and what's more, our goalie, Bower, was hurt in the fourth game and had to be replaced by Don Simmons, who hadn't played in more than two months.

Fortunately, when the series went back to Toronto for the fifth game, we got a break right at the beginning. Pulford scored a goal just 17 seconds into the game, and that took the wind out of Chicago's sails. We went on from there to win 8–4, and Pully, bad shoulder and all, had a hat trick.

Our win didn't convince many people that we were the real deal because it had been in our own rink. Sure we had a 3–2 edge in the series, but people were saying, "wait until they go back to Chicago for the sixth game."

That's the game I'll never forget: Game 6, Chicago Stadium, April 22, 1962.

It was one of the most exciting, emotional and best-played games I was ever involved in. The Chicago crowd at that time was unbelievable, the noise they made. It seemed like everybody brought something special to throw on the ice. Anytime a Chicago player made a solid body check or scored a goal the crowd noise was deafening and seemed like it would never end.

Chicago wanted to carry the series back to Toronto, and we wanted to end it right there and win the Cup.

Dick Duff chases a rebound in mid-1960s action.

It was a tough, well-skated, hard-hitting game. Nobody was giving anything away. And Simmons, as rusty as he'd been going into the series, played great goal, matching Hall save for save.

It wasn't until the midway point of the third period that a goal was scored, and it was my man to cover, Bobby Hull, who got it when he capitalized on my mistake. I had gone back in our zone to take the puck from Simmons. I misplayed it, and it went in front of the net. Hull drove it in to make it 1–0.

The crowd went mad. They threw so much stuff on the ice that it took about 15 minutes to clean it up. Sometimes the home crowd excitement of the game works to the advantage of the other team. The delay gave us a chance to recuperate —to rally—and get our composure.

Just a few seconds after the puck was finally dropped again, Bobby Nevin scored to tie the game up 1–1.

It went back and fourth for another three or four minutes until Eric Nesterenko of Chicago drew a holding penalty.

The powerplay started, and Dave Keon won a faceoff and sent the puck back to defenseman Tim Horton. Horton gave it to Armstrong, who gave it back to him in our zone. Horton gave it a rush and saw me breaking for the net. I must have been about 20 feet from the goal. The pass was slightly behind me, but I swung around and put a shot on the net. It went in past Hall to give us the 2–1 lead. I remember looking up at the clock, and I'm pretty sure it said 14:14 when the winning goal was scored.

That was the first time I'd played on a Stanley Cup winner—Toronto hadn't won it for 11 years—and I'd scored the winning goal. There are some other great games I remember, but that one really stands out.

Toronto 2, Chicago 1

FIRST PERIOD

NO SCORING

PENALTIES: Evans, Chicago (holding), 2:57; Hull, Chicago (boarding), 6:08; Pulford, Toronto (high-sticking), 12:09

SECOND PERIOD

NO SCORING

PENALTIES: Fleming, Chicago (tripping), 5:19; Nesterenko, Chicago (high-sticking), 7:42; Baun, Toronto (holding), 11:46; St. Laurent, Chicago (holding), 18:07

THIRD PERIOD

1 ▶ Hull (Balfour, Hay), Chicago, 8:56

2 ▶ Nevin (Baun, Mahovlich), Toronto, 10:29

3 ▶ Duff (Horton, Armstrong), Toronto, 14:14 (PP)

PENALTIES: Horton, Toronto (tripping), 4:30; Nesterenko, Chicago (hooking), 13:27; Horton, Toronto (tripping), 19:02

SHOTS ON GOAL

	1	2	3	TOTAL
Toronto	4	8	8	20
Chicago	13	14	8	35

GOALIES: Simmons, Toronto; Hall, Chicago

REFEREE: Frank Udvari

LINESMEN: Neil Armstrong, Matt Pavelich

SEMIFINALS
4 games to 2 over Montreal

Pierre Pilote, Bobby Hull and Glenn Hall in action versus the Toronto Maple Leafs.

ROSTER

Al Arbour	Wayne Hicks	Eric Nesterenko
Earl Balfour	Wayne Hillman	Pierre Pilote
Murray Balfour	Bobby Hull	Tod Sloan
Denis DeJordy	Ed Litzenberger (captain)	Dollard St. Laurent
Roy Edwards		Moose Vasko
Jack Evans	Chico Maki	Kenny Wharram
Reggie Fleming	Ab McDonald	Tommy Ivan (general manager)
Glenn Hall	Stan Mikita	
Bill Hay	Ron Murphy	Rudy Pilous (coach)

Blast from the Past

Coach Bill Stewart and players Mike Karakas, Johnny Gottselig, Mush March and Carl Voss from Chicago's 1938 Stanley Cup–champion team were all on hand for the final game in 1961. So was Alfie Moore, who'd been the surprise star in Game 1 of the 1938 final after filling in for Karakas in goal.

FINAL　4 GAMES TO 2

APR. 6	▶	Detroit 2 at Chicago 3
APR. 8	▶	Chicago 1 at Detroit 3
APR. 10	▶	Detroit 1 at Chicago 3
APR. 12	▶	Chicago 1 at Detroit 2
APR. 14	▶	Detroit 3 at Chicago 6
APR. 16	▶	Chicago 5 at Detroit 1

PLAYOFF SCORING LEADERS

	GP	G	A	PTS
Gordie Howe DETROIT	11	4	11	15
Pierre Pilote CHICAGO	12	3	12	15

FINAL SERIES SCORING

CHICAGO	GP	G	A	PTS	PIM
Pierre Pilote	6	2	6	8	2
Stan Mikita	6	3	4	7	2
Bobby Hull	6	2	5	7	2
Murray Balfour	5	3	3	6	4
Bill Hay	6	1	3	4	8
Ron Murphy	6	2	1	3	0
Kenny Wharram	6	2	1	3	10
Ab McDonald	6	1	1	2	0
Eric Nesterenko	6	1	1	2	2
Jack Evans	6	1	0	1	10
Reggie Fleming	6	1	0	1	2
Ed Litzenberger	4	0	1	1	0
Tod Sloan	6	0	1	1	6
Dollard St. Laurent	5	0	1	1	2
Moose Vasko	6	0	1	1	6
Al Arbour	3	0	0	0	2
Earl Balfour	6	0	0	0	0
Wayne Hicks	1	0	0	0	2
Wayne Hillman	1	0	0	0	0
Chico Maki	1	0	0	0	0
GOALTENDER	GP	W	L	MIN	GA	SO	AVG
Glenn Hall	6	4	2	360	12	0	2.00

DETROIT	GP	G	A	PTS	PIM
Gordie Howe	6	1	7	8	8
Alex Delvecchio	6	3	3	6	0
Al Johnson	6	1	2	3	0
Bruce MacGregor	6	1	2	3	6
Vic Stasiuk	6	1	2	3	4
Howie Young	6	1	1	2	18
Val Fonteyne	6	0	2	2	0
Norm Ullman	5	0	2	2	2
Howie Glover	6	1	0	1	0
Leo Labine	6	1	0	1	0
Len Lunde	5	1	0	1	0
Parker MacDonald	6	1	0	1	0
Warren Godfrey	6	0	1	1	10
Marcel Pronovost	4	0	1	1	0
Pete Goegan	6	0	0	0	14
Gerry Melnyk	6	0	0	0	0
Gerry Odrowski	6	0	0	0	4
GOALTENDERS	GP	W	L	MIN	GA	SO	AVG
Hank Bassen	4	1	2	220	9	0	2.45
Terry Sawchuk	3	1	2	140	10	0	4.29

Rebuilding the Black Hawks

Entering the 1960–61 season, the Chicago Black Hawks had not won the Stanley Cup in 23 years, marking the longest drought among the NHL's six franchises (at that time). With offensive stars such as Max and Doug Bentley, Bill Mosienko and Roy Conacher, the Black Hawks had at least managed to keep the crowds coming to Chicago Stadium during the 1940s, but by the 1953–54 season, attendance of only about 4,000 fans was not uncommon. Over the next couple of seasons, several Chicago home games were moved to Indianapolis, Omaha, St. Louis and St. Paul. Other teams began feeding players and prospects to the Black Hawks to keep the club alive.

In 1954, Tommy Ivan was hired as Chicago's new general manager. Ivan had recorded six first-place finishes and won the Stanley Cup three times in his seven seasons as coach of the Red Wings. He would rebuild the Black Hawks. A key move came in the summer of 1955, when Ivan convinced owners Arthur Wirtz and Jim Norris to purchase the Buffalo Bisons of the American Hockey League. With the Bisons, and the junior team they sponsored in St. Catharines, Ontario, the Black Hawks finally began to develop the farm system they had always lacked. Over the next few years, Bobby Hull, Stan Mikita, Ken Wharram, Pierre Pilote and Moose Vasko would all arrive in Chicago via St. Catharines and/or Buffalo. Hull would become the NHL's biggest star, but the others all had a part to play in the rebirth of the Black Hawks in the 1960s.

Still, the big story of the 1960–61 regular season took place in Toronto and Montreal, where the Maple Leafs and Canadiens battled for first place as Frank Mahovlich and Bernie Geoffrion raced to equal the recently retired Maurice Richard as hockey's next 50-goal-scorer. In the end, Geoffrion scored 50 to Mahovlich's 48, and Montreal edged out Toronto with 92 points to the Maple Leafs' 90. In the playoffs, however, fourth-place Detroit stunned Toronto in five games. Chicago upset Montreal in six and ended the Canadiens' run of Stanley Cup championships after five in a row.

In the first All-American Stanley Cup final since the Red Wings beat the Rangers in 1950, Chicago beat Detroit in six games. Glenn Hall had been solid in goal throughout the playoffs, while defenseman Pierre Pilote led the offense with Hull and Mikita.

The Semifinals

The Canadiens scored easy wins of 6–2 and 5–2 in Games 1 and 4 of their semifinal against Chicago. The Black Hawks squeaked out a 4–3 win in Game 2 and a 2–1 win in Game 3, when Earl Balfour scored with Dickie Moore in the penalty box at 12:12 of double overtime. Glenn Hall was the hero of Games 5 and 6, recording back-to-back shutouts as Chicago scored a pair of 3–0 victories.

The Final Detroit's Terry Sawchuk suffered a shoulder injury in Game 1 that would limit his action throughout the final. Bobby Hull scored twice in the game to give Chicago a 3–2 victory. The Red Wings kept the scores close in the first four games, but the Black Hawks offense broke open Game 5. Stan Mikita had two goals and an assist in the third period to lead Chicago to a 6–3 victory. The Red Wings went with Hank Bassen in goal in Game 6 and led 1–0 after one period. Reg Fleming tied the game for Chicago at 6:25 of the second period, and it was all Black Hawks from there, as they rolled to a 5–1 victory.

Are You Experienced?

It was a mild scene in the dressing room following Chicago's Stanley Cup win. The Black Hawks celebrated with only a few sips of beer. "There's no champagne," said owner Jim Norris. "I didn't order any. I was afraid of jinxing the boys."

Stranded in Detroit by a snowstorm on the Sunday night of their victory, the party got started when the Black Hawks returned to Chicago on Monday morning. A police and fire department escort led the team from the airport to city hall. Later that night, the champagne flowed freely at a party held in the lobby of a theater owned by Arthur Wirtz. When Norris was pouring champagne into the Stanley Cup, Ab McDonald, who'd won it three years in a row with Montreal, nudged him aside. "Let me do that boss, I've had more experience."

Stealing Stanley

When the Black Hawks faced the Canadiens in the semifinals again in 1962, the defending Stanley Cup champs had the Cup on display in the Chicago Stadium. During Game 3, Kenneth Kilander, a 25-year-old piano player from Montreal, stole the prized trophy. When caught by an usher and a policeman, he offered them $250 to let him take the trophy. He later told Lieutenant John L. Sullivan, head of the Stadium police detail, a couple of different stories. One was that, with the Canadiens losing, he thought the only way to get the Cup back to Montreal was if he took it. The other was that he'd been promised $400, a photograph and an interview if he delivered the Cup to a Montreal sportswriter. Kilander spent the night in jail, but the Black Hawks didn't press charges. He was still fined $10 plus court costs for disorderly conduct.

The Stanley Cup and other NHL trophies were stolen from the old Hockey Hall of Fame building on Toronto's lakefront on a couple of occasions. On April 9, 1969, the Calder, Hart and Conn Smythe Trophies were all stolen but recovered two days later after an anonymous tip to police. On December 4, 1970, the Stanley Cup, the Conn Smythe Trophy and the Masterton Trophy were stolen. At 4 a.m. on the morning of December 23rd, Police Sergeant Wally Harkness was awakened by his barking dog and found the trophies in the snow on his driveway. In January 1970, the original collar from the Stanley Cup (which had been replaced in 1963) was stolen. It wasn't recovered until September 1977, when police found it at a local dry cleaners.

The Game I'll Never Forget

STAN MIKITA
FORWARD
BLACK HAWKS
21

> **"It's hard to imagine a bunch of grown men acting like kids, but we couldn't have been happier."**

Hockey Digest: June 1973
By Stan Mikita, as told to George Vass

This is my 14th season with the Chicago Black Hawks, and you can bet there have been a lot of big moments in that time.

One of the most memorable days I recall was in 1967, when we clinched the Prince of Wales Trophy for the first time in the history of the team. We really went crazy over that one in the locker room, and though we've finished first four times since, there was never a party like that. It had taken 40 years to set up. Usually a division title isn't as big a cause for celebration as, say, winning the Stanley Cup, but all of our efforts that year had been aimed at finishing first, partly to wipe out the memory of the years in which we had just missed making it. No Hawk team had ever done it before, from the time the club started in 1926.

I've seen films of the celebration in the dressing room, and it was a wilder scene than I even remember: champagne bubbling down throats, over shirts and hair and spraying in all directions. It's hard to imagine a bunch of grown men acting like kids, but we couldn't have been happier.

Unfortunately, we didn't go on to win the Stanley Cup that year. We got knocked out of contention in the first round by Toronto, which went on to win the Cup in 1967.

We've won the Cup only once since I've been with the Hawks, in 1961, which brings me to the game I'll never forget. That was the third game of the first round against the Montreal Canadiens on March 26, 1961, in Chicago Stadium.

The Canadiens won the first game of the series 6–5, and we came back in the second game to win 4–3, with Eddie Litzenberger getting the deciding goal. That gave us a split of the first two games, both at Montreal, and our chances looked pretty good going into the third one, at Chicago.

It was a close-checking game, although there were enough chances on both sides to score in the first two periods. We had a 1–0 lead going into the last minute of play, but you knew that anything could happen with Montreal having the big bombers like Boom Boom Geoffrion, Dickie Moore and Jean Béliveau.

I don't remember what started it

now, but with about a minute or so to go in the game, I got into a fight with Bill Hicke. Both of us went to the penalty box, each getting two minutes for roughing.

We hadn't even sat down when Hicke said something uncomplimentary to me, and I answered him back. We started swinging, and it took a couple of minutes before the linesmen could separate us. And this was in the penalty box!

Referee Dalt McArthur gave us each five minutes more plus 10-minute misconducts. That was a total of 17 minutes in penalties with only a minute to go in the game. McArthur said, "You guys might as well go down to the dressing room. You won't be playing any more tonight."

I figured we had the game down. I went downstairs to the dressing room and started to change. Suddenly there was this tremendous shout, although I didn't know what it was about until my teammates came into the room a couple of minutes later.

With half a minute left, Henri Richard had scored the tying goal for the Canadiens, and we were going into a 20-minute sudden-death overtime.

"Kid, you'd better get dressed," Rudy Pilous, our coach, told me. "We might need you."

I put on a clean uniform and took a seat in the penalty box when the

March 26, 1961
Game 3, Stanley Cup semifinal · Chicago Stadium, Chicago

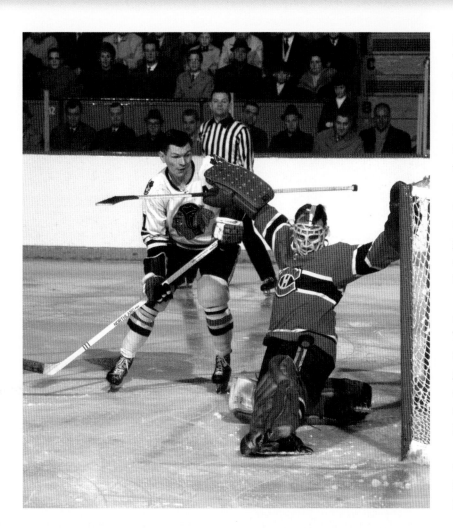

Stan Mikita looking for a loose rebound versus the Montreal Canadiens.

overtime period started. I didn't think I'd play, since I still had almost 16 minutes in penalties left. I figured a goal would come before that.

But when my penalty time elapsed we were still tied 1–1, although each team had hit a few posts. The second overtime finished the same as the first, no score, and Dickie Moore twice hit the post with shots.

Finally, in the third overtime we got a break. McArthur called a penalty on Montreal, giving us our best chance to win it.

I was playing right point on the power play, but somehow I ended up on the left side when the puck came out to me. I wound up for the slap shot but half-fanned on it in my eagerness. I got just enough of the puck to get it past the first Canadien, who was charging into me, and it reached Murray Balfour, who was standing in front of the net.

Murray wheeled around with a backhand shot and put the puck through Jacques Plante's legs, and we won the game 2–1.

Canadiens coach Toe Blake was so infuriated by McArthur's penalty call that had set up our power-play goal that he took a swing at the referee after the game. That cost him a $2,000 fine.

There were three games left in the series, but that was the "big one." The three overtimes really sapped the Canadiens. They won the next game to tie the series 2–2, but it didn't really matter. We knew we could beat them and we did, Glenn Hall shutting them out twice.

We went on to beat Detroit in six games in the final to take the Stanley Cup for the first time since 1938.

Chicago 2, Montreal 1 3X OT

FIRST PERIOD

NO SCORING

PENALTIES: Langlois, Montreal (high-sticking), 1:26; Balfour, Chicago (charging), 6:44; Richard, Montreal (roughing), 7:18; Fleming, Chicago (roughing), 7:18; Hay, Chicago (high-sticking), 11:04; Gendron, Montreal (high-sticking), 11:04; St. Laurent, Chicago (high-sticking), 18:00; Backstrom, Montreal (high-sticking), 18:00

SECOND PERIOD

1 ▸ Balfour (Hay, Hull), Chicago, 18:33

PENALTIES: Balfour, Chicago (holding), 7:47; St. Laurent, Chicago (tripping), 8:12; Johnson, Montreal (hooking), 12:59; Murphy, Chicago (roughing), 14:07; Provost, Montreal (roughing), 14:07

THIRD PERIOD

2 ▸ Richard (Goyette), Montreal, 19:24

PENALTIES: Mikita, Chicago (fighting, misconduct) 13:09; Hicke, Montreal (fighting, spearing, misconduct), 13:09; Hay, Chicago (tripping), 18:40

FIRST OT PERIOD

NO SCORING · NO PENALTIES

SECOND OT PERIOD

NO SCORING

PENALTIES: Talbot, Montreal (tripping), 4:20; St. Laurent, Chicago (tripping), 10:21; Langlois, Montreal (hooking) 14:18

THIRD OT PERIOD

3 ▸ Balfour (Pilote, Mikita), Chicago, 12:12 PP

PENALTIES: Chicago Murphy (tripping), 0:08; Montreal Moore (tripping), 11:44.

SHOTS ON GOAL

	1	2	3	1	2	3	T
Chicago	7	6	7	8	13	4	45
Montreal	13	4	13	8	10	6	54

GOALIES: Hall, Chicago; Plante, Montreal

REFEREE: Dalton McArthur

LINESMEN: George Hayes, Ron Wicks

SEMIFINALS
4 games to 0 over Chicago

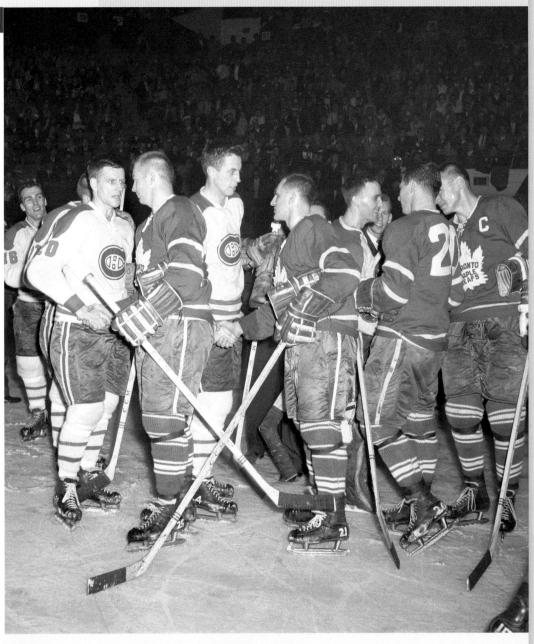

FINAL   4 GAMES TO 0

APR. 7	▶	Toronto 2 at Montreal 4
APR. 9	▶	Toronto 1 at Montreal 2
APR. 12	▶	Montreal 5 at Toronto 2
APR. 14	▶	Montreal 4 at Toronto 0

PLAYOFF SCORING LEADERS

	GP	G	A	PTS
Henri Richard MONTREAL	8	3	9	12
Bernie Geoffrion MONTREAL	8	2	10	12

FINAL SERIES SCORING

MONTREAL	GP	G	A	PTS	PIM
Henri Richard	4	3	5	8	9
Bernie Geoffrion	4	0	6	6	0
Dickie Moore	4	2	3	5	2
Jean Béliveau	4	4	0	4	4
Maurice Richard	4	1	2	3	2
Phil Goyette	4	2	0	2	2
Doug Harvey	4	2	0	2	6
Marcel Bonin	4	0	2	2	6
Albert Langlois	4	0	2	2	12
Don Marshall	4	1	0	1	0
Bill Hicke	4	0	1	1	0
André Pronovost	4	0	1	1	0
Claude Provost	4	0	1	1	0
Jean-Guy Talbot	4	0	1	1	4
Ralph Backstrom	4	0	0	0	2
Tom Johnson	4	0	0	0	2
Bob Turner	4	0	0	0	0

GOALTENDER	GP	W	L	MIN	GA	SO	AVG
Jacques Plante	4	4	0	240	5	1	1.25

TORONTO	GP	G	A	PTS	PIM
Bert Olmstead	4	2	0	2	0
Larry Regan	4	1	1	2	0
George Armstrong	4	0	2	2	2
Red Kelly	4	0	2	2	2
Bob Baun	4	1	0	1	17
Johnny Wilson	4	1	0	1	2
Carl Brewer	4	0	1	1	6
Dick Duff	4	0	1	1	2
Garry Edmundson	4	0	1	1	2
Billy Harris	3	0	1	1	0
Tim Horton	4	0	1	1	0
Gerry Ehman	3	0	0	0	2
Gerry James	4	0	0	0	0
Frank Mahovlich	4	0	0	0	0
Bob Pulford	4	0	0	0	8
Allan Stanley	4	0	0	0	0
Ron Stewart	4	0	0	0	0

GOALTENDER	GP	W	L	MIN	GA	SO	AVG
Johnny Bower	4	0	4	240	15	0	3.75

Toe Likes the Odds

"I like odd numbers. And after six comes seven."
— Coach Toe Blake, when asked how long the Canadiens could keep on winning the Stanley Cup.

Four's a Bore

"Well, when you win [the game] 4–0 and win in four games and after four Cup titles, you don't get too excited." — Doug Harvey, commenting on the quiet celebration in the Canadiens' dressing room.

Five in a Row

The Montreal Canadiens of 1959–60 reached the Stanley Cup final for the 10th straight season and won the title for the fifth year in a row. Henri Richard (who would go on to win the Cup six more times) spent his first five NHL seasons with the great Montreal dynasty and had high praise for the team that capped the streak. "That 1960 team was the best I ever played on," he said.

In truth, the Canadiens of 1959–60 had changed very little from the season before. They led the NHL in most goals for and fewest goals against for the fifth season in a row and cruised to first place with 92 points on a record of 41-19-10. Jean Béliveau, Bernie Geoffrion and Henri Richard all reached the 30-goal plateau (three of only six players in the league to do so), while Doug Harvey won the Norris Trophy for the fifth time in six years, and Jacques Plante won the Vezina Trophy for the fifth season in a row. Plante, who had been wearing a mask in practice for years, finally wore it in a game after suffering a bad cut to his face on an Andy Bathgate shot in a game against the Rangers on November 1, 1959. Though Frank Selke and Toe Blake were against him wearing it, Plante's stellar play throughout the season finally won them over.

On the eve of the regular season, Toe Blake called the Chicago Black Hawks the team he feared the most. Chicago finished well back of the Canadiens, in third place with 69 points, but Bobby Hull had emerged as the NHL's scoring champion in just his third season. When the two teams met in the semifinals, Hull and Stan Mikita both missed the first game but were back for the rest of the series, which only went four games. Close checking from Claude Provost limited Hull to just one goal in three games, while Plante notched shutouts in the final two as the Canadiens scored a sweep.

An improving Toronto team followed up its surprise appearance in the 1958–59 Stanley Cup final with a second-place finish in 1959–60, and they returned to the finals with a six-game semifinal win over fourth-place Detroit. Once again, though, the Maple Leafs provided little competition for the Canadiens. Montreal downed Toronto in four, equaling Detroit's 1952 accomplishment of winning the Stanley Cup with two sweeps—eight straight games.

MOST CAREER GAMES BY A GOALTENDER IN THE FINALS

41	Jacques Plante, Montreal (38), St. Louis (3)
38	Turk Broda, Toronto
37	Terry Sawchuk, Detroit (33), Toronto (4)
32	Glenn Hall, Detroit (5), Chicago (19), St. Louis (8)
	Ken Dryden, Montreal

MOST CAREER WINS BY A GOALTENDER IN THE FINALS

25	Jacques Plante, Montreal
24	Ken Dryden, Montreal
21	Turk Broda, Toronto
19	Terry Sawchuk, Detroit (17), Toronto (2)
18	Patrick Roy, Montreal (10), Colorado (8)
17	Martin Brodeur, New Jersey
	Billy Smith, New York Islanders

Jacques Plante

Here to Stay

After making 30 saves in a 4–0 shutout that gave Montreal the Stanley Cup, Jacques Plante raised his mask above his head in celebration as the clock wound down and his teammates began to gather around him. Plante had been brilliant throughout the playoffs, allowing only 11 goals for a 1.35 average and posting three shutouts.

"I wasn't in accord with Jacques Plante's experiments with masks," coach Toe Blake said after the game. "I wasn't sure a mask was necessary. [But] Plante's performances in the two playoff series have convinced me. I don't care what kind of a mask he wears in the future. As far as I'm concerned the mask is here to stay."

Near the End At 11:07 of the third period in Game 3, Maurice Richard backhanded a rebound past Toronto's Johnny Bower to put the Canadiens up 5–1 in a game they would win 5–2. His 544 regular-season goals, 82 playoff goals and 34 goals in the Stanley Cup final were all records at the time, but it was obvious that the Rocket was slowing down. Injuries had plagued Richard for years, and his goal in Game 3 was his only one of the playoffs that spring. When he retrieved the puck after setting up his brother, Henri, in the third period of Game 4, it fueled speculation that he was about to retire.

However, when the Canadiens opened training camp in September, the Rocket was there, and he looked good. But on Tuesday, September 13, 1960, he told his wife he was going to quit. Two days later, he announced his retirement.

Behind Hockey's Greatest Dynasty

Maurice "Rocket" Richard was the heart and soul of the Montreal Canadiens—and the idol of Quebec fans—during his 18-year career from 1942 to 1960. In an age when English culture dominated his home province, French Canadians loved that the Rocket never backed down. But his temper sometimes got the better of him.

It's often been said that Canadiens general manager Frank Selke found a replacement for Dick Irvin as coach after the 1954–55 season because of Irvin's inability to control Richard's temper.

On March 13, 1955, Richard punched referee Cliff Thompson during a stick-swinging incident with Hal Laycoe of the Boston Bruins. Richard had hit officials before, so on March 16th, NHL president Clarence Campbell suspended him for the final three games of the regular season and all of the playoffs. The next night, Campbell took his regular seat at the Montreal Forum despite death threats and warnings he should not attend. As the Detroit Red Wings jumped out to an early 4–0 lead over Montreal, the ugly mood inside the arena worsened. A fan threw a punch at Campbell, and when the period ended a smoke bomb went off. As the Forum was cleared and the game was forfeited, the streets outside erupted into a full-fledged riot.

Without Richard the Canadiens fell 6–0 to Detroit two games later on the final night of the season. The Red Wings took first place in the NHL standings, and when the teams met again in the Stanley Cup final, Detroit beat Montreal in seven games.

It's often been said that Canadiens general manager Frank Selke found a replacement for Dick Irvin as coach after the 1954–55 season because of Irvin's inability to control Richard's temper. That may be true, but when the Chicago Black Hawks hired Irvin as their new coach on Monday, May 2, 1955, Selke stated that Black Hawks owner Jim Norris had approached him about Irvin back in February.

"[Canadiens president Donat Raymond] and I decided we would let Dick make up his mind on the Chicago offer," Selke explained. "But he would have been welcome to remain here."

The Black Hawks had offered a lot more money, and Irvin said he looked forward to the challenge of rebuilding the club. Even so, "as late as last Thursday," Selke said, "I thought Dick would be with us again. But then on Friday he let me know he had decided to take the Chicago offer."

In the *Montreal Gazette* on May 3rd, Dink Carroll reported on rumors that Selke himself would soon be joining the Black Hawks as general manager.

Selke stayed in Montreal, and on June 8, 1955, he announced that Toe Blake had been hired as coach. The former Canadiens star had played left wing on the famous Punch Line with Maurice Richard and Elmer Lach in the 1940s before becoming a coach in the Montreal farm system. Blake welcomed 54 players to the Canadiens' training camp on September 21, 1955.

"I'm asking you to give everything you've got in this camp," Blake told the group. "Many of you, of course, can't make the team, but don't get discouraged. The work won't hurt you and you can do yourselves credit."

Among those who did themselves the most credit was Maurice Richard's 19-year-old brother, Henri. The "Pocket Rocket," as the stylish 5-foot-7 playmaker would become known, was spectacular at training camp and earned a spot on the team. So did fellow rookies Claude Provost, Jean-Guy Talbot and Bob Turner. The key battle at training camp was in goal, where Gerry McNeil had come out of retirement. Jacques Plante had

Hart Trophy (Gordie Howe won it three times through the era and Andy Bathgate won it in 1958–59), but the Canadiens dominated the postseason All-Star Teams: Plante, Harvey, Johnson, Béliveau, Moore, the Richard brothers, Geoffrion and Bert Olmstead combined for 15 selections to the First All-Star Team and 10 to the Second All-Star Team.

Even with their galaxy of stars, it was the depth of the Canadiens that was truly impressive. Provost made it to the Hall of Fame mainly as a defensive forward, but he had help in that job from Marshall and Floyd Curry. Ralph Backstrom, Phil Goyette, Albert Langlois, Ab McDonald, Bill Hicke and André Pronovost all arrived from the farm system to play important supporting roles. Marcel Bonin, who joined the team in 1957, was unusual in that he came to the Canadiens after playing with Detroit and Boston.

One of the rare stars to leave Montreal during the years of this great dynasty was Olmstead. The Canadiens gave up on him after their Cup win in 1958, believing the torn ligaments in his right knee would end his career. Olmstead went on to play four more years with the Toronto Maple Leafs and was a key player in their 1962 Stanley Cup victory.

replaced McNeil in 1954–55, but the roaming style of the idiosyncratic young goaltender had not won him many fans. Plante would earn the job once again at training camp, but, like Ken Dryden a generation later, he would often hear the criticism that anyone could play goal on such a strong team. When the Canadiens won the Stanley Cup in 1956, Blake defended his goalie: "Experts tried to run Jacques Plante out of the league, pointed him out as the weak link on our team. Jacques showed them."

Plante, Provost and Henri Richard were among nine future Hall of Famers who played on each of Montreal's five straight Stanley Cup–winning teams from 1955–56 through 1959–60. Maurice Richard, Jean Béliveau, Bernie Geoffrion, Doug Harvey, Tom Johnson and Dickie Moore were the six others. Talbot, Turner and Don Marshall also won the Cup five years in a row, but it's the stars who define the Canadiens of this era.

In this era Béliveau (1955–56) and Moore (1957–58 and 1958–59)

Maurice Richard gets his stick up in a scrum with the Toronto Maple Leafs.

won scoring titles as the Canadiens led the NHL in goals scored in each of their five championship seasons. Plante won the Vezina Trophy five years in a row, while Harvey won the James Norris Memorial Trophy four times and Johnson once (1958–59) as the Canadiens also allowed the fewest goals each season. Surprisingly, only Béliveau, in 1955–56, won the

SEMIFINALS
4 games to 2 over Chicago

FINAL **4 GAMES TO 1**

APR. 9	►	Toronto 3 at Montreal 5
APR. 11	►	Toronto 1 at Montreal 3
APR. 14	►	Montreal 2 at Toronto 3 OT
APR. 16	►	Montreal 3 at Toronto 2
APR. 18	►	Toronto 3 at Montreal 5

PLAYOFF SCORING LEADER

	GP	G	A	PTS
Dickie Moore				
MONTREAL	11	5	12	17

FINAL SERIES SCORING

MONTREAL	GP	G	A	PTS	PIM
Ralph Backstrom	5	3	4	7	8
Bernie Geoffrion	5	3	4	7	6
Henri Richard	5	1	5	6	5
Doug Harvey	5	0	6	6	10
Marcel Bonin	5	3	2	5	2
Dickie Moore	5	2	3	5	8
Claude Provost	5	2	2	4	2
Tom Johnson	5	2	1	3	2
Ab McDonald	5	1	1	2	0
Phil Goyette	5	0	2	2	0
André Pronovost	5	1	0	1	0
Don Marshall	5	0	1	1	0
Jean-Guy Talbot	5	0	1	1	6
Bob Turner	5	0	1	1	8
Bill Hicke	1	0	0	0	0
Albert Langlois	4	0	0	0	2
Maurice Richard	4	0	0	0	2
GOALTENDER	**GP**	**W**	**L**	**MIN**	**GA**	**SO**	**AVG**
Jacques Plante	5	4	1	310	12	0	2.32

TORONTO	GP	G	A	PTS	PIM
Billy Harris	5	3	1	4	14
Frank Mahovlich	5	2	2	4	6
Gerry Ehman	5	0	4	4	4
Dick Duff	5	2	1	3	4
Bert Olmstead	5	2	1	3	6
Ron Stewart	5	2	1	3	2
Bob Pulford	5	1	2	3	4
George Armstrong	5	0	2	2	6
Carl Brewer	5	0	2	2	18
Dave Creighton	5	0	1	1	0
Tim Horton	5	0	1	1	2
Allan Stanley	5	0	1	1	2
Bob Baun	5	0	0	0	11
Barry Cullen	1	0	0	0	0
Brian Cullen	3	0	0	0	0
Noel Price	2	0	0	0	2
Marc Reaume	4	0	0	0	0
Larry Regan	3	0	0	0	0
GOALTENDER	**GP**	**W**	**L**	**MIN**	**GA**	**SO**	**AVG**
Johnny Bower	5	1	4	310	18	0	3.48

Ab McDonald, Ralph Backstrom and Bernie Geoffrion celebrate after Game 4 of the final.

ROSTER

Ralph Backstrom

Jean Béliveau

Marcel Bonin

Ian Cushenan

Bernie Geoffrion

Phil Goyette

Doug Harvey

Bill Hicke

Charlie Hodge

Tom Johnson

Albert Langlois

Don Marshall

Ab McDonald

Dickie Moore

Ken Mosdell

Jacques Plante

André Pronovost

Claude Provost

Henri Richard

Maurice Richard
(captain)

Jean-Guy Talbot

Bob Turner

Frank Selke
(managing director)

Toe Blake (coach)

Coach's Comments

"Let's face it. They're a great team. Every man they send over the boards is an excellent shooter and skater." —Punch Imlach

"I can't say this was the greatest of Montreal teams. Not even the best I've had in the last four years. But they're not just ordinary either." —Toe Blake

Special Teams

Power-play goals were the key to Montreal's success in the playoffs. Nine of their 21 goals against Chicago in the semifinals came with a man advantage. The Canadiens went 5-for-20 on the power play against Toronto in the final (including 2-for-5 in their 5–3 Cup-clinching game) while holding the Maple Leafs to just one goal in 15 power-play chances.

The First to Four

Though a couple of clubs from the early days of the Challenge Era had come close, no team in hockey history had ever completed four straight seasons as Stanley Cup champions. After Montreal won its third in a row, Toe Blake knew the pressure would be on in 1958–59. "It'll be the same trouble," said the Canadiens coach. "We'll be picked to win by so many games and we'll be on the spot again."

On the spot or not, the Canadiens cruised to first place in the regular-season standings for the third straight year. Their 91 points had them well ahead of second-place Boston's 73, and their 258 goals broke the single-season record of 250, which they had set the year before. They also led the league with only 158 goals-against as Jacques Plante earned the Vezina Trophy for the fourth straight season. Dickie Moore led the offense and won his second straight Art Ross Trophy. His 41 goals and 55 assists for 96 points broke the record of 95 set by Gordie Howe in 1952–53. Second place in the scoring race went to Jean Béliveau, who had 45 goals and whose 91 points were both a career high and broke his own record for scoring by a center. Moore and Béliveau were the first teammates to top 40 goals in a season since Cooney Weiland and Dit Clapper had done so with Boston back in 1929–30.

Injuries were the only thing threatening to hold the Canadiens back. Maurice Richard missed 38 games after breaking his ankle in January. Béliveau, Henri Richard, Bernie Geoffrion, Marcel Bonin and Doug Harvey were also among those who missed time. Harvey would relinquish his hold on the Norris Trophy as best defenseman after four straight wins, but it would go to teammate Tom Johnson. Ralph Backstrom won the Calder Trophy as top rookie.

Injuries kept Béliveau out of the final and saw Maurice Richard play only sparingly after missing the semifinals, but Montreal would not be denied. After needing six games to overcome the goaltending of Glenn Hall in the semifinals, the Canadiens faced the Maple Leafs.

A late rally had gotten Toronto into the playoffs, where they upset the Bruins. The Maple Leafs were able to keep the games close against the Canadiens in the final, but they managed only one win, in overtime in Game 3, as Montreal took the series in five.

He Wins, He Scores!

There have been 20 times when a player has won the Stanley Cup in the same season that he led the NHL in scoring:

1925–26	Nels Stewart	Montreal Maroons
1930–31	Howie Morenz	Montreal Canadiens
1932–33	Bill Cook	New York Rangers
1940–41	Bill Cowley	Boston Bruins
1951–52	Gordie Howe	Detroit Red Wings
1953–54	Gordie Howe	Detroit Red Wings
1955–56	Jean Béliveau	Montreal Canadiens
1957–58	Dickie Moore	Montreal Canadiens
1958–59	Dickie Moore	Montreal Canadiens
1969–70	Bobby Orr	Boston Bruins
1971–72	Phil Esposito	Boston Bruins
1975–76	Guy Lafleur	Montreal Canadiens
1976–77	Guy Lafleur	Montreal Canadiens
1977–78	Guy Lafleur	Montreal Canadiens
1983–84	Wayne Gretzky	Edmonton Oilers
1984–85	Wayne Gretzky	Edmonton Oilers
1986–87	Wayne Gretzky	Edmonton Oilers
1991–92	Mario Lemieux	Pittsburgh Penguins
2003–04	Martin St-Louis	Tampa Bay Lightning
2008–09	Evgeni Malkin	Pittsburgh Penguins

Dickie Moore

Close Games

The first four games of the Stanley Cup final were tied either entering or at some point during the third period. Only the fifth game followed a different script, as the Canadiens jumped out to a 3–0 lead after one period and a 5–1 lead through two. The Leafs fired 15 shots at Jacques Plante in the third period and scored twice. With Johnny Bower on the bench for the final 2:33 of the game, the Leafs kept Plante busy — and the Forum crowd nervous — but the Canadiens held on for a 5–3 victory.

Rocket Rubs Off

Marcel Bonin was primarily known as a checker and a defensive forward during his career. He scored only 13 goals in 57 games during the 1958–59 regular season, but he then led all playoff performers with 10 goals in just 11 games. Amazingly, Bonin had never scored a single goal in 25 previous playoff games. The secret this year? Bonin was wearing Maurice Richard's gloves for luck. Bonin scored seven goals against Chicago in the semifinals, and some stories say that when the Rocket returned for the final he donned a new pair of gloves so as not to jinx Bonin.

No Shutouts

There were no shutouts recorded during the 18 playoff games played in 1959. The only other times in NHL history when there were no shutouts in the playoffs were during the first two seasons of 1917–18 and 1918–19.

SEMIFINALS
4 games to 0 over Detroit

ROSTER

Jean Béliveau

Marcel Bonin

Connie Broden

Floyd Curry

Bernie Geoffrion

Phil Goyette

Doug Harvey

Charlie Hodge

Tom Johnson

Albert Langlois

Don Marshall

Ab McDonald

Gerry McNeil

Dickie Moore

Bert Olmstead

Jacques Plante

André Pronovost

Claude Provost

Henri Richard

Maurice Richard (captain)

Dollard St. Laurent

Jean-Guy Talbot

Bob Turner

Frank Selke
(managing director)

Toe Blake (coach)

FINAL 4 GAMES TO 2

APR. 8	▶	Boston 1 at Montreal 2
APR. 10	▶	Boston 5 at Montreal 2
APR. 13	▶	Montreal 3 at Boston 0
APR. 15	▶	Montreal 1 at Boston 3
APR. 17	▶	Boston 2 at Montreal 3 OT
APR. 20	▶	Montreal 5 at Boston 3

PLAYOFF SCORING LEADER

Fleming MacKell	GP	G	A	PTS
BOSTON	12	5	14	19

FINAL SERIES SCORING

MONTREAL	GP	G	A	PTS	PIM
Bernie Geoffrion	6	5	3	8	0
Doug Harvey	6	2	5	7	8
Jean Béliveau	6	2	4	6	8
Dickie Moore	6	1	5	6	2
Maurice Richard	6	4	1	5	8
Henri Richard	6	1	2	3	9
Claude Provost	6	1	0	1	2
Marcel Bonin	5	0	1	1	10
Don Marshall	6	0	1	1	0
Bert Olmstead	5	0	1	1	0
Connie Broden	1	0	0	0	0
Floyd Curry	3	0	0	0	0
Phil Goyette	6	0	0	0	2
Tom Johnson	2	0	0	0	0
Albert Langlois	3	0	0	0	0
Ab McDonald	1	0	0	0	2
André Pronovost	6	0	0	0	10
Dollard St. Laurent	4	0	0	0	8
Jean-Guy Talbot	6	0	0	0	6
Bob Turner	6	0	0	0	2
GOALTENDER	GP	W	L	MIN	GA	SO	AVG
Jacques Plante	6	4	2	366	14	1	2.30

BOSTON	GP	G	A	PTS	PIM
Larry Regan	6	2	4	6	2
Don McKenney	6	4	1	5	0
Fleming MacKell	6	1	4	5	6
Bronco Horvath	6	3	1	4	4
Allan Stanley	6	1	2	3	4
Vic Stasiuk	6	0	3	3	0
Norm Johnson	6	2	0	2	4
Jerry Toppazzini	6	1	1	2	2
Leo Labine	6	0	2	2	8
Doug Mohns	6	0	2	2	8
Leo Boivin	6	0	1	1	9
Buddy Boone	6	0	1	1	4
Fern Flaman	6	0	1	1	4
John Bucyk	6	0	0	0	6
Larry Hillman	5	0	0	0	2
Johnny Peirson	2	0	0	0	0
GOALTENDER	GP	W	L	MIN	GA	SO	AVG
Don Simmons	6	2	4	366	15	0	2.46

Rare Road Win

Montreal's win of the sixth game in Boston marked the first time that the Stanley Cup had been won on the road since 1948. It was just the second time among their nine wins to date that the Canadiens had won the Cup on the road. The previous time had been in 1924, when Montreal beat the Calgary Tigers on neutral ice in Ottawa.

Taking It for the Team

"I have never been knocked on my pants as much as [Fern] Flaman put me there tonight. But we won and that's all that matters." —Maurice Richard after Game 6

Rough Road to Three in a Row

The status of a fledgling NHL players union dominated the off-ice news during the 1957–58 season, but the big news on the ice as the season began was Maurice Richard's pursuit of 500 goals. Richard had been the NHL's regular-season goal-scoring leader since surpassing Nels Stewart with his 325th career goal in 1952. With 493 goals entering 1957–58, the 36-year-old Rocket came out flying. He scored six goals in the Canadiens' first five games and notched No. 500 on October 19, 1957. Richard had 23 points in only 14 games when he suffered a severed Achilles tendon on November 13th. He missed 42 games over the next three months.

With a record of 43-17-10, the Canadiens' 96 points topped the NHL standings by 19 over the second-place New York Rangers, but injuries plagued Montreal throughout the 1957–58 season. Jean Béliveau, Bert Olmstead and Jacques Plante were all hurt, but the most serious incident came when Bernie Geoffrion collapsed with a ruptured bowel at practice on January 28th. It was expected that Geoffrion would need at least four months to recover, but he was back in two.

Around that same time, Dickie Moore suffered what was first thought to be a badly sprained left wrist. It was later diagnosed as a fracture. Moore played the last five weeks of the season wearing a cast, but he never missed a single game and led the NHL with 36 goals and 84 points. Henri Richard topped the league with 52 assists and finished second behind his linemate Moore with 80 points. Despite Plante's injury, he led the NHL with 34 wins, nine shutouts and a 2.11 goals-against average and won the Vezina Trophy for the third straight season. Doug Harvey won the Norris Trophy as best defenseman for the fourth year in a row.

Maurice Richard had returned to action on February 20, 1958. He was in fine form for the playoffs and led all scorers with 11 goals in 10 games. He had seven goals in Montreal's sweep of Detroit in the semifinals and scored in overtime to win Game 5 of the final versus Boston. Richard and Geoffrion scored early in Game 6, and Geoffrion scored again late in the second to put the Canadiens up 4–1. Still, it took an empty-net goal from Doug Harvey at 19:00 of the third to clinch the Stanley Cup.

Walking Wounded

"Instead of surrendering and cursing their luck … [Toe Blake] did a masterful job of keeping his cripples rolling.… In the playoffs, Toe had wounded Habs practically tumbling out of ambulances to volunteer for patrols against the Bruins. The final one was Tom Johnson, who parked his crutches and stiffened the Montreal defense after Dollard St. Laurent had suffered his second cheek fracture of the season."
— Milt Dunnell, *Toronto Star*

One of a Kind After winning the World Championship with the Whitby Dunlops in early March 1958, Connie Broden rejoined the Montreal Canadiens. He played only sparingly, but he got his name on the Stanley Cup for the second year in a row. Broden is the only player in history to win the World Championship and the Stanley Cup in the same season.

Rowdy Fans Visiting Montreal fans swarmed onto the Boston ice during the Stanley Cup presentation. NHL president Clarence Campbell was so upset by the fans' behavior that he announced after the game he would recommend future on-ice Cup presentations wait until the opening game of the following season.

Tom Johnson

The Current Cup

In 1958, the Stanley Cup was remodeled into the style we are familiar with today. Ten years earlier, the Cup had broadly taken its current shape, but there were a few key changes to come. It was in 1948 that the current "barrel" of the Cup was devised to replace the tall, gangly "stovepipe," but the new design had turned the Cup into a two-piece trophy, where the barrel at the bottom was detachable from the collar and bowl on top. Additionally, because the new barrel incorporated the many individual pieces from the "stovepipe," it did not leave a lot of room for the names of future winners. The remodeling in 1958 took care of both problems. The barrel was securely fastened to the collar and redesigned so it could accommodate five wide silver bands with plenty of room for future engravings. Each of these new bands, which began with the winners from 1927–28, had room for 13 years worth of championship names. That should have meant that the bands would not be filled until 1992 and that something new would have to be done with the Stanley Cup when it celebrated its 100th anniversary in 1993. Unfortunately, the engraving for the Montreal Canadiens in 1964–65 took up more than its allotted space, and so the Cup was actually filled a year too early, when the Pittsburgh Penguins won it in 1991. At that time, the NHL and the Hockey Hall of Fame decided that, rather than remodel a trophy whose size and shape had become so iconic, they would retire the top band to the Hockey Hall of Fame, move up the others and add a new one at the bottom.

SEMIFINALS
4 games to 1 over New York Rangers

FINAL 4 GAMES TO 1

APR. 6	►	Boston 1 at Montreal 5
APR. 9	►	Boston 0 at Montreal 1
APR. 11	►	Montreal 4 at Boston 2
APR. 14	►	Montreal 0 at Boston 2
APR. 16	►	Boston 1 at Montreal 5

PLAYOFF SCORING LEADER

Bernie Geoffrion	GP	G	A	PTS
MONTREAL	10	11	7	18

FINAL SERIES SCORING

MONTREAL	GP	G	A	PTS	PIM
Bernie Geoffrion	5	4	2	6	2
Doug Harvey	5	0	5	5	6
Maurice Richard	5	4	0	4	2
Floyd Curry	5	2	2	4	0
Dickie Moore	5	1	3	4	2
Don Marshall	5	1	2	3	2
Jean Béliveau	5	1	1	2	6
Phil Goyette	5	1	1	2	2
Tom Johnson	5	0	2	2	2
Bert Olmstead	5	0	2	2	9
Henri Richard	5	0	2	2	8
André Pronovost	3	1	0	1	0
Connie Broden	4	0	1	1	0
Claude Provost	5	0	1	1	2
Dollard St. Laurent	5	0	1	1	9
Jean-Guy Talbot	5	0	0	0	6
Bob Turner	2	0	0	0	0

GOALTENDER	GP	W	L	MIN	GA	SO	AVG
Jacques Plante	5	4	1	300	5	1	1.00

BOSTON	GP	G	A	PTS	PIM
Fleming MacKell	5	4	0	4	2
Leo Labine	5	1	1	2	12
Don McKenney	5	1	1	2	0
Larry Regan	5	0	2	2	4
Bob Armstrong	5	0	1	1	2
Leo Boivin	5	0	1	1	4
Fern Flaman	5	0	1	1	13
Doug Mohns	5	0	1	1	0
Jerry Toppazzini	5	0	1	1	2
Jack Bionda	5	0	0	0	6
Buddy Boone	5	0	0	0	10
Jack Caffery	5	0	0	0	0
Real Chevrefils	5	0	0	0	2
Cal Gardner	5	0	0	0	0
Johnny Peirson	5	0	0	0	12
Vic Stasiuk	5	0	0	0	2

GOALTENDER	GP	W	L	MIN	GA	SO	AVG
Don Simmons	5	1	4	300	15	1	3.00

Worrying Numbers Boston had seven wins and three ties in their 14 meetings with Montreal during the regular season. "I feel very, very relieved," Toe Blake said after the Canadiens won the Cup. "I was worried about this series since it started. After all, why shouldn't I have been?"

More Balanced NHL president Clarence Campbell thought the Canadiens' superior depth and condition made the difference against the Bruins. Montreal got goals from eight different players during the Stanley Cup final, while only three Boston players scored.

Second Place to a Second Straight Cup

The Detroit Red Wings had beaten the Canadiens for the Stanley Cup in 1954 and 1955, but in the 1955–56 season, Montreal ended Detroit's run of seven straight first-place finishes in the regular-season standings and beat the Red Wings in the final as well. In the spring of 1958, Detroit GM Jack Adams would offer the opinion that, "a good hockey team disintegrates about every five years," but in the fall of 1956 he resisted the urge to overhaul his roster. With Gordie Howe and Ted Lindsay finishing first and second in the NHL scoring race, the Red Wings returned to top spot in the NHL standings in 1956–57 in a close race with the Canadiens and the Boston Bruins.

Jean Béliveau, Maurice Richard, Henri Richard and Bernie Geoffrion all missed time due to injuries this season, but the Canadiens still led the NHL in scoring. Despite their injuries, Béliveau and Maurice Richard both had 33 goals to tie for second behind Gordie Howe's league-leading 44. Béliveau's 51 assists trailed only Ted Lindsay's 55, while Dickie Moore had 29 goals and 29 assists. Butch Bouchard had retired after Montreal's Cup win the previous season, but with Doug Harvey, Tom Johnson, Jean-Guy Talbot, Bob Turner and

Dollard St. Laurent in front of goalie Jacques Plante, the Canadiens remained the NHL's best defensive team. Glenn Hall played all 70 games for Detroit and led the NHL with 38 wins, but Plante led the league with nine shutouts and a 2.00 goals-against average.

In the playoffs, Boston surprised Detroit with a five-game victory in their semifinal series. The Canadiens beat the Rangers in five games as well. Bernie Geoffrion, completely recovered from the elbow injury that had sidelined him for 29 games, had seven goals and five assists. Still, it took an overtime goal from Maurice Richard to wrap up the series.

In Game 1 of the final, the Rocket exploded with four goals in a 5–1 victory over the Bruins. The tight Boston checking that had shutdown Detroit re-emerged in Game 2, but a goal from Béliveau and a shutout by Plante gave Montreal a 1–0 victory. Don Simmons, who had replaced an exhausted Terry Sawchuk for the Bruins midway through the season, kept Boston alive with a shutout of his own in Game 4, but a shorthanded goal and two assists from Dickie Moore in a 5–1 win in Game 5 wrapped up the Cup for Montreal.

Rocket's Record

Maurice Richard's four goals in Game 1 tied the NHL record for most goals in a game in the Stanley Cup final. Three others had accomplished the feat previously: Newsy Lalonde scored four in one game for the Canadiens against the Seattle Metropolitans on March 22, 1919; Babe Dye netted four for the Toronto St. Pats on March 28, 1922; and Ted Lindsay had four for Detroit on April 5, 1955.

MOST GAMES PLAYED IN THE FINALS

65	Red Kelly, Detroit (37), Toronto (28)
	Henri Richard, Montreal
64	Jean Béliveau, Montreal
59	Maurice Richard, Montreal
56	Bert Olmstead, Montreal (43), Toronto (13)
55	Gordie Howe, Detroit
	Jean-Guy Talbot, Montreal (43), St. Louis (12)

Red Kelly

Montreal Canadiens

ROSTER

Jean Béliveau

Butch Bouchard
(captain)

Floyd Curry

Bernie Geoffrion

Doug Harvey

Charlie Hodge

Tom Johnson

Jackie Leclair

Don Marshall

Dickie Moore

Ken Mosdell

Bert Olmstead

Jacques Plante

Claude Provost

Henri Richard

Maurice Richard

Dollard St. Laurent

Jean-Guy Talbot

Bob Turner

Frank Selke
(managing director)

Toe Blake (coach)

Toe Blake talks with Maurice Richard and Jean Béliveau.

FINAL 4 GAMES TO 1

MAR. 31	►	Detroit 4 at Montreal 6
APR. 3	►	Detroit 1 at Montreal 5
APR. 5	►	Montreal 1 at Detroit 3
APR. 8	►	Montreal 3 at Detroit 0
APR. 10	►	Detroit 1 at Montreal 3

PLAYOFF SCORING LEADER

Jean Béliveau	GP	G	A	PTS
MONTREAL	10	12	7	19

FINAL SERIES SCORING

MONTREAL	GP	G	A	PTS	PIM
Jean Béliveau	5	7	3	10	8
Bert Olmstead	5	0	8	8	4
Bernie Geoffrion	5	3	3	6	2
Maurice Richard	5	2	2	4	12
Floyd Curry	5	1	3	4	4
Henri Richard	5	2	1	3	11
Claude Provost	5	1	2	3	2
Doug Harvey	5	0	3	3	6
Dickie Moore	5	0	3	3	6
Jackie Leclair	5	1	1	2	4
Don Marshall	5	1	0	1	0
Ken Mosdell	4	0	1	1	0
Jean-Guy Talbot	4	0	1	1	2
Butch Bouchard	1	0	0	0	0
Tom Johnson	5	0	0	0	8
Dollard St. Laurent	3	0	0	0	2
Bob Turner	5	0	0	0	4
GOALTENDER	GP	W	L	MIN	GA	SO	AVG
Jacques Plante	5	4	1	300	9	1	1.80

DETROIT	GP	G	A	PTS	PIM
Gordie Howe	5	1	5	6	4
Ted Lindsay	5	2	3	5	6
Alex Delvecchio	5	3	1	4	0
Norm Ullman	5	1	1	2	11
Bill Dineen	5	1	0	1	4
Red Kelly	5	1	0	1	2
Al Arbour	4	0	1	1	0
John Bucyk	5	0	1	1	4
Lorne Ferguson	5	0	1	1	8
Marty Pavelich	5	0	1	1	8
Dutch Reibel	5	0	1	1	2
Cummy Burton	1	0	0	0	0
Murray Costello	2	0	0	0	0
Bob Goldham	5	0	0	0	2
Larry Hillman	5	0	0	0	2
Gord Hollingworth	2	0	0	0	2
Gerry Melnyk	4	0	0	0	0
Marcel Pronovost	5	0	0	0	2
Metro Prystai	4	0	0	0	4
GOALTENDER	GP	W	L	MIN	GA	SO	AVG
Glenn Hall	5	1	4	300	18	0	3.60

He Would

"From the first day I held a hockey stick, my great ambition was to play on a Stanley Cup team. I am very happy that it came with the Canadiens and I hope that I can play with them on a few more Stanley Cup teams."
—Jean Béliveau

Coaches Get Credit

"Toe Blake deserves all the credit in the world for what he has done with this team. And I'm not forgetting Dick Irvin, either. Some people think he's too tough. People don't always agree with him. But his discipline makes men out of boys."
—Butch Bouchard

Béliveau Leads Canadiens Breakthrough

For two years in a row, the Detroit Red Wings had beaten out Montreal for both first place in the regular-season standings and for the Stanley Cup. The 1954–55 season had been particularly disappointing. With Maurice Richard suspended for the last three games of the season and all of the playoffs after punching a linesman, Detroit passed Montreal for first place on the last night of the regular season and then used the home ice advantage they had gained to beat the Canadiens for the Stanley Cup in seven games.

Toe Blake replaced Dick Irvin as coach after the 1954–55 season. Blake would lead essentially the same team in 1955–56, but there were a few key differences. Veteran Butch Bouchard would be phased out on defense in favor of rookies Bob Turner and Jean-Guy Talbot. Claude Provost would also make his debut, as would Maurice Richard's 19-year-old brother Henri. The biggest news in the off-season came from Detroit, who sent Terry Sawchuk to Boston in a nine-player deal. Detroit had a more than adequate replacement in Glenn Hall, but Warren Godfrey would be the only player obtained from the Bruins who was still with the Red Wings when the 1955–56 season ended.

After being injured in his rookie season of 1953–54, Jean Béliveau had emerged as the star everyone expected in 1954–55. The classy center had put up with plenty of cheap shots and decided to play with more of an edge in 1955–56. Béliveau's 143 penalty minutes that year ranked third in the NHL (behind Lou Fontinato's 202 and Ted Lindsay's 161) and would remain a career high. Playing on a line with Maurice Richard and Bert Olmstead, Béliveau also led the NHL with a career-high 47 goals and was the top scorer with 88 points, winning both the Art Ross Trophy and the Hart as MVP. With the league's best offense and Jacques Plante's league-best 1.86 goals-against average, the Canadiens set an NHL record with 45 wins (45-15-10) and posted the first 100-point season in franchise history.

The Red Wings were a distant second with 76 points but easily disposed of fourth-place Toronto to reach the final. The Canadiens outscored the Rangers 22–9 in their five-game semifinal and faced the Red Wings for the Stanley Cup for the third year in a row. This time, Montreal came out on top.

The Final

Detroit had a 4–2 lead after two periods in Game 1, but goals by Jackie Leclair, Bernie Geoffrion and Jean Béliveau (his second of the game) in a span of 4:11 early in the third led Montreal to a 6–4 victory. Béliveau, Geoffrion and the Richard brothers scored to lead Montreal to a 5–1 romp in Game 2. The Red Wings got a win on home ice in Game 3, but Béliveau scored two more in Game 4, and Jacques Plante made several big saves in a 3–0 shutout. The dominance of Montreal's power play in 1955–56 resulted in a rule change the following season, allowing players serving a minor penalty to return to the ice if a goal was scored (as opposed to serving the entire penalty). The Canadiens scored all three of their goals in Game 5 on the power play, including two during the same two-minute penalty late in the second period, to wrap up the Stanley Cup with a 3–1 victory.

Le Gros Bill Jean Béliveau's 12 goals in the playoffs equaled Maurice Richard's 12 in 1944 as the highest total ever during the NHL's six-team era. His seven goals in the final were also the best of this age.

Experience Helps

Seven NHL teams have lost in the final one year and come back to win the Stanley Cup the following season:

YEAR	LOST CUP	WINNER	YEAR	WON CUP	DEFEATED
1932	NY Rangers	Toronto	1933	NY Rangers	Toronto
1949	Detroit	Toronto	1950	Detroit	NY Rangers
1952	Montreal	Detroit	1953	Montreal	Boston
1955	Montreal	Detroit	1956	Montreal	Detroit
1967	Montreal	Toronto	1968	Montreal	St. Louis
1983	Edmonton	NY Islanders	1984	Edmonton	NY Islanders
2008	Pittsburgh	Detroit	2009	Pittsburgh	Detroit

Or Not...

11 NHL teams won the Stanley Cup one year but lost in the final the following season:

YEAR	WON CUP	DEFEATED	YEAR	LOST CUP	DEFEATED BY
1925	Victoria*	Mtl Canadiens	1926	Victoria	Mtl Maroons
1928	NY Rangers	Mtl Maroons	1929	NY Rangers	Boston
1946	Mtl Canadiens	Boston	1947	Mtl Canadiens	Toronto
1953	Mtl Canadiens	Boston	1954	Mtl Canadiens	Detroit
1955	Detroit	Mtl Canadiens	1956	Detroit	Mtl Canadiens
1966	Mtl Canadiens	Detroit	1967	Mtl Canadiens	Toronto
1975	Philadelphia	Buffalo	1976	Philadelphia	Mtl Canadiens
1983	NY Islanders	Edmonton	1984	NY Islanders	Edmonton
1999	Dallas	Buffalo	2000	Dallas	New Jersey
2000	New Jersey	Dallas	2001	New Jersey	Colorado
2008	Detroit	Pittsburgh	2009	Detroit	Pittsburgh

*Victoria Cougars faced NHL teams as a member of the Western Canada Hockey League in 1924–25 and the Western Hockey League in 1925–26.

The Game I'll Never Forget

> **You know that with a club like we had with the Canadiens that you should win. So much talent and so much potential, it would be a shame for it to be wasted. It's a big test for any coach.**

Hockey Digest: March 1976
By Toe Blake, as told to George Vass

The first year as a coach, that one you remember because so often you don't know what to expect.

It's one thing to have been a player for the Montreal Canadiens; it is another to be their coach. I played for them 13 years, and I coached them 13 years. I won Stanley Cups as a player three times and as a coach eight times.

So many games, so many moments.

But I know I got a helluva thrill my first year as a coach, in 1955–56, in the first game of the Stanley Cup final. That is a game I could never forget!

When I first became coach I was worried. Not about whether we had good players. No, what I worried about was whether or not it was going to be tough to coach players I once had as teammates. Think about that and you make yourself nervous.

You know that with a club like we had with the Canadiens that you should win. So much talent and so much potential, it would be a shame for it to be wasted. It's a big test for any coach.

In those days, Detroit was the toughest club for us to beat.

Detroit had Gordie Howe. They had Ted Lindsay, Alex Delvecchio, Red Kelly, Marcel Pronovost, Glenn Hall and many other good players.

For seven straight years before I became Montreal's coach, Detroit finished in first place in the regular season. They defeated us in the Stanley Cup final the two years before I took over, each time the series going seven games.

We always had trouble with Detroit, and the boys were disappointed with what had happened the previous two years. You could see that right from training camp in 1955. They worked very hard. They knew they could win if they didn't beat themselves.

They all went out of their way to help me, knowing what was expected of me in my first year as coach. Rocket was very good that way. So were Butch Bouchard and Kenny Mosdell.

I felt that if we finished anywhere but first I wouldn't have done a good job. But you never know in hockey. Everything doesn't always go right. They played in the season as well as I could have expected. Maybe better. We won 45 games and lost

only 15 (in a 70-game season) and finished with 100 points. Detroit was second, 24 points behind us.

What a power play we had! Harvey and Geoffrion were on the points, Rocket Richard, Béliveau and Olmstead up front. Sometimes we scored two or three goals on a power play, which you could do at that time. After the season they changed the rule because of that, letting the man come out of the penalty box after a team scored a goal.

We played the New York Rangers in the first round [the semifinals] of the Stanley Cup playoffs and beat them in five games. Detroit beat Toronto in their first round.

So it was our club against Detroit again. They'd beaten us in the final two years in a row, and nobody had to tell us they'd be tough again.

The first game of the final was in Montreal on March 31, 1956.

There was a lot of animosity between the two clubs, and it showed in the first period. There were brawls and stick swinging, and the referee, Jack Mehlenbacher, handed out penalties.

Detroit scored the only goal in the first period. I think Delvecchio got one past our goalie, Plante, in the middle of the period. We couldn't score on Hall, not that we were pressuring him that much. We were being outplayed.

The second period was much worse. Béliveau tied the game 1–1

March 31, 1956
Game 1, Stanley Cup final · Montreal Forum, Montreal

Toe Blake talks with All-Star goaltender Jaques Plante.

with a goal for us early, but Detroit then scored three of the next four goals. I know Henri Richard got our other goal that period, but Detroit came out of it with a 4–2 lead.

They were checking our big guys, Béliveau, Geoffrion, Moore, the Rocket and Olmstead. When that happens you hope your other guys can come up with some goals and get you back in the game.

Maybe I said a few things to our guys between the second and third periods. I thought they could do better than be behind 4–2 after two periods in their own rink. You have to win on your own ice.

I figured maybe our third line could get us started. It worked. Floyd Curry, John Leclair and Claude Provost bailed us out.

Leclair's goal was the one that got us started, about five minutes into the third period. That made it 4–3, and we were just a goal down.

I can still see the next goal, about a minute later, by Geoffrion. He wheeled around and put a backhander past Hall that the goalie didn't see. That tied the game 4–4, and the fans went wild. It took five minutes to clear the ice.

We had it going our way now. Less than a minute after Geoffrion's goal, Béliveau skated in with Bob Goldham hanging on his back. Somehow he got a backhander away, and it beat Hall to put us ahead 5–4.

We still weren't in the clear, not against the explosive Detroit team, but we were aroused and kept up the pressure. We were checking them now, and Plante wasn't having to stop too many shots.

We got one more goal to give us room. There was a scramble around the Detroit net, and Provost banged in a loose puck to give us a 6–4 lead.

We were able to hang on to that lead and win that opening game 6–4. We went on to take the final in five games, which was the start of five straight years of winning the Stanley Cup.

A lot of people ask me which team was the greatest. I couldn't tell you, it was equally good for five years. But if we'd lost that game, who knows what would have happened?

Montreal 6, Detroit 4

FIRST PERIOD

1 ▸ Delvecchio (Reibel, Howe), Detroit, 8:17 PP

PENALTIES: Béliveau, Montreal (high-sticking), 2:13; Lindsay, Detroit (high-sticking), 2:13; Turner, Montreal (high-sticking), 3:21; Dineen, Detroit (roughing), 3:21; M. Richard, Montreal (high-sticking), 4:44; Howe, Detroit (hooking), 5:45; M. Richard, Montreal (high-sticking), 8:02; Dineen, Detroit (interference), 13:18; M. Richard, Montreal (hooking), 14:32; Ullman, Detroit (charging), 15:35

SECOND PERIOD

2 ▸ Béliveau (Olmstead), Montreal, 3:00 PP

3 ▸ Dineen (Ullman, Bucyk), Detroit, 3:45

4 ▸ H. Richard (M. Richard, Moore), Montreal, 6:40

5 ▸ Lindsay (Howe), Detroit, 8:11

6 ▸ Delvecchio (Howe, Ferguson), Detroit, 11:20 PP

PENALTIES: Prystai, Detroit (kneeing), 1:10; Johnson, Montreal (cross-checking), 11:13; Hollingworth, Detroit (roughing), 16:29; Johnson, Montreal (roughing), 16:29

THIRD PERIOD

7 ▸ LeClair (Curry, Harvey), Montreal, 5:20

8 ▸ Geoffrion (Talbot), Montreal, 6:20

9 ▸ Béliveau (Geoffrion, Olmstead), Montreal, 7:31

10▸ Provost (LeClair, Curry), Montreal, 10:49

NO PENALTIES

GOALIES: Plante, Montreal; Hall, Detroit

REFEREE: Jack Mehlenbacher

LINESMEN: Bill Morrison, George Hayes

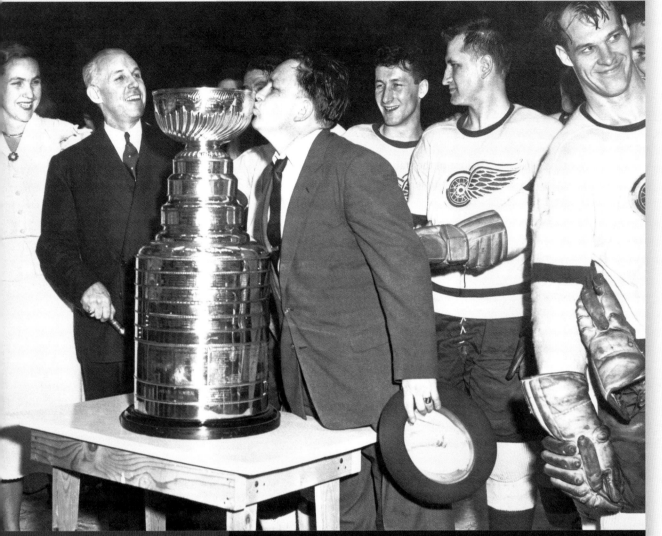

SEMIFINALS
4 games to 0 over Toronto

ROSTER

Jimmy Skinner kisses the Cup as the Red Wings celebrate.

FINAL 4 GAMES TO 3

APR. 3	►	Montreal 2 at Detroit 4
APR. 5	►	Montreal 1 at Detroit 7
APR. 7	►	Detroit 2 at Montreal 4
APR. 9	►	Detroit 3 at Montreal 5
APR. 10	►	Montreal 1 at Detroit 5
APR. 12	►	Detroit 3 at Montreal 6
APR. 14	►	Montreal 1 at Detroit 3

PLAYOFF SCORING LEADER

	GP	G	A	PTS
Gordie Howe DETROIT	11	9	11	20

FINAL SERIES SCORING

DETROIT	GP	G	A	PTS	PIM
Gordie Howe	7	5	7	12	24
Ted Lindsay	7	5	6	11	6
Alex Delvecchio	7	6	4	10	0
Dutch Reibel	7	2	5	7	2
Vic Stasiuk	7	3	3	6	2
Red Kelly	7	2	3	5	17
Marty Pavelich	7	1	2	3	12
Marcel Pronovost	7	1	2	3	2
Bob Goldham	7	0	2	2	2
Jim Hay	5	1	0	1	0
Glen Skov	7	1	0	1	4
Marcel Bonin	7	0	1	1	4
Tony Leswick	7	0	1	1	10
Bill Dineen	7	0	0	0	2
Johnny Wilson	7	0	0	0	0
Benny Woit	7	0	0	0	4

GOALTENDER	GP	W	L	MIN	GA	SO	AVG
Terry Sawchuk	7	4	3	420	20	0	2.86

MONTREAL	GP	G	A	PTS	PIM
Bernie Geoffrion	7	6	2	8	2
Jean Béliveau	7	3	5	8	12
Floyd Curry	7	5	1	6	2
Calum MacKay	7	2	4	6	2
Ken Mosdell	7	1	4	5	6
Doug Harvey	7	0	5	5	4
Jackie Leclair	7	2	0	2	2
Dickie Moore	7	0	2	2	16
Tom Johnson	7	1	0	1	16
Butch Bouchard	7	0	1	1	31
Bert Olmstead	7	0	1	1	14
Dollard St. Laurent	7	0	1	1	10
Jim Bartlett	2	0	0	0	0
Dick Gamble	2	0	0	0	2
Don Marshall	7	0	0	0	2
George McAvoy	3	0	0	0	0
Paul Ronty	2	0	0	0	2

GOALTENDERS	GP	W	L	MIN	GA	SO	AVG
Jacques Plante	7	3	3	403	24	0	3.57
Charlie Hodge	1	0	1	17	3	0	10.59

ROSTER

Marcel Bonin
Alex Delvecchio
Bill Dineen
Bob Goldham
Jim Hay
Larry Hillman
Gordie Howe
Red Kelly
Tony Leswick
Ted Lindsay (captain)
Marty Pavelich

Marcel Pronovost
Dutch Reibel
Terry Sawchuk
Glen Skov
Vic Stasiuk
Johnny Wilson
Benny Woit
Jack Adams (manager)
Jimmy Skinner (coach)

Royal Request

Rioting was not the only response Montrealers had to the suspension of Maurice Richard. On March 23, 1955, the *Montreal Gazette* reported that a telegram had been sent to Queen Elizabeth, asking her to intercede on behalf of the Rocket. Frank Selke of the Canadiens knew the fan who sent the wire, but would not to release his name.

Campbell and the Cup

There was such bitterness toward Clarence Campbell in Montreal that if Detroit had won the Stanley Cup there in Game 6, the NHL president would not have been the one to present it to them. It would have been Stanley Cup trustee Cooper Smeaton. Campbell did present the trophy to the Red Wings in Detroit after Game 7.

Red Wings and the Richard Riot

Tommy Ivan had coached the Red Wings to six straight first-place finishes and to Stanley Cup wins in 1950, 1952 and 1954, but he left Detroit to become general manager of the Chicago Black Hawks in 1954–55. Jimmy Skinner, a former Red Wings prospect who had coached in the lower levels of their farm system, took over for the defending champions. Skinner surprised observers when he put the pressure on himself and his team at training camp. "We should win it all again," the rookie coach said. "We've got the best players, haven't we?"

For most of the 1954–55 season, it was the Montreal Canadiens who had the best players. Maurice Richard, Jean Béliveau, Bernie Geoffrion, Bert Olmstead and Doug Harvey dominated the offensive statistics. But the big story in Montreal came after March 13, 1955, when Richard punched linesman Cliff Thompson after a stick-swinging incident with Boston's Hal Laycoe. NHL president Clarence Campbell suspended Richard for the season's final three games and all of the playoffs. When Campbell showed up at the Canadiens' game with the Red Wings on March 17th, a riot ensued outside the Montreal Forum. Only a radio plea by Richard the following day was able to restore peace to the city.

At the time of his suspension, the Rocket led Bernie "Boom Boom" Geoffrion by two points in the NHL scoring race, and the Canadiens were two points up on Detroit for top spot in the standings. With Richard out, Geoffrion passed him for the scoring title, and Detroit claimed first place for the seventh consecutive season when they beat Montreal 6–0 on the final night of the season. With Ted Lindsay and Gordie Howe both missing time due to injuries, goalie Terry Sawchuk had kept Detroit close in the standings. Still, it took closing out the season with nine wins in a row to take top spot. The Red Wings then won four straight to sweep Toronto in the semifinals and ran their streak to 15, with two wins at home against Montreal to open the Stanley Cup final. The Canadiens won the next two in Montreal, and through six games the home team had won them all. In Game 7 at Detroit, the checking was closer than it had been previously. After a scoreless first period, Alex Delvecchio and Gordie Howe got goals in the second, and Delvecchio scored again early in the third to lead Detroit to a 3–1 victory.

Farmhands Ineligible

Detroit's strategy for Game 7 had been to try to wear out the Canadiens by employing four lines instead of the three that were typical of this era. Johnny Bucyk and Bronco Horvath had been called up from the Edmonton Flyers, but NHL president Clarence Campbell ruled them ineligible because of an agreement with the Western Hockey League and Quebec Hockey League that banned call-ups, except in emergencies, while minor league teams were still involved in the playoffs.

MOST CAREER PENALTY MINUTES IN THE STANLEY CUP FINAL

94	Gordie Howe, Detroit	(55 games)
87	Kevin McClelland, Edmonton	(22 games)
86	Duane Sutter, New York Islanders	(24 games)
83	Maurice Richard, Montreal	(59 games)
79	Wayne Cashman, Boston	(26 games)

Kevin McClelland

Lavish Party

As they had in previous years, the Red Wings celebrated their 1955 Stanley Cup victory with a champagne party at the Sheraton-Cadillac Hotel (now the Westin Book Cadillac Hotel) in downtown Detroit. Players, relatives, friends and executives from the NHL and other league clubs were all invited. Boston GM Lynn Patrick was asked if he thought Bruins management would give the same kind of lavish party for a Stanley Cup win. "I'd sure like to have the opportunity of finding out," he sighed.

Cup-Winning Kids

Larry Hillman was 18 years and two months old when Detroit won the Stanley Cup in 1955. Though he played only six games during the regular season and three in the playoffs (none in the final), his name was engraved on the trophy, making him the youngest player ever to win it. Next youngest is Gaye Stewart, who made his NHL debut for Toronto in Game 5 of the 1942 Stanley Cup final and was 18 years and nine months old when the Maple Leafs won the Cup that year.

Home Ice Advantage
In addition to 1955, there are two other seven-game Stanley Cup finals where each game was won by the home team: Montreal versus Chicago in 1965 (Montreal won the Cup) and New Jersey versus Anaheim in 2003 (New Jersey won the Cup).

The Detroit Dynasty

Hockey history might have been very different if things had worked out better between Gordie Howe and the New York Rangers in the fall of 1943. Howe was one of about 30 players on hand in Winnipeg, Manitoba, on October 11, 1943, when Lester Patrick opened his annual hockey school for young prospects. In previous years no player younger than 17 had been admitted, but with World War II taking so many young men away for military service, boys as young as 15—like Gordie Howe—were welcomed.

With all of Adams' wheeling and dealing, only Gordie Howe, Red Kelly, Ted Lindsay, Marty Pavelich, Marcel Pronovost and Johnny Wilson were a part of all four of Detroit's Stanley Cup–winning teams from 1950 to 1955.

It's often been said that Howe was miserably homesick at the Rangers camp, and that he made a poor impression and went home early. But Howe told a very different story to New York Times sportswriter David Anderson in 1980, saying the Rangers wanted to assign him to a junior team they sponsored in Regina, Saskatchewan. Howe told them he would join the team if some of his friends from Saskatoon, Saskatchewan, would be going too. When he was told the Rangers weren't interested in any of the other Saskatoon prospects, Howe decided to go home.

New York's loss would be Detroit's gain.

A year later, Howe was offered a tryout with the Detroit Red Wings and accepted their assignment to the Galt Red Wings of the Ontario Hockey Association (OHA). He was only allowed to play in exhibition games due to an OHA limit on Western players, but the lack of playing time didn't seem to set him back. Howe was promoted to Detroit's Omaha Knights farm team in the United States Hockey League for the 1945–46 season and quickly made an impression.

In a story in the Toronto Star on December 7, 1945, the Red Wings' director of public relations, Fred Huber, hyped Howe as having the potential to become the greatest right-winger hockey ever knew. "That we'll have to see," wrote the unnamed Star columnist, but hockey fans everywhere would soon be choosing sides as to whether Howe or fellow right-winger Maurice Richard was the best player in hockey.

Howe made the Red Wings as an 18-year-old in the fall of 1946 and joined another youngster named Ted Lindsay, who had made the team at age 19 two years before. One year later they'd be joined by 20-year-old defenseman Red Kelly. The infusion of young talent, along with the successful return of veterans such as Sid Abel and Jack Stewart from military service, soon sparked a Red Wings resurgence that matched the giddy era of post-war prosperity the automobile market had launched in Detroit. The Red Wings finished first in the NHL standings seven years in a row from 1948–49 through 1954–55 and again in 1956–57. They reached the Stanley Cup final seven times in nine years from 1948 through 1956 and won the prized trophy in 1950, 1952, 1954 and 1955.

Jack Adams had been running the Red Wings as both coach and general manager since the team's second season of 1927–28, when they were still known as the Detroit Cougars. Before the 1947–48 season, Adams turned over the coaching reins to Tommy Ivan, who had coached Howe during his season in Omaha. With Ivan behind the bench, Adams the GM had more time to tinker with the roster, and he was constantly making adjustments. Adams brought in Billy Taylor from the Toronto Maple Leafs in 1946–47 and got a league-leading 46 assists out of him

role players in future Stanley Cup wins. Gaye Stewart, who also came from Chicago in the big trade, would soon be swapped to acquire Tony Leswick from the New York Rangers. Leswick won the Cup three times in Detroit, including in 1954 when he joined Babando as the only players in hockey history to score a Cup-winning goal in overtime of the seventh game.

Detroit's deep farm system continued to add star players, such as Alex Delvecchio and Marcel Pronovost, and role players such as Glen Skov, Marty Pavelich and Johnny Wilson. But with all of Adams' wheeling and dealing, only Howe, Kelly, Lindsay, Pavelich, Pronovost and Wilson were a part of all four of Detroit's Stanley Cup–winning teams from 1950 to 1955.

Adams continued to deal off stars and prospects alike over the next few years, but this time the moves backfired on him. Sawchuk, Lindsay, Kelly and young players Glenn Hall and Johnny Bucyk were all traded between 1955 and 1960 but brought little in return. In 1962 Adams was all but forced out as general manager in Detroit. After seven Stanley Cup titles in 35 years, it would be another 35 years before the Red Wings won it again.

before sending him on his way. He also acquired Roy Conacher that year and saw him score a career-best 30 goals before selling him to the Chicago Black Hawks. Other trades brought in players such as George Gee, Pete Babando and Leo Reise Jr., who all played key support roles in Detroit's Stanley Cup victory in 1950. But even victory didn't stop the transactions.

Harry Lumley had been a

17-year-old wartime replacement player when he first joined the Red Wings in 1943–44, but had proven himself to be one of the NHL's best goalies. Even so, with Terry Sawchuk garnering honors at every stop in Detroit's minor-league system, Adams dealt Lumley shortly after the 1950 Stanley Cup championship. Jack Stewart, who had been key to the team's success since the late 1930s, and

The Production Line of Gordie Howe, Sid Abel and Ted Lindsay takes a break during practice.

Pete Babando, who had scored the winning goal in overtime of Game 7 in the 1950 final, were also packaged with Lumley in a nine-player trade with Chicago. Among the four players the Red Wings got in return were Metro Prystai and Bob Goldham, two more important

SEMIFINALS
4 games to 1 over Toronto

ROSTER

Keith Allen
Al Arbour
Alex Delvecchio
Bill Dineen
Gilles Dubé
Dave Gatherum
Bob Goldham
Gordie Howe
Earl Johnson
Red Kelly
Tony Leswick
Ted Lindsay (captain)
Marty Pavelich
Jimmy Peters
Marcel Pronovost
Metro Prystai
Dutch Reibel
Terry Sawchuk
Glen Skov
Johnny Wilson
Benny Woit
Jack Adams (manager)
Jimmy Skinner (coach)

FINAL   4 GAMES TO 3

APR. 4	►	Montreal 1 at Detroit 3
APR. 6	►	Montreal 3 at Detroit 1
APR. 8	►	Detroit 5 at Montreal 2
APR. 10	►	Detroit 2 at Montreal 0
APR. 11	►	Montreal 1 at Detroit 0 OT
APR. 13	►	Detroit 1 at Montreal 4
APR. 16	►	Montreal 1 at Detroit 2 OT

PLAYOFF SCORING LEADER

		GP	G	A	PTS
Dickie Moore MONTREAL		11	5	8	13

FINAL SERIES SCORING

DETROIT	GP	G	A	PTS	PIM
Alex Delvecchio	7	2	4	6	0
Red Kelly	7	3	1	4	0
Ted Lindsay	7	2	2	4	14
Metro Prystai	7	2	2	4	0
Gordie Howe	7	1	2	3	23
Johnny Wilson	7	2	0	2	0
Tony Leswick	7	1	1	2	8
Dutch Reibel	4	1	1	2	0
Bob Goldham	7	0	1	1	0
Marty Pavelich	7	0	1	1	4
Glen Skov	7	0	1	1	10
Benny Woit	7	0	1	1	4
Keith Allen	3	0	0	0	0
Bill Dineen	7	0	0	0	0
Gilles Dubé	2	0	0	0	0
Jimmy Peters	6	0	0	0	0
Marcel Pronovost	7	0	0	0	8
GOALTENDER	GP	W	L	MIN	GA	SO	AVG
Terry Sawchuk	7	4	3	430	12	1	1.67

MONTREAL	GP	G	A	PTS	PIM
Floyd Curry	7	3	0	3	2
Maurice Richard	7	3	0	3	20
Bernie Geoffrion	7	2	1	3	16
Dickie Moore	7	1	2	3	8
Paul Masnick	6	0	3	3	4
Jean Béliveau	6	0	2	2	2
Elmer Lach	4	0	2	2	0
Tom Johnson	7	1	0	1	8
Ken Mosdell	7	1	0	1	2
Dollard St. Laurent	6	1	0	1	6
Doug Harvey	6	0	1	1	4
Calum MacKay	3	0	1	1	0
Eddie Mazur	7	0	1	1	0
Bert Olmstead	7	0	1	1	8
Butch Bouchard	7	0	0	0	4
Lorne Davis	7	0	0	0	6
Bud MacPherson	2	0	0	0	4
John McCormack	4	0	0	0	0
Paul Meger	2	0	0	0	2
Gaye Stewart	3	0	0	0	0
GOALTENDERS	GP	W	L	MIN	GA	SO	AVG
Gerry McNeil	3	2	1	190	3	1	0.95
Jacques Plante	4	1	3	240	10	0	2.50

Tough to Take

"It was a real simple goal, I'll tell you. Boy it was a long skate back to [our dressing room at] the other side of the rink. There's no way you can express how you feel at a time like that when you're a goalie. It's like the end of the world." — Gerry McNeil to Dick Irvin Jr. for his book *The Habs: An Oral History of the Montreal Canadiens, 1940 to 1980*

Red Wings Win on Leswick's Lucky Goal

After a shocking playoff loss the year before, Detroit bounced back to top the regular-season standings for the sixth straight year in 1953–54. Gordie Howe's 33 goals were second behind Maurice Richard's 37, but Howe's 48 assists topped the league, and his 81 points gave him the Art Ross Trophy as the NHL scoring leader for the fourth straight season. Ted Lindsay ranked among the NHL leaders with 26 goals, 36, assists and 62 points. Red Kelly and Dutch Reibel also finished in the top-10 in scoring, with Kelly becoming the first winner of the Norris Trophy as the league's best defenseman. Reibel was the runner-up to Camille Henry of the New York Rangers for the Calder Trophy as Rookie of the Year. Terry Sawchuk's 1.93 goals-against average and 12 shutouts ranked second behind Toronto's Harry Lumley (1.86 and 13) as the Maple Leafs surrendered 131 goals to the Red Wings' 132 to give Lumley the Vezina Trophy.

The Montreal Canadiens signed Jean Béliveau this season, but injuries limited him to just 44 games. Injuries also sidelined Dickie Moore, while a pair of suspensions forced the Canadiens to do without Bernie Geoffrion for 16 games. Still, with Maurice Richard leading the way,

Montreal held off Toronto for second place, but their 81 points in the standings left them seven back of Detroit. The Bruins grabbed fourth place, while the Rangers and Black Hawks missed the playoffs. Chicago was a woeful 12-51-7, and yet goalie Al Rollins won the Hart Trophy as the player most valuable to his team.

In the playoffs, Detroit opened with a 5–0 win over Toronto. The rest of the semifinal games were close, but the Red Wings took the series in five. The Canadiens swept Boston behind goalie Jacques Plante, who had taken over for an injured Gerry McNeil in February. When Montreal fell behind Detroit three games to one in the Stanley Cup final, coach Dick Irvin went back to McNeil for the first time in two months. McNeil matched Sawchuk save for save in Game 5 before Ken Mosdell scored at 5:45 of overtime to keep the Canadiens alive. McNeil was brilliant again in a 4–1 Montreal win that forced Game 7. After six penalty-filled affairs, Game 7 was clean, but when Tony Leswick bounced in a fluky game-winning goal at 4:29 of overtime, the devastated Canadiens left the ice without shaking hands.

Women Engraved on the Stanley Cup

As president of the Red Wings, Marguerite Norris was the first woman to have her name engraved on the Stanley Cup, in 1954. It's there again in 1955. Other women engraved on the Cup are Sonia Scurfield (Calgary, 1989), Marie Denise DeBartolo York (Pittsburgh, 1991), Marian Ilitch (Detroit, 1997, 1998, 2002, 2008), Denise Ilitch Lites (Detroit, 1997, 1998, 2002, 2008), Lisa Ilitch Murray (Detroit, 1997, 1998, 2002, 2008), Carole Ilitch (Detroit, 1997, 1998, 2002, 2008), Marie Carnevale (New Jersey, 2000), Callie Smith (New Jersey, 2000), Charlotte Grahame (Colorado, 2001), Nancy Beard (Detroit, 2002) and Susan Samueli (Anaheim, 2007).

MOST YEARS IN THE FINAL (WINS IN BOLD)

12
Maurice Richard, Montreal (**1944**, **1946**, 1947, 1951, 1952, **1953**, 1954, **1956**, **1957**, **1958**, **1959**, **1960**)

Red Kelly, Detroit (1948, 1949, **1950**, **1952**, **1954**, **1955**, 1956), Toronto (1960, **1962**, **1963**, **1964**, **1967**)

Jean Béliveau, Montreal (1954, 1955, **1956**, **1957**, **1958**, **1960**, **1965**, **1966**, 1967, **1968**, **1969**, **1971**)*

Henri Richard, Montreal (**1956**, **1957**, **1958**, **1959**, **1960**, **1965**, **1966**, 1967, **1968**, **1969**, **1971**, **1973**)

11
Bert Olmstead, Montreal (1951, 1952, **1953**, 1954, 1955, **1956**, **1957**, **1958**), Toronto (1959, 1960, **1962**)

Doug Harvey, Montreal (1951, 1952, **1953**, **1954**, 1955, **1956**, **1957**, **1958**, **1959**, **1960**), St. Louis (1968)

Jean-Guy Talbot, Montreal (**1956**, **1957**, **1958**, **1959**, **1960**, **1965**, **1966**, 1967), St. Louis (1968, 1969, 1970)

*Béliveau's Canadiens also won the Stanley Cup in 1959, but he missed the final due to injury.

The Overtime Winner

Only twice in NHL history has the seventh game of the Stanley Cup final been decided in overtime. Like Pete Babando for the Red Wings against the New York Rangers in 1950, Tony Leswick was an unlikely hero in 1954.

The 5-foot-7 forward, known as "Mighty Mouse," had twice topped 20 goals as a member of the Rangers earlier in his career, but since joining the Red Wings in 1951, Leswick had become something of a defensive specialist. He played on Detroit's checking line with Glen Skov and Matt Pavelich and had scored just six goals during the 1953–54 season. Leswick and Pavelich had managed only one assist each through six games of the Stanley Cup final, but they had done a great job of shutting down the Canadiens' big shooters.

A record crowd of 15,791 at the Detroit Olympia saw Montreal take an early lead in Game 7, when Floyd Curry scored at 9:17 of the first period. Red Kelly tied the game with a power-play goal at 1:17 of the second. Detroit was the better team for much of the night, but Terry Sawchuk had to make 12 saves in the third period to keep the game tied.

Just past the 4:00-mark in overtime, Metro Prystai cleared the Detroit zone and passed to Glen Skov, who fired the puck into the Montreal end. Doug Harvey cleared the puck behind the net and out the other side. Leswick had just got on the ice and kept it in along the boards beyond the top of the faceoff circle. He lofted a shot on goal, and the puck bounced off Harvey's glove past Gerry McNeil for the Stanley Cup–winning goal.

The Montreal-Detroit Rivalry

"**I**f I had shaken hands," said Montreal Canadiens coach Dick Irvin in the aftermath of the 1954 Stanley Cup final, "I wouldn't have meant it."

> **"We'd play them twice on a weekend and it was a 120-minute game for four points. In the second game, you'd pick up right where you left off in the first. The intensity was unbelievable."**
>
> **— Marcel Pronovost**

In the days following Tony Leswick's overtime goal that gave the Detroit Red Wings the Stanley Cup in Game 7, the fact that the Canadiens had skipped the traditional handshake became a big story.

"Did the Germans congratulate the Allied nations after the war?" complained one bitter Montreal sports writer on the train back home after the series.

"We don't know that the cases are parallel," wrote Dink Carroll in the *Montreal Gazette* on April 19, 1954. "Hockey is supposed to be a game.... Even so, we seem to recall seeing pictures of [diplomats] shaking hands when meeting to discuss terms of armistice. There was no loss of honor in the Canadiens defeat and it would have been easy to be graceful about it."

But there was little that was ever graceful about the rivalry between Detroit and Montreal in the 1950s. For seven straight seasons from 1948–49 through 1954–55, the Red Wings finished first in the NHL standings. Five of those seasons it was Montreal that finished second. They met in the Stanley Cup final in 1952, 1954 and 1955, with Detroit always coming out on top. Finally, in 1955–56, it was the Canadiens who finished first and beat the Red Wings for the Stanley Cup.

"The Canadiens were our biggest rival," the Red Wings' Marcel Pronovost told Dick Irvin Jr. for his 1991 book *The Habs: An Oral History of the Montreal Canadiens, 1940 to 1980*. "We'd play them twice on a weekend and it was a 120-minute game for four points. In the second game, you'd pick up right where you left off in the first. The intensity was unbelievable."

"I didn't hate too many players," recalled Maurice Richard, "except the guy who played with Gordie Howe. Number 7. Ted Lindsay."

"I hated 'em all," Ted Lindsay admitted.

Still, in terms of personal rivalries, the biggest one was between Gordie Howe and Richard. Both played right wing, and both had passionate supporters claiming them to be the best player in hockey. In the eight biggest years of the Montreal-Detroit rivalry, Howe won four scoring titles and earned four selections to the First All-Star Team and three to the Second All-Star Team. Richard led the league in goals three times, finished among the top three in points five times and earned four selections each to the First and Second All-Star Teams.

"I was never the best player in the league," Richard admitted to Irvin Jr. "I knew that. I was a bad skater, but I worked hard. I think there were a lot of guys who played in the NHL who could have played better than me. But I had more drive from the blue line in. That's what gave me the chance to score more goals than they did."

"Gordie didn't play the way the Rocket did," Pronovost recalled. "The Rocket had the ability to lift 16,000 people out of their seats."

"I respected him," Howe said of Richard, "but I didn't like him."

Even though hockey fans were well aware of the bad blood between the players and the teams, everyone still seemed disappointed in the handshake incident.

"It came as a considerable surprise," said NHL president Clarence Campbell. Gaye Stewart, a former Red Wing who played with the Canadiens during the 1954 playoffs, was quoted as saying that "higher ups" in the organization had forbid the Montreal players to shake hands.

Doug Harvey mauls Gordie Howe as he heads into the Montreal zone.

But Stewart vehemently denied having said so and later told reporters that many Canadiens executives felt that Detroit's general manager Jack Adams had planted the story.

"We felt so downhearted," said longtime Canadiens center Ken Mosdell, "that we just didn't feel like shaking hands. After we dressed, we couldn't get near the Red Wings' room and, of course, none of them came to see us to congratulate us on the way we came back [from a three-games-to-one deficit] to put up such a fight."

Coach Dick Irvin also pointed out that "no one congratulated us from their side" when the Canadiens had stunned the Red Wings in the 1951 semifinals.

Even so, the 1954 incident could still spark bad blood even 20 years later. In the fall of 1974, the 1954 Stanley Cup final was featured in a 13-part PBS television series called *The Way It Was*, which highlighted great moments in sports history. Toward the end of the broadcast, host Curt Gowdy asked about the handshake snub. An angry Bernie

Geoffrion of the Canadiens denied it.

"No," he said. "We all went there and shook hands with the Detroit Red Wings."

"Not that night you didn't," the Red Wings' Red Kelly said quietly.

"Nope," added Ted Lindsay. "Not that night."

"No way," said Geoffrion, still denying it. (Perhaps he was

confusing that night with the end of the seven-game series in 1955 when the Canadiens did shake hands.) "I looked and Lindsay was not in the lineup. He went in the [dressing] room right away. We shook hands with a few other guys."

Lindsay stared him down. "Didn't you see me out there kissing that Cup," he said, referencing the film clip Gowdy had just shown. "I didn't go anywhere."

Realizing he was probably wrong, Geoffrion lightened the mood: "The only thing that we didn't like is they had champagne, we had coke."

The mood had mellowed somewhat by the time Irvin Jr. did the interviews for his Habs book during the 1990–91 season.

"I try not to live in the past," Lindsay told him. "But when you ask me about the games we had with the Canadiens back then, I say there was never hockey like that before, and there hasn't been since. There'll never be hockey like that again."

SEMIFINALS
4 games to 3 over Chicago

ROSTER

Doug Anderson

Butch Bouchard
(captain)

Floyd Curry

Lorne Davis

Dick Gamble

Bernie Geoffrion

Doug Harvey

Tom Johnson

Elmer Lach

Calum MacKay

Bud MacPherson

Paul Masnick

Eddie Mazur

John McCormack

Gerry McNeil

Paul Meger

Dickie Moore

Ken Mosdell

Bert Olmstead

Jacques Plante

Billy Reay

Maurice Richard

Dollard St. Laurent

Frank Selke
(manager)

Dick Irvin (coach)

FINAL 4 GAMES TO 1

APR. 9	▶	Boston 2 at Montreal 4
APR. 11	▶	Boston 4 at Montreal 1
APR. 12	▶	Montreal 3 at Boston 0
APR. 14	▶	Montreal 7 at Boston 3
APR. 16	▶	Boston 0 at Montreal 1 OT

PLAYOFF SCORING LEADER

	GP	G	A	PTS
Ed Sandford BOSTON	11	8	3	11

FINAL SERIES SCORING

MONTREAL	GP	G	A	PTS	PIM
Maurice Richard	5	4	1	5	0
Ken Mosdell	5	2	2	4	4
Calum MacKay	5	1	2	3	6
Dickie Moore	5	2	0	2	9
Floyd Curry	5	1	1	2	0
Elmer Lach	5	1	1	2	0
Bert Olmstead	5	1	1	2	2
Doug Harvey	5	0	2	2	4
Dollard St. Laurent	5	0	2	2	2
Lorne Davis	5	1	0	1	2
Bernie Geoffrion	5	1	0	1	0
Tom Johnson	5	1	0	1	4
Paul Masnick	3	1	0	1	0
Butch Bouchard	5	0	1	1	2
Eddie Mazur	5	0	1	1	11
John McCormack	2	0	0	0	0
Paul Meger	1	0	0	0	0
Billy Reay	4	0	0	0	0

GOALTENDERS	GP	W	L	MIN	GA	SO	AVG
Gerry McNeil	3	3	0	181	3	2	0.99
Jacques Plante	2	1	1	120	6	0	3.00

BOSTON	GP	G	A	PTS	PIM
Ed Sandford	5	2	1	3	5
Fleming MacKell	5	0	3	3	2
Milt Schmidt	4	2	0	2	2
Dave Creighton	5	1	1	2	0
Leo Labine	5	1	1	2	4
Woody Dumart	5	0	2	2	0
Bob Armstrong	5	1	0	1	6
Jack McIntyre	4	1	0	1	0
Johnny Peirson	5	1	0	1	2
Real Chevrefils	5	0	1	1	6
Joe Klukay	5	0	1	1	7
Hal Laycoe	5	0	1	1	10
Frank Martin	5	0	1	1	2
Bill Quackenbush	5	0	1	1	2
Warren Godfrey	5	0	0	0	0
Jerry Toppazzini	5	0	0	0	4

GOALTENDERS	GP	W	L	MIN	GA	SO	AVG
Gord Henry	3	1	2	163	10	0	3.68
Jim Henry	3	0	2	138	5	0	2.17

First Cup Games on TV The 1953 final marked the first time that Stanley Cup games were broadcast on television. René Lecavalier, who was on the air when *Le Soirée du Hockey* (Hockey Night in Canada) made its TV debut from the Montreal Forum on October 11, 1952, called Games 1, 2 and 5 from Montreal in French. There was no English broadcast, and neither of the games from Boston was televised.

Scalpers in Action Six men were arrested for ticket scalping shortly before the fifth and final game of the Stanley Cup final. Sergeant Marcel Roy of the Montreal police confirmed the men were trying to sell $2 tickets for $16.

Canadiens Scratch Seven-Year Itch

Montreal's offense sputtered during the 1952–53 season, but a defense led by Butch Bouchard, Doug Harvey and Tom Johnson helped goalie Gerry McNeil post a 2.12 goals-against average and tie Toronto's Harry Lumley with a league-best 10 shutouts. Jacques Plante made his NHL debut when McNeil suffered a broken cheekbone and had two wins and a tie in three games played. Jean Béliveau also had a three-game trial and scored five goals.

Sid Abel left Detroit to become a player-coach with the Chicago Black Hawks this season. His place between Gordie Howe and Ted Lindsay was filled by second-year center Alex Delvecchio, who was just 20 years old. The Production Line kept on producing, as Gordie Howe led the NHL with 49 goals and 46 assists to set a new scoring record with 95 points. Ted Lindsay was second in the league with 32 goals and 71 points, while Delvecchio trailed only Howe with 43 assists. Howe won the Hart Trophy as MVP for the second straight season in addition to winning the Art Ross for the third year in a row, while Terry Sawchuk led the league with a 1.90 goals-against average and won the Vezina Trophy for the second

straight season. With a record of 36-16-18, Detroit had 90 points. Second-place Montreal had only 75.

Boston lost 10 of 14 games to Detroit during the regular season and lost 7–0 to the Red Wings to open the playoffs. Stunningly, Boston bounced back to beat Detroit in six games and reach the Stanley Cup final for the first time since 1946. Chicago, on the other hand, finished fourth in the league and reached the playoffs for the first time since 1946, and they gave Montreal fits in their semifinal series. The Canadiens won two in a row, but the Black Hawks took the next three before coach Dick Irvin reluctantly agreed to pull Gerry McNeil at the goalie's own request. Jacques Plante won Games 6 and 7 3–0 and 3–1 and also won Game 1 of the final against Boston. When the Canadiens lost Game 2, Irvin went back to McNeil, who faced only 19 shots to earn a 3–0 shutout in Game 3. After a 7–3 Montreal win in Game 4, McNeil blocked all 21 shots he faced in Game 5, and the Canadiens won the Stanley Cup for the first time since 1946 when Elmer Lach beat Boston goalie "Sugar" Jim Henry at 1:22 of overtime.

Challenge Denied

In the summer of 1952, the NHL turned down an application from the Cleveland Barons to join the league due to concerns about the team's working capital. In March 1953, Jim Hendy of the Barons issued a Stanley Cup challenge for a best-of-five series if Cleveland won the American Hockey League's Calder Cup. At a governors meeting in Montreal on March 19th, the NHL declined the challenge, saying that Cleveland had not yet won the championship and that the competition with an AHL club would not be of major-league caliber.

Bonnie's Birthday During the Stanley Cup presentation, Ken Mosdell of the Canadiens picked up his four-year-old daughter, Bonnie, and skated around the north end of the ice with her. "Tomorrow is her birthday," Mosdell explained in the dressing room later. "That's why I brought her to the game."

Sucker Bait

"Sure I predicted we'd lose four straight," Canadiens coach Dick Irvin confirmed to reporters after the Stanley Cup final. "And it worked, didn't it? I knew we could beat them. So I made them feel overconfident. The day we whipped Chicago in the semifinals I telephoned the Boston publicity chief and gave him the sob-story of the century. I told him it was fine that old guys like Milt Schmidt and Porky Dumart and Bill Quackenbush would be around in this year 1953 to lead the Bruins to the Stanley Cup. They fell for it — so did the Bruins. Call it overconfidence, call it sucker bait. It worked."

The Overtime Winner

A slick center from Nokomis, Saskatchewan, Elmer Lach battled injuries for much of his career, but when he was healthy he was one of the best players in hockey. Playing with Maurice Richard and Toe Blake on the Punch Line, Lach helped the Canadiens win the Stanley Cup in 1944 and 1946. A two-time NHL scoring champion, Lach enjoyed his last great moment when he scored the Stanley Cup–winning goal in overtime in 1953.

The Bruins took possession of the puck at the start of overtime and got the first shot when Woody Dumart lifted an easy drive at Gerry McNeil. The Canadiens quickly took over and stormed the Boston end. Lach tested "Sugar" Jim Henry with a long shot, and then rookie Eddie Mazur, called up from the minors for the playoffs, whipped a sharp backhander. Maurice Richard picked up the rebound near the net, took a step toward the end boards and then sent a pass to Lach. Reports of the goal are all a bit different, but it seems Lach whipped a backhander past Henry at 1:22 of overtime to win the game. Richard hugged him so hard that he broke Lach's nose and they both fell to the ice.

"I didn't even have time to see the puck go in before Rocket hugged me," Lach said after the game. "I just let the shot go when the puck suddenly came in front of me." For Lach, it was his only goal of the playoffs, though he also had six assists in the 12 games he played. It was Maurice Richard's only assist to go along with seven playoff goals.

SEMIFINALS
4 games to 0 over Toronto

ROSTER

Sid Abel (captain)

Alex Delvecchio

Fred Glover

Bob Goldham

Glenn Hall

Gordie Howe

Red Kelly

Tony Leswick

Ted Lindsay

Marty Pavelich

Marcel Pronovost

Metro Prystai

Leo Reise Jr.

Terry Sawchuk

Enio Sclisizzi

Glen Skov

Vic Stasiuk

Johnny Wilson

Benny Woit

Larry Zeidel

Jack Adams
(manager)

Tommy Ivan (coach)

FINAL 4 GAMES TO 0

APR. 10 ▶	Detroit 3 at Montreal 1
APR. 12 ▶	Detroit 2 at Montreal 1
APR. 13 ▶	Montreal 0 at Detroit 3
APR. 15 ▶	Montreal 0 at Detroit 3

PLAYOFF SCORING LEADERS

Ted Lindsay	GP	G	A	PTS
DETROIT	8	5	2	7

Floyd Curry	GP	G	A	PTS
MONTREAL	11	4	3	7

Gordie Howe	GP	G	A	PTS
DETROIT	8	2	5	7

Metro Prystai	GP	G	A	PTS
DETROIT	8	2	5	7

FINAL SERIES SCORING

DETROIT	GP	G	A	PTS	PIM
Ted Lindsay	4	3	0	3	4
Gordie Howe	4	2	1	3	2
Tony Leswick	4	2	1	3	14
Metro Prystai	4	2	1	3	0
Marty Pavelich	4	1	2	3	2
Glen Skov	4	1	2	3	12
Sid Abel	4	0	1	1	2
Alex Delvecchio	4	0	1	1	2
Vic Stasiuk	3	0	1	1	0
Johnny Wilson	4	0	1	1	0
Bob Goldham	4	0	0	0	4
Red Kelly	3	0	0	0	0
Marcel Pronovost	4	0	0	0	2
Leo Reise Jr.	2	0	0	0	0
Benny Woit	4	0	0	0	2
Larry Zeidel	3	0	0	0	0
GOALTENDER	GP	W	L	MIN	GA	SO	AVG
Terry Sawchuk	4	4	0	240	2	2	0.50

MONTREAL	GP	G	A	PTS	PIM
Tom Johnson	4	1	0	1	0
Elmer Lach	4	1	0	1	4
Floyd Curry	4	0	1	1	0
Bernie Geoffrion	4	0	1	1	0
Bert Olmstead	4	0	1	1	2
Butch Bouchard	4	0	0	0	6
Doug Harvey	4	0	0	0	6
Dick Gamble	2	0	0	0	0
Stan Long	2	0	0	0	0
Bud MacPherson	4	0	0	0	0
Paul Masnick	4	0	0	0	0
Eddie Mazur	3	0	0	0	4
Paul Meger	4	0	0	0	0
Dickie Moore	4	0	0	0	12
Billy Reay	3	0	0	0	0
Maurice Richard	4	0	0	0	4
Dollard St. Laurent	2	0	0	0	0
GOALTENDER	GP	W	L	MIN	GA	SO	AVG
Gerry McNeil	4	0	4	240	10	0	2.50

The Octopus Brothers

Brothers Pete and Jerry Cusimano, who owned a local fish market, snuck a dead octopus into the Detroit Olympia for Game 4 of the 1952 final. The eight tentacles were meant to symbolize the eight playoff victories needed to win the Stanley Cup in this era. Pete tossed the octopus onto the ice during the second period. The Red Wings beat the Canadiens that night to win the Stanley Cup with their eighth straight playoff win. The octopus has been a good luck charm in Detroit ever since.

Red Wings Romp Through Eight Straight

Detroit had set records with 44 wins and 101 points in 1950–51, but they were eliminated in the semifinals by a third-place Montreal team that had finished 36 points behind them in the standings. Jack Adams shook up the roster for the 1951–52 season, selling six players to the Chicago Black Hawks. Added to the lineup were junior scoring sensation Alex Delvecchio and the hard-working Tony Leswick, who was acquired from the New York Rangers.

The heart of the Red Wings was still the Production Line of Sid Abel, Gordie Howe and Ted Lindsay, who played their last year together in 1951–52. Howe had a spectacular season, leading the NHL with 47 goals and 86 points and winning the Hart Trophy as MVP for the first time along with his second straight scoring title. Lindsay finished second in the scoring race with 69 points on 30 goals and 39 assists, while Abel cracked the top 10 with 53 points. Defensively, stars Red Kelly and Marcel Pronovost were strongly supported by Bob Goldham, Leo Reise Jr., Benny Woit and tough rookie Larry Zeidel. Behind this solid group, Terry Sawchuk played every minute of all 70 games for the second straight season, bettering his impressive rookie performance of 1950–51 with a league-leading 1.90 average and 12 shutouts. Detroit allowed the fewest goals-against to give Sawchuk the Vezina Trophy and the Red Wings finished the season 44-14-12 for 100 points—22 more than the second-place Canadiens.

Montreal was without Maurice Richard for much of the season due to a groin injury, but he still managed 27 goals in just 48 games. Bernie Geoffrion led the team with 30 goals and won the Calder Trophy as Rookie of the Year. Dickie Moore joined the team in December and recorded 33 points in 33 games, while Elmer Lach led the NHL with 50 assists. In the playoffs against Boston, Paul Masnick scored an overtime goal in Game 6, and Maurice Richard recovered from a hard check and a stick to the face to score the series-winning goal in Game 7. Detroit got shutouts from Sawchuk in the first two games against Toronto in their semifinal and swept the Maple Leafs easily. In the Stanley Cup final, Sawchuk posted two more shutouts to wrap up a series sweep as the Red Wings romped through the playoffs with eight straight wins.

Sawchuk's Shutouts

Terry Sawchuk's four shutouts in the 1952 playoffs tied what was then an NHL record shared by Clint Benedict (1928), Dave Kerr (1937) and Frank McCool (1945). Sawchuk did it in only eight games, whereas the others had needed nine, nine and 13 respectively. It would take until 1975, when Bernie Parent had four shutouts for Philadelphia in 15 playoff games, for the record to be equaled again. Detroit's Dominik Hasek broke the record with six shutouts in 23 games in 2002. A year later, Martin Brodeur had seven shutouts in 24 games for the New Jersey Devils.

Sawchuk's Numbers
Sawchuk posted eight wins in eight games in the 1952 playoffs and allowed just five pucks to get past him for a goals-against average of 0.63. Save percentage was not an official statistic at the time, but Sawchuk surrendered those five goals on 217 shots for a mark of .977. He did not allow a single puck to get past him in the Red Wings' four home games at the Detroit Olympia.

Martin Brodeur

Greatest Goal?

Though no footage of the play exists, many consider it to be hockey's greatest goal. "The Rocket has scored some spectacular goals in the past," wrote Dink Carroll in the *Montreal Gazette* on April 9, 1952, "but none of them was more brilliant than his 'big one' last night."

In Game 7 of the semifinals against Boston, Richard collided hard with the Bruins' Leo Labine in the second period. The Rocket sailed through the air and fell to the ice, out cold. Labine's stick had clipped him in the face, and when Richard was revived, he was taken to the Forum clinic with blood running from a deep cut over his left eye. Six stitches and a large bandage closed the wound, but Richard was still groggy when he returned to the bench late in the second period. According to the Canadian Press report, he took his regular shift in the third.

The score was tied 1–1, and the teams were both shorthanded when Butch Bouchard fed a pass to Richard around the 16-minute mark of the third period. Richard carried the puck out of the Canadiens' zone, eluded a Bruins forward and bore down on the defense. Richard went wide around Bill Quackenbush then cut back sharply. He was nearly on top of "Sugar" Jim Henry when he whipped a low shot past him at 16:19. An empty-net goal by Billy Reay with 34 seconds remaining clinched a 3–1 victory.

The photo of Henry (with a black eye of his own) nearly bowing as he shakes Richard's hand after the game is one of hockey's classic images. Richard is said to have broken down in tears in the dressing room a short time later.

SEMIFINALS
4 games to 1 over Boston*

*6 games played; Game 2 deemed a 1–1 tie after one period of overtime due to local curfew.

ROSTER

Bill Barilko

Max Bentley

Hugh Bolton

Turk Broda

Fern Flaman

Cal Gardner

Bob Hassard

Bill Juzda

Ted Kennedy (captain)

Joe Klukay

Danny Lewicki

Fleming MacKell

Howie Meeker

John McCormack

Gus Mortson

Al Rollins

Tod Sloan

Sid Smith

Jimmy Thomson

Ray Timgren

Harry Watson

Conn Smythe (president/manager)

Hap Day (assistant manager)

Joe Primeau (coach)

FINAL　4 GAMES TO 1

APR. 11	▶	Montreal 2 at Toronto 3 OT
APR. 14	▶	Montreal 3 at Toronto 2 OT
APR. 17	▶	Toronto 2 at Montreal 1 OT
APR. 19	▶	Toronto 3 at Montreal 2 OT
APR. 21	▶	Montreal 2 at Toronto 3 OT

PLAYOFF SCORING LEADERS

Maurice Richard	GP	G	A	PTS
MONTREAL	11	9	4	13

Max Bentley	GP	G	A	PTS
TORONTO	11	2	11	13

FINAL SERIES SCORING

TORONTO	GP	G	A	PTS	PIM
Tod Sloan	5	3	4	7	7
Sid Smith	5	5	1	6	0
Ted Kennedy	5	2	4	6	2
Max Bentley	5	0	4	4	2
Harry Watson	5	1	2	3	4
Howie Meeker	5	1	1	2	10
Bill Barilko	5	1	0	1	6
Gus Mortson	5	0	1	1	0
Danny Lewicki	3	0	0	0	0
Fern Flaman	3	0	0	0	6
Ray Timgren	5	0	0	0	0
Joe Klukay	5	0	0	0	0
Cal Gardner	5	0	0	0	0
Bill Juzda	5	0	0	0	2
Fleming MacKell	5	0	0	0	2
Jimmy Thomson	5	0	0	0	4

GOALTENDERS	GP	W	L	MIN	GA	SO	AVG
Al Rollins	3	3	0	193	5	0	1.55
Turk Broda	2	1	1	129	5	0	2.33

MONTREAL	GP	G	A	PTS	PIM
Maurice Richard	5	5	2	7	4
Billy Reay	5	1	2	3	10
Doug Harvey	5	0	3	3	2
Paul Masnick	5	2	0	2	4
Paul Meger	5	1	1	2	2
Bert Olmstead	5	0	2	2	7
Elmer Lach	5	1	0	1	2
Butch Bouchard	5	0	1	1	0
Bud MacPherson	5	0	1	1	4
Ross Lowe	1	0	0	0	0
Bob Dawes	1	0	0	0	2
Eddie Mazur	2	0	0	0	0
Calum MacKay	5	0	0	0	0
Tom Johnson	5	0	0	0	2
Ken Mosdell	5	0	0	0	2
Floyd Curry	5	0	0	0	2
Bernie Geoffrion	5	0	0	0	4

GOALTENDER	GP	W	L	MIN	GA	SO	AVG
Gerry McNeil	5	1	4	322	13	0	2.42

Barilko by the Numbers

Bill Barilko scored the Leafs' first goal of the playoffs in 1951 as well as the last one. As reported by Red Burnett in the *Toronto Star* on April 24, 1951, Leafs boss Conn Smythe calculated that Barilko had been on the ice for 17 of the 30 goals Toronto scored during the playoffs and only four of the 15 goals the Leafs gave up. Plus-minus was not an NHL statistic at this time.

One and Only

For Sid Smith, Ted Kennedy, Harry Watson and Bill Barilko, the overtime goals they scored for Toronto in the 1951 final marked the only overtime goals of their career.

Working Overtime

J oe Primeau, a star center in Toronto during the 1930s, replaced former teammate Hap Day as coach of the Maple Leafs in 1950–51. Primeau had previously led the St. Michael's Majors to the Memorial Cup and the Toronto Marlboros to the Allan Cup. His Leafs would set club records with 41 wins and 95 points this season and win the Stanley Cup—Toronto's fourth title in five years.

Detroit was the defending Stanley Cup champions, but the Red Wings revamped their roster for the 1950–51 season in a nine-player trade with the Chicago Black Hawks. Goalie Harry Lumley was among the five players shipped to Detroit, but Terry Sawchuk was more than ready to step in. Sawchuk won the Calder Trophy after playing all 70 games and posting a 1.99 goals-against average with a league-leading 11 shutouts. The Red Wings set new NHL records with 44 wins and 101 points.

Gordie Howe had suffered a major head injury during the 1950 playoffs, but he returned to win his first NHL scoring title this season. His 43 goals were only one more than Maurice Richard's 42, but Howe's 43 assists for 86 points gave him a 20-point lead over Richard in the race for the Art Ross Trophy. Toronto's Max Bentley finished third with 62 points, while teammate Ted Kennedy was one of three players tied with 61. Tod Sloan's 31 goals for the Maple Leafs and Sid Smith's 30 trailed only Howe and Richard in that category. Al Rollins shared the Toronto goaltending duties with Turk Broda and earned the Vezina Trophy as the Maple Leafs allowed the fewest goals in the NHL.

Montreal finished well back of Detroit and Toronto in the standings, with only 65 points, and faced the Red Wings in the semifinals. Games 1 and 2 both went deep into overtime, with Maurice Richard scoring the winners at 1:09 of the fourth session and then again at 2:20 of the third. The Canadiens took the series in six games in a huge upset. Toronto disposed of fourth-place Boston and would dominate the Canadiens in the Stanley Cup final. Only the fine performance of Montreal goalie Gerry McNeil kept things close as, for the only time in NHL history, every game in a playoff series required overtime. Toronto won the Cup in five games when Bill Barilko netted the winner with the last goal he ever scored; he died in a plane crash on a fishing trip that summer.

Sunday Sports

It actually took six games for Toronto to defeat Boston four games to one in their 1951 semifinal series. After Boston won a rough series opener 2–0 at Maple Leaf Gardens, a fight-filled Game 2 on Saturday, March 31st, was tied 1–1 after one period of overtime. Though Toronto's ban on Sunday sports had been lifted in 1950, the new laws only allowed for games to be played on Sunday afternoons. As a result, no new period in a Saturday night hockey game could begin after 11:40 p.m. With the time approaching 11:45, the Leafs game with the Bruins was halted.

As was the case when a power failure in Boston brought an early end to Game 4 of the final between the Bruins and the Edmonton Oilers in 1988, all the stats from this game counted, but it would have to be replayed in its entirety at the end of the series if necessary. Four straight Toronto wins meant it was not.

PLAYERS WITH THE MOST CONSECUTIVE SEASONS IN THE FINAL

10	Bernie Geoffrion, Montreal (1950–51 to 1959–60)
	Doug Harvey, Montreal (1950–51 to 1959–60)
	Tom Johnson, Montreal (1950–51 to 1959–60)
	Bert Olmstead, Montreal (1950–51 to 1958–59), Toronto (1959–60)
9	Dickie Moore, Montreal (1951–52 to 1959–60)
8	Floyd Curry, Montreal (1950–51 to 1957–58)
7	Dollard St. Laurent, Montreal (1951–52 to 1957–58)

TEAMS WITH THE MOST CONSECUTIVE SEASONS IN THE FINAL

10	Montreal Canadiens (1950–51 to 1959–60)
5	Montreal Canadiens (1964–65 to 1968–69)
	New York Islanders (1979–80 to 1983–84)

The Final

The Maple Leafs outshot the Canadiens 39–22 in Game 1, yet the score was 2–2 after regulation time. Both Toronto's Turk Broda and Montreal's Gerry McNeil were called on to make tough saves in overtime before Sid Smith's second goal of the night gave Toronto a victory at 5:51 of the extra session.

In Game 2, the Leafs fired 36 shots to the Canadiens' 24. Still, after Montreal let an early 2–0 lead slip away, Maurice Richard notched his third OT goal of the playoffs at 2:55 and the series was tied.

The scene shifted to Montreal for Game 3, but the pattern was basically the same. Al Rollins, who'd been hurt during the semifinals, took over from Broda in Game 3. He played a fine game, but once again McNeil faced the heavier workload as Toronto fired 30 shots to Montreal's 24. Rollins made a tough save on Richard early in overtime, and Ted Kennedy scored at 4:47 for a 2–1 Toronto victory. Game 4 was tighter than the previous three, and the Canadiens outshot the Maple Leafs 21–19. Sid Smith scored 33 seconds into the game, but it took Harry Watson's goal at 5:15 of overtime to give Toronto a 3–2 victory.

Back at Maple Leaf Gardens for Game 5, Toronto was totally dominant. The Leafs outshot the Canadiens 41–19, but Montreal held the lead until the dying moments. Tod Sloan scored with the Leafs' net empty and only 32 seconds remaining to tie the game 2–2. At 2:53 of overtime, Bill Barilko chased a loose puck and chopped a backhander over Gerry McNeil for the Stanley Cup–winning goal.

The Legend of Bill Barilko

It may be a cliché, but if Bill Barilko's story weren't true it would be too unbelievable to be fiction. Hollywood handsome—he played for a Toronto Maple Leafs farm team in the California movie capital after leaving his hometown of Timmins, Ontario—Barilko had barely been able to skate as a boy, yet he worked hard enough to make the NHL by the age of 19. In his five years in Toronto, the Maple Leafs won the Stanley Cup four times. And then he disappeared.

The Maple Leafs put Barilko on their negotiation list after an impressive performance with the Porcupine Combines against the powerful Toronto St. Michael's Majors in the all-Ontario final of the Memorial Cup playoffs in the spring of 1945. That fall, the young defenseman went to training camp with the Pittsburgh Hornets, a Toronto farm club in the American Hockey League. He was then assigned to the Hollywood Wolves, another farm club further down the development chain in the Pacific Coast Hockey League. A year later, Barilko attended a rookie training camp with the Maple Leafs. He was sent to Hollywood once again, but before the season was over, he was recalled by Toronto and made his NHL debut.

The Maple Leafs' rookie-filled squad had made a strong start to the 1946–47 season, but it was slumping when Barilko got the call. He played his first game on February 6, 1947, and though the Montreal Canadiens beat Toronto 8–2, the young defenseman made his presence known. He laid a heavy hit on Maurice Richard early in the game and had a couple more hard checks later.

"Barilko was a bright spot in the Toronto cause with his ability to hit the opposition," wrote Jim Vipond in the Globe and Mail.

The big hits he delivered that night became Barilko's trademark. "Holy jumpin' Jehoshaphat, the guy could hit and hit like a ton," said teammate Howie Meeker according to his biography *Golly Gee It's Me: The Howie Meeker Story*, penned by Charlie Hodge.

Barilko quickly became a favorite with both Toronto fans and his teammates as the Maple Leafs became a powerhouse.

"Bashing Bill may not be the smoothest character in the NHL,"

Red Burnett of the *Toronto Star* would later write, "but I doubt if any player gets more fun out of playing for pay than the hard rock from Timmins."

Part of the fun for Barilko was firing slap shots and joining in the offensive attack, something the Maple Leafs did not encourage in their defensemen. As a result, the seven goals Barilko scored in 1949–50 would mark a career high. He had just 26 goals in 252 career games and added five more in 47 playoff contests, yet on April 21, 1951, Barilko scored one of the most famous goals in hockey history.

Early in overtime against the Montreal Canadiens, after Meeker and Harry Watson had a couple of close calls, Barilko cruised in from the blue line toward the loose puck. He lost his balance as he chopped a backhander, going briefly airborne as his shot sailed over goalie Gerry McNeil at 2:53. Barilko's goal gave Toronto the Stanley Cup and ended the only playoff series in NHL history in which every game went into overtime, but it was what happened later that made Barilko the stuff of legend.

Toward the end of the summer of 1951, Barilko went on a fishing trip with his friend Henry Hudson, a Timmins dentist. Hudson flew

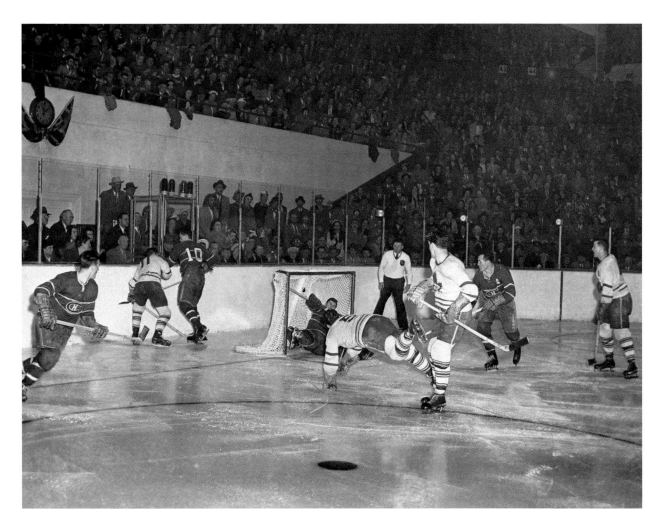

By the time the Maple Leafs opened training camp in late September, the reality began to hit that Barilko was really gone. In October, Leafs owner Conn Smythe offered a $10,000 reward for anyone who found him, dead or alive. But nobody did. Almost as if the team had been cursed, the Maple Leafs fell into a steady decline. After four Stanley Cup titles in five years, they missed the playoffs completely three times in the next seven seasons, never got past the first round when they did make it and fell into last place in 1957–58.

"Barilko was a tremendous defenseman," said former Toronto coach Joe Primeau, recalling the 1950–51 team for reporters in 1956. "The Leafs have never really found a suitable replacement."

The team finally began to recover at the end of the 1950s, and on April 22, 1962—11 years and a day after Barilko's last goal—they were Stanley Cup champions once again. Six weeks later, on June 6, 1962, the remains of Bill Barilko and Henry Hudson were finally found, still strapped to their seats in Hudson's seaplane, deep in the woods near Cochrane, Ontario, only 75 miles from home. It was an eerie coincidence, and one no fiction writer could hope to get away with.

them up to a favorite spot on the Seal River near James Bay on Friday, August 24th. After a successful weekend, they left for home on Sunday afternoon despite the warning of an approaching storm. No one was too concerned when the little yellow seaplane didn't make it home on Sunday evening, but by Monday afternoon people began to fear the worst. Six planes started a search of the bushland north of Timmins on Tuesday. By Wednesday, the story that Barilko had gone missing was in

newspapers across North America.

"As far as I'm concerned, they are not missing," Hudson's wife told reporters. "They're out of gas and down on some lake. My husband is a very careful pilot and bad weather or lack of gas may have forced him down."

The Royal Canadian Air Force launched the most extensive—and expensive—search in the country's history. It would eventually involve some 150 men covering 100,000 square miles over two months at a

Bill Barilko sails through the air while watching his shot beat Gerry McNeil for the Stanley Cup.

total cost of $385,000. As the days passed, people clung to the belief that Barilko would still be found alive in the woods somewhere, but soon strange stories began to circulate: that Barilko had been taken or defected to the Soviet Union to teach defense; that Hudson had actually been smuggling gold.

Detroit Red Wings

SEMIFINALS
4 games to 3 over Toronto

ROSTER

- Sid Abel (captain)
- Pete Babando
- Steve Black
- Joe Carveth
- Gerry Couture
- Al Dewsbury
- Lee Fogolin
- George Gee
- Gordie Howe
- Red Kelly
- Ted Lindsay
- Harry Lumley
- Clare Martin
- Jim McFadden
- Doug McKay
- Max McNab
- Marty Pavelich
- Jimmy Peters
- Marcel Pronovost
- Leo Reise Jr.
- Jack Stewart
- Johnny Wilson
- Larry Wilson
- Jack Adams (manager)
- Tommy Ivan (coach)

FINAL 4 GAMES TO 3

APR. 11 ►	NY Rangers 1 at Detroit 4	
APR. 13 ►	Detroit 1 vs. NY Rangers 3*	
APR. 15 ►	Detroit 4 vs. NY Rangers 0*	
APR. 18 ►	NY Rangers 4 at Detroit 3 OT	
APR. 20 ►	NY Rangers 2 at Detroit 1 OT	
APR. 22 ►	NY Rangers 4 at Detroit 5	
APR. 23 ►	NY Rangers 3 at Detroit 4 2x OT	

*Played in Toronto

PLAYOFF SCORING LEADER

	GP	G	A	PTS
Pentti Lund NEW YORK RANGERS	12	6	5	11

FINAL SERIES SCORING

DETROIT	GP	G	A	PTS	PIM
Sid Abel	7	5	2	7	2
Gerry Couture	7	4	2	6	0
Ted Lindsay	6	4	2	6	6
George Gee	7	2	3	5	0
Pete Babando	5	2	2	4	2
Joe Carveth	7	1	3	4	4
Marty Pavelich	7	2	1	3	6
Jim McFadden	7	2	1	3	2
Al Dewsbury	5	0	3	3	8
Red Kelly	7	0	3	3	2
Jack Stewart	7	0	3	3	10
Jimmy Peters	5	0	2	2	0
Marcel Pronovost	6	0	1	1	4
Johnny Wilson	5	0	1	1	0
Steve Black	6	0	0	0	0
Lee Fogolin	4	0	0	0	2
Clare Martin	3	0	0	0	0
Doug McKay	1	0	0	0	0
Max McNab	4	0	0	0	0
Leo Reise Jr.	7	0	0	0	8
Larry Wilson	2	0	0	0	0

GOALTENDER	GP	W	L	MIN	GA	SO	AVG
Harry Lumley	7	4	3	459	17	1	2.22

NY RANGERS	GP	G	A	PTS	PIM
Edgar Laprade	7	3	3	6	2
Tony Leswick	7	2	4	6	2
Buddy O'Connor	7	3	1	4	2
Dunc Fisher	7	2	2	4	12
Nick Mickoski	7	0	4	4	0
Allan Stanley	7	2	1	3	6
Alex Kaleta	7	0	3	3	0
Ed Slowinski	7	0	3	3	4
Don Raleigh	7	2	0	2	0
Pat Egan	7	1	1	2	4
Pentti Lund	7	1	1	2	0
Gus Kyle	7	1	0	1	14
Jack Gordon	4	0	1	1	2
Frank Eddolls	7	0	0	0	2
Jack Lancien	2	0	0	0	0
Jack McLeod	5	0	0	0	0
Fred Shero	4	0	0	0	0

GOALTENDER	GP	W	L	MIN	GA	SO	AVG
Chuck Rayner	7	3	4	459	22	0	2.88

The Circus at MSG

The Ringling Brothers and Barnum & Bailey circus made its debut at Madison Square Garden in New York in 1919. Circuses owned by P.T. Barnum already had a long association with Madison Square Garden by that time, and they would continue to be an important presence when a new Garden (the third one) was built in 1925. The circus appeared at Madison Square Garden every spring, and it often played havoc with the Rangers' playoff schedule. The circus continued to appear at the Garden after a fourth new facility opened in 1968 and would do so every year until 2010. Renovations to Madison Square Garden in 2011 caused the circus to relocate to the home of the New Jersey Devils, the Prudential Center in Newark, New Jersey.

Game 7 and Then Some

The Detroit Red Wings had lost to the Toronto Maple Leafs in the Stanley Cup finals for two straight seasons. In 1949–50, they were not to be denied. Ted Lindsay, Sid Abel and Gordie Howe, of the famed Production Line, finished one, two and three in the NHL scoring race, and third-year defenseman Red Kelly emerged as an All-Star. The Red Wings had seven wins and a tie in their first 10 games and went on to top the regular-season standings for the second year in a row.

The surprise story of this season was the New York Rangers, who improved from a last-place finish in 1948–49 to make the playoffs as the fourth-place team. The Rangers had a balanced attack led by Edgar Laprade, but their biggest star was Chuck Rayner, who became the second goalie in NHL history (following Roy Worters in 1928–29) to win the Hart Trophy as NHL MVP. In the playoffs against Montreal, Rayner allowed just seven goals in five games to lead the Rangers to the Stanley Cup final for the first time since 1940.

Detroit advanced with a tough seven-game triumph over Toronto despite losing Gordie Howe in Game 1.

Howe suffered a broken nose, a fractured cheekbone and a major concussion after a collision with Ted Kennedy and had to undergo a series of operations to relieve the pressure on his brain. Howe missed the rest of the playoffs but returned to action the following season.

With the circus making its annual visit to Madison Square Garden, the Rangers were forced to play the entire Stanley Cup final on the road. Still, they gave the Red Wings all they could handle. After letting an early lead slip away in Game 1, the Rangers evened the series on a pair of goals by Edgar Laprade in Game 2. After a 4–0 Detroit win in Game 3, the Rangers won two straight overtime contests to take a 3–2 series lead. They led Game 6 3–1 in the second period and 4–3 in the third, but Ted Lindsay and Sid Abel scored to give Detroit a 5–4 victory. The Rangers had a 2–0 first-period lead in the finale but couldn't hold it, and for the first time in history the seventh game of the Stanley Cup final went to overtime. Pete Babando scored at 8:31 of the second overtime period to give Detroit a 4–3 victory.

Hometown Heroes

Pete Babando, the 1950 overtime hero, and Bill Barilko, the 1951 hero, had both grown up in the Timmins-Porcupine district of Northern Ontario. Babando had played with future NHLers Allan Stanley and Eric Prentice on the local Holman Pluggers team that won the Ontario Juvenile Championship in 1942–43. Alex Barilko also played for that team, while his younger brother Bill served as the stick boy and a practice goalie.

Going for a Skate
There is grainy footage of Ted Lindsay picking up the Stanley Cup in 1950 after it was presented to captain Sid Abel and skating around the rink with it. This is thought to be the birth of that tradition, although there are some sources that say Lou Trudel picked up the Cup and skated around the rink with it after Chicago beat Detroit back in 1934. However, as reported in the *Chicago Tribune* the day after that game, it may have been only Stanley Cup hero Mush March that Trudel escorted around the rink, not the trophy.

Other Overtime Heroes

Though not known as a goal-scorer, defenseman Leo Reise Jr. fired two key goals for the Red Wings during their semifinal series against Toronto. The overtime winners in Games 4 and 7 that Reise netted were the only goals he scored in the playoffs that year.

Don Raleigh's two overtime goals for the Rangers against Detroit in Games 4 and 5 set a record for the Stanley Cup final. Raleigh's feat would not be matched until John LeClair scored two OT winners for the Montreal Canadiens against the Los Angeles Kings in 1993.

The Overtime Winner

The Red Wings carried the play throughout much of the overtime in Game 7, but Rangers goalie Chuck Rayner was brilliant. Just past the 8-minute mark of the second extra session, Rayner slid 10 feet out of his net to smother a point-blank drive from Detroit's George Gee. But on the ensuing faceoff, Gee beat Buddy O'Connor to the draw and fed the puck to Pete Babando. Babando, who had scored his first goal of the playoffs earlier in Game 7, slid a backhander through a maze of legs. The puck found the far corner of the Rangers' net before Rayner ever really saw it.

The Right Place at the Right Time
Doug McKay played just one game in his NHL career, but that game was Game 2 with Detroit in the 1950 Stanley Cup final. McKay, who'd been called up from Indianapolis of the American Hockey League, is the only player in history to make his sole NHL appearance with a Cup-winning team in the Stanley Cup finals.

In 1967, two members of the Maple Leafs would get their names on the Stanley Cup despite never playing a regular-season game for Toronto. Milan Marcetta suited up for three matches during the 1967 playoffs before moving on to the Minnesota North Stars the next season. Aut Erickson, who had previously played for Boston and Chicago, got into one game during the Stanley Cup final.

The Game I'll Never Forget

> **You had to admire the way the Rangers had fought us. I remember walking into their dressing room later and saying, 'Don't you guys know when to quit?'"**

Hockey Digest: March 1974
By Sid Abel, as told to George Vass

More than 30 years in hockey make it almost impossible for me to single out any game as standing alone in my memory—or even to recall the details of some of the bigger ones.

Still, I guess I could say that among the many memorable games I played with the Detroit Red Wings, the seventh game of the 1950 Stanley Cup final was one of the highlights. That game against the New York Rangers belongs right up there not just because of the way it went, but the circumstances surrounding it.

We had a powerful, well-balanced team at Detroit in 1949. We had been coming on for several seasons after falling off during World War II, although we hadn't won the Stanley Cup since 1943.

We finished first in 1949 and were to do so for the next six seasons, quite a record in a league containing such powerful teams as the Montreal Canadiens and the Toronto Maple Leafs. But in 1949 we couldn't win the Cup, losing to Toronto four straight in the final.

The next year, 1949–50, we got another shot at the Cup, and this time we weren't going to miss. We'd

finished first again under coach Tommy Ivan and had some fine players, like Gordie Howe, George Gee, Marcel Pronovost and Ted Lindsay to name a few. Harry Lumley was our goalie.

Our first round opponent was Toronto, who had won three straight Stanley Cups. We'd lost 11 games in a row to them in the playoffs, and for a couple of days it didn't look as if this playoff match would be any different. They beat us 5–0 in the opening game, but what was even more serious was that Howe was severely injured on a play with Ted Kennedy that left him with a fractured nose and skull, and he required surgery to save his life.

So we were without Howe, our top scorer, the rest of the way. Ivan put Doc Couture in at right wing with Ted Lindsay and me, and he did a fine job.

We came back to win the second game against the Leafs and then took them all the way to the seventh game. We beat them in that one 1–0 on an overtime goal by Leo Reise Jr. to go into the final against the Rangers, who had beaten the Canadiens in five games.

We beat the Rangers 4–1 on our ice the first game of the final. Then the series shifted to Toronto, which was "home ice" for the Rangers because Madison Square Garden in New York was occupied by a circus. We split the two games there, and then the Rangers beat us the fourth game in Detroit.

The fifth game was in Detroit again, and we tied the Rangers 1–1 with less than two minutes left on a goal by Lindsay. But they beat us in a couple of minutes of overtime on a goal by Bones Raleigh to take a 3–2 lead in the series.

It looked like the Rangers had the edge, two games to play and needing only one win, but we beat them the sixth game. I was fortunate enough to get the winning goal midway in the third period.

I found myself in front of Chuck Rayner, the Ranger goalie, and got off a wrist shot. Somehow he stopped it, and I was knocked to my knees at the same moment the puck hit him. The rebound came back to me, and I was able to get a stick on it and put the puck past him.

So the series was even, 3–3, and it all came down to the seventh game, the one I'll never forget, April 23, 1950, at the Olympia.

The Rangers got off to a good start,

April 23, 1950
Game 7, Stanley Cup final · Olympia Stadium, Detroit

Detroit's Sid Abel

scoring twice before we were able to get one in the net, and they still had a 3–2 lead in the middle period.

We were working hard and kept pressing them. Finally we got a break. Jim McFadden beat Ranger defenseman Allan Stanley to the puck in the Ranger zone near the boards and got off a wide-angle shot that skipped past Rayner to tie the game 3–3.

The score stayed that way to the end of regulation time. Now it was "sudden death" in overtime, but it took a lot longer in coming than most people expected.

We had, by far, the better chances. We were carrying the attack to the Rangers in the first overtime but couldn't get the puck past Rayner.

Our best chance might have come when Nick Mickoski pulled Rayner out of the net with a fine deke but then hit the post.

We went eight minutes into the second overtime before the break came. Ivan sent out Gee to take a faceoff against Buddy O'Connor to the left of the Ranger net. The other forwards out there with Gee were Pete Babando and Couture.

Gee told Babando to move directly behind him. He'd try to get the puck to him.

That's the way it happened. Gee beat O'Connor to the draw and whipped the puck back to Babando. Rayner, of course, had moved over to the near corner of the net at the faceoff. He was still there when Babando got the shot off, but he couldn't see it because Stanley was blocking his view. It went for the far side. At the last split second Rayner kicked out his left pad, but the puck went over it into the far corner of the net.

Babando's goal had won the Stanley Cup, but you had to admire the way the Rangers had fought us. I remember walking into their dressing room later and saying, "Don't you guys know when to quit?"

SEMIFINALS
4 games to 1 over Boston

ROSTER

Bill Barilko

Max Bentley

Garth Boesch

Turk Broda

Bob Dawes

Bill Ezinicki

Cal Gardner

Bill Juzda

Ted Kennedy (captain)

Joe Klukay

Vic Lynn

Fleming MacKell

Howie Meeker

Don Metz

Gus Mortson

Sid Smith

Harry Taylor

Ray Timgren

Jimmy Thomson

Harry Watson

Conn Smythe
(president/manager)

Hap Day (coach)

Ted Kennedy receives the Stanley Cup from NHL president Clarence Campbell.

FINAL   4 GAMES TO 0

APR. 8 ▸	Toronto 3 at Detroit 2 OT
APR. 10 ▸	Toronto 3 at Detroit 1
APR. 13 ▸	Detroit 1 at Toronto 3
APR. 16 ▸	Detroit 1 at Toronto 3

PLAYOFF SCORING LEADER

Gordie Howe	GP	G	A	PTS
DETROIT	11	8	3	11

FINAL SERIES SCORING

TORONTO	GP	G	A	PTS	PIM
Sid Smith	4	3	1	4	0
Max Bentley	4	2	2	4	0
Ray Timgren	4	1	3	4	0
Jimmy Thomson	4	1	3	4	4
Ted Kennedy	4	1	2	3	2
Joe Klukay	4	1	2	3	2
Fleming MacKell	4	0	3	3	2
Bill Ezinicki	4	1	1	2	10
Cal Gardner	4	1	1	2	0
Gus Mortson	4	1	0	1	2
Garth Boesch	4	0	1	1	4
Harry Watson	4	0	1	1	2
Bill Barilko	4	0	1	1	8
Bob Dawes	4	0	0	0	2
Bill Juzda	4	0	0	0	4
Vic Lynn	4	0	0	0	0

GOALTENDER	GP	W	L	MIN	GA	SO	AVG
Turk Broda	4	4	0	258	5	0	1.16

DETROIT	GP	G	A	PTS	PIM
George Gee	4	1	2	3	14
Ted Lindsay	4	1	2	3	6
Pete Horeck	4	1	1	2	4
Jack Stewart	4	1	1	2	8
Gordie Howe	4	0	2	2	2
Bill Quackenbush	4	1	0	1	0
Jim McFadden	4	0	1	1	4
Sid Abel	4	0	0	0	4
Gerry Couture	3	0	0	0	0
Lee Fogolin	3	0	0	0	0
Fred Glover	2	0	0	0	0
Red Kelly	4	0	0	0	0
Max McNab	3	0	0	0	2
Marty Pavelich	2	0	0	0	4
Nels Podolsky	3	0	0	0	0
Bud Poile	3	0	0	0	0
Gerry Reid	2	0	0	0	2
Leo Reise Jr.	4	0	0	0	2
Enio Sclisizzi	3	0	0	0	2

GOALTENDER	GP	W	L	MIN	GA	SO	AVG
Harry Lumley	4	0	4	258	12	0	2.79

Oops Bill Ezinicki played in 52 of 60 games for Toronto during the 1948–49 regular season and all nine in the playoffs. His name (William Ezinicki) was engraved on the Stanley Cup at the time, but it was mistakenly left off when the Cup was remodeled for the 1957–58 season.

One of a Kind The 1948–49 Maple Leafs were the only fourth-place team to win the Stanley Cup during the 25 years of the NHL's six-team era.

Third Straight in Four Straight

At the time, no team in NHL history had won the Stanley Cup three years in a row. After winning it the previous two seasons, the 1948–49 Toronto Maple Leafs gave little indication that they would become the first to capture a three-peat.

Despite the fact that Max Bentley had been acquired the previous season to mitigate the expected retirement of Syl Apps, the loss of their captain as well as veteran Nick Metz hurt the Leafs. So did injuries to Howie Meeker, Cal Gardner, Joe Klukay, Bill Juzda and Vic Lynn. For much of the season, the offense struggled and Toronto sat in fifth place. In February 1949, Hap Day made it known that Conn Smythe was willing to pay any price to purchase Maurice Richard from Montreal, but Frank Selke said that "all the money in Toronto wouldn't buy him." The Maple Leafs finally showed signs of life in February, but they closed out the 60-game schedule in March with five losses in their last six games to finish 22-25-13. Still, with both the Rangers and Black Hawks winning just two of their last 10 games, the Leafs managed to finish in fourth place. Chicago was fifth

despite Roy Conacher and Doug Bentley finishing one and two in the NHL scoring race.

A knee injury kept Detroit's Gordie Howe out of action for 20 games, but Sid Abel and Ted Lindsay still ranked among the league's top scorers, and Detroit finished the regular season in first place for the first time since 1942–43. Abel won the Hart Trophy as NHL MVP, while his teammate Bill Quackenbush won the Lady Byng Trophy after becoming the first defenseman in history to finish a season without a penalty. Detroit was heavily favored to beat Montreal in the semifinals, but they needed seven games to win a hard-fought series. Boston beat Toronto 7–2 on the final night of the regular season, but the Leafs had little trouble in the playoffs and beat the Bruins in five games. Toronto was only 3-7-2 against Detroit in the regular season, but with eight days off before the final, the Maple Leafs were rested and ready. Joe Klukay won the opener with a goal at 17:31 of overtime, and Turk Broda allowed just one goal in each of the next three games as Toronto swept Detroit for the second straight season.

Cinderella Stories

Fifteen teams have reached the Stanley Cup finals after posting regular-season records below .500. Only two (in bold) have won it:

YEAR	TEAM	RECORD (GP)	WIN %
1937	New York Rangers	19-20-9 (48)	.490
1938	**Chicago Black Hawks**	**14-25-9 (48)**	**.385**
1939	Toronto Maple Leafs	19-20-9 (48)	.490
1942	Detroit Red Wings	19-25-4 (48)	.438
1944	Chicago Black Hawks	22-23-5 (50)	.490
1949	**Toronto Maple Leafs**	**22-25-13 (60)**	**.475**
1950	New York Rangers	28-31-11 (70)	.479
1951	Montreal Canadiens	25-30-15 (70)	.464
1953	Boston Bruins	28-29-13 (70)	.493
1958	Boston Bruins	27-28-15 (70)	.493
1959	Toronto Maple Leafs	27-32-11 (70)	.464
1961	Detroit Red Wings	25-29-16 (70)	.471
1968	St. Louis Blues	27-31-16 (74)	.473
1982	Vancouver Canucks	30-33-17 (80)	.481
1991	Minnesota North Stars	27-39-14 (80)	.425

Ted Kennedy

Toronto Maple Leafs

ROSTER

Syl Apps (captain)

Bill Barilko

Max Bentley

Garth Boesch

Turk Broda

Les Costello

Bill Ezinicki

Ted Kennedy

Joe Klukay

Vic Lynn

Howie Meeker

Don Metz

Nick Metz

Gus Mortson

Phil Samis

Sid Smith

Wally Stanowski

Jimmy Thomson

Harry Watson

Conn Smythe (manager)

Hap Day (coach)

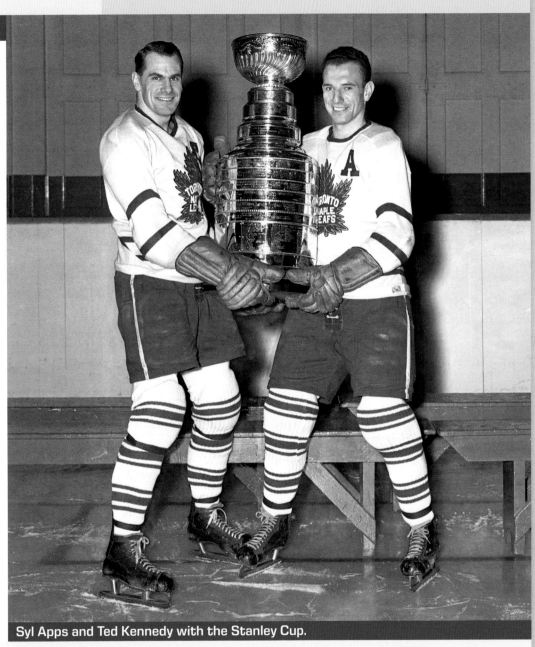

Syl Apps and Ted Kennedy with the Stanley Cup.

FINAL **4 GAMES TO 0**

APR. 7	▶	Detroit 3 at Toronto 5
APR. 10	▶	Detroit 2 at Toronto 4
APR. 11	▶	Toronto 2 at Detroit 0
APR. 14	▶	Toronto 7 at Detroit 2

PLAYOFF SCORING LEADER

Ted Kennedy	GP	G	A	PTS
TORONTO	9	8	6	14

FINAL SERIES SCORING

TORONTO	GP	G	A	PTS	PIM
Harry Watson	4	5	1	6	4
Max Bentley	4	2	4	6	0
Syl Apps	4	2	2	4	0
Ted Kennedy	4	2	2	4	0
Les Costello	4	1	2	3	0
Bill Ezinicki	4	1	1	2	4
Joe Klukay	4	1	1	2	2
Vic Lynn	4	1	1	2	18
Gus Mortson	1	1	1	2	0
Garth Boesch	4	1	0	1	0
Howie Meeker	4	1	0	1	7
Phil Samis	3	0	1	1	2
Wally Stanowski	4	0	1	1	0
Jimmy Thomson	4	0	1	1	5
Bill Barilko	4	0	0	0	13
Nick Metz	4	0	0	0	2

GOALTENDER	GP	W	L	MIN	GA	SO	AVG
Turk Broda	4	4	0	240	7	1	1.75

DETROIT	GP	G	A	PTS	PIM
Pete Horeck	4	2	2	4	8
Jim McFadden	4	1	1	2	0
Jim Conacher	4	1	0	1	0
Fern Gauthier	4	1	0	1	5
Ted Lindsay	4	1	0	1	2
Leo Reise Jr.	4	1	0	1	4
Sid Abel	4	0	1	1	9
Lee Fogolin	2	0	1	1	6
Pat Lundy	1	0	1	1	0
Marty Pavelich	4	0	1	1	2
Bill Quackenbush	4	0	1	1	0
Eddie Bruneteau	3	0	0	0	0
Al Dewsbury	1	0	0	0	0
Bep Guidolin	1	0	0	0	2
Gordie Howe	4	0	0	0	9
Red Kelly	4	0	0	0	0
Rod Morrison	1	0	0	0	0
Max McNab	3	0	0	0	2
Enio Sclisizzi	1	0	0	0	0
Jack Stewart	3	0	0	0	0

GOALTENDER	GP	W	L	MIN	GA	SO	AVG
Harry Lumley	4	0	4	240	18	0	4.50

Praise for the Captain

"I'd like to offer him so much money that he'd have to turn down that business offer he's received. But it wouldn't be fair. He's been a great hockey player—one of the greatest—and still is … but watching him out there, you know it's getting tougher for him all the time…. Syl has had one of his very best years, and that's the way he should be remembered. I hate to see him go, but I won't stand in his way." — Conn Smythe after Game 4 of the 1948 Stanley Cup final, confirming that Syl Apps would retire.

Gamble for Bentley Pays Off

The 1947–48 season began on October 13, 1947, with the first official NHL All-Star Game. Max Bentley, scoring champion of the past two seasons, lined up as a member of the All-Star Team that took on the defending Stanley Cup–champion Toronto Maple Leafs. Three weeks later, on November 2, 1947, Bentley was traded to Toronto. In what was the biggest deal in hockey history at the time, the Leafs gave up forwards Gus Bodnar, Bud Poile and Gaye Stewart along with defensemen Ernie Dickens and Bob Goldham for Bentley and rookie Cy Thomas. "I feel it's quite a gamble," said Leafs boss Conn Smythe, "but it's worth it." Smythe had been worried his team lacked depth at center. "If anything happened to captain Syl Apps, we would be desperate," Smythe explained.

With Apps, Bentley and Teeder Kennedy, the Leafs now had future Hall of Famers centering all three of their lines. Apps and Bentley both finished among the NHL's top goal-scorers with 26 apiece, while Kennedy added 25 goals and left-winger Harry Watson scored 21. Still, defense was the key in Toronto, as the Maple Leafs allowed the fewest goals with the hard-hitting crew of Bill Barilko, Gus Mortson, Wally Stanowski and Jimmy Thomson in front of Vezina Trophy–winning goalie Turk Broda. Toronto finished first in the regular-season standings with a record of 32-15-13. "This is the greatest Toronto club we've ever had," Smythe would say after the season.

The 1947–48 campaign marked the end of two legendary forward lines. The retirement of Bobby Bauer broke up the Kraut Line in Boston, and a career-ending injury to Montreal's Toe Blake marked the end for the Punch Line. Montreal's Elmer Lach won the scoring title anyway and claimed the brand new Art Ross Trophy, but the Canadiens slumped and missed the playoffs. In Detroit, the teaming of Ted Lindsay, Sid Abel and Gordie Howe gave rise to a great new scoring trio soon to be dubbed the Production Line. The Red Wings lead the NHL in scoring and finished second in the standings, behind the Maple Leafs. In the playoffs, Detroit downed the New York Rangers in six, while Toronto beat Boston in five. Though the Maple Leafs and Red Wings had clearly been the class of the NHL this season, the Stanley Cup final proved surprisingly one-sided, as Toronto swept the series.

Going Out in Style

Syl Apps had given indications that he planned to retire at the end of the 1947–48 season. He hoped to hit the 200-goal plateau (a major milestone at the time) before he did. On the last night of the regular season, Apps had a hat trick in a 5–2 win over Detroit to give him 201 goals in his career. The last game he ever played was Game 4 of the final, and Apps scored a goal in that one too.

GOALTENDERS WITH THE MOST YEARS IN FINALS (WINS IN BOLD)

10	Jacques Plante, Montreal (**1953**, 1954, 1955, **1956**, **1957**, **1958**, **1959**, **1960**), St. Louis (1969, 1970)
8	Turk Broda, Toronto (1938, 1939, 1940, **1942**, **1947**, **1948**, **1949**, **1951**)
7	Terry Sawchuk, Detroit (**1952**, **1954**, **1955**, 1961, 1963, 1964), Toronto (**1967**)
	Glenn Hall, Detroit (1956), Chicago (**1961**, 1962, 1965), St. Louis (1968, 1969, 1970)
6	Johnny Bower, Toronto (1959, 1960, **1962**, **1963**, **1964**, **1967**)
	Ken Dryden, Montreal (**1971**, **1973**, **1976**, **1977**, **1978**, **1979**)

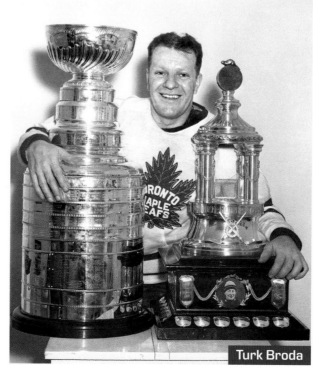

Turk Broda

Toronto Maple Leafs

The Semifinals

Toronto trailed Boston three times in Game 1 and needed two late goals from Syl Apps and Jimmy Thomson to send the game into overtime. Nick Metz scored at 17:02 to give Toronto a 5–4 victory. Ted Kennedy scored four times in a 5–3 win in Game 2. Game 3 in Boston was a rough one, and the fans became unruly as Toronto rolled to a 5–1 victory. A couple of fans took swings at Bill Barilko as he left the ice after the second period. There were further attacks on players from both teams, as well as the referees, after the game. A larger police presence, and a Bruins win, kept things under control in Game 4. Back in Toronto for Game 5, the Leafs wrapped things up with a 3–2 win on Kennedy's sixth goal of the series.

The Final Slow starters for most of the year, the Leafs had come from behind for a win or a tie 33 times during the regular season. In Game 1 of the final, Detroit went ahead at 7:20 in the first period only to see Toronto score twice in the next 1:43 to break on top. The Maple Leafs led 5–1 after two and held on for a 5–3 victory.

Toronto's Gus Mortson suffered a broken leg in the opener, but the game had been fairly tame. Game 2 was much rougher, with even goalies Turk Broda and Harry Lumley exchanging punches at the end. The Maple Leafs won 4–2 on a pair of goals from Max Bentley. Game 3 was a defensive struggle with Broda making 26 stops in a 2–0 victory. Game 4 was a romp, with Ted Kennedy and Harry Watson scoring twice each in a 7–2 Toronto victory.

SEMIFINALS
4 games to 1 over Detroit

ROSTER

Syl Apps (captain)
Bill Barilko
Gus Bodnar
Garth Boesch
Turk Broda
Bill Ezinicki
Bob Goldham
Ted Kennedy
Joe Klukay
Vic Lynn
Howie Meeker
Don Metz
Nick Metz
Gus Mortson
Bud Poile
Wally Stanowski
Gaye Stewart
Jimmy Thomson
Harry Watson
Conn Smythe (manager)
Hap Day (coach)

From left to right, the four goal-scorers from Game 3 of the Final: Vic Lynn, Gus Mortson, Ted Kennedy and Bud Poile.

FINAL 4 GAMES TO 2

APR. 8	▶	Toronto 0 at Montreal 6
APR. 10	▶	Toronto 4 at Montreal 0
APR. 12	▶	Montreal 2 at Toronto 4
APR. 15	▶	Montreal 1 at Toronto 2 OT
APR. 17	▶	Toronto 1 at Montreal 3
APR. 19	▶	Montreal 1 at Toronto 2

PLAYOFF SCORING LEADER

Maurice Richard	GP	G	A	PTS
MONTREAL	10	6	5	11

FINAL SERIES SCORING

TORONTO	GP	G	A	PTS	PIM
Ted Kennedy	6	3	2	5	2
Vic Lynn	6	3	1	4	12
Harry Watson	6	2	1	3	0
Gaye Stewart	6	1	2	3	6
Howie Meeker	6	0	3	3	6
Bud Poile	5	2	0	2	2
Syl Apps	6	1	1	2	0
Gus Mortson	6	1	1	2	6
Bill Barilko	6	0	2	2	6
Don Metz	6	0	2	2	4
Gus Bodnar	1	0	0	0	0
Garth Boesch	6	0	0	0	6
Bill Ezinicki	6	0	0	0	16
Joe Klukay	6	0	0	0	0
Nick Metz	1	0	0	0	0
Wally Stanowski	5	0	0	0	0
Jimmy Thomson	6	0	0	0	12
GOALTENDER	GP	W	L	MIN	GA	SO	AVG
Turk Broda	6	4	2	377	13	1	2.07

MONTREAL	GP	G	A	PTS	PIM
Buddy O'Connor	6	3	3	6	0
Toe Blake	6	0	4	4	0
Maurice Richard	5	3	0	3	25
Butch Bouchard	6	0	3	3	14
Leo Gravelle	4	2	0	2	2
Billy Reay	6	2	0	2	2
George Allen	6	1	1	2	6
Glen Harmon	6	1	1	2	0
Roger Léger	6	0	2	2	6
Murph Chamberlain	6	1	0	1	6
Jimmy Peters	6	0	1	1	4
John Quilty	2	0	1	1	2
Frank Eddolls	5	0	0	0	2
Bob Fillion	5	0	0	0	0
Leo Lamoureux	2	0	0	0	4
Hub Macey	3	0	0	0	0
Murdo MacKay	6	0	0	0	0
Ken Reardon	4	0	0	0	16
GOALTENDER	GP	W	L	MIN	GA	SO	AVG
Bill Durnan	6	2	4	377	13	1	2.07

End of an Era

The 1946–47 season marked the final year of the "stovepipe" Stanley Cup. The trophy was remodeled for the 1947–48 season into a size and shape that was very similar to the Stanley Cup as it still appears today. More importantly, on June 30, 1947, Stanley Cup trustees P.D. Ross and Cooper Smeaton and NHL president Clarence Campbell signed a document formalizing the NHL's control of the Stanley Cup. The NHL was granted full authority to determine and amend the conditions for Stanley Cup competition (i.e., the playoffs) and the responsibility for the Cup's safe keeping. This agreement is to remain in place as long as the NHL remains the world's leading professional hockey league as determined by its caliber of play.

After giving up day-to-day control of the team while serving in the Canadian army, Conn Smythe took over full charge of the Maple Leafs once more for the 1946–47 season. Toronto had won the Stanley Cup in 1945 only to fall out of the playoffs the following season, so Smythe and coach Hap Day decided a complete overhaul was necessary. Seven of the 21 players on the Leafs' roster from 1945–46 were traded, released or encouraged to retire. Another four were sent to the minors. The team would go with youth, and though Smythe couldn't guarantee success, he did promise that no other team in the NHL would work harder than his crew.

Ted "Teeder" Kennedy was only 21 years old, but the wartime star was already entering his fourth full season. He led Toronto with 28 goals and 60 points during the 60-game schedule. Rookie Howie Meeker, in his first full season back in hockey after being wounded during World War II, had 27 goals and won the Calder Trophy. The Leafs defense featured four rookies in Jimmy Thomson, Bill Barilko, Garth Boesch and Gus Mortson. Though the rookies occasionally showed their inexperience, Turk

Broda had returned to his pre-war form in goal. Broda could not match the numbers of Vezina Trophy–winner Bill Durnan in Montreal, but the Leafs goalie finished in a tie for fourth place in voting for the Hart Trophy and was a big reason why Toronto finished the regular season in second place.

Frank Selke had left the Maple Leafs to run the Canadiens. The defending Stanley Cup champions started out slowly, but a strong season from Maurice Richard lifted Montreal into top spot. Richard's 45 goals made him the only player in the NHL with more than 30, and only a late-season slump allowed Chicago's Max Bentley to pass him for the scoring title, with 72 points to Richard's 71. In the playoffs, the Canadiens met the Boston Bruins in the semifinal and beat them in five games to return to the final. The Maple Leafs were beaten 9–1 by the Detroit Red Wings in Game 2 of their semifinal series, but they still defeated Detroit in five. Montreal took Game 1 of the final 6–0, but the Leafs bounced back for a 4–0 win in a rough Game 2. Maurice Richard was suspended for Game 3, which the Leafs won easily. Toronto went on to take the series in six games.

Bouncing Back

NHL TEAMS WINNING THE STANLEY CUP A SEASON AFTER MISSING THE PLAYOFFS

TEAM	CHAMPIONSHIP SEASON
Montreal Maroons	1925–26
Chicago Black Hawks	1933–34
Detroit Red Wings	1935–36
Chicago Black Hawks	1937–38
Toronto Maple Leafs	1946–47
Montreal Canadiens	1970–71
Pittsburgh Penguins	1991–92
New York Rangers	1993–94
Carolina Hurricanes	2005–06*

*Carolina missed the playoffs in 2003–04, and a lockout canceled the 2004–05 season.

Syl Apps

Birth of the Rivalry

A young but determined Maple Leafs team led the NHL in penalty minutes in 1946–47. Though they were more tough than dirty, the Canadiens, led by former Leafs front-office man Frank Selke, were critical of the Leafs all season. Early in the year, Selke accused Toronto defensemen of using "wrestling tactics." The bad blood got even worse when Montreal's Elmer Lach suffered a fractured skull on February 6, 1947, after a hard hit from Toronto's Don Metz. It all boiled over in Game 2 of the Stanley Cup final. With the Maple Leafs up 3–0 in the second period, Maurice Richard took exception to the close checking tactics of Vic Lynn and cut him on the head with his stick. Richard received a major penalty, and shortly after returning to the ice, Richard and Bill Ezinicki got their sticks up. Both were called for minor penalties, but Richard swung again and cut Ezinicki on the head. He received a match penalty, a $100 fine and was suspended from Game 3 by NHL president Clarence Campbell.

Tough Team For five straight seasons from 1946–47 to 1950–51, one of Gus Mortson, Bill Barilko or Bill Ezinicki led the league in penalty minutes. The Leafs won the Stanley Cup four times during that same period.

Turning Point Game 4 was the key one in the 1947 final. After each team allowed an early goal, Turk Broda and Bill Durnan staged a goaltenders' battle that wasn't broken up until Syl Apps scored for Toronto at 16:36 of overtime.

Beating 'em in the Alley

In his 1980 autobiography, Conn Smythe admitted that he couldn't remember when he first uttered his famous motto. Though it appears no newspaper quoted him as saying it at the time, it was pretty obvious during the Toronto Maple Leafs' 1946 training camp that Smythe wanted a tough team.

Smythe "told his players he wanted a fighting team filled with the desire to mix it with anyone," wrote Jim Vipond in the *Globe and Mail* on September 27, 1946. "He further stressed the importance of team spirit and co-operation."

Gordon Walker of the *Toronto Star* wrote that same day of Smythe's "brief, forceful address on club policy," quoting Smythe directly: "If they start shoving you around, I expect you to shove them right back, harder. If one of our players should get injured by illegal tactics of the enemy, I expect the players on our team to see that the man responsible doesn't get away with it."

In other words: "If you can't beat 'em in the alley, you can't beat 'em on the ice."

Smythe also wrote in 1980 that he felt his motto had often been misunderstood. He didn't want his players to be bullies, he explained, he merely wanted them to refuse to be bullied. With that in mind, Smythe was critical of the 1945–46 version of the Maple Leafs not because they

missed the playoffs a year after winning the Stanley Cup, but because they had the fewest penalty minutes in the NHL. He vowed that would never happen again.

To reshape his team in the image he wanted, Smythe decided to rebuild around the young players in his farm system. Having missed the playoffs the year before, he reasoned that if he had to lose he'd rather lose with youngsters than with veterans. And so on September 20, 1946, a week before training camp was set to open in St. Catharines, Ontario, the Leafs held what would now be called a "prospects camp."

From that camp emerged Bill Barilko (though he would begin the season in the minors), Gus Mortson and Howie Meeker, who would all be a part of four Stanley Cup–winning teams in Toronto over the next five years. Jimmy Thomson's brief appearance with the Maple Leafs in 1945–46 had already earned him a spot at training camp, where he too made the team and won four titles

in the next five years. Three-time Cup-winners Garth Boesch and Vic Lynn both came out of the prospects camp. Tod Sloan was also among the 25 young players invited, but he needed a few more years to develop into the star he would become in 1950–51. Sid Smith was not at the prospects camp, but did make a brief debut in the NHL in 1946–47 before breaking out as a star a few years later.

Smythe and coach Hap Day were confident they had put together a team they might win with a year or two down the road, but with six rookies among the 12 new faces on the 18-man roster, Smythe downplayed his expectations for 1946–47.

"The Maple Leafs will suffer plenty of defeats this season," he admitted. But he couldn't completely hide his optimism: "We'll win plenty, too!"

With a team that refused to back down from anyone, Toronto won more games than anyone expected. The rookies blended perfectly with young veteran Ted Kennedy, newly acquired Harry Watson and older veterans Syl Apps, Nick Metz, Wally Stanowski and Turk Broda, who all dated back to the 1942 Stanley Cup champion team. Toronto went 7-3-1 to start the season and was in first place with a record of

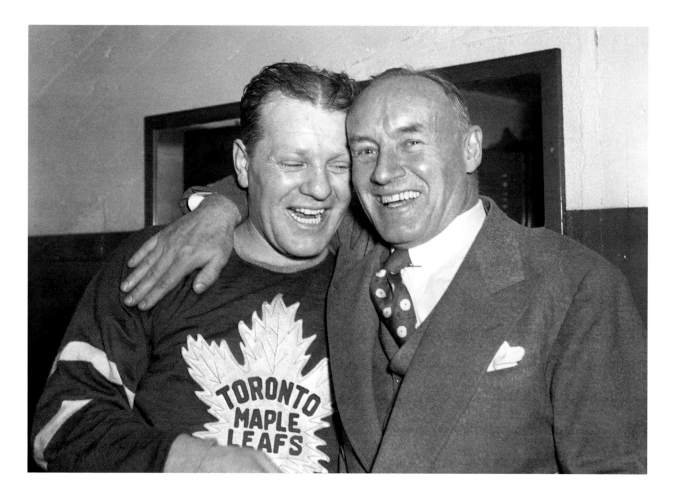

20-6-4 at the halfway point of the newly expanded 60-game schedule. Despite falling to second behind the Montreal Canadiens before the end of the season, the Maple Leafs beat them to win the Stanley Cup.

Day had been one of the NHL's best defensemen in his playing days and preached a defensive philosophy as coach, but both he and Smythe believed the strength of any team was at center and in goal. Broda was one of the greatest big-game goaltenders of all time, but in order to improve the team's depth at center behind Apps and Kennedy,

Smythe swung a huge deal for Max Bentley early in the 1947–48 season. The "Dipsy-Doodle Dandy from Delisle" might not have seemed like a Smythe favorite, but the Leafs boss respected talented players who were tough but clean. Bentley certainly fit the bill.

When Apps retired after a second straight Stanley Cup victory in 1948, Smythe acquired Cal Gardner from the New York Rangers to maintain his depth at center. The six-player swap also brought Bill Juzda to Toronto to further toughen the Leafs' defense. After a difficult

Conn Smythe and Turk Broda following Toronto's 1949 Stanley Cup victory.

regular season in 1948–49, Toronto won eight of nine games in the playoffs and became Stanley Cup champions for the third straight season.

The Leafs failed to make it four in a row in 1949–50, and after five Cup wins in 10 seasons, Day gave up his coaching duties to become Smythe's assistant general manager. Former star center Joe Primeau was brought in as coach and opened up the Leafs attack. Toronto posted a mark

of 41-16-13 during the 70-game 1950–51 season for a .679 winning percentage that remains the best in team history. By then Broda was the only player left from the 1942 Stanley Cup team and even he was being phased out by rookie Al Rollins. The team still had depth at center with Kennedy, Bentley and Gardner—and was still tough on defense with Thomson, Mortson, Juzda and Barilko—but Barilko's death in the summer of 1951 took the heart out of his Toronto teammates, and the toughest team in hockey went into a long decline.

SEMIFINALS
4 games to 0 over Chicago

Stellar defense: Ken Reardon, Bill Durnan and Butch Bouchard.

FINAL 4 GAMES TO 1

MAR. 30 ►	Boston 3 at Montreal 4	OT
APR. 2 ►	Boston 2 at Montreal 3	OT
APR. 4 ►	Montreal 4 at Boston 2	
APR. 7 ►	Montreal 2 at Boston 3	OT
APR. 9 ►	Boston 3 at Montreal 6	

PLAYOFF SCORING LEADER

	GP	G	A	PTS
Elmer Lach MONTREAL	9	5	12	17

FINAL SERIES SCORING

MONTREAL	GP	G	A	PTS	PIM
Elmer Lach	5	3	4	7	0
Maurice Richard	5	3	2	5	0
Butch Bouchard	5	2	1	3	4
Murph Chamberlain	5	2	1	3	0
Dutch Hiller	5	2	1	3	0
Glen Harmon	5	1	2	3	0
Bob Fillion	5	2	0	2	2
Ken Mosdell	5	2	0	2	2
Frank Eddolls	4	0	1	1	0
Toe Blake	5	1	0	1	5
Jimmy Peters	5	1	0	1	4
Leo Lamoureux	5	0	0	0	2
Buddy O'Connor	5	0	0	0	0
Gerry Plamondon	1	0	0	0	0
Ken Reardon	5	0	0	0	4
Billy Reay	5	0	0	0	2
GOALTENDER	GP	W	L	MIN	GA	SO	AVG
Bill Durnan	5	4	1	341	13	0	2.29

BOSTON	GP	G	A	PTS	PIM
Bep Guidolin	5	2	1	3	9
Bill Cowley	5	1	2	3	2
Don Gallinger	5	1	2	3	0
Milt Schmidt	5	1	2	3	2
Bobby Bauer	5	2	0	2	2
Terry Reardon	5	2	0	2	2
Woody Dumart	5	1	1	2	0
Herb Cain	5	0	2	2	2
Ken Smith	5	0	2	2	0
Jack Crawford	5	1	0	1	0
Pat Egan	5	1	0	1	4
Murray Henderson	5	1	0	1	0
Bill Shill	3	0	1	1	2
Jack Church	5	0	0	0	2
Dit Clapper	1	0	0	0	0
Roy Conacher	1	0	0	0	0
Jack McGill	5	0	0	0	0
GOALTENDER	GP	W	L	MIN	GA	SO	AVG
Frank Brimsek	5	1	4	341	19	0	3.34

Brother vs Brother Ken Reardon of Montreal and Terry Reardon of Boston faced off against each other in the 1946 Stanley Cup final. The next time that two brothers would oppose each other for the Stanley Cup was 2003, when Scott Niedermayer's New Jersey Devils beat Rob Niedermayer's Mighty Ducks of Anaheim.

New Trustee Though the role was now little more than ceremonial, original Stanley Cup trustee P.D. Ross announced the appointment of Cooper Smeaton as his fellow trustee on February 24, 1946. Smeaton replaced William Foran, who had passed away on November 30, 1945. Smeaton had long been prominent in hockey circles, mostly as a referee in the National Hockey Association and in the NHL from 1913 to 1937.

Canadiens Kick Off the Post-War Era

With World War II ending during the summer of 1945, more than 40 players who had been serving in the military returned to NHL rosters. Some took a bit of time to regain the skills they had displayed before the war. Many never would. Still, with higher caliber players back on the ice, the 1945–46 NHL season was much more competitive than the previous two. It would take several years (plus the expansion of the schedule to 60, and then 70, games) before the offensive explosion of the wartime years would be matched.

As defending Stanley Cup champions, the Maple Leafs looked to be much stronger with the return of Syl Apps, Gaye Stewart, Don Metz and a few others. Unfortunately, a contract dispute kept 1944–45 hero Frank McCool off the ice for five weeks at the start of the season. McCool's eventual return, followed by the later return of Turk Broda from the army, wasn't enough to offset Toronto's 3-10-1 start. The Maple Leafs fell to fifth place and missed the playoffs. The return of several pre-war stars didn't help New York much either, as the Rangers finished sixth for the fourth straight season.

The Montreal Canadiens did not get the same production from the Punch Line of Maurice Richard, Elmer Lach and Toe Blake as they had in previous seasons, but the return of Ken Reardon alongside Butch Bouchard bolstered the NHL's best defense. The Canadiens slumped in midseason when Bill Durnan missed 10 games with a broken hand, but the big goalie still led the NHL with four shutouts and a 2.60 average, and Montreal topped the standings for the third straight year. In Boston, the Kraut Line of Milt Schmidt, Woody Dumart and Bobby Bauer slowly rounded into form. Another big boost came with the midseason return of goalie Frank Brimsek from the U.S. Navy. After two seasons out of the playoffs, Boston climbed into second place, behind Montreal, and met the Canadiens in the Stanley Cup final.

The Punch Line came to life in the playoffs, with Blake and Richard each scoring seven goals in nine games and Lach recording 12 assists and 17 points. The Canadiens outscored Chicago 26–7 in sweeping the Black Hawks in the semifinals. Boston kept the scores close but still fell to Montreal in five games.

MOST CAREER OVERTIME GOALS IN THE PLAYOFFS

8	Joe Sakic (Colorado)
6	Maurice Richard (Montreal)
5	Glenn Anderson (Edmonton, Toronto, St. Louis)
4	Bob Nystrom (New York Islanders)
	Dale Hunter (Quebec, Washington)
	Wayne Gretzky (Edmonton, Los Angeles)
	Stéphane Richer (Montreal, New Jersey)
	Joe Murphy (Edmonton, Chicago)
	Esa Tikkanen (Edmonton, New York Rangers)
	Jaromir Jagr (Pittsburgh)
	Kirk Muller (Montreal, Dallas)
	Jeremy Roenick (Chicago, Philadelphia)
	Chris Drury (Colorado, Buffalo)
	Jamie Langenbrunner (Dallas, New Jersey)

MOST CAREER OVERTIME GOALS IN THE FINAL

3	Maurice Richard (Montreal)
2	Don Raleigh (New York Rangers)
	Jacques Lemaire (Montreal)
	John LeClair (Montreal)

Glenn Anderson

The Final

The Canadiens expected a tougher battle from the Bruins than they'd gotten from the Black Hawks, and they were right. Goalies Bill Durnan and Frank Brimsek were thought to be the keys to the series, and both played well in Game 1. Montreal took a 2–0 lead in the second period, but the Bruins tied it up and were leading 3–2 late in the third. Murph Chamberlain tied the score with 3:37 remaining, and Maurice Richard won it with an overtime goal at 9:08.

Toe Blake hurt his back when he crashed into the net in Game 1, but he was in the lineup for Game 2. Blake set up Maurice Richard early in the game, and when Elmer Lach punched in the rebound, Montreal had a 1–0 lead. It then took a late goal from Butch Bouchard to tie the game 2–2 and a lucky break from war veteran Jimmy Peters, who bounced in a shot off Boston's Terry Reardon at 16:55 of overtime, for the win.

With Blake playing sparingly in Game 3, Ken Mosdell took his place. Mosdell kept Milt Schmidt under wraps and scored twice himself in a 4–2 victory. Durnan and Brimsek were the stars of Game 4, as the Bruins stayed alive with a 3–2 overtime win.

Back in Montreal for Game 5, Boston battled hard. The Canadiens led 3–2 after one, but Milt Schmidt (who'd been questionable for the game with a charley horse) tied the score midway through the second. Checking was tight in the third until Toe Blake's tally at 11:06 sparked a three-goal outburst, and Montreal won the Stanley Cup for the second time in three years with a 6–3 victory.

SEMIFINALS
4 games to 2 over Montreal

ROSTER

Pete Backor

Gus Bodnar

Lorne Carr

Bob Davidson
(captain)

Reg Hamilton

Mel Hill

Ted Kennedy

Art Jackson

Ross Johnstone

Frank McCool

John McCreedy

Jack McLean

Don Metz

Nick Metz

Moe Morris

Tom O'Neill

Babe Pratt

Sweeney Schriner

Wally Stanowski

Conn Smythe
(manager)

Frank Selke
(business manager)

Hap Day (coach)

FINAL   4 GAMES TO 3

APR. 6	▶	Toronto 1 at Detroit 0
APR. 8	▶	Toronto 2 at Detroit 0
APR. 12	▶	Detroit 0 at Toronto 1
APR. 14	▶	Detroit 5 at Toronto 3
APR. 19	▶	Toronto 0 at Detroit 2
APR. 21	▶	Detroit 1 at Toronto 0 OT
APR. 22	▶	Toronto 2 at Detroit 1

PLAYOFF SCORING LEADER

	GP	G	A	PTS
Joe Carveth DETROIT	14	5	6	11

FINAL SERIES SCORING

TORONTO	GP	G	A	PTS	PIM
Ted Kennedy	7	4	1	5	2
Mel Hill	7	1	2	3	4
Babe Pratt	7	1	1	2	4
Gus Bodnar	7	1	0	1	2
Moe Morris	7	1	0	1	2
Sweeney Schriner	7	1	0	1	2
Bob Davidson	7	0	1	1	0
Nick Metz	3	0	1	1	0
Wally Stanowski	7	0	1	1	0
Lorne Carr	7	0	0	0	5
Reg Hamilton	7	0	0	0	0
Art Jackson	7	0	0	0	0
John McCreedy	4	0	0	0	0
Don Metz	7	0	0	0	0
GOALTENDER	GP	W	L	MIN	GA	SO	AVG
Frank McCool	7	4	3	434	9	3	1.24

DETROIT	GP	G	A	PTS	PIM
Flash Hollett	7	2	2	4	0
Eddie Bruneteau	7	2	1	3	0
Joe Carveth	7	2	1	3	0
Murray Armstrong	7	2	0	2	0
Ted Lindsay	7	1	0	1	4
Mud Bruneteau	7	0	1	1	2
Bill Quackenbush	7	0	1	1	2
Tony Bukovich	1	0	0	0	0
Syd Howe	5	0	0	0	2
Harold Jackson	7	0	0	0	4
Carl Liscombe	7	0	0	0	0
Jud McAtee	7	0	0	0	0
Fido Purpur	4	0	0	0	4
Earl Seibert	7	0	0	0	2
Steve Wojciechowski	2	0	0	0	0
GOALTENDER	GP	W	L	MIN	GA	SO	AVG
Harry Lumley	7	3	4	434	9	2	1.24

Low-Scoring Series Both Toronto and Detroit scored only nine goals in the 1945 Stanley Cup final. Their total of 18 makes this the lowest-scoring seven-game series in NHL playoff history. Nine goals by one team in a seven-game series was also an NHL record for many years, until the Vancouver Canucks scored only eight times in their seven-game Stanley Cup loss to the Boston Bruins in 2011.

Family Affair Elwyn "Moe" Morris won the Stanley Cup with the Maple Leafs in April 1945. His brother Frank won the Grey Cup with the Toronto Argonauts that December, and then he won it again in 1946 and 1947. Before turning pro in hockey, Moe Morris had also played football with the Argonauts, back in 1940 and 1941.

Cooling Off the Canadiens

After a record-setting season that had culminated in the Stanley Cup in 1943–44, the Montreal Canadiens ran away with the regular-season race once again in 1944–45. The Canadiens matched their record win total by going 38-8-4, and though their league-leading 228 goals were just behind the 234 of the previous season, the performance of the Punch Line was even more amazing: Maurice Richard scored 50 goals in 50 games, Elmer Lach set a new record with 54 assists and led the league with 80 points to Richard's 73, and Toe Blake finished third in scoring with 67 points.

The Canadiens had lost some players to military service, but the fact that Quebecers did not support the war as readily as English Canadians led to a lot of resentment. Many dismissed Maurice Richard as a wartime wonder, but while many wartime stars couldn't cut it in the post-war era, Maurice Richard certainly did. But despite the star power of Richard and the Punch Line, the Canadiens got a shocking surprise in the 1945 playoffs from a third-place Toronto team that had finished 28 points behind them in the standings.

Frank McCool was a 26-year-old NHL rookie with the Maple Leafs in 1944–45. Stomach ulcers had cut short his army career and kept him out of hockey in 1943–44 after an impressive training camp with the New York Rangers. In Toronto, McCool tied for the NHL lead with four shutouts and won the Calder Trophy, but it was in the playoffs that he truly stood out. In Game 1 of Toronto's semifinal versus Montreal, McCool matched the great Bill Durnan save for save before Ted Kennedy scored with 22 seconds remaining to give Toronto a 1–0 victory. The Maple Leafs raced out to a 3–1 series lead, and though the Canadiens bombed them 10–3 in Game 5, Toronto played tough in front of McCool in Game 6 and advanced to the Stanley Cup final with a 3–2 victory.

Toronto faced Detroit in the final. The Red Wings had finished a distant second behind Montreal in the regular-season standings and knocked off fourth-place Boston in seven games in the semifinal. McCool opened the series with three straight shutouts, but Detroit bounced back with three wins, including two shutouts by their 18-year-old rookie goalie, Harry Lumley. Game 7 was another low-scoring affair, with Babe Pratt breaking a 1–1 tie at 12:14 of the third period to give Toronto the Stanley Cup.

Three in a Row

Before Frank McCool, only one goalie had ever posted three straight shutouts in the playoffs. John Ross Roach of the New York Rangers blanked the New York Americans in back-to-back games in the quarterfinals in 1929 and then opened the semifinals with a shutout against Toronto. Since McCool, Brent Johnson (St. Louis, 2002), Patrick Lalime (Ottawa, 2002) and Jean-Sébastien Giguère (Anaheim, 2003) have all posted three consecutive shutouts in one playoff series, but McCool remains the only one to do so in the Stanley Cup final.

Come on, Teeder! Like Maurice Richard, Toronto's Ted Kennedy was a wartime replacement player who proved he could handle the competition in the post-war game. Kennedy made a brief debut as a 17-year-old in 1942–43 and was a star by age 19. A talented two-way player, Kennedy led Toronto with 29 goals and 25 assists in 1944–45. He performed brilliantly throughout the playoffs and led all postseason performers with seven goals in 13 games.

Ted Kennedy

Ulcers McCool

Frank McCool was a bundle of energy on the ice, twisting, bending and hollering encouragement to his teammates in an attempt to keep his nervous stomach under control. McCool would drink milk by the quart before and after games, as well as between periods, to combat his ulcers.

"McCool called weakly for his milk," wrote the *Toronto Star*'s Red Burnett of the scene in the dressing room after the Maple Leafs upset the Canadiens. "'These games are tough on a guy,' he murmured."

Off-Ice Job When his ulcers kept him out of hockey in 1943–44, Frank McCool found work in his hometown as a sportswriter with the *Calgary Albertan*. He also wrote the occasional column for the *Toronto Star* during his time with the Maple Leafs. McCool retired from hockey because of his stomach problems after the 1945–46 season. He returned to Calgary and continued to work as a sports editor and newspaper executive with the *Albertan* until his death at the age of 54 on May 20, 1973.

1943–44   Montreal Canadiens

SEMIFINALS
4 games to 1 over Toronto

ROSTER

- Toe Blake (captain)
- Butch Bouchard
- Murph Chamberlain
- Bill Durnan
- Bob Fillion
- Ray Getliffe
- Glen Harmon
- Gerry Heffernan
- Elmer Lach
- Leo Lamoureux
- Fern Majeau
- Mike McMahon
- Buddy O'Connor
- Maurice Richard
- Phil Watson
- Tommy Gorman (manager)
- Dick Irvin (coach)

Bill Durnan is flanked by Leo Lamoureux and Glen Harmon with the Punch Line (Richard, Lach, Blake) front and center.

FINAL   **4 GAMES TO 0**

APR. 4	►	Chicago 1 at Montreal 5
APR. 6	►	Montreal 3 at Chicago 1
APR. 9	►	Montreal 3 at Chicago 2
APR. 13	►	Chicago 4 at Montreal 5 OT

PLAYOFF SCORING LEADER

Toe Blake	GP	G	A	PTS
MONTREAL	9	7	11	18

FINAL SERIES SCORING

MONTREAL	GP	G	A	PTS	PIM
Toe Blake	4	3	5	8	2
Maurice Richard	4	5	2	7	4
Elmer Lach	4	2	3	5	0
Ray Getliffe	4	2	1	3	4
Phil Watson	4	2	1	3	6
Butch Bouchard	4	0	3	3	0
Murph Chamberlain	4	1	0	1	2
Mike McMahon	4	1	0	1	12
Gerry Heffernan	2	0	1	1	0
Leo Lamoureux	4	0	1	1	2
Buddy O'Connor	3	0	1	1	2
Bob Fillion	2	0	0	0	2
Glen Harmon	4	0	0	0	0
Fern Majeau	1	0	0	0	0
GOALTENDER	GP	W	L	MIN	GA	SO	AVG
Bill Durnan	4	4	0	249	8	0	1.93

CHICAGO	GP	G	A	PTS	PIM
George Allen	4	3	2	5	4
Clint Smith	4	1	3	4	0
John Harms	4	3	0	3	2
Doug Bentley	4	1	2	3	2
Cully Dahlstrom	4	0	2	2	2
Virgil Johnson	4	0	1	1	2
Bill Mosienko	4	0	1	1	2
Art Wiebe	4	0	1	1	4
Joe Cooper	4	0	0	0	6
Johnny Gottselig	2	0	0	0	0
George Grigor	1	0	0	0	0
Fido Purpur	4	0	0	0	0
Jacques Toupin	1	0	0	0	0
Earl Seibert	4	0	0	0	0
GOALTENDER	GP	W	L	MIN	GA	SO	AVG
Mike Karakas	4	0	4	249	16	0	3.68

Out of the Dark

The Canadiens' Stanley Cup win in 1944 was the team's first since 1931 and the city's first since the Montreal Maroons' victory in 1935. The intervening years of the Great Depression, which had seen the death of Howie Morenz and the demise of the Maroons, would come to be known as the *grand noirceur*, or "great darkness."

Punch Line Has Last Laugh

Military service continued to take players from the NHL in 1943–44. In an effort to keep fans coming out, the league made a move to increase the offense. Until this time, players had not been permitted to pass the puck across their own blue line. The puck had to be carried out of the defensive end. The innovation of a red line at center ice opened up the game by allowing teams to pass the puck out of their own end—provided they didn't pass it beyond center. (This rule would not be altered to create the modern "stretch" pass until the 2005–06 season.)

No team in NHL history had ever scored more than 198 goals entering the 1943–44 season. This year, four teams topped 200 goals. In addition, three players broke the single-season record of 73 points: Boston's Herb Cain topped the league with 82, followed by Chicago's Doug Bentley, who had 77, and Toronto's Lorne Carr was third, with 74. On February 3, 1944, Detroit's Syd Howe scored six goals in a single game. He was the first player in 23 years to achieve this feat (and would be the last for another 24). The Montreal Canadiens led the league with 234 goals while posting the spectacular record of 38-5-7. At the other end of the standings, the New York Rangers went a woeful 6-39-5 and surrendered 310 goals. Ken McAuley allowed every goal. He posted an average of 6.24 while playing in all 50 games and in all but 20 minutes of action.

The Canadiens were led by the Punch Line, featuring Elmer Lach at center, Toe Blake at left wing and Maurice Richard on the right. Richard had missed most of his rookie season (1942–43) with a broken right ankle. He had also missed big chunks of previous amateur seasons with a broken left ankle and a broken wrist. Richard's brittle bones had kept him out of the army when he tried to enlist, but when he was healthy he could always score goals. Richard's 32 goals ranked him among the NHL leaders in 1943–44. His 12 goals in nine playoff games set a new postseason record. Toe Blake's 18 points were also a record, and it was Blake who scored the Stanley Cup–winning goal in overtime.

The Semifinals

The Maple Leafs beat Montreal 3–1 to open their semifinal series, but there was no stopping the Punch Line in Game 2, on March 23, 1944. Maurice Richard scored three goals in the second period and two more in the third in a 5–1 victory. Though Elmer Lach had four assists and Toe Blake set up all five goals, the "Rocket" was selected as the first, second and third star after the game.

The Canadiens went on to win the series in five games. In the finale on March 30th, Montreal won 11–0. Several modern playoff records set that night still stand, including largest win by shutout, seven goals in one period (the third) and five goals by one team in a span of 3:36.

Bill Durnan
Goalie Bill Durnan made his NHL debut with Montreal at age 28 in 1943–44. He won the Stanley Cup in 1944 and 1946. Durnan was ambidextrous and wore special gloves that allowed him hold his stick with either hand. He played only seven seasons in the NHL, but he both won the Vezina Trophy and was named to the First All-Star Teams six times. Despite his success, Durnan found the pressure of playing goal to be too much for him and retired after the 1949–50 season.

Rally Time

No team has every come from more than three goals down to win a Stanley Cup game. These are the six teams who have rallied from down either 3–0 or 4–1 to win a game in the Stanley Cup final:

DATE	TEAM	GAME
March 29, 1919	Montreal 4 Seattle 3	5
April 9, 1936	Toronto 4 Detroit 3	3
April 13, 1944	Montreal 5 Chicago 4 (OT)*	4
May 22, 1987	Philadelphia 5 Edmonton 3	3
May 26, 1992	Pittsburgh 5 Chicago 4°	1
June 5, 2006	Carolina 5 Edmonton 4°	1

*Victory clinched series.
°Went on to win series.

The Final

Fourth-place Chicago had surprised second-place Detroit in five games during the semifinals, but nobody really expected them to give the Canadiens much of a battle. Montreal's 5–1 win at home in Game 1 seemed to bear that out.

With no ice available in Chicago after April 9th, the Black Hawks got the next two games at home. They played better, but Montreal still returned home for Game 4 on the verge of a sweep. The Canadiens "did the expected," as Dink Carroll wrote in the *Montreal Gazette*, "but they did it in an unexpected manner."

The Black Hawks got on the scoreboard early in Game 4, but Toe Blake set up Elmer Lach to tie the game 1–1 midway through the first period. Penalty trouble in the second period led to a couple of quick Chicago goals, and the score was 4–1 after two.

The Canadiens caught a break midway through the third period when Lach beat Mike Karakas from a bad angle after another feed from Blake. A few minutes later, Montreal's Leo Lamoureux pulled down Virgil Johnson on a breakaway. Bill Durnan turned the penalty shot aside, but Lamoureux also had to serve two minutes, and Durnan was called on to make several tough saves during the ensuing penalty kill.

Still trailing 4–2 with less than four minutes left, Blake set up Richard for goals at 16:05 and 17:20 and the game was tied. At 9:12 of overtime, Butch Bouchard sprang Blake with a pass. Swinging from the short side towards center, Blake waited for Karakas to make the first move and then banged the puck into the open net.

The Game I'll Never Forget

Richard Tests Lumley

> **The funny thing is that I don't think I had more than six or seven shots on goal all game, and each goal was scored in a different way."**

Hockey Digest: January 1974
By Maurice Richard, as told to George Vass

Hockey today isn't much different than when I was playing. The rules haven't changed, and the stars of today would have been stars when I was on the ice. The game may be a little faster now and there are a lot more goals scored, although there aren't as many nice plays. But I suppose I would have scored more goals if I were playing now. After all, there were only 50 games then and they've got 78 today.

There are a lot of games I can look back on and be proud of. In some, I set records. Others were Stanley Cup–winning games. I have never been much concerned with records, but there is one that I take special pride in. That's the record of scoring six goals in overtime play in Stanley Cup games. I'll also never forget the game in 1945 in which I scored my 50th goal.

Yet there's one game from my early years that people have often asked me about, and I know I won't ever forget that one.

It was March 23, 1944, at the Montreal Forum. It was the second game of the opening round of the Stanley Cup playoffs, between the Montreal Canadiens and the Toronto Maple Leafs. The Leafs had won the first game 3–1.

When the 1943–44 season started, coach Dick Irvin put me on a line with Elmer Lach at center and Toe Blake at left wing. We worked well together, and pretty soon people were calling us the "Punch Line." I scored 32 goals playing with those two, and when the playoffs opened the Leafs decided to shadow me with Bob Davidson, a big, good-checking forward. He must have done a good job because I didn't score in the first game.

In the second game, Davidson was all over me again, and I don't even remember getting off any shots in the first period. We didn't score and neither did Toronto, so we went into the second period tied at zero.

But soon after the second period started I got my chance. I think it was defenseman Mike McMahon who passed the puck to Lach to start the play going. Lach gave it to me, and I went in on Leafs goalie Paul Bibeault. I gave him a deke then the shot. It went in at 1:48 of the second period.

Less than 20 seconds later I scored my second goal. It was a nice line play this time, Blake and Lach setting me up for the shot.

Being ahead 2–0 meant Toronto had to open up a little. It is always good when a team opens up because it gives you a chance to take advantage of a team thinking about offense instead of defense. But it worked for the Leafs this time, as Reg Hamilton scored about halfway through the period to cut our lead to one.

We kept working. Davidson kept on me, and I wasn't getting any chances. I think my two goals had been my only chances in the first 30 minutes or so of the game. I'd been in the penalty box twice, too. But near the end of the second period Blake and Lach set me up again, this time for the hat trick, and all three goals in one period!

We had a 3–1 lead heading into the third, and in hockey you never know how safe a lead is. It may never be enough. When we came back on the ice for the final frame we were ready to go. It would be hard to come back after losing the first two games of a series, and we did not want to lose this one at home. We kept pressing for another goal—it never hurts to get one or two more if you can still play your game defensively and wait for your chances.

The crowd at the Forum was really

Maurice Richard in for a chance at the Boston goal in 1940s action.

alive, cheering us on as we took the ice. It gave us a lift. It always did. One minute in, maybe—not much more—Blake and Lach again set me up in the Toronto zone. I put a wrist shot past Bibeault for my fourth of the game. I added a fifth midway through the third.

The funny thing is that I don't think I had more than six or seven shots on goal all game, and each goal was scored in a different way. A couple of nights later, when we beat the Leafs 11–0, I scored only two goals.

But this night I got all five. And we beat Toronto 5–1.

When they picked the top three stars of the game after the final buzzer, like they always do in Montreal, they selected Richard as star number one, number two and number three. Never before had that happened to me. Later I learned that the five goals

were a Stanley Cup record. Getting them against the Leafs was something extra special. They were always a close-checking club. Davidson was always out there shadowing me. Sometimes he stayed so close that I'd get angry. Maybe that night I took it out on him and the puck.

There are a lot of other games that I could talk about. We won a lot of them at Montreal in those days. But that five-goal game in 1944, only my second season in the league, was something special.

Montreal 5, Toronto 1

FIRST PERIOD

NO SCORING

PENALTY: Lamoureux, Montreal, 6:43

SECOND PERIOD

1 ▸ Richard (Blake, McMahon), Montreal, 1:48.

2 ▸ Richard (Blake, Lach), Montreal, 2:05

3 ▸ R. Hamilton (Carr, Morris) , Toronto, 8:50 **PP**

4 ▸ Richard (Lach, Blake), Montreal, 16:46

PENALTIES: Richard, Montreal, 8:34; Webster, Toronto, 12:20; Richard, Montreal, 12:20; Morris, Toronto, 19:24

THIRD PERIOD

5 ▸ Richard (Blake, Lach), Montreal, 1:00 **PP**

6 ▸ Richard (Blake, Lach), Montreal, 8:54

PENALTY: Heffernan, Montreal, 14:57

SHOTS ON GOAL

	1	2	3	TOTAL
Montreal	5	20	17	42
Toronto	3	11	6	20

GOALIES: Durnan, Montreal; Bibeault, Toronto

REFEREE: Bill Chadwick

LINESMEN: Bert Hedges, Stan McCabe

1942-43 Detroit Red Wings

ROSTER

Sid Abel (captain)

Adam Brown

Connie Brown

Mud Bruneteau

Joe Carveth

Les Douglas

Joe Fisher

Don Grosso

Syd Howe

Harold Jackson

Carl Liscombe

Alex Motter

Johnny Mowers

Jimmy Orlando

Cully Simon

Jack Stewart

Eddie Wares

Harry Watson

Jack Adams (manager)

Ebbie Goodfellow (player-coach)

Adam Brown and Jack Adams.

FINAL 4 GAMES TO 0

APR. 1	▶	Boston 2 at Detroit 6
APR. 4	▶	Boston 3 at Detroit 4
APR. 7	▶	Detroit 4 at Boston 0
APR. 8	▶	Detroit 2 at Boston 0

PLAYOFF SCORING LEADER

Carle Liscombe	GP	G	A	PTS
DETROIT	9	7	11	18

FINAL SERIES SCORING

DETROIT	GP	G	A	PTS	PIM
Sid Abel	4	1	5	6	2
Carl Liscombe	4	2	3	5	2
Mud Bruneteau	3	3	0	3	0
Joe Carveth	4	3	0	3	2
Don Grosso	4	3	0	3	4
Les Douglas	4	2	1	3	2
Eddie Wares	4	0	3	3	2
Jack Stewart	4	1	1	2	8
Jimmy Orlando	4	0	2	2	6
Syd Howe	3	1	0	1	0
Harold Jackson	4	0	1	1	4
Alex Motter	1	0	1	1	0
Adam Brown	4	0	0	0	2
Joe Fisher	1	0	0	0	0
Cully Simon	3	0	0	0	0
Harry Watson	1	0	0	0	0
GOALTENDER	GP	W	L	MIN	GA	SO	AVG
Johnny Mowers	4	4	0	240	5	2	1.25

BOSTON	GP	G	A	PTS	PIM
Art Jackson	4	3	0	3	7
Herb Cain	2	0	2	2	0
Bill Cowley	4	0	2	2	2
Jack Crawford	3	1	0	1	2
Ab DeMarco	4	1	0	1	0
Murph Chamberlain	4	0	1	1	6
Don Gallinger	4	0	1	1	4
Bep Guidolin	4	0	1	1	8
Flash Hollett	4	0	1	1	0
Ossie Aubuchon	1	0	0	0	0
Irvin Boyd	4	0	0	0	2
Dit Clapper	4	0	0	0	0
Busher Jackson	4	0	0	0	2
Jackie Schmidt	2	0	0	0	0
Jack Shewchuk	4	0	0	0	4
GOALTENDER	GP	W	L	MIN	GA	SO	AVG
Frank Brimsek	4	0	4	240	16	0	4.00

Working Overtime Rookie Adam Brown, only recently returned from the minors to replace the injured Syd Howe, sent the Red Wings into the final when he scored at 9:21 of overtime to wrap up Detroit's semifinal with a 3–2 win against Toronto in Game 6.

Good Call

"We've been beaten for the Cup twice in the last two years, but this year we are going to win four in a row."
—Detroit coach/GM Jack Adams prior to the 1943 final

Wings Win It

With the departure of the New York Americans (who had played the previous season as the Brooklyn Americans), the NHL was reduced to six teams for the 1942–43 season. For a while, it had looked like there might be no NHL hockey at all.

World War II raged on, and in August 1942 the National Selective Service in Ottawa asked league president Frank Calder to submit a brief outlining the NHL's manpower situation. It appeared that the Canadian government was willing to give some consideration to maintaining the NHL for at least one more season to help keep national morale up. On September 16, 1942, newspaper reports confirmed that the NHL had been given the go-ahead to proceed. Word was also received from the U.S. Manpower Commission that Canadian hockey players would be welcome to play in the United States during the coming season.

The NHL still faced problems. Seventy players and/ or prospects under contract to NHL teams were already on active military service. More would follow. Rosters would have to be filled out with players under the army draft age of 20, with older married men or with those with health problems that exempted them from military service. On November 21st, three weeks after the start of the 1942–43 season, the NHL was forced to discontinue regular-season overtime due to wartime travel restrictions. It was the last major decision president Frank Calder would ever make, as he died of heart failure on February 4, 1943.

Though the product was clearly not what it had been, fans continued to flock to NHL arenas. Offense was up, and Chicago Black Hawks brothers Doug and Max Bentley battled Boston's Bill Cowley for the scoring title. Doug Bentley took it with 73 points to tie the single-season record set by Cooney Weiland in 1929–30, when the NHL first allowed forward passing in the offensive zone. Detroit had no one among the league's top scorers, but it boasted the NHL's best defense and topped the standings with a record of 25-14-11 in the newly expanded 50-game schedule. In the playoffs, the Red Wings avenged their 1942 collapse against Toronto by beating the Maple Leafs in the semifinals. Facing the Bruins in the final, Detroit turned the tables on a Boston team that had swept them in 1941 by winning the Stanley Cup in four straight games.

Pair of Threes

The Red Wings got two hat tricks during their four-game sweep of Boston. Mud Bruneteau scored three goals in Detroit's 6–2 victory in Game 1, and Don Grosso scored three in their 4–0 win in Game 3.

Four of a Kind Due to wartime player shortages, the Bruins had four teenagers in their lineup during the 1942–43 season. Bep Guidolin, who was 16 years old when the season began, is the youngest player in NHL history. When Guidolin played with 17-year-old Don Gallinger and 19-year-old Bill Shill, the trio was dubbed the Sprout Line. Boston's fourth teenager was 18-year-old Jackie Schmidt (no relation to Bruins great Milt Schmidt).

One of a Kind With shutouts against Boston in Games 3 and 4 of the 1943 final, Johnny Mowers is the only goalie in Stanley Cup history to post back-to-back shutouts on consecutive days.

Best-of-Seven Synopsis

Since the best-of-seven format was introduced to the Stanley Cup playoffs in 1939, the number of finals that have gone four, five, six and seven games has been remarkably balanced:

FOUR GAMES	▶	20 times
FIVE GAMES	▶	17 times
SIX GAMES	▶	20 times
SEVEN GAMES	▶	16 times

Johnny Mowers

The Detroit defense was far and away the best in the NHL this season, earning goalie John Mowers the Vezina Trophy. Mowers was the only goaltender in the league to post a goals-against average below 3.00 as he led the league with a mark of 2.47. His six shutouts were more than the rest of the NHL's goaltenders combined. The eight other netminders in the league this season totaled only five shutouts. Only Mowers had more than one.

Mowers had joined the Red Wings in 1940–41. The 24-year-old redhead had been impressive in his professional debut during half a season with Omaha in 1939–40 and was signed to replace future Hall of Famer Tiny Thompson. Mowers posted a 2.01 goals-against average as a rookie and finished as the runner-up in voting for the Calder Trophy, behind Montreal's Johnny Quilty. He nearly won the Vezina Trophy as well, as Detroit's 102 goals-against were just three back of Turk Broda and the league-leading Toronto Maple Leafs.

After the Stanley Cup in 1943, Mowers was one of four Red Wings (along with Sid Abel, Jack Stewart and Harry Watson) to join the Royal Canadian Air Force for World War II. With Mowers gone, 17-year-old Harry Lumley made his NHL debut in 1943–44, taking over the Detroit net in 1944–45.

When Mowers returned to Detroit in the fall of 1946, Jack Adams promised he'd have "every chance to get his old job back," but the one-time hero was never able to regain his form. Mowers played poorly in limited action during the 1946–47 season and retired after playing two games in the minors the following year.

The Stanley Cup, featuring the original bowl and collars, as it was during the 1926–27 NHL season.

NATIONAL HOCKEY LEAGUE
1917–18 through 1941–42

PACIFIC COAST HOCKEY ASSOCIATION
1917–18 through 1923–24

WESTERN CANADA HOCKEY LEAGUE
1921–22 through 1924–25

WESTERN HOCKEY LEAGUE
1925–26

NHL Teams of This Era

MONTREAL WANDERERS
1917–18

OTTAWA SENATORS
1917–18 through 1930–31,
1932–33 through 1933–34

MONTREAL CANADIENS
1917–18 through 1941–42

**TORONTO ARENAS/ST. PATRICKS/
MAPLE LEAFS**
1917–18 through 1941–42

QUEBEC BULLDOGS
1919–1920

HAMILTON TIGERS
1920–21 through 1924–25

MONTREAL MAROONS
1924–25 through 1937–38

BOSTON BRUINS
1924–25 through 1941–42

PITTSBURGH PIRATES
1925–26 through 1929–30

NEW YORK/BROOKLYN AMERICANS
1925–26 through 1941–42

CHICAGO BLACK HAWKS
1926–27 through 1941–42

DETROIT COUGARS/FALCONS/RED WINGS
1926–27 through 1941–42

NEW YORK RANGERS
1926–27 through 1941–42

PHILADELPHIA QUAKERS
1930–31

ST. LOUIS EAGLES
1934–35

Early NHL Years: 1917–18 to 1941–42

Professional hockey was nearly a casualty of World War I. With so much death and destruction in real life, few people would probably have noticed or cared if the pro game had gone out of business.

This was the reality when the owners of the clubs in the National Hockey Association announced their re-organization as the National Hockey League on November 26, 1917. The new name did little to disguise the shortage of quality players or to attract new fans, but the end of the war about one year later on November 11, 1918, would give the NHL a boost. By the time the 1920s began to roar, NHL hockey was poised to cash in on the "Golden Age of Sports." New stars such as Howie Morenz and Eddie Shore brought back the crowds, and the NHL grew from just three teams in its inaugural season to 10 by 1926–27. The growth came at the expense of the other major pro hockey leagues of this era, and after sharing the Stanley Cup with the Pacific Coast Hockey Association (as the NHA had done since 1914) and the Western Canada Hockey League, the NHL emerged as the only league standing.

The Montreal Canadiens and Ottawa Senators were the league's top teams when the NHL was formed, but during the 1920s, former hockey stars Art Ross and Lester Patrick would build great teams in Boston and New York. In Toronto, Conn Smythe bought the fledgling St. Patricks in 1927, renamed them the Maple Leafs and established a powerhouse despite the Great Depression of the 1930s. Jack Adams iced top teams in Detroit, and owner Frederic McLaughlin managed two Stanley Cup wins despite his fondness for firing coaches. But the 1930s proved to be trying times for several other teams, and three franchises were no longer operating by 1938. With the outbreak of World War II in September 1939, the NHL faced new challenges.

SEMIFINALS
4 games to 2 over New York Rangers

FINAL 4 GAMES TO 3

APR. 4	▶ Detroit 3 at Toronto 2
APR. 7	▶ Detroit 4 at Toronto 2
APR. 9	▶ Toronto 2 at Detroit 5
APR. 12	▶ Toronto 4 at Detroit 3
APR. 14	▶ Detroit 3 at Toronto 9
APR. 16	▶ Toronto 3 at Detroit 0
APR. 18	▶ Detroit 1 at Toronto 3

PLAYOFF SCORING LEADERS

		GP	G	A	PTS
Don Grosso	DETROIT	12	8	6	14
Syl Apps	TORONTO	13	5	9	14

FINAL SERIES SCORING

TORONTO	GP	G	A	PTS	PIM
Billy Taylor	7	1	8	9	2
Sweeney Schriner	7	5	3	8	4
Don Metz	4	4	3	7	0
Syl Apps	7	3	4	7	2
Wally Stanowski	7	2	5	7	0
Lorne Carr	7	3	2	5	6
Nick Metz	7	2	3	5	4
Bob Goldham	7	2	2	4	22
John McCreedy	7	1	2	3	6
Bob Davidson	7	1	1	2	14
Pete Langelle	7	1	1	2	0
Bingo Kampman	7	0	2	2	8
Ernie Dickens	5	0	0	0	4
Gordie Drillon	3	0	0	0	0
Hank Goldup	3	0	0	0	0
Bucko McDonald	3	0	0	0	0
Gaye Stewart	1	0	0	0	0
GOALTENDER	GP	W	L	MIN	GA	SO	AVG
Turk Broda	7	4	3	420	19	1	2.71

DETROIT	GP	G	A	PTS	PIM
Don Grosso	7	4	4	8	14
Syd Howe	7	3	3	6	0
Carl Liscombe	7	2	4	6	2
Eddie Bush	6	1	5	6	16
Sid Abel	7	2	1	3	4
Mud Bruneteau	7	2	1	3	4
Eddie Wares	7	0	3	3	20
Gerry Brown	7	2	0	2	4
Pat McReavy	6	1	1	2	2
Alex Motter	7	1	1	2	6
Jimmy Orlando	7	0	2	2	41
Joe Carveth	7	1	0	1	0
Adam Brown	5	0	1	1	4
Jack Stewart	7	0	1	1	6
Gus Giesebrecht	2	0	0	0	0
Doug McCaig	2	0	0	0	6
GOALTENDER	GP	W	L	MIN	GA	SO	AVG
Johnny Mowers	7	3	4	420	25	0	3.57

Turning Points

In addition to Hap Day's decision to alter his lineup, another turning point in the series occurred at the end of Game 4. Unhappy with some late penalties against the Red Wings, Jack Adams jumped onto the ice and attacked referee Mel Harwood. NHL president Frank Calder promptly suspended Adams, prohibiting him from running the team for the rest of the series.

The *Toronto Star* reported Calder as saying that his first thought after seeing the way the Red Wings had reacted to the penalties, followed by Adams' attack, was to disqualify Detroit and award the Stanley Cup to Toronto.

A Comeback for the Ages

The 1941–42 Toronto Maple Leafs pulled off the greatest comeback in the history of hockey when they rallied from a three-games-to-nothing deficit to defeat the Detroit Red Wings for the Stanley Cup. Though two other NHL teams, and Major League Baseball's Boston Red Sox of 2004, would later rally from similar deficits, nobody else has accomplished this feat in the final series to win its sport's championship.

The defending Stanley Cup–champion Boston Bruins were in first place in the NHL standings midway through the 1941–42 season, but they lost stars Milt Schmidt, Woody Dumart, and Bobby Bauer to military service with the Royal Canadian Air Force. The Rangers, led by NHL points leader Bryan Hextall and top-scorer Lynn Patrick, took over top spot from the Bruins while the Toronto Maple Leafs finished second. The Rangers were favored when the two teams met to open the playoffs, but the Maple Leafs took the first two games of the best-of-seven series en route to a 3–1 series lead. Toronto won the series in six and advanced straight to the Stanley Cup final, as per the playoff format (see Playoff Format, at right).

The Detroit Red Wings had finished fifth in the regular-season standings and needed to play a quarterfinal and a semifinal to advance to the Stanley Cup final. The Wings needed all three games to beat the sixth-place Montreal Canadiens in their first playoff series but then scored a surprising sweep over the Bruins. A bitter rivalry between Detroit and Toronto had built up through the 1939 and 1940 playoffs, and though the experts favored the Maple Leafs in 1942, the Red Wings remained on a roll and opened the final with three straight wins.

Conn Smythe was in the army and encamped at Petawawa near Ottawa when he sent word to coach Hap Day that he wanted a shake-up. Day benched Gordie Drillon, the team's top scorer during the regular season, and inserted Don Metz on the top line with his brother Nick and Syl Apps. He also replaced defenseman Bucko McDonald with 20-year-old rookie Ernie Dickens. Don Metz set up brother Nick for the winning goal late in Game 4 and then scored a hat trick in Toronto's 9–3 win in Game 5. Goalie Turk Broda was the star with a 3–0 shutout in Game 6.

This was the first time a Stanley Cup series had gone seven games, and the crowd of 16,218 at Maple Leaf Gardens was the largest ever for a game played in Canada. Detroit took a 1–0 lead, but two goals from Sweeney Schriner in the third period, and one by Pete Langelle, gave Toronto a 3–1 victory.

Playoff Format

After the collapse of the Montreal Maroons following the 1937–38 season, the NHL operated as a seven-team circuit through to 1941–42. During those four seasons, six of seven teams made the playoffs with only the last-place club eliminated. The teams that finished first and second met each year in a seven-game series to determine one Stanley Cup finalist. Meanwhile, the third-place team played the fourth-place team, and the fifth-placed met the sixth-placed in a pair of best-of-three series. The winners would then meet in another best-of-three series, with the team that won that set advancing as the other Stanley Cup finalist.

First in Ten Toronto's Stanley Cup victory in 1942 marked the Maple Leafs' first Cup victory since 1932. They had, however, reached the final six times in the years in between.

Dump and Chase Feeling that his forwards could take advantage of Toronto's slow defense, Red Wings coach and general manager Jack Adams came up with a new tactic during the 1942 Stanley Cup final. Instead of carrying the puck across the enemy blue line as teams routinely did in this era, Adams instructed his team to dump the puck into the Leafs' end and chase after it.

Grand Slam Part I

When Gaye Stewart made his NHL debut as an 18-year-old in Game 5 of the Stanley Cup final, it completed a remarkable rise through the ranks that season. Stewart had begun the year playing junior hockey with the Toronto Marlboros. He was later moved up to the Marlies' senior team, and when they were knocked out of the playoffs, he made his professional debut with the Hershey Bears of the American Hockey League. Stewart was said to be the first player in contemporary hockey history to play in junior, senior, the minors, and the NHL all in one year.

Grand Slam Part II Leafs rookie Johnny McCreedy completed his own impressive feat in 1942. McCreedy added a Stanley Cup victory to the Memorial Cup junior championship he'd won with the Winnipeg Monarchs in 1937 and to the Allan Cup senior championships he'd won with the Trail Smoke Eaters in 1938 and the Kirkland Lake Blue Devils in 1940. McCreedy had also won the World Championship for Canada with Trail in 1939.

Comeback Kids

Teams that have rallied to win after a 3–1 deficit in a best-of-seven series:

YEAR	SERIES	RESULT IN GAMES	YEAR	SERIES	RESULT IN GAMES
1942	F	Tor 4 Det 3*	1995	CQF	Pit 4 Wsh 3
1975	QF	NYI 4 Pit 3*	1998	CQF	Edm 4 Col 3
1987	DSF	NYI 4 Wsh 3	1999	CQF	StL 4 Phx 3
1987	DF	Det 4 Tor 3	2000	CF	NJ 4 Phi 3
1988	DSF	Wsh 4 Phi 3	2003	CQF	Min 4 Col 3
1989	DSF	LA 4 Edm 3	2003	CQF	Van 4 StL 3
1990	DSF	Edm 4 Wpg 3	2003	CSF	Min 4 Van 3
1991	DSF	StL 4 Det 3	2004	CQF	Mtl 4 Bos 3
1992	DSF	Det 4 Min 3	2009	CQF	Wsh 4 NYR 3
1992	DSF	Van 4 Wpg 3	2010	CQF	Mtl 4 Wsh 3
1992	DSF	Pit 4 Wsh 3	2010	CF	Phi 4 Bos 3*
1994	CQF	Van 4 Cgy 3	2011	CQF	TB 4 Pit 3

*Came back from trailing 3–0 in games.
Abbreviation Legend:
CQF – Conference Quarterfinal
CSF – Conference Semifinal
CF – Conference Final
F – Final

SEMIFINALS
4 games to 3 over Toronto

ROSTER

Bobby Bauer
Frank Brimsek
Herb Cain
Dit Clapper (captain)
Roy Conacher
Bill Cowley
Jack Crawford
Woody Dumart
Mel Hill
Flash Hollett
Art Jackson
Pat McReavy
Terry Reardon
Milt Schmidt
Jack Shewchuk
Des Smith
Eddie Wiseman
Art Ross (manager)
Cooney Weiland
(coach)

FINAL   4 GAMES TO 0

APR. 6	▸ Detroit 2 at Boston 3
APR. 8	▸ Detroit 1 at Boston 2
APR. 10	▸ Boston 4 at Detroit 2
APR. 12	▸ Boston 3 at Detroit 1

PLAYOFF SCORING LEADER

Milt Schmidt	GP	G	A	PTS
BOSTON	11	5	6	11

FINAL SERIES SCORING

BOSTON	GP	G	A	PTS	PIM
Milt Schmidt	4	3	4	7	0
Eddie Wiseman	4	3	0	3	0
Roy Conacher	4	1	2	3	0
Woody Dumart	4	0	3	3	2
Bobby Bauer	4	1	1	2	0
Flash Hollett	4	1	1	2	4
Pat McReavy	4	1	1	2	5
Terry Reardon	4	1	1	2	2
Dit Clapper	4	0	2	2	2
Jack Crawford	4	0	2	2	0
Des Smith	4	0	2	2	2
Art Jackson	4	1	0	1	0
Herb Cain	4	0	1	1	0
Mel Hill	4	0	0	0	0

GOALTENDER	GP	W	L	MIN	GA	SO	AVG
Frank Brimsek	4	4	0	240	6	0	1.50

DETROIT	GP	G	A	PTS	PIM
Carl Liscombe	4	2	1	3	5
Syd Howe	4	1	2	3	0
Sid Abel	4	1	1	2	2
Bill Jennings	4	1	1	2	0
Connie Brown	3	0	2	2	0
Mud Bruneteau	4	1	0	1	0
Gus Giesebrecht	4	0	1	1	0
Don Grosso	4	0	1	1	0
Jimmy Orlando	4	0	1	1	6
Jack Stewart	4	0	1	1	2
Eddie Bruneteau	2	0	0	0	0
Harold Jackson	4	0	0	0	0
Ken Kilrea	2	0	0	0	0
Alex Motter	4	0	0	0	2
Eddie Wares	3	0	0	0	0
Bob Whitelaw	4	0	0	0	0

GOALTENDER	GP	W	L	MIN	GA	SO	AVG
Johnny Mowers	4	0	4	240	12	0	3.00

Best-of-Seven Sweep

The Boston Bruins posted the best regular-season record in the NHL for the fourth straight season in 1940–41 and won the Stanley Cup for the second time in three years.

Shortly after the outbreak of World War II, in September 1939, the NHL announced plans to carry on as best as possible. The United States would not enter the War until after the attack on Pearl Harbor, on December 7, 1941, and though more and more Canadians, including some NHL players, were enlisting by the fall of 1940, interest was high heading into the 1940–41 season. The Bruins started slowly, but a record-setting 23-game undefeated streak (15 wins, eight ties) between December 22nd and February 23rd carried them to the top spot. Boston's Bill Cowley was the runaway scoring leader and would also win the Hart Trophy after setting a single-season record with 45 assists during the 48-game schedule. Linemate Roy Conacher tied for the NHL lead with 24 goals, and the Kraut Line of Milt Schmidt, Woody Dumart and Bobby Bauer (who were often called the Kitchener Kids amid growing anti-Germany feelings) provided a second high-scoring unit. Dit Clapper was

named to the First All-Star Team on defense, while Frank Brimsek led the league with six shutouts. His 2.01 goals-against average was only one point behind Vezina Trophy–winner Turk Broda of Toronto.

Broda's Maple Leafs finished second behind the Bruins in the overall standings. Toronto boasted the league's best defense and second-best offense, while Boston had the best offense and second-best defense. When the two teams hooked up to open the playoffs, the results (with the exception of a 7–2 Toronto win in Game 3) were just as tight as people expected. The last four games were all 2–1, with Boston taking three of them and winning the series in seven.

Bill Cowley played only two games against Toronto due to a knee injury. He would miss the entire Stanley Cup final against Detroit, who had beaten the Rangers and Black Hawks to get there. Rusty after a week's layoff, the Red Wings managed just eight shots through two periods in Game 1 but only lost 3–2. The games all remained close, and Detroit had a lead in each one, but Boston took the series in four straight for the first sweep of a seven-game series in NHL history.

End of An Era

As the Bruins sipped champagne from the Stanley Cup in their dressing room after the fourth game, general manager Art Ross proclaimed them as the greatest hockey team ever assembled. It would be years before anyone would say that again about a Bruins team.

Since entering the NHL in 1924–25, the Bruins had finished first in their division and/or the overall NHL standings 10 times in 16 years. They had reached the Stanley Cup final five times and won the Cup three times. But several key players would be lost to military service in World War II, and the team would go into a steep decline. There would be a few good years in the 1950s, but the Bruins would not begin a return to power until the arrival of Bobby Orr in 1966. It would be 29 years before Boston's next Stanley Cup victory, in 1970.

Stanley Cup Sweeps

Since the best-of-seven format was introduced in 1939, there have been 20 sweeps in the Stanley Cup final:

1941	► Boston over Detroit		1977	► Montreal over Boston
1943	► Detroit over Boston		1982	► New York Islanders over Vancouver
1944	► Montreal over Chicago			
1948	► Toronto over Detroit		1983	► New York Islanders over Edmonton
1949	► Toronto over Detroit		1988	► Edmonton over Boston
1952	► Detroit over Montreal		1992	► Pittsburgh over Chicago
1960	► Montreal over Toronto		1995	► New Jersey over Detroit
1968	► Montreal over St. Louis		1996	► Colorado over Florida
1969	► Montreal over St. Louis		1997	► Detroit over Philadelphia
1970	► Boston over St. Louis		1998	► Detroit over Washington
1976	► Montreal over Philadelphia			

Getting Too Big

Beginning in 1928, and in every year from 1930 through 1939, the Stanley Cup grew in height by an inch or so as new bands commemorating the winners were added to the trophy. This long, narrow version of the Stanley Cup that existed in this era is often referred to as the stovepipe Cup, and sometimes as "the cigar" or the "elephant's leg." Writing in the *Montreal Gazette* after Boston's victory in 1941, Marc T. McNeil speculated there was room for another five years of winners. "After that," he wrote, "it is believed some new arrangement will have to be evolved to allow for further winners' inscriptions because it is felt that [bands] cannot be added indefinitely, without making the trophy appear too tall, unsightly and unwieldy."

A Trio of Trophies

Though the Bruins had received the Stanley Cup in their dressing room in Detroit after Game 4, NHL president Frank Calder made the formal presentation to the team at a banquet in Boston on April 15th. He also announced that the Hart Trophy had been awarded to Bill Cowley, ahead of teammate Dit Clapper and Toronto's Syl Apps, in a close vote. Bobby Bauer, who had finished ninth in the NHL scoring race while accumulating just two penalty minutes for the second straight season, was named the winner of the Lady Byng Trophy. Bauer had also won it the year before.

New York Rangers

SEMIFINALS
4 games to 2 over Boston

ROSTER

Mac Colville

Neil Colville

Art Coulter (captain)

Ott Heller

Bryan Hextall

Dutch Hiller

Dave Kerr

Kilby MacDonald

Lynn Patrick

Muzz Patrick

Alf Pike

Babe Pratt

Alex Shibicky

Clint Smith

Stan Smith

Phil Watson

Lester Patrick
(manager)

Frank Boucher
(coach)

Coach Frank Boucher shakes Bryan Hextall's hand after the Rangers' Cup win.

FINAL   4 GAMES TO 2

APR. 2	►	Toronto 1 at NY Rangers 2 OT
APR. 3	►	Toronto 2 at NY Rangers 6
APR. 6	►	NY Rangers 1 at Toronto 2
APR. 9	►	NY Rangers 0 at Toronto 3
APR. 11	►	NY Rangers 2 at Toronto 1 2X OT
APR. 13	►	NY Rangers 3 at Toronto 2 OT

PLAYOFF SCORING LEADERS

| **Phil Watson** | GP | G | A | PTS |
| NEW YORK RANGERS | 12 | 3 | 6 | 9 |

| **Neil Colville** | GP | G | A | PTS |
| NEW YORK RANGERS | 23 | 30 | 18 | 12 |

FINAL SERIES SCORING

NY RANGERS	GP	G	A	PTS	PIM
Bryan Hextall	6	4	1	5	7
Neil Colville	6	2	3	5	12
Phil Watson	6	1	4	5	8
Dutch Hiller	6	1	2	3	0
Alf Pike	6	2	0	2	4
Lynn Patrick	6	1	1	2	0
Babe Pratt	6	1	1	2	6
Ott Heller	6	0	2	2	8
Alex Shibicky	5	0	2	2	2
Art Coulter	6	1	0	1	8
Muzz Patrick	6	1	0	1	6
Mac Colville	6	0	1	1	6
Clint Smith	6	0	1	1	2
Kilby MacDonald	6	0	0	0	4
Stan Smith	1	0	0	0	0

GOALTENDER	GP	W	L	MIN	GA	SO	AVG
Dave Kerr	6	4	2	394	11	0	1.68

TORONTO	GP	G	A	PTS	PIM
Syl Apps	6	2	2	4	2
Hank Goldup	6	2	1	3	0
Sweeney Schriner	5	0	3	3	2
Gordie Drillon	6	2	0	2	0
Gus Marker	6	1	1	2	2
Nick Metz	5	1	1	2	9
Red Horner	5	0	2	2	14
Pete Langelle	6	0	2	2	0
Red Heron	6	1	0	1	0
Wally Stanowski	6	1	0	1	2
Billy Taylor	2	1	0	1	0
Jack Church	2	0	1	1	2
Bob Davidson	6	0	1	1	11
Murph Chamberlain	3	0	0	0	2
Reg Hamilton	1	0	0	0	0
Bingo Kampman	6	0	0	0	19
Pete Kelly	2	0	0	0	0
Bucko McDonald	1	0	0	0	0
Don Metz	2	0	0	0	0

GOALTENDER	GP	W	L	MIN	GA	SO	AVG
Turk Broda	6	2	4	394	14	1	2.13

Pep Talk

"Well boys, you've had your fun. Now lets get down to business. I've made arrangements for a victory party in the Tudor Room of the Royal York [Hotel]. I'll see you there. Don't let me down." — Lester Patrick, according to stories, in the dressing room after two periods of Game 6.

He Ain't Heavy...

The Rangers' Stanley Cup teams of 1927–28 and 1932–33 had both featured brothers Bill and Bun Cook. The 1939–40 Stanley Cup champs featured two pairs of brothers, Lynn and Muzz Patrick and Neil and Mac Colville. Lynn and Muzz were the sons of Rangers general manager Lester Patrick.

Rangers' Road to the Stanley Cup

War had broken out in Europe before the start of the 1939–40 season, but its effects were not immediately felt in North America. Economic conditions were beginning to improve, though the NHL—which had lost three of its 10 franchises during the Great Depression—still had one problem team. The New York Americans were strapped for cash, but the New York Rangers would thrive this season.

Lester Patrick had stepped down as coach but remained on as general manager, turning over coaching duties to former star Frank Boucher. A 19-game undefeated streak (14 wins, five ties) from November 19th to January 13th had the Rangers in first place at the midway point of the season, but they would end the year in second place after a tight battle with Boston. The Kraut Line of Milt Schmidt, Woody Dumart and Bobby Bauer, who finished one, two and three in the NHL in scoring, led the Bruins. The Rangers featured two strong forward lines, with brothers Neil and Mac Colville playing with Alex Shibicky, and Bryan Hextall (who led the NHL with 24 goals in 48 games) playing with Phil Watson and Lynn Patrick. They also had Calder Trophy–winning rookie Kilby MacDonald. The defense of Muzz Patrick, Ott Heller, Art Coulter and Babe Pratt allowed a league-low 77 goals to give Dave Kerr the Vezina Trophy. The Rangers goalie had an average of 1.54 during the 1939–40 season. No one in the NHL has posted a number that low since.

In the playoffs, Kerr had three shutouts against Boston as the Rangers beat the Bruins to advance to the Stanley Cup final. The Rangers faced the third-place Maple Leafs, who had swept both the Black Hawks and Red Wings to advance. Because a circus was being held at Madison Square Garden, New York would host the first two games of the final on back-to-back nights with the rest of the series being played in Toronto. The Rangers won the opener on an Alf Pike overtime goal. They took the second behind a Bryan Hextall hat trick, but Toronto won the next two. Muzz Patrick had scored just two goals all season, but his double-overtime winner in Game 5 marked his third goal of the playoffs. In Game 6, the Rangers trailed 2–0 after two periods but won the Stanley Cup when Bryan Hextall scored at 2:07 of overtime.

According to Legend...

After their Stanley Cup victory in 1940, the Rangers would not win it again until 1994. There are two stories that have sprung up to explain the lengthy drought. One says that the "hockey gods" were angered after the mortgage on Madison Square Garden was paid off during the 1940–41 season and the papers were burned in celebration inside the Stanley Cup bowl. Another story claims that Red Dutton, of the New York Americans, cursed the Rangers when his team was forced to withdraw from the NHL in 1942.

All in the Family
Stanley Cup wins by the Patrick Family:

LESTER PATRICK	▶	Montreal Wanderers 1906, 1907
		Victoria Cougars 1925 (coach/GM/owner)
		New York Rangers 1928, 1933, 1940 (coach/GM)
FRANK PATRICK	▶	Vancouver 1915 (player/coach/GM/owner)
LYNN PATRICK	▶	New York Rangers 1940
MUZZ PATRICK	▶	New York Rangers 1940
CRAIG PATRICK	▶	Pittsburgh 1991, 1992 (GM)

What Really Happened

With the exception of Art Coulter and goalie Dave Kerr, who had been acquired in trades, every member of the 1940 Stanley Cup–winning Rangers had been a product of their farm system. But player shortages during World War II would cause the Rangers farm system to collapse. The War hurt the Rangers at the NHL level as well, with stars such as Lynn and Muzz Patrick, Neil and Mac Colville, Alf Pike and Alex Shibicky all called away due to military service. Dudley "Red" Garrett, who played part of the 1942–43 season with the Rangers before being called off to war, was killed when a German submarine sank the HMCS *Shawinigan* off the coast of Newfoundland during a destroyer escort run.

It would take the Rangers many years to rebuild their organization. The team would fail to make the playoffs 18 times in the 25 years of the six-team era, from 1942–43 through 1966–67, and only became a contender again after NHL expansion.

Overtime Winner

The Leafs had set a fast pace through the first 40 minutes of Game 6. After Syl Apps scored in the first period and Nick Metz in the second, it appeared the series was destined for a seventh game. But the Rangers came to life in the third period. Alex Shibicky, who had been taking injections in his badly injured ankle, set up Neil Colville at 8:08. Less than two minutes later, with each team playing a man short, Clint Smith set up Alf Pike and the game was tied. The Rangers scored again with under three minutes remaining, but referee Bill Stewart waved it off because Bryan Hextall was in the crease and lying on top of goalie Turk Broda.

The Leafs came out strong in overtime, and Dave Kerr had to make a couple of sharp saves. The Rangers got the break they needed when Gordie Drillon collided with teammate Jack Church in the New York end just past the two-minute mark. With the two Leafs down on the ice, Dutch Hiller passed the puck to Phil Watson in the corner. Watson fed it out front to Bryan Hextall, who backhanded the Stanley Cup–winning goal home.

Surgery Seven Rangers were hospitalized in New York within days of the Stanley Cup victory. Dutch Hiller had his appendix removed, while Kilby MacDonald and both Neil and Mac Colville underwent tonsillectomies. Dave Kerr, Muzz Patrick and Alex Shibicky all had bone chips removed from their elbows. On a happier note, Clint Smith got married.

SEMIFINALS
4 games to 3 over New York Rangers

ROSTER

- Bobby Bauer
- Frank Brimsek
- Dit Clapper
- Roy Conacher
- Bill Cowley
- Jack Crawford
- Woody Dumart
- Harry Frost
- Ray Getliffe
- Red Hamill
- Mel Hill
- Flash Hollett
- Gord Pettinger
- Jack Portland
- Charlie Sands
- Milt Schmidt
- Eddie Shore
- Cooney Weiland (captain)
- Art Ross (manager/coach)

FINAL 4 GAMES TO 1

APR. 6	▶	Toronto 1 at Boston 2
APR. 9	▶	Toronto 3 at Boston 2 OT
APR. 11	▶	Boston 3 at Toronto 1
APR. 13	▶	Boston 2 at Toronto 0
APR. 16	▶	Toronto 1 at Boston 3

PLAYOFF SCORING LEADER

	GP	G	A	PTS
Bill Cowley BOSTON	12	3	11	14

FINAL SERIES SCORING

BOSTON	GP	G	A	PTS	PIM
Roy Conacher	5	5	2	7	6
Bill Cowley	5	0	7	7	2
Mel Hill	5	2	2	4	4
Bobby Bauer	5	2	1	3	0
Eddie Shore	5	0	3	3	6
Jack Crawford	5	1	1	2	4
Milt Schmidt	5	0	2	2	0
Woody Dumart	5	1	0	1	2
Flash Hollett	5	1	0	1	0
Dit Clapper	5	0	0	0	0
Ray Getliffe	5	0	0	0	2
Red Hamill	5	0	0	0	2
Gord Pettinger	5	0	0	0	0
Jack Portland	5	0	0	0	2
Cooney Weiland	5	0	0	0	0
GOALTENDER	GP	W	L	MIN	GA	SO	AVG
Frank Brimsek	5	4	1	311	6	1	1.16

TORONTO	GP	G	A	PTS	PIM
Doc Romnes	5	1	3	4	0
Gus Marker	5	1	2	3	0
Bingo Kampman	5	1	1	2	12
Gordie Drillon	5	0	2	2	4
Syl Apps	5	1	0	1	2
Murph Chamberlain	5	1	0	1	0
Red Horner	5	1	0	1	6
Busher Jackson	3	0	1	1	2
Nick Metz	5	0	1	1	2
Jack Church	1	0	0	0	0
Bob Davidson	5	0	0	0	0
Jimmy Fowler	4	0	0	0	0
Reg Hamilton	5	0	0	0	4
Red Heron	2	0	0	0	4
Pete Kelly	4	0	0	0	0
Pete Langelle	4	0	0	0	0
Bucko McDonald	5	0	0	0	0
GOALTENDER	GP	W	L	MIN	GA	SO	AVG
Turk Broda	5	1	4	311	12	0	2.32

High Praise

"It is the best team I ever had or ever saw."
— Manager/coach Art Ross on the 1938–39 Bruins

Topping Toronto

Boston had been beaten by Toronto in all four of their previous playoff meetings (1933, 1935, 1936 and 1938) before defeating the Maple Leafs to win the Stanley Cup. Toronto native Roy Conacher scored the Cup-winning goal, breaking a 1–1 tie at 17:54 of the second period. Flash Hollett, whom Toronto had sold to Boston in 1936, got the clincher at 19:23 of the third.

Boston the Best of Seven

The Montreal Maroons suspended operations prior to the 1938–39 season, leaving the NHL with seven teams. As a result, the league reverted to a single division for the first time since 1925–26. Six of the seven teams would qualify for the postseason: the first- and second-place clubs would play a seven-game semifinal, while the third- and fourth-place teams would meet in a best-of-three quarterfinal, as would the fifth- and sixth-place teams. The quarterfinal winners would then compete in a three-game semifinal series. The Stanley Cup final would be a best-of-seven series for the first time.

The Boston Bruins were the NHL's best team in 1937–38, but they had been swept out of the playoffs by Toronto. Still, the Bruins had a powerful lineup featuring Bill Cowley and the Kraut Line of Milt Schmidt, Woody Dumart and Bobby Bauer on offense. Dit Clapper, Eddie Shore and Flash Hollett anchored the defense. Goalie Tiny Thompson had won the Vezina Trophy for the fourth time, but early in the 1938–39 season, the Bruins' coach and general manager, Art Ross, had shipped Thompson to Detroit. He replaced him with a rookie named Frank Brimsek. Another Boston rookie,

Roy Conacher, would lead the NHL with 26 goals, but Brimsek was the real hero. Brimsek earned the nickname "Mr. Zero" after twice recording streaks of three straight shutouts during his first month in Boston. He went on to lead the league with 10 shutouts and a 1.56 goals-against average. He won the Calder Trophy, the Vezina Trophy, was named to the First All-Star Team and helped the Bruins win the Stanley Cup.

The Bruins finished the season with a record of 36-10-2. Their 74 points had them well ahead of the second-place New York Rangers, who had 58 points on a record of 26-16-6. When the two teams met during the playoffs, the results were much closer than anyone had expected. Game 1 went into triple overtime before Mel Hill scored to give Boston a 2–1 victory. Hill was the overtime hero again in Game 2, but even after the Bruins won the third contest in regulation, the Rangers rallied to force a seventh game. Once again three overtime sessions were needed, and again it was Hill who scored the winner. The Stanley Cup final proved something of an anticlimax, as the Bruins avenged their 1938 loss to the Leafs with a five-game victory.

Cup Presentation

Giant fireworks thundered through the Boston Garden as NHL president Frank Calder presented the Stanley Cup to Art Ross and Cooney Weiland near center ice. This was Boston's second Stanley Cup victory, after winning it in 1929, but their first one at home.

All in the Family
Stanley Cup wins by the Conacher brothers:

CHARLIE CONACHER	▸	Toronto Maple Leafs, 1932
LIONEL CONACHER	▸	Chicago Black Hawks, 1934 Montreal Maroons 1935
ROY CONACHER	▸	Boston Bruins 1939, 1941

Last Hurrah

Eddie Shore had gone to the dressing room before the Stanley Cup presentation, but he returned to the ice amid chants of "We Want Shore." The shouts from the crowd as he posed for pictures with the trophy were reported as being louder than those for the Cup presentation.

This was the last great moment for Eddie Shore, whose veteran presence was given a lot of credit for Boston's success that season. He was named a First Team All-Star for the seventh time since the honor had been created in 1930–31, but, anticipating retirement, Shore bought the Springfield Indians in May 1939. He acted as a playing-owner in 1939–40. He also played a handful of games for the Bruins that season before being traded to the New York Americans, where he ended his NHL career.

Sudden Death

Mel Hill would be forever known by the nickname "Sudden Death" after his performance for the Bruins in the 1939 semifinals. Hill was in his first full season in 1938–39 and had scored 10 goals in an almost anonymous role as the right-winger on a line with Bill Cowley and Roy Conacher. But with the Rangers focusing so much attention on the two big stars, Art Ross advised his slick center Cowley to feed the puck to Hill.

Hill scored the winning goal at 19:25 of the third overtime period in Game 1 and then got the winner at 8:24 of the first extra session in Game 2. His goal in Game 7 came at 8:00 of triple overtime. To date, only Maurice Richard (1951) has equaled Hill's three overtime goals in one playoff year, and no one else has ever duplicated the feat of three overtime goals in a single series. Hill would never score another overtime goal in a career that lasted until 1946, but he did score two goals in the 1939 final. He also scored the series winner in Game 7 of the semifinals in 1941, and Boston won the Cup again that year.

During his big series in 1939, it became common knowledge that Lester Patrick had turned down Hill as a 20-year-old at a Rangers "hockey school" for amateur prospects in Winnipeg in 1934. "I only weighed about 130 pounds," Hill recalled after Game 7. "I don't blame Patrick for not being impressed."

"Hill was an awkward kid," Patrick remembered. "He had a fair-paying job at the time, and I thought I was doing him a favor when I advised him to forget hockey and stick to his work."

QUARTERFINALS
2 games to 1 over Montreal Canadiens

SEMIFINALS
2 games to 1 over New York Americans

FINAL 3 GAMES TO 1

APR. 5	▶	Chicago 3 at Toronto 1
APR. 7	▶	Chicago 1 at Toronto 5
APR. 10	▶	Toronto 1 at Chicago 2
APR. 12	▶	Toronto 1 at Chicago 4

PLAYOFF SCORING LEADERS

Johnny Gottselig	GP	G	A	PTS
CHICAGO	10	5	3	8

Gordie Drillon	GP	G	A	PTS
TORONTO	7	7	1	8

FINAL SERIES SCORING

CHICAGO	GP	G	A	PTS	PIM
Johnny Gottselig	4	2	2	4	0
Doc Romnes	4	1	2	3	2
Paul Thompson	4	1	2	3	2
Carl Voss	4	2	0	2	0
Cully Dahlstrom	4	1	1	2	0
Mush March	3	1	1	2	6
Earl Seibert	4	1	1	2	8
Jack Shill	4	1	1	2	4
Roger Jenkins	4	0	2	2	6
Lou Trudel	4	0	1	1	0
Virgil Johnson	2	0	0	0	0
Alex Levinsky	4	0	0	0	0
Bill MacKenzie	4	0	0	0	9
Pete Palangio	3	0	0	0	0
Art Wiebe	4	0	0	0	2

GOALTENDERS	GP	W	L	MIN	GA	SO	AVG
Mike Karakas	2	2	0	120	2	0	1.00
Alfie Moore	1	1	0	60	1	0	1.00
Paul Goodman	1	0	1	60	5	0	5.00

TORONTO	GP	G	A	PTS	PIM
Gordie Drillon	4	4	1	5	2
Syl Apps	4	1	2	3	0
George Parsons	3	2	0	2	11
Bob Davidson	4	0	2	2	4
Jimmy Fowler	4	0	2	2	0
Pete Kelly	4	0	2	2	0
Bill Thoms	4	0	2	2	0
Busher Jackson	4	1	0	1	8
Reg Hamilton	4	0	1	1	2
Red Horner	4	0	1	1	8
Murray Armstrong	2	0	0	0	0
Buzz Boll	4	0	0	0	2
Murph Chamberlain	2	0	0	0	2
Bingo Kampman	4	0	0	0	6
Nick Metz	4	0	0	0	0

GOALTENDER	GP	W	L	MIN	GA	SO	AVG
Turk Broda	4	1	3	240	10	0	2.50

ROSTER

Bert Connelly
Cully Dahlstrom
Paul Goodman
Johnny Gottselig (captain)
Harold Jackson
Roger Jenkins
Virgil Johnson
Mike Karakas ▲
Alex Levinsky

Bill MacKenzie
Mush March
Alfie Moore
Pete Palangio
Doc Romnes
Earl Seibert
Jack Shill
Paul Thompson
Lou Trudel
Carl Voss

Art Wiebe
Bill Tobin (vice president)
Bill Stewart (coach)

Wanna Bet?

When Chicago won the Stanley Cup, Mike Karakas was keen to cash in on a bet he had made with a teammate. Roger Jenkins had promised the goalie that if they won, he'd push him in a wheelbarrow down State Street. At one o'clock in the afternoon on the day after their Stanley Cup victory, Jenkins wheeled Karakas in front of thousands of cheering onlookers. Jenkins had paid off on a similar bet by rolling Charlie Gardiner through the Loop back in 1934.

Shocker in Chicago

The Boston Bruins posted a record of 30-11-7 to lead the NHL's overall standings with 67 points in 1937–38. They were six points up on the New York Rangers, who finished second behind them in the American Division standings. Both were well ahead of the Chicago Black Hawks, whose record of 14-25-9 was good for only 37 points but was still enough for third place in the division and a spot in the playoffs (Detroit was 12-25-11 with only 35 points).

Toronto was tops in the Canadian Division, with a record of 24-15-9, and faced the Bruins for a berth in the Stanley Cup final. The Maple Leafs had the league's best offense, led by Gordie Drillon and Syl Apps, who finished one and two in scoring, but it was Toronto goalie Turk Broda who sparked the upset as the Maple Leafs swept the Bruins in three straight.

Despite their poor regular season, Chicago came to life in the playoffs. The Black Hawks eliminated the Montreal Canadiens on a goal by Lou Trudel in overtime in the quarterfinals. Then, after losing their semifinal opener against the New York Americans, Chicago won Game 2 1–0 on a Cully Dahlstrom goal in double overtime. They took the series with a 3–2 win in Game 3. Unfortunately for Chicago, goalie Mike Karakas broke the big toe on his right foot during the game and was unavailable when the Stanley Cup final got under way.

The Black Hawks hoped to borrow Dave Kerr from the Rangers, but Toronto insisted they use local minor leaguer Alfie Moore. Moore was brilliant as Chicago stunned Toronto 3–1 in Game 1, but he was ruled ineligible before Game 2. The Black Hawks owned the rights to Wichita goalie Paul Goodman and had summoned him to Toronto. Goodman had arrived too late for Game 1 and, as the story goes, because everyone expected Moore to start for Chicago again, Goodman had gone to the movies. He only reported to the team about two hours before game time. The Black Hawks were beaten 5–1. Karakas then returned to action in Game 3, wearing a special skate boot with a steel guard. With a strong defense in front of him, Karakas allowed only one early goal, and Chicago rallied for a 2–1 victory before wrapping up the series with a 4–1 win in Game 4.

A Busy Guy

Bill Stewart was the first American-born coach to win the Stanley Cup. He coached the Black Hawks in 1937–38 and part of 1938–39 and was an NHL referee from 1928 until 1937 and then again until 1941. Stewart was also a Major League Baseball umpire in the National League from 1933 to 1954. In fact, just four days after leading Chicago to the Stanley Cup, Stewart was in Boston umpiring an exhibition game between the Red Sox and the Boston Bees in preparation for the upcoming baseball season.

Born in the USA
In addition to their coach, the Black Hawks featured eight American-born players in their lineup: Mike Karakas, Doc Romnes, Alex Levinsky, Carl Voss, Cully Dahlstrom, Roger Jenkins, Lou Trudel and Virgil Johnson. No Stanley Cup winner would feature more American players until the 1995 New Jersey Devils, who had 12.

Playoff Format

During the seasons from 1928–29 through 1937–38, the first-place teams in the Canadian and American divisions opened the playoffs against each other in a best-of-five series. The winner was declared NHL champion and earned a berth in the Stanley Cup final. Meanwhile, the second-place teams in each division faced each other in another series, while the third-place teams were also paired off. Then, the winners of those two series met to determine the other Cup finalist. Over the years, the series involving the second- and third-place teams changed from two games and total goals to a best-of-three series.

Pay Day
According to a Canadian Press report after the Stanley Cup final, Alfie Moore was paid $300 for his appearance in goal. He also received a gold watch from the Black Hawks and a week's holiday in Chicago at the club's expense.

Moore Makes Good

As Black Hawks captain Johnny Gottselig liked to tell it, when he was sent out to get Alfie Moore before Game 1 of the Stanley Cup final, he found him drunk in a tavern. "We took him out to the rink," Gottselig said, "and put some coffee into him and put him under the shower. By game time he was in pretty good shape."

In truth, it was Toronto's Conn Smythe who had reached Moore by telephone and told him to report to Maple Leaf Gardens. Moore was a 32-year-old Toronto boy who had played a few games in the NHL with the New York Americans the year before, but he had spent most of his time since 1926 bouncing around the minor leagues. As Moore told newspaper reporters after the game, the Black Hawks didn't even know he was there until he walked into their dressing room. Chicago had already made arrangements with the Rangers' Dave Kerr, and he was getting suited up when Moore arrived. NHL president Frank Calder had apparently ruled that Kerr was ineligible, but Black Hawks coach Bill Stewart claimed Smythe had approved him. Stewart and Smythe came to blows in the corridor outside the dressing room, but Smythe insisted that Stewart had to use either Karakas or Moore — and Karakas couldn't even stand on his broken toe.

Moore felt that Smythe had played him for a sucker. "I was so mad," he told reporters, "I told him 'I hope I stop every puck you give even if I have to eat the rubber.'" He almost did. Moore gave up a goal to Gordie Drillon at 1:53 of the first period but shut out Toronto the rest of the way.

Detroit Red Wings

SEMIFINALS
3 games to 2 over Montreal Canadiens

ROSTER

Larry Aurie
Marty Barry
Ralph Bowman
Mud Bruneteau
Jimmy Franks
John Gallagher
Ebbie Goodfellow
Syd Howe
Pete Kelly
Hec Kilrea
Wally Kilrea
Herbie Lewis
Howie Mackie
Bucko McDonald
Gord Pettinger
Earl Robertson
Rolly Roulston
John Sherf
Normie Smith
John Sorrell
Doug Young (captain)
Jack Adams
(manager/coach)

FINAL   3 GAMES TO 2

APR. 6	►	Detroit 1 at New York Rangers 5
APR. 8	►	New York Rangers 2 at Detroit 4
APR. 11	►	New York Rangers 1 at Detroit 0
APR. 13	►	New York Rangers 0 at Detroit 1
APR. 15	►	New York Rangers 0 at Detroit 3

PLAYOFF SCORING LEADER

	GP	G	A	PTS
Marty Barry DETROIT	10	4	7	11

FINAL SERIES SCORING

DETROIT	GP	G	A	PTS	PIM
Syd Howe	5	1	4	5	0
Marty Barry	5	3	1	4	0
John Sorrell	5	2	2	4	2
Ebbie Goodfellow	4	0	2	2	12
Mud Bruneteau	5	1	0	1	2
John Gallagher	5	1	0	1	8
Herbie Lewis	5	1	0	1	4
Hec Kilrea	5	0	1	1	0
Wally Kilrea	5	0	1	1	4
Gord Pettinger	5	0	1	1	2
John Sherf	5	0	1	1	2
Ralph Bowman	5	0	0	0	2
Pete Kelly	3	0	0	0	0
Howie Mackie	3	0	0	0	0
Bucko McDonald	5	0	0	0	0

GOALTENDERS	GP	W	L	MIN	GA	SO	AVG
Earl Robertson	5	3	1	280	5	2	1.07
Normie Smith	1	0	1	20	3	0	9.00

NY RANGERS	GP	G	A	PTS	PIM
Butch Keeling	5	2	1	3	0
Frank Boucher	5	1	2	3	0
Joe Cooper	5	1	2	3	12
Lynn Patrick	5	2	0	2	2
Neil Colville	5	1	1	2	0
Babe Pratt	5	1	1	2	9
Art Coulter	5	0	2	2	6
Cecil Dillon	5	0	2	2	0
Mac Colville	5	0	1	1	0
Murray Murdoch	5	0	1	1	0
Ott Heller	5	0	0	0	5
Ching Johnson	5	0	0	0	2
Alex Shibicky	5	0	0	0	0
Phil Watson	5	0	0	0	4

GOALTENDER	GP	W	L	MIN	GA	SO	AVG
Dave Kerr	5	2	3	300	9	1	1.80

Red Wings Repeat

Several NHL stars were sidelined by major injuries during the 1936–37 season. Worst of all was the injury suffered by Howie Morenz. Morenz had seemed to regain his star form after being traded back to Montreal, but he suffered a broken leg on January 28, 1937. The injury was bad enough to end his career, and Morenz never got out of the hospital. He died of an embolism caused by blood clots on March 8, 1937.

Despite the loss of their great superstar, the Canadiens hung on to win the NHL's Canadian Division in a tight race with the Montreal Maroons. Detroit, the defending Stanley Cup champions, won the American Division for the second straight year despite a rash of injuries of their own. Captain Doug Young had seen his season end early with a broken leg, as did his replacement Rolly Roulston. Then, late in the season, Larry Aurie (whose 23 goals tied Nels Stewart for the NHL lead) suffered a broken ankle. Injuries continued to plague the Red Wings, with goalie Normie Smith (who won the Vezina Trophy) hurting his shoulder in Game 3 of Detroit's playoff series with Montreal. After sitting out Game 4, he returned for Game 5 and was brilliant in a contest that was tied 1–1

until 11:49 of the third overtime period. Hec Kilrea, who had taken Aurie's spot on Detroit's top line with Marty Barry and Herbie Lewis, scored to give Detroit the victory.

Facing Detroit in the Stanley Cup final were the New York Rangers. The Rangers had finished third in the American Division with a 19-20-9 record before sweeping the Maple Leafs and the Maroons in a pair of best-of-three series. Goalie Dave Kerr was the star with three shutouts in four games.

With a circus already booked in Madison Square Garden, the Rangers played their only home game of the final in Game 1 before the series moved to Detroit for the duration. The Rangers stayed hot in Game 1, scoring a 5–1 victory. Normie Smith re-injured his shoulder and came out after the first period. Earl Robertson, up from the minors in Pittsburgh, took over for the rest of the series. He became the first rookie to post two shutouts in the finals, blanking the Rangers in Games 4 and 5 as the Red Wings became the first American team to repeat as Stanley Cup champions.

Lucky Charm

Shortly after Detroit won the Stanley Cup in 1936, Mrs. Ida Lefleur went into labor. According to a story that made the rounds after Detroit won again in 1937, Mrs. Lefleur told her friend Normie Smith that if the child was a boy, "we'll name him Stanley after the Cup and next year the Red Wings will win the Stanley Cup again on his birthday." Before Game 5 — which was played on Stanley Lefleur's first birthday — Smith advised Earl Robertson to go for a visit and pat the boy on the head a few times for good luck.

Barry Comes Up Big
Marty Barry scored the lone goal for Detroit in the third period to give the Red Wings a 1–0 victory over the Rangers in Game 4. Prior to Game 5, he was presented with the Lady Byng Trophy after finishing third in the NHL scoring race in 1936–37 while posting only six penalty minutes. He then proceeded to score two goals and set up a third in Detroit's 3–0 Stanley Cup–winning victory.

Strange Celebration

Celebrations in the Detroit dressing room fell silent when Jack Adams fainted. Bedlam broke out once again when it was determined that the Red Wings coach and general manager had suffered nothing more severe than a weak spell brought on by excitement, joy and worry. After Adams was revived, a police escort led the Stanley Cup into the dressing room, where NHL president Frank Calder presented it to the team.

Robertson to the Rescue

Earl Robertson had played for nine minor league seasons before finally getting a shot in the NHL at the age of 27. He was called up by Detroit to fill in for Normie Smith in Game 4 of their playoff series against Montreal. He played well in a 3–1 loss, and the Red Wings decided to keep him around. It was fortunate they did.

Robertson took over for an injured Smith once again with the Red Wings down 3–0 to the Rangers after the first period of Game 1 in the Stanley Cup final. He gave up just two goals over the final two periods and was brilliant in a 4–2 Red Wings victory in Game 2. The Rangers took the next game 1–0 before Robertson recorded his own shutout in a 1–0 Red Wings victory that forced a fifth and deciding game. The rookie goalie was brilliant in Game 5. "Robertson," read the Canadian Press report, "turned in an amazing performance, his sensational stops time and again robbing the Rangers of goals."

"They just can't keep you in the minors now," Red Wings star Marty Barry told Robertson. "You were great kid. Sensational."

Jack Adams, Detroit's coach and general manager, agreed. Only it wouldn't be with the Red Wings. Normie Smith would remain in Detroit, and Robertson was traded to the New York Americans. Sadly, Smith would never again be the goalie he was before his shoulder injury. Robertson wouldn't enjoy much success either, spending three full seasons and parts of two others with the woeful Americans.

SEMIFINALS
3 games to 0 over Montreal Maroons

ROSTER

Larry Aurie
Marty Barry
Ralph Bowman
Mud Bruneteau
Ebbie Goodfellow
Syd Howe
Pete Kelly
Hec Kilrea
Wally Kilrea
Herbie Lewis
Bucko McDonald
Gord Pettinger
Normie Smith
John Sorrell
Doug Young (captain)
Jack Adams
(manager/coach)

FINAL   3 GAMES TO 1

APR. 5	▶	Toronto 1 at Detroit 3
APR. 7	▶	Toronto 4 at Detroit 9
APR. 9	▶	Detroit 3 at Toronto 4 OT
APR. 11	▶	Detroit 3 at Toronto 2

PLAYOFF SCORING LEADER

Frank Boll	GP	G	A	PTS
TORONTO	9	7	3	10

FINAL SERIES SCORING

DETROIT	GP	G	A	PTS	PIM
Syd Howe	4	2	3	5	2
John Sorrell	4	2	3	5	0
Marty Barry	4	2	2	4	2
Gord Pettinger	4	2	2	4	0
Bucko McDonald	4	3	0	3	4
Wally Kilrea	4	2	1	3	0
Mud Bruneteau	4	1	2	3	0
Herbie Lewis	4	1	2	3	0
Ralph Bowman	4	1	1	2	2
Pete Kelly	4	1	1	2	0
Hec Kilrea	4	0	2	2	0
Doug Young	4	0	2	2	0
Ebbie Goodfellow	4	1	0	1	2
Larry Aurie	4	0	1	1	2
GOALTENDER	GP	W	L	MIN	GA	SO	AVG
Normie Smith	4	3	1	241	11	0	2.74

TORONTO	GP	G	A	PTS	PIM
Frank Boll	4	3	1	4	0
Joe Primeau	4	3	1	4	0
Bill Thoms	4	2	2	4	0
Bob Davidson	4	1	2	3	2
Pete Kelly	4	2	0	2	0
Frank Finnigan	4	0	2	2	0
Red Horner	4	0	2	2	8
Busher Jackson	4	0	2	2	2
Charlie Conacher	4	0	1	1	2
Art Jackson	4	0	1	1	0
Jack Shill	4	0	1	1	4
Andy Blair	4	0	0	0	2
King Clancy	4	0	0	0	2
Hap Day	4	0	0	0	4
GOALTENDER	GP	W	L	MIN	GA	SO	AVG
George Hainsworth	4	1	3	241	18	0	4.48

He Was Right

"These boys were good enough to win this year, and they'll be better next season. Don't be surprised if the Wings make it two in a row."
— Red Wings coach/manager Jack Adams

Up and Down
The Red Wings had rallied from a last-place finish in the NHL's American Division in 1934–35 to win the both the division title and the Stanley Cup in 1935–36. After repeating both victories in 1936–37, Detroit fell to last place once again in 1937–38.

Detroit Does It

The Detroit Red Wings had reached the 1934 Stanley Cup final largely on the strength of goalie Wilf Cude. Midway through the 1933–34 season, Cude was acquired on loan from the Montreal Canadiens, who had assigned the netminder to the Syracuse Stars of the International Hockey League. When the Red Wings offered to buy his contract outright after the season, the Canadiens refused to sell him and brought him back to Montreal. Forced to juggle a past-his-prime John Ross Roach and the not-quite-ready Normie Smith in goal in 1934–35, the Red Wings slumped to last place in the American Division and missed the playoffs entirely.

Smith would be a key player in Detroit's turnaround in 1935–36, as would Syd Howe, who came on board midway through the 1934–35 campaign. The biggest acquisition would prove to be Marty Barry, whom Jack Adams obtained in a deal with the Boston Bruins in the summer of 1935. Centering Herbie Lewis and Larry Aurie on Detroit's top line, Barry finished second in the NHL in scoring in 1935–36. His solid play allowed Ebbie Goodfellow to make the permanent move from center to defense, where he was named a Second Team All-Star.

The Wings emerged as the best in the league this season, winning the American Division with a 24-16-8 record. The Montreal Maroons won the Canadian Division with a mark of 22-16-10, and the two teams proved to be so evenly matched in the first game of their playoff series that it took until 16:30 of the sixth overtime period for Mud Bruneteau to beat Lorne Chabot for the only goal in the longest game in NHL history. Smith made 90 saves that night and then blanked the Maroons for 60 minutes more in another 1–0 victory in Game 2. He allowed one goal in a 2–1 win that swept the series.

Toronto had rallied from a 3–0 loss in their playoff opener to beat Boston 8–3 in Game 2 and take the total-goals series 8–6. The Maple Leafs then beat the New York Americans two games to one to advance to the Stanley Cup final. Detroit took the first two games from Toronto handily on home ice, and the Red Wings went on to win the best-of-five series in four.

City of Champions

The Red Wings, who had entered the NHL in 1926, had their first Stanley Cup victory in team history in 1936. It came just six months after the Detroit Tigers had won the World Series for the first time and four months after the Detroit Lions won their first NFL championship.

Scoring Records

MOST GOALS IN THE STANLEY CUP FINAL BY BOTH TEAMS IN ONE GAME (1918 TO 2012)

15 Chicago Black Hawks (8) at Montreal Canadiens (7) in Game 5, May 8, 1973 (Montreal won the series 4–2)

13 Toronto Maple Leafs (4) at Detroit Red Wings (9) in Game 2, April 7, 1936 (Detroit won the series 3–1)

MOST GOALS IN THE STANLEY CUP FINAL BY ONE TEAM IN ONE GAME (1918 TO 2012)

9 Detroit Red Wings in Game 2, April 7, 1936; Toronto 4 at Detroit 9 (Detroit won the series 3–1)

Toronto Maple Leafs in Game 5, April 14, 1942; Detroit 3 at Toronto 9 (Toronto won the series 4–3)

Ebbie Goodfellow

QUARTERFINALS
1 goal to 0 over Chicago

SEMIFINALS
5 goals to 4 over New York Rangers

ROSTER

Toe Blake

Russ Blinco

Herb Cain

Lionel Conacher

Alex Connell

Stewart Evans

Dutch Gainor

Bob Gracie

Gus Marker

Sammy McManus

Bill Miller

Baldy Northcott

Earl Robinson

Al Shields

Hooley Smith
(captain)

Dave Trottier

Jimmy Ward

Cy Wentworth

Tommy Gorman
(manager/coach)

FINAL 3 GAMES TO 0

APR. 4	►	Montreal Maroons 3 at Toronto 2 OT
APR. 6	►	Montreal Maroons 3 at Toronto 1
APR. 9	►	Toronto 1 at Montreal Maroons 4

PLAYOFF SCORING LEADERS

	GP	G	A	PTS
Baldy Northcott MONTREAL MAROONS	7	4	1	5
Busher Jackson TORONTO	7	3	2	5
Cy Wentworth MONTREAL MAROONS	7	3	2	5
Charlie Conacher TORONTO	7	1	4	5

FINAL SERIES SCORING

MONTREAL MAROONS	GP	G	A	PTS	PIM
Cy Wentworth	3	2	2	4	0
Baldy Northcott	3	2	1	3	0
Earl Robinson	3	2	1	3	0
Russ Blinco	3	1	1	2	0
Jimmy Ward	3	1	1	2	0
Gus Marker	3	1	0	1	0
Dave Trottier	3	1	0	1	4
Al Shields	3	0	1	1	2
Herb Cain	3	0	0	0	0
Lionel Conacher	3	0	0	0	8
Stewart Evans	3	0	0	0	4
Bob Gracie	3	0	0	0	0
Bill Miller	3	0	0	0	0
Hooley Smith	3	0	0	0	4
GOALTENDER	GP	W	L	MIN	GA	SO	AVG
Alex Connell	3	3	0	185	4	0	1.30

TORONTO	GP	G	A	PTS	PIM
Frank Finnigan	3	1	1	2	0
King Clancy	3	1	0	1	4
Busher Jackson	3	1	0	1	0
Nick Metz	3	0	1	1	0
Bill Thoms	3	1	0	1	0
Andy Blair	1	0	0	0	2
Frank Boll	2	0	0	0	0
Charlie Conacher	3	0	0	0	4
Baldy Cotton	3	0	0	0	0
Hap Day	3	0	0	0	0
Ken Doraty	1	0	0	0	0
Flash Hollett	3	0	0	0	0
Red Horner	3	0	0	0	4
Pete Kelly	3	0	0	0	0
Hec Kilrea	2	0	0	0	2
Joe Primeau	3	0	0	0	0
GOALTENDER	GP	W	L	MIN	GA	SO	AVG
George Hainsworth	3	0	3	185	10	0	3.24

All-Canadian The Stanley Cup series between the Maroons and Maple Leafs marked the first time that two Canadian teams had appeared in the final since the Maroons beat the Victoria Cougars in 1926. It would not happen again until the Maple Leafs met the Canadiens in 1947.

Beating the Best To become Stanley Cup champions in 1935, the Maroons knocked off the 1934 champions from Chicago to open the playoffs. In beating New York next, they defeated the 1933 champions. In downing Toronto in the final, they knocked off the 1932 champions.

The Maroons' Last Great Moment

The NHL, which had grown to 10 teams for the 1926–27 season, was reduced to nine in 1930–31, when the Philadelphia Quakers, after five years as the Pittsburgh Pirates, suspended operations. The league would be reduced to eight teams after the 1934–35 season, when the St. Louis Eagles, formerly the original Ottawa Senators, were terminated.

The effects of the Great Depression were being felt all over the NHL, and it would soon become obvious that Montreal could no longer support both the Canadiens and the Maroons. The Maroons would win the Stanley Cup this season, but it was the beginning of the end for Montreal's English-language team, who would play their final season in 1937–38.

The 1934–35 Maroons were led by Tommy Gorman. Gorman had resigned as coach and general manager of the Chicago Black Hawks 10 days after leading them to the Stanley Cup in 1934 and was hired two weeks later to take the same two positions for the Maroons. Gorman brought Lionel Conacher (who had played for him in Chicago) back to Montreal and had acquired Alex Connell from Ottawa before the Senators moved to St. Louis. Connell would lead the NHL with nine shutouts and post a goals-against average of 1.86.

The Maroons were a veteran team led by Hooley Smith, Baldy Northcott, Dave Trottier, Cy Wentworth and Jimmy Ward, but they also featured promising youngsters in Herb Cain and Toe Blake. They finished second to Toronto in the Canadian Division standings but beat Chicago to open the playoffs when Connell posted two straight shutouts. Northcott scored the only goal of the two-game total-goal series at 4:02 of overtime in Game 2. The Maroons then hung on to defeat the Rangers by a single goal in the next round. They met the Maple Leafs in the Stanley Cup final; Toronto having swept the American Division–champion Boston Bruins in the battle of first-place teams to get there.

Led by the Kid Line of Charlie Conacher (Lionel's brother), Busher Jackson and Joe Primeau, the Maple Leafs had been the NHL's best team, with a record of 30-14-4. Their 64 points had them comfortably ahead of the Maroons' 53. Even so, the Maroons were able to shut down Toronto's league-leading offense. After Dave Trottier scored the winner in overtime in Game 1, the Maroons went on to sweep the series.

Rare Double

Having won with the Black Hawks in 1933–34 and with the Maroons in 1934–35, Tommy Gorman is the only coach in NHL history to win the Stanley Cup with two different teams in back-to-back seasons.

Winning More Than One
STANLEY CUP COACHING VICTORIES WITH MORE THAN ONE TEAM

Lester Patrick	Victoria Cougars	1925
	New York Rangers	1928, 1933
Dick Irvin	Toronto Maple Leafs	1932
	Montreal Canadiens	1944, 1946, 1953
Tommy Gorman	Chicago Black Hawks	1934
	Montreal Maroons	1935
Scotty Bowman	Montreal Canadiens	1973, 1977, 1978, 1979
	Pittsburgh Penguins	1992
	Detroit Red Wings	1997, 1998, 2002

Lester Patrick

Fastest Two Goals

Baldy Northcott and Cy Wentworth scored at 16:18 and 16:30 of the second period to break open a 1–1 tie in Game 3 and lead the Maroons to a 4–1 victory that swept the series. Those two goals, 12 seconds apart, set a record for the two fastest goals by one NHL team in the Stanley Cup final. The record was later tied by Bernie Geoffrion, who scored twice in 12 seconds for the Montreal Canadiens in Game 3 of the 1955 final, and by Jon Sim and Kirk Muller of New Jersey in Game 1 of the 2000 final.

Golden Oldies Two days after their victory, the Maroons were presented with the Stanley Cup at a banquet at the Queen's Hotel. Among those on hand to honor the team that evening were Bob McDougal and Hartland McDougal, who had won the Stanley Cup with the Montreal Victorias in the late 1890s. Earlier in the day, at a civic reception held at City Hall, alderman W.S. Weldon had been on hand. Weldon had been secretary of the Montreal Amateur Athletic Association when the hockey club affiliated with that organization became the first Stanley Cup champions, in 1893.

New Suit Bob Gracie wore the same suit for two weeks straight during the playoffs because Maroons coach Tommy Gorman had decided it was lucky. Gorman promised to buy Gracie a new suit if the Maroons won the Cup.

Chicago Black Hawks

SEMIFINALS
6 goals to 2 over Montreal Maroons

ROSTER

Clarence Abel
Lionel Conacher
Tom Cook
Art Coulter
Rosie Couture
Charlie Gardiner (captain)
Leroy Goldsworthy
Johnny Gottselig
Roger Jenkins
Bill Kendall
Jack Leswick
Mush March
Don McFadyen
Paul Thompson
Lou Trudel
Doc Romnes
Johnny Sheppard
Tommy Gorman
(manager/coach)

FINAL 3 GAMES TO 1

APR. 3	► Chicago 2 at Detroit 1 2x OT
APR. 5	► Chicago 4 at Detroit 1
APR. 8	► Detroit 5 at Chicago 2
APR. 10	► Detroit 0 at Chicago 1 2x OT

PLAYOFF SCORING LEADER

		GP	G	A	PTS
Larry Aurie DETROIT		9	3	7	10

FINAL SERIES SCORING

CHICAGO	GP	G	A	PTS	PIM
Doc Romnes	4	1	3	4	0
Johnny Gottselig	4	2	1	3	4
Paul Thompson	4	2	1	3	0
Rosie Couture	4	1	1	2	2
Mush March	4	1	1	2	2
Lionel Conacher	4	1	0	1	2
Art Coulter	4	1	0	1	4
Don McFadyen	4	0	1	1	2
Clarence Abel	4	0	0	0	2
Tom Cook	4	0	0	0	0
Leroy Goldsworthy	4	0	0	0	0
Roger Jenkins	4	0	0	0	0
Bill Kendall	1	0	0	0	0
Johnny Sheppard	3	0	0	0	0
Lou Trudel	4	0	0	0	0
GOALTENDER	GP	W	L	MIN	GA	SO	AVG
Charlie Gardiner	4	3	1	291	7	1	1.44

DETROIT	GP	G	A	PTS	PIM
Larry Aurie	4	2	2	4	0
Herbie Lewis	4	2	1	3	2
Cooney Weiland	4	1	1	2	2
Gord Pettinger	3	1	0	1	0
Doug Young	4	1	0	1	2
Walt Buswell	4	0	1	1	2
Frank Carson	2	0	1	1	0
Ted Graham	4	0	1	1	4
Wilf Starr	3	0	1	1	2
Gene Carrigan	3	0	0	0	0
Hap Emms	3	0	0	0	2
Ebbie Goodfellow	4	0	0	0	6
Gus Marker	3	0	0	0	2
Ron Moffatt	2	0	0	0	0
John Sorrell	4	0	0	0	0
Burr Williams	2	0	0	0	0
Eddie Wiseman	3	0	0	0	0
GOALTENDER	GP	W	L	MIN	GA	SO	AVG
Wilf Cude	4	1	3	291	9	0	1.86

Chicago's First Cup

Though they'd been drawing large crowds since moving into the Chicago Stadium in 1929 and had reached the Stanley Cup final in 1931, the Chicago Black Hawks had struggled. After making the playoffs in their first season (1926–27), they missed the postseason three times in the next six years and consistently ranked among the worst offensive teams in the NHL. In 1928–29 (the lowest-scoring season in NHL history), the Black Hawks scored just 33 goals during the 44-game schedule and were shut out in eight straight games at one point. Fortunately for Chicago, the team boasted a brilliant young goaltender in Charlie Gardiner.

Despite battling injury and illness, Gardiner was sensational in 1933–34. He led the NHL with 10 shutouts and posted a 1.63 goals-against average. Chicago boasted the league's best defense, which earned Gardiner the Vezina Trophy for the second time in three years. The acquisition of Lionel Conacher from the Montreal Maroons helped to bolster the blue line corps, and though the offense was the NHL's worst by far (with just 88 goals in 44 games), Paul Thompson's 20 goals and 36 points ranked him among the top-10 scorers. Johnny Gottselig (16) and Conacher (10) were the only other Chicago players to reach double-digits goals.

Chicago had finished last in the American Division standings and missed the playoffs the year before, but coach Tommy Gorman guided them to a second-place finish, behind the Detroit Red Wings, in 1933–34. The Black Hawks opened the playoffs against the Canadiens and won the total-goals series on a Mush March goal in overtime. They then downed the Montreal Maroons to reach the Stanley Cup final. Their Cup-final opponent was the Red Wings, who had beaten Toronto 1–0 in the fifth and final game of their semifinal series, which had featured the league's first-place clubs.

Chicago opened the final on the road in Detroit and won Game 1 on a goal by Paul Thompson at 1:10 of the second overtime period. It had been more than a month since the offensively challenged Black Hawks had scored more than three goals, but they won Game 2 4–1. An ailing Gardiner played poorly in a 5–2 loss in Game 3 but vowed that he'd only need one goal to win the Cup in Game 4. That goal finally came at 10:05 of double overtime, when Mush March scored to give Chicago a 1–0 victory.

Charlie with a C

Charlie Gardiner is the only goaltender to have his name appear on the Stanley Cup as the captain of a championship team. He was named captain of the Black Hawks in a unanimous vote by his teammates prior to the start of the 1933–34 season.

Howdy, Neighbor
Charlie Gardiner and Detroit's Wilf Cude, the opposing goaltenders in the 1934 Stanley Cup final, had grown up together in Winnipeg as childhood friends. "He lived near my place over on William Street," Gardiner recalled, "and for years we went back and forth to school together."

The Overtime Hero

Mush March scored only four goals during the 1933–34 season, the lowest total of any full season during his 17-year NHL career. The 5-foot-5, 150-pound forward added just two goals in the playoffs, but both of them were series winners in overtime.

Detroit's Ebbie Goodfellow was in the penalty box (serving the first penalty called since the first period) when March scored the Stanley Cup winner. Doc Romnes had carried the puck across the Red Wings blue line and fed it to March, who was bumped off balance by Teddy Graham but still managed to drive the puck past Wilf Cude from 20 feet out. It was the second year in a row that the Stanley Cup had been won in overtime.

Death of a Hero

Two months after leading Chicago to the Stanley Cup, Charlie Gardiner was dead. He passed away on June 13, 1934, in Winnipeg, the city he had grown up in after coming to Canada from Scotland with his parents as a boy. Gardiner died of a brain hemorrhage. He was still six months shy of his 30th birthday. His death shocked the hockey world and tributes poured in from across North America. In 1945, Charlie Gardiner was among the first group of players inducted into the Hockey Hall of Fame.

Gardiner never missed a game after taking over the Chicago goal early in the 1927–28 season. He played the entire 1932–33 season while suffering from tonsillitis and was never quite able to beat the disease despite repeated hospital visits. The infection grew steadily and spread to his kidneys. His health problems would flare up throughout the 1933–34 season, often leaving him in severe pain, yet he played through it.

As the story goes, Gardiner was overcome by a wave of pain as he bent over to lace up his skates before Game 3 of the 1934 Stanley Cup final. "He's bad," coach Tommy Gorman said to Lionel Conacher, but Gardiner insisted on playing. After two periods, he faded badly and Chicago lost 5–2. Still, he was back in action two nights later. Despite battling near-constant pain, Gardiner made 39 saves and played over 90 minutes of shutout hockey in a 1–0 Stanley Cup victory.

When Gardiner passed away, the attending physician attributed the brain hemorrhage to the tonsil and kidney infections. He ruled out any link to hockey injuries.

QUARTERFINALS
8 goals to 5 over Montreal Canadiens

SEMIFINALS
6 goals to 3 over Detroit

FINAL 3 GAMES TO 1

APR. 4	►	Toronto 1 at New York Rangers 5
APR. 8	►	New York Rangers 3 at Toronto 1
APR. 11	►	New York Rangers 2 at Toronto 3
APR. 13	►	New York Rangers 1 at Toronto 0 OT

PLAYOFF SCORING LEADER

	GP	G	A	PTS
Cecil Dillon NEW YORK RANGERS	8	8	2	10

FINAL SERIES SCORING

NY RANGERS	GP	G	A	PTS	PIM
Cecil Dillon	4	3	1	4	4
Bill Cook	4	2	1	3	4
Art Somers	4	0	3	3	4
Ott Heller	4	2	0	2	4
Butch Keeling	4	1	1	2	6
Murray Murdoch	4	1	1	2	2
Bun Cook	4	1	0	1	4
Earl Seibert	4	1	0	1	2
Oscar Asmundson	4	0	1	1	2
Frank Boucher	4	0	1	1	4
Doug Brennan	4	0	0	0	2
Ching Johnson	4	0	0	0	8
Gord Pettinger	4	0	0	0	0
Babe Siebert	4	0	0	0	10

GOALTENDER	GP	W	L	MIN	GA	SO	AVG
Andy Aitkenhead	4	3	1	248	5	1	1.21

TORONTO	GP	G	A	PTS	PIM
Ken Doraty	4	3	0	3	2
King Clancy	4	0	2	2	6
Red Horner	4	1	0	1	8
Alex Levinsky	4	1	0	1	6
Baldy Cotton	4	0	1	1	2
Bob Gracie	4	0	1	1	0
Joe Primeau	4	0	1	1	4
Charlie Sands	4	0	1	1	0
Ace Bailey	4	0	0	0	2
Andy Blair	4	0	0	0	0
Buzz Boll	1	0	0	0	0
Charlie Conacher	4	0	0	0	6
Hap Day	4	0	0	0	6
Busher Jackson	4	0	0	0	2
Bill Thoms	4	0	0	0	2

GOALTENDER	GP	W	L	MIN	GA	SO	AVG
Lorne Chabot	4	1	3	248	11	0	2.66

The Ranger's top line of Bill Cook, Frank Boucher and Bun Cook.

ROSTER

Andy Aitkenhead	Butch Keeling
Oscar Asmundson	Murray Murdoch
Frank Boucher	Gord Pettinger
Doug Brennan	Earl Seibert
Bill Cook (captain)	Babe Siebert
Bun Cook	Art Somers
Cecil Dillon	Lester Patrick (manager/coach)
Ott Heller	
Ching Johnson	

Rangers Get Revenge

After losing to Toronto in 1932, Rangers coach and general manager Lester Patrick made two key changes to his lineup. One was the purchase of Babe Siebert from the Montreal Maroons. The other was the sale of goalie John Ross Roach to Detroit to open up a spot for Andy Aitkenhead. However, most of the roster had stayed intact and still boasted many of the players who had been members of the Rangers team that entered the NHL in 1926–27 and won the Stanley Cup in 1928. Among those were Ching Johnson, Murray Murdoch and the team's top forward line of Frank Boucher centering brothers Bill and Bun Cook. They also had an up-and-coming young defenseman named Earl Seibert.

Bill Cook led the NHL with 28 goals and 50 points during the 48-game 1932–33 season. Frank Boucher's 28 assists were also tops in the NHL. Even so, the Rangers, who had won the American Division in 1931–32, found themselves in a tight battle with Boston and Detroit. Their record of 23-17-8 for 54 points was only good enough for third place behind the Bruins and Red Wings, who both had 25 wins and 58 points. The Rangers opened the playoffs against the Canadiens and nearly let their 5–2 lead after Game 1 slip away, but Cecil Dillon scored two late goals for an 8–5 victory in the total-goals series. After beating the Red Wings in the next round, the Rangers returned to the Stanley Cup finals for a rematch with the Maple Leafs.

Toronto had won the Canadian Division and then beaten out Boston in a tight five-game series that saw four games go into overtime. The finale lasted until 4:46 of the sixth overtime period, when Ken Doraty finally scored to give Toronto a 1–0 victory. The Leafs then caught a 3 a.m. train to New York to open the Stanley Cup final that same night. Toronto had hoped for a postponement, but the Rangers, about to be forced onto the road by the circus, were anxious to get in their only home game. They beat the Leafs 5–1. Even with four days off before the series resumed, and the rest of the games in Toronto, the Maple Leafs never really recovered. The Rangers took the best-of-five series in four, with Bill Cook scoring the Cup-winning goal in overtime.

Don Cherry Would Agree

With Alex Levinsky already in the box for an overly aggressive hit on Oscar Asmundson, Bill Thoms accidentally shot the puck into the stands after being knocked off balance near center ice. When the Rangers complained to referee Odie Cleghorn, Thoms was penalized. The Leafs argued, but Thoms went off. Less than a minute later, Bill Cook scored. "There never was any intention to have that rule applied to any such an accident as that," wrote longtime *Toronto Star* sports editor and former NHL referee Lou Marsh. "If every rule in the hockey book was interpreted to the last letter and not in its true spirit, there would be no hockey game. This over-the-fence rule is one that will certainly be amended.... The rule was only meant to penalize teams who deliberately shot the puck into the crowd to get a breather or break up a sustained and dangerous attack."

Andy Was Dandy

Andy Aitkenhead made 48 saves to earn the shutout in the Rangers' 1–0 Cup-clinching victory. Hardly a well-known name even in his own time, Aitkenhead played 15 years of professional hockey between 1925–26 and 1940–41 but spent only two full seasons and part of a third in the NHL.

Beat the Clock Though newspaper reports list the time of Bill Cook's winning goal as 7:34 of overtime, the NHL game summary records it as 7:33.

Working Overtime

The Rangers became the first NHL team to win the Stanley Cup in overtime and the first team from any league to win it in extended play since Dan Bain had scored to give the Winnipeg Victorias a 2–1 win over the Montreal Shamrocks back in 1901.

The Maple Leafs were two men short when Bill Cook scored the winning goal. Toronto had failed to score on its own two-man advantage late in the third period and had center Joe Primeau and defensemen King Clancy and Hap Day on the ice to try to kill the overtime penalties. They had almost killed off the first penalty to Alex Levinsky when there was a faceoff outside the Toronto blue line. Primeau and Murray Murdoch got tangled up, but the Rangers' Butch Keeling poked the puck free and carried it into the Leafs' zone. Clancy moved toward him, and as he did, Keeling fed a pass to Cook, who swept in on goalie Lorne Chabot and snapped the puck past him.

Special Teams Though Bill Cook's Cup-winning goal came with the Maple Leafs two men short, it was the Rangers' penalty killing more than their power play that made the difference in the series. The Rangers scored four shorthanded goals to set a record for the Stanley Cup final that still exists.

The Game I'll Never Forget

TINY THOMPSON

66 They came early, but they didn't have any idea how late they'd stay."

Hockey Digest: December 1976
By Cecil Thompson, as told to George Vass

Hockey was a little different in the 1930s when it came to puckhandling, shooting or skating, but it was the same in one respect—the idea was to put the puck in the net, or keep it out if you were the goaltender, as I was.

My rookie year was pretty memorable. That was 1929, and we won the Stanley Cup for Boston against the Rangers in New York. That last game at New York, which we won 2–1, well, that's almost up there with my most memorable game. When your team finishes first in the league and goes on to win the Stanley Cup in your rookie season that's quite a thrill.

But the game that was the highlight of my career happened in 1933. I still think of it as the finest game I ever played on an individual basis, even if we lost.

We had some players that year at Boston, I'll tell you—Eddie Shore, Dit Clapper, Red Beattie, Nels Stewart—those are just some of them.

We went into the first round of the Stanley Cup playoffs, a best-of-five, against Toronto, and they were a strong club, too. Lorne Chabot

was their goalie, and they had King Clancy, Joe Primeau and a raft of other good players.

What a series that was! Three of the first four games went into overtime. We'd each won a pair going into the fifth game, and we had no idea what was ahead of us.

The fifth game, that's the one, April 3, 1933—the most memorable game of my career. It was at Toronto and everything depended on it. The winner would go to the final.

Hockey was just as big in those days in Toronto as it is today. The place was packed. Something over 14,500, and with everything on the line even the crowd felt the tension. They came early, but they didn't have any idea how late they'd stay.

Everybody was a little careful, naturally, so much riding on the game. But Toronto seemed to get more chances to score during regulation time than we did. They tell me I stopped 113 shots that night. I can't tell you. I was too tired to count, because after a while it seemed the game would never end.

We almost won it in regulation time, in the third period. Alex Smith broke through and flipped one past

Chabot, but he was ruled offside. Well, we argued loud and long but it didn't get us anywhere.

Now 60 minutes of playoff hockey is a long, hard grind, but that was just the start. And the ice—that was incredibly bad. In those days they didn't flood the ice between periods as they do now. It got sloppier and sloppier as the game went on.

And it did go on. Nobody even got close to scoring until the fourth overtime period. That's when Clancy rifled one past me. But I'd heard the whistle and just let it go. It was no goal, of course, because an official had blown the whistle.

At the end of the fourth overtime Frank Calder, who was president of the National Hockey League, suggested we flip a coin to decide the winner.

Well, the crowd didn't like that idea and neither did the players, as tired as we were after 140 minutes of hockey. We all wanted to play until someone won legitimately, even if it took all night. And it nearly did.

The fifth overtime was like a slow-motion film. The ice was mush, and everybody was so exhausted they were skating around listlessly. Every once in a while somebody would get a second wind and there'd be a rush on goal, but neither Chabot nor myself let anything get past.

The fans seemed just as tired. But every once in a while they'd get

April 3, 1933
Game 5, Stanley Cup semifinals · Maple Leaf Gardens, Toronto

stirred up and they'd cheer a little and it would speed up the action briefly. But then the game would die down again.

It was past 1:30 in the morning when the sixth overtime period started. We were four minutes into it when the winning play happened.

Andy Blair was playing for Toronto chiefly to shadow Shore, who was a great scoring threat despite being a defenseman. He was right on top of Shore all night and finally he got a break.

Shore tried to break away from Blair with the puck. He batted the puck ahead of him, meaning to go around Blair and pick it up. Instead he put the puck right on Blair's stick.

Blair saw his chance and made the most of it. He crossed the blue line into our zone with Shore right with him. As Shore swung around to check him, Blair passed to Ken Doraty, who was heading for our net.

Doraty picked up the pass in full stride and snapped the puck past me to win the game for Toronto 1–0. It was at 4:46 of the sixth overtime. That was the longest game ever played at that time.

They tell me that the crowd gave me a standing ovation, though we lost. I didn't hear a thing. I was just too tired. I don't think anyone cared at that point.

But that's my most memorable game. I stopped 113 shots and played more than eight periods in goal.

Tiny Thompson in net for the Boston Bruins of the 1930s.

SHOTS ON GOAL

	1	2	3
Toronto	12	20	11
Boston	9	5	15

	1	2	3	4	2	6	T
Toronto	8	19	12	15	14	3	114
Boston	8	12	12	16	13	3	93

GOALIES: Chabot, Toronto; Thompson, Boston

REFEREES: Odie Cleghorn, Eusebe Daigneault

Toronto 1, Boston 0 6X OT

FIRST PERIOD

NO SCORING

PENALTIES: Clancy, Toronto; Shore, Boston

SECOND PERIOD

NO SCORING

PENALTIES: Chapman, Boston; Shore, Boston

THIRD PERIOD

NO SCORING

PENALTIES: Lamb, Boston; Doraty, Toronto; Clapper, Boston; Thoms, Toronto; Cotton, Toronto; Day, Toronto

FIRST OT PERIOD

NO SCORING

PENALTIES: Levinsky, Toronto; Levinsky, Toronto (holding); Sands, Toronto

SECOND OT PERIOD

NO SCORING

PENALTIES: Barry, Boston; Shore, Boston; Shore, Boston

THIRD OT PERIOD

NO SCORING

PENALTIES: Stewart, Boston; Conacher, Toronto

FOURTH OT PERIOD

NO SCORING

PENALTIES: Smith, Boston; Clancy, Toronto

FIFTH OT PERIOD

NO SCORING · NO PENALTIES

SIXTH OT PERIOD

1 ▸ Doraty (Blair), Toronto, 4:46

NO PENALTIES

QUARTERFINALS
6 goals to 2 over Chicago

SEMIFINALS
4 goals to 3 over Montreal Maroons

ROSTER

Ace Bailey

Andy Blair

Lorne Chabot

King Clancy

Charlie Conacher

Baldy Cotton

Hap Day (captain)

Harold Darragh

Frank Finnigan

Bob Gracie

Red Horner

Busher Jackson

Alex Levinsky

Earl Miller

Joe Primeau

Fred Robertson

Conn Smythe (manager)

Dick Irvin (coach)

The Kid Line of Charlie Conacher, Joe Primeau and Busher Jackson.

FINAL 3 GAMES TO 0

APR. 5 ► Toronto 6 at New York Rangers 4

APR. 7 ► Toronto 6 vs New York Rangers 2*

APR. 9 ► New York Rangers 4 at Toronto 6

*Played in Boston.

PLAYOFF SCORING LEADER

Frank Boucher	GP	G	A	PTS
NEW YORK RANGERS	7	3	6	9

FINAL SERIES SCORING

TORONTO	GP	G	A	PTS	PIM
Busher Jackson	3	5	2	7	9
Charlie Conacher	3	3	2	5	2
Hap Day	3	1	3	4	4
Joe Primeau	3	0	4	4	0
Andy Blair	3	2	0	2	2
King Clancy	3	2	0	2	8
Baldy Cotton	3	1	1	2	10
Frank Finnigan	3	1	1	2	8
Bob Gracie	3	1	1	2	0
Red Horner	3	1	1	2	6
Ace Bailey	3	1	0	1	0
Harold Darragh	3	0	0	0	0
Alex Levinsky	3	0	0	0	2
Earl Miller	2	0	0	0	0
Fred Robertson	3	0	0	0	0
GOALTENDER	GP	W	L	MIN	GA	SO	AVG
Lorne Chabot	3	3	0	180	10	0	3.33

NY RANGERS	GP	G	A	PTS	PIM
Frank Boucher	3	3	3	6	0
Bun Cook	3	4	1	5	6
Bill Cook	3	0	2	2	0
Doug Brennan	3	1	0	1	4
Cecil Dillon	3	1	0	1	4
Ching Johnson	3	1	0	1	10
Ott Heller	3	0	1	1	2
Murray Murdoch	3	0	1	1	0
Vic Desjardins	3	0	0	0	0
Dutch Gainor	3	0	0	0	2
Butch Keeling	3	0	0	0	10
Hib Milks	3	0	0	0	0
Earl Seibert	3	0	0	0	6
Art Somers	3	0	0	0	4
GOALTENDER	GP	W	L	MIN	GA	SO	AVG
John Ross Roach	3	0	3	180	18	0	6.00

Tennis Anyone? Because of the scores (6–4, 6–2, 6–4) of the games between the Maple Leafs and the Rangers, the 1932 Stanley Cup final has been referred to as the "Tennis Series."

How Sweep It Is Though there had been a few sweeps of best-of-three finals in the years in between, Toronto's victory marked the first time a team had swept a best-of-five Stanley Cup series since the Vancouver Millionaires in 1915.

The success of professional hockey in Toronto was no sure thing before Conn Smythe. Amateur hockey was much more popular with local sports fans, and the city had seen one of its National Hockey Association franchises fail. Toronto was only reluctantly admitted to the NHL in 1917, when Quebec City chose not to operate its team. Despite the Stanley Cup success of the Arenas and the St. Patricks, crowds at the Mutual Street Arena were often small

Conn Smythe put together a group that purchased the St. Pats in February of 1927. He chose the Maple Leafs' name and emblem as a patriotic gesture because it had been the symbol of Canadian soldiers during World War I. It was also the emblem Smythe had worn during his days with the University of Toronto, whose blue and white colors he also adopted. Smythe hired Frank Selke, and the two men used their amateur hockey connections to build the Maple Leafs. Establishing relationships with the Toronto Marlboros and St. Michael's College soon brought in players such as Charlie Conacher, Busher Jackson, Joe Primeau and Red Horner. Prior to the 1930–31 season, Smythe purchased King Clancy from Ottawa

for two players and a record sum of $35,000.

Foster Hewitt's radio broadcasts of Maple Leafs games attracted more and more fans, and, despite the hardships of the Great Depression, Smythe built Maple Leaf Gardens for the 1931–32 season. The Kid Line of Conacher, Jackson and Primeau emerged as true stars in 1931–32, with Jackson leading the league with 53 points, Primeau leading the league with 37 assists and Conacher tied for the league lead with 34 goals. The Maple Leafs finished second behind the Montreal Canadiens in the Canadian Division and defeated the Black Hawks easily to open the playoffs. Next, they rallied to beat the Montreal Maroons on a late goal by Hap Day and an overtime tally from Bob Gracie.

The Rangers defeated the Canadiens in the playoff battle between division winners, and Toronto opened the Stanley Cup final in New York. The Rangers were favored at home, but the Maple Leafs took Game 1 6–4. A circus booked at Madison Square Garden saw Game 2 played in Boston, where Toronto won 6–2. The Maple Leafs then wrapped up the series on home ice with another 6–4 victory.

Sweet Revenge

Shortly before the 1928–29 season, the Rangers had traded goalie Lorne Chabot to Toronto for John Ross Roach. Rangers coach and general manager Lester Patrick believed that Chabot had become puck shy after being hit in the eye during the 1928 Stanley Cup final.

The Coach's Kid A day after Toronto's Stanley Cup victory, coach Dick Irvin hurriedly caught a train to Calgary upon learning that his five-week-old son, whom he had yet to see, was seriously ill. The baby was suffering from erysipelas, a rare form of bacterial infection in his leg. The boy would recover, and Dick Irvin Jr. would grow up to become a broadcasting institution on the CBC's *Hockey Night in Canada*.

Most Goals in One Period

Since NHL teams began competing for the Stanley Cup in 1918, six players have scored three goals in a single period during the finals. Those players are:

BUSHER JACKSON, TORONTO	▸ 2nd period of Game 1, April 5, 1932; Toronto 6 at New York Rangers 4
TED LINDSAY, DETROIT	▸ 2nd period of Game 2, April 5, 1955; Montreal 4 at Detroit 7
MAURICE RICHARD, MONTREAL	▸ 2nd period of Game 1, April 6, 1957; Boston 1 at Montreal 5
WAYNE GRETZKY, EDMONTON	▸ 1st period of Game 3, May 25, 1985; Philadelphia 3 at Edmonton 4
DIRK GRAHAM, CHICAGO	▸ 1st period of Game 4, June 1, 1992; Pittsburgh 6 at Chicago 5
PETER FORSBERG, COLORADO	▸ 1st period of Game 2, June 6, 1996; Florida 1 at Colorado 8

Stanley Cup Squabble

Before the start of the 1926–27 season, there had been talk of the newly formed American Hockey Association taking the place of the Western Hockey League as a Stanley Cup rival for the NHL. However, the NHL saw the AHA as a minor league and an outlaw organization. Though the *Montreal Gazette* reported on April 8, 1927, that the AHA-champion Duluth Hornets had challenged for the Stanley Cup, Ottawa was not called on to defend its championship.

At the beginning of February 1932, president William F. Grant of the American Hockey Association issued a new challenge for the Stanley Cup. At first the Stanley Cup trustees accepted, but there were immediate protests from NHL president Frank Calder. Calder promised to forfeit the trophy rather than play against the AHA champions and announced that "a prominent sportsman" had already offered another cup "valued at over $1,000" to replace the Stanley Cup. Calder also expressed his doubts that trustee William Foran would really turn over the trophy to the AHA, believing that it was more likely that the Stanley Cup would be withdrawn from competition and donated to the Dominion Archives in Ottawa.

The dispute lasted well into March before Foran finally announced that the AHA challenge had been rejected.

SEMIFINALS
3 games to 2 over Boston

ROSTER

Marty Burke

Johnny Gagnon

George Hainsworth

Aurel Joliat

Wildor Larochelle

Albert Leduc

Pit Lepine

Art Lesieur

Georges Mantha

Sylvio Mantha
(captain)

Bert McCaffrey

Armand Mondou

Howie Morenz

Jean Pusie

Gus Rivers

Nick Wasnie

Léo Dandurand
(manager)

Cecil Hart (coach)

FINAL 3 GAMES TO 2

APR. 3	▸	Montreal Canadiens 2 at Chicago 1
APR. 5	▸	Montreal Canadiens 1 at Chicago 2 **2X OT**
APR. 9	▸	Chicago 3 at Montreal Canadiens 2 **3X OT**
APR. 11	▸	Chicago 2 at Montreal Canadiens 4
APR. 14	▸	Chicago 0 at Montreal Canadiens 2

PLAYOFF SCORING LEADER

Cooney Weiland	GP	G	A	PTS
BOSTON	5	6	3	9

FINAL SERIES SCORING

MONTREAL	GP	G	A	PTS	PIM
Johnny Gagnon	5	4	2	6	2
Pit Lepine	5	3	1	4	4
Georges Mantha	5	2	1	3	4
Aurel Joliat	5	0	2	2	2
Nick Wasnie	5	1	1	2	2
Howie Morenz	5	1	0	1	6
Marty Burke	5	0	1	1	2
Wildor Larochelle	5	0	1	1	6
Albert Leduc	2	0	1	1	2
Art Lesieur	5	0	0	0	4
Sylvio Mantha	5	0	0	0	16
Armand Mondou	3	0	0	0	0
Jean Pusie	3	0	0	0	0
Gus Rivers	5	0	0	0	0

GOALTENDER	GP	W	L	MIN	GA	SO	AVG
George Hainsworth	5	3	2	379	8	1	1.27

CHICAGO	GP	G	A	PTS	PIM
Johnny Gottselig	5	2	2	4	2
Stew Adams	5	2	1	3	2
Vic Ripley	5	1	1	2	2
Ty Arbour	5	1	0	1	0
Mush March	5	1	0	1	6
Cy Wentworth	5	1	0	1	8
Frank Ingram	5	0	1	1	2
Tom Cook	5	0	1	1	7
Rosie Couture	5	0	1	1	2
Clarence Abel	5	0	0	0	6
Helge Bostrom	5	0	0	0	8
Vic Desjardins	5	0	0	0	0
Ted Graham	5	0	0	0	10
Doc Romnes	5	0	0	0	2
Art Somers	5	0	0	0	0

GOALTENDER	GP	W	L	MIN	GA	SO	AVG
Charlie Gardiner	5	2	3	379	11	0	1.74

Back to a Best of Five The decision to increase the Stanley Cup finals back to a best-of-five series after two years as a best-of-three was announced after the monthly meeting of NHL executives in Toronto on January 31, 1931. Though no reason was given in newspaper stories as to why, it's long been said that the decision was due to Montreal's shocking two-game sweep of Boston in the 1930 final.

Tulsa Time After winning the championship of the American Hockey Association on April 11th, the Tulsa Oilers issued a challenge for the Stanley Cup. Trustee William Foran ruled that it was too late in the season to order more games.

Morenz Makes It Two Straight

The 1930–31 season marked the last time that the NHL would operate as a 10-team league. Having grown to that many franchises in 1926–27, during the heady days of the Roaring Twenties, the economic depression of the Dirty Thirties began to take its toll.

The financially troubled Ottawa Senators had been selling off players since winning the Cup in 1927, culminating in the trade of King Clancy to Toronto for Art Smith, Eric Pettinger and $35,000. Now stripped of nearly all their stars, Ottawa finished the 1930–31 season a dismal 10-30-4, with their 24 points leaving them 22 behind every other team in the Canadian Division. The Philadelphia Quakers were even worse. After several poor seasons as the Pittsburgh Pirates, including a dreadful 5-36-3 record in 1929–30, the franchise had been forced to move when the stock market crash hit the steel industry hard. In their lone season in Philadelphia, the Quakers were a woeful 4-36-4.

At the other end of the standings, the Boston Bruins topped the American Division for the fourth straight year. The Bruins boasted the league's best offense while also featuring defenseman Eddie Shore and goalie Tiny Thompson. The Montreal Canadiens, led by NHL-scoring-leader and Hart Trophy–winner Howie Morenz, topped the Canadian Division. A year earlier, the Canadiens had swept the Bruins in the Stanley Cup final. This year, when they met to open the playoffs, the series went right down to the wire. Four of the five games were decided by a single goal, with three going into overtime, including the last one. Wildor Larochelle scored after 19 minutes of extra play to give the Canadiens a 3–2 victory. Montreal's opponent in the Stanley Cup final was Chicago. Under coach Dick Irvin (who would be fired after the season despite his success), the Black Hawks had finished second behind Boston in the American Division. In the playoffs, Chicago got an overtime goal from Stew Adams to eliminate Toronto and then got back-to-back shutouts from Charlie Gardiner to defeat the Rangers.

Boston and Chicago both closely guarded Montreal's Howie Morenz throughout the playoffs. He'd been banged up but had played well, though he had yet to score a goal heading into Game 5 of the final. The Canadiens were hanging on to a 1–0 lead when Morenz finally scored with less than five minutes remaining and clinched a second straight Stanley Cup title.

You've Gotta Have Hart

A player has won the Stanley Cup in the same season that he was named MVP of the NHL 16 times:

1925–26	Nels Stewart	Montreal Maroons
1930–31	Howie Morenz	Montreal Canadiens
1940–41	Bill Cowley	Boston Bruins
1951–52	Gordie Howe	Detroit Red Wings
1955–56	Jean Béliveau	Montreal Canadiens
1969–70	Bobby Orr	Boston Bruins
1971–72	Bobby Orr	Boston Bruins
1974–75	Bobby Clarke	Philadelphia Flyers
1976–77	Guy Lafleur	Montreal Canadiens
1977–78	Guy Lafeur	Montreal Canadiens
1983–84	Wayne Gretzky	Edmonton Oilers
1984–85	Wayne Gretzky	Edmonton Oilers
1986–87	Wayne Gretzky	Edmonton Oilers
1989–90	Mark Messier	Edmonton Oilers
2000–01	Joe Sakic	Colorado Avalanche
2003–04	Martin St. Louis	Tampa Bay Lightning

Coaching Records

MOST GAMES BY A COACH IN THE STANLEY CUP FINAL

77 Dick Irvin, Chicago (5), Toronto (29), Montreal (43)
58 Scotty Bowman, St. Louis (12), Montreal (25), Pittsburgh (4), Detroit (17)
48 Toe Blake, Montreal
33 Punch Imlach, Toronto
30 Lester Patrick, Victoria (11), New York Rangers (19)

Seesaw Series

Montreal opened the Stanley Cup final with a 2–1 victory in Chicago. Goalie George Hainsworth was the hero as the Canadiens withstood a late Black Hawks rally after taking a 2–0 lead.

Chicago coach Dick Irvin juggled four forward lines in an attempt to outskate the Flying Frenchmen in the second contest. The game was a wide-open affair. Only the brilliant goaltending of Hainsworth and Charlie Gardiner kept the score low, as the Black Hawks went on top midway through the second period, but the Canadiens tied it up late in the third. The two goalies were particularly sharp in overtime, and it was 4:50 in the second extra session before Johnny Gottselig scored for Chicago to even the series. Just before the start of that second overtime period, Canadiens star Johnny Gagnon learned that his father had passed away.

After three days off, the series resumed in Montreal. Gagnon got the Canadiens on the scoreboard early. They led 2–0 until Chicago scored twice in 43 seconds late in the third period. The game then stretched until 13:50 of triple overtime, when Cy Wentworth scored to put Chicago ahead in the series. Facing elimination, it was the Canadiens who had to rally in Game 4. After Chicago took an early 2–0 first-period lead, Gagnon scored early in the second and then again early in the third. Pit Lepine followed with two quick goals for a 4–2 Montreal victory. In Game 5, it was again Gagnon who got the Canadiens on the scoreboard. His goal at 9:59 in the first held up until Howie Morenz scored at 15:27 of the third for a 2–0 victory.

QUARTERFINALS
3 goals to 2 over Chicago

SEMIFINALS
2 games to 0 over New York Rangers

FINAL 2 GAMES TO 0

APR. 1 ► Montreal Canadiens 3 at Boston 0

APR. 3 ► Boston 3 at Montreal Canadiens 4

PLAYOFF SCORING LEADERS

Marty Barry	GP	G	A	PTS
BOSTON	6	3	3	6

Cooney Weiland	GP	G	A	PTS
BOSTON	6	1	5	6

FINAL SERIES SCORING

MONTREAL	GP	G	A	PTS	PIM
Albert Leduc	2	1	2	3	0
Sylvio Mantha	2	2	0	2	2
Pit Lepine	2	1	1	2	0
Nick Wasnie	2	1	1	2	6
Marty Burke	2	0	1	1	0
Aurel Joliat	2	0	1	1	0
Bert McCaffrey	2	1	0	1	0
Howie Morenz	2	1	0	1	6
Gerry Carson	2	0	0	0	0
Wildor Larochelle	2	0	0	0	8
Georges Mantha	2	0	0	0	0
Armand Mondou	2	0	0	0	2
Gus Rivers	2	0	0	0	0

GOALTENDER	GP	W	L	MIN	GA	SO	AVG
George Hainsworth	2	2	0	120	3	1	1.50

BOSTON	GP	G	A	PTS	PIM
Dit Clapper	2	1	0	1	0
Percy Galbraith	2	1	0	1	2
Eddie Shore	2	1	0	1	8
Harry Oliver	2	0	1	1	2
Cooney Weiland	2	0	1	1	0
Marty Barry	2	0	0	0	6
Bill Carson	2	0	0	0	0
Harry Connor	2	0	0	0	0
Dutch Gainor	1	0	0	0	0
Lionel Hitchman	2	0	0	0	4
Myles Lane	2	0	0	0	0
Mickey MacKay	2	0	0	0	2
George Owen	2	0	0	0	2

GOALTENDER	GP	W	L	MIN	GA	SO	AVG
Tiny Thompson	2	0	2	120	7	0	3.50

ROSTER

- Marty Burke
- Gerry Carson
- George Hainsworth ▲
- Aurel Joliat
- Wildor Larochelle
- Albert Leduc
- Pit Lepine
- Georges Mantha
- Sylvio Mantha (captain)
- Bert McCaffrey
- Armand Mondou
- Howie Morenz
- Gus Rivers
- Nick Wasnie
- Léo Dandurand (manager)
- Cecil Hart (coach)

Grueling Schedule

The Canadiens played six games in 12 nights during the course of the playoffs. With their lengthy overtime battles against the Black Hawks and the Rangers, they actually played the equivalent of eight games in 12 nights.

Heads Up

Bruins captain Lionel Hitchman suffered a broken jaw late in the season and wore a helmet throughout the playoffs. Even so, he was badly cut above the eye when he was slashed in the face during the final game of Boston's semifinal series against the Maroons.

Bruins Suffer Stunning Defeat

The collapse of major pro hockey in the West and the expansion of the NHL to 10 teams in 1926–27 had, in essence, brought all of the best players in hockey into one organization. The competition became better than ever, but overall scoring dropped drastically. In 1928–29, scoring reached an all-time low of 2.80 goals per game.

Goaltending equipment had been vastly improved from earlier days, and netminders such as George Hainsworth, Charlie Gardiner, Tiny Thompson and Roy Worters were among the best the game would ever know. Still, it was largely the rules and tactics that led to such low scores. Teams would often drop forwards back to protect their own end rather than pursue goals in a defensive system that became known as "kitty (or katy) bar the door." Before the 1929–30 season, a new rule was introduced that stated that no more than three players, including the goalie, could remain in the defensive zone when the puck went up ice. Even more importantly, forward passing was finally allowed inside the offensive zone. Early in the season, another new rule was introduced, stating that no player could precede the puck into the offensive zone, much like the modern offside rule.

Though Boston was the defending Stanley Cup champion, Art Ross was instrumental in passing these new rules, and he prepared the Bruins well. Boston posted a stunning record of 38-5-1 during the 44-game season for a winning percentage of .875, which remains the highest in hockey history. Cooney Weiland's 73 points (43 goals, 30 assists) shattered the previous NHL record of 51. Dit Clapper added 41 goals, while Eddie Shore and Lionel Hitchman anchored the league's best defense. In the playoffs, Boston needed four games to beat the Montreal Maroons in a tough, physical semifinal. The Bruins' win in Game 1 required triple overtime, but their 1–0 loss in double overtime in Game 3 marked the first time all season they were shut out.

The Bruins' opponent in the Stanley Cup final was the Montreal Canadiens. Howie Morenz scored 40 goals for Montreal, who had the NHL's second-best offense, behind Boston, but the Canadiens had lost all four games they'd played against the Bruins. During the season, Boston had enjoyed a 14-game winning streak and another streak of 17 games without a loss. They had not dropped two straight games at any point in the season—until Montreal swept them to win the Stanley Cup.

No Goal

Having rallied from a 4–1 deficit with two quick goals midway through the third period, the Bruins were desperate to salvage their record-setting season in the final moments of Game 2 of the final. With just a few seconds remaining, Marty Barry kicked the puck into the net. The red light went on, but referee George Mallinson refused to allow it. Interestingly, some newspapers reported that Cooney Weiland scored the goal, and some said it was called back due to interference.

Black Cats for Luck? Canadiens coach Cecil Hart patted a black cat at the Forum just before the fourth overtime period against the Rangers in the semifinals. He found another one at Madison Square Garden before the second game of the series. Two fans accompanying the Canadiens to Boston for Game 1 of the final gave Hart a toy black cat to carry in his suitcase.

Beaten Up

For weeks prior to the end of the NHL season, there was speculation that if the Maroons won the Canadian Division and met the Bruins to open the playoffs, the team that survived would be too beaten up to defeat anyone in the Stanley Cup final. Because of injuries suffered in the Maroons series, Art Ross could only put the Bruins through one practice in their four days off before facing the Canadiens.

Hainsworth the Hero

After his record-setting 22 shutouts in 1928–29, Montreal's George Hainsworth managed only four in 1929–30. His goals-against average jumped from 0.92 to 2.42. Even so, those numbers were among the best in the NHL under the greatly improved offensive conditions of 1929–30.

Hainsworth opened the playoffs with a shutout in a 1–0 victory over the Black Hawks. When Chicago won the second game 2–1, overtime was required to decide the total-goals series. It lasted until 11:43 of the third extra session, when Howie Morenz broke up the brilliant goaltenders' battle between Hainsworth and Charlie Gardiner.

Two nights later, the Canadiens opened their second-round series against the Rangers with an even longer overtime battle. This time it took 68:52 of overtime over four periods before Montreal scored a 2–1 victory. Hainsworth blanked the Rangers for the final 113:18 of the game, and then posted another shutout in Game 2 as the Canadiens swept the Rangers with a 2–0 victory.

The Bruins were heavily favored over Montreal in the Stanley Cup final, but Hainsworth was solid when he had to be, particularly in the scoreless first period of Game 1. Montreal ended up winning 3–0, and Boston didn't beat Hainsworth until 16:50 of the second period in Game 2, ending his shutout streak at 270:08. To this day it remains the longest shutout sequence in NHL playoff history.

Boston Bruins

SEMIFINALS
3 games to 0 over Montreal Canadiens

FINAL 2 GAMES TO 0

MAR. 28 ▶ New York Rangers 0 at Boston 2

MAR. 29 ▶ Boston 2 at New York Rangers 1

PLAYOFF SCORING LEADERS

| **Andy Blair** | GP | G | A | PTS |
| TORONTO | 4 | 3 | 0 | 3 |

| **Butch Keeling** | GP | G | A | PTS |
| NEW YORK RANGERS | 6 | 3 | 0 | 3 |

| **Ace Bailey** | GP | G | A | PTS |
| TORONTO | 4 | 1 | 2 | 3 |

FINAL SERIES SCORING

BOSTON	GP	G	A	PTS	PIM
Harry Oliver	2	1	1	2	2
Bill Carson	2	1	0	1	2
Dit Clapper	2	1	0	1	0
Norm Gainor	2	1	0	1	0
Percy Galbraith	2	0	0	0	2
Lionel Hitchman	2	0	0	0	10
Myles Lane	2	0	0	0	0
Mickey MacKay	2	0	0	0	0
George Owen	2	0	0	0	0
Eddie Shore	2	0	0	0	8
Cooney Weiland	2	0	0	0	0
GOALTENDER	GP	W	L	MIN	GA	SO	AVG
Tiny Thompson	2	2	0	120	1	1	0.50

NY RANGERS	GP	G	A	PTS	PIM
Butch Keeling	2	1	0	1	0
Clarence Abel	2	0	0	0	4
Frank Boucher	2	0	0	0	0
Leo Bourgault	2	0	0	0	0
Bill Boyd	1	0	0	0	0
Gerry Carson	1	0	0	0	0
Bill Cook	2	0	0	0	4
Bun Cook	2	0	0	0	4
Leroy Goldsworthy	1	0	0	0	0
Ching Johnson	2	0	0	0	2
Murray Murdoch	2	0	0	0	0
Russell Oatman	1	0	0	0	0
Ralph Taylor	1	0	0	0	0
Paul Thompson	2	0	0	0	4
Sparky Vail	2	0	0	0	0
GOALTENDER	GP	W	L	MIN	GA	SO	AVG
John Ross Roach	2	0	2	120	4	0	2.00

Second Team? Shortly after the Stanley Cup final, rumors began making the rounds that Boston would have a second NHL team for the 1929–30 season. These rumors had the Boston Garden Company potentially purchasing either the Ottawa Senators or the Pittsburgh Pirates.

Twice Is Nice When the Stanley Cup was redesigned in 1958 to feature the five broad bands across the barrel we're familiar with today, the top band featured all of the winners from 1927–28 to 1939–40. It included a brand-new engraving for 1928–29, meaning that until that band was retired in 1992, that year's Boston team was actually on the Cup twice because the original 1928–29 engraving was part permanent collar.

Boston was already a hockey hotbed when the Bruins became the first American-based team in the NHL in 1924–25. Amateur and college hockey had been popular for years, and though the Bruins missed the playoffs their first two years in the NHL, fans flocked to see them. With the addition of Eddie Shore from the now-defunct Western Hockey League in 1926, Boston quickly became an NHL power.

The Bruins reached the Stanley Cup final in 1926–27 and won their first American Division title in 1927–28. They moved into the Boston Garden for the 1928–29 season and celebrated with their first Stanley Cup championship. Boston brought up goalie Cecil "Tiny" Thompson from their Minneapolis farm team, and he led the Bruins to an NHL-best 26-13-5 record while posting 12 shutouts and a 1.15 goals-against average. But with 1928–29 marking the lowest-scoring season in NHL history, Thompson's numbers merely fit right in. George Hainsworth set records with 22 shutouts in 44 games and a 0.92 goals-against average, but eight of the NHL's top 10 goaltenders had at least 10 shutouts and all 10 had averages below 2.00. Toronto's Ace Bailey led the NHL in scoring with just 32 points (22 goals, 10 assists), and he and Nels Stewart (21 goals) were the league's only 20-goal-scorers. Averaging just over two per game, Boston's 89 goals were the best in the NHL. With Harry Oliver (17 goals), Dutch Gainor (14), Shore (12) and Cooney Weiland (11), the Bruins were the only team with four players who reached double-digit goals.

Opening the playoffs against the Canadian Division champions, Thompson outperformed Montreal's George Hainsworth. He recorded shutouts in the first two games, while Cooney Weiland scored in each one for a pair of 1–0 victories. Eddie Shore, whose rough play drew boos from the Forum crowd, was the hero in Game 3, scoring the winner in a 3–2 victory for a series sweep.

The defending Stanley Cup–champion New York Rangers defeated the New York Americans and the Toronto Maple Leafs en route to facing Boston in the first all-American Stanley Cup final in hockey history. Thompson registered another shutout as the Bruins beat the Rangers 2–0 in Game 1. Bill Carson was the hero of Game 2, scoring the Stanley Cup–winning goal at 18:02 of the third period in a 2–1 Boston victory.

Unusual Engravings

There are several oddities associated with the engraving for the 1928–29 Bruins when the Stanley Cup was redesigned in 1958. For instance, it includes the names of Lloyd Klein and Eddie Rodden, who were both just part-time players and not included on the team's original engraving in 1929. It also includes Frank Fredrickson, Eric Pettinger and Red Green, all of who were traded away during the season (though Green was later re-acquired). They had also been left off the original engraving. Hal Winkler has his name engraved too, with the notation "sub goaltender," even though the former starter spent that entire season with the team's Minneapolis farm club. Finally, Cy Denneny's name appears twice, once among the players and once at the top where he is noted as the coach, but there his name is misspelled as Dennenny.

King's Ransom

In a move that would likely bring tampering charges today, Bruins owner Charles Adams admitted that he would "pay any price they ask" to add King Clancy to his championship roster. "But," Adams added, "I fear that the chances of his release from Ottawa are about as remote as that of Shore from Boston or Howie Morenz from the Canadiens."

Eighteen months later, the Senators sold Clancy to Toronto for two players and $35,000.

New York Rangers

QUARTERFINALS
6 goals to 4 over Pittsburgh

SEMIFINALS
5 goals to 2 over Boston

APR. 5	▶ New York Rangers 0 at Montreal Maroons 2
APR. 7	▶ New York Rangers 2 at Montreal Maroons 1 OT
APR. 10	▶ New York Rangers 0 at Montreal Maroons 2
APR. 12	▶ New York Rangers 1 at Montreal Maroons 0
APR. 14	▶ New York Rangers 2 at Montreal Maroons 1

ROSTER

Clarence Abel

Frank Boucher

Leo Bourgeault

Bill Boyd

Patsy Callighen

Lorne Chabot

Bill Cook (captain)

Bun Cook

Alex Gray

Ching Johnson

Joe Miller

Murray Murdoch

Paul Thompson

Lester Patrick (manager/coach)

PLAYOFF SCORING LEADER

▶ Frank Boucher	GP	G	A	PTS
NEW YORK RANGERS	9	7	3	10

FINAL SERIES SCORING

NY RANGERS	GP	G	A	PTS	PIM
Frank Boucher	5	4	0	4	2
Bill Cook	5	1	2	3	16
Ching Johnson	5	0	2	2	26
Bun Cook	5	0	1	1	4
Clarence Abel	5	0	1	1	10
Leo Bourgeault	5	0	0	0	6
Bill Boyd	5	0	0	0	2
Patsy Callighen	5	0	0	0	0
Alex Gray	5	0	0	0	0
Murray Murdoch	5	0	0	0	10
Paul Thompson	3	0	0	0	19
GOALTENDERS	GP	W	L	MIN	GA	SO	AVG
Joe Miller	3	2	1	180	3	1	1.00
Lester Patrick	1	1	0	46	1	0	1.30
Lorne Chabot	2	0	1	81	2	0	1.48

MONTREAL MAROONS	GP	G	A	PTS	PIM
Merlyn Phillips	5	2	0	2	2
Nels Stewart	5	2	0	2	8
Red Dutton	5	1	1	2	13
Babe Siebert	4	1	1	2	10
Hooley Smith	5	0	2	2	13
Dunc Munro	5	0	1	1	2
Fred Brown	5	0	0	0	0
Frank Carson	5	0	0	0	0
Joe Lamb	4	0	0	0	21
Russell Oatman	5	0	0	0	12
Jimmy Ward	5	0	0	0	2
GOALTENDER	GP	W	L	MIN	GA	SO	AVG
Clint Benedict	5	2	3	307	5	1	0.98

While in New York...

The Stanley Cup went on display for a while at Cartier & Company, Fifth Avenue jewelers. Cartier would engrave the new band that was added to the Cup to mark the Rangers' victory. This was the first of the bands that would cause the Stanley Cup to grow into the tall, narrow trophy it became during the 1930s and 40s.

Though it was Conn Smythe who built the New York Rangers, it was Lester Patrick who led them to greatness. Smythe acquired most of the star talent the Rangers would need to succeed, but when he could not get along with boss Colonel John Hammond, Patrick was brought in to take over during the team's first training camp in the fall of 1926.

The Rangers finished first in the NHL's newly created American Division in 1926–27, and though they would slip to second place the following season, they would go on to win the Stanley Cup in just their second year of operation. The Rangers knocked off the third-place Pittsburgh Pirates to open the playoffs and then beat the first-place Boston Bruins with each of their top forwards, Bill Cook, Bun Cook and Frank Boucher, scoring in a 4–1 victory in Game 2, which gave them a 5–2 win in the total-goals series. The Montreal Canadiens, with Howie Morenz leading the NHL in scoring and winning the Hart Trophy as MVP, had been the best team during the regular season, but the rival Montreal Maroons defeated them in the semifinals and advanced out of the Canadian Division to face the Rangers for the Stanley Cup.

With a circus booked in Madison Square Garden, the Rangers elected to play the entire final in Montreal. After the Maroons won the opener 2–0, the second game provided a legendary moment when 44-year-old Lester Patrick was forced to take over in goal early in the second period after Lorne Chabot was badly injured by a Nels Stewart backhander that struck him just above the left eye. The Rangers played solid defense in front of Patrick, and he allowed just one goal late in the third period as New York evened the series with a 2–1 win on a Frank Boucher overtime goal. Goalie Joe Miller took over for the rest of the series, and though he had struggled with the New York Americans earlier in the season, he was brilliant for the Rangers. After a 2–0 loss to the Maroons in Game 3, Miller posted a shutout of his own in Game 4 to push the best-of-five series to the limit. He was cut and suffered two black eyes in Game 5, but he hung on for a 2–1 victory behind a pair of goals from Frank Boucher.

Previous Experience

It was widely stated at the time, and believed for a long time afterward, that Lester Patrick had not played for years, nor ever played goalie, when he took over for Lorne Chabot in the Stanley Cup final. Neither was true. Patrick had played an entire season with the Victoria Cougars just two years earlier, and he had even suited up for a game with the Rangers in 1926–27. As for going in net, Murray Murdoch later recalled that Patrick would sometimes don the pads to work with the defensemen in Rangers practices. He'd also made a few brief appearances in goal during his playing career. In fact, Patrick had even played goalie in a Stanley Cup game before. While playing for Brandon (Manitoba) against Ottawa on March 9, 1904, Patrick took over for a couple of minutes when goalie Dugald Morrison was penalized. Unlike his performance in 1928, Patrick did not inspire his teammates to victory in 1904. Though he stopped the only shot he faced, Brandon was losing 5–2 at the time and went on to a 6–3 defeat.

Beau James

Returning to New York with the Stanley Cup, the Rangers were invited to City Hall on April 16, 1928, by mayor Jimmy Walker. Walker, who had recently ridden in a ticker-tape parade with Charles Lindbergh and shaken hands with Babe Ruth after his 60th home run, posed for photos with the team and the trophy. He was said to have been surprised by the battered condition of the Stanley Cup.

All in the Family
Stanley Cup wins by the Boucher brothers:

GEORGE BOUCHER	►	Ottawa 1920, 1921, 1923, 1927
BILLY BOUCHER	►	Montreal 1924
BOBBY BOUCHER	►	Montreal 1924
FRANK BOUCHER	►	New York Rangers 1928, 1933, 1940 (coach)

Hey Joe

When Lorne Chabot was hurt in Game 2 of the final, Alex Connell of the Ottawa Senators and Hugh McCormick of the minor league London Panthers were both in the stands. The Rangers asked permission to borrow either one of them. The Maroons, however, were rare among NHL teams in that they carried a spare goaltender on their roster. Their players insisted that the Rangers use someone off their own roster to replace the injured goalie, as NHL rules stipulated.

When it became obvious that Chabot would be out for the rest of the series, it was agreed that the Rangers could fill the spot with someone else. One possibility was Abbie Cox, who played with the Rangers' Springfield farm club (and would see brief NHL action during the 1930s). The other was Joe Miller.

Miller had begun the 1927–28 season with the New York Americans, but the local press had been so critical of his play that he had requested the team farm him out to Niagara Falls. Before they could, the Bruins claimed him on waivers, though it was decided to allow him to go to the minors and make him available as a backup, if required, by any NHL club.

With Niagara Falls having failed to make the playoffs in the Can-Pro league, Miller had not seen action in four weeks. He was called to Montreal from his hometown of Ottawa and got in a light practice with the Rangers the morning of Game 3. After his heroic stint with the Rangers, Miller would spend the next three seasons with the Pittsburgh Pirates and Philadelphia Quakers, tending goal for some of the worst teams in NHL history.

SEMIFINALS
5 goals to 1 over Montreal Canadiens

ROSTER

Jack Adams
George Boucher (captain)
King Clancy
Alex Connell
Cy Denneny
Frank Finnigan
Ed Gorman
Milt Halliday
Hec Kilrea
Frank Nighbor
Alex Smith
Hooley Smith
Dave Gill (head coach)

FINAL 2 WINS AND 2 TIES

APR. 7	▸ Ottawa 0 at Boston 0 OT
APR. 9	▸ Ottawa 3 at Boston 1
APR. 11	▸ Boston 1 at Ottawa 1 OT
APR. 13	▸ Boston 1 at Ottawa 3

PLAYOFF SCORING LEADERS

Harry Oliver	GP	G	A	PTS
BOSTON	8	4	2	6

Percy Galbraith	GP	G	A	PTS
BOSTON	8	3	3	6

FINAL SERIES SCORING

OTTAWA	GP	G	A	PTS	PIM
Cy Denneny	4	4	0	4	0
Frank Finnigan	4	2	0	2	0
King Clancy	4	1	1	2	4
Hec Kilrea	4	0	1	1	2
Frank Nighbor	4	0	1	1	0
Hooley Smith	4	0	1	1	12
Jack Adams	4	0	0	0	2
George Boucher	4	0	0	0	27
Ed Gorman	4	0	0	0	0
Milt Halliday	4	0	0	0	0
Alex Smith	4	0	0	0	8

GOALTENDER	GP	W	L	T	MIN	GA	SO	AVG
Alex Connell	4	2	0	2	240	3	1	0.75

BOSTON	GP	G	A	PTS	PIM
Harry Oliver	4	2	1	3	2
Jimmy Herbert	4	1	0	1	18
Billy Boucher	4	0	0	0	0
Sprague Cleghorn	4	0	0	0	4
Billy Coutu	4	0	0	0	2
Frank Fredrickson	4	0	0	0	16
Percy Galbraith	4	0	0	0	0
Lionel Hitchman	4	0	0	0	17
Harry Meeking	4	0	0	0	0
Eddie Shore	4	0	0	0	20
Billy Stuart	4	0	0	0	0

GOALTENDER	GP	W	L	T	MIN	GA	SO	AVG
Hal Winkler	4	0	2	2	240	7	1	1.75

10-Team NHL Takes Over the Cup

Since the 1926–27 season, NHL teams have been the only ones to compete for the Stanley Cup. This situation came about following the collapse of the Western Hockey League.

From 1913–14 through 1925–26, competition for the Stanley Cup had been an East–West affair and was generally referred to as the World Series of Hockey. During that time, the league champion from the East—that is, the National Hockey Association through 1916–17 and the NHL after that—met the champions from the Pacific Coast Hockey Association, the Western Canada Hockey League or the Western Hockey League in the Stanley Cup final. However, by 1926, the successful American expansion of the NHL into Boston, New York and Pittsburgh, which had begun in 1924, had convinced Western moguls Frank and Lester Patrick that they no longer had the financial means in their smaller markets to compete with the NHL. With the agreement of five of the six Western Hockey League owners (the Saskatoon Crescents made their own arrangements), Frank Patrick sold off the WHL's players. New NHL teams in Detroit and Chicago were built from the rosters of the Victoria Cougars and Portland Rosebuds, while the New York Rangers picked up key Western stars, such as Frank Boucher and brothers Bill and Bun Cook. Other WHL stars who would make a big impression in the NHL

included George Hainsworth with the Canadiens and Eddie Shore in Boston.

The addition of the Rangers, Black Hawks and Detroit (who were known as the Cougars for five seasons before becoming the Falcons and, finally, the Red Wings in 1932–33) saw the NHL grow to 10 teams. The three new clubs played in the American Division along with the Pittsburgh Pirates and the Bruins, while Toronto, Ottawa, the Montreal Canadiens and the Montreal Maroons played in the Canadian Division along with the New York Americans (whose inclusion caused many to call this the International Division). Three teams from each division made the playoffs, and the first-place teams earned a bye into the second round.

In 1926–27, the Ottawa Senators finished atop the Canadian Division with an NHL-best record of 30-10-4. The Canadiens had come on strong late in the season and beat the Maroons in the quarterfinals on an overtime goal by Howie Morenz. Ottawa won their semifinal opener 4–0 in Montreal and, content to protect their four-goal lead at home, scored a 1–1 tie in Game 2 to take the total-goals series five goals to one. Boston reached the Stanley Cup final by beating Chicago in the quarterfinal and eliminating the first-place Rangers in the semifinal, but they fell to the Senators in the final.

Why the Ties?

Game 1 of the Stanley Cup final was played in mild weather with poor ice. Though the players were willing to play on, NHL president Frank Calder called the game after 20 minutes of overtime. Then, to ward off any speculation that the decision had been made to gain extra gate revenue, Calder announced that the series would not be extended beyond five games and that if the two teams ended the series in a tie they would share Stanley Cup honors and split the playoff revenue evenly. Poor ice also resulted in Game 3 ending in a tie, and when the Senators won Game 4 it made Game 5 unnecessary, as the Bruins could not match Ottawa's two wins.

Banned from Boston

Bad blood building throughout the series boiled over in a brawl near the end of Game 4. After the game, Boston's Billy Coutu attacked referees Jerry LaFlamme and Billy Bell. Coutu was fined $100 and expelled from the NHL by president Frank Calder. Ottawa's Hooley Smith was also fined $100 and suspended for the first month of the following season. Lionel Hitchman and Sailor Herbert of Boston were fined $50, as was Ottawa's George Boucher. All fines were taken from the players' shares of playoff money and were distributed to charities in Boston and Ottawa.

My Son Stan Frank Nighbor named his son Francis Stanley after he was born on the night of Ottawa's 1927 Cup win.

Friends in High Places

Lord Julien Byng was already well-known to Canadians before his appointment as governor general in 1921. In 1916, during World War I, he was given command of the Canadian Army Corps on the Western Front and oversaw the Canadian victory at Vimy Ridge in April 1917. Byng was a sports fan, and both he and his wife rarely missed an Ottawa Senators game during his time in office. In 1925, Lady Evelyn Byng presented a trophy to the National Hockey League, which, to this day, recognizes sportsmanship and excellence in play. The Byngs left Canada in 1926 but continued to follow the Senators from abroad. After Ottawa's 1927 Stanley Cup victory, the following message arrived via telegram at the home of team president Frank Ahearn from Thorpe-le-Soken, England: "Both of us are delighted at the splendid success of the Ottawa team. Please give our warmest congratulations to all. Evelyn Byng"

"This message so pleased the boys," reported the *Ottawa Citizen*, "that they unanimously voted to make the first toast out of the historic cup to the health of Lord and Lady Byng."

In Demand Bruins management received over 30,000 applications for tickets to the two Stanley Cup games played in Boston. The Boston Arena's seating capacity was only 7,000 with space for 2,000 more in standing room. Boston Garden replaced the Boston Arena in 1928–29.

The Original Senators

Ottawa has a long tradition of winter sports. Skating, curling and tobogganing had all been popular in Canada's capital since at least the 1870s. Hockey made its official debut on the scene during the winter of 1883.

The Senators were charter members of the National Hockey League when it was formed in 1917, and Ottawa quickly established itself as the NHL's best team.

Local sportsmen Jack Kerr and Halder Kirby had been to the inaugural Montreal Winter Carnival that January and had witnessed a series of hockey games played between two local clubs and a team from Quebec City. After returning to Ottawa, the two men started a team there. The Ottawa Hockey Club competed at the Montreal Winter Carnival in 1884 and was front and center in the formation of the country's first major hockey league, the Amateur Hockey Association of Canada (AHAC), in December 1886.

Though the team from the Montreal Amateur Athletic Association dominated play in the AHAC, it was the success of Ottawa's team during the winter of 1891–92 that inspired Lord Stanley (likely at the urging of team president Philip Dansken Ross) to donate the Stanley Cup.

It would take 10 years before Ottawa won the Stanley Cup, but the team quickly made up for lost time. The famed Ottawa "Silver Seven"—still formally known as the Ottawa Hockey Club, but best known to fans of that time as the "Ottawas"—won the Stanley Cup in 1903, 1904 and 1905. They successfully defended the Cup in two challenge matches early in 1906 before being beaten by the Montreal Wanderers at season's end in March. The team became known as the Ottawa Senators after their championship reign ended, and won the Stanley Cup under that name in 1909. They won two challenges early in 1910 before being beaten by the Wanderers again, but then won back the Cup in 1911.

The Senators were charter members of the National Hockey League when it was formed in 1917, and Ottawa quickly established itself as the NHL's best team. The Senators won the Stanley Cup in 1920, 1921 and 1923, with teams composed (as they had been throughout the club's history) mainly of players born and raised in Ottawa.

In an era when NHL rosters contained no more than a dozen players, goalie Clint Benedict, defensemen George Boucher and Eddie Gerard, and forwards Punch Broadbent and Jack Darragh were all Ottawa boys and future Hockey Hall of Famers who suited up for each of those three championship teams. Frank Nighbor from nearby Pembroke, Ontario, and Cy Denneny of Cornwall, Ontario, spent years in Ottawa and were still with the team when they won the Stanley Cup again in 1927. So was Boucher. Alex Connell was another local boy made good who replaced Benedict in goal in 1924 and won the Cup in 1927, while King Clancy—the team's super-sub in 1923—was now among the NHL's best defensemen.

But despite all their success, the Senators were in financial trouble. The NHL's expansion into the United States had left Ottawa as the league's smallest market by far. With the NHL growing to 10 teams in 1926–27 and the season stretched to 44 games, it was thought that 22 home dates were just too many for a city the size of Ottawa. Saturday night games were still drawing full houses, but weekday attendance was poor.

"As the team is largely composed of Ottawa boys, the encouragement and support of their fellow citizens is what they appreciate and value the most," said club owner Frank

The 1927 Ottawa Senators, the last great team Ottawa would ice before the franchise moved in 1934.

10 percent, but the committee's report at a December meeting rejected any increase at all.

By then Ottawa had already begun selling off its stars. On October 7, 1927, Hooley Smith was sold to the Montreal Maroons for $22,500 and the return of former Senators star Broadbent, who was now well past his prime. A year later, Broadbent was sold to the New York Americans and Denneny was sold to the Boston Bruins. But selling off stars hurt the team both on the ice and at the box office. Even with the NHL's lowest ticket prices, the Senators drew poorly at home. Things only got worse with the stock market crash in October of 1929 that signaled the onset of the Great Depression. Nighbor was sold to the Toronto Maple Leafs in January of 1930, but even the record sale of Clancy to Toronto for $35,000 before the 1930–31 season couldn't help the team.

Ottawa took a leave of absence from the NHL in 1931–32 and then returned to play two more dismal seasons before moving to St. Louis, Missouri, in 1934. In 1935 the NHL bought out the franchise and distributed its players throughout the league. It was a sad end for a team that had so often been the best in hockey.

Ahearn, announcing a reduction in ticket prices on February 8, 1927. "Naturally, having set up a very fine record this season, the team hopes for that support. It means much to the morale of the team. Put them into the playoffs with a boost and that may mean the Stanley Cup."

The Ottawa Senators did indeed win the Stanley Cup in 1927, but even the team's fourth championship in eight years wasn't enough to save the franchise. Other action had to be taken.

As a perennial power, the Senators had always been a good draw on the road and they were now attracting much bigger crowds in other cities than they were at home. At the NHL meetings in September 1927, Ahearn requested that visiting teams receive a larger percentage of the gate receipts from road games. He wanted the rate increased from 3.5 percent to 15 percent. NHL president Frank Calder opposed such revenue sharing, feeling it would make weaker teams complacent. The NHL agreed to appoint a committee to look into raising the visitor's share to

Montreal Maroons

NHL SEMIFINALS
6 goals to 4 over Pittsburgh

NHL FINAL
2 goals to 1 over Ottawa

STANLEY CUP FINAL
3 GAMES TO 1

MAR. 30 ►	Victoria 0 at Montreal Maroons 3
APR. 1 ►	Victoria 0 at Montreal Maroons 3
APR. 3 ►	Victoria 3 at Montreal Maroons 2
APR. 6 ►	Victoria 0 at Montreal Maroons 2

PLAYOFF SCORING LEADER

	GP	G	A	PTS
Nels Stewart MONTREAL MAROONS	8	6	3	9

ROSTER

Clint Benedict
Punch Broadbent
Bernie Brophy
Frank Carson
Chuck Dinsmore
Albert Holway
George Horne
Hobie Kitchen
Dunc Munro (captain)
Reg Noble
Merlyn Phillips
Sam Rothschild
Babe Siebert
Nels Stewart

Eddie Gerard
(manager/coach)

STANLEY CUP SERIES SCORING

MONTREAL MAROONS	GP	G	A	PTS	PIM
Nels Stewart	4	6	1	7	16
Babe Siebert	4	1	2	3	2
Merlyn Phillips	4	1	1	2	0
Punch Broadbent	4	1	0	1	22
Dunc Munro	4	1	0	1	6
Frank Carson	4	0	0	0	0
Chuck Dinsmore	4	0	0	0	2
Albert Holway	2	0	0	0	0
Reg Noble	4	0	0	0	4
Sam Rothschild	4	0	0	0	0

GOALTENDER	GP	W	L	MIN	GA	SO	AVG
Clint Benedict	4	3	1	240	3	3	0.75

VICTORIA	GP	G	A	PTS	PIM
Frank Fredrickson	4	1	1	2	10
Harold Halderson	4	1	0	1	8
Clem Loughlin	4	1	0	1	8
Jocko Anderson	1	0	0	0	0
Frank Foyston	4	0	0	0	2
Gord Fraser	4	0	0	0	14
Gizzy Hart	4	0	0	0	2
Harry Meeking	4	0	0	0	6
Russell Oatman	4	0	0	0	10
Jack Walker	4	0	0	0	0

GOALTENDER	GP	W	L	MIN	GA	SO	AVG
Hap Holmes	4	1	3	240	10	0	2.50

Benefit Fund

Jocko Anderson of the Victoria Cougars suffered a career-ending injury in Game 1 of the 1926 Stanley Cup final. Anderson collided with Babe Siebert of the Maroons early in the second period and broke his right leg just below the hip joint. On April 5th, hockey fans in Montreal raised $1,300 for Anderson when 3,000 tickets were sold for an exhibition doubleheader featuring the Montreal Canadiens versus the Saskatoon Crescents and the Montreal Wanderers old-timers versus NHL officials. All the proceeds from the sale of programs at Game 4 of the Stanley Cup final were also placed in a benefit fund for Anderson.

End of an Era

The defending Stanley Cup–champion Victoria Cougars, who had joined the Western Canada Hockey League (WCHL) along with the Vancouver Maroons in 1924 after the demise of the Pacific Coast Hockey Association (PCHA), found themselves playing under their third different league name in three seasons in 1925–26. Poor fan support in Regina had seen the Capitals of that city transferred to Portland, Oregon, and, as a result, the word "Canada" was dropped, and the WCHL was re-christened as the Western Hockey League (WHL). Poor fan support continued to plague cities in the league and led to speculation that major professional hockey in the West was on its last legs.

The Cougars started the season slowly and had just five wins through the first 16 games of the 30-game WHL season. However, Victoria went 10-2-2 over the final 14 games and finished the season third in the standings. In the playoffs, they knocked off both the second-place Saskatoon Crescents and first-place Edmonton Eskimos to earn the right to go east and play the NHL champions for the Stanley Cup.

A year after adding a second team in Montreal and its first American city in Boston, the NHL expanded into Pittsburgh in 1925–26 and saw the New York Americans replace the Hamilton Tigers. The Pittsburgh Pirates were stocked with players from the American amateur–champion Pittsburgh Yellow Jackets and included such stars as Lionel Conacher and Roy Worters. The Pirates finished third in the seven-team NHL to qualify for the playoffs, but the improvement of the Montreal Maroons from second last in its first season to second place in 1925–26 was an even bigger story. The Maroons added rookies Nels Stewart and Babe Siebert to a lineup that included second-year star Dunc Munro and veterans Clint Benedict, Punch Broadbent and Reg Noble. Stewart led the NHL with 34 goals and 42 points in 36 games and won the Hart Trophy as MVP.

In the playoffs, the Maroons beat Pittsburgh in the semifinals and then upset first-place Ottawa in the NHL final. Hosting Victoria in what would prove to be the last Stanley Cup final to feature a team from outside the NHL, the Maroons were too tough. Clint Benedict posted a shutout in each victory, and Nels Stewart scored twice in the first game and both goals in the last, as the Maroons beat the Cougars three games to one.

East vs West

In the years between 1914 and 1926, when the so-called World Series of Hockey pitted the champions from the East against the champions of the West, the entire best-of-five Stanley Cup final was played in one city. With trains taking nearly seven days to go from one side of the continent to the other, it would have been impractical to do anything else. The site was simply rotated every year between the East and the West with the home league's rules being used in Games 1, 3 and 5 and the visitors' in Games 2 and 4.

No Place Like Home
The 1926 series marked the first of 32 Stanley Cup finals to be contested at the Montreal Forum. Originally built as the home of the Maroons in 1924, they would lose the Cup there on home ice in 1928 but win it again in 1935. The Montreal Canadiens hosted 29 Cup finals there, and 22 of their 24 Stanley Cup titles were won while the Forum was their home arena (they were not yet tenants when they won in 1916 and 1924). Of those 29 series, the Habs lost seven, though only one was lost on home ice: 1989's 4–2 series loss to the Calgary Flames.

GOALIES WITH THREE SHUTOUTS IN ONE PLAYOFF SERIES

Clint Benedict	Montreal Maroons	1926 final
Dave Kerr	New York Rangers	1940 semifinal
Frank McCool	Toronto	1945 final
Turk Broda	Toronto	1950 semifinal
Felix Potvin	Toronto	1994 conference quarterfinal
Martin Brodeur	New Jersey	1995 conference quarterfinal
Brent Johnson	St. Louis	2002 conference quarterfinal
Patrick Lalime	Ottawa	2002 conference quarterfinal
Jean-Sébastien Giguère	Anaheim	2003 conference final
Martin Brodeur	New Jersey	2003 final
Ed Belfour	Toronto	2004 conference quarterfinal
Nikolai Khabibulin	Tampa Bay	2004 conference quarterfinal
Marty Turco	Dallas	2007 conference quarterfinal
Michael Leighton	Philadelphia	2010 conference final

Hockey Rules

The differences in the rules between hockey in the East and hockey in the West were always a point of discussion during this era. By 1926, the key differences between the rules in the NHL and the rules in the WHL were

- the WHL allowed forward passing in all three zones (though not across the blue line), while the NHL only allowed it in the neutral zone;
- kicking the puck was allowed anywhere on the ice in the WHL (though the puck could not be kicked into the net), but it was whistled for a stoppage in the NHL if it occurred outside the neutral zone;
- penalty shots were awarded for certain infractions in the WHL but did not exist in the NHL.

While everyone seemed to agree that the Western rules sped up the game, NHL executives didn't like them. After Game 2 of the 1926 series, the April 2nd edition of the *Montreal Gazette* reported that NHL president Frank Calder believed "the western type of hockey leads to a lot of fancy skating without getting the puck anywhere." Léo Dandurand, owner of the Montreal Canadiens, expressed similar views. He felt the forward pass eliminated puckhandling from the game. "Hockey," claimed Dandurand, "gives way to a skating exhibition, which may be entertaining to many, but not to real died-in-the-wool hockey fans."

WCHL SEMIFINALS
6 goals to 4 over Saskatoon

WCHL FINAL
3 goals to 1 over Calgary

MAR. 21 ► Montreal 2 at Victoria 5

MAR. 23 ► Montreal 1 vs Victoria 3*

MAR. 27 ► Montreal 4 at Victoria 2

MAR. 30 ► Montreal 1 at Victoria 6

*Played in Vancouver.

PLAYOFF SCORING LEADER

Jack Walker	GP	G	A	PTS
VICTORIA	8	8	2	10

WESTERN CHAMPIONS 1924-25

WORLD CHAMPIONS 1924-25

"HAPPY" HOLMES

CLEM LOUGHLIN CAPT.

FRANK FREDRICKSON

HARRY MEEKING

HAROLD HART

"SLIM" HALDERSON

"JOCKO" ANDERSON

GORDON FRASER

FRANK FOYSTON

MANAGER LESTER PATRICK

JACK WALKER

WALLY ELMER

W.C.H.L. CUP

VICTORIA COUGARS

STANLEY CUP

STANLEY CUP SERIES SCORING

VICTORIA	GP	G	A	PTS	PIM
Jack Walker	4	4	2	6	0
Frank Fredrickson	4	3	2	5	6
Gord Fraser	4	2	1	3	6
Harold Halderson	4	2	1	3	8
Gizzy Hart	4	2	1	3	0
Jocko Anderson	4	1	0	1	10
Frank Foyston	4	1	0	1	0
Clem Loughlin	4	1	0	1	4
Harry Meeking	4	0	1	1	2
Wally Elmer	2	0	0	0	0

GOALTENDER	GP	W	L	MIN	GA	SO	AVG
Hap Holmes	4	3	1	240	8	0	2.00

MONTREAL	GP	G	A	PTS	PIM
Howie Morenz	4	4	1	5	4
Aurel Joliat	4	2	0	2	16
Billy Boucher	4	1	1	2	13
Billy Coutu	4	1	0	1	12
Odie Cleghorn	4	0	0	0	0
Sprague Cleghorn	4	0	0	0	2
Fern Headley	4	0	0	0	0
Sylvio Mantha	4	0	0	0	2
Johnny Matz	4	0	0	0	2

GOALTENDER	GP	W	L	MIN	GA	SO	AVG
Georges Vezina	4	1	3	240	16	0	4.00

ROSTER

Jocko Anderson

Wally Elmer

Frank Foyston

Gord Fraser

Frank Fredrickson

Harold Halderson

Gizzy Hart

Hap Holmes

Clem Loughlin (captain)

Harry Meeking

Jack Walker

Lester Patrick (manager/coach)

Two Lines Beat Top Stars

The Cougars used a better-balanced attack to beat the Canadiens. While Montreal relied heavily on its big line of Howie Morenz, Aurel Joliat and Billy Boucher, Victoria made much more liberal use of its spare players than was common at the time. "Lester Patrick substituted his line every five minutes so as to give the Frenchmen no chance to catch their breath," read the report of the fourth and final game.

Western Winners

The 1915 Vancouver Millionaires (PCHA), the 1917 Seattle Metropolitans (PCHA) and the 1925 Victoria Cougars (1925) were the only Western champions during the "World Series" era of 1914 to 1926. The next West Coast team to win the Stanley Cup would be the Anaheim Ducks in 2007.

Last of Their Kind

The NHL expanded to six teams in 1924–25. The league added its first American club, the Boston Bruins, and a second team in Montreal, soon to be known as the Maroons because of the color of their sweaters. Out West, the Seattle Metropolitans folded, marking the end of the Pacific Coast Hockey Association (PCHA), which had begun operations back in 1911–12. Vancouver and Victoria from the PCHA joined Calgary, Edmonton, Regina and Saskatoon in a six-team Western Canada Hockey League (WCHL).

With expansion, the NHL extended its season from 24 to 30 games, which matched the length of the WCHL season. In both leagues, the first-place team would receive a bye into the finals, where it would meet the winner of a series between the second- and third-place teams. The Victoria Cougars added stars Jack Walker, Frank Foyston and goalie Hap Holmes from Seattle to a roster that already boasted future Hall of Famer Frank Fredrickson. Still, they finished only third in the WCHL standings, with a record of 16-12-0, but they were just one point behind the second-place Saskatoon Crescents

and just two back of the first-place Calgary Tigers. In the playoffs, Victoria defeated Saskatoon and Calgary to earn the right to host the NHL champions.

The Montreal Canadiens were the defending Stanley Cup champions but could finish no better than third in the NHL. The four established teams waged a tight battle that saw only four points separate first from fourth, while the two new expansion teams struggled. The Hamilton Tigers, who'd placed last in each of the previous four seasons, went 19-10-1 this year to finish one point ahead of the Toronto St. Pats for first place. But the Hamilton players were upset that the season had been lengthened by 25 percent without a comparable increase in their salaries. They refused to take part in the playoffs unless they received an extra $200 each. President Frank Calder suspended the players and announced that the winner of a semifinal playoff between the Canadiens and St. Patricks would be declared NHL champion.

Montreal beat Toronto to win the NHL title, but they could not defeat Victoria, as the Cougars became the last non-NHL team to win the Stanley Cup.

According to Legend...

As owner, coach, general manager and occasional player with the Victoria Cougars, Lester Patrick apparently had the Stanley Cup stored in his basement for a while. When sons Lynn and Muzz came across it one day, they decided to scratch their names onto the trophy with a nail. Is the story true? There appears to be no evidence of it on the original Stanley Cup bowl or the collars on display at the Hockey Hall of Fame. However, Lynn and Muzz Patrick would have their names engraved on the Stanley Cup properly in 1940, when they won it as players with the New York Rangers.

Police Presence Things got out of hand in Victoria when tickets went on sale for reserve seats the day before Game 3 of the Cougars-Canadiens series. The first hopeful buyers had begun lining up at 3:30 a.m., and by 6 o'clock people were lined up four deep along an entire city block. As the crowd continued to gather, people from the back began pushing those in front, and a Canadian Press report stated "women dropped to the pavement unconscious." A squad of police eventually succeeded in restoring order.

Stanley Cup and Olympic Gold

With the Cougars win over the Canadiens, Victoria teammates Frank Fredrickson and Slim Halderson became the first players in history to win both an Olympic gold medal and the Stanley Cup. Fredrickson and Halderson had both been members of the Winnipeg Falcons who had won gold in 1920, when hockey was held as part of a spring sports festival in conjunction with the Olympics later that summer in Antwerp, Belgium. In 1926, Dunc Munro joined the illustrious group, winning the Stanley Cup with the Montreal Maroons after having won gold at the first Winter Olympics with the Toronto Granites in 1924. In 1927, Hooley Smith added his name to the list, winning the Stanley Cup with Ottawa to go along with the Olympic gold medal he had also won as a member of the Granites.

Moving to Vancouver

Game 2 of the 1925 Stanley Cup final was scheduled to be played in Vancouver, as opposed to Victoria, to take advantage of the greater seating capacity of the arena there. Victoria's rink held only about 4,000 fans, while Vancouver's could hold just over 10,000. Since player bonuses and traveling expenses in this era came only out of the revenue from the first three games of the best-of-five series, it had been decided before the series started to play one of those first three games in Vancouver.

Had the Calgary Tigers beaten Victoria to win the WCHL title, they also would have played games in Vancouver, as that ice surface was chilled artificially. But, as Calgary officials attested, if they did in fact get to host the Stanley Cup final, the first game would have been played in Calgary no matter what state the natural ice was in. "[The fans] support us all through the winter," said Tigers manager Lloyd Turner, "and when there is a fine classic as the world's series, it [would be] too bad if they cannot get a chance to see even one game of it. We had to play on terrible ice at Montreal last year in the Stanley Cup series, and the NHL champions need not expect any better treatment than we were accorded."

NHL FINAL
5 goals to 2 over Ottawa

ROSTER

Billy Bell
Billy Boucher
Bobby Boucher
Billy Cameron
Odie Cleghorn
Sprague Cleghorn (captain)
Billy Coutu
Charles Fortier
Aurel Joliat
Joe Malone
Sylvio Mantha
Howie Morenz
Georges Vezina
Leo Dandurand (manager/coach)

STANLEY CUP SEMIFINAL
2 GAMES TO 0

MAR. 18 ▸ Vancouver 2 at Montreal 3

MAR. 20 ▸ Vancouver 1 at Montreal 2

STANLEY CUP FINAL
2 GAMES TO 0

MAR. 22 ▸ Calgary 1 at Montreal 6

MAR. 25 ▸ Calgary 0 vs Montreal 3*

*Played in Ottawa.

PLAYOFF SCORING LEADER

Howie Morenz	GP	G	A	PTS
MONTREAL	6	7	3	10

STANLEY CUP SERIES SCORING

MONTREAL	GP	G	A	PTS	PIM
Billy Boucher	4	5	1	6	6
Howie Morenz	4	4	2	6	4
Aurel Joliat	4	3	1	4	6
Sprague Cleghorn	4	2	1	3	2
Odie Cleghorn	4	0	2	2	0
Billy Bell	3	0	0	0	0
Bobby Boucher	3	0	0	0	0
Billy Cameron	4	0	0	0	0
Billy Coutu	4	0	0	0	0
Sylvio Mantha	4	0	0	0	0

GOALTENDER	GP	W	L	MIN	GA	SO	AVG
Georges Vezina	4	4	0	240	4	1	1.00

VANCOUVER	GP	G	A	PTS	PIM
Frank Boucher	2	1	1	2	2
Helge Bostrom	2	1	0	1	0
Joe Matte	2	1	0	1	2
Lloyd Cook	2	0	0	0	4
Charlie Cotch	1	0	0	0	0
Art Duncan	2	0	0	0	6
Mickey MacKay	2	0	0	0	0
Ernie Parkes	2	0	0	0	0
Alf Skinner	2	0	0	0	0

GOALTENDER	GP	W	L	MIN	GA	SO	AVG
Hugh Lehman	2	0	2	120	5	0	2.50

CALGARY	GP	G	A	PTS	PIM
Herb Gardiner	2	1	0	1	0
Bernie Morris	2	0	1	1	0
Ernie Anderson	2	0	0	0	2
Bobby Benson	2	0	0	0	0
Rusty Crawford	2	0	0	0	0
Red Dutton	2	0	0	0	6
Eddie Oatman	2	0	0	0	0
Harry Oliver	2	0	0	0	0
Cully Wilson	2	0	0	0	2

GOALTENDER	GP	W	L	MIN	GA	SO	AVG
Charlie Reid	2	0	2	120	9	0	4.50

Another 1924 Legend...

It's long been reported that Madison Square Garden–owner Tex Rickard was finally convinced to add ice to his planned new arena after witnessing Howie Morenz in action during the 1924 Stanley Cup final. In truth, both Rickard and Boston's Charles Adams were pretty much already sold on the idea of an NHL team in their cities.

Still, it's true that invitations were issued to a playoff game, but they were actually for the March 18th semifinal game, and while Adams was there Rickard was not. John Hammond represented Madison Square Garden's interests because Rickard had to be in Washington to appear before a congressional inquiry.

Two Straight Games Each

After winning the Stanley Cup three times in the previous four seasons, there were changes in Ottawa in 1923–24. Frank Ahearn took over ownership of the team, which would now be playing out of the new Ottawa Auditorium, which had artificial ice and room for 11,000 fans. Longtime star and captain Eddie Gerard had retired, but his departure allowed King Clancy to become a regular on the Senators defense. With other established stars such as Cy Denneny, George Boucher, Frank Nighbor and Clint Benedict, Ottawa topped the four-team NHL standings with a record of 16-8-0. The Montreal Canadiens finished comfortably ahead of Toronto and Hamilton (who finished last for the fourth straight year) with a record of 13-11-0 to qualify for the playoffs against Ottawa.

With Georges Vezina in goal and Sprague Cleghorn on defense, Montreal was the NHL's best defensive team. Billy Boucher, Aurel Joliat and a talented rookie named Howie Morenz led the offense. The Senators were favored over the Canadiens in the playoffs, but Morenz scored the only goal in Game 1 and added two more in a 4–2 victory in Game 2 to give Montreal the NHL title.

Out West, the Pacific Coast Hockey Association (PCHA) and Western Canada Hockey League (WCHL) played an interlocking schedule for the second straight year. The two leagues maintained their own separate standings, and though the Seattle Metropolitans finished first in the PCHA, the Vancouver Maroons eliminated them in the playoffs. Future New York Rangers star Frank Boucher scored the series-winning goal after 14 minutes of overtime. The only first-place team to survive the playoffs was the Calgary Tigers, who defeated the Regina Capitals to take the WCHL crown. The Tigers then defeated the Maroons in a best-of-three series played in Vancouver, Calgary and Winnipeg, but both teams continued on to Montreal to face the Canadiens.

Sprague Cleghorn and Billy Boucher starred for the Canadiens in Game 1 against Vancouver. The Boucher brothers, Billy and Frank, scored all the goals in Game 2, but it was Billy's Canadiens that won 2–1 for a series sweep. Warm weather had softened the natural ice at the Mount Royal Arena throughout the playoffs, but despite a slushy surface, Howie Morenz scored three times in a 6–1 victory over Calgary to open the Stanley Cup final. Game 2 was moved to Ottawa to take advantage of the artificial ice there. Calgary played better on the faster surface but couldn't put the puck past Vezina, and the Canadiens swept the Tigers in two games.

Name Game

A new silver band added to the Stanley Cup to record the names of winning teams had been attached beneath the original base in 1909. But after that band was filled in 1918, nothing more was engraved on the Stanley Cup for five years. Then, in 1924, the Canadiens added a brand new band, completely filling in the space between the earlier two. On it was engraved, "Canadiens of Montreal / World's Champions / 1924" along with the teams the Canadiens had defeated, "Ottawa Vancouver Calgary Two Straight Games Each." The Canadiens also engraved the names of the 11 players who had taken part in the playoffs, as well as those of the club executives. Names had only been engraved previously in 1907 and 1915, but they have been included every year since 1924.

New Logo

After winning the Stanley Cup in 1924, the Canadiens replaced the CH logo they had been wearing on their chests since 1916 with a depiction of a globe for the 1924–25 season, representing their status as world champions. They did wear the CH on their sleeves that season and restored it on their chests in 1925–26.

Stanley Cup Presentations
Stanley Cup trustee William Foran presented the prized trophy to the Canadiens at a banquet attended by 450 people at the Windsor Hotel in Montreal on April 1, 1924. It's likely that if the story is true about Canadiens players leaving the Stanley Cup by the side of the road while fixing a flat tire en route to a celebration at Léo Dandurand's home, it happened later that same night. Another possibility would be on the way to or on the road home from a University of Montreal banquet on April 3rd, where Dandurand, the Stanley Cup and the Canadiens players were all present.

The Bye Series

With the formation of the Western Canada Hockey League (WCHL) for the 1921–22 season, the NHL and the Pacific Coast Hockey Association (PCHA) agreed to let the WCHL in on their Stanley Cup playoffs. Unfortunately, there wasn't a consensus on how a three-team playoff would work.

In 1922, the PCHA champions met the WCHL champions in a series that sent the winner east to face the top NHL team. In 1923, when the NHL's Ottawa Senators went west, a new agreement saw them play a semifinal series against the PCHA champions with the winner to face the WCHL champs for the Stanley Cup. When a dispute arose in 1924, Montreal Canadiens owner/manager Léo Dandurand claimed that it was Tommy Gorman of the Senators acting on his own who had agreed to the previous arrangement.

In 1924, PCHA president Frank Patrick and WCHL boss E.L. Richardson insisted that both western-based champions, Vancouver and Calgary, would come east for a chance at the Cup. "At first," wrote Patrick in the *Boston Globe* in 1936, "I thought we could flip a coin to decide which club would play the Canadiens first. Then the thought occurred to me to play off for the bye berth."

Léo Dandurand expected just the winner of the Western series (Calgary) to come to Montreal and agreed only reluctantly to face Vancouver in a semifinal series. Before they did, Dandurand insisted that Patrick explain why Calgary and Vancouver had even played a bye series. Patrick answered calmly, "For $20,000..." meaning the gate receipts the teams had earned.

NHL FINAL
3 goals to 2 over Montreal

ROSTER

Clint Benedict

George Boucher

Punch Broadbent

King Clancy

Jack Darragh

Cy Denneny

Eddie Gerard (captain)

Harry Helman

Lionel Hitchman

Frank Nighbor

Tommy Gorman
(manager)

Pete Green (coach)

STANLEY CUP SEMIFINAL
3 GAMES TO 1

MAR. 16 ► Ottawa 1 at Vancouver 0

MAR. 19 ► Ottawa 1 at Vancouver 4

MAR. 23 ► Ottawa 3 at Vancouver 2

MAR. 26 ► Ottawa 5 at Vancouver 1

STANLEY CUP FINAL
2 GAMES TO 0

MAR. 29 ► Ottawa 2 vs Edmonton 1 OT*

MAR. 31 ► Ottawa 1 vs Edmonton 0 *

*Played in Vancouver.

PLAYOFF SCORING LEADER

Punch Broadbent	GP	G	A	PTS
OTTAWA	8	6	1	7

STANLEY CUP SERIES SCORING

OTTAWA	GP	G	A	PTS	PIM
Punch Broadbent	6	6	1	7	10
George Boucher	6	2	1	3	6
Cy Denneny	6	1	3	3	10
Frank Nighbor	6	1	1	2	10
King Clancy	6	1	0	1	4
Eddie Gerard	6	1	0	1	4
Lionel Hitchman	5	1	0	1	4
Clint Benedict	6	0	0	0	2
Harry Helman	2	0	0	0	0

GOALTENDERS	GP	W	L	MIN	GA	SO	AVG
Clint Benedict	6	5	1	361	8	1	1.33
King Clancy	1	0	0	2	0	0	0.00

VANCOUVER	GP	G	A	PTS	PIM
Art Duncan	4	2	2	4	0
Frank Boucher	4	2	0	2	0
Alf Skinner	3	1	1	2	6
Ernie Parkes	4	0	2	2	2
Smokey Harris	4	1	0	1	8
Mickey MacKay	4	1	0	1	4
Lloyd Cook	4	0	1	1	4
Charlie Cotch	2	0	0	0	0
Corb Denneny	3	0	0	0	0

GOALTENDER	GP	W	L	MIN	GA	SO	AVG
Hugh Lehman	4	1	3	240	10	0	2.50

EDMONTON	GP	G	A	PTS	PIM
John Morrison	2	1	0	1	0
Joe Simpson	2	0	1	1	0
Ty Arbour	2	0	0	0	0
Helge Bostrom	1	0	0	0	0
Earl Campbell	2	0	0	0	0
Art Gagne	2	0	0	0	2
Duke Keats	2	0	0	0	4
Johnny Sheppard	1	0	0	0	0
Bob Trapp	2	0	0	0	2

GOALTENDER	GP	W	L	MIN	GA	SO	AVG
Hal Winkler	2	0	2	123	3	0	1.46

Four the Hard Way Ottawa's Stanley Cup victory in 1923 marked the third win in four years for the team, but it was the fourth in a row for their captain, Eddie Gerard. In addition to his wins with Ottawa in 1920, 1921 and 1923, Gerard also helped Toronto win the Cup in 1922. He replaced injured St. Patricks defenseman Harry Cameron in Game 4 of that series and starred as Toronto shutout Vancouver 3–0.

Family Affair The Stanley Cup semifinal series between Vancouver and Ottawa saw two different sets of brothers opposing each other, with the Maroons' Frank Boucher and Corb Denneny taking on their older brothers, George Boucher and Cy Denneny.

Ottawa Overcomes the Obstacles

Ottawa, Toronto and Montreal waged a tight battle in the NHL during the 1922–23 season, with only two points separating those three teams, while the Hamilton Tigers were hopelessly out of contention. The Senators finished first with a 14-9-1 record, while the race for second place went down to the final night, when the Canadiens clinched a playoff spot at the expense of the defending Stanley Cup–champion Toronto St. Patricks.

Ottawa opened the playoffs in Montreal with a 2–0 victory despite the vicious play of Canadiens defensemen Sprague Cleghorn and Billy Coutu. Canadiens manager Leo Dandurand was so appalled by their conduct that he suspended both players from the second game even before the NHL could take action. Even so, Montreal had a 2–0 lead in Game 2 before Cy Denneny (who played only sparingly with his head swathed in bandages) scored early in the third period to give Ottawa a 3–2 victory in the total-goal series.

Out West, the Pacific Coast Hockey Association (PCHA), which had introduced so many innovative rules to the game, finally abandoned the rover position. The move to six-man hockey allowed the PCHA to play an interlocking schedule with the Western Canada Hockey League (WCHL), though each league maintained its own separate standings. Frank Fredrickson led the PCHA in scoring and made the Victoria Cougars a true contender for the first time in years. Still, Vancouver (now known as the Maroons instead of the Millionaires) held onto first place and beat the Cougars five goals to three in the playoffs. In the WCHL, the Edmonton Eskimos topped the Regina Capitals in the standings, but they then needed a penalty-shot goal from Duke Keats after he was tripped on a breakaway in the second overtime period to eliminate Regina in the playoffs. Edmonton's victory put them directly into the Stanley Cup final, while Ottawa played in Vancouver to determine the Eskimos' opponent.

The Senators were banged up from their series with Montreal and were without veteran Jack Darragh, who could not make the trip. Another Ottawa veteran, Punch Broadbent, played the hero, scoring the only goal of Game 1 with just five minutes remaining. Broadbent scored twice more in both of Ottawa's other victories as the Senators took the best-of-five series in four games. The well-rested Eskimos were confident heading into the Stanley Cup final against the worn-out Senators. Despite more injuries in the final, Clint Benedict played brilliantly in goal for Ottawa, and Frank Nighbor kept Duke Keats under wraps. The Senators got an overtime goal from Cy Denneny in Game 1 and then Broadbent scored the only goal of the game in Game 2 to sweep the best-of-three series.

King's Cup

A famous story about King Clancy from 1923 is that after the Senators' victory he received permission to bring the Stanley Cup home to show it to his father, who had been a star football player in Ottawa. According to legend, when the Canadiens won the Cup in 1924 and the Senators had to send the trophy to Montreal, no one could find it until Clancy admitted it was sitting on the mantle above his fireplace.

Welcome Home

The Senators arrived back home in Ottawa by train from Vancouver at 11:40 a.m. on April 6th. A huge crowd was waiting for them at Union Station. After a welcome home speech from Mayor Frank Plant, the players were hustled through the crowded station to a line of cars that would parade them through the downtown streets to the Château Laurier hotel. A similar parade had also been held when Ottawa previously won the Cup in Vancouver in 1921. "Moving picture men from the big American news feature syndicates were present," reported the *Ottawa Citizen* of the 1923 parade, "and took pictures in the station and along the route of the parade." Film footage of the parade still exists today.

Did He or Didn't He?

King Clancy is reputed to have played all six positions during the last game of the 1923 Stanley Cup final. While he definitely took over for Clint Benedict when the Ottawa goalie served a two-minute penalty, there is little indication in any newspaper accounts that Clancy played anywhere else but defense that night. The only real hint that he may have played several different positions is a remark in the *Vancouver Sun* after Benedict was penalized saying that, "Clancy, completing his utility performance of the series, replaced him."

In his autobiography written with Brian MacFarlane and originally published in 1968, Clancy admitted that the story of his goaltending in the Stanley Cup final "was given a twist here and there." He also wrote that his appearance in goal that night was the first time he had ever played that position, but that he did play all five positions other than goaltender during the third game of the semifinal series with Vancouver. The *Ottawa Citizen* of March 24, 1923, bears this out: "The Ottawas went through the entire sixty minutes of grueling hockey with only seven players, King Clancy, the youngest member of the team, being the only substitute used and he was compelled to play every position on the ice except in the nets."

Toronto St. Patricks

NHL FINAL
5 goals to 4 over Ottawa

STANLEY CUP FINAL
3 GAMES TO 2

MAR. 17	►	Vancouver 4 at Toronto 3
MAR. 21	►	Vancouver 1 at Toronto 2 OT
MAR. 23	►	Vancouver 3 at Toronto 0
MAR. 25	►	Vancouver 0 at Toronto 6
MAR. 28	►	Vancouver 1 at Toronto 5

ROSTER

Lloyd Andrews

Harry Cameron

Corb Denneny

Babe Dye

Eddie Gerard
(borrowed for one
game from Ottawa)

Stan Jackson

Ivan Mitchell

Reg Noble (captain)

Ken Randall

John Ross Roach

Rod Smylie

Ted Stackhouse

Red Stuart

Charlie Querrie
(manager)

George O'Donoghue
(coach)

WORLDS
CHAMPIONS
1972–23

PLAYOFF SCORING LEADER

	GP	G	A	PTS
Babe Dye TORONTO	7	11	1	12

STANLEY CUP SERIES SCORING

TORONTO	GP	G	A	PTS	PIM
Babe Dye	5	9	1	10	3
Corb Denneny	5	3	2	5	2
Rod Smylie	5	1	3	4	0
Lloyd Andrews	5	2	0	2	3
Harry Cameron	4	0	2	2	14
Red Stuart	5	0	2	2	6
Ken Randall	4	1	0	1	22
Reg Noble	5	0	1	1	9
Eddie Gerard	1	0	0	0	0
Ted Stackhouse	4	0	0	0	0
GOALTENDER	GP	W	L	MIN	GA	SO	AVG
John Ross Roach	5	3	2	305	9	1	1.77

VANCOUVER	GP	G	A	PTS	PIM
Jack Adams	5	6	1	7	18
Ernie Parkes	5	0	3	3	0
Lloyd Cook	5	1	0	1	6
Mickey MacKay	5	1	0	1	6
Eddie Oatman	5	1	0	1	14
Art Duncan	5	0	1	1	9
Alf Skinner	5	0	1	1	12
Charlie Tobin	5	0	0	0	0
GOALTENDER	GP	W	L	MIN	GA	SO	AVG
Hugh Lehman	5	2	3	305	16	1	3.15

Two-Sport Star Shortly after starring for the St. Pats in the Stanley Cup final, Babe Dye began his summer job—playing outfield for the Buffalo Bisons of the International League. Though Dye never made it to the majors, he hit .318 with 16 homers in 1923 and reportedly attracted attention from both the Philadelphia Athletics and the Washington Senators.

Which Season? After their championship season, the St. Patricks unveiled new sweaters the following year, reversing the previous green with white trim to white with green trim and introducing a new St. Pats logo. The sweaters also featured a commemorative patch, stating "World Champions 1922–23," which is somewhat confusing in that they wore these new uniforms during the 1922–23 season, but were actually the Stanley Cup champions of 1921–22.

St. Patrick and Lord Stanley

After the lean years of World War I, professional hockey—like so much else—began to flourish during the 1920s. A third pro league opened up to rival the NHL and the Pacific Coast Hockey Association (PCHA) in 1921–22; the Western Canada Hockey League (WCHL) featured teams in Calgary and Edmonton in Alberta and Regina and Saskatoon in Saskatchewan. In the NHL, Léo Dandurand, Joseph Cattarinich and Louis Letourneau purchased the Montreal Canadiens in November 1921 for a reported record price of $11,000.

On the ice, the NHL abandoned the split-season format it had used during its first four seasons and adopted the PCHA's playoff scheme that saw the first- and second-place teams meet for the league championship. The same format was also used in the WCHL. Ottawa came out on top in the NHL with a record of 14-8-2. Punch Broadbent led the league with 32 goals and 46 points and established an NHL record that still stands today, scoring in 16 consecutive games. Toronto was a close second at 13-10-1, and the St. Patricks surprised the Senators by beating them by one goal in the two-game, total-goals playoff.

In the West, the three teams in the PCHA were closely bunched with Seattle going 12-11-1, Vancouver finishing 12-12-0 and Victoria 11-12-1. The Vancouver Millionaires then defeated the first-place Seattle Metropolitans with a pair of 1–0 shutouts by Hugh Lehman. It was tight in the WCHL as well, with the Edmonton Eskimos coming out on top and the Regina Capitals and Calgary Tigers tied for second place. Regina then knocked off both Calgary and Edmonton before taking on the PCHA champs from Vancouver to determine which Western club would go East to face the NHL champions for the Stanley Cup. Playing their sixth game in eight nights, the Capitals beat the Millionaires 2–1 to open the series in Vancouver only to lose 4–0 at home three nights later.

Jack Adams had a hat trick for Vancouver in their Game 1 victory of the Stanley Cup final, but Babe Dye drew Toronto even with the overtime winner in Game 2. Adams starred again in Game 3, but Dye scored twice in a 6–0 Toronto win in Game 4 and had four goals in the 5–1 victory that gave the St. Pats the series in Game 5.

Penalty Shot Not Too Popular

The first penalty shot in Stanley Cup history was awarded in Game 2 of the 1922 series. Penalty shots had not yet been introduced into the NHL rule book, but Game 2 was played under PCHA rules. Babe Dye was tripped by Art Duncan on a breakaway and given the free shot, but he fired it over the net. Toronto fans were not impressed by the rule, which the *Globe* newspaper found to be "somewhat of a joke." Penalty shots in the PCHA were more like a free kick in soccer than the penalty shots of today, with players firing from a fixed spot 36 feet (about 11 m) in front of the net. "Duncan was not penalized," criticized the *Globe*, "and he can keep on tripping the attackers as long as he likes, as it is not likely the St. Patricks will win any games shooting shots at (Vancouver goalie Hugh) Lehman from the 36-foot mark."

Rover Over The fourth game of this year's Stanley Cup final, played under PCHA rules on March 25, 1922, was the last Stanley Cup game in which teams used a rover. The PCHA finally adopted six-man hockey for the 1922–23 season.

Jolly Jack

Jack Adams had begun his professional career in Toronto in 1917–18, when the Arenas won the Stanley Cup over Vancouver. Vancouver signed Adams in 1920, and when he returned to Toronto with the Millionaires for the Stanley Cup final in 1922, he scored a team-leading six goals in a losing effort. Adams returned to the NHL with the St. Patricks the very next season, and later won another Stanley Cup with the Ottawa Senators, in 1926–27. A year later, Adams became coach and general manager of the second-year NHL franchise in Detroit. He remained with the Red Wings through the 1961–62 season, guiding Detroit to seven Stanley Cups.

MOST GOALS IN A STANLEY CUP FINAL (NHL ERA)

9	Cyclone Taylor, Vancouver Millionaires, 1918 (5 games)
	Frank Foyston, Seattle Metropolitans, 1919 (5 games)
	Babe Dye, Toronto St. Patricks, 1922 (5 games)
8	Alf Skinner, Toronto Arenas, 1918 (5 games)
7	Jean Béliveau, Montreal Canadiens, 1956 (5 games)
	Mike Bossy, New York Islanders, 1982 (4 games)
	Wayne Gretzky, Edmonton Oilers, 1985 (5 games)

We're on the Air

There has been much confusion about the beginnings of radio hockey broadcasts. Foster Hewitt is often credited with calling the first game on March 22, 1923. The game that night was supposedly an OHA senior playoff to determine an opponent for the Toronto Granites. Problem is, the Granites were already OHA champions and defeated the University of Saskatchewan to win the Allan Cup that same night.

Turns out that the game that marked Foster Hewitt's first hockey broadcast was played between the Kitchener Greenshirts and the Toronto Argonauts on February 16, 1923. Hewitt was an employee of the *Toronto Star* and broadcast games for CFCA, a station owned by the newspaper. The very first hockey broadcast on CFCA was an OHA intermediate playoff between Midland and North Toronto made by *Star* employee Norman Albert on February 8, 1923.

It is very likely, however, that the first hockey broadcasts were actually made almost a full year earlier, during the 1922 Stanley Cup final. Three different Vancouver newspapers were racing to get radio stations running in March 1922 and were looking for content. It was already common for newspapers to run telegraph wires from Stanley Cup games and announce reports to fans outside their offices. In 1922, *Vancouver Sun* radio station CJCE read telegraphed reports from Toronto live on the air.

"Hockey returns were sent out to all stations within a thousand-mile radius," the *Sun* reported after Game 2, "and numerous radio 'bugs' in the district reported that it was as good as being at the game."

Ottawa Senators

NHL FINAL
7 goals to 0 over Toronto

ROSTER

Clint Benedict

George Boucher

Punch Broadbent

Morley Bruce

Sprague Cleghorn

Jack Darragh

Cy Denneny

Eddie Gerard
(captain)

Leth Graham

Jack MacKell

Frank Nighbor

Tommy Gorman
(manager)

Pete Green (coach)

STANLEY CUP FINAL
3 GAMES TO 2

MAR. 21 ▶	Ottawa 1 at Vancouver 3	
MAR. 24 ▶	Ottawa 4 at Vancouver 3	
MAR. 28 ▶	Ottawa 3 at Vancouver 2	
MAR. 31 ▶	Ottawa 2 at Vancouver 3	
APR. 4 ▶	Ottawa 2 at Vancouver 1	

PLAYOFF SCORING LEADER

Smokey Harris	GP	G	A	PTS
VANCOUVER	7	8	3	11

STANLEY CUP SERIES SCORING

OTTAWA	GP	G	A	PTS	PIM
Jack Darragh	5	5	0	5	12
Cy Denneny	5	2	2	4	13
Sprague Cleghorn	5	1	2	3	38
George Boucher	5	2	0	2	9
Punch Broadbent	4	2	0	2	0
Frank Nighbor	5	0	1	1	0
Eddie Gerard	5	0	0	0	44

GOALTENDER	GP	W	L	MIN	GA	SO	AVG
Clint Benedict	5	3	2	300	12	0	2.40

VANCOUVER	GP	G	A	PTS	PIM
Alf Skinner	3	4	0	4	14
Jack Adams	5	2	1	3	6
Art Duncan	5	2	1	3	3
Smokey Harris	5	2	1	3	6
Lloyd Cook	5	2	0	2	20
Mickey MacKay	5	0	1	1	0
Cyclone Taylor	3	0	1	1	5
Bill Adams	5	0	0	0	0
Syd Desireau	2	0	0	0	5

GOALTENDER	GP	W	L	MIN	GA	SO	AVG
Hugh Lehman	5	2	3	300	12	0	2.40

High Praise

"You have the greatest team I ever saw. Ottawa ought to be proud of those boys. Their defensive system is marvelous. They are better than the 'Little Men of Iron,' the 'Silver Seven,' or any other sextet I have ever watched. It was no disgrace to lose to that aggregation."
— Frank Patrick, Vancouver Millionaires owner/coach/manager and PCHA president

Ottawa Wins out West

After winning the Stanley Cup in 1919–20, the Ottawa Senators gave every indication that they were still the best team in hockey at the start of the 1920–21 season. The Senators ran off five wins in a row, outscoring their opponents 30–8. The offense provided by Cy Denneny, Frank Nighbor and Jack Darragh was impressive, but it was the defense of George Boucher and Eddie Gerard in front of goalie Clint Benedict that made the Senators so hard to beat.

Ottawa easily won the first half of the NHL's split-season schedule with a record of 8-2-0. The first-half win guaranteed Ottawa a playoff spot, but their slump in the second half was troubling. Ottawa lost seven games in a row at one point and finished third in the standings behind Toronto (10-4-0) and Montreal (9-5-0) with a record of 6-8-0. (The Hamilton Tigers, making their NHL debut this season, finished last in both halves of the season.) The Toronto St. Pats fans were confident of defeating the Senators in the playoffs, but Ottawa scored a 5–0 victory at home and then followed up with a 2–0 win in Toronto to romp through the two-game, total-goals series.

The Pacific Coast Hockey Association (PCHA) did not employ a split schedule. Despite having only three teams, brothers Frank and Lester Patrick had devised the modern playoff system in 1917–18, when they decided that the first- and second-place teams should face each other in a postseason showdown. The value in such a setup was borne out by the tight races in the PCHA most seasons, including 1920–21, when Vancouver went 13-11-0 to Seattle's 12-11-1 with Victoria third at 10-13-1. But despite the close finish, the playoffs were a rout. Smokey Harris scored four times in Vancouver's 7–0 win in Game 1 and added two more in a 6–2 win in Game 2.

No visiting team had won the Stanley Cup since the East-West format had begun in 1914, but Ottawa ended that trend this season. In a tight series in which four of the five games were decided by a single goal, the Senators came out on top. Vancouver led the finale 1–0 after one period, but Jack Darragh scored two goals midway through the second to give Ottawa a 2–1 victory. It was the second year in a row that Darragh had scored the Cup-winning goal.

Sweater Swap

After the final game, captain Lloyd Cook led his Vancouver teammates into the Ottawa dressing room. Honoring a bet they had made before the series, the Millionaires presented the maroon and white sweaters they had worn throughout the series to the Senators. Though they had won, the Ottawa players handed over their red, white and black sweaters to the Vancouver players.

Cyclone's Swan Song
Cyclone Taylor, who had won the Stanley Cup with Ottawa in 1909 and with Vancouver in 1915, made his final appearance in a championship series when he saw a few minutes of action for the Millionaires during Game 5. Taylor had played pro hockey since 1906. He led the PCHA in scoring five times in six seasons between 1913–14 and 1918–19 and would make one final appearance with Vancouver during the 1922–23 season.

Sibling Rivalry

Brothers opposed each other in the NHL playoffs for the first time when Ottawa's Cy Denneny faced Corb Denneny of the Toronto St. Patricks. It was the second significant occurrence for the Denneny brothers this season, as they also became the only pair of brothers in NHL history to score six goals in a game. Corb scored his six against the Hamilton Tigers in a 10–3 Toronto victory on January 26, 1921. Cy's double hat trick also came against Hamilton, in a 12–5 Ottawa win on the final night of the season on March 7, 1921.

Hizzoner
Senators players gave Ottawa Mayor Frank Plant the puck from their playoff victory over the St. Pats. Mayor Plant was not just a fan of the team but also the president of the Ottawa City Hockey League and the City Baseball League. When it seemed that Jack Darragh would not be able to leave his job to make the trip to Vancouver for the Stanley Cup final, Mayor Plant made a personal plea to the president of the Ottawa Dairy Company.

Record Attendance

It's often been reported that the attendance of 11,000 fans at the first game of the 1921 Stanley Cup final marked the largest crowd ever to see a hockey game in Canada at the time. The *Vancouver Sun* reported that there were actually 9,863 tickets sold for the game, but a crowd of more than 10,000 people inside. Crowds were big throughout the series, with the *Sun* reporting that nearly 12,000 fans filled the arena for Game 5, with another 3,000 unable to gain admittance. It's said that 51,000 fans attended the series.

Sprague Cleghorn

Sprague Cleghorn had won the Stanley Cup with Ottawa the year before, but he spent most of the 1920–21 season with the Toronto St. Pats. Ottawa reacquired him immediately after the NHL playoffs and brought him to Vancouver. Cleghorn was a talented defenseman but one of the dirtiest players in hockey history. He played well throughout the Stanley Cup final, but with two minutes to go in the final game, Cleghorn was the third man in after Eddie Gerard and Vancouver's Lloyd Cook got into a fight. All three were awarded match penalties and fined $25.

NHL FINAL
No Series Played

ROSTER

Clint Benedict

George Boucher

Punch Broadbent

Morley Bruce

Sprague Cleghorn

Jack Darragh

Cy Denneny

Eddie Gerard
(captain)

Jack MacKell

Horace Merrill

Frank Nighbor

Tommy Gorman
(manager)

Pete Green (coach)

STANLEY CUP FINAL
3 GAMES TO 2

MAR. 22 ▶	Seattle 2 at Ottawa 3
MAR. 24 ▶	Seattle 0 at Ottawa 3
MAR. 27 ▶	Seattle 3 at Ottawa 1
MAR. 30 ▶	Seattle 5 vs Ottawa 2*
APR. 1 ▶	Seattle 1 vs Ottawa 6*

*Played in Toronto.

PLAYOFF SCORING LEADER

Frank Foyston	GP	G	A	PTS
SEATTLE	7	9	2	11

STANLEY CUP SERIES SCORING

OTTAWA	GP	G	A	PTS	PIM
Frank Nighbor	5	6	1	7	2
Jack Darragh	5	5	2	7	3
Eddie Gerard	5	2	1	3	3
George Boucher	5	2	0	2	2
Cy Denneny	5	0	2	2	3
Sprague Cleghorn	5	0	1	1	4
Punch Broadbent	4	0	0	0	3
Morley Bruce	5	0	0	0	0
Jack MacKell	5	0	0	0	0
GOALTENDER	GP	W	L	MIN	GA	SO	AVG
Clint Benedict	5	3	2	300	11	1	2.20

SEATTLE	GP	G	A	PTS	PIM
Frank Foyston	5	6	1	7	7
Jack Walker	5	1	3	4	0
Bobby Rowe	5	2	1	3	13
Roy Rickey	5	2	0	2	0
Bernie Morris	5	0	2	2	0
Jim Riley	5	0	1	1	0
Muzz Murray	5	0	0	0	5
Sibby Nicholls	5	0	0	0	0
Charlie Tobin	5	0	0	0	0
GOALTENDER	GP	W	L	MIN	GA	SO	AVG
Hap Holmes	5	2	3	300	15	0	3.00

Wishful Thinking

The large crowd that greeted the Seattle team upon their arrival in Ottawa for the Stanley Cup final was a surprise to them. Some 2,000 people were on hand at the Central Station. Luggage and equipment were loaded onto a truck, and the Seattle players were taken to their hotel in limousines. While riding, defenseman Bobby Rowe spotted the Stanley Cup on display in the shop window of the R.J. Devlin Company, a furrier on Sparks Street. "It won't be there long," Rowe remarked. "We are going to take it back to the coast with us."

Ottawa Over Seattle

The NHL grew to four franchises for the 1919–20 season. After the withdrawal of the Toronto Arenas late the previous season, the franchise was purchased by the controlling interests of a senior amateur club known as the St. Patricks. Quebec would also make its NHL debut this season, after being inactive during the league's first two years. Joe Malone returned to Quebec and led the NHL with 39 goals and 49 points, but the team won just four of 24 games. (Quebec folded before the next season and was replaced by the Hamilton Tigers.)

Ottawa was easily the class of the NHL in 1919–20. The Senators won both halves of the NHL split-season schedule, negating the need for a championship playoff. The Senators had a record of 9-3-0 during the first half of the season to edge out Montreal for top spot and then finished well in front of Toronto and Montreal during the second half with a mark of 10-2-0. Frank Nighbor and Jack Darragh led the offense, but defense was the key to Ottawa's success, as it would be throughout the 1920s. Clint Benedict's five shutouts were the most to that point in hockey history, and his 2.66 goals-against average

was nearly two goals a game better than any other NHL netminder.

The race for the two playoff spots in the three-team Pacific Coast Hockey Association (PCHA) was tight all season long with just two wins separating the clubs at year's end. The Seattle Metropolitans clinched first place on the second-last night of the season and finished 12-10-0. The Vancouver Millionaires went 11-11-0, while the Victoria Aristocrats finished last with a record of 10-12-0. In the playoffs, Vancouver beat the Mets 3–1 in Game 1 in Seattle. In Game 2 at Vancouver, PCHA goal-scoring leader Frank Foyston netted a hat trick to pace a 6–0 victory that gave Seattle a 7–3 win in the total-goals series.

Warm weather and bad ice in Ottawa hampered the speedy Seattle team in the Stanley Cup final. After Ottawa won the first two games, Seattle stayed alive in Game 3 and then played their best game of the series after a move to the artificial ice of Toronto's Mutual Street Arena for Game 4. Ottawa bounced back to win the Stanley Cup with a 6–1 victory in Game 5 that was much closer than the score indicated.

Change of Venue

Fluctuating temperatures in Ottawa had people wondering about ice conditions. Though it was hoped that the ice inside the Laurier Avenue Arena would hold up, the NHL booked the Arena in Toronto for March 30th before the series even began. With the forecast calling for further warm weather in Ottawa, after Seattle stayed alive with a win on slushy ice in Game 3, the decision was made to transfer the series to Toronto.

Change of Uniforms PCHA president Frank Patrick wired Ottawa on March 19th to advise the Senators of the similarities between their uniforms and the red, white and green–striped sweaters worn by the Seattle team. The Senators agreed to switch from their usual red, white and black stripes. The Ottawa team would sport white sweaters with a woven red O crest, which were similar to what the team had worn around 1900, during the 1920 Stanley Cup final.

Frank Foyston

PCHA FINAL
Seattle 7 goals to 5 over Vancouver

NHL FINAL
Montreal 4 games to 1 over Ottawa

STANLEY CUP FINAL
2 WINS EACH, 1 TIE AND 1 CANCELLATION

MAR. 19 ► Montreal 0 at Seattle 7

MAR. 22 ► Montreal 4 at Seattle 2

MAR. 24 ► Montreal 2 at Seattle 7

MAR. 26 ► Montreal 0 at Seattle 0 OT

MAR. 29 ► Montreal 4 at Seattle 3 OT

APR. 1 ► Montreal at Seattle CANCELED

PLAYOFF SCORING LEADER

	GP	G	A	PTS
Newsy Lalonde MONTREAL	10	17	2	19

STANLEY CUP SERIES SCORING

MONTREAL	GP	G	A	PTS	PIM
Newsy Lalonde	5	6	0	6	3
Didier Pitre	5	0	3	3	0
Odie Cleghorn	5	2	0	2	9
Louis Berlinguette	5	1	1	2	0
Jack MacDonald	5	1	1	2	3
Bert Corbeau	5	0	1	1	3
Billy Coutu	5	0	1	1	0
Joe Hall	5	0	0	0	6

GOALTENDER	GP	W	L	T	MIN	GA	SO	AVG
Georges Vezina	5	2	2	1	336	19	1	3.39

SEATTLE	GP	G	A	PTS	PIM
Frank Foyston	5	9	1	10	0
Cully Wilson	5	1	3	4	6
Muzz Murray	5	3	0	3	3
Jack Walker	5	3	0	3	9
Roy Rickey	5	1	2	3	0
Ran McDonald	5	1	1	2	3
Bobby Rowe	5	1	0	1	6

GOALTENDER	GP	W	L	T	MIN	GA	SO	AVG
Hap Holmes	5	2	2	1	336	10	2	1.79

Newsy Lalonde

According to Legend...

There have been many stories dating all the way back to newspaper reports in 1919 claiming that the Canadiens caught the Spanish flu in Victoria. People likely believed this was true because it was well-known that several Victoria players had been sick with the flu during the 1918–19 season. But the Canadiens had gone straight to Seattle after playing an exhibition game in Vancouver on March 17th. According to the Canadian Pacific shipping schedule for 1919, the overnight ferry the Canadiens took went directly to Seattle without stopping in Victoria. The Canadiens were scheduled to visit Victoria after the Stanley Cup series, but their exhibition game there had to be postponed.

Optimistic Season Ends in Tragedy

Despite notice that the Quebec franchise was under new ownership and would return to operation, the 1918–19 season opened with the same three teams that had completed the league's first year: the Ottawa Senators, the Montreal Canadiens and the Toronto Arenas.

After four years of war and the more recent Spanish influenza scare, the signing of the armistice to end World War I on November 11, 1918, finally sounded a note of optimism. There was an air of excitement around hockey, and other sports, that there hadn't been in many years. When the Duke of Devonshire showed up at Ottawa's first home game of the season, it marked the fist time since before the war that a governor-general had been on hand to mark the opening of the hockey season.

The Canadiens won the first half of the NHL schedule with a record of 7-3-0. The defending Stanley Cup champions from Toronto opened with six losses in their first seven games and finished last among the three teams at 3-7-0. Ottawa raced out to seven wins in eight games to clinch the second-half title and a spot in the playoffs against Montreal. With Toronto continuing to struggle, both on the ice and at the box office, the Arenas withdrew from the league. The second-half schedule was halted early, and instead of playing a two-game, total-goals series, the Canadiens and Senators met in a best-of-seven. Ottawa had been on a roll, but the Canadiens took the first three games and went on to win the series in five. Newsy Lalonde, who had led the NHL in scoring this season, had 11 goals in the series, including five in Game 3.

In the Pacific Coast Hockey Association (PCHA), Vancouver finished first and Seattle finished second, but Seattle came out on top in the playoffs. After a 6–1 victory in Game 1, Seattle nearly let its five-goal lead slip away. Vancouver won the second game 4–1, but Seattle took the total-goal series 7–5.

In the Stanley Cup final, the Canadiens suffered two lopsided losses under PCHA rules, but they still kept the series close. Sadly, before the final game could be played, several Montreal players became sick with the Spanish flu and the series was canceled. The Canadiens' Joe Hall died of the flu on April 5, 1919.

Borrowing Players

Newspaper reports after the final game was canceled claim that Canadiens manager George Kennedy wanted to complete the series, even if his team had to borrow players from Victoria to do it. Seattle wouldn't let them. Some stories claimed the Metropolitans actually turned Montreal down because they thought that the difficulty of incorporating new players into the Canadiens lineup would have given Seattle an unfair advantage.

Winning by Default
Newspapers also stated that, because Montreal was unable to play the final game, Seattle could have claimed the Stanley Cup by default, but PCHA president Frank Patrick declined to claim the Cup on those grounds.

Why the Tie?

PCHA officials thought that NHL rules called for a game to end in a tie if nobody scored after two 10-minute overtime sessions. When it was learned the next day that their ruling in Game 4 had been incorrect, it was promised that any future overtime games would be played until the winning goal was scored.

Six Months Later...
In October 1919, stories claiming that Montreal would travel to Seattle in December to play a preseason best-of-three series to decide the unfinished Stanley Cup final made the rounds. Frank Patrick quickly stated that it would be impractical to try to get in such a series before the new PCHA season started.

Escape from Alcatraz

Bernie Morris had been a star for Seattle when they beat Montreal to win the Stanley Cup in 1917. He would not get a chance to face the Canadiens when the two teams met again in 1919.

Morris had another fine season with Seattle in 1918–19, collecting 22 goals in 20 games and leading the Mets in scoring for the fourth year in a row. But when Seattle faced Vancouver in the 1919 PCHA playoffs, Morris was not in the lineup. He had been arrested. The United States government had charged him with evading the draft for World War I.

As a Canadian citizen working in the United States, Morris had been registered under the military service act in both countries but had received exemptions in each. His status was changed in the United States, but Morris — who was working in the woods of northern British Columbia in the fall of 1918, according to a story in the *Seattle Post-Intelligencer* — claimed never to have received his notice.

On April 12, 1919, Morris was convicted of being a deserter from the U.S. Army. He was sentenced to serve two years hard labor at Alcatraz, which was a military prison until 1934. Morris appealed the decision in October, but it was upheld.

U.S. census records confirm that Morris was an inmate on Alcatraz Island in January 1920, but he did not serve a full two-year sentence. Morris was released some time before March, when he rejoined Seattle for its Stanley Cup series in Ottawa.

Canceled Cup

On October 16, 1918, the elite of Ottawa's sportsmen gathered. They met not for a game, but for a funeral. Three days earlier Samuel Hamilton Shore had passed away at the age of 32, a victim of Spanish influenza.

The 1919 showdown had all the makings of a classic. Instead, it was a tragedy.

A hometown boy, "Hamby" Shore had spent most of his 14-year hockey career in Ottawa, Ontario. He was a rookie with the "Silver Seven" team that won the Stanley Cup in 1905 and a key contributor to Ottawa's 1911 championship. Though injuries slowed him down during the NHL's first season of 1917–18, he had remained a fan favorite.

"When the whistle blows for the start of the first professional game in Ottawa this winter," wrote the *Ottawa Journal* on October 15, 1918, "sports lovers won't find things quite right when Hamby Shore fails to answer the call."

On the same day as Shore's funeral, tragedy struck the hockey world again when Bob Marshall, the 12-year-old son of future Hockey Hall of Famer Jack Marshall, died of influenza in Montreal. Shore and Bob Marshall were the first members of the hockey fraternity to die of the Spanish flu. They would not be the last.

The epidemic that canceled the 1919 Stanley Cup final is thought to have started at Camp Funston in Kansas in March 1918. From there, American soldiers carried the virus to Europe, where it mutated in the trenches of World War I and spread around the world. (The name "Spanish influenza" resulted from Spain's neutrality during the war. Unlike other European countries, Spain did not censor news of the epidemic's destruction.)

Wounded soldiers brought the disease back to North America in late August of 1918. Its spread was rapid and deadly. During September and October, about 8,500 people died in the city of Chicago, Illinois. In New York City, 851 people died in a single day. Populations weren't as big in Canadian cities, but the numbers were no less scary. In Montreal there were 16,566 cases of Spanish flu reported between October 1 and November 1, 1918. Over 2,800 people died. In Toronto more than 1,600 people died between October 9 and November 2, 1918. Across Canada that October, the Spanish flu killed nearly 1,000 people daily.

In the East, the disease seemed to disappear by December of that year, but in the West, Seattle, Washington, suffered through its worst month of the epidemic. Life finally began to return to normal in January 1919, and there was not a single flu-related death in Seattle during the month of March.

The Montreal Canadiens arrived in Seattle on March 18, 1919. They were looking for revenge. The Canadiens had won the Stanley Cup for the first time in 1916, but the Seattle Metropolitans had dethroned them in 1917. Now Montreal had come west once again to face their rivals from the Pacific Coast Hockey Association. George Kennedy, the owner and manager of the Canadiens, told Royal Brougham of the *Seattle Post-Intelligencer* that his boys were "anxious to avenge their defeat of two years ago."

The 1919 showdown had all the makings of a classic. Instead, it was a tragedy.

"Interest in the opening contest is keen," reported Brougham before Game 1. "Those who wager on the result cannot pick a favorite, all of the betting being at even money, both for the first game and the series."

Though the NHL had adopted forward passing in the neutral zone

Seattle and Montreal were now even, with two wins and one tie apiece. A victory for either team on April 1, 1919, would mean the Stanley Cup. But both sides were clearly tiring.

It wasn't merely fatigue. It was influenza.

On the morning of April 1, George Kennedy and Canadiens players Lalonde, Louis Berlinguette and Bert Corbeau were confined to bed at the Georgian Hotel. McDonald and Joe Hall, with fevers of 104°F, were removed to Providence Hospital. The game that night was canceled. There were reports that the final game might be played in Vancouver, British Columbia, once the Canadiens were healthy, but the series was officially over. No winner was declared.

News of the players' health continued to be reported across Canada. Most of them quickly got better, but not Hall. On April 5, 1919, he died at Seattle's Columbus Sanitarium.

Kennedy never fully recovered and would die in Montreal on October 19, 1921. Hall, Kennedy, Shore and Bob Marshall were among 50,000 Canadians to die during the Spanish influenza epidemic. It has been estimated that the loss of life may have been as high as 100 million people worldwide.

this season, the Canadiens still had trouble with the PCHA rules and Game 1 ended 7–0 for Seattle. George Kennedy wasn't worried.

"We lost every break," he said, "and if [Seattle goalie Hap] Holmes had not played such a sensational game, we would have scored at least half a dozen times. The boys will go into Saturday's battle with lots of confidence and I look for them to win."

Playing under NHL rules, the Canadiens did win, 4–2, with Newsy Lalonde scoring all four goals. However, Seattle's Frank Foyston scored four times in Game 3, with Seattle winning 7–2.

Game 4 on March 26, 1919, was epic. NHL president Frank Calder called it "the most remarkable effort in all hockey annals." His PCHA counterpart, Frank Patrick, described it as "the hardest-played game in hockey history." It ended 0–0 after two 10-minute overtime

Joe Hall, shown here posing for a photograph, died of Spanish flu on April 5, 1919.

....

periods. The Canadiens used all nine players on their roster to get through the game. Seattle used just seven. Mets defenseman Roy Rickey played all 80 minutes. Three nights later he was on the ice for 76 more when the Canadiens scored a 4–3 victory on a goal by Jack McDonald at 15:57 of overtime.

NHL FINAL
10 goals to 7 over Montreal

STANLEY CUP FINAL
3 GAMES TO 2

MAR. 20 ▸ Vancouver 3 at Toronto 5

MAR. 23 ▸ Vancouver 6 at Toronto 4

MAR. 26 ▸ Vancouver 3 at Toronto 6

MAR. 28 ▸ Vancouver 8 at Toronto 1

MAR. 30 ▸ Vancouver 1 at Toronto 2

PLAYOFF SCORING LEADER

	GP	G	A	PTS
Mickey MacKay VANCOUVER	7	7	6	13

STANLEY CUP SERIES SCORING

TORONTO	GP	G	A	PTS	PIM
Alf Skinner	5	8	2	10	18
Harry Mummery	5	0	6	6	21
Harry Cameron	5	3	1	4	12
Corb Denneny	5	3	1	4	0
Reg Noble	5	2	1	3	12
Harry Meeking	5	1	2	3	18
Ken Randall	5	1	0	1	21

GOALTENDER	GP	W	L	MIN	GA	SO	AVG
Hap Holmes	5	3	2	300	21	0	4.20

VANCOUVER	GP	G	A	PTS	PIM
Mickey MacKay	5	5	5	10	12
Cyclone Taylor	5	9	0	9	15
Ran McDonald	5	2	2	4	9
Lloyd Cook	5	2	0	2	12
Barney Stanley	5	2	0	2	6
Si Griffis	5	1	0	1	9
Leo Cook	5	0	0	0	6
Speed Moynes	5	0	0	0	6

GOALTENDER	GP	W	L	MIN	GA	SO	AVG
Hugh Lehman	5	2	3	300	18	0	3.60

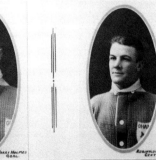

ROSTER

Jack Adams

Harry Cameron

Jack Coughlin

Rusty Crawford

Corb Denneny

Sammy Hebert

Hap Holmes

Jack Marks

Harry Meeking

Harry Mummery

Reg Noble

Ken Randall (captain)

Alf Skinner

Charlie Querrie (manager)

Dick Carroll (coach)

New Boss

When the Toronto Arena Company took control of the hockey team, former lacrosse great Charlie Querrie was put in charge. Querrie posted a set of rules in the Toronto dressing room that included the following: "It does not require bravery to hit another man over the head with a stick. If you want to fight go over to France."

The Birth of the NHL

Professional hockey was in a state of crisis in November 1917. World War I had taken its toll. Many players had become soldiers, and many that hadn't had taken jobs essential to the war effort and were not allowed time off to play hockey. Many amateur leagues across Canada had shut down, and many people wondered why the pro leagues didn't do the same.

In the early years of World War I, the National Hockey Association (NHA) had boasted six franchises. There were four in the Pacific Coast Hockey Association (PCHA). There had also been a thriving professional league in the Maritime Provinces. That league was now gone. The PCHA had moved teams from city to city and was down to just three franchises. People wondered if it would operate at all in 1917–18. There was also speculation that the NHA would go out of business, but in a series of meetings begun on November 22nd and concluded on November 26th, team owners from the NHA formed a new circuit: the National Hockey League.

Originally, the NHL teams were to have been the Ottawa Senators, Montreal Canadiens, Montreal Wanderers (who would withdraw after a fire burned down the Montreal Arena on January 2, 1918) and the Quebec Bulldogs. When Quebec chose not to operate its franchise, the Toronto franchise that had played previously in the NHA and was owned by Eddie Livingstone was offered to the directors of the Toronto Arena. Ousting the troublesome Livingstone from the NHA had been a main reason why the NHL was formed.

The star of the NHL's first season was Joe Malone of the Canadiens, who had 44 goals in just 20 games. The Canadiens won the first half of the NHL's split-season schedule, but Toronto won the second. The Arenas opened the playoffs at home with a 7–3 victory in a rough game. Toronto lost an even rougher return match in Montreal 4–3 but took the total-goals series 10–7.

The PCHA did operate in 1917–18. Seattle finished in first place and tied Vancouver 2–2 in the playoff opener. In Seattle for Game 2, Vancouver won the series with a 1–0 victory and came east to play Toronto in the Stanley Cup final. Toronto won Games 1 and 3 under NHL rules but had trouble with the PCHA rule that allowed forward passing in the neutral zone in Games 2 and 4. Game 5 under NHL rules was the closest of the series. It remained scoreless until Alf Skinner put Toronto on top early in the third period. Cyclone Taylor tied the game midway through the third, but Corb Denneny scored a short time later, and Toronto held on for a 2–1 victory.

No More Room

When Vancouver engraved its win over Seattle in the PCHA playoffs onto the Stanley Cup in 1918, it filled the last available space on the second ring that had been added to the Cup in 1909. No new names were engraved on the Stanley Cup until 1924. The wins by Toronto teams in 1918 and 1922 and by Ottawa in 1920, 1921 and 1923 (as well as information about the canceled Cup series in 1919) were not engraved onto the Cup until 1947–48, when the trophy was remodeled. These team names were added to the new "shoulder" section of the Cup that listed the names of all winning teams dating back to 1893 and would continue to do so until the space there was filled in 1992.

Name Game

What was Toronto's Stanley Cup–winning team in the inaugural season of the NHL really called? Hockey historians and researchers continue to argue over this question. During its years in the NHA, the Toronto hockey club had been called the Blueshirts, though newspapers were just as likely to refer to them as the Torontos. (In fact, Torontos is what was engraved on the Stanley Cup in 1914.) The Toronto Arena Company was given control of the team for the 1917–18 season, but most newspapers still called the team the Blueshirts or the Torontos. The name Arenas didn't really come into common usage until the 1918–19 season — though in many preseason articles in the fall of 1918 newspapers did refer to the defending Stanley Cup champions as the Arenas.

Champs or Chumps?

During the years between 1915 and 1918, three teams engraved their name onto the Stanley Cup even though it seems they hadn't really won it. Or had they?

To some historians and researchers, the fact that an agreement was signed between the NHA and the PCHA in 1913–14 to arrange an annual championship series between their two leagues, and the fact that Stanley Cup trustees quickly agreed to this new arrangement, means that the Stanley Cup ceased to be a challenge trophy and that it would no longer pass automatically to the new champion of one league if it was defeated in the regular-season standings by another team. Others, however, point to the fact that Ottawa in 1915, Portland in 1916 and Vancouver in 1918 all engraved their names on the Cup as proof that the Stanley Cup was still being passed on within a league, and that these three teams should be considered true Stanley Cup champions.

It's impossible to know for sure who is correct. Newspapers of the day offer conflicting reports. Today, an announcement as important as a change in the Stanley Cup's status would be debated endlessly. In the 1910s, the change was reported only briefly in newspapers and seemed to be forgotten each year when it came time for the playoffs.

Interestingly, when the Ottawa Senators engraved their name in 1915, they very specifically engraved the words "NHA Champions." Portland's engraving in 1916 says PCHA champions. Vancouver records only its PCHA victory over Seattle.

633

Winnipeg, on January 31'01.

Dan Bain,

Montreal.

Hearty congratulations you didn't do a thing to them.

Dr. St.John and Bro.

11:12pm

Received from Winnipeg Man 12th Feby 1900

To D Bain

Go Victoria Team

Fat oysters symbol rejoicing another

Joy Shamrock in the soup

Folks at Home

Received From Winnipeg Man 11th Feby 1900

To D Bain

Winnipeg Team

Wish you success in tonights match
is your leg better

CANADIAN PACIFIC RAILWAY COMPANY'S TELEGRAPH

Received at Winnipeg Man 12/2

To D Bain
Windsor Hotel
Montreal

Congratulations on your splendid Victory. Keep it up and bring back the Cup.

Turnock
Morning Telegram

CANADIAN PACIFIC RAILWAY COMPANY'S TELEGRAPH

Received at Winnipeg Man 12/2

To Dan Bain
Windsor Hotel Montreal

Congratulations have a high ball with me

Neilson

CANADIAN PACIFIC RAILWAY COMPANY'S TELEGRAPH

Received at Winnipeg Man 15 Feb 1899

To Dan Bain

Sorry you were hurt old man but you can do them yet, easily — all in bed but us.

Jug Wilson
Fred G Code

211-VH. N. GM. 17 Paid. 2 ex.

Victoria, B.C., February 12, 1900

D. Bain,
Capt. Victoria Hockey Team, of Winnipeg.
Montreal.

Hobble Gobble Razzle Dazzle Cis Boom Bah, Victorias Victorias Rah Rah Rah. Congratulations to all.

B. Gordon Thomson,
Ford Thomson.

11 p.m.

CANADIAN PACIFIC RAILWAY COMPANY'S TELEGRAPH

Received at Winnipeg Man 15 Feby 1900

To Dan Bain

Do not be discouraged. tell the boys Winnipeg has confidence in them. If you win next game you will own the town good luck to you

Hugh J MacDonald

CANADIAN PACIFIC RAILWAY COMPANY'S TELEGRAPH

Received at From Chapleau Ont Feby 16 1899

To Dan Bain

Rumor on train one of boys badly hurt anxious to know, please wire me on no 2 arriving Montreal tomorrow

M E Farwell

Canadian Pacific Railway Company's Telegraph

Received at Winnipeg Man 29 190

To D Bain
Captain Victoria Hockey Club
Windsor Hotel
Montreal

Association conveys warmest congratulations.

Honorary President

Canadian Pacific Railway Company's Telegraph

Received at From Smithsfalls Ont 1 Feb 190

To D Bain
Wpg Hockey Team

Congratulations am proud of you long may cup remain in Winnipeg

Ok Temple

Canadian Pacific Railway Company's Telegraph

467

Winnipeg, Man., Feb. 6, 1901.

Dan Bain,
Capt. Victoria Hockey Club of Winnipeg.
Toronto, Ont.

Trustees rule cup goes to Winnipeg without extra games if win schedule, to postpone the

8:45 p.m.

Before the NHL: 1892–93 to 1916–17

Hockey was strictly an amateur game in Canada in the 1890s. Nobody was paid to play on a team, and there certainly wasn't one big league like the NHL that controlled the Stanley Cup. Train travel meant leagues had to be regional, not national — certainly not international. There were rarely more than six teams in any league in Canada until the mid-1920s, and reliance on cold weather to freeze water into ice meant schedules could stretch only from late December to mid-March.

The Stanley Cup was first presented in 1893 to the hockey club from the Montreal Amateur Athletic Association, who had won the league title in the Amateur Hockey Association of Canada (recognized as the top league in the country). But as Lord Stanley wanted his Cup to be truly representative of a national championship, he instructed his trustees, Philip Dansken Ross and Sheriff John Sweetland, to construct a set of terms that would allow teams from across the country to challenge for the trophy. The Stanley Cup, therefore, was never the sole property of any league, and it could be competed for by the senior champion of any recognized regional association.

Because of the shortness of the hockey seasons in this era, a Stanley Cup challenge might take place at any time throughout the winter. While sometimes it was before or after, the season, often it was right in the middle of the regular schedule of games.

By the beginning of the 1900s, Canadian players were being lured to American cities, where teams could openly pay for players. In response, by the winter of 1906–07, some of the best Canadian teams began to go pro. Professionalism was a controversial issue at the time, but the trustees agreed to let the Stanley Cup go pro, too.

By the 1913–14 season, two professional leagues had emerged as the best in Canada: the National Hockey Association in the east and the Pacific Coast Hockey Association in the west. Beginning in 1914, the champions of the NHA and the PCHA met in an annual series for the Stanley Cup that was often referred to as the World Series of Hockey. In 1915, the PCHA began to expand into the American northwest, bringing cities from the United States into Stanley Cup competition for the first time.

The east–west "World Series" rivalry continued after the NHA gave way to the National Hockey League in 1917–18 and lasted through the winter of 1925–26.

Seattle World's Hockey Champions 1917.

Holmes. Rowe. Carpenter. Walker. Foyston capt. Muldoon mgr. Morris. Wilson. Rickey. Riley

PACIFIC COAST HOCKEY ASSOCIATION

	GP	W	L	T	Pts
Seattle Metropolitans	24	16	8	0	32
Vancouver Millionaires	23	14	9	0	28
Portland Rosebuds	24	9	15	0	18
Spokane Canaries	23	8	15	0	16

NATIONAL HOCKEY ASSOCIATION
First Half

	GP	W	L	T	Pts
Montreal Canadiens	10	7	3	0	14
Ottawa Senators	10	7	3	0	14
228th Battalion	10	6	4	0	12
Toronto Blueshirts	10	5	5	0	10
Montreal Wanderers	10	3	7	0	6
Quebec Bulldogs	10	2	8	0	4

Second Half

	GP	W	L	T	Pts
Ottawa Senators*	10	8	2	0	16
Quebec Bulldogs	10	8	2	0	16
Montreal Canadiens	10	3	7	0	6
Montreal Wanderers	10	2	8	0	4
Toronto Blueshirts°	4	2	2	0	4
228th Battalion^	2	0	2	0	0

*Defeated Canadiens 7–6 in two-game, total-goals NHA playoff.
°Dropped from league on February 11, 1917.
^Called overseas on February 10, 1917.

STANLEY CUP FINAL
3 GAMES TO 1

MAR. 17 ► Montreal Canadiens 8 at Seattle 4

MAR. 20 ► Montreal Canadiens 1 at Seattle 6

MAR. 23 ► Montreal Canadiens 1 at Seattle 4

MAR. 26 ► Montreal Canadiens 1 at Seattle 9

> 66 We were outclassed and you can say for me that Seattle deserved to win the championship and the Cup."
> — Montreal Canadiens owner and manager George Kennedy

> 66 The Canadiens were worthy opponents. While we did defeat them I believe that the fact they were playing under strange conditions and in a different climate had a lot to do with their being so decisively beaten. We are glad to have won the coveted honors for the Pacific Coast."
> — Seattle Metropolitans manager Pete Muldoon

ROSTER

Ed Carpenter

Frank Foyston

Hap Holmes

Bernie Morris

Roy Rickey

Jim Riley

Bobby Rowe (captain)

Jack Walker

Cully Wilson

Peter Muldoon (manager)

The Final

After a long train ride and being forced to play under PCHA rules, the Canadiens were underdogs in Game 1 but surprised Seattle with an 8–4 victory. Didier Pitre led the way with four goals, beating Hap Holmes from long range with his powerful shot. Bernie Morris had three goals in a losing effort. Game 2 was played under NHA rules, but Seattle scored a 6–1 victory. Frank Foyston scored three and Morris had two. The Canadiens had played rough in the first two games, and several penalties to Newsy Lalonde in Game 2 proved costly. Game 3 was the best of the series, with Seattle clinging to a 1–0 lead until three quick goals in the third upped the Mets' lead to 4–0 en route to a 4–1 victory. Once again, Bernie Morris scored three for Seattle. He was even more impressive in Game 4. Morris put Seattle on top at 1:56 of the first period. It was the only goal of the fast-paced first 20 minutes, but Morris scored two more in the second as Seattle pulled out to a 4–0 victory. Rather than sit on their lead, Seattle came out fast once again in the third. Morris scored at 1:20 and would add two more to finish the night with six goals in a 9–1 Stanley Cup victory.

Seattle's Stanley Cup Story

After nearly a year of planning and organizing, brothers Lester and Frank Patrick officially announced the launch of the Pacific Coast Hockey Association (PCHA) on December 7, 1911. At the time, the new league featured teams in the British Columbia cities of Vancouver, Victoria and New Westminster.

In an era when players were expected to remain on the ice for the entire 60 minutes of each game, the Patrick brothers signed only 23 players to fill out the rosters of the three teams in their league. Of the 21 players who were not Frank or Lester, 11 had played the previous season with teams in the National Hockey Association (NHA). There was plenty of friction between the two leagues during the 1911–12 and 1912–13 seasons as players jumped from league to league. A "peace treaty" was signed before the 1913–14 season, supposedly ensuring that the two leagues would recognize each other's contracts and establishing rules for player transactions. The treaty also led to an annual series between the two leagues for the Stanley Cup. But throughout the 1914–15 season, the Patrick brothers came to believe that NHA owners had reneged on the deal. That year, the PCHA had become the first Canadian-based league to place a team in the United States when the New Westminster Royals were transferred to Oregon and became the Portland Rosebuds. When the Patricks decided to add an expansion team in Washington State for the 1915–16 season, they once again raided the NHA, signing several key members of the 1914 Stanley Cup–champion Toronto Blueshirts to form the core of the Seattle Metropolitans.

With star forwards Frank Foyston and Jack Walker, plus tough guy Cully Wilson and goalie Hap Holmes from Toronto, as well as Bernie Morris, who was acquired from Victoria, Seattle was instantly competitive. The Mets drew good crowds at home, but a poor road record saw them finish the 18-game season with nine wins and nine losses.

A new treaty between the two leagues in the fall of 1916 ended the "Hockey War," but with World War I still raging, the arena in Victoria was commandeered by the Canadian army. The Victoria Aristocrats moved to Spokane, giving the PCHA three American franchises and just one in Canada. Seattle had its entire eight-man roster from the inaugural season back in 1916–17 and added Jim Riley, who had spent the previous season in Victoria (and would later become the only person in history to play both NHL hockey and Major League baseball). The Mets got off to a slow start to the newly expanded 24-game season but came on strong to beat out the Vancouver Millionaires for top spot.

Vancouver's Gord Roberts was the PCHA's top goal-scorer with 43, but Seattle's Bernie Morris had 37 goals and 17 assists to edge out Roberts by one point in the scoring race. Frank Foyston had 36 goals and 12 assists and was named the league's most valuable player in a poll of sportswriters. Jack Walker was the league's best defensive forward, and Hap Holmes was the only PCHA goalie to post a shutout (he had two), which went along with his 3.28 average, easily the league's best.

As the PCHA would not introduce a playoff system until the following season, Seattle's first-place finish entitled them to host the champions from the NHA. Seattle defeated the Montreal Canadiens three games to one and became the first American-based team to win the Stanley Cup.

After the Series

With the best-of-five Stanley Cup final wrapping up in four games, Seattle and Montreal played a final exhibition game on March 28th. Seattle won 9–7. The two teams then caught a boat for San Francisco, where they played a three-game series at the Winter Garden skating rink. Hockey teams from the University of California, Stanford and other local clubs had played at the downtown arena between Sutter and Post at Pierce Street throughout the winter of 1916–17, but the series between Seattle and Montreal (won two games to one by Montreal) marked the debut of pro hockey in California. "I'd certainly like to see the game established there," said Canadiens owner George Kennedy, who envisioned a four-team league in San Francisco, Oakland, Sacramento and Los Angeles. But, acknowledging it would cost several hundred thousand dollar to build suitable arenas, Kennedy wondered, "Who is going to take the gamble?"

The NHA Season

With more and more players enlisting for World War I and others forced to take jobs essential to the war effort, fans were beginning to turn away from hockey. People questioned why fit, young men should be paid to play games instead of joining the army. During the summer of 1916, there was talk of suspending the National Hockey Association, but come October it was clear the league would carry on. A new split-season format would introduce a postseason playoff, and it was hoped the addition of an army team would help boost attendance.

The 228th Battalion played out of the Mutual Street Arena along with the Toronto Blueshirts. Most of its 12 players had previous experience in the NHA or the PCHA, and many people thought they might win the league championship. The army team got off to a fast start with four lopsided wins but faded to finish behind Montreal and Ottawa. The Canadiens claimed top spot in the first-half standings with a better goal differential than the Senators.

Early in the second half, the 228th Battalion had to withdraw when the unit was sent overseas. In an effort to balance the remaining schedule, the other NHA owners voted to drop the Blueshirts as well and distribute Toronto's players around the league. Heading into the final night of the season, Ottawa needed to beat Quebec by seven goals to win the second half, and the Senators romped to a 16–1 victory. The Canadiens had been playing poorly, but they beat Ottawa 5–2 in the first playoff game and hung on to win the series 7–6 despite a 4–2 loss in Game 2.

THE CANADIAN HOCKEY CLUB INCORPORATED

NEWSY LALONDE Manager   G.W. KENDALL Treas.   D.P. BOUCHER President   NAP. DORVAL Secy.   DIDIER PITRE

COUPE STANLEY

BERLINGUETTE   AMOS ARBOUR   JACK LAVIOLETTE   BERT. CORBEAU   GOLDIE PRODGERS   HOWARD McNAMARA

1915   GEORGES VEZINA   1916

S. NEWSWORTHY   SKENE RONAN   G.V. POULIN   A. OUIMET

THE STANLEY CUP HOLDERS   CUPE O'BRIEN   CHAMPIONS OF THE WORLD

MONTREAL CANADA

ROSTER

Amos Arbour

Louis Berlinguette

Bert Corbeau

Jack Fournier

Newsy Lalonde

Jack Laviolette

Howard McNamara
(captain)

Didier Pitre

Skinner Poulin

Goldie Prodger

Skene Ronan

Georges Vezina

George Kennedy
(manager)

America First
Charles Uksila of the Portland Rosebuds is believed to be the first American-born player to compete for the Stanley Cup. The native of Calumet, Michigan, played just seven games for Portland during the 1915–16 season, but he saw action in all five Stanley Cup games versus Montreal. He scored two goals.

After the Series
The Canadiens and the Rosebuds headed to New York City for a two-game series at the St. Nicholas Arena. The Canadiens won 6–3 on April 4th. The next night, Portland won 4–2. The game was 4–1 after 60 minutes, but then Goldie Prodger set up Didier Pitre in overtime to give the Canadiens an 8–7 total-goals victory.

Settling an Old Score
Ernie "Moose" Johnson of the Rosebuds made his first appearance in Montreal since jumping from the Wanderers to the PCHA in 1911. Wanderers owner Sam Lichtenhein had sued him for $2,000 and threatened to garnish Johnson's wages from the Stanley Cup series, which, as a losing player, came to only $207. It's unclear if Johnson had to pay it.

❝Lalonde took the puck from Vezina and skated around the goal, yelling to Prodger as he turned away with the puck. Prodger, starting from his wing position, skated towards his corner, took the rubber from Lalonde and was off, Lalonde, meanwhile, for a moment, dribbling an imaginary puck. Prodger had, however, a rough journey. After dodging past [two] forwards, he ... beat [left winger Smokey] Harris in a rush for center ice by swinging sharply off at an angle, and a moment later with a body check toppled [defenseman Del] Irvine over. Ernie Johnson he easily outskated. Then, drawing [goalie Tom] Murray out while dribbling the puck around, Prodger skated around him and lobbed the rubber into the net for the winning score. The whole Canadiens team for the remaining four minutes confined themselves to defensive play."

—Newspaper account of the Stanley Cup–winning goal

The Canadiens' First Cup

The 1915–16 hockey season in the National Hockey Association (NHA) and the Pacific Coast Hockey Association (PCHA) didn't get started until December, but trouble off the ice began near the end of October. The two leagues had been negotiating since April to extend the "peace treaty" they had first signed in 1913, when PCHA president Frank Patrick officially informed the NHA in a letter to Sam Lichtenhein of the Montreal Wanderers on October 26, 1916, that he was breaking relations between the two leagues.

Patrick was angry that the Montreal Canadiens had never paid his Vancouver Millionaires the $750 they had agreed to when Newsy Lalonde was returned from Vancouver to Montreal prior to the 1913–14 season. He was further angered (and claimed to be in possession of "documentary evidence") that the management of the Ottawa Senators had been attempting to lure Cyclone Taylor away from Vancouver by using their friendship with members of the Canadian government to have the Department of Immigration transfer Taylor's civil service job back to Ottawa. Patrick also cited the "general failure of the NHA to transact its dealings with the PCHA in a business-like and satisfactory manner."

Though opinions were divided as to which league was really at fault, newspapers across Canada trumpeted that the "Hockey War" of previous seasons was back on. Cyclone Taylor remained in Vancouver, but the Senators signed Frank Nighbor away from the Millionaires, while Bert Lindsay (father of Ted Lindsay) and Walter Smaill left Victoria to sign with the Montreal Wanderers. The key defections going the other way were Frank Foyston, Jack Walker, Hap Holmes, Cully Wilson and Ed Carpenter, who all left the Toronto Blueshirts to join the new PCHA team in Seattle.

With the break between the two leagues, hockey fans wondered what would become of the Stanley Cup. Vancouver had won it in 1915, and Frank Patrick announced that the Millionaires would return the trophy to the Stanley Cup trustees if that was what they wanted, saying "we are through with the NHA." There were questions all season long as to what would happen, and when the Portland Rosebuds emerged as the PCHA champions, Patrick left it up to the team to decide if they wanted to face the NHA champions. Finally, on March 7,

1916, the Rosebuds confirmed they would play for the Stanley Cup. They left for the East on March 13th and arrived in Montreal on March 19th, just one day before their series against the NHA-champion Canadiens began.

The PCHA season had wrapped up on February 25th. Since then, the Rosebuds had played just three exhibition games and another during a stop in Houghton, Michigan, on their way to Montreal. They had time only for a light workout, no full practice, before the Stanley Cup series. The Canadiens, on the other hand, had just played their final game of the NHA season on March 18th and were on a roll with seven straight wins. Portland wasn't given much of a chance in Game 1, but the Rosebuds outskated and outplayed the NHA champs for a 2–0 victory that was only as close as it was because of the fine play of Georges Vezina.

With Game 2 being played under PCHA rules, Portland was expected to have the advantage this time—especially with Montreal stars Newsy Lalonde and Jack Laviolette out of the lineup. Montreal took little advantage of the forward pass allowed in the PCHA, but with Vezina again starring in goal, the Canadiens evened the series with a 2–1 victory. Lalonde and Laviolette returned for Game 3 and helped linemate and fellow future Hall of Famer Didier Pitre score three goals in a 6–3 Montreal victory. The game was marred by a third-period brawl that required police intervention to end the fighting.

Game 4 was a wide-open affair, and the Rosebuds stayed alive with a 6–5 victory. For the first time since the best-of-five format was introduced in 1914, a Stanley Cup final was stretched to the limit. In fact, outside of a few one-sided, one-game challenge matches, the 1916 series marked the first time since the Ottawa Hockey Club (Silver Seven) beat Rat Portage in a best-of-three affair in 1905 that a series had come down to winner-take-all.

After a penalty-filled first period, the two teams settled down to play hockey. Skene Ronan had put the Canadiens out front late in the first, and after a scoreless second period, Portland came out hard to open the third. Just over six minutes in, Tommy Dunderdale tied the game. Both teams had chances to score before Goldie Prodger went end to end for the winning goal with under four minutes remaining. It was the first of 24 Stanley Cup championships for the Montreal Canadiens.

America's Cup

The first official Stanley Cup inquiry from an American team came in 1907, when Pittsburgh's entry in the International Hockey League announced hopes to challenge for the prized trophy. On February 15, 1907, the *Globe* newspaper in Toronto reported that P.D. Ross would refuse the challenge. "Trustee Ross of the Stanley Cup says the trophy is for Canadian competition only," as Lord Stanley had intended.

Five years later, trustee William Foran refused to even accept the idea of two Canadian teams playing for the Stanley Cup on American ice. With talk of moving games to the artificial ice rink in Boston to allow a late challenge in 1912, Foran announced: "Defending teams may play for the silverware in any rink or in any city they may choose, but not in the United States. The Cup was donated for the championship of Canada, and we will certainly oppose any move to play for it outside the Dominion." Then, suddenly, in the heat of the dispute between the PCHA and NHA prior to the 1915–16 season, the trustees dramatically changed their tune. "The Stanley Cup is not emblematic of the Canadian honors," newspapers widely quoted Foran as announcing on December 8, 1915, "but of the hockey championship of the world. Hence, if Portland or Seattle were to win ... they would be allowed to [claim] the trophy."

No doubt this announcement was meant to ease the tension between the two leagues and help keep the peace in professional hockey.

Vancouver Millionaires

ROSTER

- Lloyd Cook
- Si Griffis (captain)
- Hugh Lehman
- Mickey MacKay
- Ken Mallen
- Johnny Matz
- Frank Nighbor
- Jim Seaborn
- Barney Stanley
- Cyclone Taylor
- Frank Patrick (player-manager)

STANDINGS

PACIFIC COAST HOCKEY ASSOCIATION

	GP	W	L	T	Pts
Vancouver Millionaires	17	13	4	0	26
Portland Rosebuds	18	9	9	0	18
Victoria Aristocrats	17	4	13	0	8

NATIONAL HOCKEY ASSOCIATION

	GP	W	L	T	Pts
Ottawa Senators*	20	14	6	0	28
Montreal Wanderers	20	14	6	0	28
Quebec Bulldogs	20	11	9	0	22
Toronto Blueshirts	20	8	12	0	16
Toronto Ontarios/ Shamrocks	20	7	13	0	14
Montreal Canadiens	20	6	14	0	12

*Defeated Wanderers 4–1 in two-game, total-goals NHA playoff.

STANLEY CUP FINAL
3 GAMES TO 0

MAR. 22 ►	Ottawa 2 at Vancouver 6
MAR. 24 ►	Ottawa 3 at Vancouver 8
MAR. 26 ►	Ottawa 3 at Vancouver 12

> 66 The Stanley Cup is going West. Coach Alf Smith says so, and Ottawa admits the corn. Why wouldn't they? The Vancouver team beat them away off under both sets of rules. It looks as if the real margin of difference lies in the fact that the Westerners play seven-man hockey. This begets real combination, something which the six-man game stultifies to a large extent. The result is that in the seven-man game the Ottawas are lost, while the Westerners bring their combination to play in the six-man game.... The Ottawas—for a wonder—have no kick. The Westerners have beaten them so decisively that they must accept defeat as gracefully as possible."
> — *Toronto Star*, March 26, 1915, prior to Game 3 of the Stanley Cup final

Name Game

As was the custom at the time, when the Vancouver Millionaires won the Stanley Cup in 1915, they had the basic facts of their victory engraved onto a silver band beneath the original bowl: "Vancouver B.C. / 1914–15 / Defeated Ottawa / 3 Straight Games." But the Millionaires also had the names of their players engraved inside the Stanley Cup bowl, within the decorative flutes around the sides of the bowl.

The Millionaires were just the second team to engrave player names on the Stanley Cup. It seems likely that Frank Patrick had his name engraved, along with the rest of the Vancouver players, because his brother Lester Patrick had been among the players whose names were engraved on the bottom of the bowl when the Montreal Wanderers became the first team to do so in 1907.

The Cup Comes to the Coast

After winning the Stanley Cup with the Montreal Wanderers in 1906 and 1907, Lester Patrick moved to Nelson, British Columbia, to help his father run the family lumber business, which had moved west from Quebec. "I was sure that all of my hockey days were now behind me," Lester would write, but there was a vibrant hockey scene in the BC interior, with strong teams in small towns such as Grand Forks, Rossland, Greenwood and Phoenix. Frank Patrick arrived in Nelson in 1908.

Lester Patrick planned for a Nelson-based team with added recruits such as former Kenora Thistles stars Tom Phillips, Si Griffis and Roxy Beaudro (who were all living in Vancouver) to challenge for the Stanley Cup in 1908–09. That challenge never panned out, nor did another challenge discussed after Nelson won the BC championship in 1909. Still, the Patrick brothers had big plans for their new hometown.

In March 1909, the *Edmonton Bulletin* reported that Frank and Lester were trying to organize a Western Canada professional hockey league with teams in Saskatchewan, Alberta and British Columbia. Nothing came of those plans, but the brothers used the sale of the Patrick Lumber Company in January 1911 to finance a new pro league. Even as late as October 1911, newspapers speculated about teams in Vancouver, Victoria, Nelson, Calgary and Edmonton. In the end, the Pacific Coast Hockey Association (PCHA) opened for the 1911–12 season with Patrick-owned teams in Victoria and Vancouver plus a third team based in New Westminster that would play at the 10,000-seat arena the Patricks built in Vancouver. (They also built a smaller arena in Victoria.)

Lester Patrick would later write that he and his brother had their former teammate Cyclone Taylor in mind for their new league "right from the beginning." However, it would take until the PCHA's second season of 1912–13 for Frank Patrick to land Taylor for the Millionaires. He had been a star defenseman in the East, but with the PCHA maintaining the seven-man game, Taylor was converted to rover. He quickly became an offensive force, but it took two more years for Vancouver to enjoy the success people had been expecting.

Several newcomers joined the Millionaires for the 1914–15 season. Goalie Hugh Lehman was acquired after three seasons with New Westminster, while Lloyd Cook, Mickey MacKay and Barney Stanley joined the team as PCHA rookies. All but Cook were future Hall of Famers, as were returning players Taylor, Frank Patrick, Si Griffis and Frank Nighbor, meaning Vancouver had seven future Hall of Famers among their 11 players this season. The Millionaires romped through the 1914–15 campaign, opening the season with six straight wins. After a brief slump, they won six in a row again before their last game was canceled. Mickey MacKay led the league with 33 goals in 17 games, though his total of 44 points had him one behind teammate Cyclone Taylor in the scoring race. (Sources list Taylor with either 23 goals and 22 assists or 24 and 21). Frank Nighbor added 23 goals, while Barney Stanley added seven in just five games.

With nearly three weeks off between their last game of the season and the start of the Stanley Cup final, Vancouver played three exhibition games against a team of PCHA all-stars. The Millionaires won all three games but lost captain Si Griffis when he suffered a broken leg. NHA president Emmett Quinn denied Vancouver's request to replace Griffis with Lester Patrick. Frank Patrick was confident of his team's ability to beat the Ottawa Senators for the Stanley Cup—even without their big defenseman.

Cyclone Taylor scored twice, and Frank Nighbor played his usual strong two-way game in a 6–2 Vancouver win in the opener against Ottawa. The Senators were uncomfortable with the PCHA rules, and coach Alf Smith said the forward pass "makes a farce out of the game." The *Vancouver Province* thought it was doubtful that Ottawa could have beaten Vancouver "under any old rules," but the Senators vowed to be better under NHA rules in Game 2. Ottawa led 2–0 after one period, but three goals from Taylor in a six-goal Vancouver second sparked the Millionaires to an 8–3 victory. Five goals from Barney Stanley (though some sources only credit him with four) and two more from Taylor highlighted a 12–3 win for the series sweep. "You have a great team here," admitted Ottawa manager Frank Shaughnessy as the Stanley Cup headed west of Winnipeg for the first time.

Toronto Blueshirts

NATIONAL HOCKEY ASSOCIATION

	GP	W	L	T	Pts
Toronto Blueshirts*	20	13	7	0	26
Montreal Canadiens	20	13	7	0	26
Quebec Bulldogs	20	12	8	0	24
Ottawa Senators	20	11	9	0	22
Montreal Wanderers	20	7	13	0	14
Toronto Ontarios	20	4	16	0	8

*Defeated Canadiens 6–2 in two-game, total-goals NHA playoff.

PACIFIC COAST HOCKEY ASSOCIATION

	GP	W	L	T	Pts
Victoria Aristocrats	16	10	6	0	20
New Westminster Royals	16	7	9	0	14
Vancouver Millionaires	16	7	9	0	12

STANLEY CUP FINAL
3 GAMES TO 0

MAR. 14 ▶ Victoria 2 at Toronto 5

MAR. 17 ▶ Victoria 5 at Toronto 6 OT

MAR. 19 ▶ Victoria 1 at Toronto 2

> 66 I knew the boys could do it, and they played with every ounce that was in them. It was a rough, hard-checking contest from start to finish, but we were always going strong, and I was sure that we would make it three straight. We will be back next season to defend the Stanley Cup, and the boys are glad the long grind is over."
> — Jack Marshall, player, coach and manager of the Toronto Blueshirts

> 66 Torontos are champions and deserve all the credit that is theirs. We never had as hard a battle in our whole Coast League season and I think the Torontos will tell you that they have had few harder battles at any time than we gave them tonight. [Dubbie] Kerr came close to tying it up right at the finish, but that is the luck of the game, and we have no excuses to offer."
> — Lester Patrick, player, coach, manager and owner of the Victoria Aristocrats

The Winner's Share Attendance was less than expected during the 1914 Stanley Cup series. It had been thought that the winner's share might come to $600 to $800 per player, but, in fact, the members of the Toronto team received only $297 apiece. The team's owners also commissioned commemorative medals, which the players received in May. The medals featured the Stanley Cup in relief with a pair of crossed hockey sticks in the background. One side of the medal was finished in dull gold while the other side bore the player's name engraved in script. "Torontos, professional hockey champions of the world," appeared in bold lettering around the Stanley Cup.

Cup on Display Senator Phillipe-Auguste Choquette, president of the 1912 and 1913 champion Quebec Bulldogs, was requested to return the Stanley Cup to trustee William Foran after the Blueshirts won the NHA title. When the Stanley Cup arrived in Toronto, it was displayed in the window of Eaton's department store.

Toronto's First Cup Title

Though Toronto had a strong reputation as an amateur hockey hotbed, the city had been among the first in Canada to ice an openly professional team during the winter of 1906–07. The Toronto team played only exhibition games, but it was instrumental in forming the Ontario Professional Hockey League in November 1907. Toronto seemed to be done with the pro game when the National Hockey Association (NHA) was formed in 1909–10, but then the city landed two franchises for the 1911–12 NHA season.

Toronto's entries into the NHA was contingent upon the completion of a new artificial ice rink, but when it became apparent that the Arena Gardens (later known as the Mutual Street Arena) would not be ready on time, the Toronto teams were dropped from the schedule. Each would make its debut in 1912–13. The two new teams were the Tecumsehs and the Toronto Hockey Club, who would be more commonly known as the Torontos or the Blueshirts (sometimes Blue Shirts) for the color of their sweaters. The Toronto entries took very different approaches to team building, with the Tecumsehs loading up on veterans while the Blueshirts went mainly with younger players out of amateur hockey or lower level professional teams. One exception was veteran Jack Marshall, who soon became the team's playing coach and manager. In addition to Marshall, the players signed for the Blueshirts included Hap Holmes, Scotty Davidson, Frank Foyston, Jack Walker (who played just one game but returned in 1913–14), Frank Nighbor and Harry Cameron, giving the team seven future Hall of Famers. Even so, the Blueshirts finished in the middle of the pack with a 9-11-0 record in 1912–13, as five of the six NHA teams were tightly bunched behind the defending Stanley Cup–champion Quebec Bulldogs, who ran away with the title with a record of 16-4-0.

The Blueshirts lost Frank Nighbor to Vancouver before the 1913–14 season, but they had most of their roster back and picked up another future Hall of Famer in George McNamara. They got off to a fast start this year with six wins in their first eight games, but they couldn't shake the Montreal Canadiens down the stretch. Scotty Davidson (23 goals, 13 assists) and Jack Walker (20 and 16) led the offense in Toronto. Hap Holmes established himself as one of the game's top goalies as the Blueshirts

tied Georges Vezina and the Montreal Canadiens for the league's best defensive record. When the Blueshirts lost and the Canadiens won on the final night of the season, the two teams finished in a tie for top spot and a playoff was necessary to determine the NHA champion. Playing on slushy ice in Montreal on March 7, 1914, the Canadiens won the opener 2–0. On the artificial ice in Toronto four nights later, the Blueshirts got three goals from Walker, two from Davidson and one from Frank Foyston. Harry Cameron and Jack Marshall proved impregnable on defense as the Blueshirts scored a 6–0 victory and won the total-goals playoff 6–2.

Before the season, the NHA and the PCHA had signed an agreement regarding contracts and player transactions that also set up an annual best-of-five postseason series between the two league champions to be played in the East and West in alternating years. There would be newspaper reports questioning the PCHA's right to play for the Stanley Cup this season, but as winners of the NHA, the Blueshirts took on the Victoria Aristocrats for the prized trophy.

The Blueshirts won the opener 5–2 under NHA rules, and though the score was only 2–1 entering the third period, it was considered to be an easy victory. Victoria was "outplayed in every department by the Torontos," according to the *Toronto World*, whose reporter thought, "The Stanley Cup is not much in danger of going west."

Playing under PCHA rules in Game 2, the general opinion seemed to be that the Blueshirts were lucky to win, but win they did. Frank Foyston scored twice in the third period to erase a 5–3 Victoria lead, and Roy McGiffin scored after 18 minutes of overtime for a 6–5 Toronto victory. Game 3 was a rough one, with plenty of slashes, elbows and cross-checks as well as a third-period "boxing bout" between Scotty Davidson and Victoria's Bob Genge. Foyston got the Blueshirts on the scoreboard early in the second period, and Harry Cameron's goal seven minutes into the third held up as the Stanley Cup–winner in a 2–1 victory. The game marked the last ever played by Scotty Davidson. The young Toronto captain would trade in his hockey blue for army green shortly after World War I began in August 1914 and was killed in action on June 16, 1915.

The PCHA Season

Though he and his brother Lester had run the PCHA since its inception (as well as played for, coached, managed and owned the teams in Victoria and Vancouver), the 1913–14 season marked the first year that Frank Patrick served as league president.

Before Frank took office, the Patrick brothers had concluded an agreement with NHA president Emmett Quinn on September 4, 1913, to form a hockey commission to oversee the pro game and stop the squabbling and contract jumping that had marked the relationship between the two leagues. Within days, there was talk of speeding up the play in both leagues with a new rule to add blue lines to the ice and allow forward passing in the neutral zone. It was decided to test the rule in the PCHA, which debuted the forward pass in an exhibition game between Vancouver and Victoria on November 28, 1913. By December 13th, Frank Patrick had written to Emmett Quinn recommending the new rule to the NHA, but forward passing would not be introduced in the East until the 1918–19 NHL season.

Lester Patrick broke his arm and did not play for Victoria until midway through the schedule. The Aristocrats were 4-5-0 and in last place in the three-team league before rattling off six straight wins en route to their second straight PCHA title. Victoria's Tommy Dunderdale tied Cyclone Taylor for the league lead with 24 goals and scored at least once in each of the Aristocrats' 16 games. Dunderdale's teammates were all on hand when he was married in Victoria on February 28, 1914, the day after the season ended.

Quebec Bulldogs

NATIONAL HOCKEY ASSOCIATION

	GP	W	L	T	Pts
Quebec Bulldogs	20	16	4	0	32
Montreal Wanderers	20	10	10	0	20
Ottawa Senators	20	9	11	0	18
Toronto Blueshirts	20	9	11	0	18
Montreal Canadiens	20	9	11	0	18
Toronto Tecumsehs	20	7	13	0	14

MARITIME PROFESSIONAL HOCKEY LEAGUE

	GP	W	L	T	Pts
Sydney Millionaires	16	11	5	0	22
New Glasgow Cubs	16	10	6	0	20
Moncton Victorias	16	9	7	0	18
Halifax Socials	16	8	8	0	16
Halifax Crescents	16	2	14	0	4

PACIFIC COAST HOCKEY ASSOCIATION

	GP	W	L	T	Pts
Victoria Aristocrats*	15	10	5	0	20
Vancouver Millionaires	16	7	9	0	14
New Westminster Royals	15	6	9	0	12

*Did not challenge for Stanley Cup.

POSTSEASON STANLEY CUP CHALLENGE
20 GOALS TO 5

MAR. 8 ▸ Sydney 3 at Quebec 14

MAR. 10 ▸ Sydney 2 at Quebec 6

> "Quebec will beat them away worse than they beat Moncton last year, because the Moncton team last year was a much better team than the Sydney outfit."
> — Former Ottawa star Alf Smith, who coached briefly in Moncton, speaking prior to Game 1 of the Sydney-Quebec Stanley Cup challenge.

> "Quebec administered a crushing defeat to the Sydney team…. Considering that the NHA furnishes a far superior organization to that in the lower provinces the showing made by the challengers was up to expectations, but few if any looked for Quebec to pile up such a score in the opening fixture."
> — *Quebec Daily Telegraph* after Game 1

ROSTER

Rusty Crawford

Billy Creighton

Joe Hall

Jeff Malone

Joe Malone (captain)

Jack Marks

Paddy Moran

Harry Mummery

Rockett Power

Tommy Smith

Mike Quinn (manager)

Bulldogs on Broadway

Between their Stanley Cup victory over Sydney and their exhibition loss in Victoria, the Bulldogs made a quick visit to New York City for a two-game, total-goals set against the Montreal Wanderers. The Wanderers took the first game 9–5 and hung on to win the series despite a 5–3 loss in Game 2.

He Ain't Heavy

Quebec's Jeff Malone was Joe Malone's older brother, but he is known to have played just eight games at hockey's highest level over five seasons and is not credited with a single goal.

The Original Rocket

Although Maurice Richard is the most famous "Rocket" in Stanley Cup history, he was not the first to win the prized trophy. James Power of the 1912–13 Quebec Bulldogs went by his middle name of Rockett, which was the maiden name of his mother, Annie Gavan Rockett. Unlike Maurice Richard in Montreal, Rockett Power didn't contribute much to Quebec's Stanley Cup victory. He only played one game with the Bulldogs that season.

Back to Back for the Bulldogs

The Quebec Bulldogs had won the Stanley Cup in 1911–12 but seemed to be in trouble as the 1912–13 season approached. There were reports in the fall of 1912 of a possible agreement to form a hockey commission between the National Hockey Association (NHA) and the Pacific Coast Hockey Association (PCHA), but it would take another year before that came to pass. When negotiations broke down, the battle for players between the two leagues became even worse than it had been the year before.

Among those who switched leagues this year were future Hall of Famers Cyclone Taylor, who signed with Vancouver after a pair of season with the Renfrew Hockey Club, and Newsy Lalonde, who left the Vancouver Millionaires to return to the Montreal Canadiens. Amid reports of players moving east and west was a rumor that the Patrick brothers had made offers to every player on the Quebec team to jump to the PCHA. Of the seven players who had seen the bulk of the action for the Bulldogs in 1911–12, the Patricks were able to sign three: Goldie Prodger, Eddie Oatman and Jack McDonald. Fortunately for the defending champions, suitable replacements were found. Bruising defenseman Harry Mummery and future Hall of Famer Rusty Crawford were acquired by Quebec after playing pro hockey in Saskatchewan. The Bulldogs also signed another future Hall of Famer in Tommy Smith, a perennial top scorer whose talent had taken him to several different professional leagues in recent years.

The new NHA season began on December 25, 1912, and by the end of January the Montreal Canadiens held top spot with a record of 7-3-0. The Wanderers and Bulldogs were tied for second at 5-4-0, but from that point on Quebec rattled off 11 straight wins, breaking Ottawa's record of 10 in a row, which dated back to the 1910–11 season. They easily won the NHA title for the second straight year and retained the Stanley Cup. Joe Malone, who had enjoyed a breakout season with a team-leading 21 goals in 18 games for Quebec in 1911–12, emerged as a true superstar this year, notching a league-leading 43 goals in 20 games. Tommy Smith was a close second with 39. Joe Hall and Harry Mummery gave the Bulldogs the league's toughest defense in front of goalie Paddy Moran.

Three days after the NHA season ended, Quebec defended the Stanley Cup against the Sydney Millionaires, and the Bulldogs romped past the Maritime champions with a pair of one-sided victories.

The PCHA Challenge

In October 1912, while in the East hunting for players, Lester Patrick, owner of the Victoria Aristocrats, spoke of his desire to do away with the Stanley Cup. Patrick saw little way to make any money from the total-goals series the Cup trustees seemed to favor. No doubt inspired by the thrilling baseball championship recently won by the Boston Red Sox over the New York Giants, Lester was quoted on October 18, 1912, by the *Globe* newspaper as saying, "My idea is to have a series of games, such as the World Series, to decide the championship — not a series of two games, but one of seven or more, which would decide beyond all question which is the better team."

The 1912–13 PCHA season got under way on December 10th. With Cyclone Taylor on their roster, many predicted a championship for Frank Patrick's Vancouver Millionaires. But as the season reached its midway point on January 31st, it was Lester Patrick's Victoria Aristocrats who were comfortably in front. Despite what Lester had said in October, he announced that Victoria would challenge for the Stanley Cup if the Aristocrats won the PCHA championship. However, with Quebec pulling away in the NHA, Lester realized he would not even be able to cover expenses if he took his team nearly 3,000 miles (4,800 km) to play a two-game series in the tiny, old arena in Quebec City. The Stanley Cup trustees would have allowed Quebec to play for the trophy on neutral ice in Toronto or out West in Victoria, but the Bulldogs would only defend the Stanley Cup at home. When Quebec did agree to travel to Victoria to face the Aristocrats, many newspapers reported that the Stanley Cup would be at stake, but the *Victoria Colonist* of March 2, 1913, had been quite clear that it would not be: "As for putting [up] the Stanley Cup as the stake, [Bulldogs manager Mike Quinn] said that was absurd. Quebec will only defend the Stanley Cup at the Ancient Capital."

Victoria defeated Quebec two games to one amid widespread speculation that this "World's Professional Series" would mark the end of the Stanley Cup as hockey's top trophy.

Maritime Disaster

The Sydney Millionaires and a large number of their fans arrived in Quebec City early on Friday morning, March 7th, the day before the start of their Stanley Cup challenge. The team had a fast workout at the Quebec rink from 1:30 to 2:30 that afternoon.

"The challengers, although not boasting," reported the *Quebec Daily Telegraph*, "are probably more confident of lifting the Cup than the Moncton Victorias were last year." Quebec fans were busy snapping up copies of a souvenir booklet the *Telegraph* was selling for 10 cents. They could also purchase a set of eight postcards depicting the Bulldogs players for 40 cents. Because the two teams had similar uniforms, the Millionaires decided to wear sweaters offered by the Quebec Sporting Association.

It became apparent shortly after the opening faceoff that Sydney wasn't going to put up much of a fight. Despite playing with a bad cold, Joe Malone scored his first of nine goals on the night just 1:30 into the first period. Sydney responded with the next two goals, but it was 4–2 Quebec after one. The Bulldogs scored seven times in the second period and then used spares Jeff Malone and Billy Creighton to replace Joe Hall and Tommy Smith in the third as they cruised to a 14–3 victory. Creighton replaced Rusty Crawford and Jack Marks played in place of Joe Malone for Game 2, but Quebec still scored an easy 6–2 victory. The most interesting play in the game came near the end, when Bulldogs goalie Paddy Moran made an end-to-end rush and nearly scored.

NATIONAL HOCKEY ASSOCIATION

	GP	W	L	T	Pts
Quebec Bulldogs	18	10	8	0	20
Ottawa Senators	18	9	9	0	18
Montreal Wanderers	18	9	9	0	18
Montreal Canadiens	18	8	10	0	16

MARITIME PROFESSIONAL HOCKEY LEAGUE

	GP	W	L	T	Pts
Moncton Victorias	18	12	6	0	24
New Glasgow Cubs	18	10	8	0	20
Halifax Crescents	18	7	11	0	14
Halifax Socials	18	7	11	0	14

POSTSEASON STANLEY CUP CHALLENGE

17 GOALS TO 3

MAR. 11	▸	Moncton 3 at Quebec 9
MAR. 13	▸	Moncton 0 at Quebec 8

A New Trophy?

At a meeting of the NHA on December 2, 1911, the league officially designated the O'Brien Trophy (donated by millionaire M.J. O'Brien of Renfrew, Ontario, in 1910) as the league's championship trophy. Though the Stanley Cup had never actually belonged to the NHA, or to any one league, some now seemed to think that the old trophy had reached the end of the line. A sportswriter at the *Montreal Herald* suggested that the Duke of Connaught (Canada's newest governor-general) be asked to put up a new trophy for the world hockey championship. Edward and Arthur Stanley, sons of Lord Stanley, who had passed away in 1908, wrote to the trustees from England to say they wished to donate $1,000 for a new trophy. In the end, the majority thought that, because of its long association with hockey, the original Stanley Cup should remain the game's championship trophy.

ROSTER

Joe Hall

George Leonard

Joe Malone (captain)

Jack Marks

Jack McDonald

Paddy Moran

Eddie Oatman

Goldie Prodger

Walter Rooney

Mike Quinn (manager)

Charlie Nolan (coach)

I'll sing you the lay of the hockey team that
    came from Moncton town,
To assail the boys of old Quebec, who'd lately
    won renown.
They came with their numerous followers,
    from "the cup of joy" to sup;
To drink the health of Moncton town from out
    of the Stanley Cup.

Chorus:
They came, they saw, on victory bent,
They brandished their sticks and grinned so,
But all they got of the Stanley Cup,
Was to view it in Renfrew's window.

Now some of the boys from Moncton town at
    that store last Monday morn,
Stood gazing fondly at that Cup that window
    did adorn.
One of them, boldly, did exclaim, you'll soon
    be our pride and joy.

I said, my dear friend, now have a good look,
    then go home and be a good boy.

(Chorus)

You know the result t'was victory of course
    for old Quebec,
And Moncton's aspirations got for the time
    an awful check.
They came like sporting boys t'is true,
    like real good sports did play;
But alas they had nothing on old Quebec,
    the "Pride of the NHA."

(Chorus)

— Song lyrics printed in the *Quebec Daily Telegraph*, March 14, 1912.

Battling like Bulldogs

The 1911–12 hockey season saw the launch of the Pacific Coast Hockey Association (PCHA) as a Western rival to the Ontario- and Quebec-based National Hockey Association (NHA). Though the PCHA would soon introduce many new rules that helped modernize hockey, it was the NHA that voted to eliminate the rover and go with the six-man alignment still in use more than 100 years later. Not everyone in the East was thrilled with the decision: "You might as well do away with the shortstop in baseball," griped star center Marty Walsh of the Ottawa Senators.

With the departure of the Renfrew Millionaires and a delay in adding two new teams in Toronto, the NHA was reduced to four clubs in 1911–12. The Senators were the defending Stanley Cup champions and were the only NHA team that had not lost any players to the PCHA. Ottawa was predicted to retain the NHA title, but the four-team race was remarkably close.

Despite a long history of top-level hockey in Quebec City dating back to the 1880s, the Quebec Bulldogs had not been included when the NHA was formed in 1909–10. When admitted in 1910–11, they finished last with a record of 4-12-0. This year, however, the Bulldogs rounded into championship form. Playing for the third straight season on a line with Jack McDonald and Eddie Oatman, Joe Malone emerged as a top scorer, with 21 goals. The acquisition of Goldie Prodger on defense helped Joe Hall recover his previous star form in front of goalie Paddy Moran. The Bulldogs finally moved into first place late in the season with a 2–1 victory over the Montreal Wanderers on Saturday night, February 24, 1912. The key game came one week later, when Quebec finished out its schedule against the defending champions in Ottawa.

A small group of fans was on hand from Quebec City, but they were drowned out by 6,000 Ottawa faithful as the Senators took a 2–0 lead after one period. Joe Hall and Joe Malone scored in the second to tie the game before Ottawa went back on top with two goals midway through the third. Again Quebec fought back for a tie, but Ottawa went ahead 5–4 with just three minutes remaining. As the final seconds were ticking down, many Ottawa fans began to take their celebration into the streets, but with only about 10 seconds to go, Joe Malone scored to tie the game. It took until three minutes into a second overtime session for Quebec to emerge with a 6–5 victory—and newspapers seem to be equally split over whether Joe Malone or Joe Hall netted the winner.

Over 10,000 people greeted the Bulldogs when their train arrived back in Quebec City on Sunday evening. There was a brass band and a bugle corps leading a parade through the streets, and players were called on to make speeches. *The Quebec Chronicle* refers to Joe Hall as being treated as the hero of heroes, though the *Daily Telegraph* credited Malone with the winner. But whoever had scored, the Bulldogs hadn't won the NHA title and the Stanley Cup just yet. The Senators now had to make up a protested game from earlier in the season. If they beat the Montreal Wanderers they would be tied with Quebec and there would be a playoff.

On the evening of March 6, 1912, the Bulldogs and their fans gathered at the Victoria Hotel in Quebec City. A special telegraph wire was set up to provide everyone with details of the game in Ottawa. When word came in that the Wanderers had scored a 5–2 victory, the celebrations started all over again. The next morning, defense partners Joe Hall and Goldie Prodger made good on a couple of celebratory promises. Prodger rolled teammate Joe Savard through the streets in a wheelbarrow, while Joe Hall pushed a peanut with a toothpick along the same route.

Moncton Is No Match

The Stanley Cup was delivered to Quebec City on Saturday morning, March 9th, and the Moncton Victorias arrived in town the following day. The Cup, decorated in the Bulldogs colors of blue and white, drew large crowds when it went on display Monday morning in a showroom window at the Holt Renfrew Company. "Whether the trophy will remain here long or not, will depend on the ability of the Moncton team," reported the *Quebec Daily Telegraph*. Joe Hall played his usual rough, two-way game in the opener, and Jack McDonald scored four times in a 9–3 victory. Reports vary as to whether McDonald scored four or five in Game 2, as Moncton faded after a strong first period and Quebec scored an 8–0 victory.

Too Late a Date

Though it's often been written that the PCHA did not, or was not allowed to, challenge for the Stanley Cup in their inaugural season, this was not the case. As early as December 2, 1911, the Ottawa Citizen reported "the Patricks intend, if possible, to wind up their season about the last week in February in order that the champion may go East to play for the Stanley Cup." However, construction delays on their arenas in Vancouver and Victoria forced the start of the inaugural PCHA season to be delayed. Still, the Stanley Cup trustees received an official challenge from the PCHA on February 22nd. Since natural ice had never been available in the East so late in the season, and it became clear that the PCHA champions wouldn't be able to play the NHA winner before March 25th, the challenge was put over until December but never played.

Never Mind...

With challenges received from both the Saskatoon Hockey Club (known as the Hoo-Hoos) of the Saskatchewan Professional Hockey League and Port Arthur of the New Ontario Hockey League, it was decided, as it had been in 1911, that the two league champions should compete to send one winner east. The games were played in Winnipeg on March 2 and 4, 1912. Port Arthur won the first game 11–1 and took the series despite a 5–1 loss in Game 2. But after their one-sided loss to Ottawa in 1911, Port Arthur decided not to make the trip to Quebec City in 1912.

NATIONAL HOCKEY ASSOCIATION

	GP	W	L	T	Pts
Ottawa Senators	16	13	3	0	26
Montreal Canadiens	16	8	8	0	16
Renfrew Creamery Kings	16	8	8	0	16
Montreal Wanderers	16	7	9	0	14
Quebec Bulldogs	16	4	12	0	8

ONTARIO PROFESSIONAL HOCKEY LEAGUE

	GP	W	L	T	Pts
Galt Professionals*	18	13	5	0	26
Waterloo Professionals	18	12	6	0	26
Berlin Dutchmen	18	10	8	0	20
Brantford Indians	18	1	17	0	2

*Defeated Port Hope of the Eastern OPHL to earn Stanley Cup challenge.

NEW ONTARIO HOCKEY LEAGUE

	GP	W	L	T	Pts
Port Arthur Lake City*	15	15	0	0	30
Fort William Forts	16	9	6	1	19
Port Arthur Thunder Bays	15	7	8	0	14
Fort William North Stars	14	5	8	1	11
Schreiber Colts	16	1	15	0	2

*Defeated Prince Albert of the Saskatchewan Professional Hockey League to earn Stanley Cup challenge.

POSTSEASON STANLEY CUP CHALLENGE 1 GAME TO 0

MAR. 13 ► Galt 4 at Ottawa 7

POSTSEASON STANLEY CUP CHALLENGE 1 GAME TO 0

MAR. 16 ► Port Arthur 4 at Ottawa 13

> "That kind of hockey passed out of the fashion books 20 years ago. We don't allow the killing of players in this part of the country."
> — Senators manager Pete Green on Galt's vicious play

> "Well, we were beaten and soundly beaten.... They're the finest all around aggregation I have ever seen in action."
> — Port Arthur manager W.H.E. Gordon

- Alex Currie
- Jack Darragh
- Horace Gaul
- Dubbie Kerr
- Fred Lake
- Percy LeSueur (captain)
- Bruce Ridpath
- Hamby Shore
- Bruce Stuart
- Marty Walsh
- Pete Green (manager)

Untimely Ends

Marty Walsh starred in football and hockey at Queen's University in his hometown of Kingston, Ontario, from 1902 to 1906 before starring with the Ottawa Senators from 1907 to 1912. Walsh was diagnosed with tuberculosis in 1914 and died at a sanatorium in Gravenhurst, Ontario, on March 27, 1915.

Ottawa native Jack Darragh played his entire career in his hometown and was a Stanley Cup champion with the Senators as a rookie in 1911 and again in 1920 and 1921. Darragh retired in the spring of 1924. Three months later, on June 28, 1924, he died of peritonitis, an inflammation of the lining of the abdomen.

Frank McGee is the best-known Stanley Cup star to have vision in only one eye, but Fred Lake, a member of the Ottawa Senators Cup-winning teams in 1909 and 1911, had lost the sight in one eye while playing in the International Hockey League earlier in his career. Lake died under mysterious circumstances in November 1937, a victim of either murder or suicide.

The Senators and the Salary Cap

The National Hockey Association (NHA) had been formed for the 1909–10 season as a rival to the Canadian Hockey Association (CHA), which had previously been known as the Eastern Canada Hockey Association and was considered the best league in hockey. But the NHA went head to head with the CHA, battling them to sign the game's top talent and to win fan support. By spending what was considered to be huge sums of money at the time, the NHA emerged as the winner.

At a time when the per-capita income in Canada stood at around $320 and a working man would consider himself lucky to earn $1,000 a year, Art Ross was paid $2,700 to play for the NHA franchise in Haileybury, Ontario. Lester Patrick left the family lumber business in Nelson, BC, to sign a $3,000 contract with the NHA team in Renfrew. Cyclone Taylor had led Ottawa to the Stanley Cup in 1909, but he was lured to Renfrew for a salary reported to be $5,250. (It was likely $4,000 plus a promotion in his off-ice job.) Renfrew paid salaries of $15,000 to the 13 men who took part in the 12-game NHA schedule. The team became known as "the Millionaires." Ottawa, stung by the loss of Taylor, paid $12,000 to keep the rest of their 10-man roster intact.

The NHA owners all suffered losses in 1909–10, so they passed several new rules on November 12, 1910: They cut their league from seven teams to five, they limited rosters to 10 men and they imposed a salary cap of $5,000 per team.

The players were angry, but the owners didn't take them seriously until they began to refuse their reduced contracts. "We are all suffering from the writers' cramp, and cannot sign up," quipped Ottawa star Bruce Stuart. With Stuart and Art Ross leading the rebellion, an attempt was made to start up a new players' league. When it became apparent that the owners of the Montreal Arena would back the NHA against the players, the plan fell apart and most players signed with their old teams. The salary cap dispute had lasted about a month. Training camps were disrupted, and some exhibition games were canceled, but the NHA season started as scheduled on December 31st. It's unclear how effectively the cap was enforced, but salaries definitely dropped dramatically in 1910–11.

The Montreal Wanderers were the defending NHA and Stanley Cup champions, but it quickly became obvious that Ottawa was the team to beat. In their home opener, the Senators crushed the Wanderers 10–5 behind four goals from rookie Jack Darragh. The Senators won 10 in a row before suffering their first defeat, and then they snapped out of a mini slump with two straight victories to close out the season at 13-3-0. During the 16-game 1910–11 season, 10 players averaged better than a goal per game, and four of them were with Ottawa. Marty Walsh led the NHA with 37 goals, while teammate Dubbie Kerr was second with 32. Bruce Ridpath scored 22, and Jack Darragh had 18. Georges Vezina and the Montreal Canadiens had the NHA's best defensive record, but Ottawa's Percy LeSueur recorded the league's only shutout, in a 5–0 win over the Canadiens in the season's final game.

As champions of the NHA, the Senators took possession of the Stanley Cup from the Wanderers and prepared to defend it.

The Galt Challenge

The Stanley Cup trustees received a challenge from the Ontario Professional Hockey League on February 21, 1911. On March 1st, Galt beat Waterloo 8–0 in a postseason makeup of a protested game, and they then defeated Port Hope of the Eastern Ontario league 12–8 in a two-game, home-and-home series played on March 3rd and 7th, winning the league title and earning the Cup challenge in the process.

The Galt Professionals had faced Ottawa for the Stanley Cup in January 1910, and when they met again for a one-game, winner-take-all series on March 13, 1911, it marked the first game in Stanley Cup history to feature three 20-minute periods instead of two 30-minute halves (the rule change had been implemented by the NHA at the start of the season). The Senators got three goals from Marty Walsh to win a rough game played on slushy ice 7–4.

The Port Arthur Challenge

With challenges accepted from both Port Arthur in northern Ontario and Prince Albert in Saskatchewan, it was decided that the two teams would meet in Winnipeg and the winner would be sent east for the Stanley Cup. Port Arthur won the games 6–3 and 6–5 on March 8th and 10th and came to Ottawa to face the Senators on March 16, 1911. Marty Walsh nearly equaled Frank McGee's feat of 14 goals in a Stanley Cup game, scored against Dawson City in 1905, when he scored 10 times to lead Ottawa past Port Arthur 13–4.

What to Do?

As was the case during the NHL lockout of 2004–05, people wondered what might happen to the Stanley Cup during the strike by NHA players prior to the 1910–11 season. On December 5, 1910, the *Toronto Star* reported that the holdout players of the defending-champion Montreal Wanderers had put in a claim for the Stanley Cup but that trustee William Foran denied it. Presumably, the Wanderers players would have liked to accept challenges for the Cup on their own or see it transferred with them to the proposed new players league. Foran, however, ruled that the Stanley Cup was the property of the club owners, not the team's players.

"The members of the Wanderers team of last year were under contract," Foran stated, "and when these articles ran out, their connection with the club ceased.... The trustees deal only with the management of different teams and the owners of the Wanderers franchise, provided they put a team on the ice ... will possess the Cup just as long as the club continues to retain the championship."

According to the Star story, other prominent sporting men also scoffed at the Wanderers players. The prevailing attitude was that hockey players were nothing more than employees of their clubs and entitled only to their salaries.

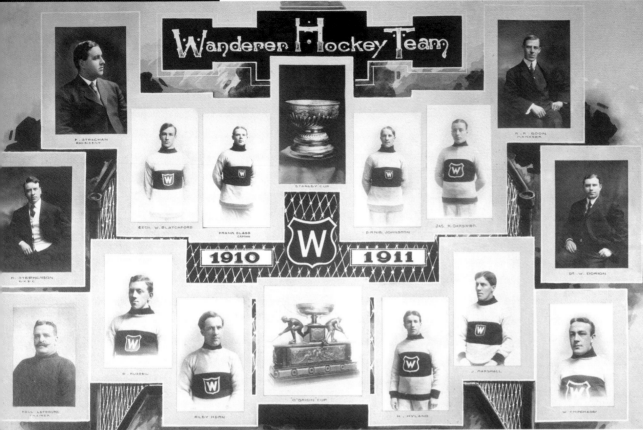

STANDINGS

NATIONAL HOCKEY ASSOCIATION

	GP	W	L	T	Pts
Montreal Wanderers	12	11	1	0	22
Ottawa Senators	12	9	3	0	18
Renfrew Creamery Kings	12	8	3	1	17
Cobalt Silver Kings	12	4	8	0	8
Haileybury Hockey Club	12	4	8	0	8
Montreal Shamrocks	12	3	8	1	7
Montreal Canadiens	12	2	10	0	4

ONTARIO PROFESSIONAL HOCKEY LEAGUE

	GP	W	L	T	Pts
Berlin Dutchmen	17	11	6	0	22
Waterloo Professionals	15	8	7	0	16
Brantford Indians	15	8	7	0	14
Galt Professionals	17	5	12	0	10

CARRYOVER STANLEY CUP CHALLENGE 15 GOALS TO 4

JAN. 5 ▶ Galt* 3 at Ottawa 12

JAN. 7 ▶ Galt 1 at Ottawa 3

*Galt (the 1908–09 OPHL champions, see pages 290–91) was awarded a carryover challenge after requesting that the original challenge of March 1909 be postponed until January 1910.

CARRYOVER STANLEY CUP CHALLENGE 21 GOALS TO 11

JAN. 18 ▶ Edmonton* 4 at Ottawa 8

JAN. 20 ▶ Edmonton 7 at Ottawa 13

*Edmonton (the 1908–09 Alberta Professional Hockey League champions, see pages 290–91) was awarded a carryover challenge, which was played in 1910.

POSTSEASON STANLEY CUP CHALLENGE 1 GAME TO 0

MAR. 12 ▶ Berlin 3 at Montreal Wanderers 7

> 66 Manager [Buck] Irving says the whole team is in the pink of condition, 'We are going to surprise Ottawa' he said. 'Let me tell you Easterners that you are underestimating this Galt team. The boys are all anxious to make a rep and will force Ottawa to the limit.'"
> —*Galt Daily Reporter*, January 5, 1910

ROSTERS

Ottawa Senators

Dubbie Kerr

Fred Lake

Percy LeSueur

Ken Mallen

Bruce Ridpath

Gord Roberts

Hamby Shore

Bruce Stuart (captain)

Marty Walsh

Montreal Wanderers ▲

Cecil Blachford

Jimmy Gardner

Pud Glass (captain)

Riley Hern

Harry Hyland

Moose Johnson

Jack Marshall

Ernie Russell

Dickie Boon (manager)

Beating Berlin Though Galt had done poorly against Ottawa in January, Berlin was quick to send in a challenge after clinching the OPHL title on February 25th. The Wanderers were not anxious to play Berlin, as the series figured to draw small crowds. They tried to have goalie Hugh Lehman declared ineligible because he had played with Galt in their challenge, but the trustees agreed to let him play because he had only filled in for Galt after their goalie developed appendicitis. The Wanderers offered Berlin only a one-game playoff, and the team accepted. It was a slow game played on soft ice, and though Berlin took an early 1–0 lead, the Wanderers were up 5–2 at halftime. The final score was 7–4, with Ernie Russell scoring four goals for the champions and Harry Hyland the other three.

What Happened? Though their team name would be added to the winners list on the "shoulder" of the Stanley Cup when the trophy was redesigned for the 1947–48 season, the name Montreal Wanderers is missing from the band it should have appeared on back in 1909–10. The reason for the omission is that the Wanderers never received the trophy that season. No one from the team ever gave the trustees the $1,000 bond for its safekeeping. Sam Lichtenheim bought the Wanderers in 1910–11 and finally put up the money late in the season. His bond was rejected because there were only 11 days left on the schedule and Ottawa was virtually assured of taking the title. An angry Lichtenheim vowed to donate a huge, expensive silver trophy to replace the Stanley Cup in 1911–12 and make it available to teams in Canada and the United States. He didn't follow through.

The Birth of the NHA

A lot had been left undecided when the 1908–09 season came to an end. A challenge from the Winnipeg Shamrocks, champions of the Manitoba Professional Hockey League, was accepted by the trustees for March 1909, but the team asked to be given dates prior to the 1909–10 season. Other challenges were received from Renfrew of the Federal Hockey League, Cobalt of the Temiskaming Hockey League and Galt of the Ontario Professional Hockey League. The trustees were concerned that all of these teams had brought in "ringers" for key games to help them win their league titles. It was decided to wait until the start of the 1909–10 season to get around any eligibility issues. As a result, the Ottawa Senators were not called upon to defend the Stanley Cup after winning it along with the championship of the Eastern Canada Hockey Association (ECHA) in 1908–09.

In October 1909, another challenge was received from Edmonton. It was also reported that Lester Patrick would challenge on behalf of the team in Nelson, BC, though it seems no formal challenge was ever made because the dates suggested were not acceptable to Nelson. On November 23rd, William Foran and P.D. Ross confirmed reports that the challenges from Winnipeg and Galt had been accepted. Edmonton was told they might be able to get games in as well. Cobalt and Renfrew were rejected, but that was not the end of the story.

The tiny town of Renfrew had been after the Stanley Cup since 1907. Now the team hoped to bypass a challenge by gaining admittance to the Eastern Canada Hockey Association. Renfrew's Ambrose O'Brien, son of wealthy mining and railway tycoon M.J. O'Brien, planned to attend the ECHA meeting in Montreal on November 25, 1909. He had the support of the Montreal Wanderers, but the Wanderers were on the outs with other ECHA officials because new owner P.J. Doran planned to move the team into the Jubilee Rink, which he owned but was only half the size of the Montreal Arena. To rid themselves of the Wanderers, the owners

of the Ottawa Senators, Quebec Bulldogs and Montreal Shamrocks voted the ECHA out of business. They reformed as the Canadian Hockey Association (CHA) and replaced the Wanderers with a French-Canadian team called the Nationals and an English team called All-Montreal.

Incensed, the Wanderers and Renfrew formed a rival league they called the National Hockey Association (NHA). It would include the northern Ontario towns of Cobalt and Haileybury (where the O'Briens had their mining interests) plus their own French-Canadian team financed by Ambrose O'Brien and called Les Canadiens. The NHA would commence play with Cobalt at the Canadiens on January 5, 1910, six days after the first CHA game. In the meantime, the two leagues went to war over the best players. O'Brien money helped to lure top talent to the NHA, especially to Renfrew, where the large contracts given to Frank and Lester Patrick, Cyclone Taylor and others saw the press dub the team "the Millionaires."

Taylor's signing gave the NHA instant credibility, and even though the CHA began their season first, they drew poorly. On January 15, 1910, representatives of the rival organizations met amid rumors of an amalgamation. Instead, the NHA offered only to take in the Senators and Shamrocks. The two teams jumped at the opportunity and abandoned the CHA, which promptly folded amid much bitterness from the teams left behind. The NHA schedule was revised and re-started with seven teams.

Since the defending-champion Senators were now in the fold, an NHA championship would mean a Stanley Cup victory as well. It was freely predicted that Renfrew was the team to beat, but the all-star aggregation was slow to blend into a team. In the end, it was a tight race between the Wanderers and the Senators. When the Wanderers beat Ottawa 3–1 late in the season, they clinched first place in the NHA and won back the Stanley Cup, which Ottawa had taken from them the year before.

January Games

Newspapers claimed the Senators had run up a deficit of $1,000 during the 1908–09 season. They were said to be anxious to fill the coffers with as many challenges as possible early in the new season. But delays in fixing the Stanley Cup dates proved costly when the Winnipeg Shamrocks announced before Christmas that they would not make the trip. So, first up was the Galt Professionals.

Despite the loss of Cyclone Taylor and the retirement of Billy Gilmour, Ottawa still had a strong team. Marty Walsh led the ECHA with 42 goals in just 12 games in 1908–09 and scored six in a 12–3 rout of Galt in Game 1. With a nine-goal lead, only a few hundred fans showed up to see Ottawa win the second game 3–1.

Edmonton was expected to put up a better fight, and this series drew larger crowds. The Senators won the opener 8–4 on soft ice, but a return of cold temperatures sped up play in Game 2. Bruce Stuart, Gord Roberts and Bruce Ridpath starred in a 13–7 Ottawa victory.

March Madness In March 1910, Moosomin met Saskatoon for the championship of Saskatchewan. It was reported that Moosomin would likely challenge for the Stanley Cup if they won, but unseasonably mild weather saw the best-of-three series canceled after one win apiece. The Wanderers faced only Berlin for the Stanley Cup before traveling to New York to play Ottawa in an exhibition series. Afterwards, Renfrew beat a combined team of Ottawa and Montreal players and was declared "Champions of America" by the New York press.

OTTAWA HOCKEY CLUB CHAMPIONS

EASTERN CANADA HOCKEY ASSOCIATION

	GP	W	L	T	Pts
Ottawa Senators	12	10	2	0	20
Montreal Wanderers	12	9	3	0	18
Quebec Bulldogs	12	3	9	0	6
Montreal Shamrocks	12	2	10	0	4

ONTARIO PROFESSIONAL HOCKEY LEAGUE

	GP	W	L	T	Pts
Galt Professionals*	20	17	3	0	34
Berlin Dutchmen	20	14	6	0	28
Brantford Indians	20	14	6	0	28
Toronto Professionals	20	11	9	0	22
Guelph Professionals°	6	0	6	0	0
St. Catharines Pros	6	0	6	0	0

*Played for Stanley Cup in 1909–10.
°A win against Toronto was credited to Toronto after Guelph folded.

ALBERTA PROFESSIONAL HOCKEY LEAGUE

	GP	W	L	T	Pts
Edmonton Pros°*	10	10	0	0	0

°Played exhibition games only.
*Played for Stanley Cup in 1909–10.

STANLEY CUP CHALLENGE
NONE PLAYED

> " The last shake of the dice brought disaster to [the] Wanderers tonight … and they emerged from the match that marked the turning point in the ECHA series at the short end of an eight goal to three score. With the defeat of the champions here tonight apparently goes beyond all chance of retrieve for at least another year the ECHA championship and the Stanley Cup, which the Wanderers have held and defended for three years in succession."
> — *Montreal Gazette*, March 4, 1909

> " Fred Taylor, the Listowel boy, carried off the honors of the night. He was the kingpin of an all-star team, and despite the hindrance of an injured foot, he swooped up and down the ice like a machine, until the big crowd marveled at his endurance."
> — *Toronto Star*, March 4, 1909

ROSTER

Edgar Dey
Billy Gilmour
Dubbie Kerr
Fred Lake
Percy LeSueur
Bruce Stuart (captain)
Cyclone Taylor
Marty Walsh

The Cup Begins to Grow The original band for engraving names beneath the bowl of the Stanley Cup was filled between 1893 and 1902. Victories by Ottawa from 1903 to 1906 filled most of the space on the bowl itself. Wins by the Wanderers in 1906 were engraved into the decorative scroll atop the bowl. Kenora left only a small inscription inside in 1907.

When Ottawa won in 1909, Senators president D'Arcy McGee (brother of Frank McGee) was shocked to find 20 names of Montreal Wanderers players and executive engraved across the bottom of the bowl to mark their 1907 victory. "Perhaps [the] Wanderers considered this their license," newspapers said, "but the liberty was never given them by the trustees."

There was no room left to engrave Wanderers' wins from 1908 or Ottawa's in 1909, so McGee suggested to the trustees that a new base be built with an additional band to continue recording the winning teams.

Sorry Cyclone At a club banquet after the season, Cyclone Taylor asked for permission to take the Stanley Cup with him at Easter to visit family and friends in his hometown of Listowel in southwestern Ontario. Taylor was denied permission, but he and his teammates obviously did get their hands on the trophy. When looking closely at the original Stanley Cup bowl in the bank vault at the Hockey Hall of Fame in Toronto, the names Fred W. Taylor and Marty Walsh can still be seen scratched into the silver near the official engraving commemorating Ottawa's 1904 series with the Wanderers.

Ottawa Finally on Top in ECHA

In 1906–07, the Eastern Canada Amateur Hockey Association (ECAHA, recognized as the top league in the sport at the time) voted to allow professional players to compete alongside amateurs. By the winter of 1908–09, the last two amateur teams in the league—the Montreal Victorias and the Montreal Hockey Club (Montreal AAA)—withdrew to play elsewhere. Since the Montreal Wanderers, the Montreal Shamrocks, the Quebec Bulldogs and the Ottawa Senators were all paying their players, the word "Amateur" was dropped from the Eastern Canada Amateur Hockey Association league title. It became the Eastern Canada Hockey Association (ECHA).

Though they lost their league title and the Stanley Cup to the Montreal Wanderers back in 1905–06, and then lost star Frank McGee to retirement, Ottawa had most of their veteran squad back in 1906–07. They again proved unable to defeat the Wanderers, so the team made changes for 1907–08. The Senators signed Tom Phillips, who had captained the Kenora Thistles to a Stanley Cup victory over the Wanderers in 1907 only to lose the trophy in a rematch. They also signed younger players Marty Walsh and Fred Taylor, who soon earned the nickname "Cyclone" due to his dazzling rushes. But once again the Senators weren't quite good enough to win the title. They lost a key late-season game to their Montreal rivals, which once again gave the Wanderers the league championship and the Stanley Cup.

Ottawa made big changes before the 1908–09 season. Harvey Pulford, Alf Smith and Harry "Rat" Westwick, who had all been playing since the mid-1890s and were key members of the "Silver Seven" dynasty, all retired or were encouraged to move on. The key acquisition was Bruce Stuart of the Montreal Wanderers, who was lured back to his hometown by an offer to captain the Senators.

With Stuart now in Ottawa, the rivalry with the Wanderers was hotter than ever. Fans of the Montreal team were pleased when their heroes downed the Senators 7–6 in overtime in the first game of the schedule for both clubs, but Ottawa would not lose another meaningful game all season. Captain Stuart collected 22 goals in the 11 games he played, but Marty Walsh was the scoring star with 42 goals in 12 games. Walsh was the Phil Esposito to Cyclone Taylor's Bobby Orr. Because assists were not tabulated by the ECHA, Taylor's name did not show up that often in statistical summaries, but Ottawa newspapers estimated that as many as half of the team's league-leading 117 goals were the result of plays led by Taylor—and he did it all while playing brilliant defense.

The key game of the 1908–09 season was the Senators' last home contest of the season, on March 3, 1909. The Wanderers had a record of 9-2-0 while Ottawa was 9-1-0. A Senators victory would clinch the league title and give them the Stanley Cup. But Ottawa fans were worried. In their previous game (an 11–2 rout of the Montreal Shamrocks), Cyclone Taylor had suffered a severe cut to his ankle. He had just four days to get ready for the Wanderers.

On game night, Taylor wrapped his injured foot in cotton and lint and wore a special skate reinforced with extra leather. The day before, he had told sportswriters, "I can stand any amount of pain when the Stanley Cup is at stake." But could he? "In the first few minutes, Taylor limped," reported the *Ottawa Citizen*, "Then, the excitement of the struggle caused Cyclone to forget his injured foot." Once he got going, he was as good as ever. Taylor set up the game's first goal and scored one himself midway through the first half. Though he slowed down in the second half after taking a puck to the head, Ottawa scored five goals to pull away for an 8–3 victory. Marty Walsh scored four goals and Dubbie Kerr had three, but it was Taylor and his defense partner Fred Lake whom most writers praised as the stars of the game. Ottawa was not called on to defend the Stanley Cup, but the team made a postseason trip to New York, where they once again beat the Wanderers, winning a two-game series 12–10.

Eligibility Issues

The Stanley Cup trustees received four challenge requests late in the 1908–09 season. Only the challenge of the Winnipeg Shamrocks, champions of the Manitoba Professional Hockey League, was accepted, though the team would later choose not to play. The requests from Renfrew of the Federal Hockey League, Cobalt of the Temiskaming Hockey League and Galt of the Ontario Professional Hockey League all presented problems.

As explained in the *Ottawa Evening Journal* on February 27, 1909, "What the trustees have done is this: In the case of every challenge so far received, they have written to the challenging club acknowledging receipt of the challenge, and pointing out that the trustees last spring wrote to the presidents of the various leagues stating that after 1908 the trustees would not consider eligible as members of teams contesting for the Stanley Cup any player who had figured on more than one senior team in Canada during the hockey season."

The trustees' letters sought assurance that none of the challenging teams had men on their roster who had played on any other senior team in Canada since January 2, 1909. Galt's challenge was to be accepted if they replaced Art Serviss and Fred Dougherty, who had also played with Berlin. Rather than drop the players, Galt asked to delay their challenge until the start of the following season. As Renfrew and Cobalt also had ineligible players, they both agreed to wait until next season for reconsideration.

Montreal Wanderers

STANDINGS

EASTERN CANADA AMATEUR HOCKEY ASSOCIATION

	GP	W	L	T	Pts
Montreal Wanderers	10	8	2	0	16
Ottawa Hockey Club	10	7	3	0	14
Quebec Hockey Club	10	5	5	0	10
Montreal Shamrocks	10	5	5	0	10
Montreal Victorias	10	4	6	0	8
Montreal Hockey Club	10	1	9	0	2

MANITOBA PROFESSIONAL HOCKEY LEAGUE

	GP	W	L	T	Pts
Winnipeg Maple Leafs	17	11	6	0	20
Portage la Prairie	15	8	7	0	16
Winnipeg Strathconas	16	6	10	0	10
Kenora Thistles*	1	0	1	0	0
Brandon Hockey Club*	1	0	1	0	0

*Withdrew after playing one game.

ONTARIO PROFESSIONAL HOCKEY LEAGUE

	GP	W	L	T	Pts
Toronto Professionals	12	10	2	0	20
Berlin Dutchmen	12	7	5	0	14
Brantford Indians	12	5	7	0	10
Guelph Professionals	12	2	10	0	4

INTERPROVINCIAL PROFESSIONAL HOCKEY LEAGUE

	GP	W	L	T	Pts
Edmonton Pros	10	7	2	1	15
Strathcona Shamrocks	9	4	4	1	9
North Battleford	9	2	7	0	4

*Withdrew after playing one game.

CARRYOVER STANLEY CUP CHALLENGE 22 GOALS TO 4

JAN. 9 ► Ottawa Victorias* 3
at Montreal Wanderers 9

JAN. 13 ► Ottawa Victorias 1
at Montreal Wanderers 13

*Ottawa (the 1906–07 Federal Amateur Hockey League champions, see pages 294–95) was awarded a carryover challenge, which was played in 1908.

Early Renfrew Efforts

Renfrew challenged for the Stanley Cup after winning the Ottawa Valley championship in 1907, but it lost a two-game series to the Ottawa Victorias (default winners of the Federal League) in December, a playoff ordered by the trustees to determine which team should get to face the Wanderers. Renfrew had offered Cyclone Taylor $1,500 to play with them against the Victorias and sign with them for the 1907–08 season. He turned it down. However, even without Taylor, Renfrew repeated as Ottawa Valley champions and once again challenged for the Stanley Cup. In September 1908, the challenge was rejected due to the lower quality of Renfrew's league.

POSTSEASON STANLEY CUP CHALLENGE 1 GAME TO 0

MAR. 14 ► Toronto 4 at Montreal Wanderers 6

POSTSEASON STANLEY CUP CHALLENGE 13 GOALS TO 10

DEC. 28 ► Edmonton 3 at Montreal Wanderers 7

DEC. 30 ► Edmonton 7 at Montreal Wanderers 6

POSTSEASON STANLEY CUP CHALLENGE 20 GOALS TO 8

MAR. 10 ► Winnipeg Maple Leafs 5
at Montreal Wanderers 11

MAR. 12 ► Winnipeg Maple Leafs 3
at Montreal Wanderers 9

Wanderers Win Again

In the early years of the 20th century, hockey had no bigger rivalry than that between the Ottawa Hockey Club (also called the Silver Seven and, later, the Ottawa Senators) and the Montreal Wanderers. In an era when teams all across Canada could challenge for the Stanley Cup, the rivalry between the Wanderers and Ottawa had the added bonus that they almost always played in the same league and faced each other several times every season. The teams finished first and second in their league standings between 1904–05 and 1909–10, and one or the other of them held the Stanley Cup for all but a few months from 1903 through 1911.

Senators players are said to have remained unpaid in 1906–07, when the Eastern Canada Amateur Hockey Association (ECAHA) first allowed professionals into the league. Ottawa joined the moneyed ranks in 1907–08, when they signed Fred Taylor and Marty Walsh, who had formerly played in the mostly American-based International Hockey League (the sport's first openly professional organization). Ottawa's biggest signing was that of Tom Phillips. The former captain of the Kenora Thistles was rumored to have signed for as much as $1,800 for the 10-game season, but he may well have been paid only $1,000 plus $60 a month for an off-ice job. (Taylor had reportedly signed for $500 plus a job in the civil service.)

The Montreal Wanderers were the defending Stanley Cup champions, but they also had some new players on their roster. Star defenseman Hod Stuart had died after diving into shallow water in the summer of 1907, and Lester Patrick had moved to British Columbia. In their place, the Wanderers signed Art Ross, who had grown up in the Montreal suburb of Westmount, and Tom Hooper of the Kenora Thistles. Hooper stayed only a short time with the team, which later added another Westmount boy in Walter Smaill. Smaill and Cecil Blachford were the only Wanderers who played as amateurs.

The Senators opened the new season with a shocking 8–1 loss to Quebec, but they then moved Taylor from forward to defense and installed Walsh at center. The improvement was instantaneous, as Ottawa trounced the Wanderers 12–2 in their first home game of the season. This is generally thought to be the night that Fred Taylor earned the nickname "Cyclone."

Despite their one-sided loss, the Wanderers were tied with the Senators for first place in the ECAHA standings when they hosted Ottawa on February 29, 1908, in the second-last game of the season for both clubs. The winner of the game would be virtually assured of winning the league title and, with it, the Stanley Cup. Tickets that normally sold for $1 were scalped for $20 as 7,000 fans jammed the Montreal Arena. Some 2,000 more were left outside, breaking windows and doors in an attempt to get in. There were already 30 or 40 policemen on site, and reinforcements had to be called in.

Like the scene outside, the game was a rough one. But it was exciting. "Perhaps the greatest game ever played in Canada," reported the *Montreal Gazette*, though newspapers of this era often made such claims. Cyclone Taylor and Art Ross each established themselves as stars this season. Both were defenseman who loved to rush the puck, but Ross had about 3 inches and 25 pounds on Taylor and used it to his advantage. He sent Taylor sprawling twice in the first half, but he also left red splotches all over the ice when he refused to go off after his nose was bloodied.

Ottawa led 1–0 at halftime, and the game got even rougher when play resumed. About five minutes in, Montreal's Bruce Stuart left the ice after a butt-end in the stomach, but he returned a few minutes later to tie the score. Then Ross put the Wanderers up 2–1. "The crowd was frantic with joy and enthusiasm. Hats, gloves, canes, rugs, ladies' hand-bags, and everything not fastened down were hurled high in the air," said the *Montreal Gazette*. Ottawa tied the score two minutes later, but Walter Smaill had the Wanderers back on top with only about seven minutes remaining. Ottawa penalties (they would blame the referees after the game) hurt the Senators as time ran out. With Tom Phillips banished, Ross went end to end for a final goal with 30 seconds left to give the Wanderers a 4–2 victory.

"The better team won," boasted Wanderers president William Jennings afterward. Ottawa secretary J.P. Dickson agreed. "A hard, close game," he said, "and the better team won." In their season finale four nights later, the Wanderers received a tough battle from the Montreal Shamrocks but scored a 6–4 victory to emerge once again as ECAHA and Stanley Cup champions.

Ringers

The Wanderers had already wrapped up their season with an easy defeat of the Winnipeg Maple Leafs and a surprisingly close call against the Toronto Professionals when the Stanley Cup trustees received a challenge from Edmonton. Eager to press their case, team president James McKinnon traveled to Ottawa in June to speak to P.D. Ross and William Foran in person. In late August, McKinnon received a letter from Foran saying that the challenge had been accepted. Edmonton captain and manager Fred Whitcroft immediately began recruiting new players.

During the fall, there were rumors that Lester Patrick and his brother Frank would sign with Edmonton. Only Lester joined, but Whitcroft also signed other future Hall of Famers Tom Phillips, Didier Pitre and Joe Hall (who didn't make the Montreal trip) as well as Steve Vair, Harold McNamara and goalie Bert Lindsay.

When asked about all the signings, William Foran reasoned that it was unfair to expect a team challenging before a new season to only re-sign its own players. "A contract lasts for a year," Foran said, "and at the expiration of that contract any club can sign up players for the succeeding season if it pays the money."

With just a single game together before they reached Montreal, Edmonton's new lineup lost 7–3 to the Wanderers in Game 1. Edmonton regulars Hay Miller and Harold Deeton suited up for Game 2 and led the team to a 7–6 victory, but the win was not enough to overcome Montreal's four-goal advantage.

Kenora Thistles & Montreal Wanderers

STANDINGS

EASTERN CANADA AMATEUR HOCKEY ASSOCIATION

	GP	W	L	T	Pts
Montreal Wanderers	10	10	0	0	20
Ottawa Hockey Club	10	7	3	0	14
Montreal Victorias	10	6	4	0	12
Montreal Hockey Club	10	3	7	0	6
Quebec Hockey Club	10	2	8	0	4
Montreal Shamrocks	10	2	8	0	4

MANITOBA HOCKEY LEAGUE
All Games

	GP	W	L	T	Pts
Brandon Wheat Kings	10	5	2	3	13
Portage la Prairie	10	5	3	2	12
Kenora Thistles	6	4	2	0	8
Winnipeg Strathconas	10	1	8	1	3

Adjusted Results*

	GP	W	L
Kenora Thistles	6	4	2
Brandon Wheat Kings	6	4	2
Portage la Prairie	6	3	3
Winnipeg Strathconas	6	1	5

*Standings adjusted to account for games missed by the Thistles for their Stanley Cup challenge in Montreal.

FEDERAL AMATEUR HOCKEY LEAGUE

	GP	W	L	T	Pts
Montreal Montagnards	11	8	1	2	18
Cornwall Hockey Club	11	6	4	1	13
Ottawa Victorias°^	11	6	4	1	13
Morrisburg Hockey Club	11	0	11	0	0

°Declared league champion after resignation of Montreal and Cornwall.
^Played for Stanley Cup in 1907–08 after defeating Renfrew of the Ottawa Valley Hockey League to earn a challenge.

CARRYOVER STANLEY CUP CHALLENGE 17 GOALS TO 5

DEC. 27 ► New Glasgow* 3 at Montreal Wanderers 10

DEC. 29 ► New Glasgow 2 at Montreal Wanderers 7

*New Glasgow (the 1905–06 Nova Scotia Hockey League champions, see pages 296–97) was awarded a carryover challenge, which was played in late 1906.

CARRYOVER STANLEY CUP CHALLENGE 2 GAMES TO 0

JAN. 17 ► Kenora 4* at Montreal Wanderers 2

JAN. 21 ► Kenora 8 at Montreal Wanderers 6

*Kenora (the 1905–06 Manitoba Hockey League champions, see pages 296–97) was awarded a carryover challenge, which was played in 1907.

POSTSEASON MANITOBA STANLEY CUP PLAYOFF
2 GAMES TO 0

MAR. 16 ► Kenora 8 vs Brandon 6*

MAR. 18 ► Kenora 4 vs Brandon 1*

*Played in Winnipeg.

POSTSEASON STANLEY CUP CHALLENGE 12 GOALS TO 8

MAR. 23 ► Montreal Wanderers 7 vs Kenora 2*

MAR. 25 ► Montreal Wanderers 5 vs Kenora 6*

*Played in Winnipeg.

ROSTERS

Montreal Wanderers December 29, 1906	Kenora Thistles January 21, 1907 ▲	Kenora Thistles March 18, 1907	Montreal Wanderers March 25, 1907
Cecil Blachford	Roxy Beaudro	Roxy Beaudro	Cecil Blachford
Pud Glass	Eddie Giroux	Eddie Giroux	Pud Glass
Riley Hern	Si Griffis	Si Griffis	Riley Hern
Moose Johnson	Joe Hall	Tom Hooper	Moose Johnson
Rod Kennedy	Tom Hooper	Russell Phillips	Rod Kennedy
Lester Patrick (captain)	Billy McGimsie	Tom Phillips (captain)	Jack Marshall
Ernie Russell	Russell Phillips	Alf Smith	Lester Patrick (captain)
Billy Strachan	Tom Phillips (captain)	Harry Westwick	Ernie Russell
Dickie Boon (manager)	Art Ross	Fred Whitcroft	Billy Strachan
			Hod Stuart
			Dickie Boon (manager)

It was widely known that Canadian hockey players were being paid to play in Pittsburgh as early as 1901, though the fact that the Western Pennsylvania Hockey League maintained these men were hired for off-ice jobs satisfied most people about their amateur status. The first openly professional organization was the International Hockey League, which began in 1904–05 with a team in Pittsburgh, three in Michigan and one in Sault Ste. Marie, Ontario.

There had long been rumors of "under the table" payments in Canadian hockey, but anyone proven to have accepted money was banned. Professional hockey was officially introduced on November 11, 1906, when the Eastern Canada Amateur Hockey Association (ECAHA) voted to allow professional players into the league. Though it was the Stanley Cup–champion Montreal Wanderers who were known to be offering salaries, it was D'Arcy McGee of Ottawa who moved the motion. "The public want good hockey," he said, "and does not care whether a player is amateur or professional as long as he can deliver the goods. To get good hockey, we must pay the players." But the issue was not that simple.

In this era, most hockey players played other sports too, and many of those sports remained strictly amateur. If a player took money to play hockey, he'd be barred from playing any amateur sport. Even if a hockey player refused a salary, he would still be considered a professional if he merely played against other pro players. This was now an important concern for Stanley Cup challengers. To those who wondered about the trophy's status, P.D. Ross (who had written about the hypocrisy of demanding so much from athletes while denying them a share of the profits in the *Ottawa Journal* on December 15, 1905) stated on November 23, 1906: "The trustees consider the Wanderers of Montreal, present holders of the Stanley Cup, still eligible to defend the trophy despite the recent action of the Eastern Canada hockey league."

In Manitoba, this led to a split in hockey circles. The Kenora Thistles, who were already slated to challenge the Wanderers in their third attempt at the Stanley Cup, had several nationally ranked amateur rowers on their roster, but they were still willing to risk their status. So were Brandon, Portage la Prairie and the Winnipeg Strathconas, who all joined the Thistles in a new pro loop.

The Winnipeg Hockey Club and the Winnipeg Victorias organized an amateur league. (The champion Winnipegs would overcome their scruples and issue a challenge for the Cup, though they never actually played for it.)

There was more trouble on the East Coast. The Maritime Provinces Amateur Athletic Association prohibited the 1906 champion New Glasgow Hockey Club from playing their challenge against the Wanderers and threatened to ban them from the Nova Scotia league. Just two days before the scheduled start of their series, the team decided to defy the ban and caught a train for Montreal. New Glasgow—who was widely mocked in the press for lacking even one local player—was beaten badly by the Wanderers and returned home to apply for reinstatement.

It was expected that the Thistles would give the Wanderers a better battle, but Kenora was having its own trouble. Matt Brown had moved away after playing with the team for years, and then Tuff Bellefeuille quit after a blowup with captain Tom Phillips following a disastrous 10–5 loss to the Ottawa Senators in an exhibition game in Winnipeg. Tom's younger brother Russell Phillips was added to the roster, and though he was good enough to help the Thistles win their first two league games, the team didn't appear to be Stanley Cup caliber. And so, after their game with Brandon on January 7, 1907, the Thistles arranged for the loan of Brandon stars Art Ross and Joe Hall. Hall saw no action with the Thistles against the Wanderers, but Ross was a star in the series.

The biggest star was Tom Phillips, who scored all four goals for the Thistles in a 4–2 victory in Game 1. "I do not see how they can beat us," he said afterward, "we are very confident of victory." Perhaps they were too confident. After racing out to a 6–2 lead midway through the second half of Game 2, the Thistles fell apart. The Wanderers put four quick goals past Eddie Giroux, and the score was tied with three minutes to go. There was only a minute remaining when Si Griffis went end to end for the Thistles. He had two shots at Riley Hern before setting up Roxy Beaudro for the go-ahead goal. Tom Hooper iced an 8–6 victory a few seconds later.

With a population of barely 6,000 people, Kenora is the smallest town ever to win the Stanley Cup. The Thistles' reign as champions would also be the shortest.

The Rematch

After going undefeated in the ECAHA, the Wanderers challenged for the Stanley Cup and promptly headed west. In their challenge, the Wanderers requested that only "bona fide members" of the Thistles team take part in the series. William Foran was not yet a trustee, but had been placed in charge by P.D. Ross, who was traveling in Europe. Foran agreed to the request. This was a problem for the Thistles.

In an exhibition game in Ottawa after their Stanley Cup victory, Billy McGimsie suffered a career-ending shoulder injury. Fred Whitcroft of Peterborough was signed to replace him. No one seemed upset with that. However, when Tom Hooper got hurt late in the season, the Thistles picked up Alf Smith and Harry Westwick from Ottawa. They played the final game of the season in Kenora, plus the playoff against Brandon, but Foran and the Wanderers insisted they couldn't play in the Stanley Cup challenge.

Public opinion favored Kenora. Before the first series there had been no protest about the Thistles adding Art Ross earlier, nor had Kenora complained about Montreal's signing Hod Stuart and goalie Riley Hern. There were also arguments about dates for the rematch, and according to Alf Smith, a frustrated Thistles executive grabbed the Stanley Cup and threatened to throw it into the Lake of the Woods.

In the end, the Wanderers agreed to let Smith and Westwick play when the Thistles agreed to move the games to Winnipeg. The teams split the two games played, but the Wanderers won the round by a total score of 12–8.

STANDINGS

EASTERN CANADA AMATEUR HOCKEY ASSOCIATION

	GP	W	L	T	Pts
Ottawa Hockey Club	10	9	1	0	18
Montreal Wanderers	10	9	1	0	18
Montreal Victorias	10	6	4	0	12
Quebec Hockey Club	10	3	7	0	6
Montreal Hockey Club	10	3	7	0	6
Montreal Shamrocks	10	0	10	0	0

CANADIAN INTERCOLLEGIATE HOCKEY UNION

	GP	W	L	T	Pts
Queen's University	4	3	1	0	6
McGill University	4	2	2	0	4
University of Toronto	4	1	3	0	2

FEDERAL AMATEUR HOCKEY LEAGUE

	GP	W	L	T	Pts
Smiths Falls Hockey Club	7	7	0	0	14
Ottawa Victorias	8	4	4	0	8
Brockville Hockey Club	7	3	4	0	6
Cornwall Hockey Club	6	2	4	0	4
Ottawa Montagnards	4	0	4	0	0

MANITOBA HOCKEY LEAGUE

	GP	W	L	T	Pts
Kenora Thistles*	8	7	1	0	14
Winnipeg Hockey Club	8	6	1	1°	13
Winnipeg Victorias	9	3	6	0	6
Brandon Hockey Club	8	3	4	1°	4
Portage la Prairie	9	1	8	0	2

*Played for Stanley Cup in 1906–07.
°Tie was replayed and won by the Winnipegs, giving them a 7-1-0 record to tie Kenora for first place. Kenora then won the league playoff with Winnipegs.

NOVA SCOTIA HOCKEY LEAGUE

	GP	W	L	T	Pts
New Glasgow Hockey Club°*	11	9	2	0	18
Halifax Wanderers	11	8	3	0	16
Amherst Ramblers	10	6	4	0	12
Truro Colts	10	5	5	0	10
Halifax Crescents	10	2	8	0	4
Windsor Hockey Club	10	1	9	0	2

°Defeated Halifax Wanderers in a tie-breaking game for Nova Scotia championship and then defeated Moncton Victorias and Summerside Crystals for the Maritime championship.
*Played for Stanley Cup in 1906–07.

ROSTERS

Ottawa Hockey Club (Silver Seven)

Coo Dion
Jack Ebbs
Billy Gilmour
Billy Hague
Frank McGee
Art Moore
Harvey Pulford (captain)
Harry Smith
Tommy Smith
Harry Westwick
Alf Smith (player-coach)

Montreal Wanderers ▲

Josh Arnold
Cecil Blachford (captain)
Pud Glass
Moose Johnson
Rod Kennedy
Henri Menard
Lester Patrick
Ernie Russell
Billy Strachan
Dickie Boon (manager)

MIDSEASON STANLEY CUP CHALLENGE 28 GOALS TO 14

FEB. 27 ▸ Queen's University 7 at Ottawa Hockey Club 16

FEB. 28 ▸ Queen's University 7 at Ottawa Hockey Club 12

MIDSEASON STANLEY CUP CHALLENGE 14 GOALS TO 7

MAR. 6 ▸ Smiths Falls 5 at Ottawa Hockey Club 6

MAR. 8 ▸ Smiths Falls 2 at Ottawa Hockey Club 8

POSTSEASON ECAHA STANLEY CUP PLAYOFF 12 GOALS TO 10

MAR. 14 ▸ Ottawa Hockey Club 1 at Montreal Wanderers 9

MAR. 17 ▸ Montreal Wanderers 3 at Ottawa Hockey Club 9

Wanderers End the Ottawa Dynasty

The Montreal Wanderers had been formed in late November 1903. The team was made up mainly of players formerly with the Montreal Amateur Athletic Association. Though they wore uniforms with the winged-wheel logo of the Montreal AAA, the players had always preferred to call themselves the Montreal Hockey Club. The reason they gave for joining the Wanderers was to escape the control of the MAAA organization. The new team also broke from the Canadian Amateur Hockey League (CAHL) and helped William Foran of the Ottawa Capitals organize the Federal Amateur Hockey League (FAHL).

The Stanley Cup–champion Ottawa Hockey Club (Silver Seven) joined the FAHL in 1904–05, but in December 1905, both the Wanderers and Ottawa quit the FAHL. They joined the four best teams from the CAHL in a brand-new league called the Eastern Canada Amateur Hockey Association (ECAHA). Ottawa had most of the same players who had helped the team win the Stanley Cup three years in a row: Frank McGee, Harry Westwick, Harvey Pulford, Alf Smith, Art Moore and Billy Gilmour. They added two more Smith brothers in 1905–06: Harry, who led the ECAHA with 31 goals in just eight games, and Tommy, who played just a handful of games. The Wanderers also made key acquisitions in Ernie Russell, Moose Johnson and Lester Patrick.

Despite playing Stanley Cup games against Queen's University and Smiths Falls late in the season, Ottawa finished the ECAHA schedule with five straight wins and a 9-1-0 record. The Wanderers won eight straight after an early loss in Ottawa and were also 9-1-0. A two-game, home-and-home, total-goals playoff would not only decide the ECAHA title but the Stanley Cup champion as well.

It was predicted that the Wanderers would be tough to beat, but nobody expected what happened to Ottawa in Game 1. Ernie Russell scored four times, and Pud Glass added three in a 9–1 Wanderers victory. "Montreal may count its chickens whenever it likes," warned a writer in the *Ottawa Citizen*, "but there is a huge amount of money in Ottawa that says the silverware will stay in the Capital, and that a lead of eight goals or nine or perhaps ten does not necessarily spell defeat to Canada's greatest sporting center."

Percy LeSueur of Smiths Falls replaced Billy Hague for Game 2, but how much difference could a new goalie make? The Wanderers played defensively in Game 2 but still scored first, when Moose Johnson beat LeSueur midway through the first half. After that, however, it was all Ottawa. They scored three quick goals before intermission and three even faster to start the second half. Ottawa took a 9–1 lead of its own, only to see it all slip away when Lester Patrick scored twice in the final minutes to salvage a 12–10 Wanderers victory.

Wanderers Cup Stories

Some of the most famous stories of Stanley Cup high jinks are associated with the Montreal Wanderers. It is said that when they defeated Ottawa in 1906 and asked to see the Cup, it was nowhere to be found. Eventually, someone remembered that Ottawa's Harry Smith had taken it home, and once the Cup was retrieved it was sent on to Montreal. Given that it took two-and-a-half weeks for the trophy to arrive in Montreal after the Wanderers' victory, this story may even be true!

It's also been said that the Wanderers left the Stanley Cup (or had it stolen from them) at a photographer's studio in 1907, and that it was used as a flowerpot, but there is little evidence to prove this story. Also, a member of the Wanderers is said to have used the trophy to hold gumballs at a bowling alley he owned after the team's victory in 1910.

If that story is true, it would have had to happen in another year because the Wanderers never actually received the Stanley Cup after their 1910 victory (see page 292).

One story that is most definitely true is that the 1907 Wanderers were the first team to have the names of all of the Cup-winning players and executives engraved onto the Stanley Cup. The names as they appear on the inside of the Stanley Cup bowl are:

James Strachan	Jack Marshall	L. Patrick
Ernie Russell	Tom Hodge	Bob Stephenson
Bob Ahern	C. Blachford	Hod Stuart
Pud Glass	Bill Strachan	Dick Boon
Geo Guile	Bert Strachan	William Jennings
Ernie Johnston	Riley Hern	R Kennedy
C McKerrow	Mr. Chipchase	

The Battered Old Mug

On April 5, 1906, the *Montreal Gazette* reported that the Wanderers had received the Stanley Cup from Ottawa the day before. A light luncheon was held to mark the event, and at this gathering the trophy was removed from the case in which it had traveled from Ottawa. The *Gazette* described it as being "a bit battered" with the "plate worn off in spots" and it "bearing the names of players of the Ottawa Hockey Club and some citizens of the Capital, not all of whom are known even in sporting fame." It appeared to be in need of "repair and refurbishing," and the *Gazette* claimed some of the names and initials carved into it were made "in a crude manner, as though done by an ordinary pocket knife."

Two weeks earlier, on March 23rd, the *Toronto Star* had written about the Stanley Cup, saying that it was "not much to look at" and that it had been "defaced during its long sojourn in Ottawa" with "names scratched everywhere."

One of the first names noticeable was that of James McGee. The brother of Frank and D'Arcy McGee had played briefly with Ottawa's 1903–04 Cup winner, but he was better known as a football player before his tragic death in a horse-riding accident in 1904. Other names on the trophy included that of Harry Westwick's infant son Thomas Stanley Westwick (who was named after the Cup), Stanley Cup trustee (and former Ottawa hockey executive) P.D. Ross, local alderman Sam Rosenthal, Miss Lily Murphy of the Ottawa Social Club and her father Denis Murphy.

Ottawa's Silver Sluggers

O n December 21, 1950, newspapers across Canada published the results of a ballot that had been released the day before. Sports editors participating in a Canadian Press poll had voted on the greatest hockey player of the last half-century, and Howie Morenz won in a romp. The late star of the Montreal Canadiens beat out the current Canadiens great, Maurice Richard, 27 votes to 4. The poll to determine hockey's greatest team was much closer, with votes cast for a variety of Stanley Cup, Allan Cup and Olympic champions. The winning teams—with four votes apiece—were the Toronto Varsity Grads and the Ottawa "Silver Seven."

No team was more rugged than the Stanley Cup champions from Ottawa. Hockey had always been a tough game, but the Ottawa team — like the Philadelphia Flyers of the 1970s — seemed to take violence to a new level.

The famous Ottawa team ruled the hockey scene in the early part of the 20th century. They won the Stanley Cup in 1903 and held it until the end of the 1905–06 season, when the Montreal Wanderers finally dethroned them. The Silver Seven nickname came from the very beginning of their championship reign. Harry Westwick, who had starred with the team, told the story to the *Ottawa Journal* shortly before his death in 1957. As Westwick recalled, the name came about after team manager Bob Shillington presented each of the players with a silver nugget following the 1902–03 season. In this era of seven-man hockey, according to Westwick, "one of the fellows said, 'We ought to call ourselves the Silver Seven' and the name caught on right there."

Today the legendary Ottawa hockey team is always referred to as the Silver Seven, but it does not appear that the nickname caught on as quickly as Westwick remembered. In his book *Win, Tie, or Wrangle: The Inside Story of the Old Ottawa Senators—1883–1935*, about the early history of Ottawa hockey, historian Paul Kitchen points out that the city's newspapers rarely used the name Silver Seven when writing about the team. Outside of Ottawa the nickname was virtually unknown. The "Senators" name was occasionally used (though it didn't become common until 1907), but officially the team was known as the Ottawa Hockey Club. To most fans and sportswriters, they were simply the Ottawas.

Percy LeSueur joined the Ottawas

in 1906, the tail end of the Silver Seven era. In commenting on the 1950 Canadian Press poll, he admitted that: "Older hockey lacked the dash of today's razzle-dazzle style." Still, he told reporters that the game of his era featured "more passing [and] more stickhandling, and the players were better shots." LeSueur also thought the hockey of his day "required a more rugged player than the present-day game."

No team was more rugged than the Stanley Cup champions from Ottawa. Hockey had always been a tough game, but the Ottawa team—like the Philadelphia Flyers of the 1970s—seemed to take violence to a new level. In writing about the 1903 playoff victory over the Montreal Victorias that gave Ottawa their first Stanley Cup, the *Montreal Herald* said: "They did not play hockey from the hockeyist's point of view. Far from it. The Gilmours [brothers Billy, Dave and Suddy] have the art of cross-checking and bodying down to a science, while [Frank] McGee has made a special study of that new terror which Ottawa has added to the game, the 'Ottawa hook.' This consists in crooking the stick around a player's neck."

During the team's championship years, newspapers in other cities

Percy LeSueur manned the Ottawa net for nine seasons, winning the Stanley Cup in 1908–09, 1909–10 and 1910–11.

Cup in nine different challenges—far more than any other team of the era. Perhaps they had merely built up more resentment over time than any other hockey team? No doubt they played a rough game, but some of the anger may have had as much to do with the changing times as with the on-ice product. Technically no one in Canada was being paid to play hockey, but as the *Montreal Gazette* pointed out after Ottawa and the Wanderers played a Stanley Cup game on March 2, 1904, "the spirit of professionalism" was creeping into the game. "There was evidenced a 'win or die' determination which resulted in a game utterly unworthy of the best spirit of honest amateurism."

Ottawa most surely exhibited that "win or die" attitude, but despite the criticism of their playing style they were a tremendously talented team. In an era when most teams still relied on the individual skills of their players, Ottawa played what was known as a "scientific" or "combination" game. While defensemen Harvey Pulford and Art Moore concentrated on protecting their goalie, the Ottawa forwards attacked as a unit. They employed short, quick lateral passes (forward passing was not yet allowed) to spring a man into the clear.

never seemed to tire of reporting on Ottawa's violent tactics. But between their first victory in 1903 and their loss to the Wanderers in 1906, Ottawa defended the Stanley

The team's biggest star was Frank McGee, who is still remembered for the 14 goals he scored in a Stanley Cup game against the Dawson City Nuggets in 1905. The performance was no fluke. McGee had lost the sight in one eye during a game in 1900, but he remained a dominating goal-scorer. Though his career of just 23 games over four seasons at the game's highest level was short even by the standards of the day, he managed to score 71 goals. (Some sources credit him with "only" 68.) McGee added 63 more goals in 22 games for the Stanley Cup. He scored eight goals in a single league game during the 1905–06 season and scored five goals in a game seven times in his career.

The Silver Seven name never really applied to just seven players, but in addition to McGee at center, the best-known Ottawa men of the day included Alf Smith at left wing, Billy Gilmour at right wing and Westwick at rover. Pulford and Moore manned the defense in front of goalie Bouse Hutton, who starred during the first two years of the Stanley Cup dynasty. Today all but Moore are members of the Hockey Hall of Fame. With that lineup, Ottawa could certainly beat other teams with their talent, but when they had to, they could beat them in other ways too.

Ottawa Hockey Club (Silver Seven)

ROSTER

Bones Allen

Dave Finnie

Horace Gaul

Billy Gilmour

Frank McGee

Art Moore

Harvey Pulford
(captain)

Hamby Shore

Harry Westwick

Frank White

Alf Smith
(player-coach)

STANDINGS

FEDERAL AMATEUR HOCKEY LEAGUE

	GP	W	L	T	Pts
Ottawa Hockey Club	8	7	1	0	14
Montreal Wanderers	8	6	2	0	12
Brockville Hockey Club	8	4	4	0	8
Cornwall Hockey Club	8	3	5	0	6
Ottawa Montagnards	8	0	8	0	0

MANITOBA HOCKEY LEAGUE

	GP	W	L	T	Pts
Rat Portage Thistles	8	7	1	0	14
Winnipeg Rowing Club	10	6	3	1	13
Portage la Prairie	10	4	5	1	9
Brandon Hockey Club	10	4	6	0	8
Winnipeg Victorias	10	2	8	0	2

CARRYOVER STANLEY CUP CHALLENGE 2 GAMES TO 0

| JAN. 13 | ► | Dawson City* 2 |
| | | at Ottawa Hockey Club 9 |

| JAN. 16 | ► | Dawson City 2 |
| | | at Ottawa Hockey Club 23 |

*Dawson City awarded challenge by trustees after years of speculation and discussion.

POSTSEASON STANLEY CUP CHALLENGE 2 GAMES TO 1

| MAR. 7 | ► | Rat Portage 9 |
| | | at Ottawa Hockey Club 3 |

| MAR. 9 | ► | Rat Portage 2 |
| | | at Ottawa Hockey Club 4 |

| MAR. 11 | ► | Rat Portage 4 |
| | | at Ottawa Hockey Club 5 |

❝ The Yukon team was defeated tonight by 23 goals to 2 and but for the splendid work of the Yukon goalkeeper the score might have been largely increased. Albert Forrest is a wonder, and is said to be the best goalkeeper that ever stood between the flags.❞
— Report from Ottawa in the *Yukon World*, January 17, 1905

❝ The game tonight was very even for 15 minutes. Then the Klondikers began to tire fast and Ottawa ran up the score.❞
— Albert Forrest's dispatch to the *Yukon World*

Other 1905 Challengers

Several other teams challenged for the Stanley Cup in the spring of 1905. They were all delayed until the start of the 1905–06 season, but none was played after Ottawa stated they would not entertain any preseason challenges.

For the second straight year, a challenge was issued from the Maritime-champion Amherst Ramblers, whose 1904 challenge had been rejected. Smiths Falls challenged after winning the Ontario Hockey Association championship, but their disputed victory was later replayed and won by the Toronto Marlboros, who then made their own challenge. There was also a challenge from the Canadian Amateur Hockey League–champion Montreal Victorias, but any need for this match was deemed unnecessary when the Victorias joined Ottawa in the newly formed Eastern Canada Amateur Hockey Association in 1905–06. There were also reports that Marty Walsh of Queen's University suggested that collegiate champions McGill challenge for the Stanley Cup, but no challenge was issued.

The Dawson City Challenge

The earliest mention of a Stanley Cup challenge from Dawson City likely appears in a letter written by former Ottawa hockey star Weldy Young to the *Ottawa Citizen* on July 27, 1900, and printed in the newspaper on August 18th. "A challenge from the Dawson Hockey club, for possession of the Stanley Cup, is now being prepared," Young wrote. "And let me further inform you 'outsiders' that if a team is sent you do not want to hold us too cheaply."

On June 7, 1901, Stanley Cup trustees P.D. Ross and John Sweetland received a letter from G.T. Kirkson and C. Shannon of Dawson City: "Gentlemen. On behalf of the Civil Service Hockey Club of Dawson, hockey champions of the Yukon Territory, we hereby challenge the Victoria Hockey Club of Winnipeg, the present holders of the Stanley Cup, to a series of matches for the championship of Canada…."

The full text of the letter appeared on page six of the *Toronto Star* on July 11, 1901. The trustees were said to be interested and had written to the Stanley Cup holders, the Winnipeg Victorias. On October 24, 1901, the *Manitoba Free Press* quoted a prominent Dawson City lawyer as saying, "The Dawson City hockey enthusiasts were quite willing to furnish funds for a team to come to Winnipeg after the Stanley Cup." Five days later, a *Toronto Star* story referred to another Dawson citizen saying, "There is much talk about the trip."

And yet there was no Stanley Cup challenge from Dawson that winter. When the *Star* reported on December 12, 1901, that a challenge by the Toronto Wellingtons had been accepted, it mentioned that P.D. Ross had never heard back from the Dawson City men after he wrote to ask about specific dates. Three years later, a team from Dawson City made a 4,500-mile trek to Ottawa to challenge for the Stanley Cup.

On September 9, 1904, P.D. Ross acknowledged receipt of the challenge from Weldy Young of the Dawson Hockey Club. Young played up his Ottawa connections and boasted that citizens of Dawson had subscribed $10,000 to send the team east. (This Dawson City All-Star team would make many stops on a lengthy exhibition tour after the games in Ottawa.) Adventurer and entrepreneur Joe Boyle, well-known in Ottawa from his many business trips to woo government officials for mining rights, was able to woo the trustees as well. Though they didn't officially sanction the challenge until December, the team had been working out for a month by then.

On December 18, 1904, the first members of the team left Dawson City by dog sled. With poor snow conditions, others followed by bicycle the next day. (Sadly, a local election meant civil service employee Weldy Young wasn't able to leave in time for the games in Ottawa.) The team arrived (mostly on foot) in Whitehorse 10 days later. Snowstorms delayed their train trip to Skagway, and they had to wait there for three days after missing their ship. They finally caught a steamer that brought them to Seattle, and it took them another day to reach Vancouver, where they boarded the train for Ottawa. The team did not arrive in the Canadian capital until January 11, 1905. Joe Boyle's last-minute request to delay the start of the series was denied, so the team had only one day to rest up from their exhausting journey before the Stanley Cup series began.

Goalie Albert Forrest and defensemen Jim Johnstone and Lorne Hannay (picked up en route in Brandon, Manitoba) played best for Dawson City, but forwards Randy McLellan, Hector Smith, George Kennedy, Norm Watt and Dave Fairburn proved no match for Ottawa, who scored a 9–2 victory in Game 1. Joe Boyle still talked about victory, but most newspaper reports slammed the poor quality of the Klondike team.

Ottawa great Frank McGee scored only once in Game 1. According to most stories, the Dawson City players publicly claimed to be unimpressed with his play. Other stories say that McGee had a personal dislike for Boyle and took it out on him in Game 2. Whatever the reason, McGee set a Stanley Cup record never to be broken when he scored 14 goals to lead Ottawa to a 23–2 victory in the second game.

Rats!

The Dawson City challenge of 1905 is the best-known series of the "challenge era," but the best-played series featured Ottawa and Rat Portage in March 1905.

The Rat Portage Thistles (the town would be renamed Kenora in May 1905) had first challenged Ottawa for the Stanley Cup in 1903. The young team was without its best player that year, as Tom Phillips was attending McGill University. Phillips returned to Rat Portage in the spring of 1904 and brought along goalie Eddie Giroux, with whom he had played on the Toronto Marlboros in 1903–04. Rat Portage, which had always played in Manitoba leagues because of its remote location in northwestern Ontario, were champions again in 1904–05. This time, they gave Ottawa a real battle.

Tom Phillips scored five goals in a 9–3 win in Game 1. Ottawa had been without injured stars Frank McGee and Billy Gilmour, but both were back for Game 2. McGee reportedly wore only a light bandage over his broken wrist while his good forearm was wrapped in a full cast to decoy the Thistles. Alf Smith scored three goals for Ottawa in a rough 4–2 win. The game was played on soft ice that many accused Ottawa of salting to slow down the speedy Thistles.

Cold weather ensured hard ice for Game 3, and it was a classic seesaw struggle. Rat Portage led 2–1 at halftime and 3–2 midway through the second half. Ottawa was up 4–3 late in the game. Phillips got his third goal to tie the score, but McGee's third in the dying moments gave Ottawa a 5–4 victory.

Ottawa Hockey Club (Silver Seven)

ROSTER

Billy Gilmour

Suddy Gilmour

Bouse Hutton

Frank McGee

Jim McGee

Art Moore

Harvey Pulford (captain)

Harry Westwick

Scott

Alf Smith (playing coach)

STANDINGS

CANADIAN AMATEUR HOCKEY ASSOCIATION

	GP	W	L	T	Pts
Quebec Hockey Club°	8	7	1	0	14
Montreal Victorias	8	5	3	0	10
Montreal Hockey Club	8	3	5	0	6
Montreal Shamrocks	8	1	7	0	2
Ottawa Hockey Club°	8	4	4	0	8

°Quebec was not awarded the Stanley Cup for the league win, as was customary. Cup trustees elected to allow Ottawa to keep the Cup.
°Ottawa was 4–0 but resigned from the CAHL on February 8th. Four remaining games were lost by default. Ottawa results did not count in final standings.

ONTARIO HOCKEY ASSOCIATION
(Senior Group 3)

	GP	W	L	T	Pts
Toronto Marlboros^	4	4	0	0	8
St. George's (Toronto)	4	2	2	0	4
Barrie Colts	4	0	4	0	0

^Defeated Perth 28–9 in two-game, total-goals series to win OHA title.

FEDERAL AMATEUR HOCKEY LEAGUE

	GP	W	L	T	Pts
Montreal Wanderers	6	6	0	0	12
Montreal Nationals	6	3	3	0	6
Cornwall Hockey Club	6	2	4	0	4
Ottawa Capitals	6	1	5	0	2

MANITOBA AND NORTH WEST HOCKEY ASSOCIATION

	GP	W	L	T	Pts
Brandon Hockey Club	12	9	3	0	18
Rat Portage Thistles	12	8	4	0	16
Portage la Prairie	12	1	11	0	2

CARRYOVER STANLEY CUP CHALLENGE

2 GAMES TO 1

DEC. 30 ► Winnipeg Rowing Club* 1
at Ottawa Hockey Club 9

JAN. 1 ► Winnipeg Rowing Club 6
at Ottawa Hockey Club 2

JAN. 4 ► Winnipeg Rowing Club 0
at Ottawa Hockey Club 2

*Winnipeg (the 1902–03 Western Canada Hockey Association champions, see pages 304–05) was awarded a carryover challenge, which was played in 1904.

MIDSEASON STANLEY CUP CHALLENGE

2 GAMES TO 0

FEB. 23 ► Toronto Marlboros 3
at Ottawa Hockey Club 6

FEB. 25 ► Toronto Marlboros 2
at Ottawa Hockey Club 11

POSTSEASON STANLEY CUP CHALLENGE

5 GOALS TO 5*

MAR. 2 ► Ottawa Hockey Club 5
at Montreal Wanderers 5

*Series awarded to Ottawa as defending champions.

POSTSEASON STANLEY CUP CHALLENGE

15 GOALS TO 6

MAR. 9 ► Brandon 3 at Ottawa Hockey Club 6

MAR. 11 ► Brandon 3 at Ottawa Hockey Club 9

Tough Times for the Stanley Cup

In the fall of 1902, there had been a long battle between the trustees, the teams and the executive of the Canadian Amateur Hockey League (CAHL) over the scheduling of Stanley Cup games. During the 1903–04 season, many came to feel that the Stanley Cup was encouraging rough play on the ice and bad sportsmanship in league boardrooms.

On-ice violence became an issue right from the start of the 1903–04 season. Ottawa had won the Stanley Cup for the first time in March 1903 and were called on to defend it in a preseason best-of-three series against the Winnipeg Rowing Club. The games were played at the Aberdeen Pavilion, which still stands on the grounds of Lansdowne Park.

Game 1 was a 9–1 rout for Ottawa, but the score wasn't the biggest news. "It was not the nicest hockey," reported the *Montreal Gazette*, "but for those who love to see strong forces clash, it was all that could be desired." The *Manitoba Free Press* referred to it as "one of the bloodiest battles ever fought on Ottawa ice," and Winnipeg captain Billy Breen called it the dirtiest game he had ever played in.

When Winnipeg won the second game 6–2, there were those who wondered if Ottawa had thrown it to guarantee the extra gate receipts, but the tight battle in Game 3 proved the Rowing Club was a worthy opponent. The *Telegram* pleaded "that brutality should not be tolerated" in Game 3, and Harry Trihey called numerous penalties in an attempt to keep the game under control. Ottawa's Frank McGee finally broke a scoreless tie when he beat Art Brown midway through the second half. Billy Gilmour (who was replacing an injured Alf Smith) combined with his brother, Suddy, for the game's only other goal, though newspaper reports seem mixed as to which of the Gilmours actually scored it. Art Moore and Harvey Pulford put up a solid defense in front of goalie Bouse Hutton as Ottawa took the match 2–0.

Off the ice, a dispute with the CAHL had already seen rival teams form the Federal Amateur Hockey League (FAHL). Further squabbles in the CAHL boardroom began after an Ottawa game against the Montreal Victorias on January 30, 1904. Ottawa had been nearly two hours late arriving in Montreal and was leading 4–1 when the game was halted at midnight. Angry about the decision over replaying the game, Ottawa resigned from the CAHL. With the consent of trustee P.D. Ross, the team finished out the winter by playing challenge matches for the Stanley Cup. They would join the FAHL the following season.

First up was a challenge from the Toronto Marlboros (formally known as the Toronto Marlborough Athletic Club), who had won the OHA senior championship in their first season in the top group. Four members of the Marlboros, including goalie Eddie Giroux, had won the junior title a year before. The key newcomer was Tom Phillips of Rat Portage. After spending the 1902–03 season playing hockey for the Montreal Hockey Club (Montreal AAA) while attending McGill University, he came to Toronto to attend the city's Central Business College.

The Marlboros wrapped up the OHA title on February 20, 1904. They caught a train to Ottawa the next day but proved no match for the Stanley Cup champions. The Marlboros started quickly in Game 1, with two goals in the first three minutes and led 3–1 at the end of the first half. Ottawa stormed back after the intermission and won the game 6–3. Toronto newspapers reacted much like those in Winnipeg had.

"In a game that was strictly hockey, [the Marlboros] would have been in the front at the finish," claimed the *Globe*, but "the hammering and jamming they got in the first part told in the second period."

The *Toronto Star* was less subtle. "Slugged and Bodied into Submission," screamed the headline. "Marlboros Beaten by Ottawa, But Not at Hockey."

The Ottawa newspapers stuck by their boys and were vindicated with an 11–2 victory in a clean game that wrapped up the series. "The squealers from Squealville-on-the-Don raised an awful howl against the alleged brutality of the holders of Lord Stanley's silverware," gloated the *Ottawa Citizen*, adding, "These men … who wrote the stuff alleged that had the champions played hockey alone the result would have been disastrous to Ottawa. But they got their answer good and hard last night."

More Trouble

When he had allowed Ottawa to keep the Stanley Cup after leaving the CAHL, P.D. Ross recalled the precedent of 1898–99: In December of 1898, the Montreal Victorias quit the Amateur Hockey Association of Canada to help form the CAHL and were allowed to keep the Stanley Cup. But this time around, Quebec (winner of the CAHL title in the wake of Ottawa's departure), felt they were entitled to the Cup, especially since Ottawa left the league halfway through the season. But under the terms of Lord Stanley's deed of gift, the trustees had the power to award the Cup as they saw fit, and the trophy stayed with Ottawa.

Trouble of another kind arose after the Montreal Wanderers opened their challenge with Ottawa with a 5–5 tie in a penalty-filled game. The Wanderers asked that the game not count and that a new best-of-three series resume with Game 1 replayed in Montreal. But the defending champions insisted on playing at home. When the Wanderers refused, the series was scrapped and Ottawa retained the Stanley Cup.

The final challenge of the year was played between Ottawa and the Brandon Hockey Club, which featured Joe Hall and Clint Bennest, but they were ruled ineligible as they had previously played with the Winnipeg Rowing Club during their challenge. Brandon also featured a promising young defenseman named Lester Patrick. Patrick had played forward while growing up in Montreal and surprised the fans in Ottawa by rushing the puck, which was quite rare for defenseman of this era. Even so, Ottawa handled Brandon with ease.

ROSTERS

Montreal Hockey Club (Montreal AAA)

Billy Bellingham

Cecil Blachford

Dickie Boon

Jimmy Gardner

Tom Hodge

Art Hooper

Billy Nicholson

Jack Marshall

Tom Phillips

George "Doe" Smith

Ottawa Hockey Club (Silver Seven)

A.A. Fraser

Billy Gilmour

Dave Gilmour

Suddy Gilmour

Bouse Hutton

Frank McGee

Art Moore

Harvey Pulford (captain)

Percy Sims

Charles Spittal

Harry Westwick

F.H. Wood

Alf Smith (coach)

STANDINGS

CANADIAN AMATEUR HOCKEY LEAGUE

	GP	W	L	T	Pts
Ottawa Hockey Club	8	6	2	0	12
Montreal Victorias	8	6	2	0	12
Montreal Hockey Club	7	4	3	0	8
Quebec Hockey Club	7	3	4	0	6
Montreal Shamrocks	8	0	8	0	0

MANITOBA AND NORTH WEST HOCKEY ASSOCIATION

	GP	W	L	T	Pts
Rat Portage Thistles	6	4	2	0	8
Brandon Hockey Club	6	3	3	0	6
Portage la Prairie	6	3	3	0	6
Winnipeg Shamrocks	6	2	4	0	4

WESTERN CANADA HOCKEY ASSOCIATION

	GP	W	L	T	Pts
Winnipeg Rowing Club*	6	4	2	0	8
Winnipeg Victorias	6	2	4	0	4

*Played for Stanley Cup in 1903–04.

CARRYOVER STANLEY CUP CHALLENGE 2 GAMES TO 1

JAN. 29 ▸ Winnipeg Victorias* 1 at Montreal Hockey Club 8

JAN. 31 ▸ Winnipeg Victorias 2 at Montreal Hockey Club 2 OT

FEB. 2 ▸ Winnipeg Victorias 4 at Montreal Hockey Club 2

FEB. 4 ▸ Winnipeg Victorias 1 at Montreal Hockey Club 4

*Winnipeg (the 1901–02 Manitoba and North West Hockey Association champions, see pages 306–07) was awarded a carryover challenge, which was played in 1903.

POSTSEASON CAHL STANLEY CUP PLAYOFF 9 GOALS TO 1

MAR. 7 ▸ Ottawa 1 at Montreal Victorias 1

MAR. 10 ▸ Montreal Victorias 0 at Ottawa 8

POSTSEASON STANLEY CUP CHALLENGE 10 GOALS TO 4

MAR. 12 ▸ Rat Portage 2 at Ottawa 6

MAR. 14 ▸ Rat Portage 2 at Ottawa 4

All-Around Athletes

Ottawa goalie Bouse Hutton was a multi-sport star who also played goal for the Ottawa Capitals lacrosse team. He played fullback for the Ottawa Rough Riders football team as well. Hutton won national championships in all three sports, though not all in one year, as has long been said of him. When he signed a pro contract to play lacrosse in 1904, he had to give up football and hockey, which were still amateur sports.

It was common for athletes to compete in many different sports in this era, but few could match the success of Hutton's teammate Harvey Pulford. In addition to his Stanley Cup wins in Ottawa, Pulford won national football titles with the Rough Riders in 1898, 1900 and 1902. While he only dabbled in lacrosse with the Capitals, he was the light-heavyweight and heavyweight boxing champion of Eastern Canada between 1896 and 1898 and also won several national titles in rowing and canoeing.

Last Win for the First Champs

The Hockey Club from the Montreal Amateur Athletic Association, the original Stanley Cup champions of 1893, had won the title again in a thrilling series with the Winnipeg Victorias in March of 1902. Almost immediately after the Montreal victory, Winnipeg began clamoring for a rematch. As champions of the 1901–02 Manitoba and North West Hockey Association (MNWHA), the Victorias officially submitted their challenge on November 10, 1902. They asked for dates in mid-January 1903. The trustees accepted and passed on the request to the Montreal Hockey Club. But there were two problems.

One problem was that in mid-December 1902, the Winnipeg Victorias had quit the MNWHA. They were not happy with the inclusion of teams from Brandon, Rat Portage and Portage la Prairie into a senior division that had long been the exclusive domain of Winnipeg teams. The Victorias and the Winnipeg Rowing Club formed a new two-team league and called it the Western Canada Hockey Association (WCHA). All of this was noted with ridicule in the Montreal newspapers, and many wondered what right the Victorias had to play for the Stanley Cup as champions of a league they were no longer a part of. But P.D. Ross explained, "the Manitoba split has no bearing on the present challenge."

The more serious problem was with the Canadian Amateur Hockey League (CAHL). Since 1900, the league had required teams to seek permission to play midseason games outside of the schedule. The CAHL had always agreed to Stanley Cup games before, but this time the league refused. They did not want the Stanley Cup trustees dictating internal league policy and argued that a Stanley Cup series in January would hurt attendance at other league games. Montreal agreed to abide by the league's decision, and the team went so far as to say they would default the series and ship the Stanley Cup west if the trustees insisted they play. No one was anxious for that to happen, and so talks continued. Negotiations between the Winnipeg Victorias, Montreal Hockey Club, the trustees, the CAHL executive and other CAHL teams dragged on—amid much press coverage in Winnipeg, Montreal and all across the country—until early January. Finally, it was resolved that a best-of-three series for the Stanley Cup would begin before the end of the month.

Despite two wins in three games to start the CAHL season, Montreal was playing poorly. When a quick trip to New York for two exhibition games failed to work out the problems on the roster, Montreal added Tom Phillips to their lineup for the Stanley Cup series. Phillips had been working out with the Montreal club, but the 19-year-old Rat Portage native had come to Montreal to attend McGill University and had to quit the school's hockey team to join his new team. Phillips had never played above intermediate hockey, which was the highest level Rat Portage had been allowed to play in prior to this season's split in Manitoba hockey, but he was a star in the Stanley Cup series. The rookie had mainly a defensive role against Winnipeg in Montreal's 8–1 win in Game 1, but the Montreal Herald noted, "Phillips will do." He played another strong defensive game and scored his first goal in a 2–2 tie in Game 2. After some discussion with the trustees, it was decided that the tie game wouldn't count. Winnipeg evened the series with a 4–2 win in the next game, but Montreal wrapped it up with a 4–1 victory in the fourth game. Phillips scored two goals and was once again instrumental in bottling up Winnipeg star Tony Gingras. "Phillips," the Herald said, "was the most conspicuous player on the ice, with body, stick and head."

After the game, the Montreal players headed to the Oxford Hotel restaurant for a celebration. "Supper was served and prominent on the table was the Stanley Cup, newly burnished for the occasion. It was filled with champagne and the players quaffed of the flowing bowl in honor of their great victory, while each one was cheered til it seemed as if the cheering would never cease."

The Montreal Hockey Club had retained the Stanley Cup, but they could not hold on to the CAHL title. Frank McGee made his senior debut in Ottawa this season, and though he played just six of eight games on the CAHL schedule, his 14 goals were second in the league. Russell Bowie of the Montreal Victorias led with 22 goals despite missing the last game of the season with an injured ankle. When the Montreal Victorias beat Quebec without their scoring star, they moved into a tie with Ottawa for first place in the CAHL standings. A two-game, home-and-home, total-goals playoff was arranged to determine the new league champion. The winner of the series would become the new Stanley Cup champion as well.

Ottawa Takes the Title

The CAHL season ended on February 28, 1903. P.D. Ross had received challenges from the Toronto Wellingtons and from the Rat Portage Thistles. He hoped the CAHL would move quickly to break the tie so that both challengers would get to play for the Cup.

Ottawa hoped to schedule the playoff with the Victorias for March 5th and 7th, but the Victorias had played two games the week before, while Ottawa had been off since February 21st. The Vics also wanted their star Russell Bowie to have a few more days to recover from his ankle injury. They held out for March 7th and 10th. After much wrangling, Ottawa agreed. The Thistles chose to wait and play the winner. The Wellingtons, with several injured players of their own, gave the Stanley Cup a pass.

With an early spring turning the ice to slush, the Victorias and Ottawa struggled to a 1–1 tie in Game 1. It was a rough game, and while Russell Bowie held up well, Ottawa's Harry Westwick suffered a broken ankle. On slightly better ice in Game 2, Ottawa scored a shocking 8–0 victory.

Ice conditions were even worse for Ottawa's series against Rat Portage. During Game 1, a puck was said to have disappeared through a hole in the ice. "Stage fright," according to the Ottawa Citizen, was the Thistles' excuse for their 6–2 loss. The young team played much better in Game 2, but the Stanley Cup remained in Ottawa. Frank McGee and brothers Billy, Dave and Suddy Gilmour combined to score all 19 goals for Ottawa in the postseason. McGee scored seven in four games.

CANADIAN AMATEUR HOCKEY LEAGUE

	GP	W	L	T	Pts
Montreal Hockey Club	8	6	2	0	12
Ottawa Hockey Club	8	5	3	0	10
Montreal Victorias	8	4	4	0	8
Quebec Hockey Club	8	4	4	0	8
Montreal Shamrocks	8	1	7	0	2

MANITOBA AND NORTH WEST HOCKEY ASSOCIATION

	GP	W	L	T	Pts
Winnipeg Victorias	4	4	0	0	8
Winnipeg Hockey Club	4	0	4	0	0

CARRYOVER STANLEY CUP CHALLENGE 2 GAMES TO 0

JAN. 21 ► Toronto Wellingtons* 3
at Winnipeg Victorias 5

JAN. 23 ► Toronto Wellingtons 3
at Winnipeg Victorias 5

*Toronto (the 1900–01 Ontario Hockey Association champions, see pages 308–09) was awarded a carryover challenge, which was played in 1902.

POSTSEASON STANLEY CUP CHALLENGE 2 GAMES TO 1

MAR. 13 ► Montreal Hockey Club 0
at Winnipeg Victorias 1

MAR. 15 ► Montreal Hockey Club 5
at Winnipeg Victorias 0

MAR. 17 ► Montreal Hockey Club 2
at Winnipeg Victorias 1

ROSTERS

Winnipeg Victorias

Dan Bain (captain)
Art Brown
F. Cadham
Magnus Flett
Tony Gingras
Rod Flett
Charles Johnstone
Fred Scanlan
Burke Wood

Montreal Hockey Club (Montreal AAA) ▲

Billy Bellingham
Dickie Boon
Roland Elliot
Jimmy Gardner
Tom Hodge
Art Hooper
Charles Liffiton
Jack Marshall
Billy Nicholson

Half Measures

During the second game of the Wellingtons' series, there was a scramble around the Winnipeg net, and the puck got broken in two. Toronto's Chummy Hill scooped up half the puck and shot it into the net. Winnipeg goalie Art Brown said afterward that he thought the play had stopped and that he was taken by surprise. The goal put Toronto ahead 2–1 early in the second half, but Winnipeg came back to win it 5–3. A few years later, referee Fred Waghorne ruled no goal in a game when a player scored with a broken puck. Waghorne figured that, since the rules said a puck was supposed to be one inch (2.5 cm) thick, if something smaller than that went into the net, it wasn't really a puck, so it shouldn't count as a goal. Ever since then, hockey rules have stated that the whole puck has to go across the goal line for a goal to count.

> Dear Sir,
> On behalf of the Wellington Hockey Club, senior champions of the Ontario Hockey Associations, I beg to challenge the holders of the Stanley Cup to play a series of matches for the Cup... I would suggest the 21st, 23rd, and 25th of January, 1902, as the dates for the games, and the best two in three to decide the winner.
>
> Trusting you can arrange this matter on the above basis, and awaiting your prompt reply.
>
> Respectfully yours, Alexander Miln, Secretary Treasurer"
> — Text of the first Stanley Cup challenge from a Toronto team, sent to P.D. Ross on December 11, 1901.

Winnipeg Beats the Wellingtons

In January 1901, the Winnipeg Victorias defeated the Montreal Shamrocks to win the Stanley Cup. The trustees advised the Vics that they would likely be called on to defend the Cup themselves later in the season, but no one came to play them for it.

On March 1, 1901, the *Toronto Star* reported that an invitation had been sent from Winnipeg asking the Ontario Hockey Association (OHA) to send its champion. In December, the Toronto Wellingtons (who had won their second straight OHA title) decided to issue a challenge.

Although the OHA was the biggest league in Canada, it was thought that the quality of play in Ontario was below that of Quebec and Manitoba. Sportswriters in Montreal and Winnipeg predicted a tough time for Toronto and thought the Wellingtons (who were used to playing in the cramped quarters of the Caledonian Rink on Mutual Street) would have a difficult time adapting to the large ice surface of the Winnipeg Auditorium. But the biggest problem the Wellingtons faced was with the Toronto weather, as a mild January meant no ice to practice on. A *Toronto Star* cartoon on January 11, 1902, showed the Wellingtons working out with weights as they watered and cut the grass growing through the arena floor. Still, the Wellingtons scored two lopsided wins to start the OHA season before boarding a train for Winnipeg.

The Victorias swept the series, but the Wellingtons still impressed the locals. "Few believed they were strong enough to give the Vics a hard game," admitted the *Manitoba Free Press* after Game 1, adding, "This was a mistaken idea." The *Winnipeg Telegram* said, "The crowd was intensely relieved when it was over and the Victorias had won." After the series, Wellingtons captain George McKay admitted, "We played as hard as we ever played in our lives, but the checking … was much harder then we were accustomed to. It was fierce."

Ottawa Outta Luck

Ottawa had won the CAHL title in 1900–01 but decided against making a trip to Winnipeg that spring to play the Cup-holding Winnipeg Victorias. In February 1902, with the new CAHL season almost over, Ottawa finally submitted a challenge. However, with Ottawa unlikely to retain the CAHL title, Winnipeg declined. They wanted to take on the new champions. The Montreal Hockey Club clinched the 1901–02 CAHL title on February 26th and issued their own challenge on March 1st. It was accepted on March 3rd.

Montreal Series Stirs Up Excitement

The Montreal Hockey Club (Montreal AAA) boasted three future Hall of Famers in 1901–02, with Jack Marshall and Jimmy Gardner joining captain Dickie Boon in the lineup. Still, the biggest star this season was Art Hooper, who led the Canadian Amateur Hockey League (CAHL) with 17 goals in eight games.

There was big excitement for the Stanley Cup series, but even in Montreal the odds were said to be 2 : 1 in favor of Winnipeg. Top-priced tickets of a $1.50 were reportedly going for as much as $25 as a full house of 4,000 fans jammed the Auditorium for each game. Crowds of people also gathered in Montreal to receive telegraphed reports. Some 600 people filled the MAAA gymnasium to listen to the updates, while thousands more gathered in the streets outside the *Montreal Star*'s downtown office and at the branch office in Point St. Charles.

The weather in Winnipeg was unseasonably mild and an inch of water over slushy ice made the going rough in Game 1. Winnipeg's Tony Gingras notched the only goal midway through the first half as the Victorias scored a 1–0 victory. Ice conditions were much improved for Game 2, and the Montrealers showed their speed. Art Hooper and Jack Marshall each scored twice, and Billy Nicholson matched Art Brown's shutout performance of Game 1 in a 5–0 Montreal victory. It was said to be the first time the Winnipeg Victorias had been shutout since the team was formed in 1890.

Game 3 was the best of the series. Hooper got Montreal on the scoreboard first, and Marshall upped the lead to 2–0 after 11 minutes. Winnipeg carried the play for the rest of the night, but Montreal held on for a 2–1 victory. Winnipeg lost the Stanley Cup, and no Winnipeg team has won it since.

The Little Men of Iron

During the thrilling final moments of Game 3 in the series between Winnipeg and Montreal, *Montreal Star* sports editor Peter Spanjaardt is said to have telegraphed that the Montreal team was standing up to Winnipeg's furious efforts "like little men of iron." Stories in other Montreal newspapers claimed the Winnipeg press had coined the phrase, but it doesn't seem to have been used in any Winnipeg newspapers. Perhaps Spanjaardt heard it spoken by Winnipeg writers during the series. Sports historian Don Morrow has speculated that the phrase may have been a way of satirizing the Toronto Wellingtons, who were called the "Iron Dukes" by Toronto newspapers after the nickname of the first Duke of Wellington, for whom the team had been named.

No matter where the phrase came from, "The Little Men of Iron" nickname stuck with the Montreal team, though it would often later be applied to the Montreal Wanderers, a team formed in 1903–04 by several former Montreal Hockey Club players who had wanted to break away from the Montreal Amateur Athletic Association.

For Whom the Whistle Blows

When the Wellingtons went to Winnipeg, OHA president John Ross Robertson came up with a way of alerting Toronto fans of the results. The Toronto Railway would blow the giant steam whistle on top of its powerhouse twice for a win and three times for a loss.

CANADIAN AMATEUR HOCKEY LEAGUE

	GP	W	L	T	Pts
Ottawa Hockey Club*	8	7	0	1	15
Montreal Victorias	8	4	3	1	9
Montreal Shamrocks	8	4	4	0	8
Montreal Hockey Club	8	3	5	0	6
Quebec Hockey Club	8	1	7	0	2

*Did not challenge for Stanley Cup this season.

MANITOBA AND NORTH WEST HOCKEY ASSOCIATION

	GP	W	L	T	Pts
Winnipeg Victorias	4	4	0	0	8
Winnipeg Hockey Club	4	0	4	0	0

ONTARIO HOCKEY ASSOCIATION
(Group 2)

	GP	W	L	T	Pts
Toronto Wellingtons^°			N/A		

^Defeated Peterborough, University of Toronto and Queen's University in playoffs to win OHA title.
°Played for Stanley Cup in 1901–02.

CARRYOVER STANLEY CUP CHALLENGE
2 GAMES TO 0

JAN. 29 ► Winnipeg Victorias† 4
at Montreal Shamrocks 3

JAN. 31 ► Winnipeg Victorias 2
at Montreal Shamrocks 1 (OT)

†Winnipeg (the 1899–1900 Manitoba and North West Hockey Association champions, see pages 310–11) was awarded a carryover challenge, which was played in 1901.

> "At last we have landed the Cup. We will certainly have a good time. Boys are all O.K. and am feeling fine myself."
> — Telegram sent home by Dan Bain after his overtime winner.

ROSTER

Dan Bain (captain) ▲

Art Brown
George Carruthers
Magnus Flett
Rod Flett
Tony Gingras
Charles Johnstone
Jack Marshall
Burke Wood

Other 1901 Challenges

Had the Shamrocks managed to defeat Winnipeg in January, Ottawa would have taken over the Stanley Cup when they won the 1900–01 CAHL title. But with the Stanley Cup now the property of the Manitoba and North West Hockey Association, Ottawa would have to head to Winnipeg for a chance to win it. A challenge was expected, but Ottawa had just completed a tough season, and the players were not thought to be in the best shape to go after the Stanley Cup. Ottawa would wait until the 1901–02 season to make a decision.

One team that did want to challenge for the Cup was the Western Ontario Hockey Association champions from Berlin (now Kitchener), but they were not looked on as serious competitors. "They couldn't beat a drum," mocked the Woodstock, Ontario, *Sentinel-Review* newspaper.

Western Road Trip

No teams came to Winnipeg to challenge for the Stanley Cup at the end of the 1900–01 season, but the Montreal Shamrocks did make the trip west for a couple of exhibition games. They beat the Winnipegs 6–2 on March 9th but lost another close game to the Victorias when they were beaten 2–1 on March 11th.

Friends in High Places

After the season, the Victorias were presented with gold watches from the club at a dinner at the home of former captain and current team president Jack Armytage. Hugh John Macdonald, the club's honorary president, made a speech. Macdonald was a prominent Winnipeg lawyer, as well as the former premier of Manitoba and the son of Canada's first prime minster, Sir John A. Macdonald.

Winnipeg Works Overtime

In February 1900, the Montreal Shamrocks successfully defended the Stanley Cup in a thrilling three-game series against the Winnipeg Victorias. It was the second year in a row that a Montreal team had defeated the Victorias, but when the Winnipeg team faced the Shamrocks again in 1901, they brought the prized trophy back west with the first Stanley Cup–winning goal ever scored in overtime.

The defending-champion Shamrocks had gotten off to slow a start in the 1900–01 season with only two wins in four league games. The Victorias weren't playing as well as their fans had hoped either. "Winnipeg papers say the Victorias are weak," reported the *Toronto Star* on January 16, 1901, "and Montreal critics count the Shamrocks out of the running. Why doesn't the Orangeville Ladies' Club challenge for the Stanley Cup."

The Victorias suffered a potentially serious blow in a game the next evening, when their captain and star Dan Bain took a puck in the eye from close range. It was feared the injury might end his season, but Bain was back at practice a few nights later and wearing a pair of goggles. He played the first game against the Shamrocks in a mask.

The Shamrocks presented basically the same lineup that had faced the Victorias in 1900, though longtime Montreal Victorias star Mike Grant replaced the ailing Frank Tansey. The Winnipeg team had added Burke Wood, who scored two goals against the Shamrocks in the first game, including the winner with just one minute remaining. The Vics had also brought newcomer Jack Marshall as a spare. He would win the Stanley Cup for the first of six times in his career and with the first of four different teams.

Game 2 was another close one with plenty of end-to-end action. Bain put Winnipeg ahead late in the first half, but Shamrocks star Harry Trihey tied the score early in the second. When Trihey was hurt late in the game, the Vics dropped Wood to even the sides, and the teams finished with six men apiece. "The absence of Trihey … was fatal for the Shamrocks," reported the *Manitoba Free Press*, "and it was quite evident that the [Victorias] would win out in time." It was still 1–1 after 60 minutes, but following a brief rest, Bain became the overtime hero. Different reports put the time of the winning goal at either four minutes or seven minutes.

Good-bye, Old Cup

Good-bye, old cup! We thought, you know,
We'd keep you here a few more seasons.
And now we've lost our grip on you,
For plain and likewise painful reasons.
But well we've fought to have you stay,
We find it hard to give you up.
We've made them fight your cause for years,
And now you go. Good-bye, old cup.

Good-bye, old cup! We've done our best,
To keep you in our fair collection.
We've slashed and played the game for fair,
As thousands have the recollection.
Yea, often have opposing teams
Assailed us, failed, and given it up,
Yet now you go to Winnipeg!
We did our best. Good-bye, old Cup!
— *Montreal Herald*, early February 1901

Welcome, Old Cup

Welcome, old cup! You are ours again,
For year after year we have sought you.
We sent our best, our ablest men,
And now, old cup, we have got you.
It's reluctant you were to come out west,
Where once you were contented.
But we entered the games with vim and zest,
And at last you have consented.

Welcome, old Cup! You are ours at last,
The Shamrocks failed to keep you.
We'll show them hockey hard and fast,
When next they come to seek you.
For it's back you are, and back to stay,
Although the east your possession crave.
We'll keep you here for many a day,
The prairie boys will the old cup save.
— *Manitoba Free Press*, February 5, 1901

66 They will take a rest. The game was the most furious I ever saw. They come on again. Winnipeg men take their places. Whistle. Six each side. Face. Off they go. Shamrocks got it. Magnus [Flett] brings it up. Two shots on Shamrock goal. Relieved. It goes up on Winnipeg goal. Dan [Bain] gets it. [Shamrocks' Art] Farrell takes it. [Frank] Wall lifts. It is on the Winnipeg goal. [Charles] Johnstone passes to Tony [Gingras], shoots. [Defenseman Mike] Grant saves. Farrell shoots wide. Dan brings it down, passes to Tony, lost it. Grant gets it. Now Tony takes it. Shamrocks take it up. Scrimmage on Winnipeg goal. Flett brings it down. Offside. Face. Dan gets it and shoots. Goes outside the post. Grant takes it up. Dan shoots. Game for Winnipeg. Bain put it in. It was a beauty."

— Play-by-play of overtime in Game 2 telegraphed to Winnipeg and re-printed in the *Manitoba Free Press*, February 1, 1901.

Montreal Shamrocks

ROSTER

Jack Brannen

Art Farrell

Joe McKenna

Fred Scanlan

Frank Tansey

Harry Trihey (captain)

Frank Wall

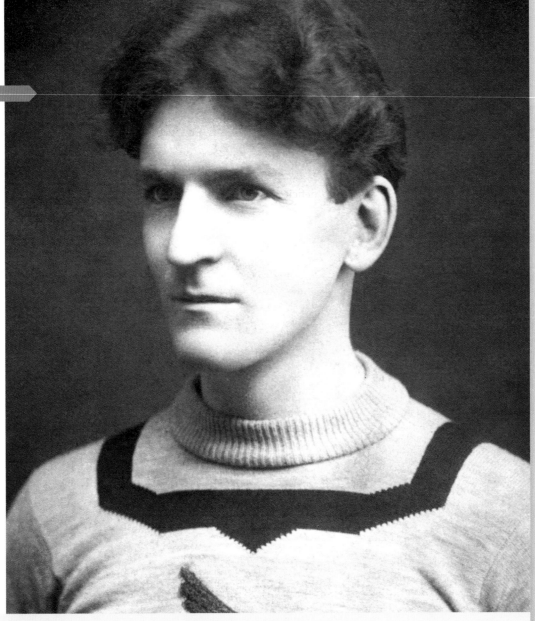

STANDINGS

CANADIAN AMATEUR HOCKEY LEAGUE

	GP	W	L	T	Pts
Montreal Shamrocks	8	7	1	0	14
Montreal Hockey Club	8	5	3	0	10
Ottawa Hockey Club	8	4	4	0	8
Montreal Victorias	8	2	6	0	4
Quebec Hockey Club	8	2	6	0	4

MANITOBA AND NORTH WEST HOCKEY ASSOCIATION

	GP	W	L	T	Pts
Winnipeg Victorias	6	4	2°	0	8
Winnipeg Hockey Club	6	2°	4	0	4

°Games were defaulted after Victorias clinched title.

HALIFAX HOCKEY LEAGUE

	GP	W	L	T	Pts
Halifax Crescents	8	8	0	0	16
Halifax Wanderers	N/A				
Dartmouth Chebuctos	N/A				

MIDSEASON STANLEY CUP CHALLENGE

2 GAMES TO 1

FEB. 12 ▸ Winnipeg Victorias 4 at Montreal Shamrocks 3

FEB. 14 ▸ Winnipeg Victorias 2 at Montreal Shamrocks 3

FEB. 16 ▸ Winnipeg Victorias 4 at Montreal Shamrocks 5

POSTSEASON STANLEY CUP CHALLENGE

21 GOALS TO 2

MAR. 5 ▸ Halifax 2 at Montreal Shamrocks 10

MAR. 7 ▸ Halifax 0 at Montreal Shamrocks 11

> ❝It was a hard blow to lose on so close a margin, but we have no complaint, we were beaten by a better team.❞
> —Winnipeg Victorias manager Abe W. Code

> ❝They were great contests; in fact, I doubt whether there has ever been three such wonderful matches played before. The Shamrocks won on their merits. They have a splendid team.❞
> —Winnipeg Victorias captain Dan Bain

Arthur, Author

In 1899, Art Farrell of the Montreal Shamrocks wrote the first book about hockey. *Hockey: Canada's Royal Winter Game* discusses the history of the game and the Stanley Cup, and it gives brief histories of the top teams at the time (complete with photographs). It is, however, essentially a handbook on how to play the game and understand its rules.

"That a book on our national winter sport has not yet appeared in Canada is a marvel," writes Farrell in his introduction. "It is our most popular winter game … and it certainly deserves a place with the other athletic pastimes that boast of a hand-book."

To assist him, Farrell turned to several other stars of his day. Quebec's Frank Stocking offered his tips on goaltending, Hugh Baird of Montreal and Mike Grant of the Victorias contributed to the section on defense, while Farrell's teammate Harry Trihey wrote about playing forward.

Shamrocks in a Thriller

The Montreal Shamrocks had dethroned the Montreal Victorias as champions of the Canadian Amateur Hockey League (CAHL) in 1898–99 to take over the Stanley Cup. The Shamrocks were led by their star center and team captain, Harry Trihey. He topped the CAHL in scoring with 19 goals in seven games in 1898–99. Ten of those goals came in a 13–4 victory over Quebec on February 4, 1899. No one has ever scored more goals in a regular-season game in a league that competes for the Stanley Cup.

Trihey, who also starred in lacrosse and football, was a slick puckhandler with a powerful shot. He centered two other future Hall of Famers on the Shamrocks in right-winger Art Farrell and left-winger Fred Scanlan. Together with rover Jack Brannen, the Shamrocks are credited with introducing a "scientific" approach to hockey. While most teams relied on individual talent, the Shamrocks pioneered a team-oriented style with the forwards attacking and defending as a unit. Sometimes defensemen Frank Tansey and Frank Wall joined in the rush as well instead of hanging back and relying on the standard practice of sending long "lift" shots down the ice to clear the puck.

As the defending Stanley Cup champions, the Shamrocks opened the new eight-game CAHL season of 1899–1900 with four straight wins. They were well on their way to another league title when they took time out from the schedule to host the Winnipeg Victorias in a Stanley Cup challenge in mid-February. It marked only the second time in the trophy's brief history that two teams would play a best-of-three series, and the winner in this one was still in doubt until the final minute of the third game.

The *Montreal Gazette* described the huge crowd of 7,000 fans for the first game as being "piled tier upon tier" into "four human walls." "The game," said the *Manitoba Free Press*, "was of the most sensational style imaginable." The Shamrocks led 2–1 at halftime before Dan Bain tied the score for Winnipeg. Tony Gingras then went end to end, beating three Shamrocks defenders in front of goalie Joe McKenna, to put the Victorias on top. Bain scored again to stretch the lead to 4–2 before Trihey got his second of the night for the Shamrocks with four minutes to go. The Montreal team pushed hard, but Winnipeg held on for a 4–3 victory. In Game 2, it was the Shamrocks who overcame a 2–1 deficit at halftime to rally for a 3–2 victory. Trihey scored the winner with about nine minutes to go. Depending on the reports, it was either his second or third goal of the game.

The third and final game of the series was even better than the first two. It was scoreless until Trihey put the Shamrocks on top late in the first half. Then the goals came quickly, with Gingras and Bain putting Winnipeg ahead only to see Trihey and Farrell make the score 3–2 for the Shamrocks at intermission. It was 4–2 early in the second half, but Winnipeg scored two to tie it by the midway point. "Then," according to the *Gazette*, "it was heart [pounding] suspense for 14 minutes."

With about a minute to go, Bain took a hard hit deep in the Winnipeg end and fell to the ice. While he was down, the Shamrocks scored, but referee Hugh Baird ruled no goal. Bain was carried off, and the game was held up for several minutes until he could return. Play resumed with a faceoff in front of the Winnipeg net, and the Shamrocks scored the winning goal right from the draw. Game stories in several newspapers refer to a fortune poke by a Shamrock forward, but the *Montreal Gazette* describes Trihey as winning the series "on a deceptive forward shot."

Shamrocks in a Romp

At the end of the 1898–99 season, the Shamrocks had traveled to the Maritimes, where they played exhibitions games in Halifax and Saint John. In two games against the Halifax Crescents, the results were a 2–2 tie and a 4–2 victory. But when the Crescents traveled to Montreal to challenge the Shamrocks in 1900, they were beaten badly. Most newspapers agreed the Shamrocks were just too fast for them. The games were also rough, but as at least one reporter noted, "If both sides had played a clean game the results would have been even more favorable to the Shamrocks." The *Montreal Gazette* offered an unusual critique: "The visitors were handicapped by excessive padding. Ponderous shin pads, knee guards … shoulder cushions … [and] a cumbersome, weighty make of skates militates against the Crescent players' natural speed and endurance."

Net Gain

In December 1899, the Canadian Amateur Hockey League appointed a committee to report on the use of goal nets. Though nets had been used for years in other sports and had been experimented with in other hockey leagues, the top leagues in Canada had employed nothing more than two iron posts embedded into the ice 6 feet apart. Not surprisingly, it was sometimes difficult to determine if the puck had actually slid between the posts or gone just wide. Shamrocks captain Harry Trihey was a member of the three-man committee that recommended the use of nets after they were tried in an exhibition game between his team and the Montreal Victorias. The CAHL adopted a design with a crossbar and net for the 1899–1900 season.

The Wellingtons Would Wait

Goal nets were used in Kingston for the first time when Queen's University hosted the Toronto Wellingtons in the final game of the Ontario Hockey Association season on March 3, 1900 — the second half of a two-game, total-goals championship series. With the series even after the third period, they agreed to play a 10-minute, total-goals overtime. No one scored in the first 10 minutes, so periods were added until the Wellingtons scored two goals in the latter half of the third extra session to win the series 6–4. Kingston papers described it as the longest game ever played in Canada.

CANADIAN AMATEUR HOCKEY LEAGUE

	GP	W	L	T	Pts
Montreal Shamrocks	8	7	1	0	14
Montreal Victorias	8	6	2	0	12
Ottawa Hockey Club	8	4	4	0	8
Montreal Hockey Club	8	3	5	0	6
Quebec Hockey Club	8	0	8	0	0

MANITOBA AND NORTH WEST HOCKEY ASSOCIATION

	GP	W	L	T	Pts
Winnipeg Victorias	4	4	0	0	8
Winnipeg Hockey Club	4	0	4	0	0

ONTARIO HOCKEY ASSOCIATION
(Kingston Group)

	GP	W	L	T	Pts
Queen's University*	2	2	0	0	4
Kingston Frontenacs	2	1	1	0	2
Royal Military College	2	0	0	0	0

*Defeated Brockville and University of Toronto in playoffs to win OHA title.

CARRYOVER STANLEY CUP CHALLENGE

2 GAMES TO 0

FEB. 15 ▶ Winnipeg Victorias* 1
at Montreal Victorias 2

FEB. 18 ▶ Winnipeg Victorias 2
at Montreal Victorias 3

*Winnipeg (the 1897–98 Manitoba and North West Hockey Association champions, see pages 314–15) was awarded a carryover challenge, which was played in 1899.

POSTSEASON STANLEY CUP CHALLENGE

1 GAME TO 0

MAR. 14 ▶ Queen's University 2
at Montreal Shamrocks 6

> ❝ Winnipeg hockey men are very much excited over the result of the Stanley Cup matches, and all sorts of anathemas are flung at the Montreal team, at the Cup trustees, and at Eastern hockeyists generally. The *Winnipeg Tribune* says the Montrealers are welcome to the Stanley Cup, which this year is the emblem of the slugging championship.❞
> — *Toronto Star*, February 22, 1899

ROSTERS

Montreal Victorias	Montreal Shamrocks ▲
Douglas Acer	Jack Brannen
Russell Bowie	John Dobby
Cam Davidson	Art Farrell
Graham Drinkwater (captain)	Charles Hoerner
Jack Ewing	Joe McKenna
Mike Grant	Fred Scanlan
Gordon Lewis	Frank Tansey
Bob McDougall	Harry Trihey (captain)
Ernie McLea	Frank Wall
Fred McRobie	
Frank Richardson	

Bowie Was the Best

In his day, there was no one who could score like Russell Bowie. In the 10 seasons he starred with the Montreal Victorias at the highest levels of hockey, Bowie scored 239 goals in 80 games. He led his league in scoring five times in eight seasons, between 1900–01 and 1907–08, and scored eight goals in a single game against the Montreal Shamrocks on January 16, 1907. Bowie was a brilliant puckhandler who attributed his success to a short stick. He played his entire career as an amateur, refusing to take money even when the game went pro

It's generally believed that Bowie began his senior hockey career with the Victorias as an 18-year-old during the 1898–99 season, but a profile of the players in the *Montreal Herald* before the 1899 Stanley Cup challenge against Winnipeg says that Bowie had been a spare player with the Vics championship team of 1897–98.

Great Series Fizzles Out

The Montreal Victorias had been champions of the Amateur Hockey Association of Canada (AHAC) since 1894–95, four straight seasons. They held the Stanley Cup for most of that time as well, except for a brief period in 1896, when they lost it to the Winnipeg Victorias. The Montreal Vics had become members of the Canadian Amateur Hockey League (CAHL) in 1898–99, when they faced the Winnipeg Vics for the Stanley Cup one more time.

About 5,000 fans filled the new Montreal Arena to see Game 1 of the Stanley Cup series. They watched nervously as the home team trailed 1–0 for most of the game. Different times are listed in various newspapers accounts, but according to the *Manitoba Free Press*, Bob McDougall scored to tie the game with just 45 seconds to go. After the ensuing faceoff, the puck was played to Montreal defenseman Graham Drinkwater, who rushed end to end and beat Winnipeg's 1896 Stanley Cup hero George "Whitey" Merritt for the winning goal. Over 7,000 fans were there for Game 2. It was another tight one, but it ended even more disappointingly for the Western team.

Winnipeg was trailing 3–2 nearing the midway point of the second half when Montreal's Bob McDougall laid a vicious slash across the knee of Tony Gingras. Referee J.A. Findlay ruled McDougall off for two minutes. Play was halted while Gingras was taken to the dressing room. His knee had been badly damaged, and the doctor who examined him said it would be impossible for him to continue. Winnipeg was already playing without Dan Bain, who'd been struck in the eye with a puck late in Game 1. To lose their second-best player was a serious blow. McDougall came to the Winnipeg dressing room

to apologize and admitted that he had hit Gingras on purpose. "I made a vicious swipe," McDougall said, according to a statement issued by Winnipeg team president Abe Code and printed in the *Ottawa Journal* on February 20, 1899. "I lost my temper and I am sorry for it."

When referee Findlay came into the dressing room to check on Gingras, the Winnipeg Vics asked him to rule McDougall off for the rest of the game for deliberately causing an injury. Findlay would not change the ruling he had made on the ice, and when the Winnipeggers continued to complain about his officiating, he refused to continue the game. He left the arena but returned about 20 minutes later and said that unless Winnipeg agreed to a new referee, the dispute would be turned over to the Stanley Cup trustees. "We accepted his ruling as to the latter," Code explained, "and at once told the players the game would not continue." Once again, Findlay left the arena.

In his own statement, Findlay admitted that was wrong to leave "and no one feels it more than I do." He returned again after another absence of about half an hour, and this time he gave Winnipeg 15 minutes to get back on the ice. But by then, the Western Vics had changed into their street clothes and some had already left the arena. Findlay awarded the game to the Montreal Vics.

The dispute was taken to the trustees, but Montreal was not anxious to replay the game, nor did Winnipeg actually wish to continue without Bain and Gingras. The trustees simply agreed to abide by Findlay's ruling and the series was over. In the Hockey Hall of Fame in Toronto, there are two sticks from 1899 with the story of the series burned into the wood, commemorating "The Great Hockey Fizzle."

AHAC Becomes CAHL

Since its formation in December 1886, the Amateur Hockey Association of Canada had been recognized as the premier league in the country. When the Stanley Cup was first presented in 1893, it was given to the Montreal Hockey Club (AAA) as recognition for winning the AHAC championship. But there was trouble brewing in December 1898. Two years earlier, the Ottawa Capitals were declined entrance to the senior division of the AHAC. After entering

and winning the league's intermediate division in 1897–98, the Capitals were admitted to the senior loop, despite the protestations of the Ottawa Hockey Club and the majority of the other senior teams. The delegates of Ottawa HC, Quebec, the Montreal Victorias and the Montreal Hockey Club resigned from the AHAC and formed the Canadian Amateur Hockey League. They soon admitted the Montreal Shamrocks, and the CAHL became the top league in hockey.

Shamrocks Are Champs

On February 24, 1899, the Ontario Hockey Association issued a Stanley Cup challenge to the Montreal Victorias of behalf of its champion, Queen's University. The school team wanted to play for the Cup right away, but with a tight battle for top spot between the Victorias and the Montreal Shamrocks in the Canadian Amateur Hockey League, the trustees wanted to see how that race came out first.

The Victorias faced the Shamrocks in a decisive game at the Montreal Arena on March 1, 1899. Nearly 8,000 people filled the stands. Harry Trihey and Jack Brannen were the stars, with Trihey scoring in a 1–0 victory that gave the Shamrocks both the CAHL title and the Stanley Cup. Queen's asked for a single game on March 8th, but the Shamrocks were headed on the road, first to the Maritimes and then to Boston. The OHA kept pushing for a game, and so the trustees declared the Shamrocks should play by March 15th or surrender the Cup to Queen's. The Shamrocks left Halifax, skipped their trip to Boston and returned home. They beat the University squad 6–2 in front of just 1,500 fans and then left for New York. On artificial ice at the Claremont Avenue Rink in Brooklyn, the Shamrocks defeated All-New York 5–2. They then played two games against the Brooklyn Skating Club, who were the American champions, first tying them 2–2 and then winning 9–4 in what the *New York Times* called "the world hockey championship."

Montreal Victorias

ROSTER

- Cam Davidson
- Graham Drinkwater
- Jack Ewing
- Mike Grant
- Gordon Lewis
- Bob McDougall
- Hartland McDougall
- Ernie McLea
- Frank Richardson (captain)

STANDINGS

AMATEUR HOCKEY ASSOCIATION OF CANADA

	GP	W	L	T	Pts
Montreal Victorias	8	8	0	0	16
Montreal Hockey Club	8	5	3	0	10
Montreal Shamrocks	8	3	5	0	6
Quebec Hockey Club	8	2	6	0	4

MANITOBA AND NORTH WEST HOCKEY ASSOCIATION

	GP	W	L	T	Pts
Winnipeg Victorias*	5	4	1	0	8
Winnipeg Hockey Club	5	1	4	0	0

*Played for the Stanley Cup in 1898–99.

STANLEY CUP CHALLENGE SERIES NONE PLAYED

> 66 It is to be hoped that during this quiet week the hockey clubs are bestirring themselves to give us a little better exhibition of the game than they have thus far this season. Spectators have put up with the rankest kind of hockey for the same price as they pay for the very best and it is about time they were getting the worth of their money. The game is gradually growing worse, and the first thing we know a bank team from Toronto will be coming down here and winning the Stanley Cup."
>
> —*Montreal Herald* commentary, reprinted in Toronto's *Globe*, January 28, 1898.

If You Can Make It There

On March 1, 1898, Toronto's *Globe* newspaper reported, "The champion Victorias of Montreal will visit New York this week and show how the game should be played."

On March 4, the Victorias beat the New York Athletic Club 6–1 at the St. Nicholas Rink. The next day's *New York Times* reported that the Vics "gave the best exhibition of hockey ever witnessed in this country." The paper added, "From the sound of the referee's whistle announcing the start of the game they made the American champions look like a team of novices. They excelled the locals in every style of play."

The following night, the Victorias beat the St. Nicholas Skating Club 8–0. "Another decisive victory," reported the *Times*, enthusing, "It is really marvelous how the Canadians play hockey.... They skate faster and dodge out of tight places. In passing the puck they are very accurate.... Scoring against them is very difficult."

The Davidson Brothers

Cam Davidson was one of three brothers to play for the Montreal Victorias, though Lyle Davidson only played in the 1893–94 season. Shirley Davidson had been a star in hockey and as a football quarterback at McGill University and played with the Victorias for four seasons, from 1892–93 through 1895–96. Though Shirley was also a champion sailor, he was presumed to have drowned after disappearing in a boating accident on the St. Lawrence River in 1907.

Aside from his one big season, in 1897–98, Cam Davidson (who studied medicine at McGill) was not considered to be the star that Shirley was. Cam was small and light, but his speed "is a puzzler to his opponents," said the *Montreal Herald* in 1899, "and his swift shots on goal have made many a goalkeeper weary."

Montreal Victorias History

The exact history of the Montreal Victorias hockey club is difficult to pin down. It's tied into both the Victoria Skating Club, which was incorporated on June 9, 1862, and the Victoria Skating Rink, which opened on December 24, 1862. Though it wasn't the first indoor rink in Montreal, it quickly became the most important. The club was named in honor of Queen Victoria and drew its membership predominantly from the city's upper class. The costume balls and skating carnivals held at the rink were important events on the Montreal social calendar.

On March 3, 1875, the Victoria Rink hosted what is recognized as the first modern hockey game with specific rules. The game was organized by James Creighton, a law student at McGill University and a member of the Victoria Skating Club. Creighton had grown up playing hockey-like games outdoors in Nova Scotia and begun organizing games at the Victoria Rink around 1873 or 1874. The ice surface at the Victoria Rink measured approximately 200 × 85 feet, which is still the standard size for an NHL arena.

As to the origins of the Victorias hockey team, a *Montreal Gazette* story from November 22, 1924, refers to the team's 50th anniversary, giving the team a startup date of 1874. Another *Gazette* story, from December 30,

1939, also indicates 1874, as it refers to the "passing into limbo of Victorias, the oldest hockey club in the world in its 65th year." However, a story in the *Gazette* on January 11, 1882, mentions the "first annual meeting of the Victoria Hockey Club," which is more in keeping with the 1881 startup date listed in Art Farrell's 1899 book *Hockey: Canada's Royal Winter Game*. Then again, in writing about the formation of the McGill hockey club in 1877 (said to be the first organized hockey club) for the second edition of *Total Hockey* (2000), Earl Zukerman notes that McGill played it first three games against the Victorias—though he says they were merely an unofficial team made up of members of other sports clubs.

Whether they were formed in 1874, 1877 or 1881, the Montreal Victorias made important contributions to the early history of the game. They were one of three teams (along with McGill and Quebec) to take part in the first Montreal Winter Carnival hockey tournament, in 1883, and were one of five teams—along with Ottawa, McGill, the Montreal Crystals and the Montreal Hockey Club (Montreal AAA)—that formed the Amateur Hockey Association of Canada (the AHAC, the game's first official league) on December 8, 1886.

The 1897–98 Season

The 1897–98 season marked the last year the AHAC would be the dominant senior hockey league in Canada. The Victorias began the winter with an easy Stanley Cup defense against the Ottawa Capitals (see page 318) and went on to win their fourth consecutive league title. Though the opposition may not have been as strong as in previous years, the Vics became the first team to go undefeated through the eight-game season since the AHAC had formally adopted a set schedule in 1892–93. Cam Davidson led the offense with a league-high 14 goals in seven games played. Bob McDougall added 12 goals, while Graham Drinkwater had 10. Mike Grant was the team's star defenseman, while Gordon Lewis and Frank Richardson shared goaltending duties.

With the AHAC title, the Victorias retained the Stanley Cup. There had been talk before the season started of a possible challenge by the Winnipeg Victorias, but the Montreal team was not called on to defend the trophy.

Game by Game

JANUARY 4, 1898	▶	Victorias 6 at Shamrocks 4
JANUARY 11, 1898	▶	Victorias 4 at Montreal HC 3
JANUARY 19, 1898	▶	Shamrocks 5 at Victorias 7
JANUARY 29, 1898	▶	Quebec 4 at Victorias 5
FEBRUARY 5, 1898	▶	Ottawa 6 at Victorias 12
FEBRUARY 12, 1898	▶	Victorias 9 at Ottawa 5
FEBRUARY 19, 1898	▶	Victorias 6 at Quebec 4
FEBRUARY 26, 1898	▶	Montreal HC 2 at Victorias 4

Graham Drinkwater

Graham Drinkwater was born into a prominent Montreal family on February 22, 1875. During the 1890s, his name often turned up in the "Social and Personal" column of the *Metropolitan*, a popular weekly newspaper. Later in life, Drinkwater was a stockbroker and the longtime vice president of the Montreal Orchestra.

Like many of his Victorias teammates, Drinkwater was educated at McGill University, where he starred at football and lacrosse as well as hockey. A brief biography in the *Montreal Gazette* on March 6, 1935, says Drinkwater joined the Victoria Hockey Club in 1889. He worked his way up through the junior and intermediate teams before making his senior debut in 1892–93. Drinkwater was a forward for most of his career, but he moved to defense for his final season of 1898–99, when he also served as captain of the team.

It's usually claimed that teammate Mike Grant was hockey's first rushing defenseman, but the 1935 *Gazette* story credits Drinkwater with popularizing the move when he went end to end to score the winning goal against the Winnipeg Victorias in the first game of a Stanley Cup series played in 1899. However, there are several inaccuracies in the story, so it's difficult to put too much stock in it.

Drinkwater was an original trustee of amateur hockey's Allan Cup when that trophy was donated in 1909 because the Stanley Cup had become a professional award. Drinkwater died in Montreal in 1946 and was elected to the Hockey Hall of Fame in 1950.

ROSTER

Cam Davidson

Shirley Davidson

Graham Drinkwater

Jack Ewing

David Gillilan

Mike Grant (captain)

Harold Henderson

Gordon Lewis

Bob McDougall

Hartland McDougall

Harry Massey

Ernie McLea

Percy Molson

66 Dear Sirs: I beg to inform you that the three clubs composing the Central Canada Hockey Association are tied for first place, each club having won two and lost two games. Two more matches will therefore be necessary to decide the championship. As the club winning the championship is desirous of challenging for the Stanley Cup, will you be good enough to inform me as to the rules governing same.

    Respectfully yours,

    Edward H. Hinchey,

    Hon. Secy. Treas., Central Canada Hockey Association"

66 Dear Sir: In reply to your letter of yesterday as to the Stanley Cup:

1. The rule followed by the trustees has been to receive challenges from the champion clubs of "recognized hockey associations."

2. For this season the trustees will accept a challenge for the Stanley Cup from the winning club of the Central Canada Association, asking the Victorias of Montreal to meet the challengers early next winter.

3. The trustees beg respectfully to add however, that they may not hold this acceptance as precedent for the future.... For the present, however, the trustees will be glad to do all in their power to facilitate a challenge from the Central Canada Association, should one be sent in."

— Correspondence with the Stanley Cup trustees, printed in the *Ottawa Journal*, March 13, 1897.

AMATEUR HOCKEY ASSOCIATION OF CANADA

	GP	W	L	T	Pts
Montreal Victorias	8	7	1	0	14
Ottawa Hockey Club	8	5	3	0	10
Montreal Hockey Club	8	5	3	0	10
Quebec Hockey Club	8	2	6	0	4
Montreal Shamrocks	8	1	7	0	2

CENTRAL CANADA HOCKEY ASSOCIATION

	GP	W	L	T	Pts
Ottawa Capitals*	4	2	2	0	4
Brockville Hockey Club	4	2	2	0	4
Cornwall Hockey Club	4	2	2	0	4

*Ottawa won playoff to break three-way tie.

POSTSEASON STANLEY CUP CHALLENGE

1 GAME TO 0

DEC. 27 ► Ottawa Capitals 2
    at Montreal Victorias 15

66 The season at the Victoria Rink is now at its height, and tonight the Hockey entertainments will be ushered in with a fine exhibition match between Montreal and Victorias.... Saturday being Christmas Day there will be an exceptionally fine musical programme, and all members have been invited to the directors' 'five o'clock tea.' Monday and Thursday of next week will see two great games for the Stanley Cup and Championship of the World."

— *Montreal Gazette*, December 23, 1897

Unclear on the Concept?

Though they had lost the Stanley Cup to the Winnipeg Victorias in a one-game midseason challenge on February 14, 1896, the Montreal Victorias completed the 1895–96 Amateur Hockey Association of Canada (AHAC) season with three straight wins to claim the league title for the second year in a row. Before the start of the 1896–97 season, they had won back the Stanley Cup in a rematch in Winnipeg on December 30, 1896 (see pages 320–21).

The Victorias played their first game of the new AHAC season on January 12, 1897, against the Montreal Hockey Club (Montreal AAA). It took a lucky goal on a long shot by captain Mike Grant in overtime to give the Victorias a 5–4 victory. Within days of their season-opening victory, the Victorias found themselves embroiled in a small controversy surrounding the Stanley Cup. The Victorias, it seemed, had written to the Stanley Cup trustees to inform them that they would not be willing to surrender the trophy at the end of the season even if they did not retain the AHAC championship—unless they were beaten for it in a specific challenge match.

The trustees interpreted the Vics' letter to mean that the team wanted the Stanley Cup to become solely a challenge trophy, and the trustees believed this to be contrary to Lord Stanley's wishes. Besides, as the *Montreal Gazette* pointed out on January 15, 1897, the Vics "would be the first to rebel if … they were called on every week" to defend the Cup against any team that asked to play them for it.

"The trustees must have misunderstood us," Victorias president Howard Wilson told reporters. "The Vics had no idea of holding the Cup as a challenge cup against all comers.… We simply maintained that we as a club are champions of Canada.… Even if we should lose the championship of the [AHAC]—which, by the way, we do not for a moment consider probable—we would still claim to be champions of Canada until a match or series of matches for the Stanley Cup had been decided adversely to us. Thus if Montreal, Shamrocks, Ottawas, or Quebec should finish first in the [AHAC] series we should still consider our claim to the championship of Canada as perfectly sound until the winners of the [AHAC] series had beaten us in the special match."

Undoubtedly, the trustees would have denied the Victorias such a "special match" if it came down to it, but there was no need to test the theory. The Vics lost only once all season (3–1 to Ottawa on February 13th) and won the AHAC title for the third year in a row.

Not Ready for Prime Time

The success of the Winnipeg Victorias Stanley Cup challenge in 1896 proved there were other top leagues in the country besides the Amateur Hockey Association of Canada and the Ontario Hockey Association (OHA). But trustees P.D. Ross and John Sweetland were leery when they received a challenge from the Central Canada Hockey Association (CCHA) on March 12, 1897.

In their return letter to Edward Hinchey of the CCHA, the trustees admitted they had never before had to consider what constituted "recognized hockey associations," and that "the nature of your association raises a new issue." The CCHA had only been formed after the Ottawa Capitals were denied entry into the AHAC for the 1896–97 season even though all three teams in the league could have played in the OHA. The trustees also outlined their fear of rapid growth, "if hockey associations were to multiply in each province, it might become impossible during the short hockey season to satisfy the best challenges."

Despite their doubts—and because they had not received any other challenges—the trustees accepted the CCHA challenge. Due to the lateness of the season and the lack of quality natural ice in the warmer weather, the champion Capitals would not face the Montreal Victorias until December 1897.

It's doubtful the Ottawa Capitals really expected they could beat the Victorias. In all likelihood, what they were hoping for was to play well enough to prove they were worthy of acceptance in the AHAC. Whatever their ultimate goal, the Capitals came up far short. "The Victorias practically scored at will," read a report from Montreal in Toronto's *Daily Mail and Empire*, "putting six goals to their credit before the whistle sounded for half-time to a large zero for the visitors. The second half was no better, as the Vics added nine goals to the Caps two, making the final score 15–2."

Though the series had been scheduled as either a best of three or two-games, totals-goals, the challengers chose not to continue after their crushing defeat.

Mike Grant

Though Mike Grant was said to have started playing hockey as a nine-year-old, it was his prowess as a speed skater that attracted the attention of the top hockey teams in his hometown of Montreal. When he was 11, Grant won speed skating titles in the under-12, under-14 and under-16 divisions.

Grant was born on November 17, 1873. He won junior and intermediate hockey titles as a member of the Montreal Crystals and Montreal Maples organizations in the early 1890s. According to stories, he was in attendance for a Victorias game when a player got hurt and a club official went up into the stands to get him. Grant agreed to play and remained with the Victorias from 1893–94 through 1899–1900. He then spent a season with the Shamrocks before returning to the Vics to end his career in 1901–02.

"Grant is a cool, clever player and one of the strongest defensemen on the ice," said the *Montreal Herald* of him in 1899. In an era when defensemen were encouraged to remain in their own zone, Grant was among the first to rush with the puck. He may well have inspired young Montrealers Lester Patrick and Art Ross, who would later be credited with this innovation.

Grant was elected to the Hockey Hall of Fame in 1950 and passed away in 1955. A fan of the game all his life, Grant was not one to dwell on the past. "We couldn't cope with shots from fellows like Geoffrion, Richard, or Howe," he told a Canadian Press reporter in 1952, adding, "Like a lot of oldtimers, I like to think we were better and be just as good now, but I'm not fooling myself."

AMATEUR HOCKEY ASSOCIATION OF CANADA

	GP	W	L	T	Pts
Montreal Victorias	8	7	1	0	14
Ottawa Hockey Club	8	6	2	0	12
Quebec Hockey Club	8	4	4	0	8
Montreal Hockey Club	8	2	6	0	4
Montreal Shamrocks	8	1	7	0	2

MANITOBA AND NORTH WEST HOCKEY ASSOCIATION

	GP	W	L	T	Pts
Winnipeg Victorias	5	3	0	2	8
Winnipeg Hockey Club	5	0	3	2	2

MIDSEASON STANLEY CUP CHALLENGE

1 GAME TO 0

FEB. 14 ▸ Winnipeg Victorias* 2
at Montreal Victorias 0

*Winnipeg (the 1894–95 Manitoba and North West Hockey Association champions, see pages 320–21) was awarded a carryover challenge, which was played in 1896.

POSTSEASON STANLEY CUP CHALLENGE

1 GAME TO 0

DEC. 30 ▸ Montreal Victorias 6
at Winnipeg Victorias 5

> 66 As to Merritt's play ... it was simply marvelous, and not one jot exaggerated. For a time the shots on goal simply rained on him, and he stopped them all."
> — Winnipeg fan W.L. Capell, giving his impressions of the game in Montreal to the *Winnipeg Tribune*, February 24, 1896.

> 66 We have never fought a harder game. It was a case of work for all we got."
> — Montreal Victorias captain Mike Grant after winning the rematch in Winnipeg.

> 66 We did our best and the best team won. We have never had a harder game and I can heartily congratulate the victors."
> — Winnipeg Victorias captain Jack Armytage after the rematch.

ROSTERS

Winnipeg Victorias ▲

Jack Armytage (captain)

Dan Bain

Tote Campbell

Rod Flett

Fred Higginbotham

Attie Howard

Charles Johnstone

Whitey Merritt

Montreal Victorias

Cam Davidson

Shirley Davidson

Graham Drinkwater

David Gillilan

Mike Grant (captain)

Harold Henderson

Gordon Lewis

Bob McDougall

Hartland McDougall

Ernie McLea

W. Wallace

Stanley Willett

Padded Protection

George "Whitey" Merritt was the goalie for the Winnipeg Victorias from 1890–91 through 1899–1900. Though the walrus-mustached Merritt was the first to wear pads on his legs in a Stanley Cup game, he was not the first goalie ever to don such protection. According to Bob Duff in the *Hockey Hall of Fame Book of Goalies*, a goalie in Dartmouth, Nova Scotia, wore some sort of shin guards in 1889. Cricket pads were commonplace for goalies in Manitoba in the early 1890s, and A.M. Stowe of an 1893 Winnipeg All-Star team caused a stir when he wore them during a tour of Eastern Canada.

Merritt's shutout in Winnipeg's 2–0 Stanley Cup win over Montreal earned him lasting fame. "Winnipeg ought to put a statue to his memory," wrote the *Montreal Herald* after the game, and "never was there such a goalkeeper." Certainly Merritt's fine play convinced other goalies to don pads as well.

Winnipeg Wins It

It's believed that hockey was first played in Manitoba around 1889—some 14 years after the modern game was born in Montreal. Art Farrell's 1899 book *Hockey: Canada's Royal Game* dates the formation of the Winnipeg Victorias to 1889, though Winnipeg hockey historian Ed Sweeney has written that the club was organized on November 3, 1890. Jack Armytage was the founder and would serve for many years as captain and president of the team.

Armytage was among a group of Winnipeggers who played an 11-game exhibition series in Ontario and Quebec in 1893. They won either eight or nine games depending on the source. Armytage brought the Victorias east in 1895 for another successful tour, with Winnipeg posting four wins in five games and outscoring its opponents 33–12. While being entertained in the clubhouse of the Montreal Amateur Athletic Association after a 5–1 win over the Montreal Hockey Club on February 4, 1895, Armytage spotted the Stanley Cup in a trophy case. During the fall of 1895, he began making inquiries about playing for it. In January 1896, a challenge was sent, and on February 14th the Winnipeg Victorias met their "sister" Victorias of Montreal in a one-game playoff for the Stanley Cup.

Given the success of Winnipeg's tour the year before, the Stanley Cup game drew plenty of attention in Montreal. Betting on the match was even, according to the *Winnipeg Tribune*, and the game proved close. Winnipeg goalie George "Whitey" Merritt played the game with white cricket pads protecting his legs and was a sensation. Winnipeg led 2–0 at halftime, and though Montreal had the better of the play in the second half, Merritt hung on for the shutout and the Stanley Cup went west.

Winnipeg Celebrates

Winnipeg hockey fans had already greeted the Victorias as world champions after their successful tour of 1895. They looked forward to making it official in 1896. A large crowd was at the station just to watch the team get on the train, and a small group of fans made the trip to see the game. Back home in Winnipeg, several hotels made arrangements to receive telegraphed reports of the game in progress. Hundreds of fans showed up to listen. "It is seldom that there have been evenings of rejoicing to equal last night," reported the *Manitoba Free Press* after the Winnipeg victory.

A huge crowd turned out to greet the Victorias when they arrived back in Winnipeg on February 24th, and several future championship traditions began: A parade took the team from the train station to the Manitoba Hotel, a large civic reception was held for them there and the Victorias toasted their victory by drinking champagne from the Stanley Cup.

Montreal Wins It Back

Until February 1896, the four-year-old Stanley Cup had not garnered much attention beyond the 500-mile (800 km) strip of land from Toronto to Quebec City. While it's true that the majority of Canada's population resided within that narrow corridor, it took Winnipeg's victory to make the young trophy a national newsmaker.

There were reports as early as May that the Montreal Victorias would seek a rematch, and when they officially submitted their challenge on November 11, 1896, it was reported in newspapers from coast to coast—even though the game would not be played for another six weeks.

A large crowd greeted the Montreal Vics when they arrived in Winnipeg on Sunday evening, December 27th. Upward of 700 people watched them practice at the McIntyre rink the next day. The *Winnipeg Tribune* reported that $1 reserved tickets to Wednesday's championship game were already being sold for as much as $5, "and chances are that by the night of the match the price will reach $10." The *Manitoba Free Press* would later write that "one man claimed to have sold 15 [pairs of] tickets at two for $25. One ticket brought two and a half tons of coal, while one gentleman who had come in from Calgary to see the match paid $15 for a reserved seat." Hundreds of fans without reserved seats lined up for hours on game day to try to buy standing-room tickets. In Montreal, the *Daily Star* newspaper had arranged for telegraphed bulletins and enormous crowds gathered in the streets to listen.

The game certainly lived up to its hype. Winnipeg went ahead early on a goal by Dan Bain and jumped out to a 3–0 lead. It was 4–2 Winnipeg at halftime, but Montreal rallied in the second half and led 5–4 with time running out. Bain's second goal of the game got Winnipeg even, but Ernie McLea's third of the night with two minutes to go gave Montreal a 6–5 victory. "The Other Vics Won," read the sad headline in the next day's *Manitoba Free Press*.

Dan Bain

Dan Bain was born in Belleville, Ontario, on February 14, 1874, but was raised in Winnipeg after his family moved there in 1880. Bain grew up to be a great all-around athlete who starred at every sport he tried. He claimed his first title at the age of 13, when he won a provincial three-mile roller-skating championship. He went on to win Manitoba and/or Canadian titles in gymnastics, bicycling, trap shooting and skeet shooting. He was a champion figure skater until the age of 56. Bain also played lacrosse and was an avid golfer, but his greatest fame came as a forward with the Winnipeg Victorias. He was the biggest star on the Winnipeg teams that won the Stanley Cup in 1896 and 1901 and was elected to the Hockey Hall of Fame in 1949.

Though there are stories that Bain joined the Winnipeg Victorias in 1895 after seeing a newspaper ad soliciting new players, statistics have been tracked for him back to the 1893–94 season of the Manitoba and North West Hockey Association. Bain became a top scorer who played the game with speed and grace but didn't shy away from the rough stuff. "Those were the days of real athletes," Bain would recall, adding, "When we passed, the puck never left the ice, and if the wingman wasn't there to receive it, it was because he had a broken leg."

Bain lived until 1962, but he was not a fan of the hockey he saw later in life. "No finesse.... We handed out hard bodychecks in our day, but we used our bodies and not our sticks, knees, and elbows as they do nowadays" he told Winnipeg reporter Al Vickery in 1955.

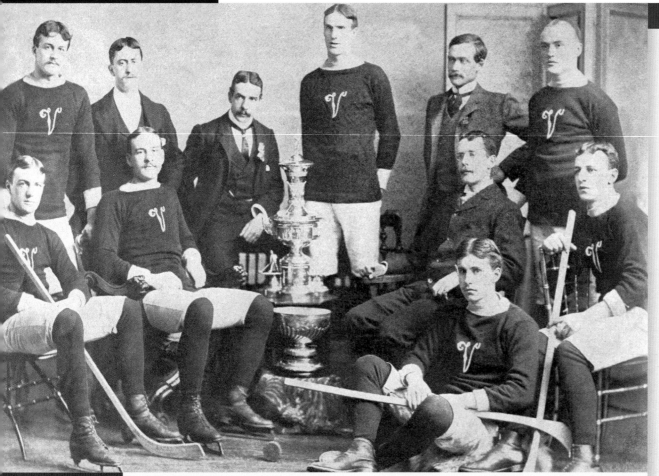

ROSTER

Shirley Davidson
Graham Drinkwater
Roland Elliot
Arthur Fenwick
Mike Grant (captain)
Harold Henderson
Robert Jones
A. McDougall
Bob McDougall
Hartland McDougall
William Pullan
Norman Rankin

Not Much of a Game

The Stanley Cup game between Queen's and the Montreal Hockey Club attracted only a small crowd to the Victoria Rink. Reports in various newspapers put the attendance as low as 400 and no higher than 600. Montreal scored an easy 5–1 victory, but neither team played very well. "Queen's was not in it from the start," reported the *Montreal Gazette*. "If the Victorias had been playing, they would have won by three times as many goals," read the game story in Toronto's *Globe*. The newspapers differed on one account though. "The game was one of the roughest of the season," said the *Globe*, but the *Gazette* reported, "no rough play worth mentioning."

The Stanley Cup would have gone to Queen's and the OHA if the university team had won, but "so sure was everyone of the result," said the *Gazette*, "that arrangements were made beforehand to hand over the trophy to the keeping of the Victorias."

Praise for the Vics

"Perhaps little could be told in these columns which would be new to admirers of the 'Vics' as they are lovingly called, but it is certain that a more popular handful of young men cannot be found in the shadow of Mount Royal. Even at this distances, when the echo of the last cheer has become a dim memory… enthusiasts will feel a glow of the old excitement as they think over the victories gallantly won by the lads in maroon and white." — *The Metropolitan*, April 13, 1895

66 The secretary of the Ontario Hockey Association has written the trustees of the Stanley Hockey Challenge cup, informing them of the final championship match in the Ontario series, which was won last week by Queen's [University]. They want a date fixed now between the Ontario and Quebec champions, something that is rather difficult, owing to the uncertainty over the final results in the East… [I]t is not improbable the trustees will call upon the Montrealers, present holders of the Cup, to play off for the trophy…. Should Queen's want a match [March 9th] is the date the trustees will suggest, and Montreal will be called upon to defend the trophy."
— *Montreal Gazette*, February 27, 1895

Victorias Win the AHAC

The 1894–95 season of the Amateur Hockey Association of Canada (AHAC) opened in Montreal on January 3, 1895, with the Victorias crushing the Crystals 7–2. The Montreal Hockey Club (Montreal AAA) played their first game two nights later. The result was a surprising 4–2 loss to Quebec. However, with wins in each of their next four games—including a 5–0 rout of the Victorias on January 26—it appeared the Montreal club was going to win another AHAC title and claim the Stanley Cup for a third straight season.

Things took a turn for the worse for Montreal when they played in Ottawa on February 16th. Montreal jumped out to a 3–0 lead, but Ottawa roared back to win 4–3 in overtime. So, instead of improving its record to 5-1-0 and taking an almost insurmountable lead in the AHAC standings, Montreal slipped to 4-2-0. With the Victorias beating Quebec 8–2 that night, both Ottawa and the Vics were clearly in contention. When the Victorias beat Montreal 4–2 and Ottawa beat Quebec 3–2 on February 23rd, the race became even tighter. The Vics and Ottawa were now tied at 4-2-0 with two games still to play. Montreal had fallen to 4-3-0 with just one game remaining.

The following week, on March 2nd, the Vics were in Ottawa. "The match from start to finish was lightning like," said the *Montreal Gazette*, though the paper also commented that both teams "seemed tired and played carelessly" at the start of the second half. Ottawa trailed 1–0 early but had the better of the play after that and tied the game before halftime. Ottawa went ahead 2–1 at the 11-minute mark of the second half, but Graham Drinkwater tied the game seven minutes later. Bob

McDougall put the Vics ahead with about seven minutes to go. "The few remaining minutes of the [game] was entirely Ottawa," said the *Gazette*, but the Vics held on to win 3–2.

The Crystals beat Montreal 4–3 in overtime that night to officially eliminate the defending champions from title contention, but even with their win over Ottawa, the Victorias—despite some reports—had not clinched the AHAC title just yet. There was still a chance of both Ottawa and the Vics finishing the season 5-3-0 if Ottawa beat the Crystals in their final game on March 6th and the Crystals beat the Victorias in the season finale two nights later. In that case though (because the Vics had won both their games against Ottawa), the Victorias might well have won the title without the need of a playoff. However, the Crystals were still very much in the mix. If they beat Ottawa (which they did, 7–3) and then beat the Victorias on March 8th, they would have a record of 4-3-0 and would no doubt continue to push to have their voided 2–1 victory over Quebec from February 2nd either replayed or (given that Quebec had been suspended by the AHAC on February 27th after their fans had attacked a referee following their loss to Ottawa on February 23rd) awarded to them. Then, a win against the Victorias would leave the two teams tied and force a playoff.

The seating capacity of the Crystal rink was expanded for the final week of the season. After their win over Ottawa, the Crystals and their fans were confident of another victory against the Victorias, but it was not to be. The Victorias won the game 5–2 to claim the AHAC title—but the Stanley Cup was not theirs just yet.

Unpopular Playoff

On February 26, 1895, the Stanley Cup trustees received a letter from the secretary of the Ontario Hockey Association (OHA) informing them that Queen's University had won the league and would like to challenge for the Stanley Cup. One year earlier, a four-way tie in the AHAC standings resulted in a round of playoffs that had left no time to play a challenge from the OHA-champion Osgoode Hall team. Facing a similar finish this season, P.D. Ross was determined to schedule a challenge. He proposed March 9th as the date (the day after the conclusion of the AHAC season), but since

it was impossible to know if a champion would have been crowned—a game was arranged between Queen's and the defending–champion Montreal Hockey Club (Montreal AAA).

Ross's decision was not popular, and even when the Victorias won the championship on March 8th and indicated they were prepared to face Queens, the game was still played as scheduled. When Montreal AAA scored an easy 5–1 victory they were not awarded the Cup, as it was given to the Victorias as the league's new champion.

STANDINGS

AMATEUR HOCKEY ASSOCIATION OF CANADA

	GP	W	L	T	Pts
Montreal Hockey Club	8	5	3	0	10
Ottawa Hockey Club	8	5	3	0	10
Montreal Victorias	8	5	3	0	10
Quebec Hockey Club	8	5	3	0	10
Montreal Crystals	8	0	8	0	0

ONTARIO HOCKEY ASSOCIATION
(Toronto Group 2)

	GP	W	L	T	Pts
Osgoode Hall*	2	2	0	0	4
University of Toronto	2	1	1	0	2
Trinity College	2	0	2	0	0

*Defeated Hamilton, Ayr and Queen's University in playoffs to win OHA title. Did not challenge for Stanley Cup.

POSTSEASON AHAC STANLEY CUP PLAYOFFS

MAR. 17 ► Montreal Victorias 2 at Montreal Hockey Club 3

MAR. 22 ► Ottawa 1 at Montreal Hockey Club 3

> As regards the whole season it will be well to remember a prediction made in the beginning of the season to the effect that Montreal [Montreal Hockey Club] could give all the others points on finishing... At the beginning it seemed as if the last year's champions would not be in the game, but, like climbing a hill, the man who reaches the summit first wins, and that is the case with Montreal...
>
> "Not only the Canadian championship, but the Governor-General's cup depended on this match, and Montreal can fly its colors in the face of any hockey breeze that ever blew...
>
> "The Victoria rink last night held the largest crowd ever packed into the rink in its history. There was 'siss-boom-ah,' 'rah-rah-rah' and several other audible tokens of imbecility and enthusiasm mixed...
>
> "It was a question of championship and Montreal had to win. There is one thing Montreal hates to do—that is to lose—and that settles it."
>
> —*Montreal Gazette*, March 23, 1894

ROSTER

Billy Barlow
Allan Cameron
Herb Collins
Archie Hodgson
Alex Irving
George James
Alex Kingan
Clare Mussen
E. O'Brien
Haviland Routh
James Stewart
Toad Wand

Before the Stanley Cup

The Montreal Hockey Club already had an impressive list of championships before the donation of the Stanley Cup. In the team's first winter of existence, they won the 1885 Montreal Winter Carnival hockey tournament. They won it again in 1887 and also won the Burlington (Vermont) Winter Carnival tournament in 1886, when no event was staged in Montreal.

The Montreal Winter Carnival is considered to be the first major hockey championship and also an important predecessor to the Amateur Hockey Association of Canada, which was formed for the 1886–87 season. The Montreal Hockey Club won the AHAC title for five straight seasons, from 1887–88 through 1891–92, before winning the Stanley Cup.

The City of Champions

Six teams representing the city of Montreal have captured the Stanley Cup: the Montreal Hockey Club (Montreal AAA), Montreal Wanderers, Montreal Victorias, Montreal Shamrocks, Montreal Maroons and, of course, the Montreal Canadiens.

Playoff Chaos

In 1893, the Montreal Hockey Club (Montreal AAA) won the Stanley Cup by finishing in first place in the Amateur Hockey Association of Canada (AHAC). It had been a close race for the title between Montreal and Ottawa, but the AHAC season of 1893–94 produced an even closer race and the first playoff in Stanley Cup history.

Montreal had many of the same players in its lineup as the previous season. Haviland Routh, who had led the league with 19 goals in eight games the season before, scored only eight goals this season, but it was still enough to tie Billy Barlow for the team lead. Five of Routh's goals came in one game, in a season-opening 7–0 win over Quebec on January 5, 1894. Montreal introduced a new goalie this season in Herb Collins, who had previously played with the Crystals but joined the MAAA club as a replacement for Tom Paton. Paton had helped form the team back in 1884 and had played goal through the 1892–93 season.

The defending Stanley Cup champions opened the new season with three straight wins, but a 4–1 loss at home to Ottawa on January 27th led to three straight losses and set up a key game in Ottawa on February 24th. With four teams bunched so closely in the standings, an Ottawa win would have been a bad blow for Montreal's chances. As the *Montreal Gazette* reported, "A victory would have placed Ottawa well in the lead for the championship, and it is doubtful if one out of the 3,000 present looked for the ignominious defeat which the Senators met with." Montreal won 5–1, and the *Gazette* led its story by saying: "The explosion of an Anarchist bomb in Rideau rink could not have caused more surprise." Barlow scored four in the Montreal victory. Routh got the fifth.

Quebec defeating the Victorias 4–3 that same Saturday night set up a huge game the following week, when Quebec visited Ottawa. Even with Montreal defeating the Crystals 2–1 the night before, Quebec could still clinch first place with a win, and the crowd of 5,000 was thought to be the largest ever at Ottawa's Rideau rink. Quebec came out quickly, trying to take the noisy gathering out of the game, but the solid defense of veteran Weldy Young and rookie Harvey Pulford in front

of goalie Albert Morel would not be beat. It was a hard-checking game played on soft ice, and Quebec "tossed the Ottawa forward line almost at will," but "Young and, especially, Pulford made themselves conspicuous in this respect" as well. Ottawa won the game 2–0 and there was now a three-way tie for first place. It became a four-way tie when the Victorias finished up the season with a pair of easy wins over the last-place Crystals.

The AHAC executive met in Montreal to decide how to break the tie, and eventually, it was decided that, in order to negate any home-ice advantage, Ottawa should play the Victorias in Quebec City, while Quebec faced Montreal in Ottawa. Everyone seemed in agreement, until Quebec's delegate announced that, should his team reach the final, they would not be willing to travel to Montreal to play against a Montreal team. The other clubs would not consent to guarantee Quebec home-ice advantage should they reach the final, so Quebec withdrew from the playoffs. After another lengthy debate, it was agreed that Ottawa would receive a bye into the finals, where they would play on the road against the winner of a semifinal between the Montreal Hockey Club and the Victorias.

Considering the warm weather in Montreal, the ice was said to be fast enough with only a thin layer of water on top for the semifinal game. The skating "was very fast," the *Gazette* reported, "but the water interfered with the passing of the heavy disk of rubber." Even so, Archie Hodgson went end to end in the game's first minute and then passed to Billy Barlow, who dodged promising young Vics defenseman Mike Grant to score the game's first goal. The Victorias went ahead 2–1 during the second half, but Hodgson and Barlow both scored late in the game to give Montreal a 3–2 victory.

Barlow and Hodgson were also the heroes against Ottawa. Montreal had the better of the play, but Albert Morel kept the visitors in it. Ottawa led 1–0 until Hodgson tied the game late in the first half. Barlow got the winner 9 minutes into the second half, and then Hodgson clinched it with about 9 minutes to go as Montreal scored a 3–1 victory to win both the AHAC title and the Stanley Cup.

No Time for Osgoode Hall

For many years, it was believed that the Stanley Cup was presented to Montreal in 1893 because Ottawa refused to travel to Toronto for a playoff game with Osgoode Hall. That dispute, however, actually took place in 1894. It had no direct bearing on the Stanley Cup, though Osgoode Hall did hope to play for it that year.

Ottawa was the only member of the otherwise Quebec-based Amateur Hockey Association of Canada that also played in the Ontario Hockey Association (OHA). Ottawa had won three straight OHA titles and seemed well on its way to a fourth in 1894. But during Ottawa's semifinal against Queen's University, the OHA announced that the winner would have to travel to Toronto to play the championship on February 24th. As reigning champions, Ottawa expected to play at home. Also, with their focus more on winning the AHAC title, and with a key game already scheduled against Montreal that same night, Ottawa withdrew from the OHA.

Queen's played Osgoode Hall in Toronto for the OHA championship on February 28th. Osgoode Hall won 3–2 and promptly challenged for the Stanley Cup. The trustees accepted, but when the AHAC season ended in a four-way tie on March 10th, and when the league waited a full week before starting its playoff, it seemed unlikely there would be time for the challenge. On March 24, 1894, Toronto's *Globe* newspaper reported that the Montreal Hockey Club still wished to play, but Osgoode Hall declined the opportunity, as they'd been inactive for nearly four weeks.

How They Won It

A 7–1 romp by the Montreal Hockey Club over Ottawa on February 18, 1893, was a key victory during the Amateur Hockey Association of Canada (AHAC) season. Ottawa had previously beaten Montreal 4–2 in an earlier game, but a surprising 4–3 loss to the Victorias in the first game of the season left Ottawa a win behind in the standings. The AHAC race went right down to the wire before Montreal officially clinched the title with a 2–1 win over the Crystals in their final

game on March 10, 1893. After falling behind early, Haviland Routh evened the score in the second half before Archie Hodgson won the game in overtime.

In addition to playing in the Quebec-based AHAC, Ottawa also played in the Ontario Hockey Association (OHA). Ottawa won the 1893 OHA title, but because Montreal beat Ottawa for the AHAC title, the trustees deemed that enough to give them the Stanley Cup.

STANDINGS

AMATEUR HOCKEY ASSOCIATION OF CANADA

	GP	W	L	T	Pts
Montreal Hockey Club	8	7	1	0	14
Ottawa Hockey Club	8	6	2	0	12
Montreal Crystals	8	3	5	0	6
Quebec Hockey Club	8	2	5	1	5
Montreal Victorias	8	1	6	1	3

STANLEY CUP CHALLENGE
NONE PLAYED

❝The possibilities of hockey, the ideality of the game were never better illustrated than last night at the match between the Montreal and Crystal clubs. It was the game of the season. For that matter it was the game of the century.... It was the fastest, hardest, best hockey ever seen in Montreal. And it was rough, too; but nobody said a word; they all gave hard knocks and they all took them silently and the referee was lenient; but there was no cause for dissatisfaction... The only drawback to the match was that the rink was not big enough to hold half the people who wanted to see it.❞
— The *Montreal Gazette*'s description of the Montreal Hockey Club's 2–1 overtime victory over the Crystals on March 10, 1893, which clinched the league title.

❝The Governor-General, in accordance with a promise made last year, has given a hockey challenge cup to be held from year to year by the winning team in the Dominion. The cup is now in Ottawa, and in two or three days will be presented to the Montreal Amateur Athletic Association, whose team defeated all comers during the late season, including the champions of the Ontario association.❞
— *Ottawa Journal*, May 1, 1893

Lord Stanley's Conditions

On May 1, 1893, the *Ottawa Journal* printed the conditions for Lord Stanley's trophy:

1. The winner to give bond for the return of the cup in good order when required by the trustees for the purpose of being handed over to any other team who may in turn win.
2. Each winning team to have at their own charge engraved on a silver ring fitted on the cup for the purpose the name of the team and the year won. (In the first instance the M.A.A.A. will find the cup already engraved for them.)
3. The cup shall remain a challenge cup and will not become property of any team, even if won more than once.
4. In case of any doubt as to the title of any club to claim the position of champions, the cup shall be held or awarded by the trustees as they may think right, their decision being absolute.
5. Should either trustee resign or otherwise drop out, the remaining trustee shall nominate a substitute.

The Trustees' Terms

Lord Stanley named Philip Dansken Ross and John Sweetland as trustees; they created nine terms for the trophy:

1. That the Cup be called the Stanley Hockey championship cup.
2. That it be held by the M.A.A.A. team until the championship of the association to which that team belongs, namely the Amateur Hockey association of Canada, be decided next year, when the cup shall go to the winning team.
3. In order, however, that the Ontario Hockey association shall have an equal interest in the cup, the Amateur Hockey association of Canada and the Ontario Hockey association be requested to each arrange its season so that there shall be an opportunity for a final match between the champion teams of the two organizations.
4. The trustees would respectfully suggest to the associations that this could be done by each association arranging to close its separate championship contest not later than the first Saturday in March. (Practically this is done now, the A.H.A. of C. for instance closing its season on March 8, and the Ontario association usually being still earlier. The first Saturday in March could not be earlier than March 1 nor later than March 7. Next year it will be March 3.)
5. If the above suggestion were adopted, the championship of the A.H.A. of C. would accordingly be settled next year on March 3, and also possession of the Stanley cup so far as that association is concerned. Then the winner might be open to challenge from the championship club of the Ontario association.
6. Then and thereafter, a challenge from the champion club of one association to a champion club of the other holding the cup might be sent under the following conditions:
   (a.) Challenge permissible either by wire or registered letter on the first Saturday or following Monday of March.
   (b.) The club holding the cup must answer within two days of receipt of challenge.
   (c.) The answer must either (1) appoint the following Saturday (the second in March) or give the challenging club the option of naming within two days any other legal day up to and inclusive of March 15. (The object of this clause is that as travelling on any but a Saturday is inconvenient, if the home club can not or will not give Saturday, the visiting club should have a choice.) The home club shall be obliged, if required, to furnish the trustees with satisfactory reasons for not giving the Saturday.
   (d.) The match shall be played on ice named by the champions, but the net gate receipts shall be equally divided between the contesting teams.
   (e.) Should the challenging club default after a date is fixed, it shall pay any advertising or other expenses gone to by the champions in preparation for the match.
7. The fact that the club winning the Ontario championship may also belong to and have been defeated in the A.H.A. of C. series shall not debar it from challenging for the Stanley cup; and vice versa, the fact that the Ontario champions may also have won in the A.H.A. of C. series shall not debar the second best team in the A.H.A. of C. from challenging the champions for a final match. (The object of this is to continue the interest in the game up to the very close of the season.)
8. Should any representative provincial Hockey association outside of Quebec and Ontario desire to compete for the cup, the trustees shall endeavor to arrange means whereby its champion team may secure an opportunity to play for it.
9. In case a senior league is ever formed representing the best hockey irrespective of local associations, the trustees may give its winning club the right to challenge for the cup, and if successful to hold it thereafter subject to new championship regulations.

Stanley Cup Dispute

The Montreal Amateur Athletic Association (MAAA) was formed in 1881, and in November 1884, Tom Paton received permission to form a hockey club within the association. It was known as the Montreal Hockey Club.

The hockey team enjoyed a strange relationship with the MAAA: It held meetings at the MAAA clubhouse and wore the MAAA's winged-wheel logo on its sweaters, but the hockey team had only "connected" status, not the "full affiliate" status enjoyed by the founding members and other new clubs. Every member of the Montreal Hockey Club had to be a bona fide member of the MAAA, but, unlike other clubs, the hockey team received no funding beyond small loans for equipment and ice rentals.

On May 15, 1893, Stanley Cup trustee John Sweetland presented the new trophy, freshly engraved with the name "Montreal AAA," to MAAA president James Taylor. Montreal Hockey Club president James Stewart was angry that the MAAA accepted the Stanley Cup before his team was informed of the conditions that came with the trophy. Stewart refused to accept the Stanley Cup, and it's not clear how many team members showed up on May 15th to receive the gold rings (engraved with the letters MHC) that had been commissioned for them. It was not until shortly before they won the Stanley Cup again in 1894 that the hockey club finally agreed to receive the trophy. After taking possession, they engraved it simply, "Montreal 1894."

Cup Winners

YEAR		WINNER	DEFEATED	YEAR		WINNER	DEFEATED
2012	▶	Los Angeles Kings	New Jersey Devils	1976	▶	Montreal Canadiens	Philadelphia Flyers
2011	▶	Boston Bruins	Vancouver Canucks	1975	▶	Philadelphia Flyers	Buffalo Sabres
2010	▶	Chicago Blackhawks	Philadelphia Flyers	1974	▶	Philadelphia Flyers	Boston Bruins
2009	▶	Pittsburgh Penguins	Detroit Red Wings	1973	▶	Montreal Canadiens	Chicago Black Hawks
2008	▶	Detroit Red Wings	Pittsburgh Penguins	1972	▶	Boston Bruins	New York Rangers
2007	▶	Anaheim Ducks	Ottawa Senators	1971	▶	Montreal Canadiens	Chicago Black Hawks
2006	▶	Carolina Hurricanes	Edmonton Oilers	1970	▶	Boston Bruins	St. Louis Blues
2005	▶	n/a	n/a	1969	▶	Montreal Canadiens	St. Louis Blues
2004	▶	Tampa Bay Lightning	Calgary Flames	1968	▶	Montreal Canadiens	St. Louis Blues
2003	▶	New Jersey Devils	Mighty Ducks of Anaheim	1967	▶	Toronto Maple Leafs	Montreal Canadiens
2002	▶	Detroit Red Wings	Carolina Hurricanes	1966	▶	Montreal Canadiens	Detroit Red Wings
2001	▶	Colorado Avalanche	New Jersey Devils	1965	▶	Montreal Canadiens	Chicago Black Hawks
2000	▶	New Jersey Devils	Dallas Stars	1964	▶	Toronto Maple Leafs	Detroit Red Wings
1999	▶	Dallas Stars	Buffalo Sabres	1963	▶	Toronto Maple Leafs	Detroit Red Wings
1998	▶	Detroit Red Wings	Washington Capitals	1962	▶	Toronto Maple Leafs	Chicago Black Hawks
1997	▶	Detroit Red Wings	Philadelphia Flyers	1961	▶	Chicago Black Hawks	Detroit Red Wings
1996	▶	Colorado Avalanche	Florida Panthers	1960	▶	Montreal Canadiens	Toronto Maple Leafs
1995	▶	New Jersey Devils	Detroit Red Wings	1959	▶	Montreal Canadiens	Toronto Maple Leafs
1994	▶	New York Rangers	Vancouver Canucks	1958	▶	Montreal Canadiens	Boston Bruins
1993	▶	Montreal Canadiens	Los Angeles Kings	1957	▶	Montreal Canadiens	Boston Bruins
1992	▶	Pittsburgh Penguins	Chicago Blackhawks	1956	▶	Montreal Canadiens	Detroit Red Wings
1991	▶	Pittsburgh Penguins	Minnesota North Stars	1955	▶	Detroit Red Wings	Montreal Canadiens
1990	▶	Edmonton Oilers	Boston Bruins	1954	▶	Detroit Red Wings	Montreal Canadiens
1989	▶	Calgary Flames	Montreal Canadiens	1953	▶	Montreal Canadiens	Boston Bruins
1988	▶	Edmonton Oilers	Boston Bruins	1952	▶	Detroit Red Wings	Montreal Canadiens
1987	▶	Edmonton Oilers	Philadelphia Flyers	1951	▶	Toronto Maple Leafs	Montreal Canadiens
1986	▶	Montreal Canadiens	Calgary Flames	1950	▶	Detroit Red Wings	New York Rangers
1985	▶	Edmonton Oilers	Philadelphia Flyers	1949	▶	Toronto Maple Leafs	Detroit Red Wings
1984	▶	Edmonton Oilers	New York Islanders	1948	▶	Toronto Maple Leafs	Detroit Red Wings
1983	▶	New York Islanders	Edmonton Oilers	1947	▶	Toronto Maple Leafs	Montreal Canadiens
1982	▶	New York Islanders	Vancouver Canucks	1946	▶	Montreal Canadiens	Boston Bruins
1981	▶	New York Islanders	Minnesota North Stars	1945	▶	Toronto Maple Leafs	Detroit Red Wings
1980	▶	New York Islanders	Philadelphia Flyers	1944	▶	Montreal Canadiens	Chicago Black Hawks
1979	▶	Montreal Canadiens	New York Rangers	1943	▶	Detroit Red Wings	Boston Bruins
1978	▶	Montreal Canadiens	Boston Bruins	1942	▶	Toronto Maple Leafs	Detroit Red Wings
1977	▶	Montreal Canadiens	Boston Bruins	1941	▶	Boston Bruins	Detroit Red Wings

YEAR		WINNER	DEFEATED	YEAR		WINNER	DEFEATED
1940	▸	New York Rangers	Toronto Maple Leafs	1908	▸	Montreal Wanderers	Edmonton Pros
							Toronto Professionals
1939	▸	Boston Bruins	Toronto Maple Leafs				Winnipeg Maple Leafs
1938	▸	Chicago Black Hawks	Toronto Maple Leafs				Ottawa Victorias
1937	▸	Detroit Red Wings	New York Rangers	1907	▸	Montreal Wanderers	Kenora Thistles
1936	▸	Detroit Red Wings	Toronto Maple Leafs		▸	Kenora Thistles	Brandon Wheat Kings
1935	▸	Montreal Maroons	Toronto Maple Leafs		▸	Kenora Thistles	Montreal Wanderers
1934	▸	Chicago Black Hawks	Detroit Red Wings		▸	Montreal Wanderers	New Glasgow Hockey Club
1933	▸	New York Rangers	Toronto Maple Leafs	1906	▸	Ottawa Hockey Club (Silver Seven)	Smiths Falls Hockey Club Queen's University
1932	▸	Toronto Maple Leafs	New York Rangers				
1931	▸	Montreal Canadiens	Chicago Black Hawks		▸	Montreal Wanderers	Ottawa Hockey Club (Silver Seven)
1930	▸	Montreal Canadiens	Boston Bruins				
1929	▸	Boston Bruins	New York Rangers	1905	▸	Ottawa Hockey Club (Silver Seven)	Rat Portage Thistles Dawson City Nuggets
1928	▸	New York Rangers	Montreal Maroons				
1927	▸	Ottawa Senators	Boston Bruins	1904	▸	Ottawa Hockey Club (Silver Seven)	Brandon Hockey Club
1926	▸	Montreal Maroons	Victoria Cougars				Montreal Wanderers
1925	▸	Victoria Cougars	Montreal Canadiens				Toronto Marlboros
1924	▸	Montreal Canadiens	Calgary Tigers				Winnipeg Rowing Club
1923	▸	Ottawa Senators	Edmonton Eskimos Vancouver Maroons	1903	▸	Montreal Hockey Club (AAA)	Winnipeg Victorias
					▸	Ottawa Hockey Club (Silver Seven)	Montreal Victorias Rat Portage Thistles
1922	▸	Toronto St. Patricks	Vancouver Millionaires				
1921	▸	Ottawa Senators	Vancouver Millionaires	1902	▸	Montreal Hockey Club (AAA)	Winnipeg Victorias
1920	▸	Ottawa Senators	Seattle Metropolitans		▸	Winnipeg Victorias	Toronto Wellingtons
1919	▸	No decision	Montreal and Seattle	1901	▸	Winnipeg Victorias	Montreal Shamrocks
1918	▸	Toronto Arenas	Vancouver Millionaires	1900	▸	Montreal Shamrocks	Halifax Crescents Winnipeg Victorias
1917	▸	Seattle Metropolitans	Montreal Canadiens				
1916	▸	Montreal Canadiens	Portland Rosebuds	1899	▸	Montreal Shamrocks	Queen's University
1915	▸	Vancouver Millionaires	Ottawa Senators		▸	Montreal Victorias	Winnipeg Victorias
1914	▸	Toronto Blueshirts	Victoria Aristocrats	1898	▸	Montreal Victorias	n/a (no challengers)
1913	▸	Quebec Bulldogs	Sydney Millionaires	1897	▸	Montreal Victorias	Ottawa Capitals
1912	▸	Quebec Bulldogs	Moncton Victorias	1896	▸	Montreal Victorias	Winnipeg Victorias
1911	▸	Ottawa Senators	Port Arthur Lake City Galt Professionals		▸	Winnipeg Victorias	Montreal Victorias
				1895	▸	Montreal Victorias	Queen's University*
1910	▸	Ottawa Senators	Galt Professionals Edmonton Pros	1894	▸	Montreal Hockey Club (AAA)	Ottawa Hockey Club
	▸	Montreal Wanderers	Berlin Dutchmen	1893	▸	Montreal Hockey Club (AAA)	n/a (no challengers)
1909	▸	Ottawa Senators	no challengers				

*The Queens University challenge was played against the Montreal Hockey Club (AAA), despite the Montreal Victorias winning the Cup. See page 323 for further explanation.

NHL Playoff Formats

1917–18 to Present

1998–99 to Present

League alignment: 27 to 30 teams in six divisions (Northeast, Atlantic, Southeast, Central, Pacific and Northwest) in two conferences (Eastern and Western).

Playoffs: Eight teams in each conference (16 teams total) with the first-place teams in each division all qualifying along with the next five best teams ranked by point totals. All series in all rounds are best of seven.

Conference quarterfinals: In each conference, the three division winners are ranked first to third based on points with the others ranked fourth to eighth. The teams are paired first against eighth, second against seventh, third against sixth and fourth against fifth in each conference.

Conference semifinals: Quarterfinal winners advance and are ranked first to fourth based on the same criteria as in the quarterfinals. The first-place team plays the fourth-place team and second plays third.

Conference finals: Winners of semifinals meet in each conference.

Stanley Cup final: Winners of conference finals meet.

1993–94 to 1997–98

League alignment: 26 teams, four divisions (Northeast, Atlantic, Central and Pacific) in two conferences (Eastern and Western).

Playoffs: The top eight teams in each conference (16 teams total) with the first-place teams in each division seeded first and second and the other six teams ranked by point totals. All series in all rounds are best of seven.

Conference quarterfinals: Teams are paired first against eighth, second against seventh, third against sixth and fourth against fifth in each conference.

Conference semifinals: Winners of the quarterfinals are ranked similarly and paired first against fourth and second against third in each conference.

Conference finals: Winners of the semifinals meet in each conference.

Stanley Cup final: Winners of the conference finals meet.

1986–87 to 1992–93

League alignment: 21 to 24 teams, in four divisions (Norris, Adams, Patrick and Smythe) in two conferences (Prince of Wales and Clarence Campbell).

Playoffs: First four teams in each division (16 teams total).

Division semifinals: In each division, the first-place team plays the fourth-place team and second place plays third place in a best-of-seven series.

Division finals: Winners of division semifinals meet in a best-of-seven series.

Conference finals: Winners in the Adams and Patrick Divisions meet in the best-of-seven Prince of Wales Conference final, and winners in the Smythe and Norris Divisions meet in the best-of-seven Clarence Campbell Conference final.

Stanley Cup final: Winners of the conference finals meet in a best-of-seven series.

1981–82 to 1985–86

League alignment: 21 teams in four divisions (Norris, Adams, Patrick and Smythe) in two conferences (Prince of Wales and Clarence Campbell).

Playoffs: First four teams in each division (16 teams total).

Division semifinals: In each division, the first-place team plays the fourth-place team and second place plays third place in a best-of-five series.

Division finals, conference finals and Stanley Cup final: Same format as outlined for 1986–87 to 1992–93.

1979–80 to 1980–81

League alignment: 21 teams in four divisions (Norris, Adams, Patrick and Smythe) in two conferences (Prince of Wales and Clarence Campbell).

Playoffs: First-place teams in all four divisions plus the next best 12 teams based on points regardless of division standings (16 teams total).

Preliminary round: All 16 teams are pooled together and ranked by regular-season points and paired first against sixteenth, second against fifteenth, third against fourteenth and so on in best-of-five series.

Quarterfinals: Eight winners advance, ranked first to eighth based on regular-season point totals and paired first against eighth, second against seventh and so on in best-of-seven series.

Semifinals: Four winners advance, ranked first to fourth based on regular-season standings and paired first against fourth and second against third in best-of-seven series.

Stanley Cup final: Winners of the semifinals meet in best-of-seven series.

1977–78 to 1978–79

League alignment: 18 teams (1977–78) and 17 teams (1978–79) in four divisions (Norris, Adams, Patrick and Smythe) in two conferences (Prince of Wales and Clarence Campbell).

Playoffs: Top three teams in each division (12 teams total).

Quarterfinals: Winners from the Preliminary round are pooled together with division winners, ranked by regular-season points and paired first against eighth, second against seventh and so on in best-of-seven series.

Semifinals: Four winners advance, ranked first to fourth based on regular-season standings and paired first against fourth and second against third in best-of-seven series.

Stanley Cup final: Winners of the semifinals meet in best-of-seven series.

Preliminary round: The first-place team in each division gets a bye into the quarterfinals. The second-place team from each division plus the four next-best teams based on regular-season point totals, regardless of their position in the division standings, are pooled and ranked first to eighth. Teams are paired first against eighth, second against seventh, third against sixth and fourth against fifth in a best-of-three series.

1974–75 to 1976–77

League alignment: 18 teams in four divisions (Norris, Adams, Patrick and Smythe) in two conferences (Prince of Wales and Clarence Campbell).

Playoffs: Top three teams in each division (12 teams total).

Preliminary round: The first-place team in each division gets a bye into the quarterfinals. The second-place and third-place teams from each division (eight teams total) are pooled and ranked first to eighth based on point totals. They are paired first against eighth, second against seventh, third against sixth and fourth against fifth in a best-of-three series.

Quarterfinals, semifinals and Stanley Cup final: Same format as outlined for 1977–78 to 1978–79.

1971–72 to 1973–74

League alignment: 14 teams (1971–72) and 16 teams (1972–73 to 1973–74) in two divisions (East and West).

Playoffs: Top four teams in each division (eight teams total).

Quarterfinals: In each division, first-place team plays fourth-place team and second-place team plays third-place team in a best-of-seven series.

Semifinals: Winners of the first-against-fourth pairing in each division cross over to meet winner of the second-against-third pairing from the other division in a best-of-seven series.

Stanley Cup final: Winners of semifinals meet in a best-of-seven series.

1970–71

League alignment: 14 teams in two divisions (East and West).

Playoffs: Top four teams in each division (eight teams total).

Quarterfinals: In each division, first-place team plays third-place team and second-place team plays fourth-place team in a best-of-seven series.

Semifinals: Winners of first-against-third pairing in each division cross over to meet winner of second-against-fourth pairing from the other division in a best-of-seven series.

Stanley Cup final: Winners of the semifinals meet in a best-of-seven series.

1967–68 to 1969–70

League alignment: 12 teams in two divisions (East and West).

Playoffs: Top four teams in each division (eight teams total).

Quarterfinals: In each division, first-place team plays third-place team and second-place team plays fourth-place team in a best-of-seven series.

Semifinals: Winners of quarterfinal series in each division meet in a best-of-seven series.

Stanley Cup final: Winners of the semifinals meet in a best-of-seven series.

1942–43 to 1966–67

League alignment: Six teams.

Playoffs: Top four teams in final standings.

Semifinals: First-place team plays third-place team and second-place team plays fourth-place team in a best-of-seven series.

Stanley Cup final: Winners of the semifinals meet in a best-of-seven series.

1938–39 to 1941–42

League alignment: Seven teams.

Playoffs: Top six teams in final standings.

Quarterfinals: First- and second-place teams get a bye into semifinals (Series A).
- Series B: Third-place team plays fourth-place team in a best-of-three.
- Series C: Fifth-place team plays sixth-place team in a best-of-three.

Semifinals:
- Series A: First-place team plays second-place team in a best-of-seven.
- Series D: Winner of Series B plays winner of Series C in a best-of-three.

Stanley Cup final: Winner of Series A plays winner of series D in a best-of-seven.

1928–29 to 1937–38

League alignment: Eight to 10 teams in two divisions (Canadian and American).

Playoffs: Top three teams in each division (six teams total).

Quarterfinals: First-place team from each division gets a bye into semifinals (Series A).
- Series B: Second-place team from each division meet in a two-game, total goals series.

- Series C: Third-place team from each division meet in a two-game, total goals series.

Semifinals:
- Series A: First-place team from each division meet in a best-of-five series.
- Series D: Winner of Series B plays winner of Series C in a best-of-three.

Stanley Cup final: Winner of Series A plays winner of Series D in a best-of-three.

Stanley Cup final expanded to best-of-five from 1930–31 through 1937–38. Series D changed to two games, total goals from 1930–31 to 1934–35 but reverted to a best-of-three in 1935–36. Series B and C expanded to a best-of-three from 1936–37 to 1937–38.

1926–27 to 1927–28

League alignment: 10 teams in two divisions (Canadian and American).

Playoffs: Top three teams in each division (six teams).

Quarterfinals: First-place team from each division gets a bye into semifinals. In each division, second-place team plays third-place team in a two-game, total goal series.

Semifinals: Winners of each second-against-third pairing play the first-place team in their division in a two-game, total goals series.

Stanley Cup final: Winners of semifinals meet in a best-of-five series.

1924–25 to 1925–26

League alignment: Six teams. (Teams in the Western Canada Hockey League also vied for the Stanley Cup.)

Playoffs: Top three teams in final standings.

League semifinal: First-place teams gets a bye into league final. Second-place team plays third-place team in a two-game, total goals series.

League final: Winner of league semifinal plays first-place team in a two-game, total goals series.*

Stanley Cup final: Winner of NHL final plays WCHL champion in a best-of-five series.

*In 1925, winner of NHL semifinal (Montreal) was declared league champion when first-place team (Hamilton) refused to play in the playoffs.

1921–22 to 1923–24

League alignment: Four teams. (Teams in the Pacific Coast Hockey League and Western Canada Hockey Association also vied for the Stanley Cup.)

League playoffs: Top two teams in final standings.

League final: First-place team plays second-place team in two-game, total goals series.

Stanley Cup final: Winner of NHL final faces PCHA and/or WCHL champion in a best-of-five or best-of-three series.

1917–18 to 1920–21

League alignment: Three teams (1917–18, 1918–19) and four teams (1919–20, 1920–21). (Teams in the Pacific Coast Hockey Association also vied for the Stanley Cup.)

Playoffs: Winner of the first half of the split-season schedule plays the winner of the second half. If the same team wins both halves they are declared the winner and no playoff is needed.

Final: The first-place team from the first half plays the first-place team from the second half in a two-game, total goals series.*

Stanley Cup final: Winner of NHL final plays PCHA champion in a best-of-five series.

*1919 NHL final was a best-of-seven.

Index

Q

Quackenbush, Bill: 1944–45 Stanley Cup final, 206; 1947–48 Stanley Cup final, 198; 1948–49 Stanley Cup final, 196–197; 1951–52 season, 187; 1952–53 Stanley Cup final, 184, 185

Quebec Aces, 128, 154

Quebec Bulldogs: 1908–09 season, 290–291; 1909–10 season, 289; 1910–11 season, 286; 1911–12 season, 283, 284–285; 1912–13 season, 280–281, 282–283; 1913–14 season, 280; 1914–15 season, 278, 279; 1915–16 season, 276; 1916–17 season, 274, 275; 1917–18 season, 271

Quebec Chronicle, 285

Quebec City, Quebec, 14, 51, 54, 239, 250, 283, 285, 319, 323

Quebec Daily Telegraph, 282, 283, 284, 285

Quebec Hockey Club: 1883 Montreal Winter Carnival, 315; 1892–93 season, 324; 1893–94 season, 322–323; 1894–95 season, 320–321; 1895–96 season, 318; 1896–97 season, 316; 1897–98 season, 313, 314; 1898–99 season, 311, 312; 1899–1900 season, 310; 1900–01 season, 308; 1901–02 season, 306; 1902–03 season, 304–305; 1903–04 season, 302, 303; 1905–06 season, 296; 1906–07 season, 294; 1907–08 season, 292

Quebec Hockey League, 177

Quebec Nordiques, 31, 51, 59, 77, 79, 93

Quebec Remparts, 115

Quebec Senior Hockey League, 154

Quebec Sporting Association, 283

Queen's Hotel, 231, 309

Queen's University: 1893–94 season, 322, 323; 1894–95 season, 320, 321; 1898–99 season, 312, 313; 1899–1900 season, 311; 1900–01 season, 308; 1905–06 season, 296–297; goal nets, 311; Marty Walsh, 286, 300

Quenneville, Joel, 22

Querrie, Charlie, 260, 270

Quick, Jonathan, 16, 17, 19

Quilty, John, 200, 213

Quinn, Dan, 76

Quinn, Emmett, 279, 281

Quinn, Mike J., 282, 284

R

Racicot, André, 58

Rafalski, Brian, 24, 26, 36, 37, 40, 42

Raleigh, Don "Bones," 192, 193, 194

Ramage, Rob, 58, 68

Ramsay, Craig, 108

Ramsey, Mike, 52

Randall, Ken, 260, 270

Ranford, Bill, 49, 64, 65, 72

Rankin, Norman, 320

Rankin Inlet, Nunavut, 55

Rask, Tuukka, 18

Rasmussen, Erik, 44

Rat Portage, 277

Rat Portage Thistles, 300, 301, 302, 304, 305

Ratelle, Jean, 98, 99, 100, 114, 115, 121

Ravlich, Matt, 142

Ray, Rob, 44

Raymond, Donat, 164

Raymond, Mason, 18

Rayner, Chuck, 192, 193, 194–195

Reardon, Ken, 29, 200, 204, 205

Reardon, Terry, 29, 204, 205, 218

Reaume, Marc, 166

Reay, Billy: 1945–46 Stanley Cup final, 204; 1946–47 Stanley Cup final, 200; 1950–51 Stanley Cup final, 188; 1951–52 Stanley Cup final, 186, 187; 1952–53 Stanley Cup final, 184; Punch Imlach and the Leafs, 154

Recchi, Mark, 18, 19, 30, 62, 63

Red Mile, the, 35

Red Square, 20

Redden, Wade, 28

Reddick, Pokey, 64, 65

Redmond, Dick, 95, 112

Redmond, Mickey, 126, 130

Reekie, Joe, 46

Regan, Larry, 162, 166, 168, 170

Regehr, Robin, 34

Regina Capitals, 253, 257, 259, 261

Regina, Saskatchewan, 178, 261

Reibel, Dutch, 172, 175, 176, 180, 181

Reid, Charlie, 256

Reid, Dave, 40, 44

Reid, Gerry, 196

Reinhart, Paul, 76

Reinprecht, Steve, 40

Reise Jr., Leo: 1947–48 Stanley Cup final, 198; 1948–49 Stanley Cup final, 196; 1949–50 Stanley Cup final, 193; 1949–50 Stanley Cup final, 192, 194; 1951–52 Stanley Cup final, 186–187; the Detroit dynasty, 179

Renberg, Mikael, 48

Renfrew Creamery Kings, 286, 288, 289, 291, 292, 294

Renfrew Hockey Club, 283

Renfrew Millionaires, 287, 289

Resch, Glenn "Chico," 85, 92

Rhéaume, Pascal, 36

Ricci, Mike, 50

Richard, Henri, 99; 1955–56 Stanley Cup final, 172–173, 175; 1956–57 Stanley Cup final, 170–171; 1957–58 Stanley Cup final, 168–169; 1958–59 Stanley Cup final, 166–167; 1959–60 Stanley Cup final, 162–163; 1960–61 semifinal, 160–161; 1964–65 Stanley Cup final, 142–143, 145; 1965–66 Stanley Cup final, 23, 140–141; 1966–67 Stanley Cup final, 134, 138–139; 1967–68 Stanley Cup final, 130–131; 1968–69 Stanley Cup final, 126; 1970–71 Stanley Cup final, 118–119; 1972–73 Stanley Cup final, 112–113; behind hockey's greatest dynasty, 164–165; the Conn Smythe Trophy, 141; Montreal's forgotten dynasty, 128; most career

goals in the finals, 65; most career Stanley Cup wins, 113; most games played in the finals, 171; most points in the final, career, 73; most years in the final, 181; Stanley Cup title games decided in overtime, 23

Richard, Maurice "Rocket," 66, 93, 104, 146, 153, 190, 197, 319; 1943–44 semifinal, 209, 210–211; 1943–44 Stanley Cup final, 173, 208–209, 210–211; 1944–45 season, 89, 91, 207; 1945–46 Stanley Cup final, 204–205; 1946–47 Stanley Cup final, 200–201; 1950–51 Stanley Cup final, 59, 188–189, 223; 1951–52 Stanley Cup final, 186–87; 1952–53 Stanley Cup final, 184–185; 1953–54 Stanley Cup final, 180–181; 1954–55 Stanley Cup final, 143, 176–177; 1955–56 Stanley Cup final, 172–173, 174–175; 1956–57 Stanley Cup final, 170–171, 239; 1957–58 Stanley Cup final, 168–169; 1958–59 Stanley Cup final, 166–167; 1959–60 Stanley Cup final, 162–163; behind hockey's greatest dynasty, 164–165; the Detroit dynasty, 178; the game I'll never forget, 210–211; Montreal versus Boston, 120; the Montreal-Detroit rivalry, 182; most career goals in the finals, 65; most career overtime goals in the playoffs and the final, 205; most career penalty minutes in the Stanley Cup final, 177; most career Stanley Cup wins, 113; most games played in the finals, 171; most goals in one period, 239; most points in the final, career, 73; most years in the final, 181; the original Rocket, 282; retirement, 159; scoring records, 123; three overtime goals in one playoff year, 223; the Richard riot, 164, 176–177; Toronto and Montreal rivalry, 137

Richards, Brad, 34, 35

Richards, Mike, 16, 17, 22

Richardson, Brad, 16

Richardson, E.L., 257

Richardson, Frank, 312, 314, 315

Richardson, Luke, 151

Richer, Stéphane, 52, 53, 68, 76, 77, 205

Richter, Mike, 56, 57

Rickard, Tex, 256

Rickey, Roy, 264, 266, 269, 274

Rideau Canal, 21

Rideau Hall, 14

Rideau Rebels, 15

Rideau Rink, 323

Rideau Skating and Curling Club, 14

Ridpath, Bruce, 286, 287, 288, 289

Riley, Jim, 264, 265, 274, 275

Ringling Brothers, 192

Ripley, Vic, 240

Risebrough, Doug, 95, 105; 1975–76 Stanley Cup final, 104, 107; 1976–77 Stanley Cup final, 100; 1977–78 Stanley Cup final, 98; 1978–79 Stanley Cup final, 94; 1985–86 Stanley Cup final, 76; the Montreal dynasty, 96

Rivers, Gus, 240, 242

R.J. Devlin Company, 264

Roach, John Ross, 239; 1921–22 Stanley Cup final, 260; 1928–29 Stanley Cup final, 244; 1931–32 Stanley Cup final, 238; 1932–33 season, 235; 1934–35 season, 229; three straight shutouts, 207

Roberge, Mario, 58

Robert, René, 108, 109

Roberto, Phil, 118

Roberts, Gary, 26, 68, 69

Roberts, Gord, 275, 279, 288, 289

Roberts, Gordie, 60, 62, 90

Roberts, Jimmy: 1964–65 Stanley Cup final, 142–143; 1965–66 Stanley Cup final, 140; 1966–67 Stanley Cup final, 134; 1967–68 Stanley Cup final, 130; 1968–69 Stanley Cup final, 126; 1969–70 Stanley Cup final, 122; 1972–73 Stanley Cup final, 112; 1975–76 Stanley Cup final, 104; 1976–77 Stanley Cup final, 100

Robertson, Earl, 226, 227

Robertson, Fred, 238

Robertson, John Ross, 307

Robinson, Earl, 230

Robinson, Larry, 17, 53, 105; 1972–73 Stanley Cup final, 112–113; 1975–76 Stanley Cup final, 104, 107; 1976–77 Stanley Cup final, 100–101; 1977–78 Stanley Cup final, 98–99; 1978–79 Stanley Cup final, 94, 95; 1985–86 Stanley Cup final, 76; 1988–89 Stanley Cup final, 68; 1999–2000 Stanley Cup final, 42–43; the Conn Smythe Trophy, 98; the Montreal dynasty, 96

Robitaille, Luc, 38, 39, 58, 75

Rochefort, Leon, 118, 129, 134, 140, 141, 147

Rochester Americans, 148

Rockett, Annie Gavan, 282

Rodden, Eddie, 244, 245

Roenick, Jeremy, 18, 23, 49, 60, 151, 205

Rogers Arena, 19, 89

Rolfe, Dale, 111, 114, 117

Rollins, Al, 181, 188, 189, 203

Roloson, Dwayne, 30, 31

Rolston, Brian, 52

Rome, Aaron, 18

Romnes, Doc, 222, 224, 225, 232, 233, 240

Ronan, Ed, 58

Ronan, Skene, 276, 277

Ronning, Cliff, 56

Ronson, Len, 147

Ronty, Paul, 176

Rooney, Steve, 76

Rooney, Walter, 284

Rosenthal, Sam, 297

Roski Jr., Edward, 17

Ross, Art: 1906–07 season, 294–295; 1907–08 season, 292–293; 1910–11 season, 287; 1914–15 season, 279; 1928–29 Stanley Cup final, 244; 1929–30 season, 243; 1938–39 Stanley Cup final, 222–223; 1940–41 Stanley Cup final, 218–219; back-to-back Stanley Cup wins with two different teams, 153; banned from hockey, 279; rushing with the puck, 317; *see also* Art Ross Trophy.

Photo Credits